TOUGH LIBERAL

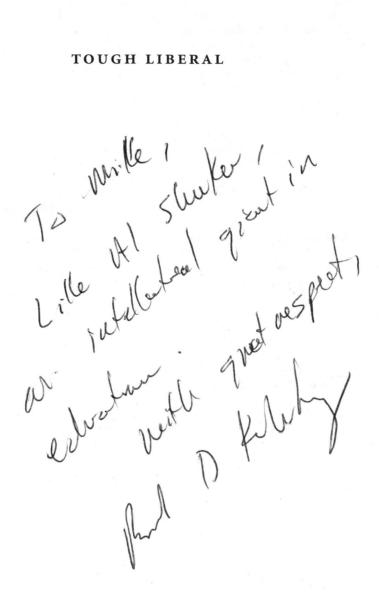

COLUMBIA STUDIES IN CONTEMPORARY AMERICAN HISTORY
ALAN BRINKLEY, GENERAL EDITOR

TOUGH LIBERAL

ALBERT SHANKER

AND

THE BATTLES OVER SCHOOLS, UNIONS,

RACE, AND DEMOCRACY

RICHARD D. KAHLENBERG

COLUMBIA UNIVERSITY PRESS   NEW YORK

Columbia University Press
Publishers Since 1893
New York   Chichester, West Sussex

Copyright © 2007 Richard D. Kahlenberg

Library of Congress Cataloging-in-Publication Data
Kahlenberg, Richard D.
Tough Liberal : Albert Shanker and the battles over schools, unions, race, and
democracy / Richard D. Kahlenberg.
p. cm. — (Columbia studies in contemporary american history)
Includes bibliographical refererences and index.
ISBN 978–0–231–13496–5 (cloth : alk. paper) — ISBN 978–0–231–50909–1 (e-book)
1. Shanker, Albert.   2. Labor leaders—United States—Biography.   3. American
Federation of Teachers.   I. Title.   II. Series.

LB2844.53.U6K34   2007
331.88′1137110092
[B]

2007005399

Columbia University Press books are printed on permanent and durable acid-free paper.
This book is printed on paper with recycled content.
Printed in the United States of America
c 10 9 8 7 6 5 4 3 2 1

To the memory of
Richard W. Kahlenberg

CONTENTS

Introduction

1

TOUGH LIBERAL

I T is the peculiar fate of Albert Shanker that he is probably best remembered for something he never did. In Woody Allen's 1973 science-
fiction comedy *Sleeper*, Allen's character wakes up two hundred
years in the future to learn that civilization was destroyed when "a man
by the name of Albert Shanker got hold of a nuclear warhead."[1] Shanker
was considered by many New Yorkers, particularly liberals like Allen, to
be a hothead and union thug for shutting down the entire New York
City school system with bitter strikes in 1967 and 1968. As head of the
United Federation of Teachers (UFT), the nation's largest union local,
Shanker led a fourteen-day strike in 1967 and a thirty-six-day series of
strikes in 1968, closing down the nation's largest public-school system and
throwing the lives of one million students and their parents into chaos.[2]
His power to disrupt the school system was bad enough for his critics, but
both incidents stirred up racial animosity, particularly between black parents and Jewish teachers. Shanker was denounced not only as a power
monger for crippling the city's schools, but also as a racist for opposing
the black community's quest for greater self-determination and control
over the schools. Because it was illegal for New York's public employees to
strike, Shanker was jailed after both incidents. When Woody Allen was
writing the script for *Sleeper* and wondered whose name to use for a joke

about a madman who had destroyed the world, he tried out a number of possibilities with people at Elaine's Restaurant. The name Albert Shanker got the biggest laugh.[3]

Almost a quarter century later, however, it was a seemingly very different Albert Shanker who was eulogized at a ceremony featuring leading dignitaries at the George Washington University in Washington, D.C. President Bill Clinton, using crutches following a recent accident, hobbled to the stage and spoke of Albert Shanker, the head of the national American Federation of Teachers (AFT) from 1974 to 1997, as an educational statesman, a personal "mentor," and "one of the most important teachers of the twentieth century." Clinton lauded Shanker as a champion of equity, recognizing that the education-standards movement Shanker led "was essential for democracy to work," because it "was the only way we could give every child, without regard to their background, a chance to live up to his or her God-given capacity."[4] Senator Daniel Patrick Moynihan, speaking in his idiosyncratic clipped tones, painted Shanker as an intellectual and a gifted writer whose celebrated "Where We Stand" column appeared in the Sunday *New York Times*. "The impact was extraordinary," Moynihan said. "Union leaders in those days rarely wrote essays, still less felicitous, thoughtful analyses of public policy."[5]

The list of speakers that day—which included Vice President Al Gore and Education Secretary Richard Riley—was evidence that Shanker was a powerful individual, as Woody Allen suggested, but speaker after speaker said Shanker exercised power well and judiciously: to upgrade the teaching profession, to promote democracy abroad, and to improve public education for American schoolchildren.

Some have hypothesized that there were two Albert Shanker's—a "bad Al" and a "good Al." The bad Al was the early, militant teachers' union leader who thirsted for power and poisoned race relations. The good Al came much later and was the statesman who led his union in the direction of education reform, even as parochial elements within the AFT fiercely resisted.

But the presence of Lorretta Johnson, one of the speakers at the ceremony that day, suggested the story wasn't so simple. A stout African American woman, Johnson was head of the AFT's division of "paraprofessionals," a group of mostly black and Latino teacher aides, many of them former welfare mothers, who were hired with federal money to help in low-income schools beginning in the 1960s.

Racial tensions ran high following the 1968 teachers' strike, which centered on the question of whether local black leaders had the right to dismiss tenured unionized white teachers and replace them, often with black
teachers, as part of an effort to give ghetto communities greater control
over their schools. Shanker was a hero of the white middle class, which
backed him for standing up to black militants, but Shanker, who had
marched with Martin Luther King Jr. in Selma, wanted to make it clear
that the issue was not black versus white, but the right of workers to be
treated with dignity. Many of the black teacher aides had crossed the
picket lines during the teachers' strike to try to keep schools open. But
when Shanker saw the opportunity to organize the "paras," who were
making as little as two dollars an hour, he jumped at the chance. Shanker
met fierce resistance from many teachers, some of whom did not want a
union of professionals to include less-educated aides, many of whom
were high-school dropouts.

But Shanker was adamant. He saw organizing the paras as a way of
proving that the UFT was a racially inclusive organization, and he laid out
a vision in which the union would negotiate a career ladder, by which paras could go back to school and become teachers and thereby better integrate the teaching profession. When some teachers continued to balk,
Johnson noted, Shanker threatened to resign as president. It was, she said,
the only time he did that in his career.[6]

Teachers eventually went along, and the UFT ended up beating out a
rival union that unsuccessfully tried to paint Shanker as a racist. The paras did not see Shanker as anti-black; they saw him as someone who went
on strike—and went to jail—in order to defend his members, and they
wanted to be a part of his organization. Johnson told the audience that
when Shanker later retired as president of the UFT, he said of all the things
he had done, he was proudest of organizing the paras and providing them
with better wages and a program in which they could go back to school
and become teachers.[7] The "bad Al" of the 1960s, to Johnson, did not
sound so bad after all.

The ceremony ended with President Clinton, Senator Moynihan, Lorretta Johnson, and hundreds of audience members singing "Solidarity
Forever."

Al Shanker was a man constantly on the go. As president of the UFT in
New York City and the AFT nationally, he was forever giving speeches,

negotiating contracts, testifying before Congress, walking picket lines, and meeting with unionist and human-rights activists abroad. He was constantly churning out new ideas, which he outlined in some 1,300 weekly columns, commenting on education reform, unions, race relations, and politics. He was passionate about his work, traveled 300,000 to 500,000 miles a year, and had little time for his family. (He took his wife, Eadie, to a union conference for their "honeymoon.")

He thought about running for mayor of New York City in the late 1960s, when polls showed he could beat Republican John Lindsay, and he was mentioned as a possible U.S. secretary of education in the early 1990s under Bill Clinton. In both cases, he concluded he was better positioned to fight for what he cared about as a leader of the UFT and AFT. As head of a union of teachers, he stood at the intersection of the two great engines for equality in the United States—public education and organized labor—and he was not about to give that up. He once told an interviewer, "If I didn't have to make a living, I would have done this as a volunteer."[8]

A Father of Modern Teachers' Unions

Shanker lived the lives of several men in a single lifetime. In 1960, when collective bargaining for teachers was generally thought impossible because it was illegal for public employees to go on strike, Shanker and a handful of other teachers in New York City convinced several thousand colleagues to break the law and risk being fired. Because the school board could not dismiss all the striking teachers, it backed down and eventually recognized the right of the UFT to bargain on behalf of teachers. Other teachers joined on, and from 1960 to 1968, union representation grew from 5 percent of New York City's teaching staff to 97 percent.[9] With collective bargaining came a huge change in the culture of teaching. Teachers were accustomed to being pushed around: they were poorly paid, forced to eat their lunches while supervising students, and told to bring a doctor's note if they were out sick. Collective bargaining brought them higher salaries and also greater dignity.[10]

"He was the George Washington of the teaching profession," said union leader Tom Mooney. "He's the one who rallied us to liberate ourselves."[11] Like George Washington, Shanker was hardly alone in helping to light the spark of teacher unionism in New York City. He was one of several leaders, including Charles Cogen, president of the UFT at the time, and David

Selden, an AFT organizer. But Shanker soon outpaced his colleagues, leading the union to far greater heights.

The influence of Shanker and his colleagues was felt far beyond New York City, as the UFT's example caught fire and teachers pushed for collective bargaining in Detroit, Philadelphia, and city after city. The nation's largest teachers' organization, the National Education Association (NEA), was adamantly opposed to collective bargaining. But as NEA leaders witnessed the AFT's dramatic gains in membership, the NEA was forced to reverse its position or risk losing its preeminent status.

With collective bargaining, membership in teachers' unions skyrocketed. During a period when the American trade-union movement saw dramatic decline, the AFT grew from sixty thousand members in 1961 to close to one million at the time of Shanker's death in 1997.[12] The NEA saw comparable growth, and schools became, after the postal service, the most heavily unionized sector in the United States.[13] Today, teachers' unions are broadly believed to be the most influential single force in American education.[14]

Influential Education Reformer

Having been one of the founding fathers of teacher unionism would have been an extraordinary legacy by itself. But then, in Act II, Shanker became the most influential education reformer of the second half of the twentieth century. He did so not by changing jobs but by utterly transforming the role of teachers' union leader.

Shanker saw that by the early 1980s the great labor agenda of the previous epoch—Social Security, Medicaid and Medicare, the minimum wage, and civil rights—had run into a political cul-de-sac. But education still had political backing, and in 1983, Shanker, virtually alone within the liberal education establishment, embraced the report of the National Commission on Excellence in Education, entitled *A Nation at Risk*, which ushered in a quarter century of education reform. While teachers' unions were being reviled as special-interest groups that blocked promising reforms, Shanker let loose with a flurry of his own reform proposals that one newspaper said made the AFT look as much like a think tank as a union.[15]

When unions were attacked for protecting incompetent teachers, Shanker backed a controversial "peer-review" plan, in which master teachers would evaluate incoming and veteran teachers, weeding out those not up to the job. He also astounded critics when he proposed a rigorous national competency exam for new teachers, a concept anathema to the NEA. When unions were attacked for opposing efforts to reward talent through "merit pay" of teachers, Shanker devised a plan to recognize superior performance with greater pay without leaving the decisions open to favoritism by principals. He proposed what would become the National Board for Professional Teaching Standards, which provides for teachers what board certification does for doctors. Each of these policies was offered not merely as a defensive maneuver against critics of teachers' unions but as part of an affirmative vision to make teaching not just an occupation but a true profession.

Shanker also proposed innovations to restructure schools and in 1988 popularized the idea of charter schools, public schools that would be set up by groups of teachers and be permitted to experiment with different educational approaches. The idea was widely embraced: in 1990, there were no charter schools; today, there are more than 3,600.[16] Over time, however, the reform went in very different directions than Shanker intended, and he grew increasingly critical of the movement he had helped to father.

Shanker's greatest impact on education reform came with his decision to embrace a system of education standards, testing, and accountability comparable to what most leading European and Asian nations had. There was enormous resistance to standards from the left (civil-rights groups, education professors, the NEA) and from the right (advocates of local control and states' rights). But Shanker broke with the education establishment and joined with governors and business leaders to push what today, remarkably, has become the leading education reform in the United States. While the movement has many participants and advocates, Shanker was generally seen as the most fervent, powerful, and consistent leader. He pounded away at the theme that educators had to give students a real incentive to do well. As a former teacher, he often told others that when he gave homework or a quiz, the class invariably shouted out, "Does it count?"[17] Although no one liked to be held accountable, Shanker argued that human nature required that public education use incentives, making it more like the private marketplace, without abandoning the fundamental public nature of schools.

Taken together—his role as a father of modern teachers' unions and his role as a leading education reformer—Shanker was arguably the single individual most responsible for preserving public education in the United

States during the last quarter of the twentieth century. Whenever private school–voucher proposals surface through ballot initiatives or legislation, the powerful teachers' unions that Shanker helped create are the most important political opponents. But if the AFT under Shanker had not transformed itself and joined the education-reform debates, the case against vouchers would have been weaker, and more forays from proponents of privatization might well have prevailed. Shanker's defense against vouchers—fighting "to change public education in order to preserve it"—was "far more effective," says education writer Thomas Toch, than those in the education establishment, who merely called "for more money to address problems that they frequently argued didn't exist."[18] While the United States economy as a whole is far more market oriented than most countries, 90 percent of students remain in government-run public schools. No individual in the past generation is more responsible for this anomaly than Albert Shanker.

Though Shanker held no public office, he became supremely influential, his name constantly invoked in education circles. "In the course of the past two decades," educator and author E. D. Hirsch Jr. wrote in 1997, "Albert Shanker made himself the most important figure in American education."[19] While secretaries of education came and went, as did presidents of the much larger NEA, Shanker endured, and he outdid and out-thought all of them. If Horace Mann was the key educational figure in the nineteenth century and John Dewey in the first half of the twentieth century, Albert Shanker has stood as the most influential figure since then. As a central thinker, writer, and player in all the great education debates of the last quarter century—whether school vouchers, charter schools, or education standards—he was, journalist Sara Mosle argues, "our Dewey."[20]

Advocate of Tough Liberalism

But that was not all. Shanker had a third life as well, as a combatant in the fight for the future of American liberalism. From the mid-1960s to the mid-1990s, he was in the thick of the great battles waged among liberals over race, unions, American foreign policy, and the direction of the Democratic Party. Shanker clashed with factions within the American left—the "New Left" and the "New Politics" movements—that jettisoned the notion of "colorblindness" in favor of racial preferences and identity politics, saw labor and working-class voters as reactionary rather than central

to the liberal coalition, and rejected muscular cold-war liberalism in favor
of a dovish, often isolationist, foreign policy. In this endeavor, unlike his
others, he and like minded advocates were mostly unsuccessful, and the
meaning of American liberalism changed dramatically.

Shanker believed in what might be called "tough liberalism," an ideology that champions an affirmative role for government in promoting social mobility, social cohesion, and greater equality at home and democracy abroad, but which is also tough-minded about human nature, the
way the world works, and the reality of evil. He remained, to the end, a
liberal, and over a thirty-year period he stood squarely for two central
pillars of liberal thought: public education and organized labor. But he
also thought liberals were wrong on many of the great issues of the day.
Shanker was a Harry Truman/Scoop Jackson Democrat and a Cold Warrior who disagreed with liberals on Vietnam in the 1960s and on detente
with the Soviet Union in the 1970s. He believed liberals did not go far
enough to support democratic forces in Poland and in Nicaragua in the
1980s, and he opposed liberal efforts to cut defense spending. An early
supporter of the civil-rights movement in the 1950s and 1960s, Shanker
stood virtually alone among union leaders in consistently raising questions about liberal support for racial preferences, arguing instead for
broad-based affirmative-action programs for economically needy people
of all races. He similarly opposed certain extreme forms of bilingual education and multiculturalism, which he saw as separatist. And Shanker disagreed with liberals on the role of organized labor in the Democratic coalition. He thought it was a grave mistake to move from a working-class
party toward one that centered around women, minorities, and upper-
middle-class white reformers.

Shanker's views on defense and quotas put him in conflict with Jimmy
Carter. For that reason, some pegged Shanker as a neoconservative, until
he decided to endorse not Ronald Reagan but Ted Kennedy for president.
As Bill Clinton noted at the memorial service, "Al Shanker would say
something on one day that would delight liberals and infuriate conservatives. The next day, he would make conservatives ecstatic and the liberals
would be infuriated."[21] People could not figure him out. They called him
a "right-wing socialist" and a "neanderthal liberal."[22]

He was a complex individual: a pacifist in his youth who became a
leading defense and foreign-policy hawk, an intellectual who was also a
populist and communicated easily with nonintellectuals, a gifted public

speaker who was unable to make small talk, a liberal whose biggest enemies were often on the left, a gifted writer who had to pay to have his
ideas published, a fierce critic of philanthropic foundations who later
served on the boards of two of them, a man who devoted his life to improving the education of children but spent little time with his own kids,
a man largely ignorant of pop culture who was cited in television shows
and movies, and a tough unionist with a gruff manner who enjoyed shop-
ping and baking bread and detested talking about sports.[23]

Throughout his life, Shanker continually rowed against the tide. He
was one of the only Jewish kids growing up in a tough Catholic neighborhood. He began as a teacher's union activist at a time when no one thought
it was possible to organize public employees and then headed a growing
union in an era when unions were in decline. He was a leading education
reformer at a time when teachers' unions were generally written off as
the greatest obstacles to reform. And he was a proponent of colorblindness, first in an era when his stance was considered radical and later in
an era when it was considered conservative. Because he did not shrink
from fights, his positions often sparked tremendous controversy. Issues of
race and issues of war are notoriously volatile. And his main passion—
education—aroused strong emotion because it deals with people's children and with society's future.[24]

Shanker's "tough liberal" philosophy was wrong on some of the major
issues of the day. It is hard to defend his relatively hawkish position on the
war in Vietnam, to take one important example. But today, when liberals
are accused of not standing for anything, it is important to note that
Shanker had a coherent ideology. He articulated a cogent rationale for his
collection of "liberal" and "conservative" views that bridged traditional
categories without merely splitting differences. For Shanker, all roads led
back to democracy.

He was for strong and free trade unions primarily because of their
democratic virtues. They gave workers a democratic voice at the workplace and in the Congress, checking the unbridled economic power of
corporations. They helped strengthen the formation of a middle class
necessary to a democracy. And they served as a crucial check against gov-
ernmental power, which is why authoritarian governments sought to
crush them. "There is no freedom or democracy without trade unionism," he said.[25] Likewise, Shanker opposed vouchers and supported strong
public schools because he believed schools were more than a place to

train future employees; they were institutions that taught democratic citizenship and helped bind diverse peoples together as Americans.

But democracy also underpinned his "conservative" positions. Shanker's support for trade unionism also translated into an unrelenting anti-Communism. Why was it "liberal" to stand by while Polish authorities crushed Solidarity, or while Nicaraguan Sandinistas beat up union leaders, or while the North Vietnamese arrested the leadership of the independent labor federation in the South, he asked. He also thought that in a democracy it was essential to have a single standard for individuals of all races, and he opposed all privileges associated with race. He recognized a need to take affirmative action to address the legacy of past racial discrimination, but he argued that extra help should be made available for economically disadvantaged people of all races. He quarreled with certain "progressive" educators who pushed fads that were soft on teaching academic content and distorted history in order to boost the self-esteem of minority groups. He believed, with E. D. Hirsch Jr., that if one really wished to be a political progressive concerned about disadvantaged kids, one needed to be an educational "conservative" who stood for teaching students certain core knowledge that was essential to upward mobility in American society.

Shanker argued that tough liberalism was not only consistent and democratic but was also politically attractive, because it addressed the central vulnerabilities of liberalism, which since the 1960s has been seen as soft, elitist, politically correct, and out of touch with the way the world works. Democrats have done fairly well in recent decades with what political scientists call the "moderate middle," upscale socially liberal and fiscally conservative citizens. But they have been trounced by voters who make up the "radical center," downscale, patriotic citizens who are concerned about right and wrong, angry about abuses of power by the wealthy, and want more government support for working families. During Shanker's lifetime, the radical center went from being the backbone of the Democratic Party to its Achilles' heel. And liberalism went from being a proud moniker to an epithet, "so reviled," as Peter Beinart notes, "that its adherents dare not speak its name."[26] Shanker believed that issues of national security and race were central to the collapse of American liberalism politically, and he articulated a different path on these questions—a path he believed was not "conservative" but, like the economic populism he also embraced, profoundly democratic. Shanker's tough liberalism was highly controversial and largely dismissed during his lifetime as being unorthodox and inconsistent. But as contemporary American liberalism struggles both for intellectual coherence and political viability, Albert Shanker's life reminds us that there is an alternative tough liberal tradition wholly worthy of reviving.

I

NEW YORK

1

The Early Years

WHEN Albert Shanker was born on September 14, 1928, he emerged from the womb with a large red birthmark on the right side of his neck running over the back of his head. His mother, Mamie Shanker, was beside herself. "What will ever become of him?" she asked.[1] In a childhood that would be marked by many struggles—deprivation and discrimination, the Great Depression and the rise of Adolf Hitler—it was not an auspicious beginning.

Albert Shanker (he had no English middle name) was the first-born child of Morris Shanker, a newspaper deliveryman, and Mamie Burko Shanker, a garment worker.[2] Both of Shanker's parents were Eastern European Jewish immigrants, coming from a part of Poland that was at times under the control of Russia.[3] Shanker's mother came to America prior to World War I, and his father just following the war, both seeking to escape the anti-Jewish pogroms and have a better life.[4]

Mamie Shanker, who was born in 1894, came from a prominent intellectual Minsk family. Her father, Abraham Yehudi Burko, was highly educated and a large landowner and timber producer. As a Jew, however, he could not own land in his own name, and when he was killed in a horrific accident, being trampled by horses, his Gentile partner, in whose name the land was held, took over the land and the family became destitute.

Mamie's mother, Rachel Burko, eked out a living by selling herbs to people who were sick.[5]

The family had little food, and it was considered a treat on the Sabbath
to have a small piece of chicken the size of a noodle. As Jews, it was a ter-
rifying time to live in Russia, and the Cossacks were a constant threat. The
leadership of Czar Alexander III and Nicholas II was particularly repressive, and during the years of their rule (1891–1917), one-third of Eastern
European Jews fled their homeland, an exodus comparable to the flight
from the Spanish Inquisition.[6] One of Mamie Shanker's half-sisters was
raped by soldiers and died soon after. During one pogrom, a Gentile
neighbor hid Mamie in a barrel underneath a pile of potatoes in order to
keep her alive. Finally, as a teenager, she walked through the forests and
made her way to Germany in order to get to the United States.[7]

When she came to America, her half-brother was already here, and he
took her on as a sewing-machine operator.[8] The occupation was common
for Jewish immigrants, because many garment industry owners were Jewish and were willing to hire other Jews, and because English was not required.[9] Though a manual laborer, Mamie Shanker was an intellectual
who liked to read poetry and discuss Yiddish books and literature. An op-
era buff, she bought standing-room-only tickets when she could.[10] She
was feisty and a tough negotiator. Al Shanker later recalled, "I'd have to
wait half an hour while she bought three tomatoes."[11] She was a strong
personality—a force to be reckoned with.[12]

If Mamie was fiery, Shanker's father, Morris, was soft spoken.[13] Born
just before the turn of the century, he studied in Europe to be a rabbi until
his family ran out of money for his education, just short of his ordina-
tion.[14] During World War I, he served in the czar's army then immigrated
to the United States, where he went to work for the Ford Motor Company
in Detroit. As the company was deeply anti-Semitic, life there was intolerable, so after a time Morris Shanker came to New York, where he later began a grueling job delivering newspapers.[15]

In December 1927, the thirty-year-old Morris Shanker and the thirty-
three-year-old Mamie Burko were united in an arranged marriage, as was
not uncommon for new Jewish immigrants.[16] Morris Shanker was considered attractive, but Mamie Shanker was not: she was overweight and
her face had been scarred by severe acne as a child. Her comparative age
was also considered a substantial deficit in a bride, but Morris Shanker's
family mistakenly believed that the Burkos had a great deal of money.[17]

The couple lived in a cramped apartment with a communal bathroom down the hallway, on Clinton Street on the Lower East Side of Manhattan.[18] To make matters worse, Mamie Shanker insisted that her mother, Rachel Burko, live with the couple, an arrangement that did not promote happiness in the family.[19]

Long Island City

Albert Shanker was born in September 1928, ten months after the couple was married. A year and a half later, a sister, Pearl, was born, and the family moved from Clinton Street to Long Island City, a neighborhood in Queens.[20] The five family members—the parents, the children, and the grandmother—lived in a small ground-level apartment a block from the Queensboro Plaza subway station.[21] The Shankers would hear the elevated subway trains going by at all hours, and the apartment's windowsills were blackened with dust from the trains and nearby factories.[22]

The Shanker apartment had three bedrooms—one for the parents, one for Pearl and her grandmother, and one for Al. Al's bedroom was roughly six feet by nine feet, with room for a bed, a tiny dresser, and a small closet, which jutted out into the room.[23] By the time he was thirteen years old, he was taller than the bed and slept with his feet sticking out of the door.[24] The bathroom had a tub and a toilet, but no room for a sink, so hands were washed in the kitchen sink.[25]

The crowded circumstances were exacerbated by the fact that Morris Shanker had to store his newspapers in the living room.[26] (He had no separate warehouse or office.) It was as if newspapers were part of the furniture.[27] In advance of the big Sunday newspapers, Pearl recalls, papers "would be piled up above our heads and there would just be a narrow aisle to walk from the bedroom to the kitchen."[28] The cramped environment added to the tension in the household. "The marriage wasn't happy," Pearl recalled years later. The parents were not close to each other, and there were many arguments and a great deal of name calling.[29]

Mamie and Morris Shanker both worked grueling jobs. Al Shanker recalled that his father, using a pushcart, would set out at two in the morning to deliver the papers, and "he'd be back at seven in the morning, totally exhausted. And then he'd have some coffee and some breakfast.

Then, at ten o'clock, the afternoon papers would come out, and he'd start all over."[30] Morris Shanker had about twenty papers to deliver in various languages.[31] Many of the deliveries were to apartment buildings, five and six stories high, none with elevators.[32] In addition, on Sundays, Morris Shanker, with the help of his family, would sell papers as parishioners came out of Mass. Through several services and in all sorts of weather, the Shankers would stand for hours selling papers from a pushcart.[33]

Al Shanker later said that as a child he hardly ever saw his father, whom he knew as "this angry, disgruntled guy who grabbed a roll and coffee and went out to work again."[34] The work was not only physically exhausting, it was dispiriting for a man who was educated and had talents that were not being put to use. Al's boyhood friend Vincent Castanza remembers wondering: why was this bright man delivering newspapers?[35]

Meanwhile, Mamie Shanker worked seventy-hour weeks at J&J Clothing in lower Manhattan to help supplement her husband's salary.[36] She would sit at work, sweating, in deep concentration.[37] One time Al went to visit her and was unable to recognize her among the essentially anonymous group of toiling women. He was horrified.[38]

Despite two incomes, the Shanker family, like many families during the Depression, had little money. They did not own a car, never owned a home, and rarely traveled or took vacations. They didn't have a telephone in the apartment until the late 1940s, and the Shanker children generally wore secondhand clothes. The Shankers did have enough food, however, which made them better off than some of the families in the neighborhood.[39] The attention to nutrition apparently paid off, for Al would grow to tower over his more diminutive parents.[40]

From a very young age, Al Shanker was a contentious child. His sister Pearl recalls that he "had his own opinions and would argue with my parents. He would argue with anybody if he disagreed."[41] When other family members pitched in to put the sections of the Sunday paper together, or to sell papers on Sundays, she says that Al refused to participate.[42]

Al ran into trouble when he began elementary school at P.S. 4 in Queens.[43] Because the family primarily spoke Yiddish in the home, Al went to school not knowing any English, and he quickly fell behind.[44] At first he could not even go to the bathroom because he did not know how to ask to do so in English.[45] One of his early teachers made fun of his accent, which only encouraged his classmates to pick on him.[46] He sometimes did not do his homework.[47] Shanker recalled, "I didn't work very hard in school. . . . There were a lot of things in school I was bored with and if I was bored with something I didn't do it and would get into trouble."[48]

His cousin Lillian Feldman said Al had "no interest in what was going on in the classroom" and would "come home with failing marks." Mamie Shanker would wring her hands over his poor grades.[49] Al got into trouble frequently, and his mother took him to counseling when he was a young child. Some relatives even suggested that he be sent to reform school to be straightened out.[50]

Pearl Shanker was more pliant and was an academic superstar who outshone her older brother.[51] She got along well with her father, in part because she was more conforming than Al. Morris Shanker was away working most of the time, Pearl says, but "what time he had, I got, and Al did not."[52] She notes, "my father was never, never close to Al. . . . Al never got any affection from my father."[53]

Al's mother had a greater influence on him than his father, but she could be overbearing. Shanker later told colleagues that his home was not a particularly loving or supportive environment.[54] After Al was married, his wife Eadie recalled, Mamie would call and "he wouldn't answer the phone. He would run from her."[55] She was controlling of Al and nagged him a lot, a boyhood friend remembers.[56]

Young Al did develop a very affectionate relationship with his grandmother. The two would go on long walks and she would tell him stories in Yiddish.[57] "She really brought me up," Shanker said, "since both my mother and father worked."[58] She treated him like a prince and would tell him: "You are very special. You're exceptional. You are going to be a great man."[59] Al's sister Pearl recalls that to Rachel Burko, "the sun rose and set on him. He was perfect." Al was named after Rachel's deceased husband, and she told young Al he would do great things.[60]

Outside the tense and crowded household, there was little benefit from escape. On top of deprivation, there was discrimination. Growing up in the 1930s, before the Holocaust, anti-Semitism was virulent and mainstream. Shanker's parents read to him about what was happening to the Jews in Germany with the rise of Hitler: the passage of the Nuremberg laws, when Al was six; the Kristallnacht, when Al was nine; and Hitler's invasion of Poland, when Al was ten.[61] At home in the United States in the late 1930s, radio preacher Father Charles Coughlin's increasingly anti-Semitic sermons drew a large audience.[62]

Many Jews sought refuge from discrimination by living in tight-knit Jewish enclaves, where there was some protection from the outer world.

Al Shanker did not have that cocoon. The newspaper route that Morris Shanker was assigned to was located in a tough working-class Irish and Italian area with few Jewish families.[63] In the neighborhood, Father Coughlin was a mainstay, and during the summer, when the windows were open, Al would hear Coughlin's anti-Semitic messages being broadcast. At the local church, one of the priests was particularly fond of Coughlin, and the Shankers always knew when he preached because anti-Semitic incidents would increase. Rocks were thrown through the Shanker's ground-floor apartment window, with notes saying "dirty Jew."[64] Pearl recalls being terrified to walk through the neighborhood in the summer, when people were out on their stoops. In the building next to the Shankers, there was a man who would call out "Jews are worse than cats" and then kick one of the stray cats that populated the neighborhood.[65] Sometimes, Mamie Shanker would share extra food with the neighbors' children, but the gesture did not bring good will and only made them hate the Shankers more.[66] Shanker recalled, "Not all the kids were anti-Semitic or all the parents, but there was enough of it there so you could really cut it with a knife; and it was very open."[67] To keep the children from having to walk past anti-Semitic neighbors on the way to the library, the Shanker parents bought a set of the *Encyclopedia Britannica*.[68]

Occasionally, a more tolerant family would move in, and Pearl would find a playmate, but Al never did. "There were no friends in the immediate neighborhood at all," she says.[69] "Most of the time, I couldn't go out and play on the street because I never knew when I would be beaten up next," Al Shanker recalled. "So I grew up sort of as an isolate at home with not much to do."[70]

Like all boys, Al just wanted to be accepted, and when he was about eight years old, it looked for a moment as though he might be.[71] A group of neighborhood boys asked Al if he wanted to join their club. He said yes, and they put a blindfold on him for what they said was the initiation process. The group took Al to an empty lot nearby and put a rope around his arms and neck and threw the other end over a branch. They were about to pull him up when Pearl came out, saw what was happening, and screamed. A bystander came over and rescued Al.[72] The group later said they had strung Al up to avenge the killing of Christ.[73]

The horrific experience left long-term scars. "It was an absolutely traumatic experience for him," says his wife, Eadie. "I think something closed in him emotionally."[74] Said union colleague Sandra Feldman, "it had a huge effect on him," making him highly confrontational. It made him never shirk a fight; "sometimes he looked for a fight."[75] Says another union official, Velma Hill: "That stayed with him throughout his life."[76]

Once the Shanker children got to school, there was no oasis from the prejudice. Pearl recalls one junior-high teacher told her Hitler was right about the Jews and discouraged her from trying to advance to a competitive high school.[77] Al Shanker recalled a teacher announcing to the class around Christmas time: "For the next few weeks, we'll be singing Christmas carols, but Albert is Jewish, so he won't have to sing them, since he doesn't believe in God." What followed were more beatings from fellow students.[78]

Because none of the neighbors would let their children play with him, young Al spent a lot of time alone, listening to music, collecting stamps, and reading.[79] "I would just go berserk because I had nothing to do," he told the *New York Teacher*.[80] He started building hi-fi equipment from sets and spent a lot of time listening to the radio.[81]

For much of Shanker's childhood, then, there was nowhere to hide. There was fighting among family members inside the cramped apartment, Shanker recalled, "and once you got out, you got the hell beaten out of you."[82] Shanker used to sit by himself, staring into the East River, wondering "what we Jews had done to make everyone so mad at us."[83]

If Shanker's childhood suggested there was abiding unfairness in life— widespread poverty, persistent bigotry—his parents also taught him that certain institutions and ideas could help. One central institution was organized labor. Mamie Shanker had a dark view of human nature and believed employers would do whatever it took to maximize profits. She often talked to her children about how 150 workers were killed in the 1911 Triangle Shirtwaist Company fire because the owners, worried that the workers would steal the garments, locked the doors from the outside. When she first came to the United States as a garment worker, she worked very long hours, had no health benefits, and worked in unsafe conditions.[84] She joined Sidney Hillman's Amalgamated Clothing and Textile Workers Union (ACTWU) and was also a member of the International Ladies Garment Workers Union (ILGWU), headed by David Dubinsky.[85] The unions made a huge difference in her life, improving her wages and working hours (eventually down to thirty-five hours a week).[86] Growing up, "unions were just below God," Al Shanker said.[87]

So was labor's champion, Franklin Roosevelt.[88] When Al was eight, he marched in parades for FDR in the 1936 election.[89] In 1940, when FDR ran for a third term against Wendell Willkie, twelve-year-old Al "stood for hours on a subway platform one afternoon arguing with grownups who didn't intend to vote for F.D.R.," wrote reporter A. H. Raskin. "A ticket he had bought for the World's Fair lay forgotten in his pocket."[90]

Though they voted for Roosevelt, the Shankers were not Democrats. In the New York circles in which Shanker was raised and schooled in the 1930s and 1940s, the question was not whether one was a Democrat or a Republican, but whether one was a Socialist or a Communist.[91] Many Jewish immigrants had been Socialists in Russia, as part of the resistance to czarist rule.[92] The Yiddish language newspaper, the *Jewish Daily Forward*, had "workers of the world unite!" emblazoned on the masthead.[93] Most writers and intellectuals in New York City leaned toward the Communist Party.[94] At City College, the Communists outnumbered the anti-Stalinist left by about ten to one.[95]

Shanker was briefly pro-Soviet in high school, but while still a teenager, he read George Orwell's *Homage to Catalonia* and saw how Orwell, who had signed up to fight the fascists in the Spanish Civil War, became disillusioned with the Communists. Shanker later recalled: "Here was Orwell, this innocent leftist, who wants to fight the fascists, but the Communists will stop at nothing, including wiping out the non-Stalinist opposition, to make sure they alone emerge in control."[96] The Spanish Civil War was something that stayed with him for years, recalls his friend Mel Lubin, who said Shanker had six or seven books on the topic.[97] Al spent many hours debating his Communist cousin, Faye Godlin, and her husband, Al Godlin, who lived fifteen minutes away in Sunnyside, Queens.[98] One boyhood friend remembers Al leading his buddies to Union Square and Al standing on a soapbox, arguing with Communists.[99]

Another important value stressed in the Shanker household was education—education as a route out of poverty and as a way of reducing prejudice and discrimination. Despite the lack of family wealth, says Pearl, "it was always just assumed that we would go to college and be something."[100] Debate and disagreement were expected, she says. "We weren't encouraged to just nod and agree with our parents' political views or other views. We were encouraged to think about it and read about it."[101]

Much to the chagrin of his parents, however, Shanker's embrace of education and intellectual questioning ran headlong into their strongly held religious beliefs. Morris and Mamie were Orthodox Jews, and Shanker's grandmother Rachel was even more observant and always wore a wig to cover her head as a sign of respect.[102] The family did not ride the subway or light the stove on the Sabbath, except for the father, who worked on Saturdays.[103] Al attended religious school in advance of his bar mitzvah, and a friend from his class, Edward Flower, recalls that for about a year following his bar mitzvah, Al took religion very seriously. Each morning he would wear Tefillin, a leather box strapped around his arm and his forehead, and read the Jewish law.[104] He would even chastise his parents for not being orthodox enough.[105] Al briefly thought about becoming a rabbi.[106]

Over time, however, Al Shanker saw a tension between his parent's emphasis on orthodox religion and their emphasis on the intellect and education. When Al was about fifteen, he began reading the New Testament. He was excited by it, he later told his wife Eadie, and told his rabbi. The rabbi said it was blasphemy and threw Shanker's copy of the book out. "For Al," she said, "anyone who would do that with a book" was suspect. "If you couldn't read a book, there was something wrong."[107] Al began exploring other religions, going to other services, and challenging the family's religious beliefs. "My parents were very upset," Pearl says.[108] It was part of a general intellectual questioning, Pearl says, noting Al was particularly interested in humanistic and Unitarian services.[109]

In his youth, Shanker's formative experience was not his religious training but rather his time in the Boy Scouts—the one group that was less anti-Semitic in his experience. Troop 277 met in a community center in a housing project located under the Fifty-Ninth Street Bridge.[110] The group would go hiking and camping for the weekend, which was an enormous escape for Al.[111] In the summer, he would attend an inexpensive Boy Scout camp for eight weeks.[112] Flower was a member of the Boy Scouts (Al recruited him), as were his friends Vinnie Castanza, Nick La Giglia, and Bill Andrietti.[113]

Boy Scouting was good for Al, not only because it got him out of the house and the neighborhood, but because it helped him demonstrate competence to his peers—something he couldn't do in the normal arena for boys, sports. He had poor eyesight: he was practically blind in one eye and began wearing glasses at age six.[114] Because he grew up to his full height of six foot, four inches at age thirteen, he was awkward and a poor athlete, skinny and not particularly muscular. In the Boy Scouts, however, he could excel at earning merit badges—based purely on ability—and he earned everything to attain the rank of Eagle Scout except the merit badge for swimming.[115]

In December 1941, the bombing of Pearl Harbor meant that many of the adult men who normally led the Boy Scout troops went away in the service, so it fell to the older boys to take up the leadership and organizing roles.[116] At age thirteen, Shanker rallied members to demand camping trips; troop membership skyrocketed from seventeen to eighty-five.[117] Shanker drew up a petition saying the troop ought to drill less and hike more. It worked: "That was sort of my first successful politically rebellious experience," he said.[118]

The Scouts did include a fair number of tough kids from the projects who would not normally take orders from someone like Al, so he had to work his way into leadership positions artfully. Instead of being appointed patrol leader, he was made the troop scribe, but he expanded the role of that position, and when it came time for parents' night, it was Al who made the address to the adults.[119] Eventually, he became senior patrol leader and essentially ran the troop. Vincent Castanza recalls "the adult leaders would come to him for information regarding the Boy Scout program."[120] Shanker would lead trips of kids for hikes along the Palisades, starting with a subway ride to the George Washington Bridge and a bus trip across the Hudson. Adults rarely went along.[121] Shanker read all the Boy Scout manuals and books on leadership. Years later, Shanker would look back and say that it was in the Boy Scouts where "I learned my leadership skills."[122]

The coming of World War II created a number of other responsibilities for Al. Mamie Shanker was an air-raid warden and Al was assigned to be a bike messenger when air-raid warnings came. He would go around during alerts and make sure people's lights were out and the window shades were drawn.[123] During the war, Al took on other jobs. In 1945, Shanker got an after-school job filing court papers for lawyers with a company called the United Lawyer Service. The position paid roughly six dollars a week, but one day, his friend Ed Flower recalls, Al decided the pay was insufficient, and he organized the twenty or so high-school students, who told their bosses they would not make their deliveries that day unless they got a dollar raise. Shanker knew he had the upper hand, Flower recalls, because there were not many adult men around to do the job. Management capitulated and the boys got their dollar raise. "That was Al Shanker's first successful strike," Flower says.[124]

Having gained confidence in his role as a Boy Scout leader and informal union activist, Shanker became a leader among a small group of friends. In the 1940s, immigrant boys tended be given great freedom by their parents, and Shanker made the most of it, said Flower. "We used to roam all over Manhattan and it was like a giant playground."[125] Flower recalls that Al would lead him and others to visit stamp shops for their collection, go to Central Park, the Museum of Modern Art (where they could also see old movies), the American Museum of Natural History, the Metropolitan Museum of Art, or inexpensive theaters.[126]

A favorite destination was the newsstands. Shanker would read six or eight papers a day. Years later, he recalled, "As a kid I'd walk over the Queensboro Bridge to the newsstands outside the library on Forty-Second Street. I discovered *The Partisan Review* when I was fifteen. My subscription to *Commentary* goes back to 1948."[127] Al also loved to buy books. As soon as he and Flower were paid by the United Lawyers, they would spend their entire paychecks mostly on books such as the Modern Library series.[128] Vincent Castanza, an Italian kid who grew up in the projects, remembers being struck visiting Al's apartment: "I would see books all over the place."[129] His reading often centered on politics, Communism, and labor unions. At age fifteen, he began reading the Socialist philosopher Sidney Hook, and in high school, Al read Irving Stone's 1943 book *Clarence Darrow for the Defense* and fell in love with the idea of defending labor leaders.[130]

While in junior high school, Shanker took a test to try to qualify for one of New York's elite public high schools. Although he had struggled in his very early years, over time he began to excel academically and was accepted to the competitive Stuyvesant High School.[131] Shanker enjoyed Stuyvesant, which drew bright students from across New York City.[132] At the school, which was heavily left-wing and working class, he graduated 160th out of a class of 635.[133]

Although not at the very top of his class, Shanker did excel in one extracurricular activity: debate. One former classmate remembers that in the predominantly Jewish high school, "Shanker got involved with the debating club and defended the Arabs. He'd win all the time."[134] The debate team also got Al in some trouble, though. Stuyvesant was all-male in those years, and some administrators thought it was improper for girls to enter the school. When Al invited a girls' team to compete in a debate tournament, he was punished by the school, which limited the number of colleges to which it would send his transcripts.[135]

University of Illinois

Shanker applied to Harvard College but he was rejected, to his great disappointment.[136] Instead, in 1946 he went off to the University of Illinois
at Urbana-Champaign.[137] While some of his friends went to City College,
which was excellent, Shanker's main objective, his friend Ed Flower said,
was "to get away from home."[138]

On Labor Day weekend in 1946, Shanker boarded a Greyhound bus to
Champaign-Urbana. At the first stop, Wheeling, West Virginia, he got off
to go to the bathroom and someone took his seat, so he had to stand all
the way to Indianapolis. Champaign-Urbana was booming, with a flood
of World War II veterans going to college on the GI Bill.[139]

A land-grant college founded in 1867, the University of Illinois was sit-
uated in the middle of the state, 140 miles south of Chicago.[140] Because of
the influx of veterans, when Shanker arrived there was a substantial housing shortage. At the University's housing bureau, many postings said
"White Anglo Saxon Protestants Only" or "No Jews or Negroes Wanted."
Shanker recalls going to places where a room was advertised as available,
being one of three people to show up, and having the landlady say, "well,
there is only one fair way of doing this. Are any of you Jewish?"[141] Shanker
eventually got a room at a farmhouse eight miles out of town, and the
first night a kid from Chicago told him, "well, it's too bad they didn't let
Hitler finish the job."[142] To avoid his roommate, Shanker spent most of
his time in the library.[143]

Shanker began college majoring in history and went so far as to write
an undergraduate history thesis on the Spanish Civil War. But in the summer of 1948, he took philosophy courses at the University of Minnesota,
and when he returned, he switched to philosophy as his major.[144] Shanker
began reading Hegel, Marx, Santayana, and Dewey. He read Dewey so
thoroughly he could cite the page number on which a given sentence was
written.[145] During that time, Shanker became particularly interested in a
philosopher named Elijah Jordan, who taught at Butler University in Indianapolis and wrote about corporate behavior. A fellow student at the
University of Illinois recalls driving with Shanker one spring to Indiana
to meet with Jordan and talk with him.[146] Shanker's high-school year-
book identified "lawyer" as his intended occupation, but that changed in
college when he began to read some law books and became bored.[147] He
began instead to consider pursuing a PhD in philosophy.

Shanker was an uneven student. He received A's in the Economic History of the United States, Contemporary European History, Contemporary Political Theory, Contemporary Sociology, and the like. In other courses he did terribly, especially languages and physical education. He earned D's in Modern Spanish, Elementary French, and Beginning German, as well as Beginning Swimming, Elementary Hygiene and Sanitation, and Prescribed Exercises.[148] Shanker explained: "The courses I enjoyed I worked like hell and did all sorts of extra things and was a straight-A student. The courses I disliked I either flunked or was on the border of flunking."[149] For the most part, he did not make a particularly favorable impression on his professors.[150]

During his time at Illinois, Shanker became active in the local civil-rights movement, and in 1947 he became a charter member of the Congress of Racial Equality (CORE).[151] He recalled that in Urbana-Champaign, "Blacks could not sit in the orchestra sections of the theaters, and no restaurant that served whites would serve blacks."[152] He engaged in sit-ins led by the local Unitarian Church to integrate the theaters and restaurants.[153] Although the nation was beginning to stir on the civil-rights issue—in 1948, Minneapolis Mayor Hubert Humphrey made his name calling for human rights at the Democratic National Convention—*Plessy vs. Ferguson*'s declaration of "separate but equal" was still the law of the land.[154] Shanker, who knew the sting of discrimination himself, believed segregation was wrong and also undemocratic—reminiscent of the totalitarian Nazi ideology the United States had been fighting.

In college, Shanker also chaired the Socialist Study Club and was a member of the Young People's Socialist League (YPSL).[155] During the 1948 presidential campaign, Shanker greeted and chauffeured Socialist candidate Norman Thomas around campus.[156] A master organizer, Shanker raised the attendance at Socialist rallies from fifteen to five hundred and garnered a larger crowd for Thomas at the University of Illinois in 1948 than for either Democratic incumbent Harry Truman or Republican candidate Thomas Dewey.[157]

The late 1940s was not an easy time to be a Socialist. The investigation of the House Un-American Activities Committee (HUAC) began in 1947, with Hollywood the first target.[158] In 1948, worried about radicalism on campuses, the Illinois state legislature passed the Clabaugh Act, prohibiting "subversive" speakers from appearing on campus.[159] Shanker had to give elaborate justifications for the various speakers he invited and went out of his way to point out the differences between Socialism and Communism. In an October 1948 letter to the Dean of Men, Shanker noted that the speakers he wanted to invite, such as Jerzy Glicksman, who had written about the Soviet gulag, and journalist Dwight Macdonald, were invited in order to make an "attack upon Communists and Wallacites. The reasons are obvious: Socialism can get nowhere until this confusion is cleared up."[160] Glicksman was approved but Macdonald was not.[161]

While a supporter of Socialism, Shanker also grew frustrated with the party's lack of action and pragmatism. In a paper he wrote for a Contemporary Political Theory class in May 1948, on "Symbolism, Mathematical Exponents, and Socialism," he wrote:

> Socialists still spend much of their time discussing the problem of the state, revolution versus evolution, etc. ad infinitum, ad absurdum, ad nauseam! This is unfortunate, for it is important that the one group which asserts the cooperative nature of man and desires to attain cooperative commonwealth cease discussing metaphysical questions which can never be solved and begin to work on an immediate program toward their end.[162]

Shanker's Socialism led him to embrace pacifism.[163] It also led him to question the establishment of the state of Israel in 1948. He was an anti-Zionist as a youth because his Socialist philosophy saw the establishment of the state of Israel as an example of nationalism.[164] Shanker initially did not want a homeland for Jews to be located in Israel, because he was concerned about what would happen to the Arabs. (Shanker later became a strong supporter of Israel given the realities of anti-Semitism and Israel's commitment to democracy in a region filled with authoritarian regimes.)[165]

In Socialist politics at the University of Illinois, Shanker also found romance. He had not dated much in high school, in part because Stuyvesant was all-male and the opportunities were limited and in part because many women found him physically unattractive.[166] But at Illinois, Al met and began to date a pretty co-ed involved in radical politics named Pearl Sabath. A year ahead of him (and almost two years older), Sabath was the daughter of Jewish immigrants who lived in Rock Island, Illinois, 150 miles west of Chicago.[167] Her father was a small businessman who sold fruits and vegetables wholesale to grocery stores; her mother was a secretary. Many men were attracted to her, and she was said to look like Rita

Hayworth.[168] If Pearl was beautiful, she was also very odd and extremely shy. Relatives described her as "a distant person," a "loner," "icy," and "very suspicious."[169]

Still, the two had a lot in common: they were both tall, they were both Jewish, they both had immigrant parents, and they were both attracted to radical politics.[170] They both also enjoyed certain cultural interests—museums, classical music, and photography.[171] And on a campus where men outnumbered women by three to one, Shanker was considered fortunate to have a female companion.[172] She was, says a friend, Shanker's first girlfriend.[173]

Shanker finished his studies at Illinois in August 1949, graduating after just three years.[174] The couple moved to New York City, and in November, Shanker and Pearl Sabath married. Shanker was just twenty-one years old.[175] They had a small religious wedding in the Shanker's synagogue in Long Island City.[176] Pearl became a teacher in the New York City public-school system, and Al signed up to pursue a PhD in philosophy at Columbia University.[177]

Columbia University Graduate School

The late 1940s and early 1950s was an exciting time to be a philosophy student at Columbia. Most of the students were Socialists and very bright. The atmosphere was intense. Columbia specialized in applied philosophy rather than analytic philosophy—philosophy had to be relevant to the events of the day—and the department was dominated by disciples of John Dewey, who had taught at Columbia for three decades until he fully retired in 1939. Because of Dewey's influence, many of the professors were pragmatists and many had a strong interest in education.[178] Some, such as John Herman Randall Jr. and Charles Frankel, were world-famous Deweyites.[179]

Shanker continued to read Dewey and heavily underlined his books, which argued, among other things, that education and democracy were inseparable: real education required democracy and freedom of thought, and true democracy required an educated populace.[180] Shanker also read theologian Reinhold Niebuhr's work; his copy of *Man and Destiny* is heavily annotated. A Socialist and unionist, Niebuhr was fiercely anti-Communist and had a dark view of human nature, which resonated with Shanker's own life experience.

At Columbia, Shanker remained active in Socialist politics and was a member of the local chapter of the Student League for Industrial Democracy (SLID).[181] The League had been founded in 1905 by Jack London, Sinclair Lewis, and other Socialists with the goal of extending "democracy to every aspect of our society." Its leading members included Dewey, Niebuhr, Sidney Hillman, and Walter Reuther.[182] As a graduate student, Shanker and other SLID members picketed the Palisades (NJ) Amusement Park, which was segregated.[183]

In 1950, while Shanker was at Columbia, the Korean War broke out. As a pacifist, Shanker did not want to serve, though his physical health prevented him from being drafted anyway.[184] Shanker had very bad eyesight and asthma, and according to one friend, just to make sure he wasn't drafted, he caused himself to have an allergic reaction and came in gasping for breath, and the recruiters told him to "get out of here."[185]

If a pacifist, he was also strongly anti-Communist. At Columbia, Shanker attended a debate between philosopher Sidney Hook, a protégé of Dewey's, and historian Henry Steele Commager, on whether or not Communists should be able to teach in the public-school system. Commager made a classic civil-liberties argument in favor of allowing Communists to teach, while Hook argued that because teachers who were members of the Communist Party were under strict party discipline to indoctrinate students, they were not fit to teach. "Hook wiped the floor with Commager," Shanker said. "These are not independent minds. These people are not looking for answers."[186]

After completing his coursework, Shanker began his dissertation on the twentieth-century American social philosopher Elijah Jordan. Shanker was intrigued by Jordan's thesis "that an individual's private feelings and intentions had no ethical significance." Said Shanker: "Jordan believed that philosophical terms gained meaning only in an institutional setting. It isn't important what I think or how I feel. Building an institution— that's important."[187]

Shanker assembled hundreds of notecards but had great trouble writing his thesis, which was tentatively entitled "Nature and Culture in Contemporary Philosophy."[188] He recalled, "I just seemed to be incapable of writing a dissertation. Every time I sat down to write one or two pages, I realized I hadn't read eight or twelve books that I needed to read."[189]

Shanker was also under intense financial pressure to finish. Funds were tight for the young married couple, and to save money, they shared apartments with other people. Relatives of Pearl would mock Al as a "professional student."[190] He had not earned a dime since the two had married three years earlier.[191] A professor from the University of Illinois suggested that Shanker teach high school for a year or two to earn money before returning to graduate school.[192] Shanker later recalled, "I ran out of money and patience," and at the age of twenty-four, he decided to try teaching on a "temporary" basis.[193]

In 1952, as he prepared to enter the adult work world for the first time in his life, Albert Shanker had learned certain things. He knew the reality of discrimination and the need to stamp it out. He understood the value of public schools as a way of providing a path out of poverty for kids who worked hard and had talent. He knew the importance of labor unions and government in defending the interests of workers. He hadn't figured everything out. He was still trying to grapple with his Socialist idealism and pacifism and his awareness of the dark side of human nature. But that would be resolved in time. And one more thing: he knew, from Boy Scouts, from the debate team, and from the Socialist Club, that he could be a leader and that people would follow him on the strength of his ideas. He left Columbia as engaged with books and ideas as ever, but also with a desire to translate thought into action.

2

Creating the United Federation of Teachers

1952–1962

T EACHING in the New York City public schools was a step back
for Shanker's career, but it set him on a path that over the next
ten years would help him change the teaching profession forever.
The poor pay and humiliation that he and other teachers faced would
lead them to risk their jobs and strike for the right to bargain collectively
in New York City, and their example would have an extraordinary influence on teachers in other parts of the country. Of course, as he began,
Shanker was mostly concerned about earning a living and knew nothing
of what was in store for him.

Teaching

Halfway through the 1952–1953 school year, Shanker took a job as a substitute math teacher in a tough East Harlem elementary school, PS 179.[1]
Shanker chose PS 179 because it had an opening and the school was not
too far from Columbia University.[2] But if the facility was geographically
close to Columbia, it was worlds away from the rarified atmosphere of an
Ivy League PhD program. "I had great doubts that I would make it," he
later wrote. "The three teachers who had preceded me that year with my

sixth-grade class had not."[3] He later admitted, "I didn't know what I was doing in the classroom."[4]

The kids in PS 179 were tough. Most were just off the plane from Puerto Rico and had difficulties with English.[5] And most were poor or working-class students, just like those in Shanker's own elementary school. Early on, Shanker was assaulted by a student, but when he asked for help from the principal he was told, "This would not have happened if you had motivated your students."[6] Shanker recalls, "One of the driving forces to going to college was to get out of that sort of violent life and be in a different kind of neighborhood and be with a different kind of people. And here I was, gone to college, very close to a Ph.D., and there I was locking myself into a room with kids who were exactly the kids I was trying to run away from."[7]

Shanker did not get much help from the adults in the school. After a week and a half of teaching, the assistant principal showed up at the door. The class was chaotic, with kids throwing things, and Shanker was thrilled that perhaps he would finally get some help. Instead, the administrator pointed and said, "Mr. Shanker, it's very unprofessional to have paper on the floor. Have that cleaned up right away. The district superintendent is coming through for an inspection."[8] The reprimand was a humiliation that Shanker never forgot.

The first week, Shanker had also been ordered by the principal to spend his lunch hour at the A&P supermarket across the street, standing near the candy because there were complaints of shoplifting.[9] A few months later, after a winter snowfall, teachers were told they should spend their lunch hour supervising the kids, to prevent snowball fights. When a faculty member asked whether everyone was needed, the supervisor said it was "unprofessional" to raise such a question.[10] It was galling, Shanker said, because adults who are with children all day need a break periodically.[11] For female teachers, there was the indignity of having to report when they became pregnant, and leave the classroom.[12] Shanker was paid $2,600 a year.[13] "There were thousands of teachers moving in and out because it was such a lousy job," Shanker recalls.[14]

In September 1953, Shanker moved to JHS 126 in Queens, also known as Astoria Junior High School.[15] He taught classes in English and social studies as well as math.[16] At JHS 126, the treatment from administrators was no better. The school building encircled a courtyard, so it was possible to look from rooms on one side of the courtyard into classrooms on the other side. The assistant principal, Abe Greenberg, took full advan-

tage of this architectural feature and would routinely spy, with binocu-
lars, on teachers across the courtyard. He obviously could not tell at that
distance whether the children were learning or how creative the teacher
was, but he could tell whether the room was messy, which is what
counted.[17] While Shanker received high marks from the principal and
from parents, he got low marks from assistant principal Greenberg.[18]
Other teachers in the school had the same experience; one remembers
Greenberg berating him publicly, in front of his students.[19]

Administrators were in a position to play favorites, Shanker said, assigning some teachers to "administrative assignments" and others to "the
most violent classes." Shanker enjoyed teaching gifted students until the
principal stuck him with the bottom classes.[20] The message from administrators was: "Be good. Be obedient. Keep your mouth shut. Don't rock
the boat. Don't do anything against the administration. Behave."[21]

Faculty meetings were held the first Monday of each month, and the
principal would typically run through a five-to-seven-page list of complaints about housekeeping items. As the meetings routinely dragged on
for three hours or more, Shanker recalled, "the teachers sat there seething.
Never, in all those hours, did we talk about anything that had anything to
do with any professional matter."[22]

Principals also had the power to approve or disapprove of transfer requests. Shanker recalled: "If you had criticized your principal once, he
might decide to punish you by never letting you transfer." Or a receiving
principal, who also had to approve the transfer, might say to a teacher,
"there are forty-five people who want this job. If you'll agree to stay every
afternoon and edit the student newspaper without compensation, you've
got it." Teachers were open to exploitation.[23]

Two things struck him, Shanker said: the "absolute power of the principal," who could play favorites and punish dissidents, and the low pay.[24]
It was said that teachers could be paid more washing cars ($72.35 a week)
than educating students (an average of $66 a week).[25]

The Teachers Guild

Soon after he began teaching at JHS 126 in September 1953, Shanker started
having lunch with another young social-studies teacher there named
George Altomare. Altomare's mother was a coworker with Shanker's
mother at J&J Clothing, where both were seamstresses and strong sup-

porters of the Amalgamated Clothing Workers Union. The two sons began discussing the working conditions under Greenberg, and they were soon joined by a third coworker, Dan Sanders, who complained about the same indignities. Looking back, Altomare says, they decided they wanted to join a union in part to get better wages, but primarily to have more dignity.[26]

At the time in New York City, there were 106 teachers' organizations from which to choose. But for Shanker, the choice was easy, since only one of them, the New York Teachers Guild, was a real union that favored collective bargaining—negotiating for higher wages and better working conditions as a united group.[27] The New York Teachers Guild was part of the American Federation of Teachers, founded in 1916, as an alternative to the much larger and older National Education Association. The NEA, founded in 1857, considered itself a professional educational organization and opposed collective bargaining. The institution was dominated by administrators, and the NEA structure had divisions of elementary-school principals, secondary-school principals, and school administrators. Although teachers constituted more than 90 percent of NEA members, more than 90 percent of the leadership and staff positions in the NEA were held by school administrators.[28] Hardly militant, the NEA was known as a "tea and crumpets" organization.[29] It also lacked a meaningful affiliate in New York City.[30]

John Dewey, the "intellectual guru" of the AFT and holder of card no. 1 in the New York City local, had a very different vision than the NEA, symbolized by the AFT's founding motto, "Education for Democracy, and Democracy in Education."[31] In 1916, Dewey did not yet envision collective bargaining for teachers. Rather, a union was needed in part to protect teachers from political meddling and preserve their independence of thought.[32] But the AFT wanted to be part of the labor movement, and shortly after its founding, it applied for and was provided with a charter from the American Federation of Labor.[33]

Shanker was also attracted to the larger social vision of the Guild and the AFT, which held that the organizations should be concerned about more than narrowly defined teacher interests and should embrace causes like civil rights.[34] In 1951, the AFT Executive Council had voted not to charter any more segregated locals, and the next year, the AFT filed an *amicus* brief supporting the plaintiffs in *Brown v. Board of Education*, the only educational group to do so. Put simply, the brief argued that segregation was undemocratic.[35] The New York Guild also filed an *amicus* brief in *Brown*.[36] By contrast, the NEA was not particularly progressive on racial issues. The NEA did not take a position in support of *Brown* until 1961—seven years after the decision was handed down.[37] And the NEA did not fully desegregate its locals until the late 1960s.[38]

As a former Columbia PhD student, Shanker was also attracted to the AFT's proud intellectual heritage. In addition to Dewey, among the other leading academics who joined the AFT were Howard University's Ralph J. Bunche, Union Theological Seminary's Reinhold Niebuhr, and political scientist Hubert Humphrey.[39] The AFT also had been led by the great Columbia University educational sociologist George Counts.[40]

Finally, Shanker was very attracted to the Guild's strong anti-Communist stance. If most Americans disliked Communism in an abstract sense, the Guild's Socialist members had first-hand experience battling Communists in New York City's Teachers Union (TU).[41] The TU, which had the AFT's original charter in New York, became a prime target for Communist infiltration in the United States. Of all sectors of life, labor unions represented an attractive means for gaining control in democratic societies. They were sympathetic to the egalitarian argument of the Communist Party and were in a good position to disrupt society.[42] While the Communists did not have much influence in the United States generally, they did make substantial inroads into American unions.[43] Moreover, teachers' unions were particularly attractive to Communists because teachers were in a position to help shape young minds and to recruit young members.

And, of all the teachers' unions in the country, New York City's represented the most fertile territory. New York City had the highest concentration of American Communists in the country—between one-third and one-half of all American Communist Party members lived in the city. New York City also had the largest bloc of unionized teachers in the nation.[44] By 1935, the Communists gained control of the Teachers Union, the AFT's largest local. It was a great victory for the Communists and represented its greatest inroad into American education.[45]

The takeover of the TU by the Communists infuriated democratic Socialists like Dewey, Counts, and Niebuhr, and in 1935, the Guild formed as an anti-Communist breakaway organization from the Teachers Union.[46] For several years, the Guild battled the Teachers Union for recognition from the AFT until 1939, when Counts won the presidency of the AFT, running on a platform that stated he would expel Communist locals from the AFT.[47] In 1940, the AFT voted 11,256 to 8,499 to expel the TU, and in 1941, the Guild received the AFT's charter.[48] The AFT constitution, which barred discrimination based on race, color, creed, or political views, was changed to add a clause: "except that no applicant whose actions are subject to totalitarian control such as Fascist, Nazi or Communist shall be admitted to membership."[49]

In sum, the Guild represented all the values Shanker treasured—it was a Socialist union, in favor of civil rights, anti-totalitarian, anti-Communist, and intellectually rigorous.

Within months of beginning teaching, Shanker and Altomare decided to join the Guild.[50] Shanker, Altomare, and Sanders, along with a couple of others, started a chapter of the Guild at JHS 126 and began having parties Friday evening at Shanker's one-bedroom apartment nearby. Altomare would play his guitar and Shanker would make whiskey sours.[51] Said Altomare: "we wanted people to join for the right reasons. But we wouldn't refuse them if they felt left out of the whiskey sour parties."[52] Within a semester, a majority of the school teachers at JHS 126 signed up with the Guild, and soon after almost the entire faculty did. The group, says Altomare, infused new blood into the citywide Guild.[53]

When Shanker joined, the Guild represented only about 2,500 of New York City's fifty thousand teachers.[54] When Shanker, Altomare, and Sanders went to the first Delegate Assembly meeting, they were not impressed. The meeting was held in the small Guild offices on 2 East Twenty-third Street, in a room that barely fit fifty people.[55] The annual budget for the Guild was just $35,000.[56] The office literally had rats in it.[57]

The president of the Guild was Charles Cogen, a diminutive high-school social-studies teacher and active Socialist, who had just been elected in 1952.[58] He had a law degree from Fordham University, an MA in labor economics from Columbia, had practiced as an attorney in the early years of the Depression, and had completed all the course requirements for a PhD in economics at Columbia.[59] Other key figures included Simon Beagle, who ran the Guild newspaper, and Jules Kolodny, a lawyer who turned to teaching during the Depression.[60]

There was one paid staff member from the national AFT, Dave Selden, a blond-haired Midwesterner who was fourteen years older than Shanker. Selden started organizing for the AFT in 1949 and came to New York City to organize in a concerted fashion in 1953, about six months before Shanker joined.[61] A Socialist, Selden immediately took Shanker, Altomare, and Sanders under his wing.[62] Shanker soon became involved in the Guild's newspaper, writing articles and eventually becoming editor.[63] The paper was delivered in unmarked brown envelopes because the government was very suspicious of leftist unions.[64]

Shanker became increasingly active in the Guild, and by the mid-1950s was elected to the Executive Board.[65] The Guild leaders would sometimes have dinner at Simon Beagle's house, and Beagle's son, Daniel, recalls that for the older generation of Guild leaders Shanker "was a God saver . . . because they were all a little burned out."[66] The group would debate civil rights, the fight against Communism, and the future of the Guild.

The mid-1950s was an exciting time for the civil-rights movement, with the 1954 *Brown* decision, Rosa Parks and the 1955 Montgomery bus boycott, and the September 1957 desegregation of Little Rock Central High School.[67] There was some debate among Socialists over whether to embrace the civil-rights movement. Some worried that the focus on race would distract from the larger class-based goal of creating a Socialist society, while others argued that the rise of the civil-rights movement could help shift the Democratic Party in a more progressive direction and break the power of the conservative southern Democrats, who were both anti-black and anti-labor. With the help of newly enfranchised blacks, the theory went, the Democratic party could become a truly progressive, pro-labor, pro-black force.[68]

Shanker and the Guild saw labor and civil-rights organizations as natural partners. Both movements were about dignity for the individual, democracy, and the right to vote. Both faced enormous obstacles in the South. Both were animated by a vision of brotherhood. (Union members and blacks both took to addressing one another as "brother.") Both employed civil disobedience against unjust laws.

In 1955, the Guild took the lead in getting the AFT to tell its large union in Atlanta it must integrate or be expelled from the organization. Atlanta left, and over time, the AFT lost about seven thousand of its fifty thousand members.[69] In 1957, the Guild gave Thurgood Marshall, then a highly controversial lawyer for his role in arguing for desegregation in *Brown*, its prestigious John Dewey Award.[70]

The Guild also debated how far it could push its strong anti-Communist stance without crossing over into McCarthyism. The Socialists in the Guild hated Communists with a passion, and for reasons different from the average anti-Communist American. The Socialists didn't oppose Communism because they were against the Communist aspiration of equality or because Communists wanted free and universal health care, but because Communists had taken the idea of democracy—which Socialists wanted to take a step further, from politics into the economy—and inverted it, destroying political democracy and ruling by violence.[71]

Shanker was outraged at Communist abuses and would pass copies of books focusing on the totalitarian nature of Communism—*The God That Failed* and *Darkness at Noon*—to Altomare between classes.[72] The Socialists also hated Communists because of what Communists did to unions, shutting them down as soon as they took over a country, even as Communists falsely claimed to represent the very people labor represented: the working class.[73]

But there was something else to the hatred. The passion against Joseph Stalin and other Communists among the Guild members was not rooted just in a contempt for totalitarianism, but also in a sense that the Communists had taken something really wonderful—a serious vision for an egalitarian society—and, by twisting it, had forever discredited not only Communism but Socialism as well.[74] As one Socialist put it, "The Stalinist movement destroyed the possibility of building a broad-based left movement in this country, and we pay the price for that every day."[75]

For all these reasons, the Guild voted in 1954 to endorse the practice under New York's Feinberg Law of barring members of the Communist Party from teaching.[76] The Guild followed the view of Norman Thomas that Fascists and Communists should not be able to teach "the children of a democracy."[77]

But the Guild drew the line at what it considered McCarthyism. In March 1955, when the School Board decided to go after those who had left the Communist Party but refused to identify coworkers who had been members, the Guild opposed the move.[78] Ultimately, the courts upheld the right of teachers not to inform on other teachers.[79] Shanker had two reasons to oppose McCarthyism. McCarthyism was "horrible," said Shanker, because teachers were afraid to bring controversial subjects up in class. It also set back anti-Communism among liberals, giving it a bad name.[80]

The Guild members saw the two great issues of the day—anti-Communism and civil rights—as the two sides of the same coin. While the abuses of McCarthy, coupled in later years with the Vietnam War, would discredit anti-Communism among many liberals, the pro–civil rights, anti-Communist positions went together in Shanker's mind, because both embraced human rights.

During these years on the Guild board, Shanker continued to teach at JHS 126, and during the summers he joined other Guild members—such as Altomare—as a counselor at Camp Hillcroft in Billings, New York, near Poughkeepsie. A small camp for about two hundred kids, Hillcroft was founded by an idealistic Austrian Socialist refugee from Hitler named Louis Buttinger.[81] Altomare recalls that the camp had a Socialist feel. It brought together wealthy children and scholarship kids, and everyone would sing folk songs and labor songs around the campfire. "It was a very idealistic period of time every summer," Altomare recalls.[82]

By 1956, Shanker was spending the eight-week summer at Hillcroft without Pearl, his wife—not a good omen for their marriage.[83] Friends remember Pearl Sabath as eccentric and odd.[84] Her brother Gerald, a psychologist, said Pearl was never institutionalized nor was she mentally ill, but she exhibited "bizarre" and "very peculiar" behavior, including paranoia.[85] Shanker later told his daughter Jennie that Pearl was "unstable." When he began to talk about divorce, she stopped using birth control and became pregnant.[86] The pregnancy confirmed for Shanker that after eight years of marriage, he needed to end the relationship. In October 1957, Altomare gave Shanker money to go to Mexico where it was easier to get a divorce than in New York.[87] Shanker got the divorce and moved to the Morningside Garden apartments near Columbia University, where Dave Selden had an apartment.[88] On November 13, 1957, a baby boy was born.[89] He was named Carl Eugene, after Karl Marx and Eugene Debs, the labor organizer and five-time Socialist presidential candidate.[90] Pearl Sabath did not want her ex-husband to see Carl much and limited visitation.[91]

At the age of twenty-nine, Shanker had hit a low point. His academic career in philosophy was in shambles. His personal life was a disaster. And although he enjoyed the intellectual stimulation of the Guild—the debates over civil rights and Communism—the truth was that it was essentially a Socialist club without any real power: in particular, no power to bargain collectively like a regular union. Shanker and the younger members of the Guild were unsatisfied with this approach, but they were not able to make much headway with the older, more conservative leaders, such as Cogen, who had reservations about Shanker and thought he was moving too aggressively.[92] In the late 1950s, all of this was about to change.

Taking Action

In the forty years since the founding of the AFT, there had been three major obstacles that made collective bargaining for teachers almost unthinkable. The biggest barrier was that public-school teachers, as public employees, were thought by virtually all parties to be outside the ambit of collective bargaining. Indeed, in most states, public employees' strikes were illegal. The founding AFL president, Samuel Gompers, strongly opposed strikes by public employees.[93] Responding to striking police officers in Boston in 1919, Calvin Coolidge, then governor of Massachusetts, famously declared, "There is no right to strike against public safety by anybody, anywhere, at any time."[94] Although teachers pushed to be included in the landmark 1935 National Labor Relations Act, the legislation limited collective-bargaining rights to the private sector, and labor's champion, Franklin D. Roosevelt, opposed strikes by public employees.[95] Because teachers did not have laws protecting the right to organize, they were open to retaliation from management for trying to organize a union. Teachers faced termination by school boards merely for joining a union in Chicago, Cleveland, Seattle, and elsewhere.[96]

A second barrier came from within the profession: most teachers were college graduates who considered unions to be for blue-collar workers of lesser educational attainment. Teachers told union organizers: "My mom and dad are union members. That's why they had enough money for me to go to college. But . . . what kind of professional joins a union?"[97]

Third, there was infighting within the teaching profession, which prevented the solidarity required for collective bargaining. In particular, elementary-school teachers, who were largely female and less well paid, wanted a single salary schedule for all teachers, while secondary-school teachers, who were more likely to be male and to be paid more highly, wanted a large differential in salary based on level of teaching.[98] Administrators often exploited these differences to prevent cooperation.[99] In some places, including New York City, teachers also divided along lines of race, ethnicity, and religion; thus New York City's 106 different teacher organizations.[100] Because of the disunity, each was powerless.

As a result of these three impediments, not much happened in Shanker's first several years with the Guild. The Executive Board, made up of brilliant old-timers, a number of them with doctorates, held intellectually stimulating meetings but did not accomplish much.[101] In the late 1950s, however, the winds of change were in the air.

One break came when the IRT and BMT, the New York subway lines, went bankrupt, and the city took them over—and with them, their unions. Said Shanker, "All of a sudden, you had government involved in a collective bargaining relationship that it had not engaged in before."[102] Another break was a decision by Mayor Robert F. Wagner to recognize public-sector labor unions in New York City. On March 31, 1958, Wagner signed Executive Order 49, known as the Little Wagner Act, which gave one hundred thousand city employees the right to join a union. Under the order, the Uniformed Sanitation Workers became the first government employees (after the transit-system workers) to sign a collective-bargaining agreement with the city.[103] In 1959, Wisconsin passed the nation's first law for public-employee bargaining.[104] (Teachers in Wisconsin did not use the law until 1964).[105]

The civil-rights movement also changed the atmosphere in the late 1950s. Across the country, blacks were violating unjust laws through civil disobedience. The development helped make Shanker and others think— it may be illegal for teachers to strike, but perhaps the law could be violated for a good purpose.[106]

The argument for action received another strong boost in January 1959, when eight hundred night high-school teachers in New York City held a wildcat strike, demanding greater pay. The Teachers Guild faced the question of whether to support the strike. Several Guild members did not wish to support a rival organization's strike. But Shanker, Altomare, Selden, and others thought the high-school teachers were right on the merits, and with an eye on eventually winning over those teachers to the Guild, thought it would be good politics to be supportive as well. Shanker, who owned a red Volkswagen bus, drove it to the strike sites outside Jamaica High School and elsewhere and gave out coffee and held signs saying "Support the strike." The strike was a success, and pay was doubled from $12 to $24 a night.[107]

Finally, the AFL-CIO began to change its attitude about public-sector collective bargaining in the late 1950s and decided to invest money in the fledgling efforts of New York City teacher organizing. Walter Reuther of the United Auto Workers provided crucial funds to help Dave Selden hire a second organizer. In 1959, Shanker, who was recognized as a good public speaker, quit his job teaching and was hired full time to be Selden's second in command.[108] The two men became extremely close. They rode to work together every day and talked on the phone when they were apart.[109]

Organizing teachers into a real union that bargained collectively was Shanker and Selden's dream. It would transform teachers' organizations like the AFT and NEA from groups that engaged in "collective begging" into groups that would bargain with school boards as equals. In their vision, teachers would become equals in the house of labor as well. In the late 1950s, with the merger of the AFL and CIO in December 1955, labor was riding high.[110] Union membership was peaking, up dramatically from Shanker's childhood in the 1930s.[111] Labor was important. It represented one-third of the private sector. Labor negotiations made national headlines.[112] Newspaper reporters wanted the labor beat, which attracted star reporters like Daniel Bell of *Fortune*. Economists chose labor as their field of interest more than any other subfield.[113] Star academics, such as James Coleman and Seymour Martin Lipset, studied labor, as would rising legal stars such as Archibald Cox and, later, Derek Bok.[114] Book stores had labor sections. The speeches of labor leaders were carried on mainstream, broadcast radio.[115]

But first, before the Guild could take action, it needed to sign up more members. Shanker's strategy was to get his foot in the door, talking about teachers' pension issues.[116] The New York State pension law was new at that time, and not well understood by teachers. Shanker studied the law and became "a pension maven."[117] Teachers would come to hear Shanker explain its provisions for half an hour, and then he would give a three-minute commercial for the union. Shanker said, "I visited hundreds of schools that way."[118]

In the meetings, when teachers told Shanker that, as college-educated professionals, they didn't need a union, Shanker responded, quite to the contrary, that unionism and professionalism were not contradictory or competing values. Shanker would always ask: As a nonunionized "professional" teacher, does the principal ever mistreat you? Do you make enough money? It was precisely because teachers were not unionized that they were able to be treated unprofessionally. He told teachers: "A professional is an expert and, by virtue of his or her expertise, is relatively unsupervised. And you are constantly supervised and told what to do."[119]

When the issue of public-sector collective bargaining came up, Shanker acknowledged that in New York, under the 1947 Condon-Wadlin Act, strikes by public employees were illegal and those who engaged in illegal strikes could be fired.[120] But, he said, sometimes people need to engage in civil disobedience to promote important goals, citing the actions of the civil-rights movement.[121] Teachers, like blacks, said Shanker, had been "treated in a second class way," and were engaged in "an honorable struggle for a legitimate place."[122]

Al Shanker met and impressed a lot of people with his speeches, but none more important than a young English teacher who had just started at Shanker's JHS 126 the fall after Shanker had left. An energetic young woman, Edith Gerber, known as "Eadie," was a City College graduate who had just dropped out of an English-literature graduate program at Lehigh

University to teach.[123] In September 1959, she went to hear Shanker speak at the urging of her union chapter leader. There was a small group of only thirteen teachers from the entire city at the shabby Teachers Guild headquarters, but Shanker spoke as if to a full auditorium. Gerber asked, "Mr. Shanker, I don't know much about the union. How many members do you have?" He said about two thousand in New York (out of some fifty thousand teachers). Gerber responded, "And what is it that you plan to do with two thousand?" Shanker shot back: "It isn't just numbers that count! It's what you stand for." Gerber said she was impressed by his answer, and afterward, when he asked her out for coffee, she agreed.[124]

Gerber and Shanker turned out to have a great deal in common. They both had a passion for union organizing and Gerber quickly threw herself into the Guild's budding efforts. They also shared interests in square dancing, folk music, medieval music, museums, theater, and hiking. Shanker found Gerber, who was five years younger than he, very attractive. And Gerber enjoyed Shanker's company and his sense of humor. On a deeper level, they also shared the bond of lost childhoods. Born in Philadelphia, Gerber was just a year and a half old when her mother died. She was placed in an orphanage and then a foster home with her siblings. Her father, whom she remembers seeing only a few times in her life, died when she was seven. Gerber worked her way through City College (which was then free) by supporting herself as a waitress. She began working on a masters' thesis on Henry James but grew to dislike scholarly work and decided to teach. After two months of dating, Shanker told Gerber, "Eadie, you are a really special person," which she says was his way of expressing his love.[125]

Meanwhile, behind the scenes, Shanker, Altomare, and others sought to address the issue of teacher disunity that plagued teachers nationally and in New York City particularly. Competing with 105 teachers' groups citywide, the Guild had only managed to organize about 5 percent of New York City's teachers.[126] There was one organization, Shanker noted, for "each division, each religion, each race, and for each grievance."[127] The groups were divided, says journalist Dennis Gaffney—Queens versus the Bronx, high school versus elementary school, Catholic versus Jew, and even Orthodox Jew versus non-Orthodox Jew. Shanker used to joke about "Female Health Education Teachers of Bensonhurst." There was competition among teachers: would money go toward science beakers or English texts, Gaffney says.[128]

Altomare and Shanker sought to address the key issue of salary, which divided the city's teachers. For many years, high-school teachers received a higher salary than elementary-school teachers. But in New York City after World War II, with the beginning of the baby boom, there was a shortage of elementary-school teachers, so the city raised the elementary-school salary to the high-school level, eliminating the differential.[129] This move infuriated high-school teachers.[130]

Historically, the Teachers Guild had been opposed to a pay differential because of the Socialist idea of equality and because the Guild represented more elementary than high-school teachers.[131] But a small group within the Guild—including Shanker, Altomare, and Selden—began talks with leaders of the High School Teachers Association at Selden's and Shanker's apartments in Morningside Gardens to see if they could find a middle ground on the issue, which would allow the Guild and the High School Teachers Association to merge.[132]

The negotiators came up with a compromise: both high-school teachers and elementary-school teachers would receive the same base salary, but teachers with a master's degree (most of whom taught at the high-school level) would get more money. This way, the differential was based on education credits earned, not level taught, so some elementary-school teachers would get extra pay and some high-school teachers would not, but in the aggregate, high-school teachers would get more.[133]

When the Shanker-Altomare-Selden group told the leaders of the Guild about the possibility of merger, some members of the Executive Board, including Jules Kolodny and Rebecca Simonson, were furious about being left in the dark and moved to censure Altomare. Simonson also questioned the merger on the merits: we know where we stand on issues of civil rights and civil liberties and separation of church and state; where do they stand? Shanker responded that this was a chance to double the size of the union; that the union was a political organization, not a religion with set dogmas; and that it was easier to educate people to the Guild's philosophy once they were inside the organization. Shanker argued that if the Guild passed up this opportunity, there might never be unity or militancy or collective bargaining. The Guild board went along by a narrowly divided margin.[134] According to Guild member Abe Levine, "Al Shanker was the most persuasive in getting many of the people in the Guild to come around" on the merger.[135]

On March 16, 1960, the Delegate Assembly of the Guild approved the merger, and some of the rival high-school teachers, who formed the Committee for Action Through Unity, joined with the Guild to create the United Federation of Teachers.[136] The new UFT represented 4,500 teachers, more than double the size of the Guild, but still less than 10 percent of the total teacher population.[137]

The newly organized UFT came up with a list of demands for the Board of Education, including collective bargaining and a single salary schedule with pay differentials for extra teacher education. The group threatened to strike on May 16, 1960, if their demands were not met.[138] On May 15, Mayor Wagner and Superintendent John J. Theobold agreed with the UFT to call a collective-bargaining election if it were requested by 30 percent of the teaching staff.[139] It was a stunning victory, made possible in part by Mayor Wagner's political roots. (His father, Senator Robert Wagner, was the key force behind labor's Magna Carta—the 1935 National Labor Relations Act, known as the Wagner Act.) Said Shanker, he "couldn't do things that would violate the spirit of what his father did in labor relations."[140]

The 1960 Strike

Over the summer and early fall, however, the mayor backed off from promises of a collective-bargaining agreement. An opinion of the Corporation Counsel disputed the legality of holding a bargaining vote.[141] So the UFT considered whether to go on strike. Within the UFT's Executive Board there was a split between the old-timers and the young Turks. Many of the older members of the UFT—Cogen, Beagle, Kolodny, and Simonson—were "radical in the Socialist-leftist terms but conservative in action," Altomare recalls. Many had twenty to forty years of teaching experience, and their pensions might be put in jeopardy if they engaged in an illegal strike.[142] Cogen and Kolodny were also trained as lawyers and cautioned others about the consequences of violating the law.[143] But Shanker, Altomare, and Selden pushed for militancy. When the older generation said, "we need to grow before we can act," the young Turks argued the opposite: "You have to act in order to grow."[144]

On October 19, 1960, the UFT voted 2,896 to 117 to set a strike deadline of November 7, 1960, the day before the Nixon-Kennedy presidential election. Henry Mayer, an attorney who was advising the UFT, said the Democrats would ensure that the strike was settled on favorable terms so as not to interrupt the election. Others said Democratic politicians who governed in New York wouldn't risk alienating voters by invoking

Condon-Wadlin on Election Day. Mayer said of John Kennedy's campaign manager, "Bobby Kennedy will be knocking on your door."[145]

With only about 10 percent of the teaching staff signed up, some feared the strike could be a disaster. The risks were considerable: The Condon-Wadlin Act provided that public employees who struck must—not may—be fired. If later restored to employment, employees could not receive a salary increase for at least three years. Superintendent Theobold and State Education Commissioner James Allen warned that teachers would jeopardize their right to teach anywhere in the entire state.[146]

The other teachers' organizations lined up against the strike in part because they did not want the UFT to succeed. The Communist-dominated Teachers Union, in particular, put out flyers saying the strike was not legitimate, and their members crossed the picket lines.[147] Meanwhile, AFL-CIO president George Meany and New York City Labor Council chief Harry Van Arsdale both opposed the teachers' strike because they worried it would be disruptive to the election. (Polling stations were often located in schools.)[148] Van Arsdale also worried that because the UFT represented such a small portion of the teachers, because competing teacher groups would actively cross the picket lines, and because teacher activists could be fired under Condon-Wadlin, the strike had a good chance of failing and the UFT could be crushed. If this happened, teacher unionism—and indeed public-employee unionism—might be severely set back.[149]

Teacher activists were prepared to lose their jobs. UFT member Vito DeLeonardis remembers that he was prepared to move to Alaska if fired.[150] As the Monday, November 7, strike date approached, Shanker, Selden, and Altomare were nervous. Because the UFT's offices on 2 East Twenty-third Street were locked on Sundays, the three plotted strategy from the Shanker and Selden apartments. Sunday night, the three barely slept.[151]

On November 7, reports came in that some five thousand teachers had not come into work. More than one hundred schools were closed.[152] Striking teachers were told over the television that they were fired, but the reality was that the board could not dismiss all five thousand teachers, so they were quickly reinstated.[153] It had been a huge gamble—teachers, some of them with lengthy service with the city—had put their jobs on the line for a leap into the unknown. "I think it was a political miracle," Shanker said. "There are very few instances in history where that kind of thing happens."[154]

George Meany called Wagner, reminded him that as the son of a great senator he should do the right thing, and urged him to set up a committee to study the issue of collective bargaining for teachers.[155] Wagner agreed to name a three-person committee of labor leaders to decide what to do—Van Arsdale of the Central Labor Council, Jacob Potofsky of the Amalgamated Clothing Workers Union, and David Dubinsky of the International Ladies' Garment Workers Union—a dead giveaway as to the expected result. Years later, Potofsky said, "The committee was not only fair but impartial," with a wide grin.[156] The UFT was fortunate to have a pro-labor mayor in Robert Wagner. Altomare says, "today, they would have smashed us," if only 10 percent had struck. "But it was a different era then, and so we got away with it."[157]

In January 1961, after due deliberation, the Van Arsdale committee recommended collective bargaining for teachers, some three decades after private-sector workers had received the right.[158] But there were a number of open questions. Should the bargaining units consist of elementary-school teachers, junior-high-school teachers, and high-school teachers, or should there be one unit for all teachers? Should there be separate bargaining units for the Bronx, Brooklyn, Queens, Staten Island, and Manhattan, or should there be a citywide group? The answers were not obvious.[159] The school board commissioned a group of experts, chaired by George W. Taylor of the University of Pennsylvania, to make recommendations about the bargaining unit. The UFT argued for a single bargaining unit and its view prevailed.[160] The decision in New York to establish a single bargaining unit for all teachers in all boroughs set a very important precedent nationally.[161]

As the drive for collective bargaining was advancing, so was Al Shanker's personal life. Eadie Gerber was active in the campaign and served as co-chair of the teachers' strike network in Queens. The two grew very close and in March 1961, they were married. The couple had little money and the wedding was small, with about thirty guests, mostly people from the union.[162] The couple's "honeymoon" consisted of going to a union workshop in Wisconsin with two fellow union members, Abe Levine and Sol Jaffe, riding in the back seat of the car.[163] Shanker could not take time off, for there were still several hurdles the UFT had to clear in order to gain collective bargaining for teachers.

In 1961, the board agreed to allow teachers to vote on whether they wished to bargain collectively. The NEA campaigned against the idea.[164] If the vote had gone the other way in New York, Shanker noted, it would have been a huge setback nationally, because if the "labor center of the world" rejected teacher unionism it would have set an important precedent.[165] Because only 10 percent of teachers had participated in the UFT's strike, Shanker and the other UFT teachers had to win over the majority, who had crossed the picket lines. But given the results of the earlier strike—no teachers had been fired, and now suddenly the board was paying attention to teachers—momentum was shifting toward collective bargaining. In the voting, which took place from June 19 to June 29, teachers voted 27,000 for collective bargaining, 7,000 against.[166]

Once the teachers had voted for collective bargaining, the UFT still had to win the right to be the collective-bargaining agent against any organization that could convince 10 percent of teachers to sign a petition.[167] The UFT had two main competitors: the Teacher Bargaining Organization (TBO), an affiliate of the NEA, and the old Teachers Union (TU), both of which opposed collective bargaining at first but now sought to represent teachers. The UFT, which occupied the sweet center between the Communist-dominated TU on the left and the administrator-dominated NEA on the right, won endorsements from labor stalwarts including Eleanor Roosevelt.[168]

The UFT committed its membership full force, and phone banks of volunteers combed through lists of teachers and called them. There were several debates scheduled between the UFT and the TU and TBO.[169] Shanker was the leading UFT debater. "Dave Selden was good," says Altomare, "but Al was, by far, the best debater of all of us."[170] Shanker pounded away at the fact that TU members had crossed the picket lines in the November 1960 strike. "That really did them in," says the UFT's Vito DeLeonardis.[171]

Nationally, the NEA membership stood at about ten times that of the AFT's.[172] And the NEA poured in between seventy-five and one hundred full-time organizers in the representation campaign.[173] In October 1961, in the middle of the campaign, Eadie Shanker gave birth to a baby boy, whom the couple named Adam. There was little time to pause, however, as Shanker worked around the clock, seven days a week, with other UFT members, writing literature and attending teacher meetings over breakfast, during the lunch hour, and after school.[174] Balloting was conducted by mail. In the December 1961 election, the UFT won 20,045 votes of 32,390 cast. The NEA won 9,770 votes, and the TU won 2,575 votes.[175]

It was a stunning transformation, Shanker said. A little more than one year earlier, 45,000 of the city's fifty thousand teachers had crossed the

UFT picket lines; now the UFT had the majority.[176] In one fell swoop, the AFT, with a national membership of fifty thousand, was selected to represent another fifty thousand teachers.[177]

On January 10, 1962, a delegation led by Cogen and including Shanker met with the Board of Education for the first time as equals.[178] But after a few months of negotiations, the Board balked at higher salaries, and on April 11, 1962, the union went on strike.[179] About 22,000 of the city's fifty thousand teachers stayed out, a huge increase from the five thousand who participated in the first strike in November 1960.[180] The strike was a success, and Governor Nelson Rockefeller and Mayor Wagner "miraculously" came up with $13 million. The penalties under Condon-Wadlin were once again held in abeyance.[181]

Winning a Contract

In June 1962, the union won its first contract, with a $995 pay increase in a single year. The total was equivalent to what teachers would normally receive over a four- or five-year period. It was the largest raise in New York City school history.[182] The contract also provided for a duties-free lunch period.[183]

More fundamentally, the contract forever changed the balance of power between teachers and principals, helping to democratize schools. The contract instituted, for the first time, a system of grievances handled under binding arbitration. Said Shanker: "Who ever heard of a government agency agreeing that some outside party is going to tell them that they are wrong and are going to have to comply."[184] More broadly, he says: "It took a whole huge patronage system, a political system which was subject to the powers and the whims of, essentially, one person within a school—the principal—and it brought it out into the open and created . . . a system of fairness and of law and of sharing rather than a system of hoarding and special rewards." The contract created, he said, "a very different world."[185]

In later years, Shanker often claimed the New York City teachers' contract was the first one collectively bargained in the United States.[186] In fact, there were contracts negotiated in Montana, Minnesota, Illinois, and Rhode Island that predated New York's.[187] But New York City was a watershed in a way that those smaller contracts were not. After New York, collective bargaining for teachers would spread across the country so quickly that within a dozen years, teaching would become among the most unionized occupations in the nation.[188]

For Albert Shanker, the decade from 1952 to 1962 had proven a thrilling one. Although the 1950s is often thought of as a placid, conservative era in American history, Shanker had begun the period as a poorly treated, poorly paid teacher and plunged himself into a militant movement that would forever change the teaching profession. Drawing inspiration from the fledgling civil-rights movement, teachers in New York City had risked their jobs in an attempt to raise their dignity—and they had won. On a personal level, Shanker had gone from a graduate-school dropout in a failing marriage to an important leader in an exciting movement, with a new wife and child. Now, at the age of thirty-three, he was ready to take on even greater challenges.

3

Rising Within the UFT

LABOR AND CIVIL RIGHTS TOGETHER

1962–1965

Having helped to create the UFT and establish the right for teachers to bargain collectively, Albert Shanker now faced new questions: Could the UFT form a coalition with civil-rights groups to promote public schools and a broader agenda of social justice? And what might his own leadership role be in the movement?

As the UFT was closing in on its first successful contract, a power struggle began emerging within the union, a struggle in which Shanker played a central role. In 1962, UFT president Charles Cogen was getting on in years and thought about handing over the reins to Roger Parente, who had been head of the High School Teachers before the organizations merged. But a few days before Cogen told Parente of his plans, some of Parente's associates began circulating false rumors about Cogen's friends crossing a picket line, and an enraged Cogen decided to run again. Shanker said of Parente, "The guy who wanted to be President had it but didn't know he had it. He made the move at the wrong time."[1]

The UFT had a system of caucuses, in which candidates did not run as individuals but as members of a party slate. The UFT's Unity Caucus, which was made up mostly of former Guild members, backed Cogen as president in the spring of 1962. And the caucus nominated Shanker to run as secretary. Shanker was seen as a rising star among the younger union members and was recognized as a persuasive debater and shrewd organizer.

The Unity Caucus slate's prime competition was the Classroom Teachers Caucus, which ran Roger Parente as president and Sol Jaffe as secretary. Shanker and Selden were concerned that under Parente the UFT would jettison the Guild's core Socialist beliefs.[2] But when the election was held in June, the Cogen/Shanker ticket of the Unity Caucus was elected by a two-to-one margin. With Cogen edging toward retirement and with Parente out of the way as competition, Shanker was well positioned to move ahead in the union.[3]

As secretary of the union, Shanker participated in the 1963 negotiations in which the school board agreed to a two-year contract even though they worked on an annual budget. This was "a big breakthrough," Shanker said, because it provided stability. Concerned about the shortage of minority teachers in New York City, the UFT also built into their 1963 contract a provision that the board would recruit more teachers from the South.[4] The UFT pushed for "Teacher-to-Teacher" recruitment centers to be opened in Washington, D.C., Atlanta, and elsewhere so that black teachers could take the entrance exam without having to travel to New York.[5]

Civil Rights

The advent of collective bargaining for teachers in New York City had an explosive effect on teachers nationally. Teachers in other cities began demanding collective bargaining. In 1964, the AFT won a collective bargaining election in Detroit, and in 1965, it won in Philadelphia.[6] Between 1960 and 1968, AFT membership nearly tripled, from 60,000 to 175,000 members, as the AFT also became the bargaining agent in Chicago, Boston, Kansas City, Cleveland, Washington, D.C., Newark, Toledo, and elsewhere.[7]

More important, though, was the effect on the much larger NEA, which was faced with an internal rebellion if it did not drop its longstanding opposition to collective bargaining. Says former NEA Executive Director Don Cameron: "Thousands of teachers and leaders would have defected to the AFT if it had become a choice between collective bargaining and no collective bargaining." He argues, "if the NEA hadn't changed its stripes, it would have become a decidedly minority organization."[8] Swarthmore historian Marjorie Murphy writes: "For the first time in forty-six years, since 1918, the AFT threatened to surpass the NEA."[9]

Following the adoption of collective bargaining for teachers in New York City, the NEA embraced the concept, taking on the tactics of its up-start rival. The effect was stunning, given the relative sizes of the organizations. "Although the AFT was dwarfed in size by the NEA, without any question the AFT tail wagged the dog," says educator Michael Usdan.[10] Teacher strikes grew in number, from nine in 1964 to thirty in 1966 and 105 by 1967.[11]

But the effects of the UFT contract went beyond teachers. In December 1961, *Business Week* asked: "How long will the government clerk go on thinking a union is below her dignity when the teacher next door belongs?"[12] In January 1962, President John Kennedy issued Executive Order 10988, establishing the right of federal employees to join unions and bargain collectively.[13] The measure was important for federal employees, but the order also served as a model for state legislatures considering public-employee bargaining legislation.[14]

Daniel Patrick Moynihan, who staffed a Kennedy task force that worked to recognize federal unions, said Shanker's role with teachers in New York City was a crucial catalyst in public-sector unionism. At Shanker's memorial service, Moynihan said, "If as Emerson wrote, 'an institution is the lengthened shadow of one man,' the public employees [unions] of our nation are singularly the mark of Al Shanker's inspired life and work."[15]

The Kennedy years were also a time of ferment on two great issues about which Shanker cared deeply: poverty and civil rights. In 1962, Michael Harrington's book *The Other America* was published, outlining the extent of poverty within the borders of the world's largest economy. At first, the book received little attention. That changed ten months later, in January 1963, when Dwight Macdonald, whom Shanker greatly admired, wrote a forty-page review of the book in the *New Yorker*. The review caught the eye of President Kennedy and attracted phenomenal publicity for the book.[16] It was extraordinary attention for a Socialist like Harrington. Meanwhile, there was growing support for federal civil-rights legislation to bar discrimination in public accommodations. The AFL-CIO was at the center of the discussions, and George Meany strongly urged the inclusion of a ban on employment discrimination as well, which JFK initially omitted for fear it would kill the bill.[17]

Among those most concerned about poverty and civil rights were two men—A. Philip Randolph and Bayard Rustin—who in December 1962 were pondering ways to celebrate the upcoming centennial of Lincoln's Emancipation Proclamation. Randolph, the head of the Brotherhood of Sleeping Car Porters, was a leading black unionist, and Rustin, an advisor to Martin Luther King Jr., was a premier civil-rights strategist with strong Socialist beliefs. The men, who in later years would play pivotal roles in Shanker's thinking about civil rights, believed that what was missing from the burgeoning civil-rights movement was an appreciation of issues of class, economic justice, and the need for jobs for all workers. They began making plans for a march on Washington that would incorporate both sets of concerns.[18]

The march was to call for "Jobs and Freedom," uniting the agendas of the labor movement and the civil-rights movement, both of which at their core were concerned about equality and dignity for individuals.[19] The march was a natural for labor, and Walter Reuther of the UAW quickly signed on as a major supporter.[20] Incredibly, AFL-CIO President George Meany bitterly opposed the march and made sure that the AFL-CIO executive committee withheld its endorsement.[21] Meany had three concerns: he disliked mass marches as a form of political participation; he was feuding with Reuther, one of the march's central supporters; and he was convinced that the march would backfire and hurt the chances for passage of the Kennedy Civil Rights Act.[22] Because of Meany's opposition, several unions refused to endorse the march.[23]

Shanker and the UFT rejected Meany's position on the march and actively promoted it among teachers.[24] In July 1963, Shanker contacted Carl Megel, the president of the AFT, and explained that the UFT planned to subsidize travel to the march for members, so it would cost them only five dollars for the round trip to Washington. He said the UFT planned to take one unemployed person for every three teachers.[25] Four busloads of New York City teachers were among those that headed to Washington.[26]

The morning of the march, Rustin was deeply concerned when at 6:30 a.m. only about two hundred participants had materialized. Early news reports discussed the sparse turnout, but then thousands upon thousands began to converge on the Mall.[27] The highlight, of course, was Martin Luther King's "I Have a Dream" speech, in which King outlined the way the horrendous treatment of black citizens violated the "magnificent words of the Constitution and the Declaration of Independence." Along with African Americans, there were many whites in the audience, including

Shanker, and King underlined this fact. Pointing to the whites in the attendance, King told his black brethren: "We cannot walk alone."

King had long urged an alliance with organized labor. Two years earlier, he had addressed the AFL-CIO convention and drew strong parallels
between the labor movement and the civil-rights movement. "Negroes
are almost entirely a working people," he said. "Our needs are identical
with labor's needs—decent wages, fair working conditions, livable housing, old-age security, health and welfare measures, conditions in which
families can grow, have education for their children and respect in the
community. . . . The identity of interests of labor and Negroes makes any
crisis which lacerates you, a crisis in which we bleed."[28]

Now, at the march, King called for an end to segregation and discrimination. He articulated a dream that his "four little children will one day live in
a nation where they will not be judged by the color of their skin but by the
content of their character." And he called for a nonviolent struggle—"we
must rise to the majestic heights of meeting physical force with soul force."
Others that day added Randolph's and Rustin's concern for an economic
agenda for blacks and whites—an increase in the minimum wage and the
creation of jobs. For Shanker, who had faced discrimination and violence
firsthand and who saw the brutal way in which blacks had been treated, the
message of the day—nondiscrimination, integration, economic equality,
and nonviolence—was thrilling. It was "a great event," he said.[29]

While King's speech highlighted Southern racism as particularly overt,
there was plenty of evidence of discrimination in the North as well, and
New York City was no exception. In the early 1960s, there were three basic
racial disparities in New York City public schools. There were very few
minority teachers (fewer than 10 percent of teachers were black or Hispanic in a city school system whose minority student population was approaching 50 percent), there was considerable de facto segregation in the
schools, and students in heavily poor and minority schools tended to get
the least experienced teachers.[30]

The UFT had proposals on all three fronts. The 1963 contract pushed
for greater recruitment of black teachers in the South, to boost the overall
number of minority teachers. And to address both the integration of
white students and experienced teachers into ghetto schools, the UFT
proposed an "Effective Schools" program (later renamed More Effective
Schools), which would provide reduced class size and extra services in a
small number of selected schools. The union argued this program would
provide a realistic way of attracting experienced teachers (while avoiding

forced transfer of teachers) and middle-class white children (while avoid-ing compulsory busing). Because the UFT members would never go along with forced teacher transfers, Shanker said "we felt an obligation to come up with a plan of our own."[31]

The concept behind the More Effective Schools program, Shanker later said, was to create "the first magnet schools."[32] By giving ghetto schools attractive features, such as smaller class sizes, and extra services, such as school psychiatrists, the program was meant to voluntarily draw in white middle-class students. In addition, the UFT supported the transfer of 12,000 to 15,000 black students over a three-year period to white schools.[33] Given the UFT's support for integration, civil-rights groups turned to the teachers for help in supporting additional initiatives.

In December 1963, Reverend Milton Galamison, the pastor of the Si-loam Presbyterian Church in Brooklyn, appeared before the UFT execu-tive board seeking support for a planned February 1964 student boycott of New York City public schools designed to call for greater integration.[34] The boycott, which was organized by Bayard Rustin from the March on Washington, was highly controversial, even among liberals and civil-rights groups, in part because of its use of children. The *New York Times* editorial page called the boycott "reckless," "violent," and "illegal" and predicted it would "alienate public opinion." The editorial also said the goal of total integration in New York was unrealistic. "You can bus chil-dren just so far."[35] Liberal columnist Jimmy Breslin and civil-rights icon Kenneth Clark opposed the boycott, and Roy Wilkins of the NAACP said: "Our organization believes it is better for children to go to school than to stay home."[36]

Galamison asked the teachers to support the boycott and not to cross the student picket lines. This was a difficult thing to ask of teachers be-cause it would have been a violation of the union contract (as well as the law) to call an official strike in support of the children's boycott.[37] In Jan-uary 1964, the union declined to endorse the boycott, but promised to protect teachers who went along with the boycott from reprisal.[38] The UFT Delegate Assembly passed a resolution declaring: "The organization will support teachers against reprisals if they respect picket lines of civil rights groups at their schools because of their individual consciences."[39] And behind the scenes, the UFT was even more supportive.[40] Altomare, with Shanker's knowledge and acceptance, went to Galamison's head-quarters and shared with Bayard Rustin information about how the UFT had organized successful strikes in the past.[41]

By saying that it would not condemn teachers who honored the boycott, said education writer David Rogers, the UFT essentially "honored"
the boycott.[42] When the Board declared that teachers participating in the
boycott would lose pay for the day and be charged with neglect, which
could disqualify them from future administration positions, the UFT responded that it would protect the rights of any teachers who participated
in the boycott.[43]

On the day of the boycott, 45 percent of students—more than 450,000—
did not attend classes, making it, according to Rustin, the largest civil-
rights demonstration in American history. About one-fifth of the demon-
strators were white, Rustin said. About 8 percent of teachers—more than
3,500—stayed out, compared to the usual 3 percent absentee rate.[44]

Following the boycott, white liberals and civil-rights groups formed
the Conference for Quality Integrated Education. Shanker was one of the
only major labor leaders to join the conference—giants like Van Arsdale,
Dubinsky, and Potofsky were absent—and Shanker also served on the
steering committee of the group.[45] The UFT also endorsed pairing schools
for desegregation—merging the student bodies of predominantly white
and black schools and sending students to one school for kindergarten
through second grade and the other for grades three through five—a
practice opposed in a September 1964 *New York Times* poll by 80 percent
of New Yorkers. The UFT opposed a student boycott sponsored by an
anti-integration group, Parents and Taxpayers (PAT).[46] And Shanker and
the UFT supported a counter-PAT group consisting of white parents who
were willing to send their children to integrated schools.[47]

Martin Luther King recognized the UFT's positive role on racial issues,
and on March 14, 1964, King spoke to UFT members, accepting the group's
John Dewey Award. In his remarks, King strongly backed school integration, saying "there is no comparison between the inconvenience some
white children may suffer and the terrible needs Negro children confront
as a tragic consequence of 300 years of inequality."[48]

The UFT Presidency

At the time of King's remarks to the UFT, Shanker was the number-two
person in the organization, but he was quickly on his way to becoming
number one. The president, Charles Cogen, was an intelligent and able
leader, but it was becoming clear that Shanker was the more commanding

and impressive figure. Like Cogen, Shanker was an intellectual, but he was equally comfortable in the world of action and power. While Cogen was mild and indecisive, Shanker was strong and self-assured.[49]

In particular, Shanker was a compelling speaker. When he rose before an audience, he was not physically impressive. He was bespectacled and ungainly, wore ill-fitting clothes, bad ties, and a generally glum expression. He didn't charm audiences with his looks. Nor did he win them over with oratorical flourishes or appeals to emotion. He had a deep voice and a thick New York accent. But he would get up before an audience, quickly size them up, and begin to present a very logical argument, carefully laid out, in easily understood terms. He relied heavily on analogies, sometimes employing humor. He almost always delivered his remarks with virtually no notes. He could speak for an hour or more, glancing down at the back of an envelope only once or twice.[50]

Unlike Cogen, Shanker was also very skilled at running meetings, giving opponents just enough rope to hang themselves.[51] And he continued to be an excellent debater. "You couldn't beat him in a debate even if he was wrong," said one UFT staffer.[52] In early 1964, a plan was hatched in which Cogen would be bumped upstairs to the presidency of the American Federation of Teachers and be accompanied by Dave Selden as a staffer, clearing the way for Shanker to take over as UFT president.[53] On April 15, 1964, the thirty-five-year-old Shanker was nominated by his caucus for the presidency of the UFT, while Cogen announced that he would seek the AFT presidency.[54]

The day of the nominations was filled with excitement of more than a professional nature. As Shanker was being nominated for president and being congratulated afterward, Eadie Shanker could feel she was going into labor with her second child. "I was crossing my legs," she recalled, and "everybody wanted to talk to him after his nomination. I went up to him and said, 'Let's go!'"[55] Shortly thereafter, a daughter, Jennie Shanker, was born.

In the general election, Shanker ran against Benjamin Mazen, a history teacher and lawyer who was part of the more militant high-school group that had opposed Cogen. On May 11, 1964, the UFT announced that Shanker was elected by a two-to-one margin in a mail ballot: 7,247 to 4,143. He took office July 1, 1964.[56] In just five short years, Shanker had moved from entry-level organizer to president of the largest local union of the American Federation of Teachers, with 28,000 members out of the AFT's ninety thousand members nationally.[57]

As president, he had several goals typical of union leaders: he wanted to increase membership, increase the union's political power, and negotiate a good contract for his members. In short order, he would accomplish all three.

In 1964, the UFT had signed up about 50 percent of the city's teachers; soon it would be 97 percent.[58] Within three years, the UFT would grow to 49,000 members and constitute the largest local union in the entire AFL-CIO.[59] He also took an organization that considered politics an undignified endeavor for teachers and built a powerful political and legislative operation, so that within a few years, politicians lined up to attend the UFT's annual John Dewey luncheon. One observer says, "it was like a wedding cake: layer after layer of politicians, all the way up. . . . You'd have congressmen and senators and mayors and assemblymen. . . . "[60] And Shanker came through on the 1965 teacher contract, skillfully negotiating not only a good salary increase and increased benefits, but also a provision that teachers no longer would have to bring a doctor's note when they were sick.[61]

But beyond these traditional union concerns, Shanker sought to do something much bigger: to make the UFT part of a larger social movement that reached beyond narrow self-interested concerns. The UFT had a strong legacy of social action—support for Martin Luther King and Bayard Rustin. Now the UFT would add political strength and resources to that endeavor, to promote the cause of civil rights and, more broadly, to promote genuine democracy for the first time to the American South.

As Shanker was making the transition to the UFT presidency, he oversaw an ongoing program to recruit teachers for Mississippi's "Freedom Schools," teaching black students whose schools had been closed as the state resisted desegregation.[62] The thirty-six UFT teachers who went to eight Mississippi cities in the summer of 1964 were well aware of dangers following the deaths of Andrew Goodman, Michael Schwerner, and James Chaney in Philadelphia, Mississippi, in the beginning of the summer of 1964.[63]

The following spring, Shanker and the UFT became very involved in the struggle to combat the repressive denial of voting rights in Selma, Alabama. On Sunday, March 7, 1965, John Lewis of the Student Nonviolent Coordinating Committee (SNCC) and others were violently beaten as they led a peaceful march across Edmund Pettus Bridge outside Selma, on a day that became known as "Bloody Sunday."[64] King called for further marches. Invoking the language of organized labor, he declared: "We must let them know that if they beat one Negro they are going to have to beat a hundred and if they beat a hundred, then they are going to have to beat a thousand."[65] And King demanded of marchers an almost superhuman resistance to violence. "If you can't accept blows without retaliating, don't get in line," he said.[66]

Shanker met with Andrew Young of the Southern Christian Leadership Conference to find out how the UFT could help and was told that the movement needed cars to help transport intimidated rural voters to register. Shanker flew to Selma and on Sunday, March 21, 1965, delivered the keys to station wagons to King in Selma and then joined him and thousands of others to march from Selma to Montgomery.[67]

Shanker's activities in Selma were controversial with some UFT members. In letters to the school page of the *New York World Telegram and Sun*, teachers complained that Shanker should stick to union issues. In April 1965, Shanker wrote a letter to the editor in response, explaining that he had marched with others in Selma and Montgomery because "it is immoral to take the position that others should speak out while we remain silent." He argued: "Teachers will earn the right to the support of the public only as they give leadership within the community on issues which go beyond narrow self-interest."[68]

Shanker pushed the UFT to become involved in other civil-rights issues of the day. In 1965, the UFT Executive Board voted to deal only with banks that had divested from South Africa.[69] Shanker sent a letter to David Rockefeller withdrawing money from Chase Manhattan because of its involvement in South Africa, and he sent a letter to Comptroller Abe Beame asking that the city divest pension moneys from Mississippi bonds.[70] Shanker was also a supporter of Cesar Chavez and his campaign to champion the mostly Latino migrant farm workers in the 1960s. Michael Harrington recalls first meeting Shanker in 1964 or 1965 in a joint effort to urge a New Jersey grape importer to honor Chavez's boycott of non-union grapes from California.[71]

The Shachtmanites

Perhaps most important to the future of the union was Shanker's decision to hire as staff a number of Socialists with strong ties to the civil-rights movement. The lynchpin was Shanker's decision, in the fall of 1965, to hire Yetta Barsh to be an assistant to the president. Barsh was hired not because she knew about education—she did not—but because she knew about politics, Socialism, and the civil-rights movement.[72]

Barsh was married to the legendary Max Shachtman, a former Communist who became a leading Socialist theoretician and mentor to a generation of Socialists active in civil rights, including Tom Kahn, Rachelle Horowitz, Sandy Feldman, Michael Harrington, and Irving Howe.[73] Shachtman was also very close to Bayard Rustin, the organizer of the March on Washington and a confidant of King's. Shachtman believed that Socialists had to embrace the civil-rights movement in part because democracy demanded it and in part because blacks in a coalition with labor could transform the Democratic Party into a far more progressive force, by freeing the Democrats of their reliance on conservative anti-black and anti-labor Southern whites.

But if Shachtman was a great theorist and thinker, he never made much money—he ran a mail-order business selling stereo equipment from his home—and had always relied on Barsh to have a "bourgeois" job to pay the bills. "The joke amongst our friends was that I was the meal ticket," said Barsh.[74] She was thrilled to have a job with Shanker because it was an opportunity to make a decent living and to be part of a political movement she cared so much about.[75]

Through Barsh, Shanker came to know Shachtman and would go out to Shachtman's home in Floral Park, Long Island, on weekends to talk about Socialist theory, the civil-rights movement, and the trade-union movement.[76] Over time, Shachtman and Shanker became close friends.[77] They even shared a hobby—stereo equipment—and worked together to build bookcases.[78] As Shanker began to put his own imprint on the UFT staff, Barsh suggested two of Shanker's most important early hires: Sandra Feldman and Eugenia Kemble.

Feldman, a New York City school teacher, grew up poor in Coney Island, Brooklyn, the daughter of a milkman, and attended Brooklyn College in the late 1950s, where she became involved in Socialist politics and civil rights. She became a member of the Congress of Racial Equality (CORE) and was arrested during the Freedom Rides for efforts to integrate Howard Johnson restaurants in Maryland along Route 40. An acolyte of Bayard Rustin, she helped organize the March on Washington before becoming a teacher in the Lower East Side of Manhattan, at PS 34. Shanker hired her to handle member grievances.[79]

Shanker also hired, on Barsh's recommendation, Eugenia Kemble, a young secretary working for Norman Thomas's Socialist Party USA. Kemble was friends with Sandy Feldman and the sister of Penn Kemble, a Socialist and civil-rights activist, and she would later marry Jervis Anderson, a writer for Bayard Rustin. Shanker hired her to be a reporter for the UFT's newspaper, *United Teacher*.[80]

Through Barsh and Shachtman, Shanker also became increasingly close to Rustin. An effective tactician—the August 1963 March on Washington and the February 1964 school boycott were both rousing successes—Rustin was a man of great ideas and principles who had persuaded Martin Luther King to embrace nonviolence. (When Rustin first went to aid King in the Montgomery bus boycott, there were guns lying around King's home for self-protection.)[81] And it was Rustin who helped ensure that King turned the principles behind the temporary Montgomery bus boycott into a permanent organization, the Southern Christian Leadership Conference (SCLC).[82] Rustin's other great effect on King was to persuade him that civil-rights groups should ally themselves with organized labor around issues of economic inequality. Rustin introduced King to many labor leaders who gave financial support to SCLC.[83]

Following the March on Washington's success, Rustin sought to form a permanent institution to follow it up—just as he had advised King to do—and he, Shachtman, and Don Slaiman of the AFL-CIO came up with the idea of forming the A. Philip Randolph Institute, to build better relationships between labor and blacks, a project to which Randolph, as head of the Brotherhood of Sleeping Car Porters, had dedicated his life.[84]

Shanker was eager to help out, and the UFT was the first union to help fund the A. Phillip Randolph Institute.[85] Shanker and Rustin made an interesting duo—a white, married Jewish New Yorker and a black, gay Quaker from Pennsylvania—but both men knew the reality of discrimination and profoundly believed that labor and blacks should be at the heart of the progressive coalition.

The idea for the Institute was to provide a two-way street of communication: blacks could learn about the activities of the AFL-CIO, and the Institute also provided a forum for blacks to communicate their concerns about the labor movement.[86] Over the years, Shanker would remain very involved in the Institute and serve as treasurer.[87]

Shanker and Rustin believed that the civil rights–labor alliance, which worked together to pass the Civil Rights Act of 1964, now needed to move beyond the legal attack on racism and confront the hard economic realities left by the wake of slavery and segregation. Having accomplished its initial goals, the civil-rights movement was at a crossroads, faced with how best to address the considerable legacy of past discrimination.

In a seminal article in the February 1965 issue of *Commentary* magazine entitled "From Protest to Politics: The Future of the Civil Rights Movement," Rustin noted that because *Brown vs. Board of Education* and the Civil Rights Act had destroyed "the legal foundations of racism," the next great challenge was to address economic inequality. "There is a widespread assumption that the removal of artificial racial barriers should result in the automatic integration of the Negro in all aspects of American life," Rustin wrote. But for blacks to advance, there had to be an enormous expenditure of money. This could not be accomplished, Rustin said, by adopting Malcolm X's strategy, to "frighten white people into doing the right thing." Instead, he said, black people needed allies. "I speak of the coalition which staged the March on Washington, passed the Civil Rights Act, and laid the basis for the Johnson landslide—Negroes, trade unionists, liberals, and religious groups." While not romanticizing the racial track record of American labor, Rustin said, the labor movement was "the largest single organized force in this country pushing for progressive social legislation." With great hope, he said, "The 1964 elections marked a turning point in American politics," and the time was right to address the remaining issues of class inequality.[88] Shanker completely agreed. "Bayard knew exactly what it was all about," he said. With the passage of civil-rights legislation, said Shanker, the next stage involved "the real hard work" of helping blacks lift themselves up on an "economic and educational" basis.[89]

Martin Luther King Jr. was making a similar argument. In his 1964 book *Why We Can't Wait*, King wrote that it was not enough to pass civil-rights legislation and expect equality to ensue. He argued that "the nation must not only radically readjust its attitude toward the Negro in the compelling present, but must incorporate in its planning some compensatory consideration for the handicaps he has inherited from the past." King said: "For it is obvious that if a man is entered at the starting line in a race three hundred years after another man, the first would have to perform some impossible feat in order to catch up with his fellow runner." But the remedy had to be race blind, King argued. He proposed a "Bill of Rights for the Disadvantaged," not a "Bill of Rights for Blacks," saying, "While Negroes form the vast majority of America's disadvantaged, there are millions of white poor who would also benefit from such a bill. . . . It is a simple matter of justice that America, in dealing creatively with the task of raising the Negro from backwardness, should also be rescuing a large stratum of the forgotten white poor."[90]

President Lyndon Johnson, too, was laying out plans for a broad-based economic program to address the next stage of the civil-rights movement. In a famous address at Howard University in June 1965, Johnson argued, in words that echoed King's: "You do not take a person who, for years, has been hobbled by chains and liberate him, bring him up to the starting line of a race and then say, 'you are free to compete with all the others,' and still justly believe that you have been completely fair." Johnson defined "the next and the more profound stage of the battle for civil rights" as one in which Americans would seek "not just equality as a right and a theory but equality as a fact and equality as a result." In the speech, Johnson did not endorse racial preferences or quotas, as some in the civil-rights community were advocating, and instead said: "Jobs are part of the answer. . . . Decent homes in decent surroundings and a chance to learn—an equal chance to learn—are part of the answer. Welfare and social programs better designed to hold families together are part of the answer. Care for the sick is part of the answer."[91]

In August 1965, riots broke out in Watts, underlining the importance of addressing the economic realities of the ghetto, and the White House gathered a group for a conference on civil rights. At a November 1965 planning session for the upcoming conference, Rustin and Randolph floated the idea for massive spending to promote full employment; a guaranteed income; better health care, education, and housing; as well as a higher minimum wage in the private sector.[92] Shachtman suggested they call the proposal the Freedom Budget for All Americans.[93] Shanker fully supported the Freedom Budget and later wrote a column in United Teacher calling for teachers to get behind it.[94] The time seemed ripe for America to address, at long last, fundamental issues of economic inequality.

As 1965 came to a close, Shanker was riding high. As head of the United Federation of Teachers, he was at the intersection of a number of exciting social movements that were coming together and reinforcing one another: education, civil rights, and labor. The concern for civil rights had helped reignite an interest in ensuring that education became an engine for social mobility. With collective bargaining, teachers were in a better political position than ever to promote both civil rights and educational equity. The UFT was seen as a strong progressive union, and unionists from across the city wanted to work there. "Dozens of union staff people all over town competed to work at the UFT," wrote union staffer John O'Neill. "The word was out that this was where things were happening."[95]

With Lyndon Johnson in the White House, money was flowing to cities through the newly authorized Elementary and Secondary Education Act. There was talk of the Freedom Budget bringing billions more to address long neglected issues of inequality. Nationally, a liberal consensus had resoundingly defeated conservative forces in the person of Barry Goldwater. It was a far cry from Shanker's childhood days, when discrimination ran rampant, millions were unemployed and had little government help, and public sector employees had no real right to unionize.

On a personal level, Shanker's life continued to blossom. In May 1965, Eadie Shanker gave birth to the couple's third child, Michael, who joined three-year-old Adam and one-year-old Jennie. And in New York City, voters elected a vibrant new mayor, John Lindsay, a liberal Republican who campaigned for civil rights and pledged an end to de facto school segregation.[96] Although the UFT did not officially endorse Lindsay in the November 1965 election, it was supportive behind the scenes.[97] Shanker wrote to Lindsay and congratulated him on his election, and Lindsay thanked Shanker for his note.[98] On one level, it seemed as though the two liberals might make excellent partners in the coming years.

4

Black Power and the 1967 Teachers' Strike

1966–1968

A s 1965 turned to 1966, American liberalism dominated the political landscape. The values that Shanker held dear—integration, nonviolence, and colorblindness—were staples of the civil-rights movement and had growing acceptance among the broader American public. Civil-rights groups and labor unions forged a powerful coalition nationally and in New York City. But almost immediately in 1966, the coalition began to splinter as core values like nondiscrimination and the importance of labor were discarded.

While Al Shanker liked John Lindsay's campaign stances on poverty, civil rights, and integration, he was immediately taken aback by Mayor Lindsay's attitude toward organized labor. On January 1, 1966, the day he took office, Lindsay was hit with a strike by the New York City Transit Workers. All mayors oppose strikes by city workers, but Lindsay went beyond the usual rhetoric about the strike's inconvenience to citizens.[1] The mayor argued that the strike was a weapon against black and Hispanic people, who relied on public transportation because they could not afford to buy cars. Lindsay's decision "to pit the unionist against blacks and Hispanics" was a nefarious tactic in Shanker's book.[2]

In May 1966, Lindsay took on another union, the Patrolmen's Benevolent Association (PBA), which represented police, by proposing a Civilian Review Board to provide citizen oversight to review cases of alleged police brutality. Police were infuriated by the move and by July 1966 gathered enough signatures to call for repeal on the November 1966 ballot.[3] Conservatives joined the PBA in pushing for repeal, arguing that Lindsay was trying to handcuff the police. The Liberal Party, the New York Civil Liberties Union, the American Jewish Committee, and Senators Robert Kennedy and Jacob Javits, citing instances of police brutality, backed Lindsay's review board.[4]

The UFT membership was split, but Shanker decided to side with the liberals and civil-rights groups against the police union and back the civilian complaint board.[5] Shanker persuaded the Executive Committee of the UFT to side with Lindsay on a vote of 30 to 2.[6] The Delegate Assembly passed the resolution by a much narrower margin, 486 to 375.[7] One of Shanker's arguments was that teachers needed to build alliances with civil-rights groups to support education.[8] The UFT was the only union to support the Lindsay position.[9]

In the end, the civilian board was crushed, repealed in November 1966 by a two to one vote, with 63 percent opposed to Lindsay and Shanker's position.[10] The vote was part of a much larger white backlash against rioting, rising crime, and disorder. From April 1965 to September 1966, the share of northern whites who said government was pushing civil rights "too fast" almost doubled, to over 50 percent.[11] On Election Day, 1966, Democrats suffered net losses to Republicans of forty-seven House members, three Senators, eight governors, and 677 state legislators.[12] On the West Coast, a conservative movie actor named Ronald Reagan, who opposed the Civil Rights Act and called for tough action against rioters, was elected governor of California. Just two years after LBJ's landslide election and a year after passage of the Voting Rights Act, the broad coalition on behalf of civil rights was fracturing.

Black Power and IS 201

If the civil-rights movement was hit by a conservative backlash in certain parts of the country in 1966, it also saw an attack from the far left, as integrationists of the King/Rustin/Shanker mode came up against a new radical call for "Black Power." In May 1966, the civil-rights movement took a fundamental turn when a young black activist named Stokely Carmichael defeated another young black activist, John Lewis, the hero of the Selma March a year earlier, to head the Student Nonviolent Coordinating Committee (SNCC). The next month, at a speech in Greenwood, Mississippi, Carmichael invoked "Black Power" for the first time, and, with it, a new phase of the civil-rights movement began. Carmichael turned the SNCC away from two of its previous commitments—class-based alliances with poor whites and the principle of nonviolence. The SNCC soon expelled whites from the organization. Carmichael argued whites should organize whites and blacks should organize blacks.[13] Whereas Martin Luther King routinely invoked documents like the Declaration of Independence, Carmichael declared: "When you talk about Black Power, you talk of building a movement that will smash everything that Western Civilization has created."[14]

In the education field, Black Power meant a rejection of school integration. "Integration," Carmichael argued, "is a subterfuge for the maintenance of white supremacy," because it required blacks to assimilate into "white culture."[15] And he called for black parents to take control of schools, over the hiring and firing of teachers, the curriculum, and the like.[16]

Carmichael, who in an earlier incarnation was a Shachtmanite, was denounced by Shachtman and Rustin, who said one-tenth of the population could not accomplish much without help.[17] Mainstream liberal and civil-rights leaders, including Martin Luther King, Roy Wilkins of the NAACP, Hubert Humphrey, Robert Kennedy, and Whitney Young of the Urban League, also rejected Black Power. Wilkins said of Black Power: "It is a reverse Mississippi, a reverse Hitler, a reverse Ku Klux Klan."[18] King called it a "nihilistic philosophy."[19]

Although Carmichael made his call for Black Power in the South, the first big battle took place in the North, in the fall of 1966, at a middle school in New York City.[20] Intermediate School 201 in Harlem was a newly built facility that was meant to be racially integrated.[21] The School Board invited whites from Queens and the Bronx to come to the school, located on 127th and 128th Streets between Madison and Park, where Spanish East Harlem and Black Harlem intersect, but none did.[22] Frustrated and insulted by the failure of integration, some black activists argued that if white children would not come to the school, white adults should not run it. On the opening day of school, parents boycotted IS 201. The boycott, academics Maurice Berube and Marilyn Gittel later wrote, "marked the end of the school integration movement" in New York City.[23]

To run IS 201, the Board of Education chose a Jewish man, Stanley Lisser, a popular liberal educator who had developed an African American curriculum. He was teamed with an assistant principal, Beryl Banfield, who was black, and the author of a biography of Marcus Garvey.[24] But neither was acceptable to protestors. Boycotters demanded a black or Puerto Rican male principal to provide a "proper image" for the mostly minority student population. One of the protesters said: "We got too many teachers and principals named Ginzberg and Rosenberg in Harlem. This is a black community. We want black men in our schools."[25] Albert Vann and Leslie Campbell, the head of the African American Teachers Association (ATA), carried signs that said, "We Want Black Teachers in Black Harlem."[26]

In mid-September, Superintendent Bernard Donovan met with local East Harlem representatives and gave what the community took to be "veto power" over personnel.[27] Lisser agreed to "voluntarily" transfer to another school, so the parents' picket line was called off. But then a group of teachers, half black and half white, began a protest of their own.[28] And Banfield, to whom Donovan offered the job, refused to take it. "I objected to being chosen on the basis of color, not competence," she said.[29] Banfield said race should be irrelevant.[30]

The teachers threatened to shut the school down if Lisser were not retained.[31] Superintendent Bernard Donovan called the teachers, Lisser, and Shanker to a meeting in the library at the Board of Education. Donovan told the teachers: "Now, you realize you're on strike and you're defying the Condon-Wadlin law. If you go back right now, I won't dock your pay." But the teachers were not intimidated. "And teacher after teacher got up, it was like a religious meeting. They got up and they said, we are not going back there. This is a great principal," Shanker recalled.

Shanker sat in the back of the room and cried. He said, "I just loved them all. It was one of those days where I felt, if the union has done nothing else, to give teachers a feeling that they can stand in front of the superintendent and state their feelings and just say we're not going back to that school unless the right thing is done." It was one thing to be among twenty thousand anonymous strikers. But "here are one hundred people, who feel so deeply and are not being cowed by the threats that the law is going to be brought down on their head. . . . It was democracy. It was solidarity. It was the individual dignity they felt. . . . It was beautiful."[32]

In late September, Donovan backed down and reinstated Lisser.[33] Shanker proclaimed a victory. "The very integrity of the school system was at stake," Shanker wrote, "for if we had not prevailed, we would enter an era where only a Jewish principal could be appointed in schools located in a predominantly Jewish neighborhood, Italians in Italian neighborhoods, Irish in Irish."[34]

Still, Shanker acknowledged that there was a problem with the lack of black principals in the school system. The union participated in a special internship program to help mostly minority teachers become principals, and Shanker criticized the principals' test as "a ridiculous exam," since it tested obscure vocabulary rather than leadership. But the union balked at the idea of matching students and principals by race or placing an absolutely racial bar on hiring for positions in a given school, as the protestors were demanding.[35]

The Lisser episode exposed a growing rift within the civil-rights community between those who embraced universal colorblindness and those who wanted color-conscious hiring. Lisser received support from Roy Wilkins and Whitney Young, who wrote columns saying the issue should be quality, not color.[36] But others were not so supportive.

During the Lisser controversy, Shanker went to Rustin and said, "you know, what's happening here is going to destroy the civil rights movement." The notion at the March on Washington "was that civil rights were civil rights for everybody." Shanker suggested to Rustin that he enlist Martin Luther King in a march on behalf of Lisser and the teachers, in which King would say just "as a black has a right to go to the University of Alabama or the University of Mississippi, a white has the right to be a principal in Harlem." Rustin wholeheartedly agreed, as did A. Philip Randolph, and they organized a meeting of black leaders in Harlem at Randolph's apartment. But none of the other leaders there wanted to be involved, and King was never invited.[37]

Lisser's return was short-lived. After he was reinstated by Donovan, some adult boycott leaders started training students to cause disruptions in the school, lighting fires and causing trouble, and after a short time, Lisser was driven out.[38]

Community Control in Ocean Hill–Brownsville

Following the IS 201 controversy, the idea of race-based hiring and community control rather than integration—notions previously considered reactionary—gained momentum nationally and in New York City.

Support often came from surprising quarters. In October 1966, one of America's leading integrationists, Dr. Kenneth B. Clark of City College, author of the famous dolls study that helped overturn *Plessy v. Ferguson*'s principle of separate but equal, called for the creation of an independent "operations board," with the authority to select staff, teachers, and principals, to run IS 201 and three nearby elementary schools.[39]

Another dramatic convert to community control was Reverend Milton Galamison, who just two years earlier had led the student boycott for integration. In December 1966, a group of community-control advocates disrupted a public hearing of the School Board. When the Board adjourned, activists occupied the leather seats of the Board and declared themselves the "People's Board of Education." Galamison was elected president of the People's Board and the group occupied the Board's seats for three days.[40] The People's Board demanded that "the school system must be decentralized to give local parents and community groups effective control over the education of their children."[41]

If some black activists were clamoring for community control, white business and community leaders began to join them. In March 1967, the Citizens Committee for Decentralization was formed, consisting of what one author called a "'who's who' of elite New York," including the president of RCA, the chairman of IBM, the president of Time Inc., and a former president of Harvard University. Some wondered whether the group was allying with angry poor blacks in order to insure stability and buy racial peace.[42]

Finally, there were important financial incentives for the city to pursue community control as a way of boosting state aid. Under the state funding formula for education, if the city's five boroughs were considered separate districts, the high property values in Manhattan would not hold down state aid for the other boroughs, and the city as a whole would receive more funds. In March 1967, a coalition of conservative Republicans and liberal black legislators in Albany said that they would provide extra money to New York City if Lindsay came back with a plan for school decentralization by December.[43]

Shanker had to decide whether to hop on the oncoming community-control train or try to stop it. The experience at IS 201 was deeply troubling, as racial demagogues and separatists had taken charge. And Shanker had his doubts that a simple change in governance would increase learning among students. But Shanker believed deeply in the importance of forming coalitions with black parents to improve schools, and he saw the chance to strike a deal. The UFT would back community control if community-control advocates backed the UFT's More Effective Schools (MES) Program of extra funding for ghetto magnet schools. The UFT began negotiations with a group of parents in the Ocean Hill–Brownsville section of Brooklyn for such a bargain.

Ocean Hill was described by one journalist as "a no-man's land between two no man's-lands," with the black ghetto of Bedford-Stuyvesant on one side and the black ghetto of Brownsville on the other.[44] It resembled, said another, "Berlin after the war: block after block of burned-out shells of houses, streets littered with decaying automobile hulks."[45] Among adults in Ocean Hill–Brownsville, fewer than one-third had finished high school.[46] There were no resident doctors or lawyers in Ocean Hill–Brownsville, and three-quarters received some public assistance.[47] The student population was 70 percent black and 25 percent Puerto Rican.[48]

Students in the community knew well the reality of racism. Integration had been tried—four thousand Brownsville children had been bused to white schools—and been made to feel very unwelcome. After a year, one half had opted to return to Ocean Hill–Brownsville.[49] It was understandable that Ocean Hill–Brownsville parents were ready to try something different.

The UFT proposed its deal: the UFT would support Ocean Hill–Brownsville's desire to be included as an experimental district for community control if the community would support the UFT's desire to have all eight schools in the district designated as MES schools.[50] Local Leader Father John Powis recalled, "the United Federation of Teachers was one of the main helps at the beginning."[51]

Shanker had one other reason to support community control, even if it did nothing educationally. Shanker understood that low-income blacks in places like Ocean Hill–Brownsville felt invisible, outside of the mainstream, and that no one was listening to them, because teachers had a similar experience.[52] He argued: "As teachers, who have only recently struggled for a voice, we support others in this struggle. The right to democratic participation need not and should not be justified on grounds of educational efficiency. It has value in itself."[53]

In April 1967, to address the growing demand for decentralization, the Board approved a compromise that allowed experimentation: the creation of three demonstration districts.[54] With UFT support, Ocean Hill–Brownsville was chosen to participate, along with the IS 201 complex in Harlem and the Two Bridges Model District on the Lower East

Side.[55] Mayor Lindsay wanted to go further than the Board was willing to go, so in late April 1967, in order to respond to the state legislature's request for a plan for decentralization, Lindsay bypassed the Board and appointed a group of leading citizens, headed by McGeorge Bundy, to make recommendations for implementing citywide community control.[56]

Bundy, the president of the Ford Foundation, the richest foundation in the country, was a former National Security Advisor in the White House who had argued for a major escalation of the war in Vietnam. He was also former dean of the faculty at Harvard University.[57] Bundy had been initially hesitant about community control, because he believed in racial integration. But he was eventually convinced by his staff, led by Mario Fantini, that since desegregation was not likely to happen in New York City, community control was a good strategy for bringing it about, because it would improve ghetto schools to the point that they would eventually attract whites voluntarily.[58]

The Bundy panel was small, and included Alfred Giardino (the president of the School Board), and four others.[59] There was no labor representative on the board, and Jules Kolodny wrote to Mayor Lindsay expressing his disappointment that Shanker was not included on the panel.[60] Shanker sent a telegram to Bundy congratulating him on his appointment and offering to help, which Bundy said, in a May 5 reply, "delighted" him.[61] In late June, Bundy's deputy at the Ford Foundation, Mario Fantini, announced a $40,000 planning grant to the Ocean Hill–Brownsville experimental project, solidifying the foundation's identification with community control.[62]

Meanwhile, Shanker's concerns about the direction community control was taking began to multiply. On June 22, a group of black separatists converged on UFT headquarters wielding signs reading "UFT, Stay out of the Black Community" and demanding that the number of black teachers be increased "to reflect the black population." The group was led by Robert "Sonny" Carson, the Executive Director of the Brooklyn Chapter of the Congress of Racial Equality. CORE had become a very different organization than the one which Shanker had been a member of at the University of Illinois. A year earlier, CORE, which had been committed to integration and peaceful protest, embraced Black Power and renounced nonviolence.[63] Carson was himself not unfamiliar with violence. As a young gang member, he engaged in street crime, and years later (in 1974) he would be convicted of kidnapping.[64]

Some twenty CORE members staged a twenty-one-hour sit-in, beginning at 3:30 p.m. on June 22 and ending at 12:30 p.m. on June 23. Shanker was out of the office at a negotiating session, and the protesters began hurling anti-Semitic statements at the staff. Shanker was reached by telephone and told his staff to let the protesters know he would meet them in the morning; in the meantime, they should be given food and coffee and be made comfortable for the night, he said. Shanker met with the protesters, had a friendly discussion, and agreed to meet with them again the following week in Brooklyn. A *Times* reporter said that "even the ultra-racists in the group went away disarmed."[65]

The following week, when Shanker met at JHS 35 with Carson and three hundred members of the black community, including members of the African American Teachers' Association, the talk was less pleasant. Shanker tried to speak but was continually shouted down by a hostile audience. He said that if he were interrupted again, he would leave, a statement that was greeted with laughter. When interrupted again, he prepared to leave. "He shuffled toward the door, with that prominent blotch on his neck that becomes very red when he gets crossed," Carson said, but was blocked by "two burly Brothers who refused to allow him to leave." Shanker, his voice rising, said, "Mr. Carson, Mr. Carson, you gave me your word." The audience laughed, said Carson, watching "this great big honky union chief standing there, blotchy with apparent fright." Shanker was ultimately allowed to leave unharmed and, Carson noted with pride, "this is the last time we were to see Mr. Shanker in The Black Community on his own."[66]

Further trouble erupted in July when the Ocean Hill–Brownsville Planning Council submitted a proposal to the Board of Education in which it dropped its call for funding of the MES program.[67] Superintendent Donovan argued that if the experiment were meant to examine the effects of community control, providing extra MES funds would taint the results.[68] Shanker was furious that the Planning Council broke the deal, removing the central reason the UFT had supported community control in Ocean Hill–Brownsville.[69] The denial of the MES funds was "the beginning of the end," said the UFT's Sandy Feldman.[70]

The planning council also issued a troubling statement with a thinly veiled threat of violence: "The ending of oppression and the beginning of a new day has often become a reality only after people have resorted to violent means. . . . The following plan . . . is acknowledged to be the last threads of the community's faith in the school system's purposes and abilities."[71]

With the substantive educational reason for supporting community control having been removed—the deal for extra resources for MES schools—the leaders in Ocean Hill–Brownsville next undercut Shanker's other rationale: that community control could promote a democratic voice for parents. Elections for the local school board were held at local schools on August 3, 1967.[72] But then, in an unorthodox procedure, voting continued, door to door, on August 4 and 5, conducted by paid canvassers. Among those elected were some who were paid to get out the vote.[73] The elections were "phony," Shanker said, because candidates for the board went door to door asking people to vote right in front of them.[74] To further cloud matters, the elected "parent representatives" in turn chose as "community representatives" the people who had hired them to conduct the election.[75]

The Honest Ballot Association, which observed and validated internal UFT elections and those of other organizations, was not brought in, and the representativeness of the Board was questioned.[76] Local black Assemblyman Samuel D. Wright challenged the election as fraudulent and was supported editorially by the *Amsterdam News*.[77] A poll of Ocean Hill–Brownsville parents in early 1968 suggested only 29 percent supported the governing board.[78]

It quickly became obvious that the experimental district was taking on a radical Black Power outlook. Over the summer of 1967, the acting unit administrator, Rhody McCoy, made clear that his eventual goal was an all-black teaching force in Ocean Hill–Brownsville.[79] The first task of the board was to choose five principals, and the board insisted that all of them be black.[80] In order to achieve this goal, they had to go beyond the traditional civil-service list of those who scored high on the principals' exam.[81] Incredibly, among those hired to be principal was Herman Ferguson, an educator who had been arrested in June for allegedly plotting to murder civil-rights leaders Roy Wilkins of the NAACP and Whitney Young of the Urban League. (He was later convicted.) When police came to his apartment, there was a large stash of weapons, including ten rifles and a machine gun.[82]

On the surface, the Ferguson appointment seemed an odd one coming from acting unit administrator McCoy. A longtime school employee, Mc-Coy was a pipe-smoking tennis player who owned a pool.[83] But in reality, McCoy was a good friend of both Herman Ferguson and Sonny Carson, with whom he would go on occasion to Malcolm X's house to talk about educating black youth.[84] Asked about Ferguson's appointment, McCoy claimed, "I chose the best man I could find." (In the end, the citywide school board suspended Ferguson, and he never became a principal.)[85] For teachers, who had been told in the spring of 1967 that they would be part of the decision making for the experiment, the events of the summer made clear that they were being bypassed.[86]

The summer had raised a number of concerns about community control for Shanker: that hiring would be based on race rather than merit, that democratic procedures would be thwarted, that violence would be condoned and employed as a tactic, and that concerns about educational programs and funding were secondary. Now, as the fall approached, the frayed working relationship between community-control advocates and the UFT would face another challenge, as a potential teachers' strike loomed over an entirely different set of issues.

The 1967 Teachers' Strike

As Shanker kept a watchful eye on the deteriorating community-control situation, he was also headed for a showdown with the Board of Education and Mayor Lindsay over the 1967 teachers' contract. The risk of confrontation for the union was high because a new law had been passed governing teacher strikes. The old Condon-Wadlin Act, which provided that public employees who went on strike would be fired, was so draconian as to be ineffective—it was never enforced, given the shortage of teachers—and both sides knew that.[87] So the state passed the Taylor Law, named after the labor expert who devised it, which provided for two days' lost pay for every one day on strike, fines against the union, and jail sentences for union leaders, among other penalties.[88] The new law was slated to go into effect September 1, 1967.[89]

Nevertheless, Shanker upped the ante in negotiations. The three previous contracts—in 1962, 1963, and 1965—dealt primarily with straightforward union issues: wages and working conditions. But in 1967, Shanker had higher aspirations and wanted to expand the scope of collective bargaining. He raised for discussion three education policy issues: smaller class size, the More Effective Schools program, and a provision giving teachers greater leeway to suspend unruly students.[90] The class-size issue was the least controversial of the three, because reducing class size could be seen as both an education policy issue and as a working condition—so it was a less clear affront to the Board's policy authority.

The More Effective Schools issue was far more contentious. The program represented the opposite vision of community control—it sought to draw white, middle-class children into ghetto schools with the lure of low class size and better services. The program had long waiting lists, and Shanker's own son attended an MES preschool.[91] One study showed the program was highly effective for students who remained in it. Poor kids move around so much that the majority who moved in and out of the program did not benefit, but the 25 percent who stayed in the program "made giant strides," Shanker said.[92] In December 1966, Shanker called for expanding the number of MES schools from twenty-one to three hundred, at a cost of $150 million.[93] The board had two concerns: MES was expensive, and including it in contract negotiations impinged on management's prerogatives to set education policy.[94]

Over the years, opponents argued that it was undemocratic to negotiate public policy with one special-interest group.[95] Teacher-unionist-turned-critic Myron Lieberman, for example, argued that it was "nonsense" to expand the scope of bargaining, saying it was like the United Auto Workers negotiating over "the price of cars, their color, and safety features."[96] Supporters of broad bargaining responded that teachers have special expertise that should be employed.[97] And Shanker said that unlike autoworkers, teachers are blamed when things go wrong. "No one dreams of going to Ford or General Motors and saying, 'Ralph Nader says my car is unsafe; I demand that you fire the following workers.' In the schools it's very different. The parent marches in and says, 'This class is behind in reading: fire the teacher.'"[98] The Board stuck to its guns and argued it could not "delegate the making of policy on this or any other experimental program to the union and exclude the participation of parents and the public."[99]

The third contested provision advocated by the UFT would make it easier for teachers to remove disruptive students from the classroom. The disruptive child provision appealed to conservatives, just as the MES proposal appealed to liberals, but the UFT argued that they were both connected: they were both aimed at addressing problems that were particularly pervasive in low-income schools. You could not do much to help kids, even with programs like MES, unless you also dealt with the discipline problem.[100]

With the two sides deadlocked, a strike appeared imminent. Shanker suddenly became the subject of intense media scrutiny, most of it favorable. Shanker was profiled in the *New York Times* as a "Man in the News" and by A. H. Raskin in a longer piece for the *New York Times Magazine*.[101] Raskin called the thirty-eight-year-old Shanker part of a "new breed of unionists" who were younger, represented dynamic white-collar industries, and would determine the future of the labor movement.[102] He noted that Shanker's 49,000-member UFT was now the single largest local in the AFL-CIO, "bigger than the giant locals at Ford's River Rouge plant or at U.S. Steel's Gary Works." Shanker was praised for his skills in negotiating with civil-rights groups and school boards and his fairness in dealing with adversaries within the union. He was described as an avid reader who was "witty and convivial." He was noted for his modest salary compared to other union presidents and his quirky habits, like making wine in his basement.[103]

On September 7, four days prior to the scheduled opening of school, Shanker reviewed for the delegate assembly the board offer, which called for $125 million in wages and other benefits, but fell short on the three educational issues the union raised—class size, the More Effective Schools program, and discipline policy. Shanker declared to the assembly that it was insufficient to "get pretty good salary and welfare provisions" if the union did not also get "anything to help the children to learn and to read." The assembly voted overwhelmingly to reject the settlement and authorized the union to go forward with a plan for "mass resignations."[104]

On September 11, nearly 46,000 of the city's 58,000 teachers stayed away from school, ignoring an injunction against striking. Pickets surrounded 740 of nine hundred city schools. Teachers urged, "We risk our job for a voice in schools"[105] and carried placards: "Teachers Want What Children Need."[106]

Lindsay stoked the racial angle, as he had in the transit strike.[107] The most sensitive issue was the attempt to make it easier to discipline disruptive children. The New York State NAACP and the Harlem Parents Committee warned that teachers would abuse the disruptive child provision to remove black children.[108] Some left-leaning intellectuals said children causing trouble in schools were not disruptive children but "revolutionaries."[109] Shanker argued that the disruptive child provision was a compromise: teachers were putting pressure on the union to come out for the power to expel, without much due process for the student. Shanker said: "We always rejected that."[110] Shanker also pointed to Mary Moore, known as the Queen Mother in Harlem, who argued that "the failure to remove violent and disruptive students was a technique by which the white power structure used some black children to destroy the education of all others." She said, "whites would never tolerate this in a white middle-class district."[111]

Some black separatists also objected to the MES funding that the UFT sought. CORE said that MES schools undercut the attempt of Black Power advocates to employ their own curriculum.[112] And Herman Ferguson and others denounced MES as racist, based on a compensatory model that suggested there was something wrong with poor and black students.[113] In Black Power circles, liberal educator Deborah Meier noted, the view was "that black children do not need anything special (not even what suburban parents take for granted). They just need unbiased teachers with the right pro-black ideology."[114]

Before the strike, Shanker had gone to Rhody McCoy and the governing board in Ocean Hill–Brownsville and reminded them that the UFT had been supportive of the experiment. He asked that they support the UFT strike.[115] But after Shanker left, McCoy told the board he would quit if the board went along with the strike.[116] In fact, all the schools in Ocean Hill–Brownsville stayed open.[117] The schools were run largely by black teachers who crossed the picket lines and local parent volunteers coordinated by Ferguson.[118] Picketing teachers were cursed by parents.[119] Community board members were so opposed to the strike that they gave the names of striking male teachers to the Selective Service, saying they were no longer employed or eligible for a draft deferment.[120]

One bright spot in the UFT's fraying relationship with members of the black community, however, was the strong support of Bayard Rustin, who appeared at a UFT rally, and of Martin Luther King, who sent a supportive telegram on September 13.[121] "I enthusiastically endorse the efforts of the teachers of New York City to improve their living and working conditions, and the quality of education they dispense," he wrote. The issue was not parents versus teachers, King said, but rather a Board of Education that does not honor the interests of teachers or students. He did urge, though, that the disruptive child provision be clarified "to avoid misunderstanding and confusion."[122]

For King, the UFT's push for greater education spending and MES schools to encourage integration made far more sense than the Black Power movement's call for community control. Though it might seem odd for a civil-rights leader like King to inject himself into the middle of a teachers' strike, particularly on the side of the largely white union at loggerheads with prominent members of the black community in New York City, siding with Shanker and the UFT was consistent with King's increasing orientation toward issues of economic inequality. In late 1966, King had told SCLC staff that "we are now dealing with class issues." In 1967, King repeated his call for a Bill of Rights for the Disadvantaged in testifying before the Kerner Commission.[123] And in late 1967, he began to plan for a Poor People's Campaign the following spring.[124]

He told leaders of the SCLC: "Gentlemen, we are going to take this movement and we are going to reach out to the poor people in all directions in this country. We're going into the Southwest after the Indians, into the West after the Chicanos, into Appalachia after the poor whites, and into the ghettoes after Negroes and Puerto Ricans. And we're going to bring them together and enlarge this campaign into something bigger than just a civil rights movement for Negroes."[125] To King, Shanker's UFT and the labor movement was not the enemy, but an indispensable ally in the fight for greater equality.

Negotiations between Lindsay, Shanker, Schools Superintendent Bernard Donovan, and School Board President Alfred Giardino continued in an effort to end the strike, which was now entering its third week—far longer than the 1960 and 1962 strikes, each of which lasted only one day.[126] The More Effective Schools issue was the toughest, because the fundamental argument was over policy, not money, Shanker said.[127]

Finally, on September 26, Lindsay, Shanker, and Donovan appeared at City Hall and announced that a written agreement had been reached. The pact called for $10 million for experimental school programs, at least half of which would be used on "intensive" projects, though no funds were specifically committed to MES, a clear setback for Shanker.[128] The final agreement also included some reduction in class size and a compromise on the disruptive pupils issue. The terms provided for the creation of local discipline review boards, consisting of teachers, board members, and outside child experts.[129] (Shanker later said the procedure for removing children proved so cumbersome that "it was never used.")[130] The annual starting salary of teachers, $5,400, was increased in the agreement by $800 in the first year and $500 more in the second year—an improvement of $150 over the prestrike offer.[131] In all, the package represented a more than 20 percent increase in pay and benefits.[132] Teachers ratified the contract overwhelmingly and returned on September 29, having missed fourteen school days.[133]

The Bundy Report

The actions of the community-control advocates during the 1967 strike left Shanker more embittered toward the idea than ever. Not only had community-control advocates abandoned nondiscriminatory hiring, integration, and nonviolence, they had also purposely tried to break the strike and hurt the union. Looking back, McGeorge Bundy said the 1967 teachers' strike was a turning point. "We were in good touch with Shanker before that, and then later on, he stopped answering our calls."[134]

On September 27, as the strike was coming to a close, Shanker appeared in the evening at a turbulent meeting of the Board of Education, and attempted to object to the appointment of Rhody McCoy, Ocean Hill–Brownsville's acting unit administrator, to a permanent position. Shanker wanted to lay out the case that McCoy's appointment was undemocratic. The board meeting was packed with two hundred black activists, many of them supporters of Herman Ferguson, whose suspension was also up for board consideration. At the outset of the meeting, Isaiah Lewis, a leader of Brooklyn CORE, shouted a threat: "Better have somebody to guard those teachers in our neighborhood from now on." As Shanker got up to speak, he was blocked by a number of community members. One yelled: "We are sick and tired of Shanker and those teachers that are not black." It was a wild meeting; chairs were thrown. Shanker was driven from the room by hecklers. After Shanker left, the Board approved the appointment of McCoy as unit administrator but upheld the suspension of Ferguson pending a hearing.[135]

The atmosphere of violence and chaos was taking a toll on teachers, and the next day Shanker met with four hundred teachers from Harlem and Brooklyn at the Americana Hotel to discuss, given community hostility, their fears of returning to ghetto schools after the strike. Teachers alleged that while on picket lines in Harlem they had been slapped and kicked.[136] Reportedly two-thirds of IS 201's teachers were asking for transfers.[137] Shanker urged the teachers to stay, saying: "We must emulate the kids of Little Rock, who kept going to school despite harassment." The teachers met for several hours and ultimately voted overwhelmingly to return to school.[138]

Amid all this chaos, the Bundy Commission had been working on its recommendations on the future of community control in New York City, and in early November it released its report. Entitled *Reconnection for*

Learning, the report recommended that a version of the Ocean Hill–Brownsville pilot be implemented citywide. The Commission called for the creation of thirty to sixty largely autonomous districts, governed by eleven-member boards (six members elected by parents and five appointed by the mayor), that would hire school personnel and set educational policy. Although the tenure rights of existing teachers would be preserved, new personnel would receive tenure from the districts. The panel also called for abolishing the Board of Examiners and allowing teachers to be hired only with state certification, a substantially lower standard, arguing that the exam limited the number of minority teachers. Although 29 percent of students were black, and 21 percent Puerto Rican, the staff was just 9 percent black and less than 0.2 percent Puerto Rican, the panel said. This imbalance, they said, had much to do with "the disaffection of large segments of the community with the schools." Finally, the Bundy panel urged that race be a consideration in hiring. "It is not unreasonable, nor is it educationally unsound, to include knowledge of, and sensitivity to, the environment of pupils as criteria for appointment and advancement. If a district board believes that otherwise qualified Negro or Puerto Rican candidates are especially likely to meet these criteria, it would be justified in staffing accordingly."[139]

Part of the theory of decentralization was that in such a large system, there was no accountability, especially for parents who lacked political muscle.[140] And part of the theory was that black students would do better academically if they had black teachers. The African American Teachers Association said that for black children, "teachers of their own race were needed to help build self-esteem and create a healthier environment for effective learning."[141]

Shanker understood the frustration that underlay the Bundy report: the ugly white resistance to integration of schools in New York City and the huge achievement gap between blacks and whites. These were very serious issues. But he believed Bundy's emphasis on community control substituted a change in governance for real reform, that it would Balkanize the city even more than it already was, would weaken teacher standards and a commitment to merit, and that it was ultimately designed as an attack on unions.

While the Bundy plan was advanced as a cutting-edge "liberal" reform, to Shanker there was nothing liberal about it. Liberals had always pushed for substantive investment in education over cheap solutions, integration against local control and states' rights, merit hiring over discriminatory hiring, and strong unions against union busting. In a series of statements, Shanker, the UFT Executive Committee, and the UFT delegate assembly tried to make the case that while blacks had a legitimate grievance about the state of New York City schools, Bundy's "radical" proposal was in fact reactionary and "would irreparably harm the educational system."[142]

Fundamentally, Shanker argued, the focus on governance changes were a distraction. "The tragedy of the Bundy proposals," Shanker said, "is that they take us away from the question of why children won't read, why they can't write, where is the money going to come from, and what can we do for these children," focusing instead on whether board headquarters should "be a little closer or a little further away."[143]

Whereas Shanker had supported the Ocean Hill–Brownsville pilot as part of a deal to get more money for MES schools, the Bundy proposal was education on the cheap—a way to be for change while also balancing the budget.[144] When business groups later argued for community control by pointing out that Scarsdale had a smaller ratio of student to school board members than New York City, Shanker responded: "The major difference in educational achievement between the children of Scarsdale and the children of Harlem is not due, as some have suggested, to local control of schools but rather to the relative effects of wealth and poverty on the lives of children." He wrote: "To try to convince the poor that by electing their own school boards their children will be enabled to read and to go to college is to perpetuate a cruel fraud or a hoax—to substitute a mere formal change for one of real substance."[145]

Nor did the Bundy proposal do anything to promote the socioeconomic integration of students, which a massive federal study, the Coleman Report, had found was the single most important school factor in promoting educational achievement. The UFT noted during the controversy that "breaking the school system up into 20 to 100 districts is a segregationist move" that would reduce academic achievement. "The Coleman Report and the Civil Rights Commission Report show that what children learn from each other and their social interaction in the classroom setting is a more important variable in academic success than textbooks (or teachers). "[146]

The Coleman Report made clear, as Shanker would later note, "that children from socioeconomically deprived families do better academically when they are integrated with children of higher socioeconomic status and better-educated families." He said, "when children converse, they learn from each other. Placing a child with a larger vocabulary next to one with a smaller vocabulary can provide a gain to one without a loss to the other."[147]

Shanker's MES program had sought to increase the interaction of poor and middle-class students, consistent with Coleman's findings that class-mates mattered. Bundy's plan, in contrast, was a step in the opposite di-rection, an attempt to make separate schools for rich and poor work, an approach unlikely to raise academic achievement.

If the institutionalization of segregation through community control was bad for educational achievement, Shanker believed it was also bad as a societal matter, for it abandoned the "common school" ideal that bring-ing students from different backgrounds together would help promote social assimilation, tolerance, and good citizenship. This was an awkward issue for Lindsay, who had run in 1965 on a prointegration platform. In-deed, as the Bundy Report was being released, Lindsay was playing a piv-otal role in the Kerner Commission, whose report, issued a few months later, warned that America was becoming two societies—black and white, separate and unequal. In fact, Lindsay penned that line.[148]

The Bundy report made a tortured argument that it was not giving up on integration: community control would so boost achievement, it claimed, that whites would want to come to ghetto schools.[149] But in franker moments, the Lindsay administration clearly saw community control as an alternative to integration, noting: "The Mayor believes that school decentralization is the most practical alternative in New York to cross-city busing of students that the state has ordered in other areas."[150]

The UFT executive board pounced on this issue, saying the Bundy pro-posal "is not decentralization, it is Balkanization."[151] Shanker argued that "the [smaller] the district, the [less] integrated it will be, and the [more] likely that it will be controlled by a small band of extremists using threats of violence."[152] He said: "We think that the smaller, the more provincial, the more bigoted, the more narrow," and the more tribal.[153]

Many advocates of community control were quite explicit about their opposition to integration. Community-control advocates carried plac-ards that read, "Black Children Need Black Culture."[154] Yes, Shanker ar-gued, but they also need American culture. The language of "community" quickly became racialized. The issue of community control, New York City civic leader Richard Ravitch notes, raised the question, "what is com-munity? How is community defined?" Advocates clearly defined commu-nity by race, and indeed, the phrase "community people" became a syn-onym for black.[155] To Shanker, the call for black control of black schools was a step backward. He noted, "there have been black schools through-out the country for more than a century," with black principals and black staff—which is "precisely the opposite" of the integration that people fought for in the South.[156]

Indeed, the original call for "community control" in New York City came from whites in Queens in 1964, seeking to stop integration of schools.[157] The argument was, said Shanker, that the local community "had the right to make final decisions in much the same way that south-ern governors demand the right to do as they wish in the name of states rights."[158]

The UFT said it was unsurprising that conservatives like Bill Buckley and Barry Goldwater favored community control.[159] Indeed, there was a strange philosophical compatibility between community-control advo-cates and those who advocated for private-school vouchers, because both upended the delicate balance between a parent's rights and society's needs. The philosophy of community control, as articulated by Ocean Hill–Brownsville Governing Board chair Reverend C. Herbert Oliver was that "it is the right (their exclusive right) and the duty of parents to educate their children. . . . No group of 'educators,' no union, or Board of Educa-tion has the inherent right to educate children."[160]

Shanker had a very different view. He did not believe that black nation-alist or white supremacist parents had the right to set up publicly funded schools that taught black separation or a KKK philosophy. Public funds were meant to teach democratic values even when they conflicted with the values of parents. The school was meant to broaden a student's out-look, sometimes exposing her to views different from her parents'. That was the delicate balance that community control sought to undermine. And in so doing, it could undermine the central rationale for public schooling, Shanker believed.

Shanker and the UFT were also concerned that Bundy's proposal to abolish the Board of Examiners and allow hiring by local school boards would mean a reduction of standards, patronage hiring, and hiring by race—all of which would end up hurting poor and minority students. In 1898, the Board of Education had centralized hiring and established an examination system in reaction to a half century of local political, ethnic-based, and corrupt hiring.[161] Many Jews felt especially passionate about the merit system and had gone into teaching because the objective examination shielded them from the discrimination that they faced in other areas of the employment sector.[162] Now this was all to be undone. Shanker conceded that the Board of Examiners did not have an unblemished history. For years, it had used the oral portion of the exam to screen out applicants with Jewish and Black accents, and Shanker himself initially failed for this reason. (He was forced to practice his diction in front of the mirror, repeating again and again: "Look at the lovely yellow lilies.")[163] But now, the exam had basically become a literacy test.[164]

Shanker said having more black teachers was desirable, and the UFT had pushed for more recruiting from the South. But the relevant measure was not Bundy's (the percentage of minority students), but rather the percentage of college-educated minority adults eligible to teach. "It is from adults, not children of school age, that teachers are recruited." Given the low percentage of blacks among New York college graduates, Shanker noted that "the percentage of black teachers in New York is considerably higher than the percentage of black eligibles."[165] Moreover, while it might be valuable for black students to have black teachers as role models, what was more important was that they be qualified. In segregated Southern schools, all the principals and teachers were black, Shanker noted, and the system did not raise black achievement.[166]

Finally, Shanker believed, if the Bundy Report was an attack on integration, merit, and nondiscrimination, it was also an assault on labor unions. Just seven years earlier, the UFT had struck for the right to collectively bargain, and a proposal for thirty to sixty school boards threatened that newly gained power.[167] Shanker knew well that unions gained their strength from unity. Their power derived from their ability to shut down the entire school system, and with up to sixty separate units, that leverage could be lost. Negotiating separate agreements would also be more cumbersome, time consuming, and would promote morale problems if some districts did better than others.[168]

The national implications were also important. Teachers' unions were still in their infancy in 1967—only 25 percent of public-school districts nationally had collective-bargaining agreements—and if big-city school systems were all broken up into tiny units, the movement might be strangled in its cradle.[169] Shanker looked at who outside the black community was backing community control—big business, Mayor Lindsay—and was suspicious of their intentions toward unions.[170]

The irony for Shanker was that labor unions held dear many of the same values the community-control advocates purported to represent. Many community-control supporters said they wanted "black values" taught in the schools, by which they meant mutuality, cooperation, and community, in contrast to self-centered individualism.[171] But what institution better exemplified those values than trade unions, which said if you fire some of us unjustly, we will all go out on strike?

In place of the Bundy proposal, the UFT recommended the creation of no more than fifteen districts (in order to promote the possibility of integration and reduce administrative costs) with the central board retaining power over salaries, working conditions, and selection of teachers.[172] To improve accountability, the UFT proposed an independent civilian review board for teachers, comparable to Lindsay's review board for police, which would adjudicate parents' complaints against teachers on nonprofessional matters such as abusing a child or using racial epithets.[173]

Civil Jail

As the battles over the Bundy Report raged, Shanker had another challenge to face: the prospect of going to jail for his actions in the September strike. In October, Shanker had been found guilty of criminal contempt, sentenced to fifteen days in jail, and given a $250 fine. The union was fined $150,000.[174]

In mid-December, an appeals court upheld Shanker's fifteen-day jail sentence, and the UFT decided not to appeal further. On December 20, Shanker presided over a two-hour meeting of 1,800 UFT delegates, some of whom urged a new strike to protest his jailing. Shanker opposed the idea, but he told the delegates, "It's a very sad thing when someone in the United States has to go to jail for fighting for smaller class sizes, [for] regular rather than uncertified teachers for our children, and for insisting that there was more money available for teachers when the city government said there was none."[175]

As the meeting ended, Eadie Shanker ran up to her husband and kissed him—a moment captured by a *New York Times* photographer for the next day's newspaper. A few minutes after 6:00 p.m., Shanker was taken by police car to the Civil Jail at 434 West Thirty-seventh Street. As Shanker entered the jail, hundred of teachers who had walked over from the Delegate Assembly at the Manhattan Center sang "For He's a Jolly Good Fellow."[176]

The jail was a one-hundred-year-old low-security redbrick facility, with dormitories rather than cells and wire mesh screens over the windows rather than bars. Prisoners were expected to do about thirty minutes of maintenance chores each day but were otherwise free to watch TV, read, or play ping-pong. While incarcerated, Shanker read two books: a serious tome by Charles Scott Benson entitled *The Economics of Public Education* and Bernard Malamud's 1966 novel *The Fixer*. Although the facility was not designed for felons, it housed some rough characters who were being held as material witnesses in murder cases. Some of the prisoners would act out and be put in solitary confinement. Shanker's job was to set the table for meals and sweep the facility. The beds had no mattresses, but rather consisted of blankets on top of springs.[177]

The other inmates enjoyed having Shanker around because he received hundreds of packages of cakes and fruit. "The prisoners loved it while I was there. They never ate so well," he said. One of the cakes had a file inside as a joke. Everyone laughed until they realized they could be seriously punished.[178] Shanker could see that outside the jail there was a round-the-clock vigil of union members, including at least a dozen picketers at all times.[179]

The jail term was hard on his family. "It wasn't an easy time," Eadie Shanker recalls. "I was alone with the kids." Adam was six, Jennie was three, and Michael was two. She says, "It was wintertime. It was the holidays. The kids wanted to know where their daddy was. And I had to tell them daddy was in jail because he believed in certain things very strongly and sometimes you have to do things that aren't right now considered lawful. . . . That daddy was in there for good reasons."[180]

On Christmas Day, Eadie Shanker planned to visit with gifts from the kids. Shanker called her when he found out that there was a policy of no visitors on holidays. Eadie got very angry and decided to visit anyway and appeared at the steps with presents in hand, at about 1:00 p.m. She was turned away.[181] Eadie told the assembled press, whom she had alerted: "A Scrooge must run this city"—a line that Al Shanker loved to repeat for years to come.[182] With cameras rolling, she said, "Michael, who is just two and a half, sent his favorite book, *The Little Engine That Could*."[183] Jennie sent a telephone so her Daddy could call her; Adam sent candy.[184]

On December 28, union leaders took out an ad, "Albert Shanker: Christmas Behind Bars," attacking the Taylor Law and arguing that public-sector strikes should be legal unless "the health and safety of the community are clearly imperiled." The signers included David Dubinsky, Michael Harrington, Irving Howe, Tom Kahn, Martin Luther King Jr., Eleanor Holmes Norton, A. Philip Randolph, Joseph Rauh, Bayard Rustin, Harry Van Arsdale, and Jerry Wurf.[185]

Shanker always argued that it was outrageous to jail public-employee union leaders for striking when private employees were free to strike without fear of punishment. The right to strike was crucial to providing employees with a means to counteract the power of the employer, and virtually all other democracies extend the right to public employees. Why would a teachers' strike in private schools be perfectly legal when public-school teachers' strikes are illegal? The issue should not be public sector versus private sector, but whether public health and safety were at stake—which a strike by private utility company employees, for example, would jeopardize and a strike by public school teachers would not.

The ban on public-employee strikes came down to "an outmoded concept of sovereignty," Shanker argued, "that the subjects may not refuse to do the bidding of the monarch." He contended that "only in totalitarian societies is a strike against the government as employer viewed as an act of rebellion. Such a view is abhorrent in a democratic society."[186]

The jailing backfired on Lindsay, says Eadie Shanker. "He made a martyr of Al" and just made him more famous.[187] The jailing of a teacher was a remarkable event for the public and it helped make Shanker a household name.[188]

Shanker was released on January 3, 1968, at 4:00 p.m., to a cheering crowd of 250 teachers. He mounted a sound truck and struck a defiant tone. Asked by a reporter what he thought he had proved by staying in prison, he responded: "I wasn't trying to prove anything. I didn't ask them to send me here. . . . The teachers are not going to give up their fight for professional dignity, and they're not going to give up the fight for good schools, and if this is the price that we have to pay periodically, then that price is gonna be paid."[189] Noting that the walkout had resulted in the loss of checkoff privileges, a substantial fine, and a jail sentence, Shanker said: "If we have to suffer these consequences one, two, five, or ten times, we will if it will lead to better schools."[190]

After Shanker was released, he received a ten-dollar check in the mail to help him pay a personal fine of $250.[191] The check, dated January 5, 1968, came from Martin Luther King.[192] "Al was truly like a kid when he found out that King had sent this ten dollar check," recalls Rachelle Horowitz. "He was very moved by that."[193] Michael Harrington remembers that Shanker carried the check around with him with great pride.[194]

The King Assassination

Four months later, on April 4, 1968, Shanker received the news that King had been assassinated while in Memphis, Tennessee, helping sanitation workers with their strike. In a statement, Shanker said:

> The sudden and violent death of Dr. Marin Luther King, Jr. places a serious and profound obligation on all Americans, black and white—an obligation to continue and broaden the now stilled efforts of Dr. King to rebuild a society where racial justice and peace prevail. . . . We have been proud to walk with Dr. King in Mississippi and in Washington and to work with him in establishing freedom schools in the South. In this tragic hour, we rededicate ourselves to his cause.[195]

Shanker pledged that the UFT would raise thousands of dollars to aid the Memphis sanitation workers whose cause had brought King to Memphis and to redouble the "effort to bring together a great civil rights coalition to work for equality of opportunity throughout America."[196] Later, Shanker went to Memphis to honor King's memory, and the UFT actively supported King's Poor People's Campaign in the spring.[197] Shanker's statement closed with a call for the Board of Education to hold memorial services in all New York City public schools on April 5.[198]

But in Ocean Hill–Brownsville, in JHS 271, the memorial service held was not of the type Shanker envisioned. The principal called an assembly to discuss the killing and said that the white teachers could leave if they wished. One teacher, Fred Nauman, recalls: "We were very disturbed by the fact that we had been segregated. This seemed to be saying to the students, 'These people should not be here for this.'"[199] Among the speakers was Leslie Campbell, vice president of the African American Teachers Association, who told the students: "Brothers and sisters, you have to stop fighting among yourselves. . . . You know who to steal from. If you steal, steal from those who have it—stop fighting among yourselves." He said, "If whitey taps you on the shoulder, send him to the graveyard." Following the assembly, one teacher was attacked for taking down a sign which read, "Martin Luther King was killed by a vicious white man—Prepare yourselves." Another teacher was knocked unconscious and sent to the hospital.[200]

Stokely Carmichael reacted to the assassination in Washington, D.C., by declaring: "White America killed Dr. King last night. . . . Black people know that they need to get guns."[201] Nationally, King's assassination led to rioting and disorder in 110 cities, resulting in thirty-nine deaths.[202] The next day in New York City, the UFT was scheduled to give its annual John Dewey award to Bayard Rustin. But Rustin, upon learning of King's death, headed straight to Memphis. Michael Harrington read Rustin's prepared speech in his stead.[203]

Rustin's speech, entitled "Integration Within Decentralization," argued that civil-rights groups and teachers' unions were natural allies. As a division of the labor movement, teachers' unions were part of an institution that was more integrated than schools or churches and the only mass institution dedicated to eradicating poverty. Likewise, as a group of educators, teachers had a strong vested interest in ensuring that student poverty was addressed so that they could do their job of teaching more effectively. Rather than fighting over decentralization, he said, parents should join teachers in advocating for better facilities and education. The emphasis on complete community control was dividing the coalition and also would further segregate students. He ended by quoting the Kerner Commission, whose vice chair was John Lindsay, on the importance of addressing "the consequences of racial isolation."[204]

For Albert Shanker, the rise of Black Power in New York City and its embrace by white establishment figures like McGeorge Bundy was a stunning betrayal of liberal principles. Within the span of just a few years, one by one, the ideals of integration, nonviolence, and colorblind hiring, along with the potent political coalition between blacks and organized labor, were diluted or even discarded. With King gone, American liberalism had lost its most eloquent spokesperson for these principles.

Bayard Rustin had been King's mentor, and now he was arguably King's leading intellectual heir. But at the UFT luncheon, protesters more attuned to Malcolm X than Martin Luther King denounced Rustin for supporting the union.[205] The fight between them and Rustin, between the disciples of Malcolm X and Martin Luther King, and between John Lindsay and Albert Shanker, was about to explode.

5

The Ocean Hill–Brownsville Strike and
the Liberal Assault on Labor

1968

A T least since Franklin Roosevelt's time, one of the core values of American liberalism has been that workers have the right to organize to fight for better wages and to protect themselves from arbitrary dismissal. Many conservatives, particularly in the South, never accepted that view. But it was a bedrock liberal principle. It was stunning, therefore, that in the topsy-turvy environment of 1968, the right to protect unionized workers from arbitrary termination would come under assault not from Southern conservatives but from New York City liberals.

The Terminations

On May 9, 1968, the Ocean Hill–Brownsville District Governing Board sent telegrams to nineteen educators (thirteen teachers and six administrators), terminating their employment in the district.[1] Of the nineteen, eighteen were white and Jewish and one was black, the latter mistakenly included in the list because his name was similar to that of a white teacher.[2] The dismissal of the single black teacher was rescinded almost immediately after the mistake was discovered.[3]

The telegrams read:

The Governing Board of the Ocean Hill–Brownsville Demonstration
District has voted to end your employment in the schools of this district. This action was taken on the recommendation of the Personnel Committee. This termination of employment is to take effect
immediately.

   In the event you wish to question this action, the Governing Board
will receive you on Friday, May 10, 1968 at 6 P.M. at Intermediate School
55, 2921 Bergen Street, Brooklyn, New York.

   You will report Friday morning to Personnel, 110 Livingston Street,
Brooklyn, for reassignment.

The letters were signed by Reverend C. Herbert Oliver, Chairman,
Ocean Hill–Brownsville Governing Board; and Rhody McCoy, Unit
Administrator.[4]

Fred Nauman, the UFT chapter leader, was among those fired. An admirer of Martin Luther King and a member of the NAACP, he was sympathetic to the plight of his black students.[5] Unlike many teachers in
ghetto schools who moved to a middle-class school as quickly as possible,
Nauman, a Holocaust survivor, started teaching at Junior High 73 (the
predecessor of JHS 271) in 1959 and stayed, because, he says, "I enjoyed the
age level and the nature of the kids. I felt you could do things with them.
And 271 had a great staff. . . . I had never planned to leave."[6]

   Nauman says that the collection of terminated teachers was odd. It included some excellent teachers and three or four who probably deserved
to be fired. It included critics of the community program, like Nauman,
and supporters of the program. Nauman says the firings were not based
on merit, ideology, or religion. "They just wanted a confrontation. It was
a push to see how much power they could get."[7]

   Shanker immediately met with the group of fired teachers and said it
was up to them whether the union should take a stand on the issue. "Al
really left that decision up to us," says Nauman. The group was virtually
unanimous in saying the union should fight.[8] Shanker believed that if he
backed down, more teachers would be terminated. Governing Board
chairman Rev. Oliver said the board really wanted to transfer "hundreds"
of teachers. The first nineteen were meant to make a dramatic statement
and to assert control.[9] The ultimate logic of McCoy's notion that minor-

ity students need minority teachers was a massive firing of whites in a system whose student body was more than 50 percent minority.[10]

Defenders of community control would later make much of the fact that the telegram suggested that teachers were only being reassigned or transferred, not fired. But that was clearly not the intent of McCoy and the Governing Board. On May 16, McCoy was quoted in the *New York Times* as saying: "Not one of these teachers will be allowed to teach anywhere in this city. The black community will see to that."[11] Members of the governing board also repeatedly said they had "fired" the teachers.[12]

Superintendent Donovan said the Ocean Hill–Brownsville District Governing Board had no authority to terminate the nineteen educators and ordered the district to take them back.[13] On May 13, when five teachers sought to return to JHS 271, black militants blocked the doors. Parents screamed, "the children will never let you stay." Extremists painted swastikas on the building.[14] McCoy refused to take back the teachers. Lindsay refused to force the issue and urged the dismissed teachers to go quietly.[15] Shanker was furious, called Lindsay "a profile in weakness," and asked Lindsay whether he would have backed down to a white mob that fired a black teacher.[16] On May 22, 350 of 556 teachers in Ocean Hill–Brownsville went on strike for the remainder of the school year.[17] Because the strike only affected a small number of schools, little attention was paid to it.[18]

If McCoy was temporarily winning in Ocean Hill–Brownsville, his move to terminate teachers proved a tactical mistake for the cause of community control. By confirming the teachers' fears that decentralization could jeopardize their job security, the move energized them to oppose a bill that at that very moment was being considered in Albany to establish decentralization along the lines recommended in the Bundy Report. Shanker brought five hundred teachers to lobby against the bill and spent hundreds of thousands of dollars.[19] Shanker pointed to the terminations without adequate cause and the vigilantism and anti-Semitism in Ocean Hill–Brownsville as evidence of what could happen under community control.[20]

As the New York state legislature moved toward adjournment in late May, it passed a watered-down decentralization bill authored by conservative state senator John Marchi that essentially deferred the issue for a year. A stronger plan, backed by the Ford Foundation, the mayor, and the State Commission of Education, was abandoned under pressure from the UFT.[21] Shanker was considered the key figure in the strong plan's defeat.[22]

One observer wrote: "Never before had a teacher trade union exercised so much power."[23]

Over the summer, hearings were held on the charges against the teachers terminated in Ocean Hill–Brownsville. The School Board asked a retired African American judge, Francis Rivers, to preside over the hearings.[24] By June, eight of the nineteen teachers had given up and requested transfers, and the one black teacher had been reinstated, leaving ten teachers to be judged. On August 26, Rivers announced his finding. In each and every case, he cleared the teachers of wrongdoing and ruled they should be reinstated. In one case, a teacher accused by McCoy of allowing kids to throw chairs was found to have taught in a classroom where chairs were nailed to the ground.[25]

Politically and morally, the Rivers decision strengthened Shanker's case immensely. Defending members from unjust dismissal went to the heart of what it meant to have a union. Under American law, nonunionized employees can normally be fired "for any reason, or for no reason at all," under the reigning "employment at will" doctrine.[26] (Now there are exceptions to the rule for discrimination based on race, gender, ethnicity, religion, disability, and age). But in this case, a union had fought for tenure protection in the legislature and was there to defend its members from unjust dismissal. If the union could not do that, what reason was there for the union to exist?

Over the summer, with the chaos rising around him, Shanker moved his family out of New York City to a distant suburb. Shanker's run-in with Sonny Carson was but one of several incidents. Shanker was threatened by militants in the spring when he and his oldest son Adam were taking a walk in Prospect Park in Brooklyn. Other threats led Shanker to be protected by police bodyguards.[27] "Try explaining that to your young children," Shanker said.[28]

Throughout his rise to prominence and power, Shanker had continued to draw a very modest salary from the UFT. While other union presidents were often making salaries ranging from $50,000 to $100,000 in the 1960s, Shanker made $14,950 in 1967, which was fixed at $3,000 above the maximum teacher salary.[29] By 1968, he was making $16,000.[30] The Shankers were living in a fairly modest home in the Flatbush section of Brooklyn, a working-class neighborhood.[31] Although Shanker was not infrequently on the front page of the *New York Times*, he was living in very close quarters, with houses squeezed up next to one another. The Shankers' home abutted an apartment building a few feet away, so neighbors overlooked the backyard.[32]

In August 1968, the family moved to a split-level home in the distant suburb of Putnam Valley, New York, where land was relatively cheap and Shanker could afford a home with a brook running behind it. In the stream, one could fish for trout and observe blue herons.[33] The home cost $31,000.[34] Given the lengthy commute, the UFT rented Shanker a studio apartment on East Twenty-fourth Street in Manhattan.[35] Ironically, while the Putnam Valley home was meant to be an escape from the tensions in the city, the conservative semirural community was hardly welcoming to the family of a big-city union chief. There were few Jews in the area and the children were subject to anti-Semitic taunts in school.[36]

Meanwhile, Rhody McCoy spent the summer lining up replacements for the 350 UFT teachers who had gone on strike in May. McCoy had pledged an all-black teaching force, but he was unable to accomplish that. Of those hired, one hundred were black. The balance were white, half of these Jewish.[37] McCoy acknowledged that the pool of black teachers to draw upon was very small.[38]

The First 1968 Strike

As teachers prepared to begin the new school year, the stage was set for a major confrontation. The disputed teachers had been cleared of wrongdoing by Judge Rivers, but McCoy had hired a new batch of replacements for them—and for all the teachers who had struck in May. Shanker believed it was time to up the ante and expand the scope of the ineffective Ocean Hill–Brownsville strike the previous spring to involve the entire New York City school system and its one million students.

On September 6, the UFT delegate assembly met to discuss whether to call a citywide strike for the beginning of the school year, September 9. When concerns were raised that the strike would be seen as anti-black, Shanker said: "This is nonsense. This is a strike that will protect black teachers against white racists and white teachers against black racists." The delegates applauded vigorously. "If we don't strike, there will be no union," he said. "Public sentiment is overwhelmingly for us. We are not fighting for a buck." The delegate assembly voted 1,914 to 254 to recommend a strike to the membership.[39]

As the talks with the school board continued in an effort to avert the strike, Shanker was threatened by about ten community-control activists, including members of the Ocean Hill–Brownsville governing board. The president of the PTA at PS 269 in Brooklyn, Carrie Raynor, yelled, "I'm going to whip you, Shanker, myself." She continued, "come on out, Shanker. I'm going to jail for you." Shanker left the board building with a police escort.[40] The chairman of the IS 201 governing board, David Spencer, said his schools would remain open. Shanker, he said, stood for "the same old racism that refuses to recognize the right of black and Puerto Rican people to control their own lives."[41]

The school board said the ten ousted teachers needed to be reinstated, but Rhody McCoy said the local governing board would not take back the teachers. "This is about the fifth ultimatum we've gotten so far," McCoy said. "We are now using ultimatums for souvenirs."[42]

On September 8, with schools slated to open the following day, UFT members voted 12,021 to 1,716 in favor of striking.[43] On Monday, September 9, the opening day of school, the UFT launched its most successful walkout, as measured by teacher participation. Some 93 percent of teachers failed to report to work, compared with 12 percent in the 1960 strike, 52 percent in the 1962 strike, and 77 percent in the 1967 strike. Some 810 of nine hundred schools were closed.[44]

Two days later, the strike was settled between the union and the school board, and teachers went back to work, having won virtually everything they sought. The settlement provided for the return of the ten dismissed teachers from Ocean Hill–Brownsville, full salary payments and return of the three hundred teachers who walked out in the spring in support of the dismissed teachers, and a promise that when decentralization plans were implemented citywide, teachers would be provided guarantees of due process in termination proceedings. The front page *New York Times* photo featured a smiling Al Shanker along with Superintendent Donovan and Board of Education president Rose Shapiro.[45]

If the union and the board agreed, Rhody McCoy and members of the Ocean Hill–Brownsville district did not. Rev. Herbert Oliver, chairman of the Ocean Hill–Brownsville board, noted: "We had nothing to do with [the agreement] and have not been asked to be part of it." Rhody McCoy said the three hundred striking teachers were welcome back, but the board would have to pay for a double staff, since new teachers had already been hired as replacements.[46] It was not a good sign of things to come.

The Second 1968 Strike

On Wednesday, September 11, Sandra Feldman arrived at McCoy's offices before 7:00 a.m. to try to ensure the safe return of the teachers. McCoy was noncommittal, and as they were talking, the phone kept ringing, and McCoy repeatedly told callers that the procedures agreed upon were to be put into effect.[47]

At JHS 271, as the disputed UFT teachers arrived around 8:00 a.m., a dozen black adults led by Sonny Carson sought to block their entrance. Fred Nauman, chairman of the school UFT chapter, announced, "we're here to teach." One demonstrator shouted at the teachers: "You're dead! We know your faces. We'll get you, your families, your children. We'll be where you live." But the school's black principal, William Harris, appeared with Lloyd Sealy, assistant chief inspector of policy, also black, and declared the teachers should be allowed to enter the school, which they did.[48]

Nauman and the other teachers, however, were not assigned to their classes. Inside, their timecards were missing, and Carson and others assailed the teachers as "pigs and faggots." The teachers received a notice saying they were to attend a meeting with Rhody McCoy in the auditorium at the nearby IS 55.[49]

When the teachers arrived, they were greeted by Sonny Carson and about fifty black men, some armed with sticks. Then the threats began. The lights were turned off and on while community members screamed: "You're going out of here in pine boxes." The crowd chanted "we don't want you," and someone began tossing .30 caliber cartridges at the teachers. Community members called Jewish teachers "Jew pig." Board members, including Chairman Oliver, stood outside the doors and banned the press from entering. McCoy did nothing to protect the teachers. After more than an hour and a half, the "meeting" ended.[50] Oliver, when asked whether community people would try to block the school entrances the following day, replied, "I think so—I hope so." Asked what role the teachers would have in the schools, Oliver replied: "Their role is to get out of the community."[51]

The gambit worked. Advocates of community control had a weapon—the ability to physically block the return of the UFT teachers. More importantly, the advocates had a mayor who was so intent on avoiding violence that he was unwilling to enforce the board's directive to return the teachers. Lindsay prided himself on the fact that New York City did not riot after the King assassination, and now he told Shanker: "If I send the police in there, they'll burn the city down."[52]

But Shanker had his own weapon. He called an emergency session of the UFT's executive board at the Gramercy Park Hotel for 6:00 p.m. on September 11. Exercising authority provided by teachers in the previous strike settlement in the event the agreement was broken, the board voted for a second citywide strike.[53] Shanker predicted that it "may be the longest teachers' strike in history."[54]

Many in the press and the public saw the dispute not as workers versus management but as white teachers versus black parents, and as the second strike entered its second week, Shanker turned to Rustin for help. Rustin went to Randolph and explained that white teachers had been terminated without cause by a black management team and sought their support. Randolph said: "So, what's the question. Of course I'll support it." Rustin explained that many in the black community were supporting McCoy, and Randolph responded, "what does that matter? It's due process."[55] Randolph told Rustin: "You have got to go to Shanker's help because if Rhody McCoy can get away with firing teachers without giving them any reasons, without due process, without seniority lines, and there's ever established a precedent for this, the ones who are ultimately going to suffer the most under the conditions will be blacks."[56]

On September 17, Randolph and Rustin held a press conference at the Commodore Hotel and argued: "It is the right of every worker not to be transferred or fired at the whim of his employer. . . . It is the right of every worker to job security. These are rights that black workers have struggled and sacrificed to win for generations."[57]

On September 19, an advertisement appeared in the *New York Times*, coordinated by Rustin, in which a group of black trade unionists voiced their support of the UFT. Rustin warned that local control would mean that in conservative white areas, local boards could fire black and white liberal teachers. Rustin also noted that in a stratified society, segregated education would never mean equality. "After all the years of our struggle," Rustin said, "we are now being asked to accept the idea that segregated education is in fact a perfectly respectable, perfectly desirable, and perfectly viable way of life in a democratic society."[58] Community control, Rustin said, was "the spiritual descendant of states' rights."[59]

For their support of the UFT, Rustin and Randolph were pilloried in the black community.[60] Rustin later said: "You'd think we had committed a heinous crime from the insulting telephone calls, vulgar letters, and general denunciation in the press we received from a number of black people."[61] James Farmer of CORE was particularly caustic. "Bayard has no credibility in the black community," he said of the organizer of the March on Washington. Farmer asserted, "Bayard's commitment is to labor, not to the black man. His belief is that the black man's problem is economic, not racist, runs counter to black community thinking now."[62] Eleanor Holmes Norton said that after Ocean Hill–Brownsville, Rustin was "read out of the civil rights movement."[63]

The attacks on Randolph and Rustin were appalling. In 1968, Randolph was almost eighty years old, and he had more than paid his dues in the civil-rights arena. In his prime, he had been, says his biographer Jervis Anderson, "the number-one black political figure in the country." He had succeeded in getting Franklin Roosevelt to ban discrimination in the defense industries, had conceived of the 1963 March on Washington, and had fought tirelessly to make labor more progressive on racial issues. He had taken on George Meany over segregated unions, prompting Meany to famously reply at one convention: "Who the hell appointed you as guardian of the Negro members in America?"[64] Rustin, too, had more than paid his dues in the civil-rights movement and had literally been beaten on a number of occasions for the cause.

But now, the two were being pilloried as sycophants for labor. Both stood firm. In a letter to a critic, Randolph explained: "I could not very well refuse to support the teachers' right to due process and job security since it is not only a basic part of our democratic life but is indispensable for the ability of workers to hold jobs."[65] Randolph and Rustin believed in nonviolence, nondiscrimination, integration, and the need for a coalition with labor, and would not go along with the casual dismissal of these bedrock principles simply because they had gone out of fashion.

Critics said that given the UFT's financial support for the A. Philip Randolph Institute, Rustin had no choice but to support Shanker. But the Randolph Institute actually received more money from the local affiliate of AFSCME than from the UFT, and Rustin's support for Shanker created a "cleavage" between Rustin and the affiliate's chief, Victor Gotbaum, who was opposed to the strike. "Life would have been much easier" if Rustin had stayed out of Ocean Hill–Brownsville, says Rachelle Horowitz, who worked for Rustin at the time. "Bayard was losing friends hand over fist," and while New Yorkers as a whole were supportive of the teachers, in liberal circles only "a beleaguered few" supported the UFT.[66]

Rustin's support meant a great deal to Shanker. Referring both to the Lisser affair and Ocean Hill–Brownsville, Shanker later noted Rustin "fought for the right of a white man to be principal of a Harlem school and for the rights of black and white teachers to due process in New York City, just as he had fought for the rights of black students to enter the University of Mississippi and for the end of Jim Crow in the South." He "faced down white mobs in the South and black mobs in the North."[67] Years later, Shanker identified Rustin as his biggest hero.[68] Said Shanker: "The great thing about Rustin was that he didn't put up his finger to see which way the wind was blowing. He had the guts to say what he felt was right, no matter how unpopular it was."[69]

Shanker's other bulwark of support on the left were the Shachtmanites. Michael Harrington and Tom Kahn formed the Ad Hoc Committee to Defend the Right to Teach. On September 20, the group took out a large advertisement in the *New York Times* entitled "The Freedom to Teach," in which the group argued:

> Decentralization is not the issue. . . . The real issue now is job security. It is the right not to be fired arbitrarily by your employer, because he doesn't like the color of your skin, or the way you wear your hair, or the political opinion you hold.
>
> It is the right to a contract that protects the interests of both the employer and the employee—not a contract that can be violated or torn up by the employer whenever he feels like it.
>
> It is right to due process on the job. If an employee is to be fired, he is entitled to a list of specific reasons, and he is entitled to answer the charges against him. . . .
>
> It is the right of freedom from harassment, intimidation and violent assault on the job. . . .
>
> These are not subtle or disputable rights. They are elementary. . . .

Recounting the dismissals, and the refusal of the community to allow teachers back in, the ad went on to say: "Some people have urged the United Federation of Teachers, in the interests of peace, to yield on this issue. We believe that they fail to understand that more than a matter of abstract principle is at stake. The future of teacher unionism is at stake."

Those joining Harrington and Kahn in signing the ad included a collection of Socialists and liberals such as Daniel Bell, Robert Heilbroner, Irving Howe, Dwight MacDonald, Reinhold Niebuhr, Martin Peretz, and Arthur Schlesinger Jr.[70]

Shanker's core support, then, came from the old coalition behind the 1963 March on Washington—Randolph, Rustin, Harrington, and Kahn—people who believed that economic justice was a crucial ingredient in the civil-rights movement. But five years later, King was gone and a different movement, ranging from what was called the New Politics to the more extreme New Left, was emerging. Rhody McCoy, the disciple of Malcolm X, drew far more support from white liberals than Malcolm X ever had.[71] At the center of the liberal support for community control was the New York chapter of the American Civil Liberties Union, led by Aryeh Neier and his second in command, Ira Glasser.

Neier had been at one time executive director of the League for Industrial Democracy, a strong supporter of unions as an engine for making the economy more democratic.[72] The New York chapter of the ACLU, as Diane Ravitch notes, "might have been expected to defend the teachers' academic freedom and the right to due process"—they were terminated in part for their political views—but instead the group became a "prime defender" of the governing board.[73]

During the controversy, Neier's group issued a blistering attack on the UFT entitled "The Burden of Blame."[74] The report, written by Glasser, charged that the UFT "has used 'due process' as a smoke screen to obscure its real goal, which is to discredit decentralization and sabotage community control. . . . The major burden of blame for the chaos in Ocean Hill–Brownsville must fall on the central Board of Education and the UFT."[75]

Many white liberals, like academics Maurice Berube and Marilyn Gittel, painted the issue not as labor versus management but as "the poor" against "middle-class school professionals." They argued that while the fights of the 1930s were about protecting the rights of workers, now the question had become about the right to hold unions "accountable to an urban alienated poor." They said that American labor was no longer on the side of social justice and that community control was about truly democratizing American education.[76] Many whites were concerned about the small number of black teachers and saw the union's insistence of keeping a system of tests in place as discriminatory. Some liberals charged that the teachers had been eager to join the civil-rights movement in the South, but once it involved their jobs, the alliance was off.[77] Moderate black leaders also began siding with McCoy and his colleagues. Whitney Young of the Urban League declared that the need for community control outweighed the rights of labor.[78]

Many saw Shanker's talk of standing up to black vigilantism as racist. Jimmy Breslin said Shanker's tone was but "an accent away from George Wallace."[79] Sol Stern, writing in *Ramparts*, accused the UFT of engaging in a "racist strike."[80] Stern, who in later years became a conservative, quoted a young liberal teacher as saying that "in six years, the UFT has become middle-aged," going from civil-rights pioneer to part of the backlash.[81] Liberal writer Murray Kempton called Shanker a "goon."[82] Other liberal writers became caught up with the notion of participatory democracy, which took them to strange places. Jason Epstein, writing in the *New York Review of Books*, said that liberals should embrace not only community control but also Milton Friedman's vision of school vouchers for private schools, because both were consistent with "participatory democracy."[83]

To Shanker and other unionists, these arguments represented the liberal betrayal of long-held principles. Moderate black leaders, who had deplored Black Power just two years earlier, had now switched sides, leaving once mainstream black figures like Randolph and Rustin marginalized. Meanwhile, Michael Harrington noted, liberal white Democrats were trying to keep schools open during the strike, "an action that the entire Left would have denounced as 'scabbing' only a few years before."[84] The labor movement was used to being attacked by corporations and right-wing interests, but this was something different: an assault on labor in labor's capital, New York City, from the left, both militant black and liberal white.

Sandra Feldman, who had been so active in civil rights and union affairs, said: "It kills me to see white liberals supporting separatism. I don't understand how you can be progressive and anti-union at the same time."[85] Harrington also argued that the right of a group to annul a democratic agreement with the threat of violence was "inimical to democracy itself" and was the province of groups like the KKK.[86]

As the strike entered its third week, with close to one million students stranded, pressure built on all sides to find a settlement. On the evening of September 28, Shanker entered a lengthy sixteen-hour negotiation with the school board and Mayor Lindsay on the final terms of an agreement. The talks went through the night at Gracie Mansion, with Shanker stretching out on the floor at one point for a twenty-minute nap. It was his only sleep in thirty-six hours. On Sunday, September 29, Mayor Lindsay came out to announce that an agreement had been reached. He appeared with Shanker, superintendent Donovan, and Council of Supervisory Association president Walter Degnan. All four appeared unshaven, the *Times* said.[87]

The terms provided that all 110 disputed teachers would be returned to Ocean Hill–Brownsville, with adequate police protection. Teams of observers—from the superintendent's office, the mayor's office, and others appointed by the UFT—would report on any threats or violence. Teachers would make up most of their lost wages during the strike through pay for additional makeup days. In Ocean Hill–Brownsville, UFT teachers would be returned, but the replacement teachers hired by the district would be allowed to stay. And the demonstration project in Ocean Hill would be allowed to continue.[88] The UFT rank and file voted 5,825 to 592 to support the settlement and end the strike. On Monday, September 30, teachers returned to work, having missed the first eleven of thirteen school days.[89]

The Ocean Hill–Brownsville governing board, which had not been a party to the negotiations, ordered McCoy to fire the disputed UFT teachers. With the UFT poised to call another strike, Donovan reassigned McCoy, along with seven principals hired by the governing board who went along with McCoy and failed to give the disputed teachers regular teaching assignments.[90]

The Third 1968 Strike

Over the course of the next two weeks following the September 30 return to school, there were varying levels of disturbance in Ocean Hill–Brownsville, particularly at JHS 271. Two teachers at JHS 271 loyal to the governing board threatened a Board of Education observer and a UFT teacher: "You are going to die, and they are going to put you six feet under." Union teachers were shouted at: "We don't want you in this school." They were called "white racist pigs." And they were asked, "who's going to protect you when the police leave?" Other teachers were told, "you are the enemy of my people." Children were heard chanting "we will die for Rhody McCoy."[91]

Nevertheless, on October 11, Superintendent Donovan reinstated the seven principals he had suspended, which Shanker said gave them the "green light" to assign disputed teachers to nonclassroom duties. Shanker denounced the move as a "betrayal" of teachers.[92] On October 13, teachers voted to strike and Monday, October 14, 48,000 teachers returned to the picket line for the third time that fall.[93]

Shanker upped the ante. He had had enough broken promises and failed guarantees. Now he said the teachers would not return to work until the Ocean Hill–Brownsville demonstration district was dissolved.[94] And he was willing to stay out a long time to do so. The strike, he said, could last "a month or longer."[95]

In pushing the new strike, Shanker knew he was taking something of a gamble. Public tolerance was waning. The UFT felt the need to spell out its position further and on October 15, the *New York Times* carried a full-page UFT ad declaring: "We would rather teach than picket. But we have no choice." Explaining that many of the teachers were parents, too, with children in the public schools, the UFT put the blame on Superintendent Donovan for "changing his line again and again." The ad said: "We are determined to defend sanity in our schools. We will not tolerate capitulation to small groups who use the threat of violence to have their way."[96] If the first strike was about due process, and the second strike added the issue of violence and vigilantism, the third strike layered on top of these two a concern that had been simmering for some time: black anti-Semitism.

It was said that of the five white people a New York City ghetto resident meets, the cop was Irish and the landlord, store owner, social worker, and teacher were Jewish.[97] For many blacks, Jim Sleeper explains, "everyone in authority seemed Jewish," whether one sought an apartment, a job, credit, or a passing grade at school. Jews were to blacks what the WASPs had been to the Irish. Jewish liberals, Sleeper said, were "the closest of strangers" and "the easiest targets."[98]

In 1967 about two-thirds of New York City's teachers, supervisors, and principals were Jewish.[99] Jews had flocked to teaching in part because they faced less discrimination in hiring than in the private sector. Many Jews were mystified and deeply hurt by black anti-Semitism, since Jews had been far more heavily involved in the civil-rights movement than other whites. But precisely for this reason, Sonny Carson and other black militants believed it was a sign of authentic radicalism to be not only anti-white but anti-Semitic. "Part of becoming the most militant was telling whites to shove it, and part of it was to tell Jews, who had been your allies . . . to shove it too," says Arch Puddington.[100]

During the teachers strike, Shanker learned that an anonymous leaflet had been distributed in teacher mailboxes at JHS 271 and PS 144. It read, in part:

> If African-American History and Culture is to be taught to our Black Children it Must Be Done by African-Americans Who Identify With And Who Understand The Problem. It is Impossible For the Middle East Murderers of Colored People to Possibly Bring to This Important Task The Insight, The Concern, The Exposing of The Truth That is a Must If The Years of Brainwashing and Self-Hatred That Has Been Taught To Our Black Children By These Blood-sucking Exploiters and Murderers Is To Be Overcome . . . Cut Out, Stay Out, Stay Off, Shut Up, Get Off Our Backs, Or Your Relatives In The Middle East Will Find Themselves Giving Benefits To Raise Money To Help You Get Out From Under The Terrible Weight Of An Enraged Black Community.[101]

The leaflets were highly inflammatory, and Shanker had to decide what, if anything, to do with them. On the one hand, it would be unfair to try to discredit the entire community-control movement based on the actions of a few racists. On the other hand, Shanker saw growing evidence of anti-Semitism during the strike. The most recent was a demonstration outside his office in which protestors placed a Menorah on a coffin, a frightening anti-Semitic ritual.[102]

The *African American Teachers Forum* had been particularly notorious. In one newsletter, John Hatchett wrote: "We are witnessing today in New York City a phenomenon that spells death for the minds and souls of our Black children. It is the systematic coming of age of the Jews who dominate and control the educational bureaucracy of the New York Public School system and their power-starved imitators, the Black-Anglo Saxon."[103]

Shanker decided to have five hundred thousand copies of the fliers made and distributed, giving them far more circulation than they originally received.[104] The flier was cut and pasted with a separate circular with the statement: "Is this what you want for your children? The UFT says NO!"[105] Tactically, the move was brilliant, because it changed the terms of the debate and undercut the moral authority of community-control advocates.[106] But there were also problems. Even Shanker's defenders acknowledge that he overreached. It was unfair to paint the entire Ocean Hill experiment with the tar of anti-Semitism, as Shanker implied.[107] And distributing the flyers proved inflammatory, contributing, says Diane Ravitch, to a "hate-filled atmosphere."[108] Jimmy Breslin called the duplication of the fliers and the attempt to blame the governing board "a smear tactic reminiscent of the days of Senator Joseph McCarthy."[109] Twenty-five years later, Ira Glasser said, "I have always blamed Shanker for whipping up the anti-Semitism issue. I think the union manufactured much of it. It caused a rupture between blacks and Jews that hasn't healed and I think it's unforgivable."[110]

Shanker defended the distribution of literature, saying we shouldn't "make believe this garbage doesn't exist."[111] He asked, why condemn "the people who put the searchlight on it," rather than those who actually wrote it?[112] He noted Martin Luther King reproduced KKK literature and no one had cried foul. "He was trying to mobilize the conscience of the country by showing the kind of garbage and the kinds of minds that some people had, and what he did was perfectly proper."[113]

At first, critics appeared right to accuse Shanker of trumpeting the ravings of a lunatic as if they were representative of the leaders in Ocean Hill–Brownsville. The Governing Board issued a statement saying it "has never tolerated nor will it ever tolerate anti-Semitism in any form. Anti-Semitism has no place in our hearts or minds and indeed never in our schools. . . . We disclaim any responsibility for this literature and have in every way sought to find its source and take appropriate action to stop it."[114] But then, astoundingly, Rhody McCoy confirmed Shanker's hunch that the feelings extended beyond the fringe. McCoy refused to condemn the fliers. "I have to work in both worlds," he said.[115] "We have more things to be concerned about than making anti-Semitism a priority," he said.[116]

The issue of anti-Semitism energized many in the Jewish community to take action. On October 15, Mayor Lindsay, who had received strong Jewish support in his first election, was booed and heckled by an audience at the East Midwood Jewish Center in Brooklyn, an audience that included many teachers. Outside, a mob of two thousand people shouted "Lindsay must go" and "we want Shanker." Inside, Lindsay was jeered. When Rabbi Harry Halpern scolded the crowd, "Is this the exemplification of the Jewish faith?" many shouted back, "yes, yes." As Lindsay left, the mob, now numbering five thousand, pounded on his limousine.[117]

A few weeks later, reacting to the charges of anti-Semitism and racism during the teachers' strike, Lindsay appointed a commission headed by

Justice Bernard Botein to examine the issue.[118] As October turned to November, with no end in sight for the strike, racial tensions flared.

On November 3, community-control supporters took their protest to Shanker's home in Putnam Valley. Riding in two chartered buses and seven cars, about 150 protesters picketed outside Shanker's house, noting that Shanker's children lived in a school district with local control. Shanker, his wife Eadie, and the children were not home at the time of the protest, which lasted from about 3 to 4 p.m., but the protesters left their signs in Shanker's yard. One was entitled "Albert Shanker's Report Card" and gave him an F in "Works and Plays Well with Others" and an F for "Emotional Stability," while giving him an A for "Racism." They warned they would return: "Neighbors, you had better kick Mr. Shanker out. We're going to bring blacks and Puerto Ricans out here and the property values will drop by morning."[119]

The charge of racism stung Shanker, though he was not intimidated by it.[120] In an interview with the *New York Times*, published on November 9, Shanker called the racial polarization "a horrible, tragic thing." In the early days of the strike, Shanker said, when he walked from Grand Central Terminal to his office on Park Avenue South, black and Puerto Rican people would "reach out and say 'Good luck, Al,'" but in the previous two weeks, he said, that had stopped happening.[121]

"The really tragic thing," Shanker said, "is that our union, of all the unions in the country, has tried to create an alliance with the black community, going back many years. Now appeals for racial solidarity have become so great that all of that is lost."[122] Part of what made Shanker's plea for racial harmony difficult to penetrate was that much of organized labor was not particularly enlightened during that era. The racist charge hit Shanker "very hard," says UFT staffer Naomi Spatz, because "one of the distinguishing characteristics about Al [was that] he was not a racist nor a sexist. And in that particular year and time in leadership in trade unions to find someone who was neither sexist or racist, it was really quite wonderful."[123]

And some of Shanker's public support did come from racists. Fred Nauman recalled that people would say: "You got the guts. You put the blacks in their place. . . . It was disturbing."[124] Some teachers began calling those sympathetic to community control "Nigger lover."[125] Liberal journalist Nat Hentoff, who was very critical of Shanker and the UFT during the strike, nevertheless said he was told by a community-control supporter: "Shanker's the best you can get. You have no idea what the majority of that membership is like."[126]

In mid-November, Shanker had a private meeting with Rustin at the Commodore Hotel, in which Rustin pleaded that the UFT not insist on an all-out victory. Rustin argued that if hardliners in the UFT had their way, hatred in the black community for labor would grow intolerably. Rachelle Horowitz says, "Bayard said to Al, 'You gotta go back. We can't keep this up.'"[127] Afterward, one union leader present said: "No one could listen to this man, who had been martyrized by his own people for standing up for the legitimate rights of the union, without coming away tremendously impressed."[128] Shanker later said, "Bayard did help moderate the situation because we were aware of how he put his head on the block."[129]

From the very beginning, there had been a tension for Shanker between doing what was right in principle—protecting his members from unlawful dismissal, preserving the union, standing for nondiscrimination, and not rewarding violence and threats—and doing what would preserve the coalition between progressive forces, blacks, and labor. For several weeks, Shanker had sided with principle. This was a defensive strike, and the survival of the union depended upon it. And as a practical matter, he had to protect his members or he would have been voted out of office.[130] Now, as victory appeared close, the importance of the coalition began to weigh more heavily on the separate question of when to end the strike.

On November 16, Shanker joined Mayor Lindsay, Harry Van Arsdale, Rhody McCoy, Rev. C. Herbert Oliver, Kenneth Clark, and Whitney Young of the Urban League, as well as two labor mediators, to begin round-the-clock negotiations.[131] After twenty-seven hours, at 1:50 p.m. on Sunday, November 17, an agreement was reached. The pact provided for the transfer, at least temporarily, of three Ocean Hill–Brownsville principals to the central office, the appointment of a trustee to run the district, and the establishment of a special committee to protect the rights of teachers and supervisors. Ten days were added to the schedule, along with extended school days for fourteen weeks, so that students would make up their work and teachers would only lose six days of pay. In addition, the superintendent temporarily removed three teachers accused of harassing UFT members at JHS 271, pending a hearing—Albert Vann, Leslie Campbell, and Lilly Curtis. The state commissioner said he would continue the suspension of the governing board and Rhody McCoy until he received assurances they would carry out the directions of the trustee.[132] In return, the UFT gave up its demand to entirely dissolve the Ocean Hill–Brownsville district.[133] Governing board member Rev. John J. Powis said the pact "looks like total capitulation to the demands of the union."[134] Some teachers, however, were not happy for the opposite reason. When Shanker met with the delegate assembly, he was repeatedly interrupted by irate teachers who denounced the agreement as a sellout. Shanker said the delegates' behavior was an "atrocity" and a "disgrace." "The constitution does not require me to conduct a mob," he said, "it requires me to conduct a meeting."[135]

Shanker was being attacked by a right wing—the superhawks at the delegate assembly that said he had sold out to community control—and by a left wing that said he was racist for pushing too hard. But as the votes of the membership were counted, it was clear that the center held. By a vote of 17,658 to 2,738—a six to one margin—the membership approved the settlement. The five-week strike, together with the first two strikes, had kept more than one million students out of class for thirty-six of the first forty-eight school days, one-fifth of the school year. It had been the longest and largest teachers' strike in the nation's history.[136]

During the strike itself, Shanker argued the costs to students were small. "What has not been learned today can be learned tomorrow."[137] But Shanker later conceded that the length of the strike had an effect on children's learning and "resulted in a dramatic decline in citywide reading scores."[138]

The Ocean Hill–Brownsville strikes of 1968 left an indelible mark on New York City and to a certain degree on American liberalism itself. In an iconic year that saw the assassinations of Martin Luther King and Robert Kennedy, Ocean Hill–Brownsville represented something new in America: the liberal assault on organized labor. The old liberal idea that unions should protect individuals from arbitrary dismissal and the idea that race should play no part in who is hired and fired were abandoned by many who considered themselves liberal. Albert Shanker stood firm against this turn away from longstanding liberal principles and as a result, he won praise from many white working-class people but was also pilloried with vicious personal attacks from those who wanted liberalism to move in a very different direction.

The strike was ended and students returned to school. But the issues raised by the strike—bigotry, the future of community control, and the lessons for liberalism—remained to be sorted out.

6

Ocean Hill–Brownsville

THE FALLOUT

1969

WITH the picket signs put away, the community-control dispute would move to the New York State legislature in Albany. In the coming months, Shanker would argue that the fight was not between liberals and conservatives, but between two versions of liberalism—his tough liberalism, which embraced full funding of integrated schools, nonviolence, nondiscrimination, and the rights of organized labor; and Lindsay's limousine liberalism, which favored community control, tolerated violence, explained away anti-Semitism, and held labor unions in low regard. In the short term, Shanker would ally with conservatives in Albany to defend his union, but it was clear he believed the alliance was temporary and that he longed for something better.

Continued Anti-Semitism

During the strike, Shanker was widely criticized by liberals for inflating black anti-Semitism in order to win sympathy for the UFT, but in the post-settlement period, a steady drumbeat of anti-Semitism continued to sound, suggesting the problem was not a phantom of Shanker's imagination. If anti-Semitism was a ploy to curry sympathy for the UFT, community-control activists appeared oddly willing to help out.

In early December 1968, Shanker was denounced in Harlem in an anti-Semitic leaflet from Jesse Gray's Tenants Rights party. Headlined "Shanker This Is Not Egypt—You Ain't Coming in Here," the leaflet said: "Zionists kill black people in their own land in the Middle East. They run the people out of their own communities. . . . Harlem will not stand by while these racist ruthless Zionist bandits [Shanker and the UFT] and his puppets, the police, run us out of our own communities."[1]

In late December, in an incident that received far more attention, Leslie R. Campbell, a twenty-nine-year-old black teacher at JHS 271, appeared on the "Julius Lester Program" on WBAI-FM, owned by Pacifica Radio Foundation. Campbell, who had been suspended on charges of harassing UFT teachers but was subsequently reinstated, set off a firestorm when he read a poem written by a fifteen-year-old black student and dedicated to Albert Shanker. The poem began: "Hey, Jew boy, with that yarmulke on your head / You pale-faced Jew boy—I wish you were dead." The poem went on to link New York schools to the Middle East.

When the U.N. made Israel a free independent state
Little four- and five-year-old boys threw hand grenades;
They hated the black Arabs with all their might
And you, Jew boy, said it was all right.
Then you came to America, land of the free,
And took over the school system to perpetuate white supremacy.[2]

The show's host, Julius Lester, a field secretary of the Student Nonviolence Coordinating Committee, praised the poem on the air, and in a later appearance, he and Campbell called it "beautiful" and "true." Shanker denounced Campbell, saying "Leslie Campbell's proud reading of his student's anti-Semitic poem is an indication of his teaching approach."[3]

Particularly disturbing to many was the idea that the poem would come from a student, who may have been learning hate from teachers. One of the great hopes for public education was that an educated populace would be more tolerant; now, in certain schools that aspiration was being stood on its head.

As the controversy over the anti-Semitic poem grew, Mayor Lindsay called for an investigation of Campbell. The ATA's Vann, by contrast, defended the poem, saying it was "critical of Jews" but had "no anti-Semitic overtones." Adding fuel to the fire, Vann, who claimed to represent six thousand black educators, said Lindsay had trampled on Campbell's rights and was seeking "to appease the powerful Jewish financiers of the city."[4] The New York Civil Liberties Union sided with Campbell and Vann, saying their free-speech rights were guaranteed outside of the classroom.[5]

More troublesome, in some ways, was the tolerance of anti-Semitism by certain public officials. On January 3, at a School Board public hearing on community control at Prospect Heights High School in Brooklyn, William O. Marley, chairman of the Brownsville Model Cities Committee, stood up and denounced Jewish dominance of the school system. He accused Jews of "gross negligence and misguidance of black and Puerto Rican children" and accused Jewish leadership of attempting "to perpetuate their greedy rape of the city under the guise of unionism and 'teachers' rights.'" The board members, John Doar, Hector Vasquez, and Aaron Brown, responded with silence until a reporter later asked them about it, at which point the group issued a general denunciation of bigotry.[6]

On January 5, the *New York Times* reported an anti-Semitic editorial in the latest issue of the bimonthly *African American Teachers Forum*. The editorial asked: "How long shall the Black and Puerto Rican communities of New York City sit back and allow the Jewish-dominated United Federation of Teachers to destroy our every effort to rescue our children from those incompetent teachers whose only goal—aside from receiving fat paychecks—is stifling our children's intellectual growth?" The editorial continued: "Don't tell us any more about the 6 million slaughtered by Hitler. Tell us instead about the 12 million Blacks slaughtered in 300 years of Black genocide." The editorial charged: "And the Jew, our liberal friend of yesterday, whose cries of anguish still resound from the steppes of Russia to the tennis courts of Forest Hills, is now our exploiter. He keeps our women and children from becoming teachers and principals and he keeps our children ignorant." The "truth," the editorial charged, was that "most Jewish teachers and administrators here have failed a grave public trust: they have kept us functionally illiterate." The piece attacked the Board of Examiners for turning the teaching profession into a "private Jewish club by systematically failing or disqualifying Black and Puerto Rican applicants for license as teachers and principals." (The *Times* noted that in fact, the Board's civil-service procedures provided that papers were graded without the reader knowing the identity of the test taker.) The hate-filled editorial concluded by saying: "It is time to declare that Albert Shanker and all who support his racist diatribes do a disservice to the entire Jewish community."[7]

Many blacks disdained this form of anti-Semitism, and in early January 1969, Whitney Young Jr. of the National Urban League denounced anti-Semitism, declaring, "religious prejudice has no place among people who have been the victims of racial prejudice." He argued, in particular, that black anti-Semitic statements "damage the cause of community control."[8] Likewise, in mid-January, the *Amsterdam News* devoted a front-page editorial to condemning bigotry of any kind.[9]

On January 16, a panel appointed by Mayor Lindsay released a report that found that "an appalling amount of racial prejudice—black and white—surfaced in and about the school controversy." The nine-member Special Committee on Racial and Religious Prejudice, headed by retired judge Bernard Botein, included Robert Carter of the NAACP and David Dubinsky of the International Ladies Garment Workers Union. The report said the prejudice appeared on both sides, with a difference:

> The prejudice emanating from blacks generally takes a form somewhat different from that which has emerged among whites. The countless incidents, leaflets, epithets and the like in this school controversy reveal a bigotry from black extremists that is open, undisguised, nearly physical in its intensity—and far more obvious and identifiable than that emanating from whites. On the other hand, anti-black bigotry tended to be expressed in more sophisticated and subtle fashion, often communicated privately and seldom reported, but nonetheless equally evil, corrosive, damaging, and deplorable.[10]

On January 22, the Anti-Defamation League of B'nai B'rith issued a report on the schools crisis, finding that "raw, undisguised anti-Semitism is at a crisis level in New York City schools where, unchecked by public authority, it has been building for more than two years." In addition to documenting instances of anti-Semitism among black-power extremists, the report noted that anti-Semitism was being taught to students in public schools. "There is a clear and present danger that schoolchildren in the city have been infected by the anti-Semitic preaching of Negro extremists who, in some cases, are teachers and to whom these youngsters increasingly look for leadership."[11]

On January 26, a front-page story in the *New York Times* outlined the fears of some Jews that "anti-Semitism, which seemed safely out of the way after World War II, is on the increase and must be vigorously countered." It quoted Norman Podhoretz, who called black anti-Semitism "the most serious crisis confronting American Jews since World War II."[12] Others argued that anti-Semitism had to be considered in context. At a rally in support of community control on February 16, Dr. Benjamin Spock said Jews and other whites shouldn't overreact to racial slurs from blacks, who have "suffered much worse for much longer."[13]

Polling suggested a worsening problem—on both the Jewish and black sides. Polls commissioned by community-control supporters, the Ford Foundation, and the Institute for Community Studies in April and May 1969 found both increased anti-Semitism among blacks and racism among Jews, who had previously been considered more tolerant than other whites. For example, among Jews in New York, 43 percent said blacks have less ambition than whites, compared with 32 percent of non-Jewish whites. On the other hand, blacks had higher levels of anti-Semitism than non-Jewish whites: 71 percent of blacks (compared with 23 percent of non-Jewish whites) said that between money and people, Jews will choose money; 62 percent of blacks (and 17 percent of non-Jewish whites) said Jewish businessmen will try to put over a shady deal on you; and 52 percent of blacks (and 18 percent of non-Jewish whites) said Jews are more loyal to Israel than to America.[14]

Class Warfare

To some, the alliance between black militants and WASPs such as Mayor Lindsay and McGeorge Bundy of Ford suggested that old WASP anti-Semitism was part of the mix. (The original Henry Ford, the benefactor of the Ford Foundation, was a notorious anti-Semite.) But Shanker rejected the idea—floated in *Commentary* magazine—that "WASPs are exercising residual anti-Semitism by encouraging blacks to attack Jews." Said Shanker: "I don't buy it."

To Shanker, the alliance was not a matter of ethnicity or religion, but class:

> What you have is people on the upper, upper economic level who are willing to make any change that does not affect their own position. And so it is the middle-class interests that are narrow and selfish, and the civil-service teacher who must be sacrificed. I'm not sure that is a WASP

attitude. I think it is only human. But what if you said give 20 percent of Time Inc. or U.S. Steel to the blacks? Who would be narrow then?[15]

Henry Ford, Shanker noted, was not only an anti-Semite; he was also anti-union.[16] While the press reported the story as a fight between blacks and Jews, and blacks and whites, Shanker saw that at a deeper level this was also a fight about class, a theme he pounded away at in speeches and interviews. Appearing at a conference of principals on February 1, Shanker charged that there is "a great alliance against us: Time-Life, big business men, department stores and others, who feared massive demands for more school money and decided to turn responsibility over to local groups." These business groups were allied with "black separatists, Students for a Democratic Society, the lawyers' association, and white liberals who are racists because they always say yes to black demands."[17]

Shanker was particularly critical of the role of wealthy foundations in the alliance, which he saw not only as wrong on the merits of community control but also fundamentally undemocratic and unaccountable. So angered was he by the Ford Foundation's role in funding and supporting community control that he launched a nationwide speaking tour on the topic.[18] Shanker argued that foundations exercise immense power in a way that was completely unaccountable, "responsible neither to elected public officials nor to stockholders." They distort the public debate about issues, he suggested, because academics might be reluctant to criticize foundations for fear of jeopardizing future support.[19] By dispensing their largesse, they created a built-in political lobby to support their special tax status, he argued.[20]

In February 1969, Shanker testified before the House Ways and Means Committee in their investigation of tax-exempt organizations.[21] The upshot of the hearings was the Tax Reform Act of 1969, which sought to reign in foundations and was in large measure targeted at Ford.[22] The legislation restricted the scope of political activity that foundations can participate in and narrowed the tax exemptions provided to foundations.[23]

Lindsay and Bundy's brand of liberalism was something quite different than the liberalism with which Shanker had been raised. While they shared Shanker's concern for civil rights and the plight of blacks, they seemed to have utter disdain for, and little understanding of, white working-class concerns and fears. Shanker's life experience was shaped by New York public schools and the University of Illinois, Bundy's by Groton

and Yale, and Lindsay's by Buckley, St. Paul's, and Yale.[24] Bundy was chauffeured to work in a limousine and sent his four children to private prepa-
ratory schools, Groton and Collegiate. These experiences disposed him to
the idea of private-school vouchers, a policy Shanker saw as anathema to
democratic liberalism.[25]

Lindsay was the original "limousine liberal" (so labeled by his mayoral
opponent Mario Procaccino),[26] and his wife had utter disdain for Shanker.
"Mary Lindsay hated Al and the union people so much," Eadie Shanker
recalls. "Al and the negotiating team were at Gracie Mansion for endless
hours, even overnight [and] she wouldn't even give them a cup of coffee."[27] Shanker was the only municipal leader whom Lindsay would not
invite into his personal living quarters during negotiations.[28] Like young
members of the rising New Left, Lindsay and Bundy's version of liberalism grew out of an environment of affluence, and white working-class
people were viewed as backward and even reactionary.[29]

The Shachtmanites, by contrast—Bayard Rustin, Michael Harrington,
Tom Kahn, and Paul Feldman—put the working class of all races at the
center of the progressive coalition. The four men, wrote Sol Stern, "are
all personally close to Shanker and serve as a kind of 'kitchen cabinet' for
his union."[30] Yet in this new environment, even some of the Shachtmanites were defecting. Especially wounding to Shanker was the loss of
Dwight Macdonald.[31] Macdonald, whom Shanker had invited to speak to
the Socialist Club at the University of Illinois, had served as publicity director of Max Shachtman's campaign for the House of Representatives
years before and was the author of the famous *New Yorker* review of Michael Harrington's *The Other America*. At Harrington's urging, Macdonald had signed the September 1968 advertisement in support of the teachers.[32] But after the strike, Macdonald wrote an open letter to Harrington,
published in the *New York Review of Books*, in which Macdonald said he
was "ashamed" that he had signed the pro-UFT advertisement. It was
wrong, Macdonald said, because Shanker had since engaged in "racist
demagogy." In fact, he asserted, the Ocean Hill–Brownsville schools are
impressive.[33]

Harrington responded in the *New York Review of Books* in January
1969, in an "Open Letter to Men of Good Will (with an Aside to Dwight
Macdonald)." He noted that Macdonald had embraced a very conservative form of education reform, backed by business interests, which substituted a change in governance for investment in schooling, housing,

and employment. It was not surprising that Barry Goldwater and William F. Buckley Jr. had signed on to community control, Harrington wrote. "What is surprising is that people on the Left should join in the chorus."[34]

To Shanker, Lindsay/Bundy liberalism was preferable to Goldwater/Buckley conservatism, because Lindsay and Bundy had a concern for the plight of disadvantaged blacks. But he thought that sympathy took them to irrational places. Said Shanker: "In Bundy, you have, too, the phenomenon of the guilty white liberal. Since society said 'no' [for] so long [to blacks], he now says 'yes' to everything. This is still responding on the basis of the color of the skin."[35]

Albert Shanker, of course, was no guilty white liberal. At a time when chaos was reigning—with rioting following the assassination of Martin Luther King and student protests at the Democratic National Convention in Chicago and at Columbia University in New York—Shanker was one of the few liberals to stand up against threats and violence and vigilantism, which he viewed as essentially antidemocratic. For that, he became a working-class folk hero.

He was, said the *New York Times'* labor reporter A.H. Raskin, "the darling of New York's battered middle class."[36] Shanker later recalled, "every place I went, taxicab drivers wouldn't charge me a fare, newspaper vendors would give me a free copy of the *Times* in the morning."[37] Although Shanker was the anti-Lindsay—and hardly glamorous—many considered him charismatic. Polls found that Shanker could beat Lindsay if he ran for mayor of New York City in the 1969 election.[38] He briefly considered running, but his wife Eadie told him, "Al, what do you know about being mayor? You only hear the people who tell you you should run for mayor. Think of all the enemies you have out there."[39] Sandra Feldman says it would never have worked out: "He was too argumentative. I don't think he could pander at all."[40] Shanker soon dropped the idea.

The Fight in Albany

Though Shanker did not take Lindsay on directly in a mayoral contest, the two soon went head-to-head in Albany, as the state legislature considered decentralization legislation following the teachers' strike. The contest was fierce, pitting Lindsay, Bundy, and McCoy's top-bottom coalition against Shanker's labor/middle-class coalition allied with conservatives.

In late March, 1969, Shanker brought five hundred teachers to lobby the UFT's position, while community-control activists chartered forty-five buses to Albany, carrying two thousand activists.[41] Community-control advocates backed a bill drawn up by the State Board of Regents, calling for community school districts to have substantial powers over personnel, curriculum, and fiscal matters and for an abolition of the Board of Examiners. The UFT backed Senator John Marchi's bill providing for limited powers to local boards and maintaining the Board of Examiners.[42]

After five weeks in which the state legislature was fixated on the decentralization issue, the legislature passed on April 30, 1969, a version of the Marchi bill, with the support of Governor Rockefeller, that created roughly thirty community school districts but retained most power for the central board.[43] The law also eliminated the existing New York City school board, dominated by Lindsay appointees, and created a new seven-member board, five elected, and two appointed by the mayor, a move Shanker strongly favored.[44] By setting a minimum district size of twenty thousand students, the agreement effectively ended demonstration projects in Ocean Hill–Brownsville and the two other experimental districts.[45] The legislation also kept in place the New York City Board of Examiners.[46]

The legislation also provided, however, that in low-scoring districts (that is, almost half of them), teachers who had not passed the Board of Examiners test could still be employed.[47] Also, under the deal, local school boards would have control over patronage through nonprofessional hiring, while the central board and union contract would continue to govern professional hiring.[48]

Lindsay said the bill had "very basic weaknesses," and Rhody McCoy called the law a "prelude to the destruction of public education." Meanwhile, Shanker called the final bill "a good piece of legislation."[49] Shanker said: "We got a decentralization law about 80% of which is consonant with what we wanted."[50]

In the end, the teachers had beaten a powerful coalition of the mayor, the state board of regents, civil-rights groups, and upper-class reformers.[51] McCoy, having lost his job, went on to write a PhD thesis at the University of Massachusetts in which he attacked "racist capitalist America" for making "the education of black, poor white and Third World children in this country impossible. A violent revolution is necessary to have America's public institutions serve all its people."[52]

Postscript

In the years that followed, the decentralization law was considered a mixed bag at best. On the one hand, the requirement for regulated, local school-board elections cut down on the extreme radicalism that grew out of Ocean Hill–Brownsville's unorthodox election procedures.[53] And the number of minority teachers did increase substantially through the waiver on the Board of Examiners hiring in low-scoring districts. The proportion of minority teachers increased from 10 percent to 19 percent in the decade following decentralization, and the percentage of minority principals jumped from 9 percent to 27 percent.[54]

But ultimately, as an educational matter, decentralization did little good, as Shanker had predicted. While some liberal writers and columnists including Dwight Macdonald and Nat Hentoff had predicted great increases in student achievement from community control, three years in, the reading test scores in Ocean Hill–Brownsville were lower than they had been before the experiment began.[55] Ten years after decentralization was adopted, Kenneth Clark, one of its leading advocates, conceded that "the schools are no better and no worse then they were a decade ago. In terms of the basic objective, decentralization didn't make a damn bit of difference."[56] In December 1996, after a quarter-century of decentralization, the New York State Legislature decided to cut back on the powers of the local boards.[57] In 2002, the state legislature agreed to eliminate community-control boards altogether.[58]

Albert Shanker emerged from Ocean Hill–Brownsville victorious, powerful, famous—and tainted. He was victorious to the extent that the union contract protections against arbitrary dismissal were preserved, the extremists were defeated, the teachers returned, and the threat of community control to the union diminished. He emerged powerful in two senses: Internally, within the union, Shanker's position was stronger than ever. Before Ocean Hill, he had modest control over the UFT, said former UFT vice president John O'Neill. After Ocean Hill, Shanker had total control.[59] Shanker's victory margin over the opposition staff caucus went from 1.7 to one in 1964 to 2.4 to one in 1966 to almost nine to one in 1968.[60] Externally, Shanker also emerged from the strikes as an extremely powerful figure. He had shown that the union, as journalist Robert Braun wrote, could close down the schools and no one could do anything about it— "not the mayor, not the courts, not the governor, not the Chief Justice of the State Supreme Court." Shanker, Braun wrote, "may not possess a seat on the school board, but little of importance is done in the schools of New York without his, or his union's, assent."[61] After Ocean Hill, writes Sol Stern, the UFT became "the most powerful lobbying group in Albany and was able essentially to write entire sections of the state's education law." In New York City, it became the "800 pound gorilla of the school system."[62] The union had grown from 2,500 members in 1960 to seventy thousand members in 1969.[63] The strikes also made Shanker famous nationally, and he began receiving invitations to speak across the country.[64] "Ocean Hill–Brownsville is what catapulted him into national recognition," says Myron Lieberman.[65]

The paradox, however, was that while the UFT's power was greater than ever, its reputation was in shambles in many circles. After Ocean Hill–Brownsville, writes historian Diane Ravitch, the UFT's "image as an idealistic and socially progressive union was tarnished among the liberal intelligentsia and many black leaders." The UFT had political power, "but the price of victory was high."[66]

In just four years, Shanker went from being castigated by some UFT members for spending too much time on civil-rights matters to being routinely called a racist by members of the black community. It was an extremely unfair accusation, but it nevertheless stung. Shanker later told his sister Pearl that the false charge of racism "hurt him more than anything negative that was said about him."[67]

During the strike, the UFT was the subject of sympathetic comments from vice presidential candidate Spiro Agnew, presidential candidate Richard Nixon, and some bigoted whites who supported "putting blacks in their place."[68] In Albany, Shanker found himself allied with conservative State Senator Marchi. These alliances obscured the fact that Shanker's battle was not one of liberal versus conservative, but rather one between two forms of liberalism—one pro-labor, pro-integration, and color-blind, the other anti-labor, pro-community control, and race-conscious.

Shanker believed that Nixon, Agnew, and Marchi were not his long-term allies—poor and working-class blacks were. White and black parents and teachers should be united in fighting for more resources for education, he believed, which is why he had supported Lindsay's Civilian Review Board. Shanker never viewed the 1968 strikes as "blacks versus

Jews." "It wasn't the blacks and the Jews, but it was some blacks," Shanker argued, black extremists who had little support in what they were doing in education among mainstream black parents.[69] There was also a larger strategic reason for Shanker to reopen communications with the black community. Ocean Hill–Brownsville had hurt the AFT's reputation with blacks nationally, interfering with the AFT's plan to take a run at the NEA in the South.[70]

Needless to say, Ocean Hill–Brownsville demonstrated that Shanker was not simply willing to concede to extremist black demands for the sake of the coalition. To do so would be morally wrong, even racist, he believed. "To take the view that anything a black leader does is automatically correct is racist," he argued. "Blacks have to be judged on right and wrong and good and bad and so forth, the same as whites do and the same as anybody else does. Nobody is pure, and nobody is without sin."[71]

In Ocean Hill–Brownsville, Shanker had not put organized labor above his concern for civil rights; he had chosen an integrationist and color-blind vision of civil rights over a new Black Power movement that sought neither. Shanker rejected the lazy path of symbolic politics that looked no further than the question of which parties were involved. White liberals at the Ford Foundation and the *New York Times*, "said it doesn't make any difference who's technically right, you should always support the underdog" according to Shanker.[72] But sometimes, he said, the underdog is wrong.

While Shanker could understand the impulse to say "yes" to blacks no matter the consequence—for two hundred years, whites had been saying "no" to any black demand based on race—the new form of "liberal white racism," he said, "does not offer the decency and respect for the black man to be willing to argue with him when you feel he's wrong."[73] Likewise, to give in to threats of violence coming from a small number was undemocratic and unacceptable, Shanker argued.

The Ocean Hill–Brownsville controversy was a tragic episode for the education of poor children, who gained nothing from a system of trying to make "separate but equal" work. And it was a tragedy for American liberalism more generally. The fight unleashed ugly racial and ethnic attitudes between old-time liberal allies: members of the black and Jewish communities. And, for Shanker, it meant the advent of a new, morally unsound and politically disastrous direction for liberalism: a coalition between wealthy whites and angry blacks, an alliance that alienated the broad white working class that once was the core component of the lib-

eral coalition. Shanker and his Shachtmanite friends believed that limousine liberalism was untenable and that giving into unreasonable demands
from Black Power advocates was political suicide, because it would deliver
the white, working-class vote to Richard Nixon and George Wallace. Black
rage, as Bayard Rustin noted, backfired, because it simply fed white fear.[74]
The two phenomena were mutually reinforcing: a white backlash against
integration fed Black Power, which fed a more furious white backlash,
which helped conservative politicians.

But Rustin believed the white working class was neither liberal nor
conservative—it was both, and it would vote for either a liberal Robert
Kennedy or a segregationist George Wallace, depending on how issues
were framed.[75] Shanker and Rustin wondered whether it was possible, in
New York City and nationally, to rebuild the progressive black-labor-
liberal coalition of the March on Washington, which King had appealed
to through universal American values—nonviolence, nondiscrimination,
integration, and workers' rights. Was there a way to move American liberalism away from the top-bottom Lindsay-McCoy position that alienated working-class voters and some said represented "the seeds of the
Democratic Party's decline"?[76] An alliance of middle, working-class, and
low-income voters of all races was much more potent, and Shanker and
Rustin were determined to find a way to rebuild it.

7

Rebuilding

RECRUITING THE PARAPROFESSIONALS,

LAUNCHING THE "WHERE WE STAND" COLUMN,

AND SEEKING TEACHER UNITY

1969–1972

DURING Ocean Hill–Brownsville, Albert Shanker believed he was fighting for the survival of the UFT. With the mayor, the business community, many liberal intellectuals, the elite press, and most in the black community against him, he took on a bunker mentality and could be pugnacious and appear narrow minded. Around the time of the controversy, Shanker spoke at Oberlin College and someone asked him, "Mr. Shanker, what about the children?" Weren't they hurt by teacher strikes? Shanker responded: "Listen, I don't represent children. I represent the teachers."[1]

He noted on another occasion: "My view of the leader of the union was a fairly traditional view, that I was elected by the teachers, the members of the union, and my responsibility was to keep them happy, and it did not make any difference if the newspapers liked me or parents liked me or if the public liked me or agreed with me or disagreed with me."[2] After Ocean Hill–Brownsville, Shanker's view changed radically.

Following the war over community control, Shanker was out of favor with key groups whom he needed and wanted to work with: parent groups, blacks, liberals, intellectuals, the press, and people in the NEA in New York State. Over the next four years, he made concerted efforts to reach out to each of these, for if pugnaciousness was one of his character attributes, building coalitions was one of his intellectual tenets.

The period of 1969 through 1972 was one of rebuilding for Shanker, as he would forge a new contract for teachers that sought to include parental concerns about accountability, attempt to organize a group of heavily minority teacher aides, reach out to minority groups and attempt to counteract a white backlash against civil rights, launch a paid education column in the *New York Times* that sought to present his forward-looking views on education, and work with his rivals in the NEA in New York to seek teacher unity.

The 1969 Teacher Contract

Following the fight over decentralization in the state legislature, in April 1969, Shanker turned his attention to negotiating a new contract for teachers, as the old one was due to expire in September. As talks began in earnest in June, both sides had incentive to settle.[3] Lindsay, up for reelection in the fall, had strong reason to push for an early agreement. And Shanker knew that teachers and parents were in no mood for another strike.[4]

On June 24, the two sides agreed on a generous settlement, which included several key provisions that were designed to help teachers and minority students simultaneously. The contract provided for hefty salary increases, moving the existing salary range—from $6,760 to $11,150—up to $9,400 to $13,950 by the third year. School Board Chairman Joseph Monserrat said the contract provided "the best teacher salary and working conditions of any city in the country." Shanker agreed.

But coupled with the salary increases was a provision for the development of "objective criteria of professional accountability." The program opened the door for a system where teachers might be evaluated by student test scores, against classes or schools with comparable students, teacher materials, and communities—an idea considerably ahead of its time. Discussing the idea on a radio program, Shanker said, "those who can't be improved and who are functioning at a very poor level, we're going to have to have the courage to say that, well, you may be good at some other thing, but you're not good at this."[5]

Likewise, Shanker proposed and received a commitment to create twenty early-childhood centers in certain slum schools, which could be used both by the parents in the community and by teachers for their children.[6] Shanker said the centers not only provided a benefit for teachers and parents, they also created the type of economically integrated education that the Coleman Report suggested could boost the learning of low-income students without hurting middle-class kids.[7]

The board agreed to add ten new MES schools to the existing set of twenty-one to benefit ghetto students and teachers looking for smaller class sizes. And the UFT negotiated a college-scholarship program for the children of teachers as well as for disadvantaged children. (The scholarships were later named for Shanker.) Finally, the contract established a $500,000 fund for national teacher recruitment, with an emphasis on minority areas.[8]

Shanker argued that teachers passed up $10 million in salary and benefits that they probably could have gotten in order to provide money for the ghetto program—amounting to $160.00 per teacher.[9] Both the minority-teacher recruitment and the child-care proposals were applauded by the editorial page of the *New York Times*.[10] The entire three-year pact cost more than $400 million, including $260 million in new money.[11]

The Paraprofessionals

If the 1969 contract was a big step for Shanker—in bettering the lives of his members, enhancing the education of children, and in improving relations with the minority community he was about to take an even larger step. Beginning in the mid-1960s, New York City had received an influx of federal money to hire teachers' aides, known as paraprofessionals, in high-poverty schools. Mostly welfare mothers, many lacking a high-school degree, the predominantly black and Hispanic "paras" were very poorly paid—receiving about $2.00 to $2.25 an hour.[12] Shanker thought they should be organized in a union and that the UFT ought to represent them.

For Shanker, organizing the paras would serve several purposes. It would add to the union's membership, strengthening its power. It would put the lie to the myth that Shanker and the UFT did not care about blacks and Hispanics and integrate the largely white union. And it would remove a weapon against the UFT. In future teacher strikes, Shanker needed the paras to be supportive, or they might cross the picket lines and undercut the effectiveness of teacher strikes.[13]

But Shanker's vision for the paras did not end there. In the long run, he did not want a system of college-educated white teachers and poorly educated minority paraprofessionals. For one thing, that was bad for kids. "Children learn from what they see," Shanker argued, "and what children are going to see in New York City is that almost every classroom has a white teacher and a black maid or assistant or helper. . . . And what does that tell people? Unless you find a way to get the black assistants to move up, you're creating a permanent, visible class structure of the white professional with the black servant."[14] Shanker envisioned the UFT negotiating not only better wages for paras, but also a career ladder—a stipend so that paras could go back to school, earn a high school and college degree, and become full-fledged teachers. He said, "the way to think about this is, this is going to be a generation of black teachers in the future."[15]

But as Shanker began talking about this idea, there were three major hurdles: hostility from teachers, many of whom did not want the paras in the union; hostility from the paras, many of whom saw the UFT and Shanker as racist; and the plans of the head of another crusading public-employee union, Victor Gotbaum of AFSCME, who thought his union, not the UFT, should represent the paras.

UFT teachers had several concerns about organizing the paras. Some teachers had opposed the idea of having teacher aides at all because they thought only trained professionals should be in the classroom with students.[16] Other teachers simply didn't want any other adults in the classroom with them, regardless of their educational credentials.[17] Many thought the AFT should stick to its skilled "craft-type" union structure of the old AFL, and thus opposed organizing the paras, which drew from the CIO model of "industrial-style" organizing.[18]

There was also lingering racial tension from the strikes. Many of the paras were hired by community school boards. Some teachers felt the paras were hired to spy on them in the classroom and then talk with the other mothers in the neighborhood about what the teachers were doing wrong. Some, though not all, of the paras crossed the teachers' picket lines during the 1968 strike.[19]

Opposition was so strong that Shanker was forced to lay his job on the line. He told teachers that he would not want to be part of a union that rejected the paras. It was the only time in his career that he threatened to resign.[20] The teachers went along, grudgingly. Meanwhile, among the paras, there were some grave concerns about Shanker and the UFT. The media had written about Ocean Hill–Brownsville as a race war, and now the paras were being asked to sign up with an organization that had been vilified by many in their communities.

As the representation campaign began in 1969, Victor Gotbaum of local District Council 37 of AFSCME sought to capitalize on the idea that Shanker was a racist and that the 1968 strike was against minorities. "It was a vicious campaign," recalls Eugenia Kemble.[21] Paras were told that if they went to the UFT, they would be treated like "colonial subjects" of the teachers.[22] Meanwhile, AFSCME could rightly point to a very positive civil-rights record. Jerry Wurf, the national president of AFSCME, had been side by side with Martin Luther King Jr. in AFSCME's fight to organize the mostly black sanitation workers in Memphis, where King had been shot the previous year.[23]

To lead the UFT campaign, Shanker turned to Velma Hill, a black civil-rights activist who had worked for CORE and was also active in Socialist politics. A protégé of A. Philip Randolph and Bayard Rustin, Hill had paid her dues in the civil-rights movement; she was, in fact, hit over the head while trying to integrate a beach in Chicago, leaving her paralyzed for a number of months. But Hill, who was married to Rustin's aide, Norman Hill, also had a larger Socialist vision that transcended race and addressed issues of class inequality. In 1968, with a newly minted degree from Harvard School of Education, Hill talked with both Gotbaum and Shanker about organizing the paras, but she went with the UFT because she liked the idea of paras being part of an education union and advancing to become teachers.[24]

Some on the UFT staff suggested that Shanker be kept hidden, and at first his role in the campaign was downplayed, but Shanker soon concluded that there was no way to hide the fact that he was president. Instead, he actively campaigned on the theme of "what we did for the teachers, we can do for you"—that is, boost wages and benefits.[25]

Voting began in June 1969, but the initial vote was thrown out because AFSCME had stuffed the ballot box. The ballots were not fully counted until November.[26] In the final tally, the vote was extremely close. The UFT was thirty votes behind, and there were about three hundred to four hundred ballots left to be counted, all from Ocean Hill–Brownsville and from paras who had been hired by McCoy. Amazingly, virtually all the Ocean Hill paras voted for the UFT, giving Shanker the victory.[27] While many predicted that the pull of race would prove stronger than the pull of class, says Velma Hill, the organizing of the paras was the ultimate example "of what can be done."[28]

In December 1969, Shanker laid out several demands on behalf of the paras, including a large wage hike, pensions, vacations, and holiday pay.[29] The board responded that the paras should not receive too much of a raise because "the inherent value of these people is that they live in these poor communities" and if they were paid too much, they might move out. It was quite a justification "to keep people in poverty," Shanker noted.[30]

Shanker believed that the paras needed to show their muscle by threatening to strike, and called for a vote in April 1970. In Ocean Hill–Brownsville, McCoy and Oliver sent a letter to paras in the district saying, "Shanker hopes to win friends again with the Black and Puerto Rican people whom he really hates."[31] But on April 22, the paras voted overwhelmingly to authorize a strike.[32] A key question remained, however: would the city's sixty thousand UFT teachers respect the picket lines of four thousand paras?[33] Rustling up that support was proving difficult, and a vote of the teacher membership on whether to respect the paras' strike was delayed. Teachers were weary of walkouts and many were still angry that some paras had crossed their picket lines during the 1968 strike.[34] Finally, a vote was set for June 3.

Meanwhile, in mid-May Shanker began a fifteen-day jail term for violation of the Taylor Law during the 1968 strike—his second incarceration in three years. His sentence was appealed all the way up to the Supreme Court, but he had lost and now had to suffer the consequences of his decision to break the law. Even as Shanker arrived at the jail on West Thirty-seventh Street in Manhattan, however, he sat down and crafted a defiant eight-page letter to the union members, urging them to authorize another strike.

Shanker later recalled, "I wrote a letter from jail to the members saying that there was no future for the union in New York City if we did not help the paraprofessionals and support them." Shanker recalled arguing:

> There is nothing that we could do that would more demonstrate that all these people who tried to paint us with a white racist brush [were full of] nonsense; and that we were unionists and we were fighting for due process and we were fighting for all sorts of benefits. It didn't have anything to do with being white. And that we would do the same thing for black and Hispanic paraprofessionals as we did for teachers.[35]

On May 26, unionists rallied outside Shanker's jail cell, protesting his imprisonment, and his letter to members was read aloud by UFT Secretary Jules Kolodny to a crowd of two thousand. Ocean Hill–Brownsville, Shanker said, was part of an effort to "break union solidarity through racial strife. There is nothing new in this technique. Black and white workers in the South have been exploited for years because race hatred has been used to keep workers weak and un-unionized." Supporting the paras, Shanker said, provided "a great opportunity to end this tragic and divisive racial conflict." A "no" vote would be disastrous, Shanker wrote. It would mean, he said, "an escalation of teacher-community conflict in which neither the union nor our educational system can survive."[36] On June 3, six thousand teachers lined up to vote at the Madison Square Garden center. The next day, Shanker, who had been released from jail, announced the vote: three to one (4,418 to 1,554) in favor of backing the paras.[37]

The threat of another strike, backed by teachers, resulted in serious and intense negotiations over the summer, and ultimately a three-year contract calling for a 140 percent salary increase for the paras and significant new benefits. The raise meant the average salary went from about $2,000 to $4,600. The agreement also included a career-ladder provision, in which paras would be granted two-and-a-half hours of release time with pay per week to attend college or a high-school equivalency program. The paras ratified the contract by a vote of 1,461 to 42 on August 3, 1970.[38]

Velma Hill recalls that the Board of Education was shocked when thousands of paras took advantage of the career-ladder program, enrolling either in high-school equivalency or college courses.[39] By the time of Shanker's death, the career-ladders program had brought more than eight thousand paras to teacher status, making the program the largest source of minority teachers in New York City.[40] Shanker argued, "I think this is the most successful affirmative action program anywhere in the country."[41]

Over the years, Shanker had a special place in his heart for the paras. Lorretta Johnson, who later led the paraprofessionals within the AFT, said: "We'd invite him to our conferences and he came to every one. . . . One year he flew back from overseas" to attend.[42] A colleague recalls that Shanker "would just melt" every time a paraprofessional gave a speech explaining how she had worked hard to receive a degree and moved up.[43]

Shanker also made sure that paras were fully integrated into the life of the union, providing training programs in parliamentary procedure so they could participate in the governance of the union.[44] The NEA, by contrast, did not treat the paras so well. Because the NEA considered itself a "professional" union, it did not even try to organize paras until 1977—seven years after the AFT—and in doing so they also voted to prohibit paras from holding elective office.[45] To this day, some NEA locals continue not to give paras full voting rights within the union.[46]

Years later, Shanker would say that his ability to organize the paras and negotiate a contract for their advancement was his "proudest moment."[47] Organizing the paras, he said, was "the greatest thing the union ever did."[48]

Battling the Backlash

During this period, Shanker also became active in an organization called Frontlash, headed by his Socialist friend Penn Kemble. Frontlash was meant to counteract the prevalent view that the labor movement was reactionary and populated by middle-aged white men with large salaries and who cared not a whit about poor and minority Americans.[49]

Frontlash was designed to work with working-class and minority youth to register voters and engage in political education. Part of the idea was to engage working-class blacks, a group whom Bayard Rustin felt had been bypassed by the mainstream civil-rights organization, which tended to draw their ranks from the middle-class black population.[50] And part of the idea was to reach working-class white youth who were turned off by the counterculture and were in danger of going for Wallace or Nixon.[51] Shanker served on the Advisory Council of Frontlash,[52] and he was an active speaker for the group.[53] Penn Kemble recalls, "We would always get him to come and talk about this because he was the great pedagogue."[54]

The AFL-CIO did not have an unblemished record on civil rights. Meany's failure to endorse the March on Washington was a mistake, and there were plenty of individual unions that were resistant to integration, particularly in the building trades. But Kemble and Shanker emphasized that in 1964, labor had been a crucial backer of the Civil Rights Act. Kemble cited the statement of Clarence Mitchell of the NAACP that without labor, federal civil-rights legislation would likely not have passed.[55]

They noted that labor pulled out all the stops to move white working-class backlash votes from Wallace to Humphrey in 1968, and nearly succeeded.[56] Labor was not a rácist institution, Kemble and Shanker argued;

in fact, the great "black-and-blue" coalition—blacks and blue-collar whites—was found within organized labor itself. "With a non-white membership of nearly two million and with non-whites making up one-third of new recruits," they argued, "the labor movement is the most integrated mass institution in the country."[57]

Independent of Frontlash, Shanker increasingly talked about the importance of rebuilding the civil rights–labor coalition. In July 1969, in an annual conference of superintendents at Teachers College, Shanker called for a moratorium on confrontational politics and a revitalization of the traditional alliance between labor unions, civil-rights groups, and liberals. Shanker told the audience: "The tragic thing about the recent confrontations is that the people of the traditional liberal coalition are at each other's throats and are fighting each other. While they were at each other's throats, their pockets were picked by the [New York] State Legislature. The education budget was cut. Medicaid aid was killed. There has been no new housing for three years." Reflecting on the Ocean Hill–Brownsville controversy, Shanker said, "There ought to be a moratorium to rebuild the alliance because without it, we won't be able to solve any of our problems."[58]

Likewise, in a January 1970 op-ed in the *New York Times*, Shanker outlined the need for teacher cooperation with community groups in education reform. Teachers could either choose to "narrowly defend the traditional school system and fight for their own betterment" or they could take the "more difficult but wiser route" of attempting "to build an alliance with parent and community groups" and accept "greater participation by parents and students in school affairs."[59]

On a number of occasions in this period, Shanker allied himself with civil-rights figures and sought to address minority concerns. In October 1969, Shanker and other New York union leaders joined Cesar Chavez in a demonstration of one thousand unionists, in support of the California grape boycott.[60] And in March 1970, the UFT gave Chavez its John Dewey award.[61]

Around this time, the UFT issued a series of lesson plans devised by staffer Eugenia Kemble on black history for fifth-grade through high-school students. The 204-page curriculum, entitled "Lesson Plans on African American History" covered topics from ancient Africa to slavery, Reconstruction, and contemporary struggles for freedom. Shanker called it "the first comprehensive work on African American history prepared by teachers and specifically designed for use by teachers."[62] The UFT also

published a teachers' guide on Puerto Rican culture and history with lesson plans for middle- and high-school students.[63] It was an early form of
what would later be called multiculturalism, though the UFT insisted
that the contributions of minority groups not be distorted as a form of
therapy, as sometimes later occurred.[64]

In December 1969, Shanker was honored at a labor dinner sponsored
by A. Phillip Randolph and Harry Van Arsdale at the New York Hilton for
his work on human rights. In a sign that hostilities had thawed, Mayor
Lindsay, who had just been narrowly reelected, stopped by to pay tribute.
He told the audience: "If any of you had told me a year ago that I'd be at
Albert Shanker's dinner, I'd have said you were crazy. On the other hand,
if any of you had told Albert Shanker a year ago that I'd still be Mayor,
he'd have said you were crazy. So it all balances out."[65]

Slowly, Shanker began to gain more favorable press coverage from liberal sources. In October 1971, three years after Ocean Hill–Brownsville,
New York Magazine published a lengthy and flattering profile of Shanker
by then liberal writer Midge Decter, entitled "Is It Still Ok to Hate Al
Shanker?" The answer was a resounding no.

Decter noted that in Ocean Hill–Brownsville, Shanker "had managed
to earn himself probably the worst press in living memory." He had made
enemies not only of black community-control activists, Lindsay, and
Bundy, but also "most of the literary intelligentsia, virtually all of the literary establishment," and leading education theorists.[66] But in Decter's
account, Shanker was neither racist nor power hungry. He was a staunch
integrationist, she said, citing his success in organizing the paraprofessionals. And he was an intellectual who read the *New York Review of Books*,
Commentary, and *Encounter*. The misunderstanding of Shanker, she said,
stemmed in part from a worldview that emphasized class inequality over
race. "Insofar as he has an identifiable political ideology, Shanker would
have to be termed a social democrat," Decter wrote.[67] (In February 1971,
he told the *New York Times* he was a "Democratic Socialist.")[68]

On the question of integration, for example, she noted that Shanker
said the key issue was class, not race. Wrote Decter: "It is middle-class
white children, Shanker claims, not white schools as such, who might
have something to offer blacks in the realms of the use of language and of
attitudes to the world and especially school."[69] The piece was so sympathetic to Shanker, Decter recalls, that it "occasioned certain funny rumors
about our relationship, which were certainly not true."[70]

Shanker also made a point to distance himself from white backlashers who supported him during the 1968 strike. In March 1972, when the Jewish Teachers Association (JTA) invited Rabbi Meir Kahane of the Jewish Defense League (JDL) to speak, Shanker boycotted the luncheon and withdrew the UFT's support. Shanker wrote to the organizer that the UFT "in no way wants to be associated with any individual or group that preaches violence or creates an atmosphere in which violence becomes permissive."[71] The JDL, founded in May 1968, had been active in supporting the teachers in Ocean Hill and in protesting against black anti-Semites like Leslie Campbell and John Hatchett.[72] Shanker received many angry letters from members of the JTA. The president of the JTA wrote: "We can only express our extreme disappointment that the UFT has mistakenly elected to lecture us about temperance and freedom in a manner both distasteful and spurious."[73]

Likewise, in a school busing dispute in the fall of 1972, Shanker sided with black students from Brownsville against white backlash parents in Canarsie, Brooklyn. The controversy in Canarsie, a working-class Jewish and Italian neighborhood, began when the central board assigned thirty-two black and Puerto Rican students from a housing project in Brownsville to Canarsie's John Wilson Junior High School 211.[74] In the beginning, only a handful of parents protested, but as the schools' chancellor Harvey Scribner vacillated, the small group developed into a large mob.[75] Mothers threw stones at school buses and raised a banner that declared: "Canarsie Schools for Canarsie Children." A boycott was launched in the first two weeks of school, and 90 percent of students participated. Scribner decided to transfer the Brownsville students to another school, but the central board reversed him. On October 30, 1972, Shanker issued a statement in opposition to the boycott and called on families to accept and welcome the new children to the school. He said he was "shocked and horrified by the actions which took place in Canarsie last week."[76]

The issue was different than the one in Little Rock, where white parents sought to keep a school all-white, Shanker conceded. The Canarsie school involved, JHS 211, was already integrated, and parents feared that an influx of additional black students would "tip" the school toward segregation. Nevertheless, a local mob should not dictate policy, he argued. "Mob-rule is mob-rule." Moreover, on a practical level, Shanker said, it was unlikely that thirty students in a school of 1,500 would tip the balance.[77]

On October 30, the thirty minority students were escorted into the school, and Shanker escorted the staff. Although many of the teachers were worried about the school tipping, the staff supported the UFT position that groups of parents should not decide which students or teachers were assigned to any given school.[78] What the teachers did was "truly heroic," Shanker later said. The Canarsie teachers, Shanker said, "walked through a picket line of their friends and neighbors, their husbands and wives, with tears in their eyes. I was very proud of them. I always feel the union does well to make people richer rather than poorer, more and not less secure, but the greatest thing it can do is to bring out the heroism of people. A union can make people rise above themselves."[79]

In a subsequent rally, protesters reacted angrily to Shanker's statements.[80] Canarsie parents complained that liberals had been for community control in Ocean Hill–Brownsville but were unsupportive in Canarsie. At one rally, Rabbi Alfred Cohen told a crowd of 2,200 white Canarsie parents, "we want the decentralization law upheld." If decentralization was good for minority areas, it was good for white areas, he argued, adding, "what's good for the goose is good for the gander."[81] It was precisely the argument Shanker feared would be made by white communities as well as black. This time, however, liberals saw the merit of his concern.

"Where We Stand"

Of all the steps Shanker would take to restore his reputation following Ocean Hill–Brownsville, surely the most important was his decision in 1970 to begin writing a weekly paid column. The feature, entitled "Where We Stand," began running in December 1970, in the Sunday *New York Times*' Week in Review section. Its impact was monumental.

In the late 1960s, Shanker had grown frustrated that his attempts to be published in various magazines and newspapers had been rebuffed. One day, while he was having lunch with Arnold Beichman, an academic and former unionist with the electrical workers, Beichman suggested that Shanker buy an advertisement in the *Times*. "Just buy the space like General Motors buys space," Beichman said.

While paid columns are today quite common, "Where We Stand" appears to have been the first paid column of its type in the *Times*.[82] The placement in the *Times* was ideal, because Shanker felt he was not getting fair coverage in the newspaper. In fact, UFT members had picketed the

Times over unfair coverage during the Ocean Hill–Brownsville strike. Bill Moyers noted, "Shanker and the *Times* are New York's answer to the Mc-Coys and Hatfields. They've been feuding for years."[83] Initially, Beichman says, Abe Rosenthal, managing editor of the *Times*, refused to sell space to Shanker, but Shanker appealed to the publisher, Punch Sulzberger, who overrode Rosenthal.[84] Jennie Shanker remembers her father coming home and being very excited and happy that the *Times* had agreed to accept the ad.[85]

The column was a key part of Shanker's rehabilitation project. "In 1968," Shanker recalled, "I became convinced that I had been dead wrong in believing that the public's opinion of me didn't matter. Public schools depend on public support. And the public was not likely to support the schools for long if they thought the teachers were led by a madman."[86] Shanker explained, "I decided to devote some time and energy to letting people know that the union's president was someone who read books and had ideals and ideas about how to fix schools."[87] The UFT agreed to sponsor the space for thirteen weeks, with the option to extend for a year. The annual cost was $100,000.[88] Shanker's ability to get the union to spend an extraordinary sum for something so unfamiliar to unions was a sign of his clout within the organization.[89]

Not only did he have the pull to get the union to pay for the column, but he also had the clout to get the Executive Council to allow him to say what he wanted without clearing it first. "There aren't many organizations where the organization will allow the president to do that," Shanker later said, noting that because of the strikes, "I had a tremendous amount of leeway."[90]

The AFT column was "Al's column," while a column later purchased for NEA presidents was referred to as the "NEA column," says Diane Ravitch. The latter "reads as though it were written by a committee. Al spoke for Al, who spoke for the AFT."[91] Although the document was titled "Where We Stand," some, including Shanker's colleague E. D. Hirsch Jr., noted that it was often a "royal 'We.'"[92]

The column lasted more than thirteen weeks—indeed, it lasted many more than thirteen years. It always appeared with his picture. For more than a quarter of a century, Shanker's face—adorned with "black horn-rimmed glasses and a mournful cast, like Eyeore in 'Winnie the Pooh,'" said the *Times*—appeared at the head of more than 1,300 eight-hundred-word columns.[93] If his columns were compiled in average-size books of 150,000 words each, the columns would fill seven volumes.

The gambit worked because Shanker was a font of ideas, and he was a font of ideas because he was forever reading. The view of intellectuals, at the time of Ocean Hill–Brownsville, that Shanker was a union thug who fought with black people and thought nothing of throwing one million children out of school was completely misinformed, and "Where We Stand" let Shanker's intellect shine through, week after week.

Shanker's childhood love of books never left him, and he was constantly reading, even though he was practically blind in one eye.[94] He loved history, philosophy, and politics, and his favorite authors included George Orwell, Edmund Wilson, Irving Howe, Arthur Koestler, Bernard Malamud, and Ignazio Silone.[95] He also loved to read magazines like *The New Republic, Dissent, Commentary, Encounter, The Public Interest, The Economist, Politics, Foreign Affairs, Scientific American, The Paris Review,* and *The Partisan Review,* and he would save all the back issues.[96]

His library was tremendously broad, from philosophy to religion, from education to politics, from Aquinas and Aristotle to Zinsser and Zimoviev. In his four-thousand-book collection, he had several books on Orwell, fourteen books by Dewey, twenty-two books by or about Sidney Hook, and books by George Counts and Lawrence Cremin. His office, says writer Ronald Radosh, "wasn't like what you expect your regular union leader's office to be," he said. "It was like an academic's office: papers, books, every kind of book."[97]

He read a lot on planes, where he had a period of time in which he would not be interrupted.[98] When he traveled, he brought along what he called a "heavy industrial-type schlepper," which allowed him to take one suitcase with clothes and a second with letters, books, articles, and other reading material.[99] One union official remembers meeting Shanker at the airport and offering to carry Shanker's satchel, which turned out to be full of books. "That thing must have weighed one hundred pounds."[100] He would return from trips, Adam Shanker recalls, with clippings stuffed in his shirt pocket.[101] At home, he would read more. "He hated television," says Jennie Shanker, "it was just something he despised." Instead, he read in a Scandinavian stressless chair in the living room, with the hi-fi speakers aimed specifically for listening in that chair.[102]

Shanker also encouraged his staff and union officials to read. Velma Hill recalls that she would come into the office to talk about a particular issue and Shanker would say, "Velma, did you read this article? Well, what did you think of this article?" Staffers felt pressure to keep up on their reading.[103] Lorretta Johnson remembers the AFT vice presidents receiving loads of reading materials from Shanker, which would take a whole week to read. He "wanted his vice presidents to read and to understand."[104] Says Eugenia Kemble: "Al was so intent on having people read stuff and for him it was a provocation too, because it would create the basis for a conversation."[105]

One side benefit of the column was that Shanker was sent many of the latest writings on education in advance of publication, because authors knew that a mention in "Where We Stand" could bring invaluable attention to their work.[106] In this way, the column kept him up to date on all the latest literature. The column also provided a discipline that helped Shanker think through issues, forcing him to arrive at positions.[107] The topics ranged widely, from education reform to human rights to labor unions to civil rights. What tied together the various columns, one colleague says, were "the requirements of a democratic society."[108]

Many of the columns sought to make readers understand what it is like to be a teacher.[109] And he would return to time and time again to outline a "liberal" opposition to school vouchers and a "conservative" concern about school discipline.[110] "He was a real teacher," says one colleague. "You couldn't approach a lesson you wanted people to learn in too many different ways."[111] He sometimes had guest columns from a variety of authors— from Arthur Schlesinger Jr. and Bayard Rustin to Diane Ravitch. But most columns he wrote himself, with the help of a succession of writers.

While the typical op-ed of a senator or business official is ghostwritten, Shanker was intimately involved in the column.[112] In the early years, he wrote it himself, every Thursday morning.[113] He wrote pieces typing hunt-and-peck style, while Naomi Spatz helped check facts and fill in blanks.[114] Even in the late 1970s and early 1980s, Linda Chavez remembers him using his old manual typewriter, closing his office door on Thursdays and knocking the column out in three hours.[115] But as he got busier, he received help from a succession of people, including Sue Glass, Bella Rosenberg, Edmund Janko, and Marcia Reecer.[116]

Shanker never really liked to write, said Reecer, which probably helps explain why he never finished his PhD dissertation. Sue Glass's role, she says, was largely to force Shanker to sit down and write the column, which he generally put off until the last possible moment.[117] Reecer, who was hired by Shanker from the *American School Board Journal* in 1989, described her role as "midwifery." With a PhD in English literature, her job was not to generate education ideas (Shanker had plenty) but to translate Shanker's thoughts and notes into prose. "It was always Al's column," she

said. "I never told anybody I wrote Al Shanker's column because it
wouldn't have been true." In a typical week, Reecer would meet with
Shanker on Monday morning to discuss possible column ideas. They
would work on drafts together, with the goal of getting the column in
Thursday evening. (The drop-dead deadline was Friday at 4:00 pm, so
last-minute changes occasionally were made on Friday mornings.)[118]

Shanker always reviewed the columns before they were published. Recalls his wife Eadie, "Even when he was overseas, he'd have them faxed or
they'd read them over the phone when he was ill." She would hear him tell
them, "'no, that's not the position we have to take,' and 'this doesn't make
sense.'"[119] Sometimes, before a trip, she says, he would bang out three columns so they would be lined up for the next three weeks.[120] Reecer says,
"no matter where he was, if he was in some little hotel in Africa, he had to
see it and make changes and sign off on it."[121]

He had high standards for the column, Reecer recalls. "If he didn't like
it, it got done again and that made for some very late nights."[122] She recalls:
"I can remember writing the column when I had to lie down on the floor
because I was so sick. . . . But you just did it. He did it and you did it." [123] If
Shanker was not happy with a draft, he would write it himself. "He could
do a column in less than two hours," Eadie Shanker says.[124] Reecer remembers one occasion when she and Bella Rosenberg could not get a column to
Shanker's liking, "so in disgust he sat down and in half an hour, between
12:00 midnight and 12:30 a.m., he wrote the damned thing."[125]

Reecer says Shanker had certain rules about the column. "I learned
that he didn't like long sentences. He didn't like sentences that began with
concessions" and "he didn't like any kind of cheap-shot criticism." The
columns could not get bogged down in insider's minutiae, says Reecer.
"One of his devastating criticisms was, 'That's inside the beltway stuff.'"
Finally, the ideas had to be very pragmatic. "He didn't like pie-in-the-sky
stuff. There was no point in suggesting something high flown just because
it would be good in a world that was different than the one that he believed we were living in. He didn't have a lot of sympathy for untethered
idealism."[126]

The column was famous for taking complicated scholarly ideas and
presenting them in readable form.[127] Bella Rosenberg recalls going over
columns and Shanker saying, "Well, you got it down to an 8th grade level.
I need 6th grade." But you could not do it by dumbing it down. "That was
not acceptable," she says. He relied heavily on analogies to make the message more accessible to people. "If people didn't understand something, it

wasn't because they were too stupid, it's because you did not explain it well," she said. It was the opposite of an academic style, in which the author cares only about reaching a select few. "That was just another way he was just the most profound 'small d' democrat."[128]

Like George Orwell, Shanker avoided the intellectual's fondness for abstraction and instead paid attention to concrete realities.[129] The column avoided "educationese." "People never understand what comes out of the mouths of educators," says Rosenberg. "There's all this jargon gobbledly gook." Shanker's column was different.[130] The columns also took definite positions, "stands," as the column's title suggested, reflecting Shanker's character.

Over time, the cost of the column kept rising, and it imposed "a huge financial burden for the union," Shanker acknowledged. (The expense was shared by the UFT and AFT.)[131] By 1992, when Shanker wrote his thousandth column, "Where We Stand" had expanded to include both the *New York Times* and the *New Republic* and cost the union more than $500,000 a year.[132] In 1996, it cost $700,000.[133] By 1997, the cost exceeded $750,000.[134]

But Shanker told Beichman that "it was the greatest investment he'd ever made."[135] The column became a phenomenon in education circles. It made Shanker, said the *Washington Post*, "the best-read educator in America."[136] His column was, says education professor Maurice Berube, "the only column on national education dealing with national issues that was read by everybody."[137] It made him famous in union circles as well. A *Times* reporter said, "Where We Stand" provided Shanker "an exposure enjoyed by no other union leader."[138]

Its success was measured by the fact that people did not view it as a paid column, but rather as a part of the *Times*. Rare among advertisements, it was indexed alongside stories.[139] People frequently wrote letters to the editor in response to the columns. And *Times* editorials sometimes responded to the column. A *Times* reporter told the UFT's Naomi Spatz that readers considered the column to be editorial content. "Everyone thought Albert Shanker was a *New York Times* columnist," he said. "I cannot tell you what confusion there was."[140] One summer, the union took a break with the advertisement because it was very expensive. In the fall, the *Times* came back to Shanker with a lower price because the column had such a wide readership.[141]

Some readers subscribed to the Sunday *Times* in order to get Shanker's column.[142] Others said they first turned to the Week in Review for his column.[143] Claudio Sanchez, who began reporting on education for National Public Radio in the late 1980s, says "reporters on this beat get so much stuff . . . columnists and writers and think-tankers and all these people who are writing something everyday. . . . But you kind of sift through the whole thing and you pulled out Shanker and read him first."[144]

New York State United Teachers (NYSUT)

Having reached out to education and minority groups with the 1969 contract, to blacks and Hispanics by organizing the paras and participating in Frontlash, and to intellectuals and opinion makers through his "Where We Stand" column, Shanker now reached out to one last adversary in the early 1970s: The National Education Association.

The late 1960s and early 1970s saw a dramatic transformation of the NEA, from an organization opposed to collective bargaining and dominated by administrators to one that was becoming a true union of teachers. Shanker came to believe that the fights between the NEA and the AFT were hurting teachers and that it was time to begin talking about a merger of the organizations.

Shanker's strategy was to begin with a merger of NEA and AFT in New York State. In New York, the membership numbers were more evenly matched than nationally: the NEA state affiliate, the New York State Teachers Association (NYSTA), had 101,000 members; the AFT state affiliate, United Teachers of New York (UTNY), had 85,000.[145] Shanker told Walter Tice, president of the Yonkers Teachers, "If we could merge in New York State, we could start a wave that would flow throughout the country and mergers would occur in other states, like Michigan and Illinois and California." Ultimately, all of these state mergers would put pressure on the national NEA to merge with the national AFT.[146]

The opportunity for a statewide merger came in 1971, when the New York State legislature passed a bill extending the number of years it took for a teacher to secure tenure from three to five.[147] Shanker argued that as an educational matter, you could tell whether a teacher was qualified after three years, and extending the probationary period to five years was instead meant to allow districts to lay off highly paid teachers and replace them with cheaper, inexperienced ones.[148] The defeat infuriated teachers and proved a catalyst for the two statewide organizations to begin talks.

A merger could combine NEA's upstate, suburban, and rural strength with AFT's downstate and urban core.[149] But putting together those diverse interests also presented a challenge: in parts of upstate New York, you could not use the word "union," and Jews from New York City were not particularly popular.[150] NYSTA's staff was also opposed to the merger. Executive Secretary Francis J. White called the United Teachers "our enemies" and said that the smaller group would swallow up the larger organization.[151] But as the case for merger grew after the tenure fight in the state legislature, a thirty-four-year-old pro-merger candidate, Thomas Hobart from Buffalo, won election as president of NYSTA, and in November 1971, merger talks between Shanker and Hobart were announced.[152]

When merger talks began, the main stumbling block was whether the merged group would be affiliated with the AFL-CIO.[153] Although the NEA was now in favor of collective bargaining, there was still deep distrust of and disdain for organized labor. Shanker was adamant that teachers should be part of the larger labor movement, and when a merger agreement was announced in April 1972, the deal provided that the new organization would pay dues to the NEA, the AFT, and the AFL-CIO.[154] The NEA state affiliate board was not sold on the package, and voted thirty-three to four to advise delegates to oppose the merger. But when the issue went to the NYSTA convention, the delegates voted overwhelmingly in favor of merger.[155] The issue then went to a referendum of the entire membership, and in May, Shanker and Hobart engaged in a six-day, four-thousand-mile tour to gather support for the merger.[156]

On June 5, 1972, Shanker and Hobart announced the results: United Teachers approved the merger by 34,171 to 1,706, and the NYSTA approved the measure by 45,635 to 19,477. Shanker and Hobart were named co-presidents of the New York Congress of Teachers (later renamed New York State United Teachers—NYSUT).[157] Hobart was subsequently elected president and Shanker executive vice-president, though most observers believed Hobart served at Shanker's pleasure and Shanker held the real power within NYSUT.[158]

The merger between NEA and AFT state affiliates was the first of its kind in the country, and the new merged organization was the largest state teachers' organization in the nation.[159] The development was cause for jubilation among many New York teachers and for Hobart and Shanker. But others were not so happy. Leaders of the NEA nationally now had Al Shanker as a member of their organization. Because all NYSUT members took on dual affiliation—with the AFT and NEA—Shanker could now attend NEA national conventions and many worried, said the *Times*, that the merged New York group would be "a Trojan horse from which Mr. Shanker can be expected to leap at the first opportunity."[160]

A few weeks after the statewide merger, Shanker spoke to the national NEA convention in Atlantic City. As he walked into the room, boos and hisses were heard. As Shanker spoke to delegates, members of the NEA's black caucus walked out of the convention to protest what they called Shanker's "racist" views. And, as Shanker sat in the audience fewer than twenty yards away, the NEA's top ranking staff official, Dr. Sam M. Lambert, told delegates that the New York merger would mean "one-man control" by the president of the UFT.[161] In a rebuke to Shanker and the New York merger, the NEA passed a resolution that henceforth any state-level mergers should not require AFL-CIO membership.[162]

There was one other person who worried about the implications of the NYSUT merger: Shanker's friend and mentor David Selden. Selden, who had gone with Cogen to the national AFT in 1964, replaced Cogen as president of the AFT in 1968. Selden, who had no real independent power base, had watched Shanker's control over the UFT in New York City tighten. Now, the statewide New York merger doubled the number of teachers from New York who were AFT members and put the New York membership within the AFT above the combined membership of the other forty-nine states.[163] Selden knew that with the merger, "for all intents and purposes, New York would be the Federation."[164]

In the three years following Ocean Hill–Brownsville, Shanker did much to rehabilitate himself in the eyes of his critics. He successfully began building bridges to parent groups, the black community, intellectuals, and even members of the NEA. But he did so without pivoting away from the principles he stood for in Ocean Hill–Brownsville: a commitment to fair treatment of labor, to integration, and to nondiscrimination. In organizing the paras and in opposing whites in Canarsie, Shanker's actions suggested he was motivated by those same principles whether they had the effect of benefiting whites or blacks. His thoughtful, intellectual side also began to become apparent to critics who read his paid column in the *New York Times*. Shanker's battles with fellow liberals over the direction of liberalism would continue in coming years, but even his critics were less able to dismiss him as the villain they had imagined him as during the 1968 teacher strikes.

8

Becoming President of the American Federation of Teachers and Battling the New Politics Movement

1972–1974

B Y 1972, Albert Shanker and Dave Selden had long since ended their student-mentor relationship, and a rift had developed between the former close friends. The two men, who together had helped build the first powerful teachers' union local in the country, divided on a number of issues that were also splitting liberals and the New Politics movement (a more moderate version of the New Left) across the country. The four biggest divisions between Selden and Shanker involved the Vietnam War, the uses of political power, George McGovern's presidential campaign, and the importance of the AFL-CIO. In the early to mid-1970s, these issues, and competing ambitions, set the two former friends on a collision course that would end with only one standing.

Vietnam

No issue split the country more powerfully during the late 1960s and early 1970s than American involvement in the war in Vietnam, and as a Socialist, Shanker was himself torn in two directions. He was, on the one hand, a pacifist in his youth and remained an anti-imperialist. On the other hand, as a democratic Socialist, he hated Communists and knew what they were capable of. These competing impulses would pull Shanker initially to the left and later to the right, as events shaped his views and he sorted out the issues in his own mind.

Early on, in 1965, Shanker's anti-imperialist strain led him to oppose the American invasion of the Dominican Republic.[1] Following the invasion, Shanker and other Socialists and liberals—including Norman Thomas, William Sloan Coffin, John Kenneth Galbraith, Arthur Schlesinger Jr., Victor Reuther, A. Philip Randolph, and Michael Harrington—set up a Committee on Free Elections in the Dominican Republic to ensure that left-of-center candidate Juan Bosch was treated fairly.[2] In May 1966, Shanker traveled to the Dominican Republic with Bayard Rustin and Leone Schull, executive director of the Americans for Democratic Action, as part of an advance group pushing for free elections.[3]

Early on, Shanker also had doubts about the Vietnam War. In late April 1966, Shanker was among seventeen New York City labor officials who invited others to a May 3 founding conference of the Trade Union Division of SANE. SANE was, at the time, a moderate antiwar group, which was anti-Communist and called for "de-escalation," rather than unilateral withdrawal, from Vietnam. At the May 3 gathering, the founding members unanimously adopted a statement that read, in part:

> The war in Viet Nam daily involves more Americans on the field of battle and steadily increases the toll of lives of Americans and Viet Namese in that unhappy land 9,000 miles away.... It becomes increasingly clear that the simple solution to the Viet Nam war offered again and again—"victory through escalation"—cannot succeed. It is clear also that negotiations must take place among all those involved in the armed struggle. We urge steps to bring about such negotiations, rather than further escalation of the conflict.[4]

AFL-CIO President George Meany did not take kindly to the Trade Union Division in SANE. The AFL-CIO had a long history of helping to build an independent, democratic trade-union movement in Vietnam, dating back to 1950, when Irving Brown, the federation's point man abroad, told the International Confederation of Free Trade Unions that he could "think of no more pressing task than organizing in Southeast Asia."[5] In 1953, the Vietnamese Confederation of Labor (CVT) was legally recognized, and until the bitter end, Meany and the AFL-CIO fought to protect the vulnerable organization from the repressive regimes of, on the one hand, both South Vietnamese presidents Ngo Dinh Diem and Nguyen Van Thieu, and, on the other, the anticipated bloodbath for union leaders if the North Vietnamese took over. The Federation believed that free trade unions in Vietnam would at once serve as a check on repression by the right-wing leaders in South Vietnam and also provide some economic benefit to workers, undercutting the appeal of the Communists.[6] It was against this backdrop that in August 1966 the AFL-CIO Executive Council unanimously adopted a strong statement on Vietnam which read, in part: "Those who would deny our military forces unstinting support are, in effect aiding the Communist enemy of our country—at the very moment when it is bearing the heaviest burdens in the defense of world peace and freedom."[7]

As lines were drawn between Meany and SANE, Shanker decided to mute his opposition to the war. In early March 1967, a major fight erupted within the UFT's executive committee over whether the UFT should disassociate itself from the AFL-CIO Executive Committee's uncritical support of Johnson's policy in Vietnam. Shanker pushed for defeat of the resolution, arguing in a statement along with others that the organization should take "no position" on Vietnam. Shanker had won over conservative teachers to the UFT by providing them bread and butter, but he warned that taking a position on Vietnam might split the union.[8] Shanker's stance was defeated on a twenty-one to twenty vote.[9] At an emotional Delegate Assembly meeting on March 11, 1967, the UFT adopted an anti-Vietnam resolution that Shanker objected to because it did not couple the call for the United States to stop bombing with a call on the North Vietnamese to push for peace. After the vote, Shanker said: "The UFT Delegate Assembly placed the entire burden for peace on the United States." Shanker opposed any call for unilateral withdrawal, saying, "I, for one, do not believe that a United States withdrawal—leaving Vietnam to the North and the Viet Cong—would further" the goals of democracy.[10] Shanker believed that the delegates' vote was not representative of the union membership as a whole and placed the issue of the Vietnam War on a referendum. In the referendum vote, held a few months after the Delegate Assembly, the membership sided with Shanker and rejected the Delegate Assembly's antiwar position.[11]

At the national level, however, antiwar forces within the union gained the upper hand. At the summer 1967 AFT convention, Shanker's old friend George Altomare offered a resolution criticizing the AFL-CIO's pro-war stance. Altomare's argument prevailed over Shanker's opposition. "I never saw Al Shanker glare at me as badly as that," Altomare recalls.[12] At the December 1967 AFL-CIO convention, Charles Cogen, following his union's resolution, was one of the few union leaders to speak out in opposition to the AFL-CIO's pro-war stance and to argue for neutrality. In a voice vote, only about thirty to forty of the one thousand delegates supported Cogen.[13] The AFT was clearly becoming an outlier within the AFL-CIO.

The see-saw continued, and two years later, at the 1969 AFT convention in New Orleans, Selden, having replaced Cogen as president of the AFT, pushed a strong antiwar resolution in his own right. Shanker was once again opposed, but this time he had a stronger following within the UFT. In a rebuke to the new AFT president, the convention voted for Shanker's position over Selden's.[14]

Critics, including Selden, saw Shanker's shifting position on Vietnam as evidence that he was trying to curry favor with Meany.[15] A. H. Raskin of the *New York Times* charged: "Once a boat-rocker as a young Socialist rebel, Shanker has moved steadily rightward inside organized labor until he now ranks among the most orthodox of union establishmentarians, a highly articulate defender of almost everything George Meany does."[16] Once the "darling of liberals" and an intellectual who was "steeped in the philosophy of Spinoza, Hegel and John Dewey," Raskin said, Shanker had transformed into "a favorite with the hardhat conservative elements of organized labor."[17] Shanker himself repeatedly argued that one reason not to oppose the Vietnam War was that given that the AFL-CIO had been so helpful to the AFT and UFT, "how would it look if we spit in their eye" and broke with them on Vietnam?[18] It was widely believed that George Meany used Vietnam as a litmus test among labor-union leaders.[19] The AFT would not be taken seriously within the labor movement so long as it took a position on Vietnam far outside of labor's mainstream. Taking a position different than Selden's was not a bad career move for an ambitious young labor leader.

But Shanker's position on Vietnam cannot be laid solely, or even primarily, at the door of AFL-CIO politics and ambition. Even his critics say there were other factors. One was the rising radicalism of the antiwar movement. Altomare, who clashed with Shanker on Vietnam, observed that Shanker was very uncomfortable with the peaceniks who opposed it.[20] And, indeed, there was much about the New Left's opposition that was distasteful.

One early disagreement came over the antiwar movement's reaction to the Randolph Institute's "Freedom Budget for All Americans." The Freedom Budget, backed by Randolph, Rustin, Shachtman, Shanker, and others, called for national health insurance, repeal of Taft-Hartley, a boost of the minimum wage, an increase in social security and welfare benefits, and a guaranteed minimum income.[21] Meant as a follow-up to the March On Washington, the program sounded like a liberal dream, but after its official release in October 1966, it ran into a buzz saw from the New Left because it argued for guns and butter and lacked a critique of the Vietnam War.

A program of a strong defense and a robust domestic program had been the mainstay of successful Democrats from FDR and Truman to Kennedy and Johnson, but now it was under attack. Michael Kazin of Harvard's SDS chapter, for example, attacked the Freedom Budget as promoting "imperialism." He said, "They're willing to keep all the defense money intact just so they can get George Meany on their side."[22] Irving Howe, Norman Thomas, and others criticized the Freedom Budget for refusing to condemn the Vietnam War and defense spending.[23] (Some also attacked the Freedom Budget for its declaration that "The war against want must be colorblind.")[24] The Freedom Budget was quietly shelved, and Rustin and his assistant Rachelle Horowitz blamed its demise primarily on friendly fire from the New Left.[25]

Concerns about the direction of the New Left antiwar movement multiplied in May 1967, when Israel's Arab neighbors amassed thousands of troops on the Israeli border and Cairo Radio declared a "total war which will result in the extermination of Zionist existence." On June 5, when Israel attacked its enemies during the Six Day War, many in the antiwar movement sided with the Soviets and the Arabs, something defenders of democracy found hard to understand.[26] Although Shanker was not originally a Zionist, he became a strong supporter of Israel, identifying with the struggle of the Jewish people, but at least as important, wanting to defend a strong democracy in a region where totalitarianism flourished.[27]

Increasingly, the antiwar movement showed a newfound willingness to work with Communists. SANE, which since the early 1960s had a strong anti-Communist position, reversed itself in 1967 and began allowing Communists into the organization.[28] Mary Temple, the Executive Director of SANE, resigned, as did one third of the forty-five-member SANE board of directors. Among those splitting with SANE were Walter Reuther, Irving Howe, and Helen Gahagan Douglas.

The moderates said that younger radicals had not lived through the Moscow purge trials and the Hitler-Stalin Pact and did not appreciate the methods of the Communists. Temple and many of the moderate SANE board members allied themselves with a new group, Negotiations Now.[29] Shanker was a part of the moderate new group, which included Rustin, Walter Reuther, Pat Moynihan, Scoop Jackson, Penn Kemble, Hubert Humphrey, Sandy Feldman, and Rachelle Horowitz.[30] The group did not call for immediate withdrawal, which it believed ignored the true character of the North Vietnamese Communists, but for a way to end the war with democratic guarantees for the future.[31]

Shanker was disturbed to see the increasingly radical demands of many New Left antiwar leaders. Whereas the SANE trade unionists initially called for negotiation to replace escalation, now there was a call in many quarters, including from one of Shanker's favorite leaders, Norman Thomas, for unilateral withdrawal from Vietnam.[32] Worse was the way some of the antiwar faction went beyond criticizing the American war and romanticized the Communists. Tom Hayden and Staughton Lynd, for example, declared after their visit to North Vietnam: "We knew too what the Vietnamese contribution to a humane socialism would be; it was evident in the unembarrassed handclasps among men, the poetry and song at the center of man-woman relationship. . . . Here we began to understand the possibilities for a socialism of the heart."[33] Shanker was put off by the left's insistence that Ho Chi Minh, a Stalinist dictator and murderer backed by totalitarian states, was in some fashion a democrat.[34] And during the 1968 presidential campaign, Shanker was annoyed by the decision of antiwar New Leftists to abandon Hubert Humphrey.

Within the UFT, Shanker saw the way his old adversaries from the Communist-dominated Teachers Union were using the Vietnam War issue, creating a Teachers Committee for Peace in Vietnam. And, during the Ocean Hill–Brownsville controversy, he was aware of the growing alliance between Teachers for Community Control and the antiwar movement among teachers in New York City.[35] The same New Leftists who supported community control were opposed to the war.

Meanwhile, the people who came through for Shanker during Ocean Hill–Brownsville, Max Shachtman, Bayard Rustin, Tom Kahn, and the Shachtmanites, were all coming down against unilateral withdrawal. Even Shanker's critics, such as Maurice Berube, say what influenced Shanker more on Vietnam than his desire to be in good graces with George Meany was that all his Shachtmanite friends were opposed to withdrawal.[36] Shachtman, who was twenty-four years Shanker's senior, had a strong influence on Shanker, says Shachtman biographer Peter Drucker.[37] "Max's influence on Al was quite significant," amplifying Shanker's intellectual understanding of Communism, says Eric Chenoweth, who knew both men.[38]

The Shachtmanites had a unique brand of anti-Communism different than conservative anti-Communism and they echoed what Shanker had learned from his friends in the Teachers Guild in the 1950s. Max Shachtman's view of Communists was shaped by his own experience as a former member of the Communist Party. He knew Stalin's brutal methods firsthand. In a famous debate in 1951 with American Communist Party leader Earl Browder, Shachtman recounted a list of Stalin's victims in Europe and declared: "There but for an accident of geography sits a corpse."[39]

Although Shanker himself did not have Shachtman's experience in the Communist Party, growing up and working in New York, Shanker was constantly battling Communists. "He knew what the hell it was all about," says Myron Lieberman, compared with people in Nebraska who had never met a Communist.[40] This firsthand experience toughened his resolve on the Vietnam War. His wife, Eadie, recalls that Shanker would tolerate most groups he opposed, but he "would not tolerate Communists." He saw what Stalin had done; he saw what happened in the Spanish Civil War. "So if you were a Communist, you were outside the pale; he could hardly talk to you."[41]

In particular, Shachtman and Shanker knew what the Communists in Vietnam would do to the labor movement there, and this concerned them more than it did either the New Left, the New Politics movement (antiwar Democrats who were more willing to work within the system than the New Left), or conservatives. Shanker argued that withdrawal would "abandon millions of union workers in South Vietnam who now do have the right to unionize and strike, to the Vietcong and the North Vietnamese government which tolerate no strikes, and no free trade unions."[42] In this sense, labor's anti-Communism in Vietnam and elsewhere was hardly "conservative"; it was pro-worker.[43]

Shanker came to believe that the New Left was making the same mistake in Vietnam that earlier leftists had made; that, in the words of George Orwell, the "sin of nearly all left-wingers from 1933 onwards is that they have wanted to be anti-fascist without being anti-totalitarian."[44] In the long view of history, of course, Shanker's opposition to the withdrawal in Vietnam is not easy to defend. Vietnam turned into a quagmire that split the country and arguably set back Shanker's cause—anti-Communism—for a generation.[45] But if Meany and Shanker and other supporters of the war were mistaken in their belief that further American escalation would turn the tide, they were not mistaken about the consequences of the North Vietnamese victory: reeducation camps, the institution of a Vietnamese Gulag, and a general bloodbath.[46] To Shanker, Selden's opposition to the Vietnam War stemmed from a fundamental misunderstanding of Communism.

Power

If Shanker had disdain for Selden's position on Vietnam, as insufficiently pro-labor and anti-Communist, Shanker also had a very different view than Selden on the proper exercise of political power, and the rift between the two men widened on that question. The New Left's view of power bordered on anarchic, and Selden's more moderate New Politics ideology was similarly suspicious of power. Shanker, by contrast, toughened by the rough-and-tumble battles with Communists and community-control activists, had a more hard-nosed New Yorker's approach to power: within the broad confines of running a democratic union, he would do what it took to gain and retain control.

Shanker first moved to impose a system of "party discipline" on the UFT's ruling Unity Caucus. The AFT and UFT had long had a system of party caucuses, similar to political parties, which would put forth a slate of candidates and take substantive positions on important issues. This was seen as preferable to a system in which candidates ran as individuals and won on the basis of personality or personal popularity. In the spring of 1970, at Shanker's urging, the Unity Caucus adopted a rule under which Unity members were free to fight out positions within the caucus, but once the caucus took a position, members had to support it publicly outside the caucus or risk expulsion. By 1970, the Unity Caucus had grown so powerful that expulsion from Unity was tantamount to expulsion from power within the union.[47] Over the coming years, Unity Caucus members were ousted for openly opposing caucus policy on a number of issues.[48] Shanker took a harder line than applies to national parties, like the Republicans and Democrats, where mavericks are disciplined but not expelled.

The problem with a disciplined caucus system, critics said, is that a small minority can rule the whole union. Suppose, for example, a ruling caucus has 60 percent of the votes of the union. With caucus discipline, 51 percent of the ruling caucus (in this example, totaling 31 percent of the convention) can dictate what the entire convention decides, because the other 49 percent within the ruling caucus are bound to support them. Ironically, the practice of caucus-discipline policy that Shanker imposed was once used by the Communist Party, though, of course, Shanker, once he gained control, didn't suspend democratic procedures the way the Communists had.[49]

If Shanker's Unity Caucus was in firm control of the UFT by 1970, the national analogue, the Progressive Caucus of the AFT, had a more tenuous grasp. Although Shanker had clashed with Selden over Vietnam at the 1969 convention, he decided to back Selden for reelection as AFT president in 1970.[50] A field organizer, Ken Miesen, was Selden's opponent. Aligned with the AFT's Black Caucus on the left and anti–New York conservatives on the right, Miesen came within a whisker of beating Selden. The final tally was 1,567 to 1,462.[51] Selden almost lost control of the AFT to the very type of coalition that governed the NEA. "That was quite serious," Sandra Feldman says. "It would have changed the AFT."[52]

The near loss was a surprise to Shanker, who thought he had the votes lined up to support Selden. It was clear that some caucus members who had pledged to vote for Selden when they ran as delegates had, under the cover of a secret ballot, voted differently than they said they would.[53]

Shanker did not wish this to happen again, and in March 1972 he urged AFT members to support a referendum to amend the AFT constitution to require a roll call rather than a secret ballot at conventions. Shanker noted that while the right of individual members to elect local officers and delegates by secret ballot would be preserved (and was protected by law), delegates should be required to vote openly, so members back home could know whether to reelect them the next convention.[54] An analogy was made to voters electing members of Congress by secret ballot but then requiring that members of Congress themselves should vote openly in their representative capacity. Critics noted that the open ballot also made it possible for leaders like Shanker to retaliate against dissidents—though there is little evidence that he did.[55]

Shanker's final move to consolidate power, opposed by Selden, was to abolish the AFT's Public Review Board, a group of outside citizens who heard grievances about union leadership from members. Selden had helped establish the Public Review Board in 1965, modeled after a similar board created by the United Auto Workers.[56] But at Shanker's urging, delegates at the August 1973 AFT convention voted to abolish the board.[57] Union democracy activist Herman Benson complained to Shanker about the decision to dissolve the board. Why abolish it when you have no real opposition anyway? he asked. Shanker responded, "Yeah, but Herman, you never know what's going to happen in the future when it's some crisis."[58]

Shanker and Selden's differing views on power were paralleled by differences in their personal presence and manner. Selden was a brilliant strategist and organizer, but he had a weak public presence.[59] Al Fondy, president of the Pittsburgh local, says meetings of the AFT were chaotic under Selden. "The AFT convention was a mess. You could go until three o'clock in the morning debating about nothing."[60] As a speaker, says Mary Ellen Riordan, the Detroit AFT president, "Dave Selden appeared a little disorganized."[61] Pat Daly, president of the Dearborn, Michigan, local and a friend of both Selden and Shanker, says Selden "was a terrible administrator." Although he was a talented strategist, he was also "impulsive" and "not well organized."[62]

Part of Selden's problem was that after Ocean Hill–Brownsville, the president of the AFT's New York local was far better known than the president of the AFT itself. In a book on the AFT published in 1972, Robert Braun entitled a chapter about Selden, "On Not Being Albert Shanker," and recounted a meeting Selden had with teachers in which they were disappointed that Shanker was not coming. "Not being Albert Shanker persists as David Selden's number-one leadership problem," Braun wrote.[63]

Selden tried his hardest to compete with Shanker but sometimes ended up looking pathetic. In February 1970, Selden flew to Newark to join a teachers' strike and went out of his way to get arrested. Says Braun: "with considerable advance notice, he appeared on the picket line in Newark; county sheriff's officers were waiting. Once arrested, Selden refused bail. Once convicted, he refused to appeal." He was sentenced to sixty days in jail, and was released May 1, 1970.[64] Over time, under intense pressure, Selden developed alcohol problems, according to a number of union sources.[65] "Locals became hesitant to invite Dave to speak," recalls Pat Daly. "He would arrive for a speaking engagement or a meeting perfectly sober, but in the course of the meeting and greeting he might finally arrive at the podium to deliver a disorganized presentation that showed the effect of a few too many drinks."[66]

Shanker, by contrast, cut a much more commanding presence. He was an agile debater, physically larger than Selden, with a tough demeanor, blunt style, and New York accent. He was argumentative, says James Kelly, who worked with Shanker on education issues years later, "sometimes bordering on rudeness when he wanted to be."[67] Says Kelly: "He may have loved a good fight a little more than he needed to."[68] "People were a little bit afraid of him," says journalist John Merrow, "because here's this huge bear of a guy . . . and you knew that he'd gone to jail."[69] Journalist Claudio Sanchez recalls, "He was just not one of these cautious people who say, 'I'm not going to say this because it's gonna hurt so-and-so's feelings or it's gonna hurt my standing here or there.' He just spoke his mind."[70] Shanker had great admiration, says Lieberman, for the take-charge style of Chicago mayor Richard Daley.[71]

George McGovern

One of Selden's heroes, meanwhile, was George McGovern—which caused yet another split with Shanker, who had grave misgivings about the Democratic senator from South Dakota. In the 1972 presidential race, Shanker was eager for a candidate who could beat Richard Nixon. In an April 1972 conference of the League for Industrial Democracy, Shanker said the Nixon administration "has done everything to fight against those at the bottom and in the middle."[72]

The 1972 Democratic field of candidates was politically diverse, from George Wallace on the far right to McGovern on the far left.[73] Shanker was sympathetic to the centrists—candidates like Hubert Humphrey and Scoop Jackson—who were pro-labor, strong on defense, and for civil rights but opposed to racial quotas, a brewing issue within the Democratic Party.

As the McGovern candidacy sprouted wings, Shanker, Shachtman, Meany, and their allies were increasingly alarmed. The central concern was McGovern's views on the war in Vietnam, the threat of Communism, and America's role in the world. No one questioned McGovern's patriotism—he had been a bomber pilot in World War II. But he did have a worldview, associated with Henry Wallace, that was thought to have been quashed by the Americans for Democratic Action years earlier. Wallace, who ran for president in 1948, had repudiated the Truman Doctrine, was an apologist for the Hitler-Stalin pact, and was seen by many as an appeaser, drawing the sharp rebuke of liberals like Arthur Schlesinger Jr.[74] McGovern had supported Henry Wallace in 1948 and agreed with Wallace that Americans had overreacted to the Soviets. In April 1972, McGovern said, if "we had listened to some of the things that Henry Wallace said, we might have avoided Korea and the Vietnam War."[75] Shanker, like many others in labor, saw in McGovern's "Come Home America" theme a repudiation of the cold war and a left-wing version of traditional right-wing isolationism.[76]

Shanker had other concerns about McGovern as well. McGovern said employers should hire minorities in proportion to the population. And as chair of the Democratic Rules Reform Committee in September 1969, he advocated quotas in delegate selection for women, racial and ethnic minorities, and youth, a suggestion adopted by the Democratic National Committee on a ten to nine vote, with labor opposed. McGovern told the *National Journal*, "the way we got the quota thing through was by not using the word 'quotas.'"[77]

Shanker believed quotas were undemocratic and opposed them on those grounds alone. But it was also bad politics for the Democratic Party to publicly embrace quotas. And it represented the endorsement of a new form of "identity politics" that said your ascribed characteristics mattered more than what you believed. Finally, labor saw the new rules as a way to effectively disenfranchise working-class interests, since there were no economic quotas to go along with race, gender, and age. In a powerful way, the rules symbolized an attempt by the New Politics movement to replace working-class people of all races at the heart of the Democratic coalition.[78]

If Shanker was concerned by McGovern's candidacy, Selden was delighted, and he invited McGovern to make a speech at the AFT's summer 1972 convention in St. Paul. At the gathering, Selden arranged for McGovern to have a small breakfast with AFT leaders. McGovern was seated between Shanker and Selden. According to Selden, Shanker was uncommunicative and appeared uninterested in anything McGovern had to say. Selden finally asked Shanker, "Al, don't you have any questions for the Senator?" Shanker asked, "how do you stand on quotas?" McGovern said he supported affirmative action but opposed quotas.[79] Shanker later recounted, "When I met with Senator McGovern and raised the question [of quotas], his answer to me reaffirmed his public position: that he strongly opposed rigid quotas but believed that minorities should be hired 'in reasonable relationship' to their proportion in the population—which is to say that McGovern is willing to abandon the word 'quota' but still endorse the practice."[80]

But the delegates at the convention were very favorably disposed to McGovern's speech and on the spot, Selden called for a vote to endorse McGovern for president, without any input from local leadership.[81] Shanker strongly opposed the proposal and moved that the question of endorsement be submitted to the larger membership for a referendum, but the motion was rejected by the delegates.[82] The delegates overwhelmingly gave McGovern their formal endorsement.[83]

Shanker was not done fighting, however, and in a September 1972 column, he outlined his own reasons for being unenthusiastic about McGovern. He did not mention Vietnam and instead talked primarily about McGovern's position in support of quotas. Shanker also condemned McGovern for endorsing tuition tax credits for private and parochial schools.[84] Although support for such measures is today associated with the right wing, there was at that time interest in private-school initiatives on the left as a way of promoting the types of alternative education sought by proponents of community control. In mid-October 1972, the UFT held a member referendum of whether to endorse McGovern and voted against it by a tally of 21,181 to 15,565.[85]

At bottom, Shanker saw the McGovern candidacy as embodiment of the "New Politics" movement—a John Lindsay–type coalition of minorities and wealthy liberals taken from New York City to the national scale. These were the people who had tried to break the 1968 UFT strike and supported community control in the state legislature. Regular Democratic voters, Shanker said, could not abide the New Politics' "contempt for their values, dilettantish approach to economic problems, reverse racism, and anti-American foreign policy."[86] The New Politics movement had crippled the chances of labor's 1968 candidate, Hubert Humphrey, by sitting on the sidelines, and now Shanker saw little reason to help the New Politics candidate, George McGovern.[87]

Shanker's feelings about McGovern were reinforced by his Shachtmanite friends, who were going through their own civil war within the Socialist Party over Vietnam and the McGovern candidacy. In October 1972, Michael Harrington resigned as co-chair of the Socialist Party because he was upset about the group's failure to enthusiastically support George

McGovern and because of its views on the Vietnam War.[88] Harrington formed a splinter group, the Democratic Socialist Organizing Committee (DSOC), which later became Democratic Socialists of America (DSA). The group came to include Harvey Cox, Gloria Steinem, James Farmer, Ron Dellums, William Wimpsinger, and Jerry Wurf.[89] Dave Selden became associated with the Harrington faction.[90]

The remaining group, which was later renamed Social Democrats USA, included Rustin, Penn Kemble, Tom Kahn, Rachelle Horowitz, Carl Gershman, and a number of other anti-McGovern Socialists who were close to Shanker. The name change reflected the fact that the group was no longer an independent third "party" but would work with the Democrats, was no longer "socialist" in the sense of advocating state ownership of industry but rather pro-labor and egalitarian, and that the group's larger emphasis was on promoting democracy.[91]

Just a few weeks after Harrington's resignation, on November 4, 1972, Max Shachtman died of heart failure.[92] Shanker had lost a good friend and advisor, someone who had helped him think through issues of war and Communism. But Shachtman's influence over Shanker and the AFT would be felt for decades to come, as Shanker's association with the Social Democrats USA and various Shachtmanites would grow.

On November 7, 1972, Nixon crushed McGovern in the general election. New Politics activists blamed labor. But one unnamed Shachtmanite told the *Wall Street Journal,* "if anyone is doing the work of Richard Nixon, it's George McGovern." Nixon's strategy "is to have the Democratic Party taken over by the New Politics. This will force the main base of the Democratic Party, the working class, to defect to the Republicans, because it can't stand that stuff."[93]

AFL-CIO Executive Council

Shanker and Selden's differing views of Vietnam and McGovern had not gone unnoticed by AFL-CIO president George Meany, who had a great liking for Shanker but did not take Selden seriously.[94] In early 1973, following the McGovern debacle, Shanker openly challenged Selden by saying that he would seek a seat on the prestigious Executive Council of the AFL-CIO. This would be an almost unprecedented move, since the Council was normally made up of union presidents, and Shanker was but a local president and one of twenty AFT vice presidents. So Shanker moved to be made a "first vice president" of the AFT. Selden objected, but Shanker held more power, and the AFT Executive Council approved the move and proposed Shanker as its nominee for the AFL-CIO Executive Council.[95]

Given Selden's disagreements with Meany, the AFT Council believed it would never get a seat on the AFL-CIO Council as long as Selden was the candidate.[96] Shanker, by contrast, had become a favorite of Meany's. On one level, the two men, separated by almost thirty-five years, were quite different. Meany, a high-school dropout, was an anti-intellectual, ungrammatical, homophobic leader of the plumbers' union, while Shanker, ABD at Columbia, was a fluent speaker who led college-educated, mostly female teachers.[97] But they both hated Communists, quotas, limousine liberals, and George McGovern.[98] Says Victor Gotbaum, "George loved Al."[99]

The idea of elevating Shanker, a mere local union president, to the august Executive Council ran into strong opposition, led by AFSCME's Jerry Wurf. Wurf, who, like Shanker, was an admirer of Norman Thomas, a civil-rights proponent, and a representative of public employees in New York City, considered himself to be the young public-employee rising star and had little use for Shanker.[100] AFSCME and the AFT had been through bitter battles over the representation of paraprofessionals in New York City in 1969, and the two men disagreed on the Vietnam War. AFSCME had even formed a public-employee coalition with the AFT's rival, the NEA, a move that embittered both Shanker and Meany. Wurf convinced eight of the twenty-six members of the Council to vote against Shanker, but a majority supported the move.[101]

At forty-five years of age, Shanker was elected as the youngest member of the Council.[102] There was a fair amount of speculation that the aging Meany might one day look to Shanker to head the entire AFL-CIO. Shanker himself tried to discourage such talk, and colleagues and friends say it was not something he aspired to. Nonetheless, his rising star with Meany drew considerable attention within the AFL-CIO.[103]

The NEA Merger

There was one final issue that drove the split between Selden and Shanker in 1973—how far the AFT should bend to accomplish a goal both men shared: merger with the NEA. Both were in principle in favor of merger; indeed, Shanker had executed the New York state merger as a prelude to a national merger. It was a dream, Shanker said, to create a powerful organization of more than three million teachers. It would be a huge union, Shanker argued, and its influence would be "magnified by its vast geographic spread," he said, with "members in every political election district in the nation."[104] With 2 percent of the entire U.S. workforce, teachers represented the largest single occupation in America.[105] The high education level of teachers, in a country where only one-fourth of adults have a college degree, amplified their influence. Because they were more educated than most Americans, teachers were, said Shanker, more vocal and more likely to be active in politics.[106] Selden said that if the teachers could be united, they "would be the largest, most articulate, and most influential organization in the nation."[107]

But if Selden and Shanker shared the dream of the merger, Shanker was much more cautious about moving quickly, because the NEA embodied in many ways what Shanker viewed as the worst elements of the New Politics movement: it was anti-labor, pro-quota, and suspicious of the exercise of power. At its July 1973 convention, the NEA agreed to pursue merger talks with the AFT, but outlined three non-negotiable positions: members of the merged organization would not be part of the AFL-CIO, any governing bodies of the new organization would have to have minority representation in proportion to the overall membership, and elections of officers must be by secret ballot.[108]

To Shanker, each of these provisions was troublesome. Shanker believed strongly that teachers be affiliated with the AFL-CIO. There were so many critics of teachers' unions, from foundations and liberal academics on the left to anti-tax and voucher supporters on the right, that teachers needed allies. While the NEA tried to isolate itself from other working people, Shanker believed being part of the larger movement was absolutely essential. He argued: "The very idea of unionism is solidarity. It means, 'I'm not strong enough to do things alone. I've got to band together with brothers and sisters.' And you can't just do it with teachers, you're not strong enough. And so you're in a general labor movement with other workers."[109]

On education matters, Shanker said, labor was a natural ally, because unions represent the working class, "to whom the promise of education has always been the most real and meaningful."[110] Workers had championed the public schools for many years.[111] Back in 1820, it was the Workingmen's Party in New York which called for free and universal public education.[112] Shanker argued that teachers needed allies in labor not only to lobby for education, but also for related social programs. In order for teachers to do a good job, he reasoned, students need good housing, nutrition, and health care, and labor could help bring about those goals.[113]

Shanker saw behind the opposition to affiliation some of the same class snobbery that had kept the NEA from embracing collective bargaining in the first instance. In representation contests, the NEA was sometimes blatant in its class appeal. One NEA flier in a Buffalo race in 1967 asked members: "Who would you rather be affiliated with?" On one side were doctors, lawyers, engineers. On the other side were plumbers, carpenters, and sheet-metal workers.[114] Within the NEA there was also a strange anti-AFL-CIO coalition of conservative southerners who thought that unions were somehow un-American and African Americans and New Politics adherents who saw the AFL-CIO as reactionary.[115]

Shanker was also strongly opposed to the NEA's insistence on racial quotas: that minorities should represent a minimum of 20 percent of the membership on each NEA committee and the NEA board of directors, and that at NEA's representative assembly, "allocations of ethnic-minority representation shall be at least equal to the proportion of identified ethnic-minority populations within the state."[116] The quotas, which were adopted when the American Teachers Association, a largely black organization in the South, merged with the NEA, were arguably more extensively used than in any other major U.S. organization.[117]

To Shanker, this was appalling. The NEA had been wrong not to endorse *Brown v. Board of Education* and to permit segregated locals, and now it was wrong to endorse quotas. It had gone from discrimination against minorities to discrimination in favor of minorities, without really pausing in between to consider nondiscrimination. "The NEA has gone from one form of racism to another," Shanker argued.[118]

Shanker was not oblivious to race at the AFT and made sure that there was racial diversity on his executive council.[119] In fact, Shanker said that without quotas, "we have a better percentage of minority groups on our national executive board than the NEA does."[120] Leading AFT figures included African Americans such as Nat LaCour of New Orleans, Sandra Irons of Gary, Indiana, and Lorretta Johnson of Baltimore. But Shanker drew the line at explicit quotas.

Finally, Shanker objected to the NEA's insistence that all votes at representative assemblies be taken by secret ballot. All election of delegates to conventions, strike votes, and referenda were already done by secret ballot. On the merits, when an individual casts her ballot for herself, the vote should be secret, but when she casts a vote as a representative of others, it should be public, Shanker argued.[121]

The secret-ballot issue was directly tied to the NEA's fear of Albert Shanker. Would Shanker use his power, his smarts, and his disciplined followers, under an open ballot system, to take over the much larger NEA? In an article entitled "Who's Afraid of Shanker," *Times* editorial board member Fred Hechinger said Shanker was seen by many within the NEA as "the big bad wolf" whose 375,000-member organization might swallow up the 1.4-million-member NEA.[122] Shanker's "dominating personality" was a "red flag" to several NEA constituencies, Hechinger said: liberals and blacks suspicious of his views on racial matters, conservatives concerned about his views on unions, and middle Americans "suspicious of a takeover by a pushy New York and East Coast arrogance."[123]

Concerns about Shanker surfaced at the national NEA convention in Portland in July 1973, where Shanker came under harsh attack from author Jonathan Kozol. In remarks that landed on the front page of the *New York Times*, Kozol, the author of a *Death at an Early Age*, a brilliant prize-winning account of teaching in a Boston public school, charged that Shanker fed animosity between blacks and Jews during Ocean Hill–Brownsville and damaged the old liberal alliance. Kozol said that during the 1968 strike, "Mr. Shanker openly encouraged and exaggerated the animosity that was developing between Jewish and black people."[124]

Shanker, as a member of NYSUT, was a delegate to the NEA convention and requested, and was given time, to respond to Kozol two days later. Shanker attacked Kozol as a self-identified Marxist and a supporter of private-school vouchers, both of which he was.[125] Many of the NEA delegates, says Selden, "unaccustomed to the rough and tumble New York style of public speaking, were repelled and frightened by Shanker's tirade."[126]

To Selden, none of these issues—AFL-CIO affiliation, quotas, or the secret ballot—mattered as much as the merger.[127] In late August 1973, when the AFT held its convention in Washington, D.C., Selden called for "unity by Christmas." Shanker, by contrast, said unity might not happen in five or ten years.[128]

The AFT Presidency

In late October 1973, shortly after being elected a vice president of the AFL-CIO, Shanker publicly announced he would be a candidate for the presidency of the AFT the following summer. Shanker said he would remain as UFT president.[129]

As the merger talks with the NEA began to pick up speed, Shanker heard that Selden was going around the democratically arrived at position of the AFT Negotiating Committee on the question of AFL-CIO affiliation. Selden was proposing a three-year trial affiliation with the AFL-CIO, a proposition that the AFT committee had rejected. Shanker pushed for a special meeting of the AFT Executive Council on December 7, 1973, laid out the charge, and asked, "Dave, why did you do it?" With Shanker's support, the AFT executive council voted sixteen to three to demand that Selden resign.[130]

Selden, noting the date of the meeting, likened Shanker's actions to the Japanese sneak-attack in Pearl Harbor.[131] On December 19, Selden announced he would not resign and formed the Teachers Caucus to fight Shanker's bid to unseat him. Selden denied that he had mishandled the merger talks and attributed the coup to Shanker's "thirst for power." Selden said that Shanker, whom he had first hired in 1959, "has been a good leader but now he's too big for his britches."[132] In a January 1974 column in *American Teacher*, Selden blasted Shanker as power hungry and antidemocratic. Shanker responded that it was Selden who had refused to put aside his personal views about AFL-CIO affiliation when he was voted down by the negotiating committee. "That is the nature of a democratic organization. Otherwise, why . . . have hundreds of locals send people to the convention? Why have a referendum of the membership?"[133]

As for the charge that Shanker was power hungry, the Executive Council issued a statement saying: "Power has been the objective of teacher unionism; of the AFT. We want power to achieve collective bargaining, decent salaries, and improved educational conditions. We have fought against teacher powerlessness."[134] On a personal level, having been powerless—and victimized—as a child, Shanker never wanted to be in that position again.[135] By late February 1974, it was clear that merger talks between NEA and AFT were going nowhere and negotiations collapsed. The NEA said the power struggle between Shanker and Selden hampered the negotiations.[136]

On April 15, 1974, Selden announced he would run for reelection, though he conceded that he faced an "uphill battle" against Shanker.[137] At the AFT convention in August 1974 in Toronto, Selden's forces offered a resolution to amend the AFT constitution to prevent the president from holding other offices simultaneously. (Shanker planned to maintain his

UFT and NYSUT offices while running the AFT.) Shanker noted that it was common for union officials to hold several titles, and the convention voted overwhelmingly against changing the constitution.[138]

Shanker knew what happened when Cogen and Selden decamped to the national level without holding on to their base in New York, and he did not wish to suffer the same fate. The UFT was critical to controlling NYSUT, which in turn controlled the AFT. If the UFT fell to unfriendly leadership, control of the entire AFT could be lost.[139] Of somewhat lesser concern was the matter of money. The AFT president's salary was only $33,000, while Shanker's salary at the UFT ($25,000) and NYSUT ($25,000) totaled $50,000.[140] The UFT was a much richer organization than the AFT. Giving up the UFT and NYSUT offices would have meant a substantial pay cut.[141]

On August 21, 1974, Shanker was elected president of the national AFT, defeating Selden with 87 percent of the vote (258,911 to 38,087).[142] It was a poignant moment, as Shanker took the reigns from his old friend and mentor, who had given Shanker his first break when he tapped him as a union organizer. The two men, who had commuted together to work and talked constantly on the phone, had once had an almost father-son relationship.[143] To his critics, Shanker's defeat of Selden confirmed all that they did not like about the man. Writers Jack Newfield and Paul Du-Brul saw in Shanker's willingness "to axe his old friend Selden" a certain ruthlessness.[144]

By contrast, Shanker's friends and colleagues said it pained him to take on his mentor but he felt he had to.[145] Shanker, says one friend, was not a "sentimentalist."[146] "Al was like a warrior," Velma Hill says, not a romantic.[147] He believed in friendship and loyalty, but he believed even more strongly in the union, and in his own capacity to do a far better job for teachers. And he believed firmly that Selden's willingness to ally the AFT with the New Politics movement—on Vietnam, on its view of the AFL-CIO, on McGovernism—was a grave mistake. Shanker's fight with Selden, says Pat Daly, "was a painful experience but one that he felt he couldn't avoid."[148]

In the early 1970s, Shanker was increasingly dismayed with the direction of American liberalism. George McGovern, the NEA, and even Dave Selden seemed willing to soften the cold war liberal commitment to anti-Communism, opposition to racial preferences, and the centrality of organized labor in the Democratic coalition. It was as if the community-control advocates in Ocean Hill–Brownsville and the limousine liberalism of John Lindsay had prevailed nationally.

Within the American Federation of Teachers, however, Shanker's tough liberalism remained strong. Shanker now found himself with four powerful platforms—president of the UFT, a leader of NYSUT, a vice president of the AFL-CIO, and now president of the AFT. But whereas American liberalism had once been quite comfortable with exercising power for good ends, muscular liberalism, at home and abroad, would come now under increasing attack, with Albert Shanker as a prime target.

9

"A Man by the Name of Albert Shanker"

SLEEPER *AND THE CONTROVERSY OF POWER*

1973–1975

SINCE the days of Franklin Roosevelt, American liberalism had sought to check private-sector corporate power with the countervailing power of two institutions: government and organized labor. Standing firmly within that tradition, Albert Shanker, as the new leader of the AFT, sought to broaden and expand the union's power on behalf of teachers. But instead of receiving support, in the mid-1970s he would be attacked by liberals—from Woody Allen to Bill Moyers—as American liberalism took another surprising turn from Shanker's tough liberalism.

When Shanker arrived in Washington, the AFT he inherited from Cogen and Selden was a small operation with two dozen administrative staff, located in a red-light district next to a strip joint.[1] Prostitutes ambled back and forth in front of the building, located on Fourteenth Street.[2] The AFT was very poor, selling debentures to its members in thousand-dollar increments to stay afloat.[3]

But Shanker, now forty-five years old, had big ideas for transforming the AFT. At a press conference following his election, he identified two main goals: organizing more teachers, especially in the South, and getting teachers more involved in politics. As he put it, organizing for "massive teacher power at the national level" was his primary goal. He said that among southern targets, Texas was particularly promising.[4] Education reform was not mentioned as a high priority.

Building Political, Legislative, and Organizing Operations

To build the AFT into the political, legislative, and organizing powerhouse he envisioned, Shanker turned to three people from Shachtman's Social Democrats USA. Rachelle Horowitz, a top aide to Bayard Rustin and a good friend of Sandra Feldman's, was hired to build a political operation. (She would later marry Tom Donahue, the secretary-treasurer of the AFL-CIO.) On the recommendation of the AFL-CIO, Shanker elevated Greg Humphrey to help build a legislative operation.[5] And to strengthen the organizing effort, Shanker relied first on John Schmid, a holdover from Selden's presidency, followed by Chuck Richards, and finally turned to Phil Kugler, a young Social Democrat whose father, Israel Kugler, had been active in the Teachers Guild and Socialist politics.[6]

Teachers had long been involved in lobbying for more money for education, but for many years, the AFT and NEA did not support particular political candidates because it was seen as unprofessional.[7] At the UFT, however, Shanker had long been an advocate of teacher involvement in politics. Teacher unions had a strong self-interest in electing friendly school boards, and teachers also had an interest in supporting candidates sympathetic to education and broader social spending at all levels of government, he said. At first, Shanker was unsuccessful, as an effort to get the UFT to endorse Hubert Humphrey in 1968 was rebuffed by those who said teachers should stick to collective bargaining.[8]

But over time, Shanker had transformed the UFT into a powerful political machine, electing community school members and endorsing mayoral candidates in New York City. Shanker made the UFT especially known for its phone banks.[9] By 1973, the *Times* said, Shanker wielded influence over school policy "at least equal to that of the Mayor and the Board of Education."[10] Kenneth Clark, a Shanker foe, said, given his power, "the only honest thing to do would be to designate Shanker as [Schools] Chancellor."[11] Nelson Rockefeller remarked that there was only one old-fashioned political machine left in the country: the New York City teachers.[12]

When Horowitz took over AFT political operations in 1974, she says she was expecting that each of the AFT locals would have a political apparatus like the UFT; in fact, none did.[13] And nationally, the AFT had essentially no political operation. (The AFT national headquarters had moved from Chicago to Washington only seven years earlier.)[14] The AFT would host receptions on Capitol Hill but not offer alcoholic beverages to save money. Early on, the AFT contributed fifty dollars to Joe Minish, who was running for Congress in New Jersey, and he returned the money, saying, "you need this more than me."[15]

Shanker appointed Ed McElroy, an AFT vice president from Rhode Island, to be chair of the AFT's Committee on Political Education (COPE). "He put an awful lot of spark in that committee," says McElroy.[16] And at the staff level, Shanker asked Horowitz to build a COPE operation similar to the AFL-CIO's. Horowitz says Shanker stressed member involvement through phone banks and other institutions, rather than just by writing checks. She says Shanker believed if members were personally involved in political action, it made for a stronger union, because members who understood what the union was about and were accustomed to being active were more likely to participate when the union called a strike or a demonstration at city hall. This was very unusual within the labor movement, Horowitz said, because many union leaders feared that an active membership only meant trouble for leadership.[17]

As the AFT grew, Shanker initially moved the headquarters from Fourteenth Street to Dupont Circle, but he later moved to offices near the Senate side of the Capitol. The staff was upset about moving from Dupont Circle to the relatively undeveloped area near Union Station, but Shanker thought it important that a political player in Washington be located near the halls of power.[18]

As the AFT's political power grew, Shanker beefed up the legislative department, and in the early years took a tack quite different from the NEA's. Whereas the NEA stuck to lobbying on education issues, Shanker pushed the AFT to lobby not only on education, but also health care, labor reform, civil rights and affirmative action, and minimum wage and tax issues, all of which affected education.[19]

Ultimately, however, Shanker knew that the AFT's political and legislative power would rest on its ability to continue organizing and growing—something the labor movement as a whole had been doing a fairly poor job of since the mid-1950s, when its membership peaked at one-third of the national workforce. Shanker developed a three-part strategy for the AFT: replace NEA locals where they existed, organize workers in hostile "right-to-work" states, and grow by organizing professionals outside of teaching, something the NEA was hesitant to do.

In city after city, the NEA and AFT went after each other's locals, seeking to convince teachers that each union would do a better job. If the AFT's initial argument against the NEA was "we're for collective bargaining and they aren't," by the 1970s, the main AFT platform was "we bargain better than they do," said Kugler.[20] In the early years, the AFT threw everything into organizing—perhaps 70 percent of the budget—and most of that went to fighting the NEA.[21]

As of 1973, about 40 percent of school teachers nationally were not covered by collective-bargaining contracts from either the NEA or AFT, particularly in the South, so Shanker also devoted substantial attention to organizing that region.[22] The battle was a tough one—the same strong cultural traditions that had nurtured racial segregation had left the South, although the poorest section of the country, particularly hostile to unions. But Shanker remembered when people had said organizing New York City teachers would be "impossible" too, and there were counterexamples—places like New Orleans, where bargaining was won through militant action despite the absence of a state law protecting the right to bargain.[23]

Even in states where collective bargaining for public employees was outlawed, like Texas, Shanker worked with local teachers to push for bargaining under another route known in the trade as "meet and confer."[24] The strategy was to work to elect a sympathetic board that would agree to make the AFT local an exclusive "consultant." Local Corpus Christi, Texas, union leader John Cole (later president of the Texas Federation of Teachers) recalls that Shanker was supportive of their efforts to organize against all odds. "This is a guy who understood what it was like to stand by a mimeograph machine and turn the handle and crank out your newsletter that you had just written. . . . He understood organizing at every level."[25]

In later years, drawing on his experience in New York City, where he pulled in teachers with his knowledge of pension legislation, Shanker sought to lure Southern teachers with "associate memberships," in which teachers would not initially become full members of the AFT but would pay reduced fees and get certain benefits (discount tickets to Disney World, insurance against lawsuits).[26] Associate members would also receive information from the AFT about what was going on in Austin and Washington, which would counter the anti-union information they normally received, and some would eventually sign on as full AFT members.[27]

The third part of Shanker's strategy involved a controversial move to organize other professionals outside of schools—health-care workers and municipal and state employees, for example—areas the NEA chose not to organize.[28] In August 1977, Shanker persuaded AFT members to vote to change the constitution to expand membership in the union beyond educators to "other workers" including nurses, librarians, park employees, and lawyers. Shanker argued: "It's simple, the more members, the more political influence."[29] Over time, non-teachers would constitute nearly half of AFT members; Shanker would joke that the AFT should really be called "the American Federation of Creatures."[30] Shanker's decision to organize professional employees outside of education became another defining distinction between the AFT and the NEA.

Child Care

Not all of Shanker's organizing efforts were met with open arms, and his first big effort—a proposal to organize child-care workers—met fierce resistance from his old adversaries in the community-control world.

In his first major address after being elected president of the AFT, Shanker, in a September 24, 1974, speech at the National Press Club, proposed an "Educare" program, which included a national program of early-childhood education. Preschool programs, he argued, would respond to growing research on the importance of intellectual development in the early years and would also help address a teacher surplus that had reached 250,000 people.[31] In his proposal's most controversial provision, Shanker said it would be better for early-childhood education to take place within the public sector, through public schools, which are well suited to administer such programs.[32]

The proposal that public schools be the presumed "prime sponsor" of child care—that schools administer these programs unless they choose not to—provoked outrage from two groups: civil-rights advocates, like Marion Wright Edelman, who saw schools, particularly in the South, as racist institutions; and from the National Association for the Education of Young Children (NAEYC), which worried that by involving the public schools, early-childhood education would become focused on academic content too early in children's lives. They saw Shanker's call for public-school involvement as a grab for jobs.[33]

In June 1975, Shanker testified before a joint House and Senate hearing on legislation sponsored by Senator Walter Mondale and Representative John Brademas, which provided prime sponsorship not to schools but to state and local governments, with the opportunity for profit-making and community groups to operate programs. Shanker said that provision was problematic: "The sorry record of profit-making organizations, especially in the nursing home, health care and education fields, has led the AFL-CIO to strongly oppose any involvement of profit-makers in human services programs." He said putting child care under the prime sponsorship of the public schools would ensure higher quality and public oversight of the centers. At the hearing, Shanker clashed with Rep. Shirley Chisholm, who accused teachers' unions of denigrating daycare centers. "Your teachers with all of their degrees and certificates are less than perfect too," she charged. Shanker responded that in New York, the state had cut off funds to a number of storefront child-care centers that failed to meet standards. There was yet another benefit to making schools the prime sponsors: doing so would provide the political strength to override a Republican presidential veto that had killed daycare legislation in 1971, he argued. Finally, the legislation must be aimed at all children, not just those from low-income families, Shanker argued, because means-tested programs tend not to have strong political support and often were of low quality.[34]

Shanker's arguments, however, did not win the day, and the coalition for child care fragmented as the AFT and minority groups once again found themselves in warring camps.[35] The legislation's failure represented a major missed opportunity.

Child care, as Shanker argued, was a place where teacher "self-interest and public interest" came together.[36] While placing child care in public schools could be seen as a power grab for Shanker—because he wanted to unionize daycare workers—the change might have harnessed several other developments: higher wages for preschool workers and less turnover in staff, a powerful political constituency to push for ever expanding access to daycare for all students rather than a Head Start poverty program vulnerable to slow growth, and higher standards than are currently employed in our haphazard, fairly underregulated system. Had Shanker succeeded, we might have had a child-care program like some European countries, where teachers are highly educated and well paid and the achievement gap between rich and poor is narrowed.[37] If Shanker had been able to massively unionize the child-care workers, we might not have the terrible turnover we see today, and we would have seen "a very different evolution of childcare in this country," Stanford professor Michael Kirst says.[38]

Criticisms About Power

To many in the New Politics movement, and many in the media, however, Albert Shanker's continual rise in power—and grabs for more power—from Ocean Hill–Brownsville to the fight over child care were deeply disturbing. Gene Maeroff, writing in the *Times*, noted: "Power is what some critics contend Mr. Shanker is after. And whether or not it is his goal, he seems to have gathered a lot of it."[39]

Shanker's growth in power, from the UFT presidency in 1964, to the NYSUT co-presidency in 1972, to a vice presidency of the AFL-CIO in 1973, and now the AFT presidency in 1974, happened to coincide with a number of public incidents that made the Left, in particular, suspicious of power—the abuse of power by the military during Vietnam, by the Nixon Administration during Watergate, and by the CIA in Latin America and elsewhere. Liberals came to believe, writes journalist Michael Tomasky, that "power was not a good to be sought but an evil to be confronted."[40] The New Left saw many existing centers of power as illegitimate and sought to tear them down.

Whereas liberals like Franklin Roosevelt had felt very comfortable wielding power in order to fight the Depression and the Nazis, some modern liberals had adopted a skepticism toward power, even among unions, which historically had served as an important check on the power of corporations and authoritarian regimes. Shanker believed, like Robert Kennedy, in the marriage of power and moral concern—a view that was becoming increasingly unfashionable.[41] Shanker's relatively hawkish position on the American use of power in Vietnam only fueled the Left's suspicion of his accumulating power over education.

December 1973 saw the release of Woody Allen's *Sleeper*, the science-fiction comedy in which Allen's character wakes up two hundred years in the future to learn that a madman named Albert Shanker has destroyed civilization with a nuclear warhead. The line epitomized New Left thinking about Shanker and his use of power to shut down the New York schools and cripple the community-control experiment in Ocean Hill–Brownsville. But the attitude went far beyond Allen. In April 1974, Bill Moyers made a similar charge in a one-hour portrait of Shanker on a public-television broadcast entitled "Albert Shanker = Teacher Power."[42] Shanker was expecting a positive piece, and in his "Where We Stand" column on April 14, 1974, he urged viewers to tune in.[43] Jennie Shanker remembers that the family all gathered around to watch the show together, but as the program aired, her parents grew disheartened, upset, and angry.[44]

Moyers began with a clip from *Sleeper*, and in the introduction, noting Shanker's positions as head of the largest union local in the country and his service as the youngest member of the AFL-CIO executive council, commented: "And that gleam in his eye. Is that just the sparkle of a flashbulb or a reflection of a beckoning image of power that only a man sees who aspires to be the leader of three million American schoolteachers? Who is this man who in Woody Allen's imagination could bring the world to an end? Albert Shanker equals teacher power."[45]

For the next hour, Moyers featured Shanker critics like Dave Selden, who said, "what motivates Shanker and has for many years is simply that he has achieved power. People that achieve power never seem to have enough of it." Rival Victor Gotbaum of AFSCME told Moyers, "Al's personal belief is: Don't get angry. Get even. Very vindictive man. . . . Al has to get you. He can't help himself. He involves himself in overkill."[46] Moyers said that during Ocean Hill–Brownsville, Shanker was "accused of ruling and winning by sheer terror."[47]

Moyers ended the piece with this thought on Shanker: "There comes a moment when power has the goal of justice and must find new outlets or fester, and, perhaps explode. Studying Albert Shanker, one remembers Abigail Adams writing to her husband: 'I am more and more convinced,' she said, 'that power, whether vested in many or a few, is ever-grasping, and like the grave, cries: Give. Give.'"[48] The Moyers show was followed by other articles with similar themes, including a March 1975 profile in *Phi Delta Kappan* entitled "Albert Shanker: A Portrait in Power"[49] and a September 1975 *Time Magazine* article entitled "Albert Shanker: 'Power Is Good.'"[50]

There can be no doubt that Shanker had accumulated a great deal of power and that he wanted even more. In early 1975, Shanker openly declared that his next ambition was "to be head of whatever comes out of a merger with the National Education Association." It was his goal, he said, "to be head of a union of three to four million teachers, which would be one of the largest unions in the world."[51]

But for Shanker, the attacks on his power, particularly by people from the Left, like Allen and Moyers, raised a question: since when did liberals think that it was bad for the elected representatives of workers to exercise power? Attacking union power was akin to criticizing David against the Goliath of corporate America. "Power is a good thing; it's better than powerlessness," he said.[52] Shanker did not want power for its own sake, Eugenia Kemble says, but to accomplish certain ends. "Al knew you couldn't do a whole lot if you didn't have power."[53] Power, as Michael Tomasky notes, is "neither inherently good" nor "inherently evil. . . . It is a tool."[54] The real questions boiled down to these three: was Shanker's power democratically obtained? Was it democratically exercised? And toward what ends did he use it?

Although Shanker ran a tighter ship than Dave Selden, it would be hard to make the case that Shanker ran undemocratic unions in the AFT and UFT. All truly major decisions, such as whether to ratify contracts or go out on strike, were subject to a referendum of members. Shanker told Moyers, "I can't think of another organization in this country that's had referenda on who should be endorsed as President of the United States; on dues increases; on positions on the Vietnam war; or on almost everything that's any sort of a controversial issue, we say: let the members decide."[55]

In addition, the UFT gave the opposition slate the right to full coverage in the UFT newspaper, distributed at union expense, an openness "almost unique" in the labor world, says union democracy advocate Herman Benson.[56] In their classic book on union democracy, Seymour Martin Lipset, Martin A. Trow, and James S. Coleman noted that most union officials strictly control the formal means of communication with workers.[57]

Shanker was also known for giving opponents at conventions ample time to make their case against his position. Shanker's allies within the union felt he was too lenient with opposition speakers, bending over backward to give them extra time to speak.[58] Says AFT Vice President Sandra Irons, who was on the opposite side from Shanker on many race issues, "Al never attempted to stifle debate on issues that were in opposition to what he believed."[59] Herb Magidson, another AFT vice president, said people around Shanker used to chastise him: "Al, why are you always calling on the opposition to speak?"[60]

And the AFT had two other features that Lipset, Trow, and Coleman associate with democratic unions: a highly educated active membership and an unusual amount of autonomy for locals.[61] In sum, says Herman Benson, "the AFT is one of the most democratic unions in the United States. You don't get thrown out for opening your mouth. You run for office, you get complete coverage. You have access to the membership. . . ."[62]

But even if Shanker's union was democratic, was the power he exercised through strikes—shutting down an entire public-school system for weeks at a time, over the objection of the mayor, the school board, and other elected officials—itself undemocratic? Teachers might have elected him, but the general public did not. To Shanker, this line of thinking misunderstood the role of independent groups in a democratic society. Teacher strikes were disruptive, but so were many other activities. If the president of General Motors shuts down a factory—permanently—it can plunge a town into turmoil, far more devastating than a temporary strike. But closing a factory is considered a legitimate use of private power. Why was the decision of teachers to band together and exert themselves considered illegitimate? It was certainly new and different. Teachers were supposed to be people "at home with a cat and a geranium," says Naomi Spatz.[63] Shanker observed of the Woody Allen joke that Allen must have believed it was the end of the world for teachers to have some power.[64] After all, Shanker could never have called strikes by himself; he only had power insofar as teachers voted to strike and agreed not to cross the picket line.

In Ocean Hill–Brownsville, moreover, teachers were striking essentially to enforce the decision of democratically elected officials—the mayor and school board—who were demanding the return of UFT teachers to certain schools and were blocked by a handful of unelected vigilantes. Moreover, while the decision to strike was illegal, Shanker had not run from the consequences; he had served time in jail for what he regarded as civil disobedience.

If the source of Shanker's power was legitimate, maybe it was the way he exercised his power within the union that critics found objectionable. Maybe it was Shanker's style—an imperious or authoritarian manner that rubbed people the wrong way. But Shanker did not have the personal arrogance that often is associated with those who exercise power—among leaders of unions, corporations, or government. "Shanker's power was recognized, but there was no widespread feeling that it was exercised arbitrarily," says Shanker critic Myron Lieberman.[65]

Shanker was not a prima donna. Everyone called him "Al," never "Mr. Shanker."[66] While many union leaders had drivers and people to carry their bags, Shanker drove himself, and he put his bags—often stuffed with books—on rollers.[67] At hotels he usually got a regular hotel room, not a suite.[68] Sally Muravchik, who handled conventions for the AFT, says Shanker was "totally low-maintenance, totally non-demanding," compared to other union leaders. "He wasn't fussy." Judy Bardacke, who supervised the support staff, said they "loved him because he was down to earth. He didn't have any airs. He dressed funny," donning awful ties.[69]

With staff, Shanker's management style was nonhierarchical, and he had an open-door policy rare among union chiefs. Burnie Bond, who moved back and forth from the AFL-CIO to the AFT, was struck by the contrast. At the AFL-CIO, there were channels and large slow-moving bureaucracies, and the federation's president, Lane Kirkland, was unapproachable; whereas at the AFT, if you had an idea, you would stick your head into Shanker's office and discuss it, often over a bottle of wine.[70] Eric Chenoweth also worked in both places. When you went into Kirkland's office, Chenoweth remembers, "trying to talk to him was like talking to Buddha. He had an enormous capacity to make you feel uncomfortable, like you were invading his space, and you'd better justify why you'd invaded his space." With Shanker, by contrast, you could have a real conversation, and did not have to feed him questions so he could answer them.[71]

His management style, says Horowitz, "might be chaotic, but [it was] definitely not imperial."[72] In fact, some thought Shanker's accessibility and lack of hierarchy was a problem. In the early 1980s, AFT staffer Linda Chavez proposed to Shanker that he create a more hierarchical system and appoint her as executive director. "Everybody should not be able to run to Al and have Al make decisions," she said.[73] Shanker approved the idea, but it quickly proved to be a disaster. "All hell broke loose," Chavez said. No one abided by the plan; everyone continued to go directly to Shanker. "There was really no stopping it."[74]

In meetings with staff, Shanker encouraged debate and disagreement.[75] Burnie Bond recalls: "You could go and argue with him and if he thought you had a good point he was willing to change his position. I had never worked for the 'big boss' being that open to argument before."[76] Bella Rosenberg says there was a New York Jewish atmosphere, even among staff members who were neither from New York nor Jewish, in which "you could be vehement and people understood you weren't yelling at them, you weren't attacking them personally."[77] "If you didn't argue with him," says Greg Humphrey, "I think he figured there was something wrong with you."[78] Shanker really wanted to argue and convince his staff on matters, not just hand down an edict, says Eugenia Kemble. "He wanted you to be convinced. He cared about the idea. He didn't want to just be the boss." In that sense, "he ran the organization like a teacher."[79]

Also rare among union leaders, Shanker relied heavily on a group of very strong women—Sandy Feldman, Rachelle Horowitz, Eugenia Kemble, Velma Hill, and later Linda Chavez and Bella Rosenberg. Rosenberg says: "He was very comfortable with women, certainly big-mouthed women. . . . Actually some of the men groused, they thought that Al preferred women."[80] Shanker promoted numerous women to positions of leadership in the AFT, far more than any of his predecessors.[81] "There are some places where the guys go off and play golf," says Horowitz. "In the AFT, the president cracked out the wine."[82]

Indeed, there was a softer side to Albert Shanker that was hard to square with the hard-charging power-obsessed leader that critics like Moyers and Allen saw. To be sure, Shanker was a hard bargainer and a tough negotiator who wanted more power, but he was more complex than that. He did not enjoy sports and could not carry on a "how-about-those-Redskins" conversation if he tried. Instead, he loved to shop—for wine, African art, and Native American jewelry—and was particularly proud when he got a bargain.[83]

Also belying the image of the tough union "thug" was Shanker's fondness for making gourmet bread and pasta and his penchant for whipping up a Moroccan meal. He had hundreds of cookbooks, even exceeding his education collection.[84] While critics saw a ruthless, driven unionist, others saw a more playful side in Shanker's enthusiasm for finding a good meal, whatever the time and distance involved. Educator Milt Goldberg recalls attending with Shanker a national convention of lieutenant governors at Lake Tahoe. After the two men had given their speeches, Goldberg was preparing to attend the next session, when Shanker asked: "Did you ever play hooky?" He, Goldberg, and their wives set off in a car to find a two-star Mobile restaurant.[85]

Sandy Feldman remembers she and her husband being invited to go with Al and Eadie Shanker to a restaurant that Shanker had discovered "just outside the city." Feldman says: "We drove for three hours. I'm not exaggerating. But we had a terrific meal, great wine, good conversation, all in lovely surroundings, and inexpensive too."[86] Tom Hobart recalls,

"He would mislead you in going to a restaurant to eat. He would say it was fifteen minutes away and it would be an hour and a half."[87]

Shanker also had a great enthusiasm for stereo equipment and was constantly upgrading his system for what others saw as a marginal and barely perceptible level of improvement. But what really impressed friends and colleagues was his desire to share his enthusiasm. "Some people have hobbies, it's strictly for their own pleasure," says Rosenberg. "Al shared his enthusiasms . . . and he wanted you to be enthusiastic and he wanted to share the products of it." He did not just want the best stereo for himself; he wanted you to have one too.[88] Says Marcia Reecer: "I'm sure he installed stereo systems for half the people who worked at AFT."[89]

Finally, there was a vulnerability and shyness to Shanker that belied the tough-guy image. "His social skills were far less developed than his intellectual skills," says his wife Eadie. "Al wasn't one for small talk. . . . He was a shy person."[90] People used to hate riding with him in elevators or in the car because he had no use for chit chat and was comfortable with silence. Bella Rosenberg recalls that when Shanker had to attend a reception, she would have to "drag him kicking and screaming" and then keep him company the whole time. "I was negotiating social space for Al, filling in the empty" spaces.[91]

Shanker's colleagues at the AFT were incredibly loyal to him. Myron Lieberman, a Shanker critic, wrote that in forty years watching the AFT and NEA, he had "never met an NEA officer who commanded the respect and loyalty among staff as Shanker did in the AFT."[92] Don Cameron of the NEA was struck that at the AFT Shanker "was revered. He was almost sanctified."[93] Part of this had to do with the external Al Shanker, who was visionary and articulate, and part had to do with the personal side that was softer, more vulnerable, and more endearing than his gruff public persona.

To what end did Shanker accumulate power? He clearly wanted to champion the interests of his own members, but even in the early years at the AFT, he went beyond that to talk about education reform. He created an Education Issues Department headed by Eugenia Kemble, which helped local unions and state federations take positions on important education-policy questions. In the 1970s, the AFT received a grant from the Ford Foundation, ironically, to begin a quarterly magazine on education reform called *American Educator*.[94] And he greatly expanded a biennial conference on education reform, the Quality Education Standards in Teaching (QuEST) meeting. Begun under David Selden, the QuEST conference originally attracted about 150 teachers, but over time, under Shanker, QuEST grew to the point that it drew thousands—more educators than the AFT convention.[95]

Critics of Shanker's power must also ask: If teachers have too much power in education, who should have more? Parents? Principals and administrators? Corporations? Parents are often narrowly focused on their own child's interests rather than the interests of other children, and in places like Ocean Hill–Brownsville and Canarsie, parents may be most interested in excluding others—white teachers in the first case, black students in the second. Principals, administrators, and school boards may be charged with representing the broader interests of students, but conflicts often pop up. A well-disciplined environment may be good for kids, but a principal may not want to put up with the headaches associated with expelling a disruptive student. A particular education reform may be promising, but if it was initiated by a previous superintendent or school board, the new regime may abandon it, hoping to garner public support, and approval with their own "pathbreaking" reform. Corporate interests, meanwhile, owe ultimate allegiance to stockholders, and may be more concerned about short-run profits than the long-term educational success of students.

There is little doubt that Albert Shanker was good at accumulating power for the union and wanted even more of it. But liberal critics like Woody Allen and Bill Moyers were wrong to disparage Shanker for this. Shanker's power was more democratically obtained and more democratically exercised than is most power in American society. And while more power for teachers was not always good for kids, it usually was. The New Left's anti-authority ideal, where no one held power and no one could abuse it, was a worthless and naïve fantasy. Enhancing teacher power was a noble cause—one consistent with Franklin Roosevelt's belief that enhancing the power of workers was good for society, and one consistent with the view that those adults closest to the classroom were likely to be the most reliable advocates for kids. Shanker was not setting off nuclear warheads, he was raising the dignity of teachers, pushing for more spending on education for children, and seeking to make preschool education available to all. That he was condemned by liberals for this in the mid-1970s says more about liberalism in that era than it does about Albert Shanker.

10

Losing Power

THE NEW YORK FISCAL CRISIS

AND THE DECLINE OF LABOR

1974–1976

I F Al Shanker was one of a declining breed of liberals who was quite comfortable exercising power, there was a terrible irony, because the next period of his life in the mid-1970s was marked by losses and threats to his power, along with other setbacks. In New York City, Shanker and the UFT would take an awful hit as the city's finances deteriorated, a teachers' strike failed, and thousands of UFT members were laid off. In New York State, NYSUT would face an assault from the NEA, which sought to splinter the newly merged organization. At home, Shanker would face new difficulties as his absence began to take a toll on his family. And in Washington, Shanker's brand of New Deal Cold Warrior Liberalism would decline, as attempts by him and many others to reclaim the Democratic Party from McGovernism failed, and a new force within the Democratic Party, indifferent to organized labor, beat back Shanker's favored candidate.

The New York Fiscal Crisis

Shanker's biggest and most dramatic setback came in New York City. Shanker had risen to power at the AFT in no small measure based on his fabulously successful first decade as president of the UFT. Between 1962 and 1973, starting salaries increased 81 percent, from $5,300 to $9,700, while maximum salaries increased 93 percent, from $9,970 to $19,250. "By 1973," writes UFT historian Jack Schierenbeck, "New York City's public school teachers were the highest paid in the country."[1] The length of time it took to make the maximum was reduced from fifteen years to seven and a half, and benefits exploded. Noting the provision for orthodontia, Shanker said: "You can tell New York City teachers by their good teeth."[2]

Shanker's original plan, he says, was to negotiate the 1975 contract, arrange for friendly and secure leadership at the UFT, and become the president of the AFT full time.[3] But things did not work out so smoothly, for Shanker did not foresee that in 1975, one of the world's greatest cities would teeter on the edge of bankruptcy and Shanker's members would suffer layoffs in amounts not seen since the Great Depression.

The election of Abe Beame as mayor of New York City in 1973 and of Hugh Carey as governor in 1974 was meant to usher in good times for Shanker and the UFT. (The UFT helped elect both candidates.) But the combination of recession and declining student enrollment soon led Shanker's friends Beame and Carey to call for emergency cuts, including substantial layoffs of teachers.

In June 1975, to address a growing fiscal crisis in New York City, the state created the Municipal Assistance Corporation, known as Big Mac. The group was chaired by investment banker Felix Rohatyn, and of the nine original MAC members, eight had banking or brokerage connections (Donna Shalala being the only exception).[4] The New York Times editorial board warned that in order to avoid bankruptcy, municipal labor costs had to be brought under control. Bankruptcy might mean "an indefinite period of payless paydays for city workers, and the abrogation of all union contracts." It singled out the UFT as a problem: "If the all-or-nothing, city be damned attitude of such leaders as Albert Shanker of the teachers union prevails, a staggering number of municipal workers will end up with nothing."[5]

In mid-August 1975, Mayor Beame signed legislation giving him the authority to impose a wage freeze on municipal workers, irrespective of union contract provisions. In a "Where We Stand" column on August 17, Shanker called the law "the worse piece of anti-labor legislation which has ever been adopted in the United States"—worse than Taft-Hartley, because "it totally destroys the process of collective bargaining by asserting that one of the signatories to the contract has the right to break it."[6] The times were extreme. By early September 1975, some seven thousand school employees were laid off.[7] The cuts were devastating for those laid off, but even those teachers lucky enough to have jobs would face huge classes of students.

With the level of frustration rising among teachers, on September 4, Shanker led a dramatic march of twenty thousand from the Board of Education headquarters, at 110 Livingston Street in Brooklyn, across the Brooklyn Bridge to City Hall. As the demonstration began in Brooklyn around 4:00 p.m., Shanker asked: "Are you ready to go out [on strike] if you have to?" The crowd shouted its approval. The march caused massive traffic jams.[8]

Privately, Shanker had grave doubts about whether a teachers' strike, a tactic that had worked so successfully in the past, would do any good when the employer was nearly bankrupt. Yes, it would be nice to hire back all the laid-off teachers to get class sizes back to where they were, but it would cost $220 million to do so, something the city could not afford. But on this issue Shanker, who had been in firm command during the strikes of 1967 and 1968, lost control of his union.[9]

As teachers returned for the first day of school on September 8, they were met by confusion and disorder in classes that had ballooned in size. At a Delegate Assembly meeting, teachers lined up to complain about chaotic schools. One teacher said he had sixty students in his classroom.[10] Shanker thought he could convince the assembly not to strike, but emotions were so strong among teachers that Shanker was unsuccessful.[11] That evening, when the vote went to the membership, those favoring a strike overwhelmed opponents: 22,870 to 900.[12]

On September 9, teachers went out on strike. The problem, Shanker said later, was that the city had no real incentive to end the strike. Caught in a fiscal crunch, the strike was actually saving the city considerable amounts of money in unpaid teacher salaries. And since the city had to convince the bankers that they were being fiscally prudent, they needed to show how tough they would be on the unions. Shanker recalled that usually when you go on strike, "the governor calls, the mayor calls, the mediator calls. Everybody wants to settle it. This was exactly the opposite. . . . Nobody would talk to us. . . . We could have stayed out for two years. They were not interested in opening the schools."[13]

The next day, on September 10, as part of the state's financial bailout of the city, the state legislature created an Emergency Financial Control Board, made up of the governor, the mayor, the city and state comptrollers, and three private citizens appointed by the governor, with the authority to review all contracts.[14] The creation of the emergency board, made necessary by the failure of MAC to market the city's bonds, say journalists Jack Newfield and Paul DuBrul, involved "a revolution in the governance of New York City," where bankers effectively took over the running of the city.[15] There was still some democratic accountability, but the relationship between democracy and capitalism had shifted.[16]

In this new environment, Shanker pushed for a quick settlement, and on September 16, he came to an agreement with the school board for a plan that sought to maintain classroom maximum size through various concessions. Teachers would waive their two forty-five-minute preparation periods but would gain them back by shortening the student day by forty-five-minutes twice a week. Teachers would lose $30 million in wages under the Taylor Law provision that subjected teachers to lose two days of pay for every one day of strike, but that money would be used to hire back some 2,400 of the 4,500 teachers laid off. And teachers would probably receive a small salary increase.[17] Shanker told teachers: "We've gotten the most we can possibly get, given the financial situation of the city. . . . A strike is a weapon you use against a boss that has money. This boss has no money."[18]

The response of the UFT was grudging acceptance. Whereas in the past, bargaining agreements had been ratified by healthy margins, this time the executive board voted forty-nine to thirteen for approval, the delegate assembly voted 662 to 359, and the general membership voted 10,651 to 6,695 to call off the strike. The New York Times noted that Shanker, who was usually treated like "something of an idol" by members, often enjoying standing ovations, instead received a mixed reception from members, the applause leavened with boos, hisses, and calls of "sell out."[19]

But if teachers thought the contract was too stingy, the newly created Financial Control Board thought it too generous. On October 7, the control board rejected the UFT contract on the recommendation of the UFT's erstwhile ally, Governor Hugh Carey, who said the agreement's cost "gravely violates" fiscal constraints placed on the city. Shanker reacted angrily: "The action strikes at the very heart of collective bargaining. A more antilabor act will be hard to find."[20] The New York Times editorial page lauded the decision of the Financial Control Board, saying it should put other unions on notice as well not to violate fiscal constraints.[21]

Shanker appeared to have little leverage—he was not going to take the teachers out on strike again—until a state court of appeals handed him some. As part of New York State's bailout of New York City, the state legislature had passed a bill requiring that city unions invest their pension funds in the city's MAC bonds. The New York City Teachers Retirement Fund was mandated to purchase $150 million in bonds. But then a state court of appeals declared the mandatory purchases illegal, and on October 12, Shanker raised some reservations about voluntarily purchasing the bonds.[22]

On Thursday, October 16, events came to a head. In order to trigger the state's investment of money to meet the city's obligations for the next day, the city needed to raise its agreed-to $1.5 billion in nonstate resources. The teacher's $150 million in pension funds was part of that required threshold. The city needed Shanker to give his approval to the Teachers Pension Board to invest the $150 million in teacher pension funds, or the whole deal would fall apart and the city would default. Thursday evening, Governor Carey and others went off to the annual Alfred E. Smith dinner, a white-tie affair at the Waldorf-Astoria, believing the situation was under control.[23]

Shanker, who at that point held all the cards, issued a press release indicating that teachers had invested enough in the MAC bonds, and other sources would have to be found to buy the bonds. Privately, Shanker demanded that the new teachers' contract be honored and there be no further layoffs. Governor Carey, still in white tie, met with aides and rejected the deal, because it would set a precedent that would make eventual default inevitable. Carey then summoned Richard Ravitch, the chairman of the Urban Development Corporation and a longtime friend of Shanker's, gave him a police escort, and told him, "go find Al Shanker and get him to change his mind." Ravitch found Shanker in his apartment around midnight. They met for two hours. Ravitch says Shanker was privately worried about his fiduciary responsibility, and the discussions were inconclusive.[24]

President Gerald Ford was notified of the situation when he woke up at 5:30 a.m. A Bank of America vice president told *Newsweek*: "For that brief period, Albert Shanker was the most powerful man in the United States."[25] The pressure on Shanker and the teacher trustees was enormous. MAC Board chairman Felix Rohatyn said that "the future of the city is in their hands," a message conveyed by television and radio.[26] That morning, Shanker met with Mayor Beame at Gracie Mansion, but Beame took a hard line, refusing to make any contract concessions, and Shanker said he would stay firm.[27]

By 10:30 a.m., the situation had still not been resolved, and note holders who came to the Municipal Building to cash their bonds were told to come back in the afternoon.[28] State Supreme Court Justice Irving Saypol signed a writ prepared by city attorneys to outline priorities in the event of a default, placing city payrolls above repayment of city debts.[29]

Shanker wanted a private meeting with Governor Carey, so they agreed to meet at Ravitch's apartment.[30] Governor Carey, Ravitch, and the MAC counsel, Simon Rifkind, met with Shanker at Ravitch's Manhattan apartment to convince him to okay the purchase. Shanker brought along Harry Van Arsdale and former Mayor Robert F. Wagner. Rifkind argued that if the city defaulted and was put in the hands of a federal bankruptcy court, laws governing pensions—and even the state constitution—might be suspended. Shanker was for a long time unconvinced that the city was unable to find funds elsewhere. The meeting lasted for three hours. Carey told Shanker, in essence, that "the city is in your hands for better or for worse," and asked Shanker if "he wanted to go into the history books as the man who triggered default of New York City." Shanker eventually relented, went back to the governor's office, and told the trustees to vote yes.[31]

At 2:07 p.m., Shanker announced at the governor's office the decision to purchase the bonds. At the press conference, both Shanker and Carey denied that any deal had been struck on the teachers' contract in exchange for the bond purchase.[32] Shanker told Newsweek: "Woody Allen said if I had a nuclear weapon in my hand I would use it. Here I had it and I didn't use it."[33] He complained to the New York Post that "it was blackmail," because the teachers would be blamed for the default if they did not come through.[34] Newfield and DuBrul say Shanker was "bullied" into buying the bonds.[35]

By the time the agreement was settled, the banks were due to close.[36] The state superintendent of banks issued an order to keep Manufacturers Hanover Trust Company open past its 3 p.m. closing time, and the Federal Reserve Bank of New York also extended its hours.[37] The banner headline in the Times the next morning read "City Avoids Default by Hours as Teachers Relent, Buy Bonds; Financial Markets Disrupted."[38] In his "Where We Stand" column that Sunday—an especially long one— Shanker explained his decision. Teachers, he said, had already more invested in MAC bonds than any of the city's other retirement systems, and the announcement that the city would default if the teachers did not invest more, he said, "amounted to little more than extortion." He went along, however, because default would have meant "economic, social and political catastrophe."[39]

Shanker's decision was not popular with some union members, who thought Shanker was bailing out the boss and putting worker pensions at risk.[40] Shanker's response was simple: "If the city goes down, you don't have a system."[41] In the end, it turned out the bonds were a good investment.[42]

In the short term, however, there was considerably more pain in store for teachers, for Shanker's investment of teacher pension funds postponed immediate default but did not address the underlying fiscal realities. The federal government was generally unsympathetic to New York's plight, and on October 29, President Ford said he would veto a proposed bailout.[43] The next day, the *New York Daily News* printed its famous headline: "Ford to City: Drop Dead."[44] Shanker reacted angrily. Ford, he said, "sought to rally the people of the United States against the people of New York."[45]

In all, during the fiscal crisis 15,000 New York City teachers and paraprofessionals were laid off.[46] The effect was devastating to New York City's schools and to Shanker's union, locally and nationally. Class sizes skyrocketed. The UFT lost 20 percent of its membership, and the AFT lost 10 percent—losses that would take time to restore.[47] Teachers who remained received an almost 19 percent pay cut compared with 3 to 8 percent for other city services.[48] The UFT did not receive favorable treatment in its contract following Shanker's decision to bail out the city with teacher pension funds. Indeed, the 1975 contract was not fully approved by the Emergency Control Board until seventeen months later, in February 1977.[49]

Shanker tried to fight back in the state legislature, pushing a bill that required that schools be given the same percentage of overall spending in New York as in the past—that is, that they not bear a disproportionate share of the cuts.[50] Shanker used all his political muscle to get the legislation passed, and when Governor Carey vetoed the bill, Shanker got the legislature to override a veto for the first time in 104 years.[51] But the law was later struck down as a violation of New York City's home-rule authority.[52]

The glory days for New York City teachers were clearly over. The fiscal crisis gave rise to a new group of politicians, epitomized by New York

City's mayoral candidate Ed Koch, who ran against the power of the public-employee unions, including the UFT, arguing that teachers were overpaid.[53]

The biggest lesson of the fiscal crisis for Shanker was that friends in politics were not enough; the teachers also needed to build alliances with the business community. Shanker recalled that all the other public-employee groups had ties with business—the police, fire, and hospital workers had relationships with businesses on issues of public safety, tourism, and health. The business community leaders saw the public school system in New York as a place "for other people's children," and the school system, likewise, was wary of business involvement for fear they would "teach business ideology" in the classroom.[54] The UFT had helped elect a friendly mayor in Abe Beame. But with the city in receivership, "the mayor wasn't running the city anymore." The bankers, the business community, and the control board were. "You might as well lock the mayor up in some jail or send him to some foreign country," Shanker said.[55]

For Shanker, who had been flying so high just a year before, with teacher salaries at their peak and his power and influence growing, the episode was sobering. In the new world, even in labor's stronghold—New York City—labor was not in charge, nor were elected officials fully in control: bankers were.

NYSUT Disaffiliation

As Shanker was battling with bankers and a new crop of anti-labor politicians in New York City, he faced a second threat to his power statewide: an effort to undermine and split the NYSUT merger. Shanker's vision, that a merger in New York would spawn a wave of state mergers across the country, had been turned on its head. The national merger talks between the NEA and the AFT had gone nowhere, and the temporary arrangement under which NYSUT members would pay dues to both the NEA and AFT until a national merger was consummated made little sense. The NEA gave NYSUT an ultimatum: conform to NEA procedures on quotas and the use of the secret ballot or be expelled.[56]

As it became clear the split was coming, the NEA began preparing the groundwork to set up a rival NEA structure in New York. Shanker was concerned that the NEA could siphon off a significant chunk of NYSUT teachers. A February 1976 poll found that one-third of teachers might be willing to go with the NEA if there were a split. The NEA had one particularly powerful weapon in its arsenal: with superior resources, it could hire away NYSUT staff members with higher salaries. At one point, the entire Rochester staff defected. The blood drained from Shanker's face when he learned the news.[57] It was, says NYSUT's Toni Cortese, "the only time I think I've ever seen Al be really concerned. . . . It was a very scary time." If the local leaders followed the staff, it could start a movement away from the AFT.[58]

Shanker argued that rather than sit by while the NEA was actively trying to take members away from NYSUT, the organization should officially disaffiliate, since the NEA had made clear it would eventually expel NYSUT anyway.[59] In March 1976, at NYSUT's convention, delegates voted overwhelmingly to disaffiliate from the NEA.[60]

The day following the vote, Shanker gave what teachers remember as the most famous address in his entire career.[61] Tom Hobart recalls that Shanker usually asked him what he should talk about at NYSUT conventions, but this time he did not. And there was another difference: while he usually spoke from the back of an envelope, this time, he had something written out.[62] Speaking to delegates, Shanker argued that "the NEA cannot build a united organization in this state." The best they could do is to hurt NYSUT. "They can destroy, they can weaken," but they had "absolutely no chance of having even a majority organization in this state." Shanker then read a fairy tale by Hans Christian Andersen called "The Most Unbelievable Thing."[63] The story had been invoked by a Harvard professor shortly after radical students had forcibly taken over and occupied University Hall, and Shanker said the tale applied to the NEA in New York.

Shanker's cadence slowed.[64] He read the story, in which a king announced that he would give his daughter in marriage to the man who accomplished the most unbelievable thing. There was a tremendous competition, and on the day for judgment, everyone agreed that the most marvelous accomplishment was a handsome clock that depicted leading intellectual and spiritual leaders throughout history. The judges were about to pronounce him the winner when a thug carrying a sledgehammer arrived. With three blows he smashed the clock, and everyone had to admit that was the most unbelievable thing. Shanker said: "Our organization is a wonderful work of art. It has been put together. If destroyed, it will never be put together again. To each of us goes the responsibility of seeing that it is the clock that survives and not the sledgehammer."[65]

Shanker received an ovation that lasted for five minutes. Men in the audience had tears running down their face.[66] "Keep the clock" buttons were printed up and passed around.[67]

It was a great victory. Although the UFT was weakened by the fiscal crisis, Shanker had brilliantly defended NYSUT against attack. After NYSUT withdrew from the NEA, dissidents representing something fewer than 20,000 of NYSUT's 211,000 members walked out and claimed they would have thirty thousand members by June, fifty thousand by September 1976, and would crush NYSUT over time. In fact, thirty years later, the NEA affiliate had 35,000 members in New York State, while NYSUT grew to 525,000.[68] In 2006, the two groups were reunited in a merger.[69]

The Home Front

The tough time that Albert Shanker was having with the fiscal crisis in New York City and the distraction of having to defend NYSUT in New York State were mirrored by difficulties in the Shanker household in Putnam Valley, New York. Having failed in his first marriage with a troubled woman, Shanker was now causing difficulties, largely of his own doing, for his family. In 1975, *People* headlined a story about Shanker, saying: "The man who rules New York's Teachers wishes he could see his own children more often." In the mid-1970s, he was working an estimated ninety-eight hours a week. Shanker told *People*: "If I spend one night a week at home, that's a lot."[70] He expressed his guilt about not having more time for his family to union colleagues.[71]

Eadie Shanker knew from the beginning that her husband was very committed to the work of the union. Three years after she and Shanker were married, and Dave Selden told her Shanker needed to run for UFT president, she pleaded, "don't take my husband away from me," but she knew he was happiest in his union work and it would have been impossible to deny him that.[72]

Over time, the situation grew worse, as Shanker's additional roles at NYSUT, the AFL-CIO, the AFT, and eventually the International Federation of Free Teacher Unions (IFFTU) put more demands on his time. The commute to the distant suburb of Putnam Valley proved burdensome, and Shanker spent more time at the New York City apartment the UFT rented. When Shanker became AFT president, he would spend many nights at a hotel in Washington. In Putnam Valley, Shanker was only home about once every other weekend—roughly twenty or thirty hours a month. It was virtually unheard of for him to come home during the middle of the week. He was not around for his kids' sporting events and generally would not call or write when they went away to camp. To see their father, the children had to make appointments with his secretary, Yetta Barsh.[73]

In October 1976, when Adam was fifteen, Jennie twelve, and Michael eleven, the family moved from Putnam Valley to Mamaroneck, New York, a Westchester County suburb located much closer to New York City. The family could now afford a nice home in this community, which was more accepting of Jews and had better schools than those in Putnam Valley. The hope was that the much shorter commute would allow Shanker more time with his family.[74]

But if anything, his travel schedule accelerated. Over time he began logging between 300,000 and 500,000 miles per year, making about three hundred public appearances annually.[75] He basically "lived in the hotel in D.C. or on the road," says Mary Farran, who handled finances for Shanker.[76] When he was home, Eadie Shanker recalls, he could get up at dawn, take a flight down to Washington, and "be there before a lot of the [Washington] employees."[77] One year he missed Thanksgiving and another year he missed Jennie's college graduation.[78] Shanker himself later conceded, "I was the distant outside relative who was dropping in once and a while."[79] "He would come in and he'd be the stranger and pop in for a weekend," says Michael Shanker. "After a while," he says, "we all just gave up trying to keep track of him. Where's dad? . . . He was always on a tour."[80]

Perhaps even harder on the children was Shanker's behavior when he was home. He did not read to the kids at bedtime or go to ballgames.[81] When his father was home, "he was very preoccupied," says Adam Shanker. "He was there but he wasn't there." He was exhausted from his union work and would spend most of his time reading and listening to music at a very high volume, designed to create his own private space.[82] Jennie Shanker recalls: "A typical day where my dad was home in the Shanker family household was sitting in the living room—my dad blaring his music, it was so loud it was really hard to hold a conversation if you wanted to—and we'd all be sitting around and reading something. . . . There was a lot of silence in the family."[83] (The stereo system, which was such a source of amusement for his coworkers, was not so loved by the children.)

In addition, when Shanker was home, Michael says, "the phone would ring off the hook. . . . There was no time that he was not engaged in his job." The union was his life. "Almost all of his friends were in the union."[84] A fascinating parade of people came through the house—Max Shacht- man, Bayard Rustin, and the like—but in general the kids were not brought into the discussions.[85]

When Al Shanker did engage his children directly, it was generally done on his terms. Shanker loved to spend time in the basement darkroom de- veloping photographs, which Adam enjoyed doing with him.[86] Michael recalls: "If he was interested in something and you were interested in it, you'd have something in common, but if you weren't, you were kind of left in the dark a little bit."[87]

Given his intense work schedule, family vacations were also often taken on Al Shanker's terms. Vacations were frequently combined with work, like the AFL-CIO annual meeting in Florida.[88] Shanker sometimes took his children on business trips, but often they were on their own for large portions of the time.[89] Eadie Shanker recalls: "Wherever we went, it was never a full vacation."[90]

Shanker acknowledged that his distance from his children caused "a lot of resentment. I later had to pay a price in terms of getting to know my own kids, because of a lot of resentment and a lot of anger that built up." He said in 1985, "it's still something that we're working on."[91]

He was closest to his daughter, Jennie, who excelled at school and went on to earn an MFA at Yale. They shared an interest in art and in reading. The two would perform duets together on the recorder.[92] But he had very difficult relationships with his sons. For many years, Shanker had virtu- ally nothing to do with his son from his first marriage, Carl, in part be- cause of his first wife and in part his own doing.[93] And he did not forge a close relationship with Adam and Michael. "He was on a different plane," says Adam, who, like Michael, was dyslexic and struggled in school.[94] "I think he found it very difficult to relate to us," says Michael.[95] "If you could say anything about my dad, the thing that he liked were intelligent people. He really loved people who were smart. And I don't think he liked people who weren't." Michael says, "I think it was frustrating to him in that situation that we weren't smart like he was, or smart in the same way, and that we struggled."[96]

In fact, many of the bright young staff members at the AFT, whom Shanker chose and recruited for their intelligence, received the type of at- tention that Michael and Adam Shanker say they craved. "He always wanted to teach. He always wanted to educate. He always wanted to be a mentor," says Eric Chenoweth. He was "a father-like person to many people, and it's among the reasons why there was so much affection for him."[97] Just as Al Shanker enjoyed teaching advanced classes of students more than slower-paced ones, he often seemed more devoted to his union family than his biological one. Part of the issue, Eadie Shanker says, goes back to the distant relationship Al Shanker had with his own father. "He didn't know what it was to be a father," she says.[98]

Shanker's absence took a toll not only on his children but also on his wife. "My mom was lonely," says Jennie Shanker. "She waited a long time for his retirement, which never came."[99] With Shanker on the road constantly, there were widespread rumors that he had affairs with women, inside and outside of the union, including with Sandra Feldman, a charge she denied.[100] Whether or not the rumors were true, few doubted that Albert Shanker had a deep love for his wife, and she for him. For thirty-six years, even as he traveled constantly, the two spoke by phone virtually every day and shared many wonderful times together.[101] And despite all their complaints and anger toward their father, the children also recall bright spots.

While Shanker was traveling he would bring back stamps and buttons for collections. For Michael, he brought matches from all over the world.[102] He insisted that his contract with the union include a provision that his wife and children could travel with him when possible, and they sometimes did at his urging.[103] And all of Shanker's children were influenced by his interests: Adam as a photographer with his own video business, Jennie as an artist and teacher, Michael as a chef, and Carl as a computer expert.[104]

Even if the children wanted more time with their father, they understood that he was doing good work for the union. The downside, says Adam, was "I was just kind of a spectator that got in the way a little bit of his mission."[105]

Labor and the Democrats

Shanker's final setback during the mid-1970s had to do with one of his public missions: to push labor's agenda on economic and education policy, on civil rights, and on international affairs within the Democratic Party. Following McGovern's debacle in 1972, labor had reason to be confident that it could take back the Democratic Party from the New Politics movement. Not only had Nixon received 61 percent of the popular vote, in 1972, he won a majority of the white union vote, which was unprecedented for a Republican.[106] Between 1960 and 1964, white working-class voters gave Democrats 55 percent of the vote. In 1968 and 1972, that dropped to 35 percent. Says political analyst Ruy Teixeira, "the Republicans suddenly became the party of the white working class."[107] Shanker and others in labor had every reason to believe that the New Politics' electoral repudiation would strengthen labor's role in the Democratic Party. But they were wrong.

Immediately following McGovern's defeat, Shanker received a letter from Midge Decter, the writer who had penned a favorable profile of Shanker in *New York Magazine* and was now plotting the revival of the Democratic Party. In the letter, she explained that the previous spring, after a League for Industrial Democracy luncheon, she and Ben Wattenberg, Scoop Jackson's chief strategist, had talked about creating a new ADA, a strong liberal anti-Communist group called the Coalition for a Democratic Majority (CDM). (The original ADA had reduced its commitment to fighting the cold war and endorsed McGovern.) She asked for Shanker's involvement and support.[108] The group's agenda included a restoration of the traditions of FDR, Truman, and Kennedy, on the themes of nondiscrimination, a fairer distribution of wealth, equal opportunity for the disadvantaged, a strong American role in the world, and a rejection of the New Politics.[109] Shanker's friend Penn Kemble was named executive director. Shanker readily agreed to become involved and he hosted an early meeting of CDM, in February 1973, with Decter and several members of the Social Democrats, including Sandra Feldman, Carl Gershman, Judy Bardacke, Rachelle Horowitz, and Bayard Rustin.[110]

Part of the vision that animated CDM was the Shachtmanite notion that labor must be the center of the Democratic Party's coalition, rather than the various constituencies—minorities, youth, and feminists—that were central to the New Politics movement. Unions represented minorities and women as part of a broader coalition based on common concerns about class inequality and could unite Democrats rather than Balkanize them. And one of CDM's first challenges was to persuade the Democratic National Committee (DNC) to revise the McGovern delegate rules that favored New Politics backers.

In September 1973, in a statement to the DNC's Commission on Delegate Selection and Party Structure, Shanker said the rules set up by the

McGovern Commission had essentially helped New Politics voters and allowed "an elitist upper middle class movement" to take "over the party" that working-class and poor voters "had always thought of as their own." Shanker called on the Commission to eliminate quotas. Most of the youth, minority, and female delegates were affluent, he said. "Their interests, organizational affiliations, and political orientation were not the same as those of the majority of blacks, youth, and women who live in different socioeconomic circumstances. In fact, the only group in the Democratic Party which benefited from the quotas was the New Politics movement."[111] Others noted that at the 1972 convention the Iowa delegation had only one farmer and the New York delegation had only three representatives of organized labor. Some 39 percent of delegates had postgraduate degrees compared with 4 percent nationally.[112]

Shanker concluded by pleading that the Watergate scandal then consuming the Republican party not keep the Democrats "from realizing that their party too is in crisis." Will the Democrats regain the mantle of the party of the people or become "the exclusive preserve of a self righteous upper middle class elite," Shanker asked. He said: "What is really at stake then is the future of poor and working people in the United States. The Republican party, the party of big business, offers them no hope. The Democratic party can—but only if it starts taking steps now to ensure them positions of power in the party."[113]

The battle over quotas came to a head at the Democrats' midterm convention in Kansas City in December 1974, where Shanker was a delegate. Black, female, and liberal delegates, led by Bella Abzug, Charles Rangel, and Basil Patterson, called for stronger language ensuring racial and gender representation at future conventions. The NEA also supported the convention quotas.[114] The support for quotas grew out of a long history of discrimination against minorities in delegate selection: as recently as 1964, the Mississippi Freedom Democratic Party had been rebuffed in its attempt to better integrate the state's delegates.

Shanker rose to address delegates on the CDM position. CDM's Penn Kemble and Josh Muravchik wrote a draft address, but Shanker instead gave an impromptu speech that Kemble said was much better.[115] In his speech, and in a subsequent column, Shanker argued that "the central question" of quotas was tearing the Democratic Party apart. Quotas, Shanker argued, "impelled millions of white working-class 'ethnics,' as well as middle-class whites, to move over to the Republican line" in 1972. And as a practical matter, quotas among delegates were disenfranchising labor.[116] Shanker's speech was greeted with hoots of disagreement from some at the convention.[117]

Shanker backed a compromise calling for affirmative action but no quotas. Then, at the last minute, he said, after rumors of a threatened walkout by minority, women, and youth caucuses, party chairman Robert Strauss caved in and the Kansas City convention ended up ratifying the McGovern rules.[118] The whole experience was dispiriting for Shanker. "What happened at Kansas City foreshadows insurmountable problems for the Democratic Party," Shanker predicted.[119] He later joked: "What the Republicans need is a reform group. Look what it did for the Democrats."[120]

If the issue of racial quotas in delegate selection struck many Americans as somewhat obscure (how many people wanted to be delegates to a party convention?), the question hit the public more forcefully when the U.S. Supreme Court took up a concrete case of racial preference in higher education, the 1974 case of *DeFunis v. Odegaard*.

The litigation involved a white student, Marco DeFunis, who worked his way through college and did well academically but was rejected by the University of Washington Law School, while many minority students with lower scores were admitted. The Law School had a completely separate admissions procedure for whites and minority students, and thirty-six of the thirty-seven minority students admitted had scores lower than DeFunis's.[121]

Shanker wrote a column in support of DeFunis, and quoted a lower court judge who argued: "To admit some, solely because of race or ethnic origin, is to deny others that privilege solely for the same reason."[122] Shanker was also concerned about the class-blind nature of quotas. "The particular woman or black who gets the job may have come from an affluent, advantaged background and may have pushed out an economically poor, disadvantaged white male."[123]

The *DeFunis* case split the liberal coalition straight down the middle. Labor had long been wary of racial preferences, something that had earlier united the feuding chieftains George Meany and Walter Reuther. Meany called preferences by race "discrimination in reverse."[124] And Reuther had coined the phrase "reverse discrimination."[125]

In the *DeFunis* case, the AFL-CIO joined the American Jewish Congress and the Anti-Defamation League of B'nai B'rith in opposing preferences, while civil-rights groups, including the NAACP Legal Defense and Education Fund, the Lawyers' Committee for Civil Rights Under Law, and

the Mexican American Legal Defense and Education Fund, supported the
University of Washington's program. They were joined by the higher-
education establishment: Harvard University, the Association of American Law Schools, and the Law School Admissions Council.[126] Bayard Rustin, in a guest "Where We Stand" column, decried the way racial preferences
were dividing the liberal coalition.[127]

When the *DeFunis* decision came down in April 1974, Justice William
O. Douglas, the great liberal lion, made an impassioned argument for a
compromise. Rather than providing a preference on race, taking on all
the dangers inherent in that step, why not give a leg up to economically
disadvantaged students of all races?

> A black applicant who pulled himself out of the ghetto into a junior
> college may thereby demonstrate a level of motivation, perseverance,
> and ability that would lead a fair-minded admissions committee to
> conclude that he shows more promise for law study than the son of a
> rich alumnus who achieved better grades at Harvard. That applicant
> would be offered admission not because he is black but because as an
> individual he has shown he has the potential, while the Harvard man
> may have taken less advantage of the vastly superior opportunities of-
> fered him.[128]

For labor, a class-based program open to all races could unite the coalition of civil rights and labor, just as Martin Luther King Jr. had suggested
with his Bill of Rights for the Disadvantaged and Shanker had advocated
in the form of a career ladder for paraprofessionals in New York City. But
Douglas's and Shanker's voices turned out to be lonely ones. A majority
of the U.S. Supreme Court ruled that the *DeFunis* case was moot (Marco
DeFunis was about to finish law school). The question of whether racial
preferences were constitutional would be deferred to another day.

In the mid-1970s, the old New Deal Democratic coalition was also torn
by the contentious issue of busing for school desegregation, and Shanker
sought a middle position that was fully satisfactory neither to those on
the left nor the right. On the one hand, Shanker believed strongly in the
integrated "common school," which brought together children from all
different backgrounds and taught them tolerance and the meaning of
American citizenship. This vision of schooling was central to his opposition to community control and his opposition to private-school voucher
schemes, which he feared would Balkanize people. In the early 1970s,

Shanker had opposed Nixon's anti-busing crusade and the efforts by Canarsie residents to block black students from Brownsville.[129]

But in the mid-1970s, as the nation focused its attention on an experiment with busing in Boston, Shanker began to raise some concerns.
Shanker condemned violent white resistance to busing, which revealed
northern racism in sharp relief. But as with the issue of affirmative action,
Shanker said the exclusive focus on race ignored the larger issue of class.
As an educational matter, the Coleman Report had found that poor blacks
did better when they attended school with middle-class whites. It was socioeconomic integration, not racial integration, that improved the scores
of low-income students. In Boston, however, Judge W. Arthur Garrity had
implemented a citywide plan that mixed poor and working-class whites
and poor and working-class blacks. Shanker told a reporter: "When I look
at Boston, and think of black kids being bused out to South Boston High
School, which is a school that sent almost nobody to college and had no
academic record, I can't get particularly enthusiastic about the notion
that something educationally worthwhile was accomplished."[130]

There was also an issue of fairness in Boston. Those liberal whites advocating desegregation—the federal judge, the editors of the *Boston Globe*,
the professors at Harvard—tended to live in the suburbs, and their own
children were not attending desegregated schools.[131] It was working-class
whites, who had very little control over their lives as it was, whose children were being sent to schools that were considered dangerous. In Boston, one AFT staffer said that Shanker saw the elites, "in service of their
so-called ideals," using working-class people, who were "hanging on by
their fingernails."[132]

Shanker also had a pragmatic concern: because busing was generally
limited to city boundaries, it was spawning white flight to the suburbs,
among those who could afford it, leaving poor whites and poor blacks in
the city. This was bad for cities and bad for education, but it was especially bad for the AFT, which tended to serve urban areas. Shanker understood human nature: people were looking for what was best for their kids,
and part of that was to be surrounded by middle-class peers who were on
average higher achieving and less likely to cause discipline problems.[133]

Finally, there was a very real political concern. In a 1975 interview,
Shanker said he favored busing "in principle" but noted that "a majority
of blacks and whites are against it," which presented a problem. A pragmatist, Shanker said that to be unrealistic about busing was "to play into
the hands of George Wallace."[134] Shanker's nuanced position, which

sought to balance the imperative for integration with the flaws of compulsory busing, did not sit well with everyone at the AFT. At the July 1975
convention in Honolulu, members of the Black Caucus pushed for a resolution that called for the AFT to "endorse and support the desegregation
of Boston schools by means of busing." In what was described as some of
the convention's "tensest moments," delegates fiercely debated both the
Black Caucus resolution and an alternative that condemned the violence
in Boston but did not use the word "busing." In a sign of the issue's importance, Shanker gave up the gavel to come down to the floor and participate in the debate. Shanker argued against the Black Caucus's resolution, saying the AFT "is not united on the question of busing" and arguing
that "we do not have a mandate from our membership to say that we have
researched what is the best way to desegregate schools." In the end, the
Shanker-backed resolution prevailed over the resolution from the Black
Caucus.[135]

Within the AFT staff, there was also intense debate about busing.
Shanker wanted to raise his profile on the issue, but in a meeting at
Shanker's house, Sandra Feldman argued that he should just keep quiet
about the issue apart from his speeches at conventions. "He wanted to do
some major national thing and I was opposed," she said, not on the substance but because it would hurt relations with the black community. Bayard Rustin, Rachelle Horowitz, and Velma Hill agreed with Feldman.
They prevailed, and Shanker kept quiet, something he never let Feldman
forget in later years.[136]

Shanker's relatively low profile on the busing question might have
helped the AFT with the coalition with civil-rights groups, but it also kept
Shanker from articulating a powerful alternative that went back to his
early days in New York City: the MES program of enriched school offer-
ings to entice middle-class white families into tough schools. That approach, which seeks to meet the realities of human nature (white families
will integrate if there is something special offered at the end of the bus
ride), never became a consistent theme for Shanker, which was a serious
hole in his education and civil-rights agenda.

Carter Versus Jackson

The issue of quotas and busing became part of the larger struggle between the New Politics and labor factions for control of the Democratic

Party as it moved into the 1976 election. Following the McGovern debacle, many in the labor movement had high hopes that an anti–New Politics candidate would win the 1976 Democratic presidential nomination. They had reason to be confident that their candidate, Washington Senator Henry "Scoop" Jackson, would prevail.

Shortly after he declared his candidacy, Jackson appeared on the cover of *Time* as the frontrunner.[137] Shanker had long been a fan of Jackson, who embodied for Shanker the best of cold war liberalism. Jackson was a foreign policy hawk, who introduced Soviet dissident Aleksandr Solzhenitsyn to Senate colleagues while President Gerald Ford refused to invite him to the White House.[138] He was sponsor of the Jackson-Vanik Amendment to put pressure on the Soviets to allow Jewish emigration, and in 1974, Jackson received the UFT's annual John Dewey Award for his work on behalf of Soviet Jews.[139] He also stood for human rights at home and had confronted Joseph McCarthy over his tactics in the U.S. Senate.[140]

Unlike Southern Democrats, who were pro-defense but anti-labor, Jackson was also staunchly pro-labor and had a strong affirmative economic agenda. He was for repealing Taft-Hartley, for boosting federal aid to education, and for increasing Social Security benefits.[141] And Jackson was where Shanker was on civil-rights issues as well. He had been a strong proponent of virtually all civil-rights legislation in the 1950s and 1960s, but he opposed racial preferences and mandatory busing and was tough on crime.[142]

Early on in the race, Jackson made a strategic decision to skip the January Iowa caucuses and February New Hampshire primary and to focus on bigger states like Massachusetts in March and New York and Pennsylvania in April. In the vacuum, a little-known former governor of Georgia, Jimmy Carter, racked up early victories in Iowa and New Hampshire, with an appeal based on his honesty and his status as an outsider unspoiled by Washington. Scoop Jackson won Massachusetts, in part because of his opposition to busing. (He was not, however, strongly opposed enough to satisfy the diehard anti-busing crowd, which voted for George Wallace.) But Carter bounced back and won primaries in Florida, Illinois, and North Carolina.[143]

Next came the showdown in the New York Democratic primary, slated for April 6, pitting Jackson, Carter, and a third candidate, Arizona Congressman Mo Udall. On March 24, Shanker met with Jackson for more than an hour at UFT headquarters. When the men emerged, Shanker per-

sonally endorsed Jackson, though he said the UFT had not taken an official position. He also noted that "people [from the union] have a very
large role in the campaign."[144]

The evening of Shanker's endorsement, Jackson spoke at a Social Democrats USA dinner and blasted Carter's anti-Washington campaign. "Call
it what you will, it represents an attack on the idea that government can
do things to help people," he said. "The attacks on big government re-
mind me of the attacks on big labor. I would like to see a federal government that does as much to advance the welfare of its people as some of
the unions do in advancing the welfare of their people."[145] Jackson was,
then, to the left of Carter on economic policy, the role of government, and
unions, and to the right of the rest of the Democratic field on foreign
policy and defense—precisely where Shanker was.

Two days before the primary, Shanker wrote a column endorsing
Jackson over Carter, focusing on Jackson's more liberal domestic program. Jackson was for aid to New York during the fiscal crisis, for the
Humphrey-Hawkins bill for full employment, had a detailed national
health insurance plan, and wanted to boost the federal share of education
financing from 7 percent to 33 percent. Carter, by contrast, was waging a
campaign against Washington, was opposed to federal aid that singled
out New York City, was opposed to Humphrey-Hawkins, and had no specific plan for national health insurance.[146] On primary election day, Jackson won with 38 percent of the vote, compared to Mo Udall's 25 percent
and Carter's 13 percent, but the margin was lower than expected and actually dealt Jackson a setback.[147]

Scoop Jackson's combination of tough foreign policy, populist economic policy, and color-blind social policy was potent politically: Gerald
Ford considered him the most formidable possible opponent, as had
Nixon four years earlier.[148] But Jackson proved a poor candidate on the
stump. And Jackson's cold war stances were considered outside the mainstream of Democratic primary voters. He had almost been Kennedy's
choice as vice presidential running mate in 1960, but sixteen years later,
his brand of tough liberalism was considered out of fashion.[149]

In a series of primaries, Carter defeated Jackson. For Shanker, Carter's
victory over Jackson was deeply troubling. Carter was no George McGovern—indeed, he had supported the Vietnam War.[150] But he was no Harry
Truman either, and no Scoop Jackson. He was neither a cold war liberal
nor a New Politics liberal. He was an unknown. But it was clear that with
Scoop Jackson's defeat, the era of tough liberalism—running from FDR

to Lyndon Johnson—was over. From now on, Shanker's vision of a strong government role at home and abroad would have to swim upstream.

All in all, the mid-1970s were not a particularly good time for Shanker. Just as he was elected president of the AFT, the situation in New York City imploded. Shanker led his first unsuccessful strike and saw bankers replace organized labor as the city's key power brokers. His dream of a merger with the NEA was gone, and small portions of the NEA in New York defected from NYSUT. Constantly on the road, his relationship with his family suffered. And he and his colleagues at the Coalition for a Democratic Majority proved unable to redirect the Democratic Party away from the disastrous New Politics approach on issues including quotas and busing. Shanker's dream candidate, Scoop Jackson, stumbled as the front-runner for the Democratic presidential nomination as liberalism took yet another turn in the person of James Earl Carter.

II

WASHINGTON

11

Jimmy Carter and the Rise of the Reagan Democrats

1976–1980

I F Jimmy Carter was something of an enigma to Shanker, he was bound to be better than Gerald Ford, who had presided clumsily over an economic recession and been of little help to New York City in its time of need. In August 1976, the AFT convention, meeting in Bal Harbour, Florida, overwhelmingly endorsed Carter over Ford. The NEA followed suit at its convention, for the first time endorsing a presidential candidate. The AFT delegates were particularly enthusiastic about Carter's choice of Minnesota Senator Walter Mondale as vice presidential nominee. At the convention, Mondale returned the praise, calling Shanker the "ablest union leader in America today."[1]

The election of Jimmy Carter in November 1976 was a welcome change for Shanker. And it ushered in a new, deeper involvement in Washington politics and legislation for Shanker and the AFT. During Gerald Ford's presidency, Shanker's primary involvement with federal legislation was his ill-fated attempt to push public-school sponsorship of child care. Much of Shanker's time had been consumed by New York politics—the fiscal crisis in New York City and the battles with the NEA over NYSUT. During the Carter presidency, Shanker would increasingly turn his attention to national matters and legislation. He would become intimately involved in battles over labor-law reform, tuition tax credits, the creation of the U.S. Department of Education, bilingual education, affirmative action, and human rights and refugee matters.

Sometimes Shanker worked with Carter, but as often he worked against him, as he found himself to the right of Carter on race and international affairs and to the left on economics. So did many blue-collar whites, who would abandon the Democratic Party four years later and vote for a deeply conservative Republican hardly committed to their economic interests. For Shanker, American liberalism continued during the Carter era to drift from its earlier Roosevelt-Truman-Kennedy moorings.

After eight years of Nixon and Ford, organized labor was eager to move forward on a series of liberal initiatives from education spending to healthcare reform. But Shanker's fears about Carter were confirmed almost immediately. As a Southern Democrat with few ties to labor, Carter's relatively conservative economic agenda consistently disappointed Shanker.

In June 1977, Shanker excoriated the new president on his proposal to raise the minimum wage by a mere twenty cents an hour, to $2.50. Millions of Americans had supported Carter because of his promise to address poverty, Shanker said, and are "sharply disappointed" with Carter's inadequate proposal.[2] Shanker also criticized Carter's proposed education budget in 1977 for failing to cover the costs of inflation. "In real dollars, the nation's schools would get less money next year than this," he said.[3] (Over time, Carter would prove more generous on federal education spending.)[4]

Shanker also attacked Carter's proposals to fight inflation through wage and price controls as inequitable. Shanker argued that while Carter set a clear and inflexible goal of freezing wages and benefits at 7 percent, he did not set the same hard standard for prices and provided no controls over income from dividends or capital gains or on interest rates.[5] George Meany said Carter had the most conservative economic policy since Herbert Hoover.[6]

On some issues, Shanker thought Carter was on the right side, but was not passionate enough. This was the case with labor's biggest priority during the Carter term: labor-law reform.

Labor-Law Reform

For many years, unions had been waiting for a chance to rectify what they viewed as a major imbalance in labor law: that when unions violated the

National Labor Relations Act, immediate sanctions followed, but when private employers violated the law by firing union activists, they were subject only to weak penalties applied after a long, drawn-out process.

The 1935 Wagner Act had made it illegal for private-sector employers to fire workers for organizing, because the authors knew that such tactics could stop union organizing in its tracks.[7] But the sanctions applied by the National Labor Relations Board (NLRB) were extremely weak— back pay, without the chance for compensatory and punitive damages such as were available for unlawful firing under the civil-rights laws.[8] In some ways, the penalty scheme was backward, for if it was generally irrational for employers to fire productive employees because of their race or gender, employers had a strong financial incentive to fire employees involved in union organizing, thereby avoiding the prospect of having to negotiate a wage and benefit increase. As labor lawyer Thomas Geoghegan noted: "An employer who didn't break the law would have to be what economists call an irrational firm."[9] Over time, employers began exploiting the weak penalties of the law and paid subsequent awards as a cost of doing business. In 1957, there were 872 NLRB cases of firing employees for union activity; twenty-some years later, the number shot up to ten thousand.[10] By the mid-1970s, labor was winning fewer than half its representation elections, compared with 80 percent back in the 1950s, and organized labor declined from 35 percent of the workforce to 20 percent.[11]

Of course, there were many factors contributing to labor's collapse, involving changes in the economy, patterns of world trade, and labor's own missteps. But labor law was part of the problem, and it was no accident that the public sector, where employers felt more bound by laws forbidding the firing of union sympathizers, saw large increases in organizing while the private sector saw large declines.[12] Labor-law reform called for expedited hearings, double back pay, and denial of federal contracts for repeat violators.[13]

Although the AFT was not directly affected by private-sector labor-law reform—almost all of its members were public employees—Shanker argued that a strong labor movement was vital to teachers because it would help pass progressive legislation on education spending and health care. Labor-law reform, he said at the 1977 AFT convention in Boston, would "change the entire politics of the Congress of the United States."[14] A stronger labor movement might change the nature of politics in the South, too, where teachers had trouble organizing. He argued, "if we manage to get the labor laws of this country reformed, we will have done the greatest single thing we could do to bring about massive improvements in education in this county."[15]

Even though the NLRA only affected the private sector, the AFT became very involved in lobbying for labor-law reform, says staffer Greg Humphrey: "We had some Senators that we could get to" that others could not.[16] The AFL-CIO's Tom Donahue recalls that the AFT "played a very serious role and didn't regard [it] as somebody else's fight."[17]

In his "Where We Stand" column, Shanker emphasized that the labor-law reform bill was really aimed at lawbreakers. "There is nothing in the reform measure which changes the thrust of the law or makes it more difficult for law-abiding employers to do business," he said. Bayard Rustin, writing as a guest columnist for Shanker, argued that violators of the law were equivalent to those who discriminated on other impermissible bases. "Government contracts should no more be awarded to companies that violate labor laws than to those that violate laws against discrimination on the basis of race, creed, color or sex."[18]

On October 6, 1977, the legislation passed the House by a healthy margin, 257 to 163. With President Carter's support, all that was needed was passage in the Senate, where Democrats held a strong majority, 61 to 39. Business interests—the Business Roundtable, the National Association of Manufacturers, and the Chamber of Commerce—all lined up in strong opposition. On June 14, 1978, Democrats fell two votes short of killing a filibuster mounted by Orrin Hatch and Richard Lugar, with a fifty-eight to forty-one vote.[19] Despite Democratic control of all three branches of government, labor-law reform was dead.

In the crucial vote, seventeen Democratic Senators defected. In fact, the biggest predictor on the vote was not political party but union density—the percentage of workers in a state who were members of unions. According to professors Richard Freeman and James Medoff, those from states in the top quintile of union density voted eighteen to two in favor of ending the filibuster. The next quintile was seventeen to three, and the middle quintile was sixteen to three. But then the vote shifted dramatically. In the second least union-dense quintile, the vote was six to fourteen, and in the least dense quintile, it was one to nineteen.[20]

The picture was clear: labor was on its own. Labor-law reform, at bottom, was a civil-rights issue—the right to vote in a union election was essentially nullified because the fear of being fired kept elections from taking place. Yet labor's liberal allies had not gone to the mat. Labor was central to the liberal coalition, but liberals did not see it. Shanker wrote:

> There is not a single piece of [social] legislation, whether it be minimum wages, whether it be safety standards, whether it be advances in rights to unionize and organize, whether it be health and medical care, whether it be civil rights or the non-acceptance of certain appointees to the Supreme Court, or whether it be leadership in the impeachment of a president of the United States—that would have been accomplished without the strength of the AFL-CIO.[21]

There was a direct link between the decline of labor and rising inequality, he said. Shanker argued: "Business and industry have plenty of money and power and a strong voice in American politics. They will continue to do so. And labor unions are the only large organized force to speak for the others, to provide a democratic balance, to represent those who work for a living, the poor, the minorities."[22]

President Carter, while being on the right side of the labor-law issue, had no passion for it. "On labor issues, Carter's people were absolutely no help on the Hill at all," recalls former Bricklayers president Jack Joyce.[23] Shanker expressed annoyance that while Carter lobbied very hard for other issues, the effort to pass labor-law reform had been a failure.[24]

And so labor unions were caught in a political box: they would have difficulty growing until they achieved labor-law reform, but they could not win labor-law reform until they grew and had greater power, because their allies did not fully back them. An historic opportunity had been missed.

Tuition Tax Credits

The second big legislative fight of deep concern to Shanker during the Carter administration was over tuition tax credits. In this instance, Shanker's disappointment was not with Carter, who supported the AFT's position, but with a man Shanker had helped elect to the Senate the previous fall in New York: Daniel Patrick Moynihan. Shanker and Moynihan had much in common: they were both intellectuals comfortable with power and champions of civil rights who were falsely accused of racism

(Moynihan's Ocean Hill–Brownsville was the Moynihan Report on the Black Family). They both took a hard line on the Soviets but parted with neoconservatives on the rights of organized labor and on core issues concerning economic equality.

But upon arrival in the U.S. Senate, Moynihan introduced legislation, cosponsored by Bob Packwood (R-OR), to provide up to a five-hundred-dollar tax credit to parents using private and parochial schools. Chester Finn, who was Moynihan's legislative director, recalls that the effort was essentially aimed at reviving America's Catholic schools, which had seen a steep decline in enrollment.[25]

Shanker was furious. He saw the proposal as a direct attack on two institutions he cared about more than practically any others: unions and public schools. Any effort to boost private schools would hurt teacher unions, because private schools are harder (though not impossible) to organize. The AFT had organized some Catholic lay teachers, but the vast majority of members were public-school teachers. Shanker suspected that part of the appeal of tuition tax credits to conservatives was that they would weaken teacher unions. More importantly, tuition tax credits would weaken public education, which, along with unions, were critical to democracy. Shanker's commitment was both philosophical and personal. Public education had allowed Shanker, the son of a newspaper deliveryman, to rise to a position of power and influence.

"He always felt that if there hadn't been good public education then certainly we would never have been able to do what we did," his sister Pearl notes.[26] His boyhood friend Ed Flower says that for Shanker personally, everything he achieved was not through any personal contacts that his parents had—they were poor people without influence—it was through public education. As the head of the teachers' union, Flower says, Shanker wanted to do well for his members. But education "was a be all and end all," because Shanker believed "what these kids are going to learn in school, what they are going to achieve mentally, are going to set the rest of their lives."[27] Years later, Shanker would write: "Whenever the problems connected with school reform seem especially tough, I think about this. I think about what public education gave me—a kid who couldn't even speak English when I entered first grade. I think about what it has given me and can give to countless numbers of other kids like me. And I know that keeping public education together is worth whatever it takes."[28] He worried, too, that aid to private schools would mean Balkanization even worse than the kind that resulted from community control in New York City.

In June 1978, the same month the Senate defeated the labor-law reform bill, the House passed a tuition tax credit on a vote of 209 to 194.[29] The bill had already sailed out of the Senate Finance Committee on a vote of fourteen to one, and Finn recalls that there was a real feeling that the tuition tax credit legislation might pass.[30]

To defeat the proposal, Shanker put together the National Coalition to Save Public Education. Shanker was smart enough to make the PTA the most visible organization heading the group, but, says Eugenia Kemble, "it was known that Al was the key power behind this."[31] Shanker attacked the Moynihan proposal piece by piece. While proponents referred to the tuition tax "experiment," Shanker said the proposal was radical, with far-reaching consequences. The amount of spending—roughly five hundred dollars per pupil—was far in excess of what the federal government provided for public-school students (which was along the lines of $128). Worse, he predicted, it would result in "a huge exodus from the public schools." Although some argued that only a small number of families would shift at first, Shanker said, "it does not need a majority in order for the effects to be destructive." Ever the chess player, Shanker spelled out the likely results. A five hundred dollar credit was just the beginning; as more parents took advantage of it, the pressure would grow to increase it to seven hundred or one thousand dollars. "It will be the beginning of the end for American public education," he warned. "The tuition tax credit is not just a simple experiment which will allow us to see what will happen and, if we don't like it, to go back to our traditional ways. It is more like dropping an egg. Once it breaks, it will not be put back together again. The process is irreversible."[32] The most motivated families—the children who serve as role models and the parents who attend the school-board meetings and demand education funding—were likely to leave the public system.[33] The following year, scores in public schools would decline, political influence would decline, and an irreversible downward spiral would begin.[34] Under the plan, he argued, "Eventually the public schools will be left only with those students who cannot be accepted by any private schools, or those expelled from private schools, or those too poor to pay tuition."[35]

When proponents of aid to private schools noted the long history of supporting private higher education, Shanker argued K–12 was different, because primary and secondary education are meant to provide a common education to students.[36] Shanker argued:

> Our public schools have played a major part in the building of a nation. They brought together countless children from different cultures—to share a common experience, to develop understanding and tolerance of differences. The public schools "Americanized"; they taught our language and our history. . . . Only public schools are designed to educate every child; only public schools serve to bring many diverse groups together.[37]

While the supporters of tuition tax credits talked about injecting healthy competition, Shanker said, the competition would be unfair, because private and parochial schools have the power to reject and expel difficult students, while the public schools take all comers.[38] When private-school advocates pointed to studies finding that test scores rise when children attend private schools, Shanker would say it only showed that "putting a poor minority child into a different setting, a middle class setting is beneficial," which was an argument "for a good pupil mix in schools, public or private."[39]

Being right on the merits took you only so far in Congress, so Shanker made a decision, controversial within the AFT, to make tuition tax credits a litmus-test issue: the AFT declared it would not help or contribute to any candidate who voted the wrong way on tuition tax credits. His position was: "This is it. If you're not right with us on this issue, you're not right with us period." While the AFT frequently disagreed with particular votes of members of Congress and continued to support them, tuition tax credits were different. "Tuition tax credits is not just another bill," he said. "It's the whole ball game, the existence of public education in this country."[40] Had Shanker not taken the hard line, staffer Greg Humphrey says, "I'm almost certain it [the vote] would have gone the other way."[41]

In August 1978, the proponents of tax credits flooded Congress, providing a greater volume of mail than on any issue since Watergate. Nevertheless, on August 15, after three days of debate, the Senate voted fifty-six to forty-one in favor of an amendment sponsored by Senator Fritz Hollings to strip the tuition tax credit bill of the K–12 credit while retaining a credit for higher-education spending.[42] Carter's threatened veto may also have helped with the vote.

The U.S. Department of Education

While Shanker was allied with President Carter on the tuition-tax fight, he was at loggerheads on a third major legislative battle, this one over the creation of the U.S. Department of Education, which would be carved out of the existing Department of Health, Education, and Welfare.

In later years, after the Department of Education was established and Ronald Reagan and Newt Gingrich sought to abolish it, the department became a symbol of commitment to a federal role in education, because conservatives who sought to abolish the department also supported deep cuts in federal education spending.[43] But the battle in the late 1970s was more complicated. There were, of course, conservative reasons to oppose the department, having to do with states' rights and the creation of federal bureaucracy. But Shanker, who had always backed a strong federal role and supported high levels of education funding, had other reasons— liberal reasons—to oppose the department. And he was in fact joined by several other liberals—in Congress, the administration, the media, and the education community.

The NEA had for years supported the creation of a Department of Education separate from the Department of Health, Education, and Welfare, and in 1976, in exchange for receiving the NEA's first presidential endorsement ever, Jimmy Carter pledged to back the idea.[44] When Carter was elected, some within the AFT argued for going along to be friendly with the new administration, but Shanker worried that the NEA would dominate the new department.[45] The same concerns were articulated by the editorial boards of the *Washington Post* and the *New York Times* and by most higher-education groups.[46] The *Post* said: "The bill is an inspiration of the NEA, an organization that has the same relation to the public schools as the plumbers union has to the plumbing business."[47] *Post* editorial cartoonist Herblock lampooned the department idea.[48] Higher-education groups mostly opposed the department, fearing it would be dominated by the NEA.[49] And Common Cause weighed in, accusing the NEA of trying to buy Department of Education votes with political donations.[50] Shanker also feared that a big political victory for the NEA would hurt the AFT in its battles for control in various local representation fights.[51]

Apart from the parochial concern about the NEA, Shanker had three other reasons to oppose the department. First, Shanker argued, if education was going to get something from the new Democratic administration, it should be something significant.[52] Shanker argued the creation of the department "could well be the big thing the next President does for education" and serve as "a substitute for additional federal financial aid."[53] Shanker had seen this before, when McGeorge Bundy and others argued for a change in governance over substantial investment in Ocean Hill–Brownsville, and he did not want to see it happen again. Shanker was right to be concerned. In a June 1977 memo to Carter, one of Walter Mondale's reasons to support the department was: "Because of budget constraints, there may not be much we can offer education and its advocates, except fulfillment of our campaign pledge for a separate department."[54] With the 1978 passage of California's Proposition 13, limiting tax revenues available for education and other social services, the importance of federal spending was heightened.

Second, apart from the political concerns, there was a substantive argument for keeping education with health and welfare programs in a single department—the issues of health, education, and welfare went together.[55] Kids needed adequate health care and nutrition to learn. Marian Wright Edelman of the Children's Defense Fund argued: "Children's health, education and social service needs cannot be separated out and still serve the whole child."[56]

Third, Shanker argued that there was a strong political argument for keeping education in HEW. Appropriation bills normally were organized along department lines, and the HEW bill often proved controversial. During the Nixon-Ford years, the HEW–Labor Appropriations bill was vetoed seven times, and four times, a coalition of education, labor, health, and welfare groups muscled the votes to override the vetoes.[57] Shanker argued that a separate Department of Education would weaken the coalition with health and welfare groups and leave education isolated.[58] Many civil-rights groups also argued that isolating education would cut off natural allies.[59] In Congress, Shirley Chisholm (D-NY) said that lobbying efforts of liberal groups worked best when liberal, labor-backed programs were in a single department.[60] Likewise, David Obey, a liberal Congressman from Wisconsin, opposed the legislation, arguing, "I think we are in much better shape if the unions, which are backing the jobs programs, and the scientific community, which is supporting health research programs, stand shoulder to shoulder with education groups in lobbying to override those vetoes. In unity there is power." He argued, "I would trade visibility for power any time."[61]

Early on in the administration, Shanker met with Carter and announced to reporters that Carter might reverse himself on the Department of Education.[62] Within the administration, OMD director Burt Lance and HEW secretary Joseph Califano were opposed, Carter was in the middle, and Mondale, whose brother was an official with the NEA, was a driving force in favor.[63] Califano said that a Department of Education would become a constituency-oriented institution whose narrow focus would make it more responsive to interest groups and less responsive to the president.[64] Lance's OMB conducted a study and came out in opposition to the department. Education Commissioner Ernest Boyer opposed the department, as did National Institutes of Education Director Pat Graham. Mondale aide Bert Carp said the department would pit elements of the liberal coalition against one another. But with strong NEA pressure, on January 19, 1978, Carter formally called for the creation of the department.[65]

On April 30, 1979, the Senate approved legislation 72 to 21, and the action turned to the House, where Shanker led higher-education groups and others in the fight against the department. The coalition in opposition included several conservative groups, such as the U.S. Catholic Conference, with whom Shanker had crossed swords over school vouchers.[66] Congressional staffer Robert Heffernan, who supported the department's creation, noted the "supreme irony" of Shanker's alliance with the U.S. Catholic Conference, since Shanker had called tuition tax credits "the gravest threat to public education we have witnessed in years."[67] On the other side were education's "Big Six": the NEA, the Council of Chief State School Officers, the National School Boards Association, the National PTA, the American Association of School Administrators, and the National Association of State Boards of Education.[68]

The House Government Operations Committee represented the best chance for the AFT to kill the legislation. A number of Democrats were opposed, including liberals Henry Waxman and John Conyers. But Carter pushed hard and told House Speaker Tip O'Neill he needed help with Democratic swing votes on the committee. On May 2, 1979, the House Government Operations Committee approved the legislation by twenty to nineteen.[69] As the legislation moved to the House floor in June 1979, the AFT-led coalition figured it needed 120 Republicans and one hundred Democrats to kill the legislation.[70]

A complication developed for Carter as a fight broke out over who would be appointed the interim commissioner of education to replace the outgoing Ernest Boyer. The stakes were high, because people believed the acting commissioner might become the first secretary of education. On June 15, Califano appointed the assistant education commissioner for policy studies, Marshall "Mike" Smith, to the post. One of the other leading candidates was Mary Frances Berry, the assistant secretary of HEW for education, and an African American. [71]

To torpedo Smith's candidacy, the Congressional Black Caucus attacked him for his contributions to a scholarly volume produced with Christopher Jencks entitled *Inequality*, which concluded, among other things, that the academic benefits of racial desegregation were modest. Smith met with the head of the Black Caucus, Parren Mitchell, and said he could explain his findings. Mitchell told Smith: "No, I believe the data, but I don't believe you should have said that." Smith was denounced as a "racist."[72]

Shanker, who knew something about the misuse of the race card, championed Smith's candidacy and called Mondale to register his support for Smith. "Shanker was dynamite in the whole thing," Smith says. The *New York Times* and *Washington Post* editorial boards both supported Smith against the scandalous charges of racism. The *Post* called the allegation of racism a "breathtakingly false charge" and the *Times* called the charges "absurd." Califano said there was "an element of McCarthyism" in the attack on Smith. But, says Smith, "Mondale caved."[73] When the Black Caucus threatened to withhold their block of votes for support for final passage of the Department of Education bill in July, Smith withdrew, and Mary Frances Berry became commissioner.[74]

With the Congressional Black Caucus back on board, the legislation passed the House by four votes, 210 to 206.[75] Carter had gone to the mat for the department using the power of the presidency, some argue, as he did only one other time—for the Panama Canal treaty.[76] Shanker wished he had done something similar for a truly important bill, like labor-law reform.

Over time, Shanker came to accept the reality of the Department of Education and did not fight for its repeal. Separating education probably did not hurt funding as Shanker had worried, because in Congress, appropriations for education remained in the same bill with health and welfare despite education's separate status within the executive branch. But neither did it help. Today, federal revenues remain about the same small level—under 10 percent of total local, state, and federal education spending.[77] Indeed, following creation of the department, William Rasp-berry, writing in the *Washington Post*, noted that the NEA, having cut a deal, could not criticize Carter's budget, which was disastrous for educa-tion.[78] Shanker, by contrast, blasted Carter's 1980 proposed cutbacks in education.[79]

Affirmative Action

Shanker saw Carter's economic, labor, and education agenda as mixed at best, but on racial matters, Shanker was disappointed by the new presi-dent's pursuit of racial and ethnic identity politics over the old liberal universalistic civil-rights vision. Shanker split with Carter on two key affirmative-action cases in the Supreme Court and on the assignment of teachers by race in New York City.

In 1977, liberals were split by a new case involving racial preferences in higher education. While the Supreme Court had ducked the issue in *De-Funis*, the question came roaring back in the celebrated case of *Regents of the University of California v. Bakke*, which riveted the nation. Allan Bakke, like Marco DeFunis, was a working-class white applicant (he was the son of a milkman) who charged that he had been the victim of reverse dis-crimination.[80] Bakke was rejected from the University of California Med-ical School at Davis even though he had academic credentials superior to the minority students admitted under a quota system, which set aside sixteen of one hundred seats for minorities.

Civil-rights groups generally supported the University of California, as did some labor unions, such as the UAW.[81] Two of Shanker's major rivals, the NEA and McGeorge Bundy of the Ford Foundation, also supported quotas.[82] Several Jewish groups—the American Jewish Committee, the American Jewish Congress, and the ADL—supported Bakke, saying race should not be a factor in admissions, but overcoming hardship should be.[83]

The liberal California Supreme Court sided with Bakke in a six-to-one decision. Justice Stanley Mosk echoed Justice Douglas's argument in *De-Funis* that special consideration should be given for economic disadvan-tage but not for race.[84] Many liberals, like Bayard Rustin, worried about what the case would do to the liberal coalition.[85] The AFL-CIO was so di-vided it did not file an *amicus* brief on either side.[86] The Leadership Conference on Civil Rights, which included black, Jewish, and labor groups, also ducked *Bakke*.[87]

Shanker and the AFT weighed in with an *amicus* brief supporting Allan Bakke. In a "Where We Stand" column entitled "Help for Disadvantaged, But Not Quotas," Shanker argued that while he opposed quotas, he strongly favored aiding the disadvantaged. UC-Davis's special admissions, he argued, quoting San Jose State University President John Bunzel, "is not designed to benefit the economic or educationally disadvantaged, regardless of race, but is in fact a program based on race." Shanker, again quoting Bunzel, suggested Americans would be willing to support "a state and national search program at the high school level, where talented young people—blacks, Chicanos, poor whites, and all those disadvantaged who otherwise become locked into a life of inequality—can be found and helped." Class was the real divider, not race, Shanker argued, and providing preferences based on race was the surest way to divide a progressive, class-based coalition. Racial quotas were adopted by Nixon, Shanker said, because they "pitted one group against another over limited and declining jobs and places in colleges." And it was cheap, an aspect that conservatives liked: "It required little initiative from government—no jobs, no recruitment, no training."[88]

Shanker worried about the further splits that racial preferences would cause. "There is no issue in American society today that is as divisive as preferential treatment along racial and ethnic lines," he argued.[89] Shanker predicted, with some prescience, what would happen should preferences be upheld. "If this case is not resolved in favor of Bakke, we will have a permanent conflict in this society," Shanker argued. "The overwhelming majority, 85 percent, oppose giving preference on the basis of race. Once you decide race is going to be a factor, you're entering a 50-year battle."[90]

There was division within the Carter Administration on where to come down, but in August 1977, Carter announced the administration would weigh in with a brief that backed UC-Davis. Shanker denounced the move.[91]

When the decision was handed down by the Supreme Court, Justice Lewis Powell, the swing vote, struck down the sixteen-seat quota but said that race could be used as one factor in admissions. Shanker worried about this distinction and wrote that "the fact that race can be taken into account may lead to hidden quota systems."[92]

Powell also provided a disturbing new rationale for racial preferences. The program was justified not as a temporary measure to eliminate the vestiges of past discrimination; instead, preferences would promote racial diversity in education in order to increase the learning of other students. This notion had a much longer shelf life than the temporary remedy for past discrimination. And the idea of diversity, as opposed to integration, essentially adopted the Black Power view that differences between races were greater than similarities. As historian John Diggins notes: "Now race, gender, and ethnicity, instead of being provincial hindrances that one must escape in order to free the mind, were social categories that one must embrace to discover the self."[93] Shanker warned about the analogy between preferences based on race and preferences based on geography or athletic ability. "They choose whether or not to play football," he said. "About race there is not choice. Race is an incident of birth. It cannot be changed."[94]

The *Bakke* case received a tremendous amount of attention, but for the traditional Democratic coalition of working-class whites and blacks, a second Supreme Court case during the Carter Administration posed an even more direct danger: *U.S. Steelworkers of America v. Weber*. Whereas *Bakke* dealt with the rarified issues of admissions to medical school, *Weber* dealt directly with the question of racial preferences among blue-collar workers. At issue was a quota system under which 50 percent of openings in an on-the-job training program to become a skilled craft worker at the Kaiser Aluminum and Chemical Corporation were set aside for black employees. The plan was negotiated as part of a collective-bargaining agreement between the union, the U.S. Steelworkers, and Kaiser.

The case for some sort of remedial action in Weber was strong. Prior to the agreement, only 1.83 percent of skilled craft workers were black, even though 39 percent of the local work force was black. Normally, under civil-rights laws, black workers would sue, establish liability against the union and the employers, and victims of discrimination would be made whole. But in this case, the union and the employer set up a prospective quota and paid no damages for past discrimination.

Openings in the training program were highly coveted, and Brian Weber, a white worker, felt aggrieved when he was bypassed for a slot in the program even though he had more seniority than black workers who were accepted into the program under the 50 percent quota.[95] Why should he have to pay for the discrimination, Weber asked, when the guilty parties—the union and the employer—got off with no penalties? The plain language of the 1964 Civil Rights Act suggested that the quota was illegal. Title VII said it was unlawful to "discriminate . . . because of . . . race" in hiring and in selection of apprentices for training programs. The lower courts sided with Weber, but as the case made it up to the U.S. Supreme Court, the Carter Administration took the other side. The decision was not surprising given Carter's position in *Bakke.*

But then, in December 1978, the press reported that the AFL-CIO would weigh in on the case against Weber.[96] Shanker, who sat on the AFL-CIO Executive Council, was furious. He recalled: "When I read about this in the newspapers, I blew up." A meeting was called with Shanker, George Meany, Lane Kirkland, the chief counsel Larry Gold, and some people from the Steelworkers. They argued the AFL-CIO had to support this racial set-aside because it was part of a collective-bargaining agreement negotiated by the union. Shanker said the union was hardly on the side of the angels—its agreement to impose quotas was a maneuver to avoid massive liability. And Shanker asked, "suppose they had agreed not to hire any blacks, would you be here taking the same position?" But the decision was already made.[97] The AFL-CIO had gone from opposition to quotas in *DeFunis* to neutrality in *Bakke* to support in *Weber.* "It was a turning point," Shanker says.[98] The shift, says writer Max Green, came "quite unexpectedly" and "without any public explanation."[99]

When the U.S. Supreme Court handed down its decision in the case in June 1979, the court ruled, by a five-to-four vote, that the 50 percent set-aside was legal. Although the plain language of the statute made discrimination by race illegal, the spirit of the law was intended to help blacks, the majority argued, so a temporary program of this type was legal. The dissent argued that ignoring the language of the law—saying that the "literal construction" was not dispositive and that Title VII did not mean what it said—was truly Orwellian.

For Shanker, the irony was that the dissent was written by William Rehnquist, whose nomination Shanker had opposed and who could rightly be accused of consistently siding with whites on civil-rights questions. The majority, which included civil-rights heroes like Thurgood Marshall, had been right about civil rights in the 1950s and 1960s but now rejected universalism and the nondiscrimination principle in favor of policies that would benefit black people *per se,* whatever the means involved. Where were the leaders who were for civil rights across the board?

In 1979, one of those leaders, A. Philip Randolph, died at the age of ninety. Shanker, who revered Randolph and all he stood for, wrote a column in which he declared "no American in this century has done more to eliminate racial discrimination in our society and to improve the condition of working people than did A. Philip Randolph." Shanker argued that Randolph had an enormous effect on the AFL-CIO and "transformed the labor movement into a powerful ally of the drive for racial equality." Unlike those who focused on helping the most advantaged African Americans—W. E. B. DuBois's "talented tenth"—Randolph looked to the masses of blacks, Shanker said. And unlike those Black Power advocates who turned on labor during the Ocean Hill–Brownsville crisis, Randolph had stood firm. He had a universal vision, Shanker noted. "He was a friend and counselor to me, as well as a teacher and a leader. The proudest moment of my life was when he nominated me to serve on the Executive Council of the AFL-CIO."[100]

But now, Randolph and Shanker's vision of universal nondiscrimination was clearly out of fashion among elites. Polls suggested that the vast majority of Americans opposed discrimination against minorities or racial preferences for them. But the Supreme Court, the Carter Administration, and now even the AFL-CIO had taken a different route, suggesting the goal was to elevate the black population even if it meant that principles of nondiscrimination and universality were set aside. The problem, of course, was that if civil rights became a matter of advancing certain interests rather than universal values, the majority white population might well seek to advance *its* interests, a dangerous recipe for liberals, labor, and advocates of civil rights.

Shanker also clashed with the new race-conscious liberalism of the Carter Administration over a plan to assign New York City teachers to schools based on race. In the mid-1970s, the federal government found that New York City minority teachers taught disproportionately in minority schools. In the 1974–75 school year, 76 percent of minority teachers taught in schools with more than 90 percent minority populations, compared with 40 percent of non-minority teachers.[101]

Ironically, the disproportion resulted from the decentralization law pushed by civil-rights advocates, which provided that in districts with poor reading scores, local school boards could deviate from hiring based on teacher test scores in order to provide more minority role models for students.[102] Shanker argued: "The de facto segregation of minority teachers is a direct result of the philosophy of community control."[103]

The Carter Administration's Office for Civil Rights (OCR) within the Department of Health, Education, and Welfare demanded mass transfers of teachers to remedy the racial imbalance between schools. Under an agreement negotiated between OCR, New York City, and the UFT, the parties agreed on the goal that each of thirty-two community school districts should reflect the percentage of minority teachers in the system over time, to be achieved not through forced transfer of current teachers but through the assignment of newly hired teachers.

In the fall of 1977, Shanker said he was displeased with the settlement but that "they held a gun to the head of both the union and the school system and threatened disastrous cutbacks until the system capitulated to demands that amount to illegal and unconstitutional quota hiring." Shanker said: "Either President Carter doesn't know what's going on, or he has broken a campaign promise to the American people to oppose quotas."[104] The school board adopted a policy (not required or advocated specifically by OCR) in which new black and Hispanic teachers picked their assignments from one box, and white teachers from another.[105]

The procedure drew the ire of Senator Moynihan. On September 23, 1977, in an extraordinary speech, Moynihan denounced the settlement, comparing it to the Nuremberg racial laws in Hitler's Germany. Noting that he had been the author of Lyndon Johnson's famous 1965 speech at Howard University calling for affirmative action to help the runner who was "hobbled by chains," Moynihan said the practice of separate hiring lines based on race was not at all what he had in mind. "A better prescription for division and hostility among Americans could not be devised," he said, arguing: "Nothing could more surely impede [the struggle for equality], or damage the cause of brotherhood among men, than the establishment by the government of strict and lasting legal divisions among the races." Accusing OCR of having "inflicted moral carnage on the civil rights movement," he concluded: "In the name of moral sanity, I call upon President Carter to void this wretched contract." Shanker reprinted portions Moynihan's speech in his "Where We Stand" column on October 2.[106] The rhetoric of the speech itself was hard to defend—the goal of OCR's program was integration, not racial annihilation, as in Nazi Germany. But it caught the attention of the public and made the issue more salient.

In December 1, 1977, Shanker and the UFT challenged in federal court the consent agreement in New York as unconstitutional.[107] In court papers, the UFT backed several race-neutral alternatives to increasing racial integration among teachers: the state should eliminate the provision in the decentralization law that allowed districts with low reading scores to hire teachers on their own, the state should restore free tuition to City University, the paraprofessional career-ladder program should be strengthened, and a retirement incentive program should be adopted to create room for more new teachers.[108]

Given the uproar over the racially explicit teacher assignments, the New York City Board of Education backed an alternative of achieving integration indirectly by assigning teachers to schools based on neighborhood. Those newly hired teachers living in predominantly white residential neighborhoods would be assigned to predominantly minority schools and vice versa. Shaker said, "It is certainly far better than assignment by race."[109]

Bilingual Education

Finally, late in Carter's term, Shanker clashed with the administration on the contentious issue of bilingual education. As someone who entered school not knowing English, Shanker was sympathetic to the need to offer special help to non-English-speaking students, and he supported the 1974 *Lau v. Nichols* Supreme Court decision that said schools must provide extra help to such children.[110]

But Shanker was also deeply concerned about a new movement—the Hispanic equivalent to Black Power and community control—that sought to keep Hispanic children in separate bilingual programs for years. Such programs aimed not at easing the transition to English but rather at providing employment to Hispanic teachers and instilling ethnic identity and Latino nationalism. Shanker had three concerns with this new form of "maintenance" bilingual education.

First, given the tough economic times and declining student enrollment, Shanker had to be sensitive to the job issue for his mostly black and white membership. If students were permanently placed in "maintenance" bilingual programs, that meant less employment for non-bilingual teachers in an era of declining enrollment.[111]

Second, Shanker was worried that extensive use of maintenance bilingual education undercut the assimilating role of public education—which was a major argument he used to defend against tuition tax credits and vouchers. Shanker wrote:

Will federal programs lead the U.S. to become another Quebec? The American people come from many cultures, many language backgrounds. One of the major purposes of the American public schools has been to "Americanize" waves of immigrants—most of whom did not speak English. . . . Ethnic groups had their foreign language newspapers and neighborhoods where their language was spoken, their culture preserved. But in the schools, as in public life in general, English was used. That policy worked. It brought many together to forge a nation.[112]

Third, as a matter of educational achievement, Shanker was angered by the lack of scientific evaluation of the effectiveness of bilingual programs, which the bilingual lobby strongly resisted. "Al was appalled by the fact that there was no research base," Humphrey says.[113] Shanker's concern about the educational validity of bilingual programs was compounded by the practice of hiring "bilingual" teachers who in fact knew very little English, so that "many children in 'bilingual' programs learn no English whatsoever."[114]

In 1980, in the midst of a tough reelection campaign, Carter's Department of Education proposed a set of regulations to require all schools to teach limited-English-proficient students in the child's home language. Carter pushed the regulations, according to Califano, because Mondale wanted to appease Hispanic interest groups.[115] Shanker called the regulations "an unmitigated disaster" and helped lead the fight against them.[116] The idea was not a proven educational strategy, he said, and as a societal matter, Carter's program "threatens the fabric of American education and the future of our country."[117] The NEA, by contrast, supported Carter's position. In Congress, Shanker prevailed, and an amendment was added to the Department of Education's appropriations bill prohibiting implementation until at least June 1981.[118] The proposed regulations died in the next administration.[119]

International Affairs

Shanker's disagreements with Carter on social issues like racial preferences and bilingual education were mirrored by disagreements on foreign policy, where he regarded Carter as weak and ineffectual. Although Carter was a supporter of the Vietnam War and an Annapolis graduate, it quickly became clear that he was substantially to the left of Shanker and his friends in the Coalition for a Democratic Majority. When Scoop Jackson and Pat

Moynihan, CDM co-chairs, presented Carter with fifty-three candidates for national security positions, only two received appointments, and both were peripheral. Key appointments instead went to New Politics–type candidates, such as Andrew Young as ambassador to the United Nations and Paul Warnke as chief arms negotiator with the Soviets.[120]

Carter's decision to make human rights a key priority of the United States was something Shanker long supported, but to CDM members, Carter's emphasis on human rights was selective and did not adequately highlight abuses by Communists as well as right-wing dictatorships.[121] Shanker was appalled when Carter made a speech in May 1977 at Notre Dame calling for Americans to transcend "our inordinate fear of Communism."[122] Shanker and his allies were also stunned by Andrew Young's decision to commend Cuban troops in Africa for providing stability and order.[123]

Shanker denounced what he saw as a double standard on the Left. He noted in 1977: "Some people are for human rights but only in Chile or in Spain when Franco was there; or in Greece under the dictators. But they are not for human rights when those rights were violated by Cambodia or when they were violated by Cuba or by the Soviet Union."[124] He argued: "When men and women are imprisoned, tortured, and killed because they dare to speak, write or organize, it makes no difference whether they were silenced by leftists or a rightist dictator. The action must be condemned."[125] In the late 1970s, when the Vietnamese government was causing mass starvation in occupied Cambodia, Shanker asked: "Where are the expressions of outrage? Where are the demonstrations? How can it be that there are protests only against American support for the Shahs and the Somozas—whose crimes may be real enough and surely merit exposure—and none at all against the Soviet Union and Vietnam, who are within weeks of annihilating and wiping out an entire culture from the face of the earth?"[126]

Shanker was also critical of Carter's handling of the post–Vietnam War Southeast Asian refugee crisis, which Shanker saw as an important matter of human rights. He was appalled when candidate Jimmy Carter said the refugees would be better off in Asia. The AFL-CIO, which in a time of high unemployment had reason to be concerned about immigration, Shanker said, was taking a much more open stance, "because there were larger principles at stake." Shanker asked: "Can those who want to close America's doors to the oppressed be called 'liberals?'"[127]

In March 1978, to underline the importance of the refugee issue, Shanker invited Leo Cherne, president of the International Rescue Committee, to receive the UFT's John Dewey Award. In his speech accepting the award, Cherne talked about the history of liberals like John Dewey and Reinhold Niebuhr, who created the IRC to help refugees after the rise of Hitler in Germany, and he criticized the Carter Administration for not doing enough to help refugees from Cambodia.[128]

In the summer of 1978, Shanker, with Cherne, Bayard Rustin, and other members of the IRC's Citizens Commission on Indochinese Refugees, visited Thai refugee camps.[129] Shanker, who also brought members of his family, met with hundreds of refugees, who told of escaping the Communists in Vietnam, Laos, and Cambodia. He supported Senator James Buckley's call to open U.S. doors to those refugees who had "risked death to give their children a chance to live and work in freedom. They have paid an initiation fee for a life of liberty that few Americans can honestly say they would have had the courage to meet, and they cannot turn back."[130]

Likewise, Shanker became very involved in the cause of Soviet dissidents. In September 1977, Shanker participated in and wrote about the third international Sakharov hearings to dramatize the plight of Soviet dissidents and complained that the media mostly ignored the hearings.[131] He was disturbed that the issue, a basic question of human rights, did not seem to excite his fellow liberals.

Shanker was deeply concerned that the New Left's anti-anti-Communism had moved into the mainstream of the Democratic Party. What many liberals knew most about anti-Communism was its excesses— McCarthyism in the 1950s and the Vietnam War in the 1960s and early 1970s. At home, their egalitarian vision made them worry about defense expenditures diverting money away from social problems. And abroad, some even identified with what was perceived as the egalitarian aspirations of Communists, in contrast to the corporate agenda of the United States. Finally, many liberals had pacifist tendencies and worried about ethnocentrism, which made them want to withdraw from the world and not impose American values on other societies.

Shanker fiercely disagreed with the growing anti-anti-Communism and worried that many liberals were drawing the wrong lessons from Vietnam: that Communism wasn't so bad after all and that the United States should stick to domestic concerns. Shanker wanted to rescue anti-Communism from Nixon and McCarthy and emphasize that it was a part of the human-rights agenda, as Truman and Kennedy and Humphrey had believed. "Al's big contribution was in constantly keeping a very highly tuned beam of what Communism was all about," Eugenia Kemble says: repression of human rights, free speech, intellectual freedom, and trade unionism.[132]

Carter had little understanding of the true nature of Communism, Shanker believed, which is why he pursued detente and cuts in defense spending.[133] Carter seemed "incapable of responding to the threats which the Soviet Union posed," Shanker later said. In December 1979, the Soviets invaded Afghanistan and Carter expressed shock and surprise. Shanker said: "He received his education at that very late date."[134] To Shanker, Carter was at once naïve about the intent of Communists and unduly pessimistic about beating the Soviets. The malaise that infected the Carter Administration's foreign policy was never felt by Shanker, whom associates say always believed the Soviets could be toppled.[135]

Kennedy Versus Carter

Al Shanker's deep disenchantment with Jimmy Carter over foreign policy, social issues, and his economic program left Shanker searching for an alternative. Ideally, he would have liked to see a Scoop Jackson emerge, but when the challenge came instead in the form of Massachusetts Democratic Senator Ted Kennedy, Shanker was willing to take a close look.

Labor was divided on the Kennedy-Carter fight, with the Steelworkers, Communications Workers of America, and NEA breaking for Carter, and more liberal unions like the machinists, the UAW, and AFSCME breaking for Kennedy.[136] With labor split, the AFL-CIO decided to stay neutral.[137]

For Shanker, there was little reason to stay with Carter, who had been a disappointment on quotas, bilingual education, the Department of Education, the Soviets, the minimum wage, and a host of other issues. Nor was there a personal tie. "Carter didn't give us the time of day," Phil Kugler recalls. "It was awful."[138] Rachelle Horowitz says the relationship with Carter was essentially "nonexistent."[139] After their meeting in July 1977 about the Department of Education, there was no further contact between Shanker and Carter prior to the presidential race.[140]

From Shanker's perspective, Kennedy was not much better than Carter on social issues or international affairs.[141] But Kennedy was far superior on meat-and-potato economic issues: education spending, jobs, health care, minimum wage, and the like.[142] And Kennedy would not have hanging over him a general ineptness on issues like the taking of American hostages in Iran, which came to symbolize Carter's weakness on international matters.

Ironically, the taking of the hostages in November 1979 initially boosted Carter's campaign, as Americans rallied around the president. Missteps by Kennedy and questions about his personal character also hurt his prospects, and Carter won several early primary victories.

In mid-March 1980, prior to the New York primary, Shanker publicly endorsed Kennedy, even as Kennedy was being peppered by questions about how long he would stay in the race.[143] In a column backing Kennedy, Shanker focused on Carter's betrayal of liberal economic policies—his failure to deliver on national health insurance and his proposal for large cuts in social services to balance the budget. Shanker said: "We don't want a Democratic candidate running on a program which we expect from a conservative Republican."[144]

In the New York primary, thousands of teachers volunteered for Kennedy.[145] The AFT's endorsement helped put Kennedy over the top in New York, Pennsylvania, New Jersey, and California.[146] But Carter had too much momentum, and the NEA's endorsement of Carter proved crucial in his renomination.[147]

At the Democratic convention in New York City, which Shanker attended, Kennedy gave a spirited defense of liberalism in a speech that is remembered years later. Avoiding for the most part discussion of foreign policy and social issues, Kennedy spoke of renewing "the commitment of the Democratic Party to economic justice." He said: "Our cause has been, since the days of Thomas Jefferson, the cause of the common man and the common woman. Our commitment has been, since the days of Andrew Jackson, to all those he called 'the humble members of our society—the farmers, mechanics and laborers.' On this foundation we have defined our values, refined our policies, refreshed our faith." He concluded: "For me, a few hours ago, this campaign came to an end. For all those whose cares have been our concern, the work goes on, the cause endures, the hope still lives and the dream shall never die."[148]

This was the Democratic Party Shanker had signed up for years earlier, not one that fought inflation with unemployment and balanced the budget with cuts to the poor. And it was a Democratic Party that had a shot at winning over working-class voters with a powerful economic message that might counter perceived weaknesses on social and foreign-policy questions.

Two nights later, Kennedy famously appeared with Carter on the podium at the Democratic National Convention, avoiding an enthusiastic physical embrace with the president that Carter so badly wanted.[149] Shanker, meanwhile, met with Congressman John Anderson, who was running as a third-party candidate.[150]

Carter Versus Reagan

A week later, however, both Kennedy and Shanker fully embraced Carter's candidacy. On August 21, in his first public appearance since the Democratic convention, Kennedy spoke to the AFT delegates at their convention in Detroit and urged teachers to work hard for Carter in the fall. Kennedy thanked AFT members for their "extraordinary effort" on his behalf in the primaries and urged them to extend "that same extraordinary effort to President Carter." Now it was not the soaring inspiration of Kennedy's convention speech but the fear of Republican presidential nominee Ronald Reagan that animated the members. Shanker said there were "big differences" between Carter and Reagan, whom he described as "terrible." Delegates responded with a vote to support Carter by a margin of three to one.[151]

The next day, on August 22, Carter spoke to the AFT convention and was cheered enthusiastically when he described Kennedy as "a great man," the AFT as "a fighting union," and said of Shanker, "you couldn't have a finer man." Carter won strong applause highlighting issues where he differed from Reagan, such as his opposition to tuition tax credits and his support for the Equal Rights Amendment. Carter also received an enthusiastic response when he acknowledged the AFT's political power. He told delegates of the union, now 550,000 members strong, "I learned a lesson this year about the value of AFT endorsements. It's inscribed very clearly in mind, the classrooms where I was taught, places like New York, Rhode Island and Pennsylvania."[152]

Because of Reagan's position on the Soviet Union, quotas, and the like, a number of Shanker's social democratic and CDM colleagues broke with the Democrats in 1980. Midge Decter, Linda Chavez, Jeanne Kirkpatrick, Richard Perle, Max Kampleman, Elliot Abrams, Sidney Hook, and other intellectuals made the shift to Reagan. But Shanker, says Chavez, "voted for Carter as much as he disliked him."[153]

For Shanker, supporting Reagan was out of the question. Carter might not have been as good as Kennedy on issues like the minimum wage, health care, and education spending, but at least Carter was on the right side on core issues of democracy: defense of public schools and the right of labor to organize collectively. Reagan, by contrast, wanted to cut funding to public schools and supported tuition tax credits to undermine them. Reagan was also a bitter foe of unions and an enemy of the safety net; he was a figure who would vastly increase inequality. Reagan saw government as the problem, while Shanker saw government as "the indispensable instrument of human progress."[154] While Shanker shared some ground with neoconservatives on issues like affirmative action, bilingual education, and anti-Communism, friends note that he always identified himself fundamentally "on the liberal left side."[155]

If Shanker's dark view of human nature led him to be a foreign-policy hawk distrustful of what Communist and authoritarian governments would do, it also fundamentally made him an economic liberal who believed wealthy employers had little incentive to be just in sharing their profits with workers unless forced to by a union. There was also, dating from his childhood, a feeling of alienation, a sense of not belonging to the privileged segments of society, and an identification with the underdog and the outsider.[156]

While Shanker shared Reagan's concerns about issues like quotas, he was also suspicious, for Reagan had come very late to the principle of nondiscrimination. He had opposed the Civil Rights Act of 1964 and the Voting Rights Act of 1965, both of which Shanker had supported, and while Shanker had sent teachers to Mississippi to teach in Freedom Schools, Reagan opened his 1980 presidential campaign in Neshoba County, where civil-rights workers had been killed, and defended "states' rights."[157]

Some neoconservatives argued Reagan's foreign-policy strength should trump disagreements over domestic policy. George Will argued: "If the housing program failed, you could fix it. But if you lost the Cold War, you lost the country."[158] But Shanker thought Reagan would prove inconsistent even on Communism. It was true, Reagan battled Communists firsthand in the Screen Actors Guild, so like Shanker, he knew what they were about. But Shanker worried that Reagan's allegiance to big-business interests would dilute his ideological anti-Communism. Whereas the AFL-CIO was rock-solid in opposing Communism because free unions could not survive under Communism, some business leaders wanted to work with Communist regimes if a profit was to be had.[159]

Shanker's view did not win the day and in November 1980, in a landmark election, Ronald Reagan, whom the cognoscenti viewed as too right-wing to win, did just that. The victory was unlike anything seen since FDR's New Deal. Eisenhower, Nixon, and Ford were moderates by comparison; with Reagan, it was as if Barry Goldwater had been elected.[160] To add insult to injury, the victory was delivered by what had been FDR's core constituency: white working-class voters.

Twenty years earlier, Seymour Martin Lipset had observed in *Political Man: The Social Bases of Politics* that workers in America supported the Democratic Party more consistently than workers in Britain supported the Labor Party.[161] Now, astoundingly, a candidate who called for cuts in social programs, tax cuts for the wealthy, and an anti-labor agenda had won the white working-class vote, a group dubbed "Reagan Democrats."[162] Some of Shanker's own teachers moved over. In his book on the Canarsie section of Brooklyn, Jonathan Rieder noted that Reagan "ran well in precincts full of Jewish teachers, the kind of people who had chosen Adlai Stevenson, John Kennedy, and Lyndon Johnson by margins of eight to one."[163]

Shanker had been warning for years that the New Politics embrace of racial quotas, weak national defense, and tepid economic policies were not only wrong but deeply unpopular. There was a cost to saying that civil rights was not about universal principles of nondiscrimination and instead was about advancing group interests. There was a cost to an unwillingness to exercise power—in Iran or against the Soviet Union. Shanker believed a Kennedy candidacy might have worked by appealing to white working-class voters on core economic concerns, but Carter had largely given up even on those issues, appealing instead to "moderate" voters concerned about the budget deficit. The Democrats' shift from class-based New Deal policies to race-based programs had a predictable result.[164]

The swing voters turned out not to be what political scientists called the "moderate middle," the John Anderson voters whose upper-middle-class views suggested the need to avoid a populist economic message. The numbers lay with a different group—"the radical center"—working-class

"Reagan Democrats" who were patriotic, opposed to quotas, and wanted a better economic program.

As the Carter Administration came to an end, Shanker was deeply disappointed with the direction that American liberalism continued to take. The Carter Administration had not fought hard enough for labor-law reform, had chosen form over substance in creating a Department of Education, had backed racial preferences and a separatist form of bilingual education, had shown weakness toward Iran and the Soviet Union, and had run against activist government on core issues such as the minimum wage. This record was a far cry from the liberalism of FDR and Harry Truman. Reagan's election made clear that the support of white working-class voters for Richard Nixon in 1972 was not an aberration; if anything, Carter's 1976 victory was the anomaly, following Watergate.

The people who would have to pay the price of Ronald Reagan's presidency were not the New Politics crowd or the heads of civil-rights groups with whom Shanker had battled over policy and politics. It was ordinary poor and working-class Americans of all races, the very people Shanker and like-minded Democrats had sought to unite.

FIGURE 1. Albert Shanker's parents, Mamie Shanker, a seamstress, and Morris Shanker, a newspaper deliverer, at their wedding in December 1927. The arranged marriage did not make for a happy household. *Credit: Eadie Shanker photo collection.*

FIGURE 2. Young Al Shanker with grandmother Rachel Burko, mother Mamie Shanker, and sister Pearl Shanker, in photo from the 1930s. Al was especially close with his grandmother, a Russian Jewish immigrant. *Credit: Walter P. Reuther Library, Wayne State University.*

FIGURE 3. Shanker in Boy Scout uniform, pictured with his mother. Scouting was a formative experience for Shanker, enabling him to escape the anti-Semitism of the immediate neighborhood and exercise leadership skills. *Credit: Walter P. Reuther Library, Wayne State University.*

FIGURE 4. Shanker, speaking at the University of Illinois, where he was a student from 1946 through 1949. At Illinois, Shanker was active in the civil rights movement and socialist politics and coordinated Norman Thomas's appearance on campus. *Credit: Walter P. Reuther Library, Wayne State University.*

FIGURE 5. Shanker as a young teacher, working with a New York City student in the 1950s. *Credit: Walter P. Reuther Library, Wayne State University.*

FIGURE 6. Shanker with his wife, Eadie, a fellow teacher and labor activist, at a labor dinner in the 1960s, after Shanker was elected president of New York City's United Federation of Teachers (UFT). *Credit: Eadie Shanker photo collection.*

FIGURE 7.   Shanker, handing check to Martin Luther King Jr., Selma, Alabama, 1965. King in turn supported Shanker and the UFT during the fourteen-day New York City teachers strike in 1967. *Credit: Walter P. Reuther Library, Wayne State University.*

FIGURE 8.   Shanker, marching with labor leader and civil rights pioneer A. Philip Randolph of the Brotherhood of Sleeping Car Porters, during the 1967 New York City teachers strike. *Credit: Walter P. Reuther Library, Wayne State University.*

FIGURE 9.   Shanker with New York City mayor John Lindsay and schools superintendent Bernard Donovan, settling the 1967 teachers strike. The three men would be at loggerheads again the following year during the divisive Ocean Hill–Brownsville teachers strike. *Credit: Walter P. Reuther Library, Wayne State University.*

FIGURE 10.   Shanker being greeted by his wife, Eadie, and members of the press after leaving Civil Jail in January 1968. Shanker was sentenced for fifteen days for violating the law against striking by public employees during the 1967 teachers strike. *Credit: Walter P. Reuther Library, Wayne State University.*

FIGURE 11.   Shanker speaking to teachers during the 1968 Ocean Hill–Brownsville teachers strike, which pitted mostly white Jewish unionists against black community control activists. *Credit: Walter P. Reuther Library, Wayne State University.*

FIGURE 12.   Shanker with socialist friend Michael Harrington, the author of *The Other America* and a staunch supporter of the UFT during the 1968 Ocean Hill–Brownsville strikes; he broke with white liberal supporters of community control. *Credit: Walter P. Reuther Library, Wayne State University.*

FIGURE 13. Shanker, with friend and supporter Bayard Rustin during the Ocean Hill–Brownsville strikes. Rustin was reviled in the black community for siding with Shanker. *Credit: Robert F. Wagner Labor Archives, New York University, United Federation of Teachers Photographs Collection.*

FIGURE 14.   Shanker, with Bayard Rustin, during a 1970 rally on
behalf of paraprofessionals, a
group of mostly black and Latino
teacher aides who became an important part of the teacher union
and helped resuscitate Shanker's
reputation in minority communities after Ocean Hill–Brownsville.
*Credit: Walter P. Reuther Library,
Wayne State University.*

FIGURE 15.   Shanker was the
author of the legendary "Where
We Stand" column in the Sunday
New York Times, a paid advertisement that was widely read in education circles and ran from December 1970 until Shanker's death
in 1997. *Credit: Walter P. Reuther
Library, Wayne State University.*

FIGURE 16.   Shanker, pictured with David Selden, Shanker's one-time mentor, whom Shanker defeated for the presidency of the American Federation of Teachers in 1974 after the two men split over the Vietnam War, George McGovern's presidential candidacy, and relations with the NEA. *Credit: Walter P. Reuther Library, Wayne State University.*

FIGURE 17.   Shanker with AFL-CIO president George Meany (smoking cigar) in the 1970s. Meany agreed with Shanker's distaste for communism, racial quotas, and George McGovern, and he elevated Shanker to the prestigious AFL-CIO Executive Committee in 1973, passing over president of the AFT Dave Selden. *Credit: Walter P. Reuther Library, Wayne State University.*

FIGURE 18.   Shanker shaking hands with President Jimmy Carter, with whom Shanker battled over creation of the Department of Education, racial quotas, and bilingual education. Others pictured include (on left) former NEA president Richard Batchelder and New York State United Teachers president Thomas Hobart, in undated photo. *Credit: Walter P. Reuther Library, Wayne State University.*

FIGURE 19.   Shanker with Senator Ted Kennedy, whom Shanker supported for president against Jimmy Carter, pictured at the AFT Convention in 1980. *Credit: Walter P. Reuther Library, Wayne State University.*

FIGURE 20. Shanker, with President Ronald Reagan, at the 1983 AFT Convention. Shanker fought with Reagan over union rights, school vouchers, and civil rights, but the two men found common ground on anticommunism, racial quotas, and school discipline. *Credit: Walter P. Reuther Library, Wayne State University.*

FIGURE 21. Shanker with President George H. W. Bush, with whom Shanker worked on education standards but opposed on school vouchers, in undated photo. *Credit: Walter P. Reuther Library, Wayne State University.*

FIGURE 22. Shanker, protesting apartheid at the South African Embassy, December 1984. *Credit: Walter P. Reuther Library, Wayne State University.*

FIGURE 23. Polish Solidarity leader Lech Walesa, being given an award in 1989. Shanker was a staunch supporter of Solidarity, leading to unsubstantiated Soviet accusations that Shanker was a CIA agent. Pictured, from left to right: Shanker, AFT vice president Herb Magidson, Walesa, NYSUT president Thomas Hobart, UFT president Sandra Feldman, and New York governor Mario Cuomo. *Credit: Walter P. Reuther Library, Wayne State University.*

FIGURE 24. Shanker shaking hands with South African leader Nelson Mandela at the AFL-CIO headquarters in 1990, shortly after Mandela was released from jail. The AFT was strongly supportive of teacher unions attempting to overthrow apartheid in South Africa. AFL CIO president Lane Kirkland is pictured in background. *Credit: Walter P. Reuther Library, Wayne State University.*

FIGURE 25. Shanker with President Bill Clinton, who called Shanker a personal "mentor" on education issues. Shanker developed a closer relationship with Clinton than with any other president. *Credit: Walter P. Reuther Library, Wayne State University.*

FIGURE 26. Shanker, relaxing with family members; from left to right: son Michael, wife Eadie, daughter Jennie, son Adam, daughter-in-law, at the time, Caren, and grandson Adrian, in 1988. *Credit: Walter P. Reuther Library, Wayne State University.*

FIGURE 27. Shanker, with wife, Eadie, laughing during his sixty-fifth birthday party in 1993. *Credit: Walter P. Reuther Library, Wayne State University.*

FIGURE 28. Shanker baking bread, a favorite hobby of his along with wine making. His bread was usually a success; the wine was not. *Credit: Walter P. Reuther Library, Wayne State University.*

FIGURE 29. In 1998, Shanker was posthumously awarded the Medal of Freedom, the nation's highest civilian honor. Pictured at the ceremony, from left to right: President Bill Clinton, Albert Shanker's daughter Jennie Shanker, son Michael Shanker, sister Pearl Harris, son Carl Sabath, wife Eadie Shanker, son Adam Shanker, and Hillary Clinton. *Credit: Eadie Shanker Photo Collection.*

FIGURE 30. Albert Shanker (1928–1997). *Credit: Walter P. Reuther Library, Wayne State University.*

12

Being a Social Democrat Under Ronald Reagan

DOMESTIC POLICY

1980–1988

WITH Ronald Reagan's election, Shanker geared up to fight the administration on what he viewed as two central bulwarks of American democracy: public education and organized labor. At the same time, Shanker would find himself partially allied with Reagan on several other issues, including quotas, bilingual education, values in education, and anti-Communism, positions Shanker also believed were linked to the promotion of democracy. Many saw these alliances as contradictory in the face of the threat Reagan posed, but Shanker argued his unique version of tough liberalism was perfectly consistent and animated by a vision of social democracy—and that it was mainstream liberals and conservatives who were contradicting themselves.

Defending Public Schools

Right out of the box, President Reagan proposed a series of large tax cuts aimed at the wealthy, along with a number of domestic spending cuts, including serious cutbacks in education funding. In February 1981, Shanker joined with civil-rights groups to oppose Reagan's economic program. "Robin Hood in reverse," he and others called it. "The money is going to come from those who have the least and it's going to those who have the most." Shanker said: "The President justifies this on the sort of 'trickle down' theory that should have gone out with the Hoover Administration."[1]

For Shanker, tax cuts for the rich were anathema, mostly because they starved the government of necessary funds for education and other important programs. But Shanker had long argued that taxes were more than just a source of revenue. Just as public schools promote equal opportunity, Shanker argued, "taxes are designed to place limits on the economic advantage each citizen starts with."[2] In particular, progressive taxation was meant to blunt the political power of the wealthy in a democracy. He argued, "The American tax structure, with its heavy emphasis on the progressive income tax and on large inheritance taxes, is based on the assumption that since money brings with it political power, the amassing of huge fortunes must be counteracted in order to preserve political democracy."[3]

Reagan's spending cuts hit education particularly hard. In March 1981, when Education Secretary Terrel Bell announced a 25 percent cut in education spending for the disadvantaged and disabled and a 20 percent cut in loans and grants for students in higher education, Shanker called it "a disaster for public education."[4] The students of AFT teachers, who were mostly located in urban districts, were hit especially hard, because they relied disproportionately on federal aid.

On top of the tax cuts and spending cuts came a third problem: a proposal to give states more flexibility in how they spent federal education funds. In 1981, Reagan proposed that most federal education aid go through general "block grants" rather than through targeted programs like aid for disabled and poor children. Shanker blasted Reagan's idea, arguing that the reason the federal government first became involved in education was that states were not doing a good job of meeting special needs on their own—"the education of children who do not speak English, the education of the handicapped, and the education of poor and minority children."[5]

All these cuts to education also ultimately meant lower teacher salaries, Shanker said. Given that Reagan's justification for tax cuts was the need to create incentives for job creation, Shanker asked: "Why is Reagan so certain that economic incentive is the key to success everywhere else, but fails to see it when it comes to education?"[6]

Reagan's education cuts were devastating, Shanker said, but even worse were proposals Shanker believed would not just weaken but might kill public education altogether: tuition tax credits. In 1978, Senator Moynihan's tuition tax credit proposal came dangerously close to passing, but Shanker knew that he could count on Carter to veto the legislation. Now, with Reagan's election, Shanker faced a president who would gladly sign—and actively campaign for—the tuition tax credit proposal. In addition, several key senators opposed to tuition tax credits had been defeated in the Reagan landslide.[7]

Reagan had every reason to push hard for tuition tax credits, because the proposal united three key elements of his constituency. Economic conservatives liked efforts to privatize government programs, and many of Reagan's wealthy backers who sent their children to private school would personally benefit from tuition tax credits. Moral and religious conservatives, another key constituency, were also strong backers of aid for religious schools, which they saw as important institutions for fostering the moral awakening of children.[8] Finally, Reagan had done well with racially conservative Southern voters, some of whom wanted tuition tax credits to escape public-school desegregation orders, which were in full swing in the early 1980s.[9] But Shanker was ready for the battle. "We plan to fight like hell against it," he said.[10]

In June 1981, Shanker joined with civil-rights leaders and other education groups in a coalition to stop tuition tax credits. Shanker argued: "If I don't like the public drinking water, I can't ask you to help pay for my Perrier."[11] In testimony before Congress and in columns in the *New York Times*, Shanker argued that tuition tax credits would mean further stratification, as well-off parents used the tax credit to leave the public schools.[12]

He also hit on the issue of democratic control of schools. "There is no reason for the taxpayer to pay for schools which are not subject to control by voters through their elected representatives," he argued. "Voters don't elect private school boards or determine the curriculum of private schools or the languages of instruction or which students are accepted or rejected."[13] Under the tuition tax credit proposal, he argued, taxpayer dollars could go to "schools run by cults such as the Moonies or by political extremists such as the Nazis."[14]

In April 1982, Reagan formally outlined legislation for tuition tax credits and invoked nineteenth-century educator Horace Mann to say that education, "beyond all other devices of human origin, is a great equalizer

of the conditions of men—the balance wheel of the social machinery."
Shanker pounced on Reagan's use of Mann. "Horace Mann would have
turned over in his grave at being used in this way," Shanker said. Quoting
Columbia education historian Lawrence Cremin, Shanker noted that
Mann's commitment was to a system of inclusive public schools that was
precisely the opposite of what Reagan was proposing. Fearing that religious, political, and class conflict would tear Americans apart, Mann envisioned public schools as the key instrument for creating "a sense of
community to be shared by Americans of every background and persuasion." Mann said a system of "common schools," which would be "open to
all," nonsectarian, and educate "children of all creeds, classes and backgrounds" would promote social harmony.[15]

While others emphasized that tuition tax credits would divert public
funds to private schools, Shanker went further and homed in on the more
fundamental rationale for public schooling.[16] The issue of tuition tax
credits was not just about schools—it was about all of society, Shanker
argued. "Without public education, there would be no America as we
know it." He noted:

> Unlike other peoples and nations, we are not one or two "tribes." We
> came from all over the world and we are still coming to these shores.
> We came with different religions, different languages, different skin
> complexions, different cultures, different economic status. . . . The
> public schools, more than any other institution in our society . . .
> have brought together different groups—groups which in other societ-
> ies would always be at war with each other—and taught them to re-
> spect and work with each other. And, they have given children from
> all backgrounds a chance to make it. It's no exaggeration to say that
> the public schools helped to bring about a political, social and cultural
> miracle.

Under a system of tuition tax credits, by contrast, Shanker argued that we
might end up with separate schools for different religions, different races,
and different economic classes, very different than the public schools,
which "take all children."[17]

Shanker also dismissed the argument that private-school parents are
taxed twice—paying for their children's education as well as for the public schools for other people's children. He responded: "We all pay for pub-

lic services—even those who have no children—because they serve all of us, directly or indirectly." By analogy, he said, "we give no tax credits to those who avoid public parks and grow their own gardens or to those who believe that police protection is inadequate and employ their own bodyguards."[18]

The other major argument for tax credits—they would spur competition—was also specious, Shanker said. "The 'competition' that would be fostered between public and private education would be patently unequal since private schools observe none of the mandates placed on public schools," he said. "Children with expensive educational and behavioral problems usually never make it past the first screening in most private schools."[19]

Under the weight of the argument, and strong lobbying efforts, the Senate rejected Reagan's tuition tax credit proposal in November 1983, in a vote of fifty-nine to thirty-eight.[20]

In his second term, Reagan proposed a clever and more politically sophisticated variation on his failed tuition tax credit proposal: a proposal for school vouchers, limited to low-income students. Whereas the tuition tax credit was a very big step, vouchers for the poor could be presented as more moderate and even soften up Reagan's image of being uncaring for the poor.

In fact, Shanker had himself flirted with a related idea: vouchers for the most difficult-to-educate children. In 1981, he embraced a proposal by author and civil-rights activist Barbara Lerner, who called for private school vouchers limited to public-school children who failed minimum competency tests for three or four years in a row. He called the proposal "ingenious" and "brilliant," though he also said it was probably "naïve" to think that private schools would take in the lowest performing students.[21]

But Shanker was critical of the Reagan proposal for a six-hundred-dollar voucher for poor children. He worried that private schools would skim off the brightest poor children, leaving the others worse off. "What will be the effect of taking some of these best and brightest students out of public school?" he asked, noting those remaining in public schools might not have any "models of children from similar circumstances who have succeeded." Worse, he argued, the means-tested vouchers were likely to be "merely the nose of the camel in the tent," and would eventually lead to vouchers for all students.[22]

Shanker also questioned the premise of voucher advocates: that we should give parents and kids whatever they want. Maximizing choice, he said,

> may be the point of shopping malls. But it is not the point of education, and it is certainly not the reason the public—parents and nonparents alike—pays taxes to support education. We do so not to satisfy the individual wants of parents and students but because of the public interest in producing an educated citizenry capable of exercising the rights of liberty and being productive members of society.[23]

Reagan's voucher proposal was widely debated but made little progress in Congress.

Although President Reagan's tuition tax credit and voucher proposals failed, his presidency did result in substantial cutbacks in education funding. Overall, between 1980 and 1988, the federal share of education spending declined from 9.9 percent to 6.9 percent, a 30 percent cut.[24] In 1983, Shanker gave Reagan's education program an F+.[25]

Defending Organized Labor

If Reagan was unsuccessful in pushing tuition tax credits and school vouchers, he made far more progress attacking Shanker's other cherished institution: organized labor. Whereas Nixon and Ford had simply opposed the expansion of organized labor, Reagan actively wanted to roll back its power.[26]

Reagan's opening came early in the administration. On August 3, 1981, the nation's air traffic controllers went on strike, an act illegal under federal law. Technically, Reagan had the right to fire all the workers, but that sort of action was considered inconceivable. When 200,000 postal workers struck in 1970, Nixon brought in the National Guard to deliver the mail, but he had not sought harsh penalties against workers. In the UFT's strikes, the worst that had happened was a jail term for Shanker; no teachers were fired. But in 1981, Reagan did just that.[27] After giving the controllers forty-eight hours to reconsider, Reagan fired all 11,000 workers, impounded the strike fund, and barred strikers from returning in the future. Not until Bill Clinton's administration did blacklisted members of the union—the Professional Air Traffic Controllers' Organization (PATCO)—get to return to work.[28]

Reagan had set a devastating precedent. If the mayor of New York City had done what Reagan did, there would have been no UFT, the NEA might not have come around to collective bargaining, and teachers might have remained impotent, nationally and locally. To Shanker, Reagan's actions raised the more fundamental question: why was it illegal for public employees to strike? The notion went back to the monarchical idea that subjects should not rebel against the sovereign, Shanker said. The United States, he said, was one of the few democracies in which public employees were not allowed to strike.[29] Yes, strikes that endanger public health and safety should be curtailed. But why is shutting down a public school illegal when striking in private schools is legal? Why is a strike by private-sector airline pilots legal, but not by public-sector air controllers?[30]

But the law was what it was, and Reagan made the inconceivable conceivable. In the private sector, emboldened employers began to "permanently replace" striking workers, even though the strikes were legal, sometimes with the express purpose of crushing the union.[31] The number of strikes involving at least one thousand workers declined from 424 in 1974 to only forty-five twenty years later.[32] With the strike weapon essentially neutered, workers lost bargaining power. For Shanker, Reagan's actions were unforgivable.

Race and Ethnicity

Even as Shanker gave Reagan a failing grade on education and labor, he found himself in partial agreement with the conservative president on a number of issues—including race, values (for example, discipline and teaching right from wrong), and national security.

One area of common ground was bilingual education. Early on, the Reagan Administration rescinded Carter's proposed regulations requiring that students be taught in their native tongue. And Shanker joined William Bennett, Reagan's education secretary, in his criticism of "maintenance" programs that sought to promote ethnic pride and self-esteem rather than to ease the transition to speaking English. "I happen to think he's dead right on this one," Shanker said in October 1985.[33] Shanker said that if as a child he had taken a separate class for Yiddish speakers, he probably would not have learned English as well as he did.[34] Shanker also agreed with Bennett's democracy argument in favor of learning English: "Government by consent means government by discussion, by debate, by discourse, by argument. Such a common enterprise requires a common language."[35]

Shanker also shared broad common ground with Reagan on opposition to racial preferences. While the AFT was not a direct party in the *DeFunis*, *Bakke*, and *Weber* cases, now, during the Reagan administration, a major case involving the AFT came before the courts. The case— what one Reagan Justice Department official said might become "the next *Bakke*"—actually involved something much more explosive than graduate school admission or even hiring and promotion: could an employee be laid off based on race? The case arose in Boston, where the School Committee was found guilty of hiring discrimination against blacks. As part of Judge Arthur Garrity's desegregation order, he said one black teacher must be hired for every one white teacher until the percentage of black teachers rose from 5 percent to 20 percent—the city's overall black population. By 1981, blacks had reached 19 percent of the teaching population in Boston when the board ordered layoffs. The contract with the union called for layoffs based on seniority, but if Boston employed the last-hired, first-fired protocol, doing so would wipe out the gains made by blacks and revert to an 8 percent black teaching force, the board said.[36]

In 1981, the Boston school board announced it would not lay off any black teachers and instead would lay off 1,100 more senior white teachers. The AFT local in Boston sued, but a lower court judge sided with the city. In February 1982, the First Circuit Court of Appeals affirmed the decision.[37]

In June, 1982, Shanker announced that the AFT would support an appeal in the case to the U.S. Supreme Court. Shanker said "The national AFT has decided to become involved in this case because we believe that colorblind, race-neutral seniority systems are perhaps the most important safeguard won by the American labor movement in its 100 years of struggle for job equality for all Americans." Shanker said that if the lower court decision were upheld, "it will be the first time in U.S. history that a federal court, acting in the name of the Constitution, has ruled that people must lose their jobs on the basis of race." The AFT argued that white teachers did not perpetrate the discrimination and should not have to pay for it. Teachers with up to eighteen years of experience were being laid off even though there was no contention that the newly hired black teachers had themselves been discriminated against. Shanker noted that "on the very day the layoff notices went out, the school board . . . announced a recruitment drive for new black teachers."[38]

From the perspective of Boston's schoolchildren, Shanker said, while it is educationally beneficial for all children to see black teachers in the classroom, teacher experience is also important. And the larger picture was important as well. "Every time we hire by race, black or white, or fire by race, black or white, we surrender a little piece of what we're all about," he wrote.[39]

Shanker and the AFT argued that seniority was worth preserving. Seniority "has proven to be the most effective mechanism for protecting workers—regardless of race, religion, sex or age—against capricious and arbitrary actions of their employers," the union said. Seniority prevented racist employers from firing blacks first. And it also protected workers "from the whims and prejudices of their employers" not related to race. Finally, seniority was important as a union principle because it "prevents divisiveness among working people by distributing scarcity in a way that is objectively fair and therefore perceived to be fair. The courts have termed seniority a vested right."[40]

Not everyone within the AFT was happy with Shanker's position, and in July 1982, at the AFT convention in New York, members of the Black Caucus challenged the AFT's role in the Boston case. On the convention floor, teachers from Boston pleaded their case. One teacher, Tom Gosnell, argued, "the layoffs are now affecting teachers hired almost as long ago as 1967, people approaching the age of 40." By contrast, "the individuals retaining their jobs were not even in college when Judge Garrity issued his original order." Shanker argued in a news conference called before the debate that it was in the interests of all members to protect seniority. "Once you play with seniority, blacks now protected can never be sure that 15 years from now their jobs will be secure if there is then a large population of Mexicans or some other group in Boston." The Black Caucus's resolution was defeated by a show of hands.[41] The NEA meanwhile, took the opposite side in the case, and argued that less senior minority teachers should be retained. In the end, the Supreme Court decided not to take the case.[42]

The issue did not go away, however, and a few years later, the AFT, NEA, the Reagan Administration, and others were back in court, contesting the validity of a plan in Jackson, Mississippi, in which less senior white teachers were laid off while minority teachers were retained. The case, *Wygant v. Jackson Board of Education*, involved the validity of the race-based layoffs as part of an agreement negotiated between the Board of Education and the NEA-affiliated Jackson Education Association, which had the goal of having "at least the same percentage of minority representation on each individual staff as is represented by the student population of the Jackson Public Schools."

The AFT objected to the proposal, in part because it was geared toward the percentage of minority students (not the percentage of eligible teachers in the pool). The AFT also noted that the Jackson plan was based not on remedying unlawful employment discrimination but on the theory that black teachers provided good role models for students. The problem with the idea that black students need black teachers, the AFT noted, is that "the logical extension of the race-alike role model concept is segregation." Indeed, "carried to its end," the AFT said, the theory "would justify the resegregation of American public schools, where students may be properly taught only by teachers of their own race. Or gender. Or religion. Or ethnic group."[43] On June 24, 1985, the AFT submitted an *amicus* brief to the U.S. Supreme Court opposing the NEA layoff plan and supporting the Reagan Administration's position.[44] The NEA filed a brief on behalf of the Jackson Board of Education.[45]

In May, 1986, a five-to-four Supreme Court struck down the race-based layoffs. It expressed concern, among other things, that the "role model" rationale could justify race-based decision making long beyond the limits of a remedial affirmative-action program. And the justices were concerned about the burden placed on innocent white teachers. "Denial of a future employment is not as intrusive as loss of an existing job," the court said.[46]

During Reagan's presidency, Shanker also found himself in agreement with the administration's attempt to appoint three pro–civil rights but anti-quota Democrats to the U.S. Civil Rights Commission and to appoint Linda Chavez, from the AFT staff, to be the commission's executive director. The move to nominate three Democrats, lawyer and former Brandeis president Morris Abram, Hoover Institution fellow John H. Bunzel, and Catholic University law professor Robert A. Destro, as commissioners drew the ire of civil-rights groups, in part because the nominees opposed racial preferences and in part because Reagan fired three sitting Democratic commissioners to create the vacancies.[47]

Shanker argued that the nominees were "Democrats of the JFK–Hubert Humphrey stripe with strong pro–civil rights credentials" and were, like most Americans, opposed to racial quotas.[48] Reagan had made his share of mistakes on civil rights, Shanker said, but in the nominations of Chavez, Bunzel, Destro, and Abram, Reagan had proposed "four liberal Democrats with strong civil rights commitments." Chavez worked for the AFT, Bunzel was a Kennedy and Humphrey supporter, and Abram had been president of the United Negro College Fund. Shanker asked: "Was the Democratic Party really going to make support for racial quotas a litmus test?" and "do Democrats really want to win in 1984?"[49]

Appearing on Meet the Press in May 1983, Shanker described his position on the nominees—who were opposed to discrimination and opposed to quotas—as "what we used to call the liberal stand. It used to be called taking ability into account and being fair to all people, and not discriminating against people or for people on the basis of race. That's also the Constitution, as I read it," he said.[50]

In late July 1983, Shanker was the lead witness before the Senate Judiciary Committee in favor of the appointments. Shanker distanced himself from Reagan, saying he objected to most of the administration's civil-rights policies and would "like to see this administration replaced in 18 months." In particular, Shanker criticized Reagan's move to provide tax-exempt status to Bob Jones University, which forbade interracial dating. But Shanker said that despite his many criticisms of Reagan's civil-rights record, "if a President does 200 bad things, we oppose him on the 200 bad things, and if he occasionally does something right, we ought to support him on that one."[51]

Moreover, politically, it made no sense to oppose the nominees and their positions on quotas. "I wish that the Democrats would make the issue in the next election Bob Jones University, and not quotas," he argued. Shanker told committee member Senator Joseph Biden: "What is being done here to prevent these appointments will do more to reelect this Administration than almost anything else that has happened."[52]

Shanker grew increasingly frustrated and isolated. On the one hand, Democrats seemed wedded to interest-group politics that required them to support racial preferences. On the other hand, the Reagan Administration stood firm against quotas but had an otherwise unsavory racial agenda, showing a willingness to court outright bigots.[53] Shanker was appalled by the racist jokes in the Reagan White House and Budget Department, where middle managers called Arabs "sand niggers" and Martin Luther King Jr. "Martin Lucifer Coon."[54]

Shanker was also deeply troubled by Reagan's lack of a race-neutral program to overcome the devastating effects of past segregation and discrimination. In testimony before the Civil Rights Commission, Shanker said: "The real problem is that programs of outreach, of training, of education are being ripped to pieces by this Administration."[55] Shanker favored what he called "affirmative action without quotas."[56] He fought hard for the paraprofessional career-ladder program in New York City and supported the A. Philip Randolph Institute's Recruitment and Training Program, which helped blacks get trained to compete in the building-trades industry. Reagan, by contrast, terminated federal support for the Recruitment and Training Program and also cut education aid for the poor.[57] While Shanker applauded Reagan's efforts to end quotas, he said "calling a halt to affirmative action which seeks to help the disadvantaged develop their potential as individuals would be a disaster." Although quotas were unfair and divisive, he said: "Funding for programs that help to close the gap created by years of poverty and discrimination are absolutely essential."[58]

Likewise, while Shanker agreed with Reagan that certain forms of perpetual bilingual education were divisive, he opposed Reagan's decision in 1981 to reverse the Carter Administration's position on the need to educate the children of illegal immigrants. The Carter Administration argued in court that a Texas law withholding education to the children of illegal aliens was unconstitutional, but as a case made its way up to the U.S. Supreme Court, the Reagan Justice Department changed its position to neutrality. Whatever one thinks of the parents' illegal actions, Shanker said, "there is no argument for failing to educate the children who are here."[59] If one reason to oppose extreme forms of bilingual education was the need to assimilate immigrants, how could the Reagan administration possibly justify a program that would create a "subclass of illiterates within our boundaries?"[60]

Shanker's differences with Reagan on racial and ethnic issues were as fundamental, then, as his differences with liberal supporters of quotas and bilingual nationalism. Shanker believed that there was a lot of space between racial preferences on the left and bigotry on the right—morally and politically—and yet among the leadership class, Shanker's position was a lonely one.

In August 1987, toward the end of the Reagan Administration, the pro–civil rights, anti-quota space became a little lonelier when Shanker's good friend and colleague, Bayard Rustin, died. King had been cut down in the 1960s, Randolph had died in the 1970s, and now, at the tail end of the 1980s, Rustin was gone.

In a column, Shanker wrote that Rustin was "the last of the great giants . . . who brought us a grand, humane social vision and a dream of an integrated, democratic nation." Rustin "believed in the necessity of co-alition politics," Shanker wrote, and was—the ultimate compliment—"a true democrat in a world of pretenders." Shanker said: "What needs to be remembered above all is the line Bayard pursued all along. As C. Vann Woodward said, it 'is the line of civil rights, equality, and integration, and the strategy of the ballot, the union card, and coalition politics.'"[61]

Rustin had been true to this vision to the very end. In a March 1987 article in *The New Republic*, Rustin, reflecting on Martin Luther King, wrote: "Any preferential approach postulated on racial, ethnic, religious, or sexual lines will only disrupt a multicultural society and lead to backlash. However, special treatment can be provided to those who have been exploited or denied opportunities if solutions are predicated on class lines, precisely because all religious, ethnic, and racial groups have a depressed class who would benefit." He concluded: "Today's struggle must be a non-racial program for economic justice that would facilitate the formation of coalitions based on mutual need."[62]

The evidence suggested, however, that neither side was listening. One party represented the interests of whites, the other party the interests of minorities, and neither seemed fully committed to the principles that had inspired Rustin and continued to inspire Albert Shanker.

The Values Debate

Ronald Reagan also made inroads with white working-class "radical center" Reagan Democrats on so-called values issues, which in the education realm involved a concern for discipline and the need to teach right from wrong. Shanker believed liberals needed to move to the center on those issues, though he thought Reagan and groups like the Moral Majority were flat wrong in endorsing practices like compulsory school prayer and the teaching of creationism.

Shanker had long been an advocate of tougher school discipline policies, going back to the 1967 New York City teachers' strike, and the need to remove chronically disruptive students was a constant theme in his "Where We Stand" column and in testimony before government agencies.[63] As a student and as a young teacher, Shanker had seen the effect of disruptive students on the learning process, and he continually called for greater use of high-quality alternative school settings for such students.[64]

In the Reagan administration, Shanker found an ally on the discipline issue. In February 1984, Reagan spoke to the National Association of Secondary School Principals about restoring "good old-fashioned discipline." The NEA president, Mary Futrell, reacted negatively. "Our public schools today are not blackboard jungles," she said. "We can't solve discipline problems by throwing kids out on the streets." By contrast, Shanker said, "This is not a liberal or conservative issue. Nobody likes to have their children beat up or hurt."[65]

Shanker also agreed with Reagan on the need to teach students right from wrong, a view unfashionable with some liberals who were suspicious of "imposing values." In fact, not long after creating a new quarterly publication called *American Educator*, a journal of ideas, the editor Shanker appointed, Linda Chavez, began running articles opposing the creeping relativism of the 1970s. The publication included pieces by William Bennett, then a little-known educator, calling for the teaching of virtues to children.[66] *American Educator* urged teachers to teach universal values and to avoid "moral relativism."[67] Shanker said he detected a "yearning" for values, and the AFT prepared curriculum guides on five themes: honesty, loyalty, responsibility, compassion, and courage.[68]

At the 1984 AFT convention, Shanker invited Bennett, who was by then heading Reagan's National Endowment for Humanities, to speak.[69] And Shanker announced that he planned to reach out to evangelical Christian groups. "If we let Ronald Reagan be the only one talking to them they will say, 'He is the only one who cares about us.' We can get just as many of these groups to support public education as we can get businessmen to do it," he said.[70]

In August 1985, Shanker spoke to the Christian Congress for Excellence in Public Education in Kansas City and argued that the AFT had "many things in common" with evangelical Christians. "We agree with you and the majority of the American people on school discipline, high educational standards, testing of students and teachers, and the teaching of basic values," Shanker argued. "The AFT stands with the American people in the belief that it is the job of our schools to teach our children right from wrong, honesty from dishonesty, loyalty from disloyalty." AFT staffer Mark Chaykin recalls that the message from the New York Jew about traditional values and discipline and how a good education could help people rise out of poverty was very well received. "They ate it up."[71]

At the same time, Shanker frequently disagreed with Reagan and Jerry Falwell's Moral Majority, which he said was "a small organization, not the majority."[72] Shanker never supported organized prayer in public schools as Reagan did, and noted that "voluntary" prayer in public school happens all the time, "especially before a tough test."[73] Part of the problem was the effect on religious minorities. Shanker said he remembered starting school saying the Lord's Prayer. "This was hard for many of us."[74] And part of the rationale for opposing prayer in schools was that it undercut social unity. Public schools were meant to teach people what it means to be an American and what unites us, and the use of particular religious prayers undermined that goal. Likewise, Shanker opposed creationism, which he said "has no place in the science curriculum."[75] Shanker also opposed "gay bashing" by the religious right.[76]

Still Shanker rejected politically correct efforts to rid religion from the curriculum altogether, and he said that while public schools should not teach a particular religion, they should teach about religion in history class. He ridiculed one popular textbook in the 1980s that defined the Pilgrims as "people who made long trips" and Christmas as a "warm time for special foods."[77]

Shanker's disdain for relativism was particularly strong when it came to teaching about democracy. In the past, Shanker said, the teaching of absolutes went too far, but he worried that the old absolutism was being replaced with a view that "there is nothing correct, nothing better, nothing worse." Students were being taught, for example, that the Soviet system of freedom was not worse, it was just "different." Shanker said, "the pendulum has swung too far."[78]

As he thought about the problem, Shanker was deeply influenced by an article in the July 1984 issue of *Commentary* by Sidney Hook entitled "Education in Defense of a Free Society." In the piece, Hook proposed a program of study in schools that would not just teach the intellectual skills necessary to make choices in a democracy but would also instill loyalty to the process of self-government "by learning its history, celebrating its heroes, and noting its achievements."[79]

Hook's argument, which was brought to Shanker's attention by staffer Sally Muravchik, had a great influence on Shanker.[80] Shanker believed one had to be serious about educating students about the importance of democracy in each generation; it could not be taken for granted. Shanker contacted Hook, then eighty years old, and convinced him to co-chair a meeting in New York City to plot a strategy with educators Diane Ravitch and Chester Finn of the Educational Excellence Network and Leonard Sussman of Freedom House.

Shanker had long admired Hook, a democratic Socialist who hated Communism, and he had begun reading Hook at an early age. The two men shared a reverence for John Dewey and both studied philosophy at Columbia.[81] As the younger Shanker rose to power and began writing his column in the New York Times, Hook took notice of him and congratulated him on his writing.[82] Hook and Shanker loved being together at the meeting. "I remember both of them just really enjoyed each other," Ruth Wattenberg says. "For Al, Hook was just such an intellectual icon. And for Hook, Al was this guy who was really doing things" and could translate ideas into action.[83]

The group decided to sponsor a project on "Education for Democracy." As a first step, the three groups decided to seek a diverse collection of leaders to sign onto a statement suggesting that schools should explicitly teach that democracy is "the worthiest form of government ever conceived" and move away from relativist and "values-free" education. The document, which criticized a teaching guide on human rights that gave equal footing to the right to take vacations as the freedom of speech and the right to vote, contended: "It is absurd to argue that the state, or its schools, cannot be concerned with citizens' ability to tell right from wrong . . ."[84]

Ravitch said: "The idea is that history should be taught with objectivity, but not with neutrality." While some might reject the statement as "ethnocentric," Shanker said: "We believe that values of freedom and democracy . . . are preferable to their alternatives. And we believe the curriculum should reflect this."[85] The Education for Democracy statement received wide notice, with two hundred articles appearing in the press.[86]

The groups commissioned University of Massachusetts historian Paul Gagnon to review five major textbooks in world history. The report, released in 1987, found that the texts were bland and so fearful of not indoctrinating students that they neglected the development of democratic institutions. None of the textbooks analyzed gave more than passing mention to Plato and Aristotle. And Gagnon concluded that "the basic ideas of Judaism and Christianity, which inform every debate over right and wrong and the place of the individual in society, are all but ignored in some of these texts and only feebly suggested in the rest." There was much more discussion about non-Western religions, and non-Western societies were presented in a noncritical way as if "human failings were not common to all mankind." The report called for revising curricula and textbooks to focus on the struggle for democratic ideals.[87]

Education for Democracy was on one level an example of Shanker's willingness to work with conservatives when there was common ground. The project received funding from Reagan's Department of Education.[88] And the project's broad political spectrum of sponsors included conservative supporters of private-school vouchers. But to Shanker's way of thinking, the project underlined the importance of and rationale for public schools. By asserting that public schools could and should teach values, teach right from wrong, and reject relativism, the document undercut one of the right's arguments for vouchers: that only private (particularly religious) schools were capable of teaching moral values.[89] At the same time, by emphasizing that schools are about teaching democracy—not just building skills—the project underscored the historic rationale for a system of public education: that public schools, which took all comers and charged no fees, were uniquely positioned to "Americanize" students and to teach them the meaning of democracy. Fundamentally, Shanker argued, it was public education that could best reflect American "values," which were shared by all and were by no means the exclusive province of the right wing.

During the Reagan years, Albert Shanker found himself in the strange position of being at war with the administration on many issues—tax cuts for the wealthy, education spending, tuition tax credits, the PATCO strike, school vouchers, prayer in school, and cuts to broad affirmative-action programs like Bayard Rustin's Recruitment and Training Program—but also sharing important areas of agreement, on racial quotas, separatist bilingual education, school discipline, and moral relativism. Some liberals found any agreement with Reagan inconsistent, but Shanker had an answer to that complaint, rooted in a well-thought-out social democratic ideology. That ideology will become clearer once we examine, in the next chapter, Reagan and Shanker on foreign policy.

13

Being a Social Democrat
Under Ronald Reagan

FOREIGN POLICY

1980–1988

T
o many observers who saw Albert Shanker and Ronald Reagan
fight tooth and nail on issues including school vouchers and organized labor, it was striking—even bizarre—that Shanker often
saw eye to eye with President Reagan on international affairs. Indeed, it
was questionable to some that the head of a teachers' union would even
take positions on foreign policy. But to Shanker, the seeming contradic-
tions and the involvement in international issues were all explained by a
coherent and cogent social democratic vision that placed a premium on
the value of democracy.

Shanker's Involvement in Foreign Affairs

Shanker had long been interested in international affairs, and during
the 1970s he had joined the board of the International Rescue Committee and traveled abroad to meet with union leaders in Japan, Kenya,
Israel, and Thailand. In the 1980s, during the presidencies of Ronald
Reagan and George H. W. Bush, Shanker became increasingly engaged
in foreign-policy issues, primarily through three institutions: the AFL-

CIO, the International Federation of Free Teachers Unions (IFFTU), and the AFT.

Shanker and George Meany had been close allies on international affairs, sharing strong anti-Communist views. In 1979, Lane Kirkland was elected as Meany's successor and continued in Meany's hard-line mode. Kirkland and Shanker shared a passion in fighting Communists, and Kirkland, unlike Meany, was a fellow intellectual.[1] They were "intellectual companions," Tom Donahue recalls.[2] Shanker became, says critic Paul Buhle, Kirkland's "foremost ally" on foreign affairs.[3]

Beyond their shared outlook, Shanker was particularly valuable to Kirkland for two reasons. For one thing, Shanker was an effective communicator who understood the importance of symbols and taught unionists about foreign affairs in plain and simple language.[4] He would send young labor leaders to Germany, says the AFT's David Dorn. "There was never a better educational tool than the Berlin Wall."[5] For another, Shanker was able to make intelligent arguments against Communism that went beyond the America-right-or-wrong attitude of some other unions. The AFT was not filled with red-baiting anti-Communists, as were the hardhats. "We were intellectual anti-Communists," George Altomare argues, and therefore more effective.[6] During the 1980s, Kirkland recognized Shanker's importance on foreign affairs within the AFL-CIO by asking him to chair the AFL-CIO's International Affairs Committee.

In 1981, Shanker gained a second major platform from which to engage in foreign affairs: the presidency of the International Federation of Free Teachers Unions (IFFTU), the teachers' division of the International Confederation of Free Trade Unions (ICFTU), an organization set up after World War II by the AFL-CIO to compete with the Communist-dominated World Federation of Trade Unions (WFTU).[7] In addition to the Communist teachers' group, IFFTU competed with the World Confederation of Organizations of the Teaching Profession (WCOTP), which was controlled by its largest affiliate, the NEA, and was not part of a larger labor international. WCOTP took in nonunion education groups and was neutral on the cold war, welcoming Communist and non-Communist unions.

IFFTU, in sum, stood for free democratic organizations against the Communist-dominated front unions on the one hand, and for trade unionism against the nonunion WCOTP on the other.[8] As president of IFFTU, Shanker argued that teachers' organizations ought to be part of the trade-union movement and that they ought to support democracy (and nondemocratic teachers' trade unions should not be part of IFFTU).[9]

On the issue of trade unionism, Shanker's argument largely carried the day, says Fred van Leeuwen, the secretary general of IFFTU and its successor, Education International.[10] Over time, teachers' organizations, which overwhelmingly were outside of the labor movement in the early days, became a part of organized labor throughout the world. On the issue of democracy, Shanker made sure that the IFFTU helped finance and strengthen free education unions in places such as Chile, South Africa, and Poland, and he banned nondemocratic, state-sponsored trade unions from the organization, even though accepting them would have meant more dues for the organization.[11]

Shanker strengthened his third platform—the AFT itself—when in 1981 he created an International Affairs Department and hired David Dorn to head it. Over time, he nourished and fed the department to make it the leading international affairs unit among American unions.[12] While the NEA generally had departments two to three times the size of the AFT's, AFT's International Affairs Department grew to be three times the size of the NEA's.[13]

Initially, there was substantial opposition to Shanker's push to get the AFT heavily involved in international issues. Union officials in AFT's predominantly urban districts were busy fighting for greater resources in turbulent districts and had little interest in getting involved in foreign affairs.[14] Some asked, "why were we overseas dealing with international education when we had all these problems over here?"[15] In the beginning, many within the union considered AFT's international work "Al's hobby."[16] When Shanker decided to bring Dorn to the AFT in 1981 to head up an international affairs division, he was not sure whether the Executive Council would support it.[17] How do you explain to a teacher in Ohio why they should care about teachers in Poland or El Salvador or Chile? But Shanker sought to educate union leaders and delegates about the importance of international affairs through a steady stream of speakers and debates at conventions and Executive Council meetings. Shanker argued that teachers' unions had special reasons to be involved, both self-interested and humanitarian.

It was in the interests of American teachers to promote teacher unionism abroad because what happened overseas reverberated at home, he said. Countries with weak teachers' unions, for example, were more likely to adopt school-voucher plans, which would then be used to push for similar plans in the United States.[18] But even more powerful was the civic argument for teacher involvement abroad.[19] Teachers' unions, Shanker argued, were uniquely positioned to promote democracy abroad. As a part of organized labor, teachers' unions are key political actors in societies seeking to democratize, Shanker said. As mass organizations that train people to vote and help create a strong middle class, they are crucial agitators for democracy.[20]

Shanker knew the heroic role that trade unions had played after World War II—that promoting trade unionism and democracy abroad was not an exercise in tilting at windmills. After World War II, the Soviet Communists argued that they were the wave of the future. Much of Europe was in chaos, and trade unions had been destroyed by Hitler in Germany. Stalin's plan was to control the democracies of Western Europe and Japan through puppet labor unions, and he began to make some significant headway in places like Italy, France, and Germany.[21] The AFL-CIO's Jay Lovestone and Irving Brown were instrumental in setting up free trade unions in Western Europe to counter the Communist unions.[22] When Communist workers tried to thwart President Truman's Marshall Plan by blocking the delivery of goods, the AFL-CIO worked with free local unions to ensure the aid was unloaded.[23] Shanker, who came to know Brown well, wanted the AFT to continue in that proud tradition, and Brown saw Shanker as a key ally.[24]

Moreover, among unionized occupations, teachers had an especially important role to play, Shanker argued. Unlike, say, steelworkers, teachers mold young minds and are therefore positioned to challenge the orthodoxies of dictatorships. Intimately involved in any nation's future, said Shanker, "teachers are on democracy's front lines."[25] As a highly educated group, teachers are often an important source of dissent in totalitarian societies. And from a strategic standpoint, teachers are spread across the country, unlike, say, dockworkers, who are concentrated in certain regions.[26] Democracy's opponents understood the strategic value of teachers' unions and targeted them for infiltration.[27]

Through the AFL-CIO, the IFFTU, and the AFT, Shanker actively engaged in foreign affairs in the 1980s, supporting elements of Reagan's program—the defense buildup, the National Endowment for Democracy, and supporting anti-Communist groups in Central America. Shanker was also active in promoting democracy where Reagan was not: the Philippines, South Africa, and Chile. But first came the dramatic developments in Poland, where if anything, Shanker was more hard-line than Ronald Reagan.

Poland

Dramatic change in Poland began in August 1980, late in the Carter Administration, when workers in the Lenin Shipyard in Gdansk struck against higher food prices, but also against Communism itself.[28] In a delicious irony, it was precisely the opposite of what Marx had predicted, and put the lie to the claim that Communists were the champions of the working people. Shanker wrote: "According to Marxist theory, workers are supposed to revolt against their oppressors in capitalist countries, but in Poland we have the very first revolution in the world conducted by the working class, directed not against a capitalist system—but against a communist dictatorship which claims to be a 'workers' state."[29] The other aspect of the Polish uprising that was so encouraging was the number of people involved. Individual dissidents and intellectuals in the Soviet Union could be exiled or jailed. It was difficult to imprison an entire working class.[30]

The foreign-policy establishment, including Ed Muskie, Carter's secretary of state, said the West should not aid the Polish union, Solidarity, because it would give the Soviets a pretext to invade Poland.[31] Shanker disagreed, and in a column strongly argued that the Polish struggle should not be viewed as just an internal affair, since repression of the union would violate the Declaration of Human Rights, Convention 87 of the International Labor Organization, and the Helsinki agreements.[32]

Shanker urged an active role for American unions in supporting Poland's Solidarity movement, and in September 1981, Solidarity's managing director of press and information, Zygmunt Przetakiewicz, set up an American office at the UFT headquarters in New York City.[33]

The Soviets were furious with Shanker, and Radio Moscow accused him of being a stooge of the Central Intelligence Agency. Moscow Radio said the Solidarity press operation was being run by the CIA and "Albert Shanker, president of the United Federation of Teachers, funnels agency money to it." The report further charged: "A CIA agent, Albert Shanker is responsible for materiel supplies. He uses the cover of leader of the teachers labor federation. This organization annually receives $100,000 from

the CIA for international contacts and activities to stimulate the formation of so-called free trade unions in other countries."[34]

Communists had long alleged that Shanker was connected with the
CIA. In 1978, Communist George Schmidt published an eighty-one-page
pamphlet entitled *The American Federation of Teachers and the CIA*, which
charged that the UFT "had served as a base for CIA-related labor activities" and that "direct links between the 430,000 member American Federation of Teachers (AFT) and the United States Central Intelligence Agency
(CIA) have been forged and strengthened since the election of New York's
Albert Shanker as AFT national president in 1974."[35]

The charge was not ridiculous on its face. Over the years, the CIA had
provided funds to the AFL-CIO, the NEA, AFSCME, and groups like the
Congress for Cultural Freedom, as part of the fight against Communism.[36] But the CIA link to labor was for the most part severed in the late
1960s, when the U.S. government began overtly providing funds to labor
to fight Communism through the Agency for International Development
(AID).[37]

Shanker vehemently denied the accusation that the CIA was financing
him. "These charges are outrageous and untrue," he said. "Anybody who
believes that I am a CIA agent can also believe in the tooth fairy," Shanker
added. "We haven't received a penny" from the CIA, Shanker contended.
The AFT did receive money from the U.S. Agency for International Development, Shanker acknowledged, but the funds went to help teachers'
unions in third-world countries.[38]

Shanker's associates—David Dorn and Eugenia Kemble—say the AFT
never took CIA money, in part because it would discredit AFT anti-
Communist efforts, confirming the charges of the critics.[39] Moreover, the
critics who allege a CIA-Shanker connection—George Schmidt, Paul
Buhle, and William Blum—offer no concrete evidence to back up the
charges.[40]

The CIA charge, Shanker argued, stemmed from the embarrassment
of having the Polish union revolt against a workers' paradise. Free trade
unions were the mortal enemy of Communism, Shanker noted, because
they could not be dismissed as right-wing corporations and "more than
any other free institution, threaten Communist claims to legitimacy."[41]

In December 1981, Polish authorities had had enough of Solidarity. Solidarity's leader, Lech Walesa, and thousands of others were arrested and
jailed. Martial law was declared and Solidarity was banned. With Reagan
now president, anti-Communists hoped for a stronger response than

from Carter, but they were disappointed. Reagan was a passionate anti-Communist, but he was also cautious, Shanker believed, because of his ties to the banking community, which worried that unrest in Poland would lead to default of outstanding bank loans.[42] Thomas Theobold, the chief of Citibank, remarked after the declaration of martial law: "Who knows what political system works best? All we ask is: Can they pay the bills?"[43]

In a column, Shanker lashed out at Reagan for being soft. "There was no expression of outrage at events in Poland, no demand for the release of Lech Walesa and thousands of others imprisoned." Shanker argued that the military crackdown in Poland was "clearly one of the historic moments of the Twentieth Century. Many voted for a President they thought would be tough. So far, all they have heard is tough talk during an election campaign. But when it really counts, we get silence, then mushiness and evasion."[44]

In the next week's column, Shanker again pounded away on Poland. "Under the eyes of the people of the world, freedom is being crushed in Poland; Solidarity, the national free labor union, destroyed," he wrote. "So far, the United States has done little more than express sympathy and threaten to take diplomatic and economic action unless martial law is eased—not ended, but eased," he said. "It is a weak position." Shanker outlined five key demands put forth by the International Confederation of Free Trade Unions:

1. Free Lech Walesa and all others imprisoned under the martial-law decree.
2. Abolish martial law.
3. Resume negotiations among the government, Solidarity and the Catholic Church.
4. Set up procedures to guarantee that aid sent to Poland goes directly to those who really need it.
5. Recognize that any help to Poland by government or banking sources is contingent on meeting these trade-union demands.

Shanker further argued: "Instead of merely denying new loans to Poland, we should call in those already in place, which are now due."[45] To Shanker, the crackdown on Solidarity made clear what he had been trying to communicate to fellow liberals for years: that anti-Communism was not a "conservative" cause—it was humanitarian and, indeed, pro-labor and pro-worker.

Following the Communist crackdown on Solidarity, many people assumed that Walesa's rebellion would go the way of earlier quashed revolts in other countries. But the American labor movement continued to support Solidarity, and the UFT was among the first to provide money.[46]

Solidarity needed many things, including funds for imprisoned families, printing materials for an underground press, and money to support strikes.[47] The AFT helped Polish unionists with their underground newspapers, smuggling in items including copiers and fax machines.[48] Dorn recalls: "The only way we knew Solidarnosc received the funds we sent them was that they would print 'Thanks, Al' in the middle of one of their newspaper stories."[49]

In the late 1980s, Shanker and other AFT members traveled to Poland and met with human-rights activists and labor leaders. Plainclothes agents monitored the discussion.[50] Sandra Feldman recalled: "There were risks because we were clearly not friends of theirs. We could have been picked up . . . maybe they would have thrown us in jail for a while. Who knows?"[51]

After nine long years of struggle, Solidarity wore down the opposition and in a stunning turn of events came to power following a defeat of the Communists in democratic elections.[52] In November 1989, Lech Walesa appeared at the AFL-CIO convention, received fifteen minutes of sustained cheering, and thanked the unionists for their strong support.[53] The Solidarity experience, Shanker said, was an important reminder that unions not only provide better economic conditions, but they also provide a voice that can criticize both the boss and the government.[54]

If Solidarity should have underlined for liberals that anti-Communism was a pro-worker stand, Shanker argued that the experience should make clear to conservatives that unions were not just economic instruments—they were civic associations. As critical mediating institutions that stood between the government and the individual, unions allowed people to organize as a counter to the power of government and needed to be nourished in the battles for democracy.

Defense Spending

Shanker's hard line on Communists also led him to support Ronald Reagan's defense buildup in the 1980s. Many liberals opposed the spending, in part because they thought that the Soviet threat was overblown and in part because they thought defense spending would squeeze out spending on social programs. In December 1982, in a speech to the Social Democrats USA, Shanker noted that every year, the AFT debated a transfer amendment, proposing that defense cuts pay for increases in food stamps and other social programs. Shanker's response was that "you won't have very much education if you don't have a free country."[55]

In October 1984, Shanker argued that the country needed guns and butter. "Our position was that our country need not choose between the two—that we can do both. Our Constitution says that we shall 'provide for the common defense' and 'promote the general welfare'—not either/ or." But Shanker differed from Reagan in saying the programs should be paid for by everyone, including the wealthiest, who were receiving large tax breaks from Reagan.[56]

The National Endowment for Democracy

Shanker was also very supportive of Reagan's first-term initiative to create a National Endowment for Democracy (NED). In June 1982, Reagan, in what became known as the Westminster Address, delivered a speech to the British Parliament in which he said the United States must help other nations "foster the infrastructure of democracy—the system of a free press, unions, political parties, universities—which allow a people to choose their own way."[57] He proposed a federally funded group that would work through four institutions—the Democratic and Republican parties, the AFL-CIO, and the Chamber of Commerce—to develop democratic counterparts internationally.[58]

While many liberal Democrats were skeptical of the endeavor, the AFL-CIO and particularly the AFT lobbied hard to support legislation creating the NED, which passed in 1983.[59] The NED fit with Shanker's belief that freedom and democracy were universal yearnings and that for the United States to promote them was neither ethnocentric or elitist.[60] Kirkland and Shanker were appointed as the two labor representatives on the fifteen-member board.[61] Carl Gershman, a longtime friend and colleague of Shanker's, was named executive director of the NED.

Gershman, a former aid to Bayard Rustin at the Randolph Institute, got to know Shanker when the Institute rented space from the UFT, and in fact helped Shanker write a few of his "Where We Stand" columns.[62]

Gershman went on to serve as president of the Social Democrats USA (1974–1980), as a resident scholar at Freedom House, and then as senior counselor to Jeanne Kirkpatrick at the United Nations.[63] Some noted the irony that a conservative Republican had named a Socialist to head his new democracy program, but careful students of SDUSA and labor understood the strong overlap on issues of totalitarianism. Another Social Democrat (and former AFT staffer), Eugenia Kemble, was named by the AFL-CIO to head up the labor recipient of NED funds, the Free Trade Union Institute (FTUI).[64]

With Shanker's fingerprints all over the NED, he was distressed when some grants, including one for $20,000 to a presidential candidate in Panama and another to a right-wing French organization, raised serious questions about NED's legitimacy.[65] In large measure because of the Panamanian grant, the House of Representatives voted in May 1984 by 226 to 173 to deny the endowment's appropriation for the 1985 fiscal year.[66] After the NED lost the vote, says Gershman, "it looked for a while like we might not survive."[67] In June 1984, Shanker wrote a column urging the Senate to rescue the fledgling NED, and with the help of many others it did.[68]

Central America

If Shanker's support for the National Endowment for Democracy was mildly controversial among liberals, far more troubling for them was his sympathy for elements of Reagan's Central American policy. Nicaragua was the center of the debate. Shanker was highly critical of the way Nicaragua's Sandinista government was moving to crush free trade unions and setting up government-sponsored unions in their place. Shanker complained that the pro-democratic forces who helped the Sandinistas overthrow the dictator Anastasio Somoza were in turn jailed by the Sandinistas.[69] It was reminiscent of what Orwell had seen the Communists do to democratic forces battling Franco during the Spanish Civil War.

Shanker signed on to the National Council of Prodemca, the Committee for Democracy in Central America, founded by Penn Kemble, to promote a middle ground between the Communist Sandinistas and the former supporters of the dictator Somoza.[70] Shanker supported Reagan's plan to aid the anti-Communist contras in Nicaragua, a strategy that he thought would put pressure on the Sandinistas to make changes.[71] With the support of some Democrats, including New Jersey Senator Bill Bradley, aid to the contras was provided.[72] Shanker's priorities in Nicaragua were different than Reagan's: Shanker supported land reform and wanted to build a democratic left through trade unions, ideas not high on Reagan's agenda. But they allied on their opposition to the Sandinistas.

At the AFT convention in 1986, Shanker said he supported those fighting for freedom in Nicaragua, "where you would not have a right to stand up and speak your mind or join a union that was not government approved or buy a newspaper that was uncensored by the government. It is a dictatorship, and people who are fighting for freedom, in my personal view, need the help and support of the United States."[73] The NEA, by contrast, was a strong opponent of U.S. military involvement in Nicaragua.[74]

There was certainly reason to be skeptical of Reagan's policy in Nicaragua, particularly the outrageous and illegal funneling of aid to the contras by Oliver North. But Shanker was astonished by the willingness of some liberals to ally themselves with the Communist Sandinistas. In April 1987, Shanker strongly opposed a planned "Mobilization for Justice and Peace in Central America and Southern Africa," which was supported by the NEA, UAW, AFSCME, and others, even though some of the sponsors, the Nicaragua Network and the Quixote Center, supported the Sandinistas.[75] In a column, Shanker denounced the march, noting that "the Sandinistas have repressed independent trade unionism since the very beginning of their rule, using intimidation, harassment and violence to force workers to join government-created unions."[76] Liberals would not march with totalitarians on the right, like neo-Nazis, so why were they willing to march with totalitarians on the left?

Right-Wing Dictatorships in the Philippines, South Africa, and Chile

But if liberals were too forgiving of dictatorships on the left, Shanker believed Reagan was too forgiving of dictatorships on the right, including in Central America, where right-wing death squads in El Salvador murdered organizers for the AFL-CIO's American Institute for Free Labor Development (AIFLD). Likewise in 1984, Shanker attacked the Reagan administration for supporting the Marcos regime in the Philippines. "This leads not only to loss of the support of the American people," Shanker said, "but to demoralizing the democratic non-Communist groups in the Philippines."[77]

Shanker was also tougher than Reagan on the apartheid regime in South Africa. Shanker began sending help to black trade unionists in South Africa in the 1970s—everything from office supplies to legal aid.[78] Through IFFTU, says Fred van Leeuwen, Shanker played an important role in helping South Africa's multiracial teachers' union, one of the largest unions in the country. Shanker was willing to work with the organization, bending an AFL-CIO rule against working with groups that had alliances with Communists. Shanker drew a distinction between South Africans allying with Communists as a tactical way of overturning apartheid and state-sponsored Communist unions in places such as Eastern Europe, which were antidemocratic tools of the government.[79] While Reagan was pursuing "constructive engagement" with the South Africans, Shanker demonstrated against apartheid.[80] Because of the AFL-CIO's support for anti-apartheid forces, Nelson Mandela met with Kirkland, Shanker, and other members of the AFL-CIO Executive Committee on his first trip to the United States after his release in 1990.[81]

Unlike the Reagan Administration, Shanker also took a hard line against the right-wing dictatorship of Augusto Pinochet in Chile. Like many left-wing dictatorships, Pinochet saw unions as a threat to his power, and he outlawed independent unions and fired twenty thousand teachers, with the activists being the first to be laid off.[82]

Teachers were very active in Chile's anti-Pinochet movement, which culminated in a nationwide referendum in 1988 on whether Pinochet should stay in power. Shanker provided support to Chilean teachers' union president Osvaldo Verdugo, whose organization was instrumental in the campaign to vote "no" in the referendum.[83] About one-third of the activists in the "no vote" campaign were teachers.[84]

Shanker headed an international delegation of public-sector unions to Chile prior to the referendum, and he dispatched David Dorn to Chile for four months.[85] Again, Shanker took a flexible approach on the AFL-CIO's rule against working with any group that had ties to Communists.[86] At the time of the plebiscite, Shanker sent down more than twenty AFT teachers to serve as election observers.[87] In October 1988, the "no" vote on Pinochet prevailed by 55 percent to 45 percent.[88]

Promoting Democracy During and After the Cold War

The late Reagan Administration and the administration of his successor, George H. W. Bush, witnessed a great flourishing of democracy, as repressive regimes fell on both the right (Chile, South Africa, the Philippines) and the left (Poland, East Germany, and the Soviet Union). The American victory in the forty-five-year-long cold war with the Soviets was of monumental importance, on scale with the defeat of Nazi totalitarianism in World War II.[89] In the 1970s, few would have predicted this astonishing accomplishment.

President Reagan surely deserves a share of credit, as does Pope John Paul II, for their hard-line anti-Communist stances. Lech Walesa and Vaclav Havel were enormously important, as was Soviet Premier Mikhail Gorbachev, in his own way. In the United States, a long line of Democratic hawks, from Harry Truman to John Kennedy to Scoop Jackson can claim their share of the credit. But so can the American labor movement. While American business was an unreliable ally in the fight against the Communists, labor was unfailing in its opposition.[90] The American Enterprise Institute's Joshua Muravchik argues that George Meany "as much as any American" helped bring down Communism.[91]

Shanker, in turn, was a crucial supporter of George Meany and then Lane Kirkland in holding the anti-Communist line within labor circles.[92] In places like Eastern Europe, for example, the AFT stood out, along with just a few others, as leading supporters of workers.[93] Even as the cold war liberal tradition began to waver, Shanker stood firm against the fashions of the time.

In 1989, the year the Berlin Wall fell, Shanker was named chair of the AFL-CIO International Affairs Committee.[94] He was reunited with his old friend from Social Democratic circles, Tom Kahn, who had succeeded Irving Brown as international-affairs director of the AFL-CIO.[95] The irony was that Shanker took on the title just as Communism was collapsing all around him. In the United States, the vestiges of Communism were all but eliminated. Shanker joked with the head of a major British teachers' union. "You're a lucky man," said Shanker. "You really still have a reason to live. You still have Communists to fight."[96]

Shanker knew that the fall of the Berlin Wall was only the beginning of the effort to promote democracy. He warned that while people should be exhilarated by the expansion of freedom, the spread of democracy was not inevitable, reminding readers that when the colonies won independence in Africa and elsewhere, democratic institutions did not necessarily follow.[97] It would be a mistake, he said, to assume that "we are now moving effortlessly toward a world in which everyone will live in a free society."[98] Democracy is much more than about voting, Shanker said, and in places like Eastern Europe, nongovernmental democratic institutions—independent political parties, churches, unions, newspapers, business groups, and universities—had atrophied and needed rebuilding.[99] While most conservatives focused on creating market economies, Shanker argued, "free enterprise alone will not lead to a free society. People need . . . direct contacts with trade unionists, lawyers, teachers, journalists and community leaders from democratic nations."[100] Shanker argued: "What we've seen are the beginnings of democracy. We haven't really seen democracy yet. We've seen the overthrow of dictatorship. Democracy is going to take generations to build and we have to be a part of that building because they won't be able to do it alone."[101]

Two months after the Berlin Wall fell, Shanker announced the formation of a new AFT initiative, Education for Democracy International, to help in that effort. While the AFT expected teachers' unions in places like Hungary and Bulgaria to be most concerned about how to bargain contracts, establish teacher transfer policies, and the like, the word came back that they really wanted help in transforming schools.[102] Education for Democracy International sought to help teachers in Eastern Europe and elsewhere to do just that. It began with a pilot delegation to Poland.[103] The AFT also sent field staff and AFT organizers to Eastern Europe and Chile to help build independent trade unions by teaching people how to run democratic meetings and put together a union structure.[104]

Reagan's AFT Address

Although Shanker's position on the cold war was largely vindicated by history, his periodic alliances with Ronald Reagan were highly controversial at the time—a fact best highlighted during the first term of the Reagan Administration, when Shanker invited the president to speak at the AFT national convention and Reagan agreed to do so.

The invitation to speak at the July 1983 AFT convention in Los Angeles split the AFT staff in two.[105] Rachelle Horowitz, the AFT's political director, said, "I nearly quit my job."[106] Phil Kugler, the labor organizer, thought the idea was nuts.[107] Why would the AFT give a platform to an anti-labor, anti–public school, tax-cutting Republican? Shanker, however, strongly believed one could work against someone on certain issues and then turn around and work with them on others. Moreover, he thought Reagan's speech could help the AFT in its fights with the NEA. In the South, in particular, Shanker knew the AFT had an image of strike-happy unionists and thought that if people saw Reagan giving a speech to the organization, some of that negative image might be reduced.[108] As a compromise, Shanker agreed to balance the invitation to Reagan by inviting New York Governor Mario Cuomo to address the convention.[109]

Shanker went out of his way to make clear to delegates that he did not endorse Reagan's anti–public school agenda. The day prior to Reagan's speech, Shanker issued his F+ grade to Reagan on education.[110] Faced with the difficulty of how to introduce Reagan to an audience that was likely to be hostile, Shanker gave Reagan no introduction and instead said, "Mr. President, I want to introduce you to 3,000 of the best teachers in the whole United States." It was a brilliant reversal, says David Dorn.[111]

As Reagan began to speak, about 150 of the three thousand AFT delegates walked out in protest, but most of the crowd was respectful. In a speech that lasted twenty minutes, Reagan said that unlike the NEA, his administration may "disagree on some matters with the AFT but can still work together in mutual respect and understanding to serve a higher common goal. . . . I know there's a pretty big education organization out there. But it's my experience that dedication, open-mindedness, and initiative count for just as much as size and it seems to me that in all three categories the AFT, like Avis, tries a lot harder."[112]

Reagan acknowledged differences on tuition tax credits and vouchers, but also identified several areas of agreement with the AFT: standards, testing, student discipline, bilingual education, and national defense. Of these, the issue of school discipline got the biggest applause from the audience.[113] Then he attacked the NEA for booklets it helped produce on issues of nuclear war and racism. The nuclear-war curriculum was said by some to put too much blame on the United States for the arms race, and the curriculum on racism suggested that America was a fundamentally racist society and the Ku Klux Klan was just "the tip of the iceberg."[114] Shanker had earlier dismissed the nuclear curriculum as "lopsided propaganda."[115] And he called the Klan piece wrong on the merits and damaging to teacher credibility.[116] Reagan said, "I also want to commend the

AFT . . . for its ringing condemnation of those organizations who would exploit teaching positions and manipulate curriculum for propaganda purposes."[117]

NEA leaders were furious that Shanker had given Reagan a platform from which to attack them. NEA Executive Director Don Cameron accused Shanker of "dancing political pirouettes with his ultra-conservative paramours."[118] At a press conference following the speech, Shanker found himself in the sweet political space between the NEA on the left—with whom, he said, he had "vast philosophical differences"—and Ronald Reagan on the right, with whom he also had significant differences, "not mild disagreements."[119]

The larger question was whether or not he could reconcile his unconventional constellation of views. For Shanker was not simply a moderate, a centrist who split the difference between the NEA and Reagan, always coming down in the middle. On some issues—such as labor unions—he was to the left of the NEA. And on some issues—such as Poland—he was more hard-line than Reagan. Keith Geiger of the NEA said: "There are times when I think he's one of the most liberal people I've ever talked to and times when I think he is one of the most conservative. And I always wonder which Shanker I am going to get."[120]

The two publications the AFT published exemplified the strange juxtaposition of traditionally "liberal" and traditionally "conservative" views that Shanker simultaneously held in his head. *American Teacher*, a nuts-and-bolts publication for members, emphasized the need for strong unions and labor-law reform, public education over vouchers, more spending on public schools, a higher minimum wage, and national health care. *American Educator*, a quarterly ideas magazine aimed at a broader audience, meanwhile, emphasized the need for tough discipline in the schools and high academic standards and opposed quotas, Communism, maintenance bilingual education, extreme forms of multiculturalism, and cultural relativism.

Most people, on both the left and right, had a hard time reconciling these views. When Linda Chavez, the editor of both *American Teacher* and *American Educator* from 1979 through 1983, was nominated for her post in the Reagan Administration, she was grilled by a staffer for conservative Republican Senator Jessie Helms. "Which Linda Chavez are you, the one who edits this magazine?" he asked, holding up *American Educator*, with a cover story about values and morality. "Or are you the editor of this rag?" he added, holding a copy of *American Teacher*, with a picture of

Ronald Reagan and the headline "Headed for Disaster." Chavez said the first reflected her true views, not the second.[121] But she acknowledged that Shanker's views were reflected by both publications.[122]

The Social Democrats

The group Shanker most closely identified with politically—the Social Democrats USA—were called "right-wing socialists," a very odd mix indeed. Were Albert Shanker and the Social Democrats he allied himself with inconsistent and incoherent, or was there an underlying philosophy to explain his and their disparate set of views?

Throughout his life, Shanker and other Social Democrats argued that their strange mix of traditionally liberal and conservative views was part of a well-thought-out ideology that put democracy at the core. In a classic 1976 address to Social Democrats USA, Sidney Hook, the Social Democrats' honorary chair (and Shanker's hero), put it this way: "For the Social Democrat, democracy is not merely a political concept but a moral one. It is democracy as a way of life."[123] Shanker rarely gave a speech that did not mention democracy.[124] His columns returned time and time again to democratic ideals.[125] For many conservatives, the marketplace is the touchstone; for Shanker it was democratic values that drove everything else.

Shanker's "liberal" positions—on unions, public education, economic inequality, and civil rights—all found their roots in a democratic ideology. Shanker could not abide Reagan's attack on unions because to Shanker they were society's ultimate democratic institution. "A union," he said, "is a school for workers to become leaders."[126] Unions brought together regular employees of all different ethnic backgrounds and provided them what Robert Putnam calls "schools for democracy," where members learn how to run meetings, debate one another, and organize for political action.[127] Unions to Shanker were not merely economic actors, they were institutions to democratize capitalism, provide a voice to workers in their occupations, and counter the strong influence of corporations.

Shanker's justification for public education, likewise, fundamentally came back to democratic principles. His opposition to Reagan's tuition tax credit proposals always returned to the public-school mission of providing two ingredients central to a well-functioning democracy: social mobility and social cohesion.

Shanker's support for policies promoting greater economic equality (minimum wage, health care, and the like) also had a democratic justification, because it was widely recognized, going back to Aristotle, that democracy can only work well when there is a strong middle class.[128] In an overwhelmingly poor and uneducated society, dangerous demagogues can manipulate the masses more easily, and extreme economic inequality skews political power through the use of money in politics.[129] Shanker and the Social Democrats opposed inequality not just because it was the compassionate thing to do, but also because it eroded democratic principles. Sidney Hook told the Social Democrats: "It is possible for human beings to be politically equal as voters, yet so unequal in educational, economic and social opportunities, that ultimately, even the nature of the political equality is affected. . . . The Social Democrat therefore is interested in extending the area of equal opportunity beyond the political sphere to all other areas of social life."[130] By the same token, he said in another address, the Social Democrats oppose "large concentrations of private property" that can have "oppressive effects," just as concentrations of government authority can.[131]

Finally, Shanker's strong support for civil rights—long before it became fashionable—had democratic roots. Treating people differently because of race undercut democracy's promise of equality. Likewise, Shanker's support for non-quota-based affirmative action—programs like the career ladder for the paraprofessionals—was important in a democracy. The Reagan approach of leaving the legacy of past discrimination unaddressed undermined the social unity required in a democracy and tore at the social fabric. To Shanker, it was not surprising that the American South had been so hostile to both unions and civil rights, because opposition to both was rooted in a common antidemocratic ideology. Shanker sided with liberals on South Africa and Chile because rightwing support for apartheid and opposition to unions was fundamentally antidemocratic, no matter how these countries tilted during the cold war.

But Shanker's seemingly "conservative" positions on issues from racial preferences and anti-Communism to education issues such as discipline, bilingual education, multiculturalism, and relativism had the same philosophical justification as his support for liberal programs that nourished democracy. On the issue of quotas, for example, Shanker said in testimony before the U.S. Civil Rights Commission:

> What we have here is a conflict between an effort, which I think is good, to undo the effects of slavery and racism on the one hand and, on the other hand, to try to impose a method which is really antidemocratic and may become basically totalitarian. I would not want to live in a country where everybody was in every job or every profession or every neighborhood in proportion to their proportion of the population.[132]

While most people desire the ends of an integrated workforce and university student body, he said, in a democracy there were limits on the means to getting there. He drew an analogy to the rights of criminal defendants, saying that sometimes we forego the goal of convicting criminals because the means such as wiretaps are unacceptable.[133] The issue of civil rights and quotas was not about who benefited—the lens through which many politicians on the right and left viewed those issues—it was far more fundamentally about the role of race in a democracy.

Likewise, for Shanker and the Social Democrats, the basis for anti-Communism was not the lens of Capitalism versus Communism or the United States versus Russia, it was democracy against totalitarianism.[134] Shanker agreed with the cold war liberals of the Americans for Democratic Action that the fight for civil rights at home was consistent with the fight against Communism abroad because both were about democracy.[135]

Shanker's "conservative" positions on education issues could also be tied to democracy. Tough discipline policies were about keeping public schools truly public spaces. Just as yielding to disorder in public parks undercut their democratic nature, so yielding to disorder in the classroom led to middle-class flight from public schools and increased pressure for school vouchers, both of which undercut the democratic function of schooling. Failing to hold students to high standards undercut the democratic role of schools in promoting social mobility. And extreme forms of bilingual education and multiculturalism undercut the social cohesion necessary in a democracy. Finally, Shanker's "conservative" view of cultural relativism was rooted in a passionate belief in human freedom, that democracy was a superior form of human governance, and that teaching this in the schools was not merely ethnocentric.

To Shanker and the Social Democrats, it was the traditional liberals and conservatives who were inconsistent on the question of democracy.

While Reagan was agitated about discrimination against whites, and the NEA about discrimination against blacks, neither would oppose discrimination across the board.[136] On unions, likewise, Shanker pointed to Reagan's inconsistency: it was difficult to square his support for Solidarity in Poland with his "crusade to weaken unions in America."[137] Reagan was inconsistent in applying his human-rights campaign to Soviets but not to the Philippines and South Africa, while people on the left, such as the leaders of the NEA, were active in South Africa but silent on abuses by the Soviets, Cubans, and Sandinistas. Shanker argued: "For so many years, Social Democrats USA was the only group that was not a right-wing group, that dared to talk about the violations of human rights, the Gulag, the imprisonments, and therefore it was alone in its part of the political spectrum."[138]

On education, likewise, Reagan invoked the need for assimilation in a democracy when siding with Shanker on bilingual education and multiculturalism, but he then undercut the argument by backing anti-assimilation initiatives like tuition tax credits for private schools and Texas's decision not to educate the children of illegal immigrants. The NEA was inconsistent for the opposite reason: backing public schools as a way to promote social unity but then supporting particular programs such as extreme bilingual education and multiculturalism, which undercut that very goal.

In a speech accepting the Social Democrats Eugene V. Debs award in 1990, Shanker acknowledged that he and his audience were "out of step," invoking Sidney Hook's phrase, for being on the left and anti-Communist.[139] Indeed, the Social Democrats had a tiny membership, well below one thousand.[140] The Socialist Party split and split, said Sandra Feldman, until "it finally got down to this small group that sort of agreed with each other."[141] But Shanker did not mind being out of step. His biggest heroes—people like Bayard Rustin, A. Philip Randolph, Sidney Hook, and George Orwell—were essentially figures on the left who often disagreed with others on the left.[142]

Indeed, Shanker believed the Social Democrats made more sense than any other political group, and the senior staff he hired were virtually all Social Democrats. Beginning with Yetta Barsh at the UFT, the earliest key hires, including Sandra Feldman, Eugenia Kemble, and Velma Hill, were Socialists. At the AFT, many of Shanker's department-head appointments—Greg Humphrey (legislative), Phil Kugler (organizing), Rachelle Horowitz (politics), and Eugenia Kemble followed by Ruth Wattenberg (education issues)—were from the ranks of the Social Democrats. They were hired to edit *American Educator* (Linda Chavez, then Liz McPike and Ruth Wattenberg), to work on international affairs (David Dorn, Eric Chenoweth, and Burnie Bond), to provide legal advice (Bruce Miller), to run the travel department (Sally Muravchik), and to supervise the support staff (Judy Bardacke). In later years, Shanker would hire Social Democrats to serve as in-house intellectuals (Ronald Radosh) and in the office of the president (Rita Freedman—a former executive director of the Social Democrats).[143] Other unions hired Social Democrats too, but Shanker hired the most, and virtually all the top-tier posts went to them. There was broad agreement on first principles. "It was people with whom you could talk shorthand," Ruth Wattenberg says.[144]

Shanker served on the National Advisory Council of the Social Democrats, and the AFT provided financial support to the organization. "The SD is one of our regular causes," Shanker said when he received the Debs award. "I can't think of an organization that more deserves the support of trade unions in this country," he said.[145]

For a time, the AFT regularly purchased seventy copies of SDUSA's newsletter, *New America*, for the executive council and staff of the AFT.[146] Although Shanker was not technically a member of the Social Democrats and did not pay dues, said Midge Decter, "he was more than a part of it; he was an anchor."[147] Says Bruce Miller: "We were the only group that reflected his own politics." Arch Puddington, a longtime Social Democrat, said Shanker was "the public figure that best articulated" the Social Democratic vision. "He was the one public figure who could stand up and talk about why it was important for liberals to have an anti-totalitarian, anti-Communist . . . pro-defense perspective; why it was important to defend Israel from a democratic not a Jewish perspective; and why it was important to have a social democratic domestic economy and culture."[148]

Social Democrats were so prominent in the AFT that at one point some raised the concern that they were "taking over."[149] After Michael Massing wrote an article in the *New Republic* in 1987 on the strange alliance between the Social Democrats and Ronald Reagan, and noted that the AFT employed many SDers, the issue was raised at an AFT executive council meeting. Walter Tice, a vice president from Yonkers, asked whether it was true that 90 percent of top staff positions were held by Social Democrats.[150] Shanker said the number was smaller but made no apologies for hiring Social Democrats, whose strongly anti-Communist, pro-labor, and egalitarian vision had long fit together in the coherent puzzle of cold war liberalism.[151] Now, Shanker complained, that consensus had eroded, and "the political parties have forced us to choose between pro-labor and pro-defense candidates, between social welfare and an anti-Communist foreign policy."[152]

Shanker's social democratic philosophy helped guide him through a confusing thicket of issues in the 1980s—from race to values to economics to foreign affairs—landing him in opposition to Ronald Reagan on some occasions and in surprising alliance with the president on other issues. While his critics called him inconsistent, Shanker made a convincing case that it was not he who was inconsistent, but rather contemporary American liberalism and conservatism.

In the coming years, Shanker would continue to fight for the Social Democratic philosophy, but he would sharpen his focus and apply it increasingly to a realm central to the promotion of democracy: reform of American public education. In the last decade and a half of his life, this would become his primary and consuming passion.

14

Education Reform

A s a Social Democratic thinker, Albert Shanker took a number of positions that made his fellow liberals uneasy. As an education reformer, he would ruffle many feathers among his fellow advocates of public education. Beginning in the early 1980s, he began taking risks on education reform—building alliances with business, acknowledging shortcomings in public education, and proposing innovative ideas on teacher pay and the firing of bad teachers—all of which shocked the education establishment. The difference between Al Shanker the Social Democrat and Al Shanker the education reformer was this: if in politics he and his colleagues largely lost out and became marginalized by the left on issues like foreign policy, racial quotas, and social values, in the realm of education reform, Shanker became a central figure, arguably the most influential American educator of the last quarter of the twentieth century.

A Nation at Risk

Education reform has been around as long as there has been education, but if there was a turning point in recent times, it came on April 26, 1983, with the publication of a report called *A Nation at Risk*. Against the backdrop of declining American dominance following the war in Vietnam, the Iran hostage crisis, and the collapse of the American automobile industry, the Reagan Administration's National Commission on Excellence in Education warned that poor test scores compared to other developed countries threatened to further undermine American economic competitiveness with Japan and West Germany.[1] *A Nation at Risk* was different from the numerous other education reports released each year: people listened. Education historian Diane Ravitch called *A Nation at Risk* "the most important education reform document of the twentieth century."[2] And Albert Shanker's role in the report's reception was pivotal.

Pointing to the lack of serious curricula in American public high schools, the report said: "The educational foundations of our society are presently being eroded by a rising tide of mediocrity that threatens our very future as a nation and as a people." In military language meant to resonate in the Reagan era, the report stated: "If an unfriendly foreign power had attempted to impose on America the mediocre educational performance that exists today, we might well have viewed it as an act of war. As it stands, we have allowed this to happen to ourselves." The report charged: "We have, in effect, been committing an act of unthinking, unilateral educational disarmament."[3]

The report then made five key recommendations: High schools should require four years of English; three years each of math, science, and social studies; and one half-year of computer science. Schools should end "social promotion," a system under which some students move to the next grade based on age rather than academic accomplishment. The American school day should be extended from six to seven hours, and the school year from 180 to 220 days. Teachers should be paid more and paid on an eleven-month salary contract, so they could spend time developing the curriculum and engaging in professional development when students were not in school, and merit-pay programs should be adopted to attract outstanding teachers into the teaching profession and to fill slots in certain fields that were experiencing shortages. Finally, while local and state governments bear the "primary responsibility for financing and governing the schools," the federal government has "the primary responsibility to identify the national interest in education."[4]

The report said nothing about Ronald Reagan's pet issues—school vouchers, prayer in school, and abolishing the Department of Education—and Reagan advisor Ed Meese tried to convince Reagan not to receive the report publicly.[5] In a compromise, Reagan formally received the report in the State Dining Room at the White House but nevertheless spoke of his commitment to school vouchers and prayer in school. He was widely ridiculed in the press for making an argument so disconnected from the content of the report.[6]

Shanker had to decide how to react to the report. There was a great deal of pressure, both within labor and education circles, to be critical of anything associated with Ronald Reagan.[7] Recalls education-policy expert Jim Kelly, "The first reaction from . . . almost all education leaders was to trash the report."[8] The major educational organizations—the National Association of Secondary School Principals, the National Association of State Boards of Education, the American Association of School Administrators, the Council of Chief State School Officers, and the National School Boards Association—were all cool to the report. The NEA's Don Cameron called A Nation at Risk and other similar reports "the usual doom and gloom."[9] Milt Goldberg, the executive director of the National Commission on Excellence in Education recalls that the NEA "didn't like it at all" and that he was hissed at when he spoke to an NEA convention audience about the report.[10] The NEA executive committee, Cameron later said, "believed that the Nation at Risk report and its attendant publicity had no legs, and that this latest incarnation of education reform was just another passing fad that would fade like the morning haze."[11]

Many supporters of public education saw A Nation at Risk's harsh criticism of public schools as an attack meant to lay the foundation for private-school vouchers. Others saw the report's language as "hyperbolic."[12] To the extent problems existed, it was with disadvantaged students, not the entire system. And many objected to the report's call for "merit pay," a concept long anathema to teachers' unions.

Based on Shanker's education-reform record from the 1960s and most of the 1970s, one would have expected him to denounce the report in harsh terms. Shanker had consistently argued that public schools were doing fairly well, not a surprising stance for a teacher's union leader. In 1971, he called the so-called failure of public schools "the big lie," saying, "our public schools have, by any reasonable standard, enjoyed great success.[13] In 1974, he argued "American schools are performing much better than the critics would have us believe," noting that "top students in the U.S. do as well as top students in other countries." He made similar statements in 1975, 1979, 1980, 1981, and 1982.[14] Shanker defended teachers from critical editorials, complaining: "No human being is going to stand very long for doing a tough job under difficult circumstances only to be regularly vilified in editorials which shape public opinion."[15]

Nor had Shanker been particularly open to two controversial reforms contained in the *A Nation at Risk* report. He had been an ardent opponent of merit pay.[16] And far from calling for a longer school year and school day, he had endorsed a proposal for a four-day work week for teachers, with teacher aides taking over the fifth day in elementary schools and high-school students doing independent research on those days.[17]

Neither had Shanker fostered particularly good relations with a major group that was backing the *A Nation at Risk* report and education reform: the American business community. As a labor leader, Shanker had been on the opposite side of business on major battles involving the minimum wage, health care, social security, and labor-law reform. Business groups had often been unfriendly to efforts of teachers to bargain collectively, had often opposed local ballot initiatives for property-tax increases to finance schools, and opposed federal aid for education because each of these meant increased taxes.[18] And Shanker was particularly bitter about business support for community control in New York City, which he saw as a way to avoid real investment in education and as a form of "riot insurance."

But Shanker's attitudes toward business and the need for education reform began to change over time—first, as he saw the crucial power that business held during the 1975 fiscal crisis in New York, and more importantly, as he saw the way in which tuition tax credits had evolved from an obscure idea to a genuine threat. The tuition tax credits fight underlined for Shanker the need to engage in public-school reform as never before. If public schools were not performing, they could not be moved to Mexico, like auto plants, but they could be virtually put out of business by private schools, left to educate only the most disadvantaged students. As a result, the interests of teachers and children were more closely aligned than previously. If public education did not improve, his members' jobs were on the line.

When the *A Nation at Risk* report was released in 1983, Shanker and a group of top union officials sat together and read the document. Sandra Feldman recalled: "We all had this visceral reaction to it. You know, 'This is horrible. They're attacking teachers.' Everyone was watching Al to hear his response. When Al finished reading the report, he closed the book and looked up at all of us and said, 'The report is right, and not only that, we should say that before our members.' "[19]

Shanker prepared his reaction and on April 30, four days after the re-lease of the *A Nation at Risk* report, Shanker was ready to deliver a speech to the convention of NYSUT teachers in Albany, New York. Shanker aide Naomi Spatz of the UFT recalls that he knew very well that embracing the report would be controversial and newsworthy and talked a bit with *New York Times* reporter Michael Oreskes beforehand about what he was go-ing to say. Oreskes called the *Times*, and his editors said they could hold the front page until 1:00 p.m. Shanker was due to come on around 11:00 a.m., says Spatz, "and all of a sudden, they started bringing in all these children's choirs, and each time we thought it was the last one, another one would come up. Then the mayor of Albany came out and wanted to present tulips. The feeling was, 'We're going to lose the front page because of these bloody tulips. Get those kids off the stage.'" Then, she says, "Al started and it was kind of like a bombshell, and nobody moved for an hour and ten minutes."[20]

In the speech (which did garner front-page news coverage the next day), Shanker urged teachers to cooperate with education reform, as out-lined in *A Nation at Risk* and other reports from business groups. Teach-ers should not dismiss reforms they had long resisted, so long as reforms are tied to higher teacher salaries and an infusion of new funds into edu-cation. Shanker told NYSUT delegates: "These people are not in the same class as the critics that existed before."[21]

In the speech and in subsequent interviews and columns, Shanker broke with the liberal education and labor establishments on five signifi-cant issues, which had important ramifications for the education reform debate in years to come.

First, Shanker said, advocates of public education needed to acknowl-edge that the *A Nation at Risk* report was right to say American education had serious problems. Acknowledging problems, Shanker argued, would not inevitably pave the way to vouchers; on the contrary, it was the first step to improving public education.[22] Simply wishing problems away was no longer credible. Teachers knew there were problems, Shanker said, as anyone who listened to the talk in teachers' lounges across the country recognized.[23]

Second, Shanker said, the report's recommendations—including the controversial call for merit pay—should not be dismissed out of hand. The bigger picture was that the report pointedly omitted Reagan's bad proposals from its recommendations.[24] "Nowhere in the commission's report is there mention of the Reagan Administration's major 'ideas' with

respect to education: tuition tax credits, vouchers, school prayer, etc.,"
Shanker said.[25]

Third, Shanker said, educators should reject their historic animosity
toward business groups and work with them to improve American public
education. While in the past business had often resisted spending on public education, changes in the economy had altered this calculus and put a
new premium on an educated workforce. Much more than in the past,
business needed employees who were well trained and educated. If government did not do it right the first time, business would have to pay for
it themselves. And, in particular, businesspeople had a mindset that understood incentives, so they could be an ally for increased teacher pay;
they knew the basic rule of capitalism: to draw talent, you have to pay for
it.[26] In his NYSUT speech, Shanker warned that if teachers uniformly dismissed the A Nation at Risk report, business might become disgusted and
throw in their lot with voucher advocates.[27]

Fourth, Shanker argued, teachers should embrace the report because it
put the issue of public-education reform on the front burner. While not
all public-school advocates wanted education placed front and center—
many argued that the real problems of academic achievement were rooted
in larger economic inequities and that the traditional "labor" agenda of
improving health care, housing, and wages should take a higher priority
than improving public schools—Shanker argued that the labor-versus-
education question represented a false choice. Moreover, in the Reagan
era, the labor agenda was stuck, so liberals needed to change gears and
put an emphasis on education. Indeed, Shanker welcomed the commission's finding that the federal government "has the primary responsibility
to identify the national interest in education,"[28] and commented, "I like
the phrase 'a nation at risk' because those words put education on the
same par as national defense. A nation at risk means that a country can go
down. It can fall apart."[29]

Shanker's fifth and final controversial point was that liberals should
embrace the report's focus on excellence for all children, which represented a shift from the plight of minority and poor students as the major
rationale for federal involvement in education. Many liberals opposed
this reorientation from equity to excellence on the theory that poor children would be lost in the shuffle. On the merits, Shanker believed that
there was a problematic slippage in achievement at the top levels. He argued, "we face just as great an educational crisis with our top and 'average'
students as we do with our bottom ones."[30] And politically, in a point

hotly debated within the union, Shanker argued that it was essential to frame the problem as a "nation" at risk, not just poor kids at risk. "Al believed that the agenda for poor kids . . . was stuck in the mud," said one aide. Shanker remained deeply concerned with low-income students, but he believed that the Jonathan Kozol–style hand-wringing about the poor had yielded few concrete results and that "you had to change the dynamic." The broad-based emphasis in A Nation at Risk just might do that.[31]

Shanker's embrace of A Nation at Risk represented an enormous departure from past AFT policy. Here was a major labor-union leader endorsing a report that said public education was in trouble, proposed merit pay, had the strong backing of business, deemphasized the importance of labor's equality agenda, and put emphasis on all kids rather than the poor. It was "absolutely momentous, a watershed moment" for the AFT, says Greg Humphrey.[32] Said Sandra Feldman: "It was very significant. The union hadn't thought that way before."[33]

Shanker's endorsement made an enormous difference. The NEA's Bob Chase later said Shanker's "bold" decision "changed everything." Chase argued: "Without Al's unwavering support, the report's call for educational reform and renewal would have languished."[34] The executive director of the commission, Milton Goldberg, says the report might have been crippled if there had been unanimous opposition from the education establishment. "It was vital that someone with stature step up. . . . Al Shanker never wavered on that issue and the rest of the education community and public finally caught up to him."[35]

A Nation at Risk, in turn, helped launch a new era in public-education reform. It galvanized people the way the Russian launch of Sputnik had in 1957.[36] In the year prior to the release of the report, governors barely mentioned education; by 1984, they were all "education governors."[37] Among the stars were Bill Clinton (D-AR), Bob Graham (D-FL), Jim Hunt (D-NC), Lamar Alexander (R-TN), and Dick Riley (D-SC). Over the next fifteen months, forty-four states would increase graduation requirements, forty-five would increase teacher certification and evaluation standards, and twenty-seven would increase instructional time.[38] More importantly, the report launched a quarter-century of continuing focus on improving public schools.[39]

At the time, many educators and unionists were furious with Shanker's decision to endorse A Nation at Risk. The vast majority of the NYSUT board was upset.[40] And the debate would continue for many years, as

Shanker kept up the drumbeat in columns, speeches, and articles, arguing that American public education was in severe trouble.[41]

A number of researchers, including Gerald Bracey, Richard Rothstein, David Berliner, and Bruce Biddle, argued that Shanker and the *A Nation at Risk* report were wrong and that American public-school failure was a myth.[42] Rothstein also said it was bad politically for Shanker to run down the public schools in his "Where We Stand" columns. "If a teachers union goal is to mobilize support for public education and its employees, denunciation of public school performance is a questionable strategy," he wrote.[43]

Shanker responded by arguing that denying the problems in public education—or blaming low achievement entirely on the home environment—was simply not credible. In one column, he argued that defenders of American public education should follow the BBC's example during World War II, when the nightly news accurately reported the defeats and daily retreats. He said: "Some listeners thought the BBC was crazy for reporting all the bad news, but when the tide eventually turned, people had confidence in BBC reports. If the BBC told the truth when times were bad, it could be trusted now. We need leaders in American education who can establish that kind of trust," he said.[44]

While members of the education establishment did not agree at the time with his criticism of public schools, some, though not all, later came to believe that he took the right tack. In retrospect, the NEA's Don Cameron says, the AFT was "right" to support the *A Nation at Risk* report, and it was "a mistake for the NEA" to raise so many questions.[45] The report did help stem education cuts at the federal level. After the report was published, OMB director David Stockman stopped calling for cuts in federal aid to education.[46] And after *A Nation at Risk*, some states increased taxes to put more money into education.[47]

Moreover, the AFT's embrace of *A Nation at Risk* gave Shanker a seat at the reform table that might not have been available had he simply been obstructionist. Says education reformer Marc Tucker: "He saw the future coming and he thought that teachers could lead it and not get rolled over by it."[48] Shanker knew that by becoming part of the debate, he could seek to help influence it and shape it.[49] Governors and others with creative ideas would often go to the AFT for their input, because there was a possibility the AFT might be open. The NEA, by contrast, was seen as inflexible.[50] Educator Michael Usdan says Shanker's embrace of *A Nation at Risk* helped him navigate the new "politics of education" in the early 1980s.

Education groups had always been fairly isolated as a community, but that changed when governors and businesspeople became for the first time intimately involved in education in the 1980s. Only one leader from the education community fully recognized this change, Usdan says. "Shanker was really kind of the prime ambassador" of the education community to business people and governors.[51]

Shanker could let governors and business leaders know where teachers were coming from, and share their concerns. Businesspeople did not understand the insecurities of teachers and why the education establishment was so defensive, something Shanker could explain without making excuses. He "brokered those worlds," says Usdan.[52] By 1987, Shanker noted with pride that businesspeople, for the first time ever, joined civil-rights groups, labor unions, and teachers in support of increased federal aid for education.[53]

To prepare himself better for the engagement in education reform following *A Nation at Risk*, Shanker decided he needed to beef up the intellectual capital at the AFT, and created a new position for a "reader/writer/thinker." The AFT already had many smart staff members, but Shanker was looking for someone who had familiarity with major policy research and could help him communicate it effectively. In November 1983, he hired Bella Rosenberg, a researcher from the National Institute of Education with a degree from the Harvard Graduate School of Education.[54] Among other things, Rosenberg helped Shanker on his "Where We Stand" column, which began to focus much more on education-reform issues and less on labor, quotas, and New York City contract disputes.

In the coming months leading up to the 1984 presidential election, Shanker would make headlines, tackling three controversial issues related to the improvement of education and, particularly, the improvement of teaching: merit pay, teacher tenure, and teacher testing.

Merit Pay

Of the various proposals to come out of *A Nation at Risk*, perhaps the most explosive was the call for "merit pay." Advocates of merit pay said that in order to attract and retain high-quality teachers, school officials should be allowed to pay higher salaries to exceptional teachers. Without that option, extraordinary teachers were likely to leave for the higher pay in administration, and talented candidates might not even enter teaching in the first place. In addition, advocates said, it made sense to pay higher salaries in areas with teacher shortages, like math and science.

Over the years, Shanker and other teachers' unions had consistently resisted merit pay, based on reasons both self-interested and educational. As a matter of self-interest, unions need solidarity among their members. In 1970, looking back over the UFT's ten-year history, Shanker said: "Our greatest enemy is division within our own ranks, our greatest weapon is our unity."[55] A union leader has different constituencies within his union, constituencies that want different things, Myron Lieberman explains, and throwing merit pay into the mix just exacerbates those tensions. "If you start allowing differentials, the union will be divided. . . . The way to keep peace in the union is, as much as possible, make the rules apply to everybody."[56] Teachers' unions also opposed the idea of paying more to address teacher shortages in areas like math and science because by maintaining one salary for all teachers, the increase required to attract teachers in shortage areas would go to everyone.[57]

As an educational matter, Shanker said, merit-pay plans in which principals made the judgments were subject to abuse. Principals might reward "obedient" teachers rather than the best ones. Such plans simply increased the power of supervisors, "reminding the employee of his dependence on management for rewards," he noted.[58] Likewise, there was the issue of principal competence. Would a principal who formerly taught physical education know what makes for a good French teacher? Furthermore, by making teachers compete with one another, merit-pay plans would discourage collaboration among teachers and the sharing of effective lessons.

Finally, Shanker argued that teacher performance was hard to measure, unlike, say, "an encyclopedia or vacuum cleaner salesman who sells twenty items" and "is probably twice as good as one who sells ten."[59] Shanker said that when merit pay was tried in about half the nation's school districts in the 1920s, it was dropped, largely because it was hard to devise defensible criteria.[60]

Following the publication of *A Nation at Risk*, President Reagan began making merit pay a big issue in the upcoming presidential campaign.[61] Merit pay appeared to work as an issue for Reagan on a couple of levels. For one thing, it was a question that involved reform of the public schools and did not alienate voters in the same way that private-school voucher plans did. For another, the merit-pay issue underlined a burgeoning theme in Reagan's campaign that the Democratic party was beholden to "special-interest" groups that opposed common-sense reforms.

With the publication of *A Nation at Risk*, Shanker softened his position on merit pay, and in his NYSUT speech he said proposals to combine pay for performance with higher overall education spending should be something teachers could "talk about." He also noted that the UFT and the New York City Board of Education had reached an agreement under which math and science teachers were paid more money in exchange for teaching during preparation periods.[62]

At the July 1983 AFT convention, Shanker invited not only Reagan but also the Republican Governor of Tennessee, Lamar Alexander, the author of an innovative twist on merit pay. Alexander, with the help of Vanderbilt University's Chester Finn, proposed a career-ladder system, in which master teachers, who would be involved in developing curriculum and serving as mentors to younger teachers, would receive greater pay. This career-ladder approach was more palatable to Shanker than traditional merit-pay schemes, because it involved differential pay for different jobs, not bonuses for people doing the same job as others. Under the plan, master teachers would be identified by panels that included teachers and principals from different districts, to avoid the problem of favoritism traditionally associated with merit-pay plans, in which principals reward obedient teachers. And under the proposal, 87 percent of all teachers would be eligible for raises ranging from one thousand to seven thousand dollars a year, paid from new education funds that did not subtract from the pay of some teachers to reward others.[63]

The NEA fiercely opposed the Tennessee legislation, arguing "everyone is a master teacher." The previous spring, it had killed the career-ladder bill. But Shanker said the idea should be "open for discussion."[64] Polling showed that the public did not support teachers receiving a flat across-the-board salary increase, but they might be more supportive of Alexander's plan, Shanker said. And Shanker found attractive the provision calling for committees of teachers and supervisors to make evaluations, rather than principals alone.[65] In due time, Shanker would have much more to say on the merit-pay question.

Teacher Tenure and Peer Review

If educators and policy makers were concerned about attracting and retaining high-quality teachers, they were also interested in getting rid of bad teachers. Critics were complaining that the system of tenure, backed up by union lawyers, made it virtually impossible to fire inadequate teachers. As with merit pay, Shanker was willing to rethink the issue and eventually backed a contentious program to weed out incompetents in the teaching workforce.

As the issue of teacher quality gained salience following the publication of *A Nation at Risk*, conservatives redoubled their complaint that tenure rules made it very difficult to remove bad teachers once they had passed the probationary period (usually after three years). In New York City, for example, critics complained that firing a teacher required a principal to document inadequacies for six months and then sit through union grievance proceedings that could last for years.[66] Critics said teachers were fired much less often than employees in the private sector, in part because it cost six figures to fire a teacher.[67]

Shanker was opposed to abolishing tenure. Given the low pay provided to teachers, tenure was an important tool for attracting good-quality teachers. More fundamentally, tenure was essential to protecting academic freedom. Tenure had been established in New York City back in 1917 to protect against political firings of teachers.[68] Under tenure, said Shanker, "an elected politician can't say, 'I'm going to fire you because you didn't support me in the last election.'"[69] Before tenure, it was also common for districts to fire senior teachers and hire younger cheaper ones in lean times.[70] If teachers did not have tenure, unions argued, teachers would have an incentive to give students good grades for fear that a bad grade might trigger an effort by parents to fire them. Tenure does not guarantee a job, Shanker emphasized, it only guarantees due process before someone is dismissed—the right to know why the discharge is being sought and the right to have the issue decided by an impartial body.[71] Finally, Shanker pointed out, places like Texas and Mississippi lacked tenure protection for teachers but could hardly be said to provide superior education.[72] He noted that in many high-quality education systems—in Germany, France, Sweden, and Japan—the tenure protections were even stronger than in the United States.[73]

But Shanker also recognized that teacher incompetence was a growing problem and began to say so, publicly and repeatedly. The supply of great teachers was declining, he said, because schools could no longer count on artificial outside influences to channel bright candidates into teaching. In the past, the Great Depression had encouraged many high-quality candidates to choose teaching, gender discrimination had led many highly qualified women into teaching, and exemption to the draft had fed other

promising candidates into the system. By the 1980s, those incentives were
gone.[74]

Shanker told the press that "a lot of people who have been hired as
teachers are basically not competent."[75] Lorretta Johnson recalls that after
a report found that many Baltimore teachers failed a math and writing
test and could not write a simple letter, Shanker wrote a column about it.
"Al went around the country pointing that out. You think we liked that?"
she asks. But for Shanker, "facts were facts."[76] NEA officials were astounded at Shanker's blunt statements. Don Cameron recalls: "He in effect said there are a lot of dumb teachers in American's classrooms," and
"our folks thought union leaders shouldn't be saying [that] about their
own members, even if it's true."[77] Shanker's wife, Eadie, worried about
her husband's statements and asked, as a union leader, "how can you
come out and constantly attack teachers and say that they're substandard?" He would joke that "every teacher who is reading it never thinks
I'm talking about them."[78]

Tenure, then, presented a conundrum for Shanker. Eliminating tenure
was out of the question, but defending teacher incompetence was equally
intolerable and politically unacceptable. Was there a third way? In 1984,
Shanker embraced an explosive alternative: peer review. Two years earlier,
Shanker had come across a new, highly controversial plan used in Toledo,
Ohio, in which expert teachers were involved in reviewing new and veteran teachers, providing assistance, and in some cases recommending termination of employment for colleagues. The notion struck at the heart of
what unionism stood for—solidarity and job security—but Shanker was
intrigued.

The plan was the brainchild of Dal Lawrence, the union president in
Toledo, an AFT affiliate. Like Shanker, Lawrence had strong union credentials, which gave him credibility with members to try innovative
things. Elected president of the Toledo union in 1966, Lawrence negotiated the first contract for the union in 1968, and in 1978 he led a violent
strike in which cars were destroyed and criminal charges were filed against
union members. But Lawrence, who had an MA in history, also had a
maverick side to him, and for a number of years he pushed the idea of
improving teacher professionalism by having expert teachers mentor new
teachers, the way doctors mentor interns. He conducted a referendum
among the members about the concept of peer assistance, and there was
overwhelming support.[79]

Administrators in Toledo initially balked at the idea, because they viewed it as the job of principals to mentor and train new teachers. Principals worried that if they did not have an evaluation to hang over teachers, they could not get them to do what they wanted. But at one collective-bargaining session, in March 1981, the attorney for the school district suggested: "If we can use these expert teachers to also work with our veteran teachers who are having severe difficulties, you've got a deal." Lawrence shook hands, knowing it was going to be controversial. "Here we were, a teachers union, and we were evaluating and even recommending the non-renewal and terminations of teachers," Lawrence recalls. But when he went to the teachers, they supported him on the idea.[80]

Under the plan, Toledo set up a nine-member advisory board (consisting of five teachers and four administrators) to make decisions on assisting, and if necessary, terminating the employment of new and veteran teachers. Six votes were required for action.[81]

With the program fully in operation in 1982, Lawrence was having a conversation with Marilyn Rauth, who was in charge of the AFT's Education Issues Department, when he mentioned in passing the Toledo peer-review program. Rauth expressed concern, saying she thought the idea was against AFT policy, because the union could not be involved in evaluating and firing its own members. There was also a legal concern about the implications of peer review under the 1980 Supreme Court *Yeshiva* decision, which held that higher-education faculty were not covered by the Wagner Act, because they had control over hiring and firing. Would peer review make teachers ineligible for collective bargaining under state statutes? A couple weeks later, Rauth telephoned Lawrence to say that Shanker wanted him to come to a meeting of the Executive Council of the AFT in Washington. Lawrence, who had never met Shanker, was apprehensive. "This did not sound like a friendly invitation."[82]

Lawrence and a couple of teachers traveled to Washington to explain their program of teacher evaluation, and many members of the AFT Executive Council were livid. "There were people cursing; they were pounding the table," Lawrence recalls, arguing the Toledo plan violated AFT policy. "It was a really bad scene," he says, "worse than I expected." No one spoke in favor of the plan until Shanker stepped in and said, "I think there's something you're missing." Lawrence says, "that was the first clue that maybe he was on our side." Shanker proceeded to point out that teachers in other countries—including Canada and Great Britain—had similar programs and were more highly regarded than in the United States. If teachers acted like doctors and lawyers and other self-regulated professions, they might win greater respect. Shanker did not win over the Executive Council, Lawrence recalls. "There were a lot of quiet, sullen people who left that room, and not a one of them came over and shook my hand," but Shanker had planted the seed.[83]

After publication of *A Nation at Risk*, Shanker needed to be able to point to AFT districts that were taking dramatic steps to improve quality, and in November 1983, when Liz McPike, the new editor of *American Educator*, asked Shanker and other AFT leaders if she could do a story on Toledo, Shanker readily approved the idea.[84] McPike was dispatched to Toledo for several days to write up a major story for the magazine.[85] When McPike arrived, she looked Lawrence in the eyes and said, "Dal, you're going to be famous." He had no idea what she meant.[86] She told him: "You're not going to have many weekends at home."[87]

On February 5, 1984, Shanker went public with his openness to peer review and devoted a "Where We Stand" column to the Toledo plan. He spelled out how it worked, and while acknowledging the novelty and controversy of a system in which unions are involved in dismissing teachers, he said the program had been successful in reinforcing public confidence in the school system. "After a period of failures to pass bond issues, the 1982 large bond issue was passed with 70% of voters, the largest margin in the history of the city—a sure sign of public confidence in the schools."[88]

McPike's eight-page interview with Lawrence appeared in the Spring 1984 issue of *American Educator*, going out to 600,000 educators.[89] Shanker began referring reporters to Toledo. "All of a sudden," says Lawrence, "I started getting inquiries from every major news outlet in the United States: All the major newspapers, the *New York Times*, the *Washington Post*, the *Los Angeles Times*, the *Chicago Tribune*," NBC News and others. Union leaders started phoning to find out more about the program—including Rochester, Cincinnati, Minneapolis, and Columbus. Over the years, Lawrence says he would receive some four thousand to five thousand requests for information from all over the world.[90]

But if there was strong interest from some local unions, there was substantial opposition from most. A 1984 Louis Harris poll found that a majority of teachers would rather be evaluated by principals and superintendents than by their fellow teachers.[91] Peer review was viewed as divisive for the union, a sure way to undercut solidarity. The union was there to protect teachers, not to jeopardize their livelihoods. "Talking about getting rid of bad teachers," Lorretta Johnson recalls, "was not a good subject for a teacher union president" to raise.[92] But Shanker decided to make a forceful speech in favor of peer review at the August 1984 AFT convention in Washington, D.C.

As he prepared his remarks, Jennie Shanker remembers her father telling her the leadership in the union was opposed to the ideas to be delivered in his speech the next day, but he seemed unconcerned.[93] In his state of the union speech at the convention and in subsequent interviews and articles, Shanker laid out the case for the Toledo plan. He began by acknowledging that peer review was unpopular with teachers. "I know I am sticking my neck out," Shanker said, estimating that "no more than 10 or 20 percent of the teachers favor" peer review.[94] Shanker also acknowledged that under traditional labor-management relations, there is a bright line between workers and supervisors to avoid dual loyalties.[95] In his speech, he said: "We get a lot of questions—like how can teachers who are members of the union be involved in saying that another union member shouldn't be retained as a teacher?"[96] But it was time to acknowledge, he said, "that some teachers are excellent, some are very good, some are good, and some are terrible."[97] Given that reality, if teachers wanted to protect basic tenure rights, they needed to come up with a way of weeding out bad teachers. Shanker argued: "Either we are going to have to say that we are willing to improve the profession ourselves or the governors are going to act for us."[98]

But peer review was not merely a defensive measure to preserve tenure, Shanker argued. It was a way of advancing two long-held union objectives: democratization of the workplace and increasing professionalization. "We really have to do in education what General Motors is doing with the United Auto Workers on the Saturn project," Shanker argued. "They have said that the workers are going to be involved in everything at every level, from how the plan is built to what the car looks like. I think it is time we ask the same questions."[99] Peer review and assistance would make teachers' unions more like craft guilds, which have apprenticeships and job-placement programs.[100] Peer review would also strengthen the case for teacher involvement in other areas, like textbook selection and curriculum development. If teachers implied that only administrators were smart enough to be able to determine who is a good teacher, that undercut the argument that teachers should be involved in these other areas, Shanker said.[101]

Peer review was common among professors, doctors, and lawyers, who police themselves, Shanker said: "It would be the first time in the history of American education that teachers would govern themselves."[102] Finally, teachers have a strong self-interest in favoring a system that weeded out substandard colleagues. "Teachers have to live with the results of other people's bad teaching—the students who don't know anything," he wrote.[103] In fact, because teachers more than administrators had to live with the consequences of incompetent colleagues and knew what others were doing wrong, peer review led to more dismissals than had occurred when administrators were in charge. In Cincinnati, which was the second city in the country to adopt peer review, 10.5 percent of new teachers were found less than satisfactory by teacher reviewers, compared to 4 percent by administrators, and 5 percent were recommended for dismissal by teachers, compared with 1.6 percent of those evaluated by principals.[104] The same was true in other cities.[105]

In subsequent years, peer-review programs spread from Toledo and Cincinnati to Rochester, Columbus, Minneapolis, Seattle, Pittsburgh, Hammond, and elsewhere, some thirty cities in all.[106] Toledo's peer-review program was recognized by the Rand Corporation and the Harvard Kennedy School of Government as a model for teacher evaluation.[107] In Toledo, peer review proved to be exceedingly popular, with teacher support on the order of ten to one.[108]

Yet nationally, the plans came under attack from both management and the NEA. In Rochester and Cincinnati, school principals sought to end peer review, in part because it encroaches on the prerogatives of management and in part because it is expensive to invest in serious evaluation and development of teachers. In Ohio, the NEA sought to scuttle Toledo's plan in the state legislature.[109] Years later, despite its spread to a number of cities, Lawrence says the program is "still in its infancy stage."[110]

Testing Veteran Teachers

Leading up to the 1984 presidential election, Shanker expressed a willingness to consider another highly controversial measure to rid the schools of bad teachers: a movement, in Arkansas and Texas, to test all teachers, including veterans.

The proposals, in both states, came not from right-wingers seeking to punish teachers' unions, but from Democratic governors—Mark White in Texas and Bill Clinton in Arkansas—who included testing of veteran teachers as part of a larger package of increased education spending. In Texas, Governor White's plan was based on recommendations from a commission headed by billionaire businessman Ross Perot. Along with competency tests for teachers, the program included a major tax increase, a 33 percent raise in teacher salaries, and equalization of school spending.[111] In Arkansas, Governor Clinton's job-related competency exam for veteran teachers was coupled with a tax increase to fund education and reduce class sizes.[112] The NEA strongly opposed both the Arkansas and Texas plans.[113]

Shanker was torn by proposals to test veteran teachers. On the one hand, it was insulting for teachers who had been teaching for many years to have to take a test. Teacher unionism was about dignity as much as salary, and such testing was demeaning and not required of veterans in other professions. On the other hand, he said, "there is ample evidence that states—through past hiring practices—have hired people who are illiterate." Shanker said: "If a person has been teaching for twenty years and they are illiterate, then they ought not be teaching."[114]

Moreover, veteran-teacher testing seemed to be the pill required to create the political will to get the resources needed for education. So in Texas, John Cole, president of the AFT affiliate, with Shanker's strong support, went along with reading and writing tests for veteran teachers in a bargain for a major increase in salaries and a package of reforms, including reduced class size, extra planning periods for teachers, duty-free lunches, and state tests to measure student progress.[115] The legislation passed in July 1984.[116] At the 1984 AFT convention in which Shanker endorsed peer review, he invited Governor White to speak, underlining the constructive role the AFT played in Texas. White said: "When others were ready to call it quits, the Texas Federation of Teachers remained at the negotiating table."[117]

Shanker astonished Cole by bringing him onto the AFT executive council in 1984, signaling his support for education reform. Around the same time, Shanker brought on Adam Urbanksi of Rochester and Dal Lawrence of Toledo, and the three of them pushed for reform within the Council.[118] Shanker's message, Cole says, was "You can think the unthinkable and it's all right."[119]

At a later AFT conference, Shanker invited Arkansas Governor Bill Clinton's wife, Hillary Clinton, who was the point person on education reform, to debate Rand researcher Linda Darling-Hammond about the testing of veteran teachers. In the debate, Hillary Clinton argued that the tests were elementary. The writing test, she said, required teachers to write a two-hundred-word essay, such as a letter to a parent or colleague. "Nobody should have failed our test," she said. "The fact that 10 percent failed is very significant. Those 10 percent touch thousands and thousands of children's lives." Politically, Clinton said, the weeding out of incompetent teachers helped create the political environment in which the public would support new taxes and further investments in education.[120] Clinton praised Shanker for his willingness to discuss the issue. "Under Albert Shanker's leadership, questions once considered forbidden have been given the right to see the light of day," she said.[121]

The 1984 AFT convention marked Shanker's tenth year as president of the AFT and his twentieth as head of the UFT. In a profile entitled "Shanker's Bold New Image," *New York Times* education reporter Gene Maeroff wrote that Shanker's embrace of reform had given the AFT "an enormous boost in prestige" and made "Shanker, once widely perceived as a militant union boss, appear very much the educational statesman in many people's eyes."[122] It was quite a transformation in Shanker's public image since the days of Ocean Hill–Brownsville.

In the early 1980s, in the age of Ronald Reagan, Shanker made an important and shrewd decision that the old strategy of achieving greater equality—through a labor agenda of economic redistribution and an education agenda centered around greater spending—needed rethinking. While much of the educational establishment resisted reform, Shanker saw that it was necessary to acknowledge difficulties in public education and to form alliances with the business community for constructive change. He was willing to bend on key policy initiatives—merit pay, teacher tenure, and testing of veteran teachers—so long as reform could be shaped in a way to enhance the professionalization of teaching. He was lauded widely for his new approach.

But his career as education statesman had only begun.

15

Beyond Special Interest

MAKING TEACHING A PROFESSION

1985–1987

I N November 1984, Ronald Reagan was reelected in a crushing forty-nine-state landslide over Walter Mondale, a drubbing on the scale of Nixon's defeat of McGovern in 1972 and Johnson's defeat of Goldwater in 1964. For Shanker, even though he agreed with Reagan on a few issues, the president's reelection was far worse than Nixon's, for Reagan came from the far right—essentially reversing the 1964 election, in which Reagan's candidate, Barry Goldwater, had been buried. Shanker saw how organized labor was branded as a "special interest" during the campaign. While he mostly disagreed with the charge, he saw the allegation as an opportunity both to promote a new agenda of making teaching a profession and to dispel the idea that teacher's unions were unconcerned about quality education.

Special Interests

For Democrats, the 1984 defeat prompted a period of serious rethinking, and just as the Coalition for a Democratic Majority (CDM) arose after the McGovern debacle, now a new organization, the Democratic Leadership Council (DLC), was formed in the wake of the Mondale disaster.

Mondale's key weakness, the DLC argued, was that he was seen as captive of "special-interest" groups, and the Democratic agenda had become merely a sum of those interests.

Shanker agreed with the underlying theory of the DLC—that the left needed to view issues based on the principles at stake rather than based on whose ox was gored. That had been the great liberal mistake in Ocean Hill–Brownsville: siding with black activists because of who they were rather than what they stood for. To Shanker, "identity politics" also helped explain why Democrats had taken indefensible positions in support of quotas and maintenance bilingual education. Early on in the campaign, Shanker had questions about Mondale, in part because of his support of racial preferences.[1] On the substance, Shanker and the CDM also were aligned with the DLC on the need for Democrats to become the party of international strength. The DLC's Will Marshall said he admired the CDM for keeping "the flame of liberal internationalism, or Cold War liberalism, burning."[2]

But there was one profound difference between members of the CDM and the DLC: their views of organized labor. While Shanker and the CDM, with roots in the Northeast, saw labor as a bulwark for working-class liberalism against the elitist New Politics liberalism, the DLC, with roots in the South, carried with it that region's bias against organized labor. For DLC "New Democrats," a defining moment of Mondale's candidacy came in a debate in Iowa with Gary Hart, in which Hart challenged Mondale to "cite one major domestic issue where you have disagreed with organized labor." Mondale refused to name one.[3]

Shanker mostly disagreed with the Reagan/DLC/Hart critique of labor as a "special interest." Reagan's charge was particularly outrageous given his close alliance with paradigmatic special interests like big business and the wealthy. The DLC also drew funding and significant support from private business interests that some believed undercut its claim to be above interests.

Indeed, despite his misgivings, Shanker and the AFT ended up supporting the AFL-CIO's decision to endorse Mondale early in the Democratic primaries.[4] When Hart attacked Mondale's association with labor, Shanker objected to the idea of speaking of big labor and big business as equally suspect. Labor represented the interests of its members, of course, but it had gone far beyond its early days, when it only did that. Early on, unions opposed unemployment insurance because it would undercut their own appeal, but for many years labor had supported a number of broad interests—from Medicare to Social Security—that benefited non-union "free riders."[5] In that sense, unions had essentially come around to Walter Reuther's view that labor must look beyond its own narrow interests (business unionism) and embrace larger progressive goals.[6] To Shanker, individual unions were not just narrow interest groups; they were part of a broader movement of ordinary working people, fundamental to democracy itself. In response to Hart, Shanker wrote:

> If you look at the strongest force for Social Security half a century ago (and, recently, for protecting benefits), the biggest organized battler for civil rights legislation, the fighter for elementary, secondary and higher education, the prime mover for loans and grants that have turned a generation of poor and working class students into so-called "Atari Democrats" by providing access to college, you'll find that the answer to these and many similar questions is: the American labor movement.[7]

To Shanker, Gary Hart's neoliberal view of labor was but a variant on the New Politics' anti-labor stance, epitomized by Hart's former boss, George McGovern.[8]

But while Shanker generally bridled at the "special interest" charge, he also conceded that labor leaders could sometimes be lazy and engage in their own form of identity politics, not emphasizing how they improved the quality of the product they produced and instead relying on raw political power to advance their interests. The famous labor slogan "Which Side Are You On?" suggested people should side with labor, irrespective of the merits. AFL-CIO chief Lane Kirkland used to say, only half in jest, that it is easy to be with labor when it is right, but "a true friend is someone who will support you when you're wrong."[9] Teachers' unions were themselves seen by critics as protecting incompetent members and invoking the "work to rule" principle, refusing to help students before or after class and refusing to meet with parents more than twice a year.[10] This mindset had to change, Shanker argued.

Shanker had already begun to demonstrate that the AFT was concerned about quality by showing an openness to certain versions of merit pay and the testing of veteran teachers and endorsing peer review. But now, with Reagan's reelection and labor under attack from all sides—the New Right, neoliberals, and New Democrats—and with the threat of school vouchers greater than ever, Shanker was ready to move into high gear with his agenda to promote the professionalization of teaching, and, more than that, to reinvent teacher unionism. In 1985, he gave a trio of speeches—at the National Press Club in January, at the NYSUT convention in Niagara Falls in April, and at an AFT education-issues convention in July—that offered a radically different vision for teachers and would be remembered as among his most famous.

A National Teachers' Exam

In the January 1985 speech at the National Press Club, Shanker proposed a rigorous national exam for new teachers, something that "no national organization in American education" had ever done, Shanker noted.[11] The existing system of state-by-state teacher standards, supported by the NEA, was not working, Shanker said. Twelve states did not even have tests, and while many of the rest used the Educational Testing Service's National Teachers Examination, each state set its own passing score.[12] Shanker said the existing standards "would be considered a joke by any other profession," noting that a Florida test for math teachers required only a sixth-grade proficiency. "That's equivalent to licensing a doctor on the basis of elementary biology."[13]

Shanker also dismissed the NEA's position on teacher testing, which said such tests should not be determinative. This meant, in effect, "if the teacher has other wonderful attributes, the fact that the math teacher flunks the math test shouldn't disqualify the math teacher."[14] Shanker had long argued that while passing the test did not mean a candidate would be a good teacher, a teacher who did not know basic content was unlikely to be effective.[15] This was a position with deep roots for Shanker, who had supported teacher competency standards going back to the Bundy Report's attempt to abolish the New York City Board of Examiners during the Ocean Hill–Brownsville dispute.

Shanker said the national teachers' exam would help professionalize teaching, making teachers more like doctors and lawyers, who must pass licensing examinations. And he backed up the proposal with a declaration that the AFT would limit membership to those who passed.[16] After Shanker's speech, the NEA's president, Mary Futrell, released a statement opposing a national test, saying the NEA believed in "the basic right of states to determine who is qualified to teach."[17]

The differing position of the AFT and the NEA had two philosophical underpinnings. For the NEA, says Bella Rosenberg, the main qualification for teaching was to have a love of children and a desire to nurture them. Shanker disagreed. "I'm not saying teachers shouldn't care for or love children, but the first thing a teacher has to be is a person who is very knowledgeable about how to get children to learn."[18] For Shanker, poor kids were not necessarily receiving a lot of education at home, so the public school was their one chance for social mobility. And for poor children, teachers were "representatives of what it meant to be educated," says Bella Rosenberg, which was "why he was just absolutely a bear about" teachers having a solid liberal-arts education and being literate and numerate.[19] It was a tough view but also a liberal one.

The NEA's other major concern was that a rigorous national teaching exam might decrease the number of minority teachers. On ETS's National Teachers Examination, under the varying state cutoff scores, whites passed the communication-skills section of the test ranging from 86 percent of the time on the toughest cutoffs to 98 percent on the easiest. Among Hispanics, the figure was 55 percent to 85 percent; for blacks, it was 30 percent to 69 percent of the time.[20]

Shanker said that this issue raised a legitimate concern, given that minority candidates are "frequently the victims of segregation, discrimination and a substantially inferior education." But going back to his stance on the New York City Board of Examiners, Shanker argued that the answer was not to lower standards, but rather to provide intensive help to ensure that large numbers of minority and low-income prospective teachers passed the test.[21] Furthermore, he argued, if low cut scores were adopted in order to boost the number of minority teachers, it would end up hurting minority children disproportionately. Because minority teachers often teach the next generation of minority students, lowering the standard would perpetuate inequality. "The last thing children of color need is to be taught by teachers who don't meet a minimum standard," he said.[22]

Most of the reaction to Shanker's call for a tough national teaching exam was very positive. Education Secretary William Bennett praised Shanker's proposal as "a good idea."[23] The proposal was endorsed by nearly two hundred editorials.[24] Shanker was praised for his courage, though in fact the proposal was in the self-interest of his members, who would not be subject to the test (which was for prospective teachers) and who would benefit from a move to restrict the supply of teachers and thereby drive up wages.[25]

All the positive press for Shanker put pressure on the NEA to reverse course, and later, in 1985, at the NEA's convention, Mary Futrell urged the NEA to vote to end its opposition to testing of new teachers and put aside its concerns about the racially disparate impact of such tests. She said: "As a black woman . . . I resent it. If we set clear and demanding expectations and then help all potential teachers reach those expectations, we can have both quality and equality."[26]

The convention followed Futrell's lead and approved of a resolution favoring tests for first-time teachers. Shanker's name "was not mentioned in the official proceedings," the New York Times noted, but "it was clear that he had an influence on the deliberations," having "upstaged the association largely because many Americans thought of him as the main spokesman for the nation's teachers."[27] The resolution, the Times said, was one way for the NEA to "move itself out of the shadow of Albert Shanker."[28]

Shanker's call for a rigorous national test was never enacted, though experts say that state testing of teachers is somewhat more rigorous today than it was in 1985.[29] But Shanker's Press Club speech had an important effect on one of the members of the audience, Marc Tucker, of the Carnegie Forum on Education and the Economy. Carnegie, at the suggestion of former North Carolina governor Jim Hunt, was seeking to do something in response to the A Nation at Risk report. Tucker was convinced that any education reform needed to include teacher professionalization as a key component, but did not want to publish yet another education report that had good solid ideas but was ignored. Shanker's Press Club speech suggested a new political opening: the possibility of buy-in from teachers' unions. Shanker and Tucker would become important collaborators on teacher-quality issues in the near future.

Teaching as a Profession

In April 1985, Shanker delivered his second major address of the trio at the NYSUT convention in Niagara Falls. In the hour-long speech, entitled "The Making of a Profession," Shanker argued for a "new professionalism." It was one of Shanker's most important speeches not because it contained a number of new policy proposals but because it provided a conceptual framework that tied together much of what he had been pro-posing—a national teacher test, peer review, career ladders—and some that were still to come, under a rubric of teacher professionalization.

For many years, the NEA had claimed the mantle of being the profes-sional organization, while the AFT was the "union." Years earlier, Shanker had challenged that dichotomy, arguing that only the union could make teaching a true profession by increasing wages and giving teachers a greater voice in education. In the speech, Shanker did not back away from any of that. But he said, just as the AFT had revolutionized teaching by introducing collective bargaining twenty-five years earlier, it was now time for "a second revolution," in which teachers would "take a step be-yond collective bargaining" to improve education.[30] Limiting action to collective bargaining made teachers appear unprofessional, he said. "We tend to be viewed today as though we are acting only in our own self-interest, wanting better salaries and smaller classes so our lives can be made easier. That image is standing in the way of our achieving profes-sional status, for not only must we act on behalf of our clients, we must be perceived as acting that way."[31] The message, coming from one of the fathers of collective bargaining, won the attention of the media. The *New York Times* featured the speech in a front-page story, "Shanker Urging Shift in Strategy to Aid Teachers."[32] Thomas Toch says the speech stunned its audience and "rocked public education," given Shanker's role in start-ing collective bargaining for teachers.[33]

In the speech, Shanker outlined a classical definition of what it meant to be a professional. A professional receives a liberal-arts education, then specialized training, and then must pass a rigorous exam before begin-ning to practice. She participates in an internship, is guided by mentors, and participates in reviewing the performance of colleagues. Once these professional responsibilities are met come the reciprocal set of rights: greater autonomy and higher compensation.[34] In Shanker's vision, poli-cies like a rigorous national test, peer review, and career ladders were not just defensive moves against critics of public-school teachers, they were prerequisites to the professionalization of teaching.

Finally, in order to be treated as an organization of professionals, he said, teachers' unions had to be not only concerned with self-interest but also with their members' "clients"—the students.[35] Here, Shanker added a new wrinkle: that students should be free to choose among public schools and should no longer be treated as "captive clients." Choice was linked to professionalism: "you choose a lawyer or doctor," he said. Choice within the public-school system would also reduce the pressure for private-school vouchers and tuition tax credits, he argued.[36] Endorsing public-school choice was another "huge and revolutionary" departure, says Toch.[37]

The National Board for Professional Teaching Standards

If Shanker's Niagara Falls speech made professionalism the organizing principle, his third added a new plank of tremendous importance. In a July 11, 1985, address to the AFT's Quality Educational Standards in Teaching (QuEST) conference in Washington, D.C., Shanker again made front-page news by backing an innovative compromise on the merit-pay issue: a system under which excellent teachers could receive national board certification, akin to doctors—and extra pay.[38] He told the conference: "We've heard the arguments about merit pay for at least 50 years and the issue does not go away. Most people in this country believe hard work and better work ought to be rewarded, and opposing this makes us look like we are not interested in quality. So we ought to think about ways of handing the issue while avoiding the pitfalls."[39]

Based on an idea proposed a quarter-century earlier by academic Myron Lieberman, Shanker called for the creation of a series of new national boards, made up largely of teachers and set up in different areas of the curriculum, like math and science and history, to certify "super-duper" teachers who passed a rigorous test and other evaluations. Local school boards and states would then have an incentive to pay board-certified teachers salary premiums. Shanker estimated that about 20 percent of the nation's two million teachers might become board certified.[40]

The proposal was meant to satisfy the key goals of merit pay: attracting and retaining high-quality teachers. Because teachers reach their top salary level by their mid-thirties, precisely when people in other professions see their salaries take off, the main way to increase one's salary was to move into administration. Board certification offered a way to keep excellent teachers in the classroom.[41] At the same time, a national board, using objective criteria, would avoid the problems of favoritism that plagued traditional merit-pay schemes. And because there was no fixed quota limiting who could qualify, national board certification would not pit teachers against one another and discourage cooperation the way many

merit-pay schemes did.[42] Likewise, teachers would not be penalized for
out-of-school influences, because extra pay was linked to extra qualifica-
tions, not student achievement.

Though the idea of national boards addressed some of the objections
to merit pay, it did not address all of them. How, exactly, would teacher
effectiveness be measured? (Shanker himself had raised this objection in
the past.) And the proposal had the potential to be divisive and threatened union solidarity. The NEA came out in opposition to Shanker's
proposal. "We need to increase the base salary of all teachers before we
start talking about special arrangements for some teachers," Mary Futrell
said in an interview. Futrell said she did not believe Shanker's proposal
"will fly."[43]

But Shanker had a strategy for moving forward with the proposal. Following Shanker's earlier Press Club speech, Marc Tucker of the Carnegie
Forum on Education and the Economy had created a "Task Force on
Teaching as a Profession."[44] The panel was chaired by Lewis M. Brans-
comb, a chief scientist and vice president of IBM. The fourteen-member
group included a number of luminaries, from former North Carolina
governor Jim Hunt to New Jersey Governor Thomas Kean and California
Superintendent of Instruction Bill Honig. Mary Futrell and Al Shanker
represented the teachers' unions. Tucker served as executive director.[45]

For Shanker, says Tucker, the Carnegie Task Force provided a neutral
vehicle through which the NEA might eventually sign on to Shanker's
idea of a national board. Shanker knew that if the board remained a
Shanker/AFT idea *per se*, the NEA could never embrace it. But if the proposal became a Carnegie plan, they just might support it. Shanker also
knew that Carnegie had the deep pockets to actually launch a national
board if it wished to.[46]

The Carnegie Task Force was a first point of collaboration for the two
warring teachers' union leaders. Education panels usually consisted of
AFT or NEA presidents, but not both. As the task force began its deliberations, Futrell and Shanker took very different roles. The NEA had enormous political power and was accustomed to simply stating positions and
watching legislators fall into line, Tucker says. Futrell treated the panel the
same way and would periodically make pronouncements about NEA
policy, as if letting the other board members know NEA's priorities would
automatically mean these priorities would prevail. Meanwhile, Shanker
astutely said little during the meetings, says Tucker. Everyone was aware

that Shanker's speech had helped launch the task force, and Shanker did not want to alienate the NEA by playing a highly vocal role in the proceedings.[47]

As the committee deliberated, the panel came down with several recommendations that were much closer to Shanker's view than Futrell's, Tucker says.[48] The key recommendation was the establishment of a private, nongovernmental National Board for Professional Teaching Standards (NBPTS), which would certify superb teachers who could receive extra pay. The board would be run by teachers, enabling them to take responsibility for their profession in the way that lawyers and doctors do.[49] (The panel made other recommendations—to eliminate the undergraduate degree in education so teachers would major in a subject area, such as math or history, and then take an additional one-year masters in teaching degree, for example—but these suggestions went nowhere.)[50]

A 140-page report, *A Nation Prepared: Teachers for the Twenty-First Century*, was released on May 16, 1986, in San Diego. The title was meant to be a direct response to *A Nation at Risk*.[51] Shanker was thrilled with the report, calling it "the first major move toward professionalism in teaching." He argued that the report would move the United States away from a system that invests heavily in paying supervisors to monitor low-paid teachers and toward one that hires high-quality teachers up front, teachers who "need fewer inspectors." Futrell, by contrast, provided a "statement of support with reservations" at the end of the report.[52] Futrell's statement included an attack on the lead-teacher concept, which "suggests that some teachers are more equal than others." Shanker responded saying: "This report deserves full support."[53]

The report made a big splash, and the Sunday following the report's release, Shanker appeared on "Meet the Press" with Bennett, Futrell, and Tennessee Governor Lamar Alexander.[54] Bennett said he was "generally very favorable" toward the recommendations in the report.[55] Carnegie's involvement also added prestige, because over the years it had introduced the concept of high-school credits, helped form the Educational Testing Service, and reorganized American medical education.[56]

The report's positive reception put the NEA in a difficult position at their upcoming annual convention in July.[57] On the one hand, the NEA was philosophically opposed to the National Board. A majority of the executive board of the NEA, says Don Cameron, saw the National Board as a form of merit pay that would single out certain teachers.[58] Internal polls showed the NEA Representative Assembly was opposed by an 80 percent to 20 percent margin. But Futrell knew that if the NEA flatly opposed the board, it would look obstructionist, and she devoted her whole speech at the convention to the National Board. In the end, the NEA supported it, with reservations.[59] At its Chicago convention, the AFT strongly supported the National Board.[60] Tucker called the support of the teachers' union crucial. "It's a real milestone," he said. "There was no way we were going to get education reform over the dead bodies of teachers."[61]

In May, 1987 a sixty-three-member National Board for Professional Teaching Standards was named. Two-thirds were teachers or educators, with the balance consisting of public officials, parents, and business leaders. Initial members of the board included Hunt (named as chair), Kean, Futrell, Shanker, Honig, and several others from the original Carnegie panel. The $50 million cost of setting up the board and the work of devising a set of standards and assessments over the coming several years would be picked up in part by Carnegie.[62] Shanker was elated by the progress, and in a May 1987 column he predicted that in fifty or one hundred years, the establishment of the NBPTS might be seen as "a major turning point in the history of our system of education," because it provided a bold step toward making teaching a full profession.[63]

In 1987, the National Board hired a president, James Kelly, and began the hard work of creating actual standards for teachers. Lloyd Bond, a consultant to the National Board on testing issues, remembers that Shanker pounded away at two themes over and over. The first was that the certification process must include a strong and clear content component as well as a pedagogical component. "If you don't know chemistry, you can't teach chemistry," he would argue.[64] The second theme was that standards had to be set very high. "This cannot be a thing that all teachers pass," Shanker said. Although it was arguably in the interests of a teachers' union to push for lower standards, so more members could qualify for extra money, Shanker insisted that board certification be very rigorous. When the process first began, Bond says, 65 percent of teachers failed; only half succeed today.[65]

At the meetings, Shanker was enormously influential. "It was a sixty-three-member board, but they weren't sixty-three equal people," Bond recalls. If Shanker had not spoken on an issue, Kelly would turn to him and say, "Al, surely you have something to say here."[66]

After a year and a half of work, the group unanimously agreed to a document called "What Teachers Should Know and Be Able to Do." Shanker's next column celebrated the event: "They said we couldn't do it and we did it." Says Kelly: "It had to be invented each step. It had never been done before anywhere in the world."[67] In order to take the NBPTS to scale, the group decided to seek congressional funding, and Shanker's influence on Capitol Hill was critical.[68] Shanker did a lot of personal lobbying on the project, AFT lobbyist Greg Humphrey says, and without him, "that never would have happened in a million years."[69]

Roughly a decade after Shanker first proposed a national board, the first eighty-one teachers were certified by the NBPTS.[70] Over the next decade, some forty thousand teachers would be certified.[71] This figure was significantly below the 20 percent mark Shanker had suggested, but it was forty thousand more than had existed before Shanker's speech.[72] According to Hunt, "more than any other single person, Al Shanker was the founder of the [organization]."[73] The National Board was among Shanker's most significant legacies.

Leaving the UFT

Shanker's three speeches—on the national teachers' test, the new professionalism, and the National Board for Professional Teaching Standards—thrust Shanker into the education-reform movement more substantially than ever, and he began to pull back from his duties as president of the United Federation of Teachers in New York City. Shanker had been for years slowly turning over the reins to Sandra Feldman, his longtime aide at the UFT. In 1981, he had named Feldman executive director of the union, and in the summer of 1983, she was elected secretary of the union, the second-highest position.[74]

The UFT was finally emerging from its dark days following the New York City fiscal crisis, and in September 1985, with the city back on good financial footing, the UFT won a 38 percent increase in pay over three years.[75] In December 1985, Shanker announced that he was stepping down as UFT president effective January 1, 1986. Feldman was appointed to fill out Shanker's term. Shanker said of his dual UFT-AFT presidencies: "The claims of both jobs have just been too much."[76]

Shanker announced his decision on the same day that the UFT held a celebration marking the organization's twenty-fifth anniversary.[77] In twenty-five years, the UFT had grown from two thousand members to 85,000, making it the largest local in the world.[78] The organization Feldman took over had become a major power broker, with the ability to veto chancellor appointments.[79] Shanker said his biggest achievement had been "giving power and voice and dignity to teachers," while his biggest regret was that "some of the basic things that are needed for teachers to get the job done are still not there."[80]

Education Statesman

Shanker's increasing emphasis on education reform opened a new battleground with the NEA over organizing. For years, in contested elections, the NEA presented itself as the professional organization that cared more about children and education, while the AFT presented itself as more militant and argued, "we bargain better than they do."[81]

But by the 1980s, the American Enterprise Institute's Denis Doyle said that Shanker's new emphasis on education reform, coupled with the NEA's resistance, presented a very different picture. "The AFT was always the scrappy, streetwise, bare-knuckles union," Doyle told the *Washington Post*, "and the NEA was the prim and prissy bunch of professionals who wouldn't dare think of themselves as union types. It's been a total transformation, a total role reversal."[82] On virtually every issue—teacher testing, peer review, differential pay, and public-school choice—Shanker was ahead of the much larger NEA. "Over the years," wrote Ted Fiske in the *New York Times*, "David has consistently outwitted Goliath."[83]

In battling the NEA, says Michael Kirst, Shanker was caught, organizationally, with a weak AFT state structure and a much smaller organization, so he tried to compensate for that "through the power of ideas."[84] Unlike the NEA, the AFT could not simply state a position and have it accepted in state legislatures because of its raw power. Instead, AFT leaders had to make an argument with logic. It was widely said that of the two teachers' unions, the NEA had the money and the AFT had the brains.[85] Going back to John Dewey and George Counts, the AFT had a strong intellectual tradition, one that became even more firmly rooted under Shanker. "It was a life of the mind here," says Bella Rosenberg.[86] Michael Usdan says the AFT outpaced the brainpower of not just the NEA but other education groups as well. "Intellectually, it's a much more talented group than you'll find in most of the other associations," he says.[87] Kelly argues that Shanker created a union in which bright, ambitious, vocal teachers could become union officials instead of school administrators, and his recruits continually outfoxed the managers.[88]

In organizing campaigns, Shanker's blunt talk about the need to reform education and improve teacher quality had its risks. AFT organizer Phil Kugler says some saw Shanker as "bashing" teachers.[89] At the same time, by the mid-1980s, polls were showing that younger members in particular were less concerned about bread-and-butter issues and more concerned about teacher professionalism.[90] During recruitment drives, AFT organizers would wave the *American Educator*—with its thoughtful articles on cultural literacy and phonics—and emphasize the AFT's strong professional development department to point out differences with the NEA.[91]

In Texas, for example, Shanker's emphasis on professionalism helped counter local distrust of unions. The Texas literature emphasized professional issues and made no mention of the AFL-CIO.[92] Education reform also increased the AFT's power in the halls of Congress, where Shanker was seen as more credible than the NEA.[93] Across the country, AFT literature would emphasize Shanker's meetings with the business groups to try to deflate the old reputation of the AFT as the militant organization and the NEA as the professional group.[94]

Shanker's embrace of education reform won him plaudits from the very institutions that had reviled him during Ocean Hill–Brownsville: the press, the academy, foundations, the business community, and leaders in government. The *New Republic* ran the story "Albert Shanker, Statesman: The Fiery Unionist as Educational Leader," while the *Wall Street Journal* declared: "Shanker, Once-Militant Head of Teachers' Union, Now Is Called Original Thinker in Education."[95] A *U.S. News & World Report* story on the New American Establishment named Shanker as one of ten key voices on education, along with the U.S. Secretary of Education, the presidents of Harvard, Yale, Princeton, the University of Chicago, New York University, the University of California, and the Carnegie Foundation for the Advancement of Teaching—and the then-governor of Arkansas, Bill Clinton. The NEA president was notably absent.[96] The *Boston Herald* called Shanker "the Mikhail Gorbachev of American labor leaders."[97] Shanker was invited to appear on prominent shows and was a guest on "Meet the Press" and "This Week with David Brinkley."[98]

In the academy, Shanker began receiving honorary degrees from places including the Graduate Center at the City University of New York and

Adelphi University.[99] There were also invitations to teach. At Hunter College, Shanker co-taught with the institution's president, Donna Shalala, a course called "Politics of Education."[100] He also taught a course on "Education Policy in the 1980s" at Harvard.[101]

Liberal writers such as Jonathan Kozol, who had gone head to head with Shanker over Ocean Hill–Brownsville, gained new respect for the union leader. In a letter, Kozol wrote to Shanker: "There aren't many voices as clear as yours these days; the media has, by and large, succumbed to right-wing lacerations of the teachers and the public schools. I'm glad you're there."[102]

While Shanker had gone to war with the Ford Foundation in the 1960s and had testified in favor of great restrictions on foundation activity, two decades later he was now asked to join the boards of the Spencer Foundation in Chicago and the Twentieth Century Fund in New York, "one of only a handful of labor leaders to serve as a foundation trustee," one expert noted.[103]

In the 1980s, Shanker's openness to education reform also caught the attention of the business community. Initially, many were wary. At one meeting of the Committee for Economic Development (CED), a business group, Bella Rosenberg recalls that when Shanker walked into the room of heavy-hitting businessmen "you could literally feel the air stiffen."[104] Fletcher Byrom, the chairman of the Koppers Company, Inc., a chemical manufacturer, said of Shanker, "I thought he was a reprehensible character," calling strikes and shutting down the schools. But the two began to work together on education issues through the CED and forged a strong relationship. Byrom said, "Al Shanker understands the problems facing public schools better than any other person in the country."[105] Alexander J. Trotman, the British CEO of Ford Motor Company, told Sol Hurwitz, the president of the CED, that after hearing Shanker speak at a Business Roundtable meeting on education, "Shanker made more sense than any of the business leaders in the entire room."[106] Shanker forged an especially strong relationship with Owen "Brad" Butler, the Republican chairman of Procter & Gamble. Donna Shalala, who served with Butler and Shanker on a CED committee in the early 1980s, said the businesspeople on the committee were quite sharp, but Shanker "was their intellectual match," which is why he had credibility with them.[107] In addition, Shanker knew how to communicate with them. "The business community has never really been able to understand what comes out of the ed schools," particularly the lack of emphasis on incentives and rewards, says Diane Ravitch, "but they understood Al and he could talk to them. . . . And they listened to him because he spoke their language."[108]

Finally, Shanker's openness to education reform gave him a special credibility with education-minded governors, such as Bill Clinton of Arkansas and Tom Kean of New Jersey.[109] Education reformer Ted Kolderie remembers attending a meeting of the Education Commission of the States in the early 1980s and hearing leading governors such as Chuck Robb of Virginia, Bob Graham of Florida, and Al Quie of Minnesota saying that Shanker was "the only real statesman" in the teachers' union movement.[110] When groups like the National Governors Association sought speakers, says Stanford's Michael Kirst, they asked "Al, not the NEA" to speak.[111] While the DLC was generally very critical of labor, Shanker was seen as an exception—someone concerned about quality—and was invited to participate in discussions.[112]

The stunning transformation—from the man who was labeled a madman in *Sleeper* and was now embraced by the press, foundations, academics, and governors—was on one level genuine. There was a shift in emphasis over time from a leader who said he would represent children when they started paying union dues to the man who talked about students as cherished clients. But in two important senses, the old Shanker and the new Shanker were deeply connected.

For one thing, Shanker's early militancy gave him the credibility to push education reform in a manner unorthodox for a union leader. He could say things that were perceived as at variance with established teacher interests and yet be continually reelected, says Marc Tucker, because "at some point he had established his credentials with them as a union leader so firmly that his constituency was willing to let him do those things."[113] Keith Geiger, former president of the NEA, agrees. The fact that Shanker had been to jail and led strikes meant "he never had to prove to anybody he was a unionist. And so he could branch out on the less safe issues without having to worry about anybody cutting the branch off."[114] And at a more basic level, of course, if Shanker had not built the union into a powerful force in the early years, he would not have had the platform to talk about education reform in the 1980s.[115]

Moreover, at a philosophical level, the "bad Al" of the early years and the "good Al" of the later years fit together as one piece. Throughout his career, Shanker was guided by the related goals of democracy in education and the professionalization of teaching. In 1960, 1962, 1967, and

1968, Shanker led militant strikes to raise the status of the profession and promote and defend a voice for teachers. That call for greater teacher voice continued to sound in his education proposals in the 1980s, albeit in a different political and educational environment. Peer review not only answered an argument for abolishing tenure, it gave expert teachers a greater voice in determining who would remain in the profession and who should leave. Likewise, the National Board was not only an answer to merit pay, it strengthened democratic control over the profession by ensuring that rewards would be determined not by the whims of supervisors but by objective criteria and an evaluation conducted mostly by fellow teachers.

Albert Shanker always rejected the idea that labor unions, including teachers' unions, were just another special interest like cigarette manufacturers or oil companies. But he understood that teachers' unions could sometimes look like they were unconcerned about educational quality, and in the mid-1980s, during an era of major rethinking within the Democratic Party, Shanker launched some of his most innovative proposals, from the National Teacher Exam to the National Board for Professional Teaching Standards. In doing so, he not only engaged in a defensive maneuver, blunting the effectiveness of the "special interest" charge, but he also affirmatively engaged in a long-term project of marrying trade unionism and the professionalization of teaching.

Now, toward the end of the 1980s, Shanker would challenge the education establishment once again, this time with a new idea for democratic and professional reform of the schools: school restructuring and teacher-led "charter" schools.

16

Charter Schools and School Restructuring

1988–1997

Iɴ the mid-to-late 1980s, Shanker helped launch another important education reform—teacher-run "charter schools." In Shanker's original vision, these publicly financed schools would give teachers greater freedom to experiment with innovative teaching techniques, student groupings, and other education reforms. The experiments would be time-limited and subject to rigorous evaluation. Having propelled the idea forward, however, he would watch with increasing alarm as the movement transformed into something quite different than he originally intended, with many—though not all—charter schools actually undercutting his initial vision.

School Restructuring

Shanker's concept of charter schools grew out of his belief that schooling needed to be "restructured," to move beyond the old factory model of education. Fundamentally, the factory model—in which principals barked orders to teachers who lectured students who were passed from classroom to classroom and expected to learn at the same pace—was not working well for many kids and many teachers.[1] As a political matter, focusing on "restructuring" also allowed Shanker to sidestep the growing call for longer school days and years, something his members despised, by emphasizing quality over quantity.

Shanker argued that the top-down reform movement that left the basic factory model in place was working for perhaps 15 to 25 percent of students, but a bottom-up restructuring of education was required for the other 80 percent who do not learn well in a traditional school setting.[2] Many students are not able to sit quietly and listen to others talk for five hours a day, he said. "Most adults can't do it; most kids can't do it."[3] Some of these students might in fact be very bright. He argued, "what we say to kids is either you will learn one way by sitting there and listening to me, otherwise we're going to label you as being stupid and we'll give you bad marks."[4] Shanker had in his early years been a nontraditional learner who sometimes behaved poorly because he was bored. Shanker knew that his sons Adam and Michael were bright but struggled in school and that different approaches were needed to reach children like them.[5] "You have to be like a doctor," Shanker said. "If the medicine doesn't work, he doesn't bawl the hell out of you because you didn't respond to his pill. You've got to try a variety of things."[6]

In restructuring schools, Shanker suggested specific Deweyite ideas on how to make learning more interesting for kids. Shanker was particularly intrigued by his October 1987 visit to the Holweide Comprehensive School in Cologne, Germany, where teachers had moved away from lecturing toward cooperative learning among students. Shanker noted that in America, the school structure—grouping by age, forty-to-fifty-minute periods on different subjects—assumed that students learn at the same pace. But at the Cologne school, a diverse group of students including Turkish and Moroccan pupils relied on cooperative learning, in which mixed-achievement-level groups sit at tables and learn through interaction with peers. There was a minimum of teacher lecturing.[7] Cooperative learning, he argued later, was the way students learned in the one-room schoolhouse, where older students helped younger students. Moving toward less lecturing and more learning in small groups is a superior way of raising achievement, he argued.[8] Cooperative learning also reflected the way things work in the adult world. "On the job," he said, "we are expected to ask those close to us to show us, to explain, to help. The important thing is to get something done right, and usually that means doing it together with others. In school, asking others for help is called cheating."[9]

Shanker was also intrigued by Dewey's notion of following a child's interests and learning by doing. In his columns and speeches, Shanker often talked about how, as a Boy Scout, he learned about birds by going out early in the morning to fields and studying them in a manner that stuck with him for longer than if he had memorized the different species from flash cards in a classroom. Shanker believed the way in which he earned his birdwatching merit badge was more interesting and engaging.[10] Shanker also pointed to the Japanese example, noting their success in using mixed-achievement-level classes in elementary school and in-depth learning about a narrow range of topics.[11]

The factory model was also hard for teachers because it suggested that they were an undifferentiated mass of line workers who had little to contribute in the running of the enterprise. In Shanker's thinking, school restructuring was linked to his quest for the professionalization of teaching through differentiated staffing, in which certain highly talented teachers took on greater responsibilities and were paid more, accordingly.[12] At the Holweide Comprehensive School, teams of six to eight teachers made important decisions about how their cohort of eighty-five to ninety students were educated, such as how the students would be grouped and who would teach which subjects.[13]

Advocating restructuring also answered a political problem Shanker had. The *Nation at Risk* called for American schools to lengthen the school day and the school year to match America's competitors—England and many other industrialized countries—an idea that many teachers hated.[14] Polling found that teachers opposed a longer school day by 77 percent to 21 percent and a longer school year by 71 percent to 26 percent.[15] The restructuring focus allowed Shanker to argue that a longer school day or school year was not worth the extra expense.[16] He picked up an analogy from IBM executive Jack Bowsher, who said: "If 25% of the computers were falling off the assembly line before they reached the end, and if 90% of the completed ones didn't work 80% of the time—the last thing in the world the company would do would be to run that same old assembly line an additional hour each day or an extra month each year. Instead, IBM would rethink the entire production process."[17]

Shanker's discussion of school restructuring came in the context of a burgeoning movement toward public-school choice. In the mid-to-late-1980s, more and more parents were being given choice among public schools. In 1986, the National Governors Association endorsed public-school choice in its "Time for Results" report. Legislatures passed laws permitting greater choice within the public schools, and in the decade of the 1980s the percentage of Americans who agreed that parents should have public-school choice shot up from 12 to 62.[18] The question became: could the idea of school restructuring be married to the movement toward public-school choice?

The Charter-School Proposal

Shanker's thoughts about restructuring and choice came together in a landmark address he gave at the National Press Club on March 31, 1988, five years after *A Nation at Risk* was released, in which he proposed the idea of "charter schools." In the speech and in subsequent articles, Shanker suggested that small groups of teachers and parents (as few as six) submit research-based proposals for schools (or schools within schools) to a panel consisting of the local school board and union officials. The teachers would say: "We've got a way of doing something different. We've got a way of reaching the kids that are not being reached by what the school is doing." Once given a "charter," a term first used in education by educator Ray Budde, the school would then be left alone—for five or ten years, as long as parents and teachers continued to support the experiment and there was no precipitous drop in achievement. Shanker also made clear that the charter schools should not draw from the pool of the most advantaged children, but rather should reflect the general school population.[19]

In his speech, Shanker said schools should be able to bend collectively bargained rules in certain circumstances, pointing to a UFT program under which changes to the teacher contract could be made in schools where 65 percent of the teachers, the principal, the union representative, and the superintendent agreed.[20] For example, in one school principals and teachers waived certain clauses of the contract in order to conduct evening meetings with parents and hold workshops for themselves. In another, class-size requirements were waived in order to merge two classes so teachers could team-teach.[21]

But in keeping with the teacher-led vision for charter schools, the union would remain a central player, Shanker said. He called for districts to "create joint school board–union panels that would review preliminary proposals and help find seed money for the teachers to develop final proposals."[22] Indeed, Shanker noted that the places where education reform and restructuring were occurring most actively were those areas where unions were strong. "You don't see these creative things happening where teachers don't have any voice or power or influence," he said.[23]

As a model for charter schools, Shanker often referred to the Saturn auto plant in Nashville, Tennessee. At the Saturn plant, teams of workers made suggestions to one another and to management about how best the job could be accomplished. Shanker argued, "if Saturn were a school, it would be a charter school." Workers were listened to and had dignity. Shanker said: "It isn't just about a couple extra bucks to somebody. And it's not just a way of making a better car. It is a way of fulfilling a mission of how human beings should be treated."[24]

Conservatives were skeptical of Shanker's concept of having teacher-led schools engage in widespread experimentation. William Kristol, then chief of staff to William Bennett, said the department "didn't have problems" with the proposal, but also said, "we think there is lots of evidence that traditional methods are working."[25] Bush's Assistant Secretary of Education Chester Finn attacked the charter-school proposal, saying it suggested that we did not already know what works in education.[26]

But the charter-school concept soon picked up momentum. At the July 1988 AFT national convention in San Francisco, Shanker elaborated on his call for restructuring and charter schools in his keynote address, and delegates voted to endorse the controversial idea.[27] Reformers in Minnesota, a pioneer state in public-school choice, were particularly enthusiastic about Shanker's charter-school idea. Early after the Press Club speech, the Citizens League, a local policy group, began developing a charter program for Minnesota. In October, after hearing Shanker present the idea at the Minneapolis Foundation's Itasca Seminar, two Democratic-Farmer-Labor (DFL) legislators, State Senator Ember Reichgott and Representative Ken Nelson, became interested. Their bill, enacted in 1991, created the nation's first chartering law.[28]

The idea of charter schools became especially appealing to centrist Democrats as an alternative to the growing movement toward school vouchers. In the spring of 1990, the Wisconsin state legislature voted to establish the nation's first publicly funded school-voucher program in Milwaukee. The plan was meant to pull on the heartstrings of liberals by aiding low-income, mostly African American students stuck in bad Milwaukee schools. Students began using the vouchers in the fall of that year.[29] The year 1990 also saw the publication of a seminal pro-voucher book, by John Chubb and Terry Moe, researchers from the Washington-

based Brookings Institution. The book purported to scientifically demonstrate why the use of the private-school market would produce achievement gains superior to those seen in democratically controlled public
schools. The volume received wide attention and reinvigorated the movement toward vouchers.[30] (Shanker and others attacked the volume as
flawed.)

In November 1990, the Democratic Leadership Council published a
paper by education reformer Ted Kolderie entitled *Beyond Choice to New
Public Schools*, which elaborated on the concept of charter schools. Reviewing the developments in Milwaukee and the sensation caused by the
Chubb and Moe book, Kolderie argued that charters could offer the benefits of vouchers while avoiding the drawbacks.[31] The idea of charter
schools was picked up by another centrist Democrat, California State
Senator Gary Hart, who sponsored a law that passed in 1992.[32] And, most
importantly, charters received the strong backing of DLC chair and presidential candidate Bill Clinton. In 1992, when George H. W. Bush began
championing a thousand-dollar voucher program for all students with
family income below the median, Clinton responded with public-school
choice and charter schools.[33]

The Charter-School Reality

In the coming years, however, as state after state adopted charter-school
laws and the federal government pitched in with seed money, Shanker,
the man who was called the "godfather," the "initiat[or]," and "de facto
creator" of charter schools, watched with alarm as the concept he put forward began to move away from a public-school reform effort to look
more like a private-school voucher plan.[34] In a similar reversal, conservative educator Checker Finn, who initially opposed charter schools, became their great champion.[35] Shanker came to believe that the charter-
school movement was largely hijacked by conservatives who made many
charter schools vulnerable to the same groups that made voucher schools
so dangerous: for-profit corporations, racial separatists, the religious
right, and anti-union activists.

First came the issue of privatization. Shanker became quite exercised
when state laws were written to allow private, for-profit corporations to
enter the charter-school business. When Chris Whittle's for-profit Edison
Project announced it would contract with communities to manage indi-

vidual schools, especially charter schools, Shanker warned that for-profit companies in education would care more about looking after their share-holders than educating children.[36] Wall Street saw a $300 billion business possibility, says Bella Rosenberg, and Shanker watched with dismay as "those who had tremendous contempt for public education" jumped on to the charter-schools bandwagon.[37] Shanker told the DLC's Al From, says Rachelle Horowitz, that we have to be very careful about the way that charter schools are structured "or else they will become things for huck-sters."[38] Another problem with privatization, said Sandra Feldman, is that companies would promote "cookie-cutter schools which are the ex-act opposite of what he was suggesting, where teachers would have a lot more say."[39]

Shanker began referring to the charter-schools movement as a "gim-mick" comparable to school vouchers and private management of public schools. "Vouchers, charter schools, for-profit management schemes are all quick fixes that won't fix anything," he wrote.[40] While some charter schools were good, he wrote in 1994, "there are other supporters of char-ter schools whose real aim is to smash the public schools."[41] (Today, roughly 20 percent of charter schools are privately run.)[42]

The second way in which charter schools began to resemble private schools was the way in which some state laws allowed segregation and Balkanization.[43] In particular, Shanker pointed to the charter law in Cali-fornia, which allowed schools to use contracts with parents to skim the most motivated families and exclude others. Contracts, which required parents to volunteer in school and attend meetings or be subject to fines, discriminated against students based on their parents' actions. "The par-ent contract serves as a kind of sorting device," he said, in which "children whose parents are scared off by the contract's tone, or don't have the time to volunteer, or can't read, or don't understand what is being asked, won't be enrolling in one of these schools."[44] Worse was a charter school proposal in Virginia, backed by Republican Governor George Allen, which Shanker attacked for allowing schools to "set their own admissions policies."[45]

Likewise, Shanker was worried that some charter schools were pro-moting racial separatism. Shanker devoted one column to an article by Michael Kelly in the *New Republic*, which recounted the goings-on at the Marcus Garvey Public Charter School in Washington, D.C. When a white reporter from the *Washington Times* went to write a story about the Afro-centric school, she was assaulted and told to get her "white ass out of this school."[46] Kelly noted that charter schools were popular both with some conservatives, who want to teach traditional values in their charter schools, and some liberals, who want to teach Afrocentrism in theirs. But, said Kelly,

> this bi-ideological popularity is, as the Garvey case shows, exactly why such things as charter schools and school voucher programs cannot in the end succeed. A pluralistic society cannot sustain a scheme in which the citizenry pays for a school but has no influence over how the school is run. . . . Public money is shared money, and it is to be used for the furtherance of shared values, in the interests of *e pluribus unum*. Charter schools and their like are definitionally antithetical to this American promise. They take from the *pluribus* to destroy the *unum*.[47]

The segregation of the charter-school market—with affluent students at one end and racial minorities at another—was exactly what Shanker had sought to avoid when he proposed in his Press Club speech that charter schools have representative populations.

Third, Shanker was concerned that some private religious schools were being closed and then reopened in somewhat different form as charter schools, with taxpayer money.[48] Shanker wrote about one Michigan charter school, Noah Webster Academy, which received public funds to establish a computer network to educate a group of Christian home-schooled students. Shanker said: "The students will continue to study at home the way they do now, but every family will get a taxpayer-paid computer, printer and modem, and there will be an optional curriculum that teaches creationism alongside biology."[49]

Fourth, Shanker was deeply concerned that instead of empowering teachers, as he had envisioned, charter schools were becoming a way to avoid having to deal with protections provided to teachers by their unions—again, just like private schools. Shanker had proposed that under certain circumstances charter schools be able to waive certain collective-bargaining rules, such as the length of meetings, but teachers would remain unionized, and indeed, unions would be part of the body that approved the charter-school applications. But once the charter movement took off, conservatives were quite open about the fact that charter-school laws provided a critical end-run around teacher unions. Chester Finn argued that "the single most important form of freedom for charter schools is to hire and fire employees as they like and pay them as they see fit."[50]

Shanker "was pretty disgusted with it," says Bella Rosenberg. The charter-school movement "became anti-union, and that was its main thing, anti-union."[51] In Michigan, for example, all 583 public-school districts in a recent year had unionized teachers, compared with only five of 139 charter schools.[52]

In a February 1996 AFT Executive Council meeting, Shanker was quite candid about what he thought of what had become of the charter-school movement he helped start. Republican legislation in Congress creating charter schools in Washington, D.C., he said, was "anti-union" and "anti-teacher." Shanker noted: "It sets up a charter commission which can empower all sorts of groups to issue charters. What is very clear is that they're not going to be required to hire certified personnel. They're not going to be under any collective bargaining agreement." Across the country, from Pennsylvania to California, Shanker said, the charter-school movement was being used in a way "designed to undermine unions and collective bargaining, to destroy them. . . . " He expressed frustration that "it is almost impossible for us to get President Clinton to stop endorsing them in all of his speeches." While there can be good charter schools, ones set up with the consent of teachers, "that isn't what's happening for the most part," Shanker said. "For the most part, what's happening is this is a way of breaking up the union. . . . "[53]

This was hardly teacher democracy, Shanker said, and it would also ultimately limit the effectiveness of the charter-school movement. If charters became an explicitly anti-union weapon, he said, their growth would be opposed by unions, and the lessons learned would be resisted by teachers in the unionized sector, undercutting a chief rationale for experimentation in the first place.[54]

Shanker soured on the charter-school movement primarily because of dramatic changes in the movement itself. But in part, Shanker changed his own mind about what type of education reform was most likely to improve the academic achievement of children. He rethought the issue and became increasingly convinced that reforms like school restructuring and charter schools put the cart before the horse, because there was no general agreement on the goals to be pursued.[55] First, you needed outcome standards, so you could evaluate whether or not the reforms were helping or hurting.[56] A system of public-school choice and charter schools without a system of standards made little sense. Shanker asked: how could parents judge schools without a system of standards in place to give a basis for comparison?[57] The reason innovative schooling in places like the

Holweide School in Cologne worked well was that Germany had in place standards and a common curriculum.[58]

Shanker began intensively examining systems abroad and came to the conclusion that having a high-quality national curriculum was critical. In a March 1992 speech, Shanker argued: "What the Canadians and the Germans and the French and the Dutch and the Swedes and the Japanese and others have shown is that you can, in a pretty traditional system, do things that bring about substantially better results than the results that we produce."[59] Shanker later argued that the countries that did well on the Third International Mathematics and Science Study (TIMSS) were not those with "vouchers or charter schools or any of the other jazzy schemes that we are being urged to try. Nearly all of these nations have clear and rigorous national or state curriculum standards, and everything they do in the schools is hitched to these standards."[60]

In 1988, Shanker had spoken favorably about the idea of allowing teachers the autonomy to "set their own curriculums, select their own textbooks," and have greater flexibility.[61] Reforms like school-based management and charter schools could find out what worked best. But by the early 1990s, he had come to reject that approach. Without a common, consistent core in the curriculum, Shanker said, given the amount of student mobility in America, charter schools could be a recipe for "educational chaos."[62] He argued: "The do-your-own curriculums that are a feature of charter schools are poorly suited to our mobile society."[63] Shanker attacked Governor Allen's charter-school proposal in Virginia for allowing schools to set their own curricula, which might allow a school to concentrate on self-esteem, for example, and not mathematics, English, and history proficiency.[64]

While Shanker continued to worry about equity—reaching students who struggled with traditional teaching approaches—he argued that standards and a common curriculum would do a better job of accomplishing the goal than experimentation, which allowed a thousand flowers to bloom—including many weeds.[65] And he began to talk less and less about innovative pedagogical approaches that gave choices to students about what to focus on, shifting instead to the idea that students needed to be exposed to a common core of knowledge. The "Bird Merit Badge" phase was "a pre-standards Al looking at education," says Marcia Reecer.[66]

Finally, Shanker shifted because he said there was no evidence that school restructuring and charter schools as a whole were working. Shanker argued in July 1996: "In the charter schools we now have, there is no re-cord with respect to achievement or meeting standards."[67] The system of "bottom-up" accountability—parents will withdraw their students if achievement goes down—was flawed, Shanker said, because schools could thrive on "popularity rather than quality."[68]

Shanker recognized, of course, that while on average the charter-school movement was a disappointment, there were good charter schools and bad charter schools. Some charter schools had high standards, provided union protection for teachers, had diverse student populations, were run by secular nonprofits, and were producing positive achievement results. (Indeed, the UFT itself later created two charter schools based on these types of principles.)[69] In the February 1996 AFT Executive Council meet-ing, in which Shanker was highly critical of many charter schools for pro-moting an anti-union agenda, he said he was not willing to give up on the idea altogether. He said the AFT should "put out a careful analysis of the range of types of charter schools and what's good and what's bad about different provisions in them and how they work." Such an analysis "could have a tremendous impact on influencing good legislation and getting rid of lousy legislation."[70]

In general, however, Albert Shanker largely repudiated a major reform he had helped launch. The charter-school movement was turning out to look like the two central nemeses he had battled throughout his career—school vouchers on the right and "community control" on the left. Many charter schools were involved in private "contracting out" on the one hand and "decentralization" to the point of Balkanization on the other. Charter schools were not empowering teachers; they were trying to un-dercut teachers' unions. They were not providing innovative and creative ways of teaching an agreed-upon curriculum; they were creating their very own curriculums. And there was no evidence that the experiments were raising student achievement, the ultimate test. So in the final years of his life, Shanker turned away from charters to a very different idea, where he would make his biggest mark yet: education standards.

17

The Early Education-Standards Movement

1989–1994

TODAY, the education-standards movement—the call for educators to outline content standards of what students should know, to test them to see how well they know it, and to make students and adults accountable for failure—is the leading and most notable feature of the American education-policy landscape. Differing versions of the approach have been at the center of education policy in the last three presidential administrations, including the controversial federal No Child Left Behind Act of 2001. Virtually all discussions in education ultimately tie back to standards, testing, and accountability.

This was not always the case. For years, the United States was the outlier in the world, resisting a system of standards, assessment, and consequences. (The United States continues to be an outlier in favoring local control and resisting national standards.) But in the years after *A Nation at Risk*, a group of governors and business leaders outside the world of education sought to have states adopt standards-based reform. While most of the education establishment fought the effort, reformers found a surprising ally—indeed, leader—in Albert Shanker.

The standards movement began in the late 1980s, out of a growing frustration with "school restructuring." The idea begged the question: restructuring to achieve what specific goals?[1] *A Nation at Risk* had done a good job of outlining what courses students should take and for how many years they should take them, but there was still a big hole at the center of American education: the lack of agreement on what skills and knowledge students should master. Teachers had textbooks but no real guidance on what to prioritize, so they were, essentially, asked to create their own curricula. Teachers ended up choosing very different topics to pursue, based on personal interests, creating incoherence and confusion. A teacher could not assume to know what students had learned the year before, so just to be safe, many teachers ended up repeating material that some students had already learned, which was a waste of time and also induced boredom and created discipline problems. Given an incoherent curriculum, teachers had little ground on which to collaborate and improve their skills. Since teachers were not on the same page content-wise, professional development tended to focus on vacuous topics such as learning styles, rather than on how best to teach, for example, the French Revolution.[2] Likewise, although testing had long existed, too often, like an SAT test, they assessed general skills, rather than curriculum knowledge (like an AP test would assess).[3]

In an influential paper, Marshall Smith and his coauthor Jennifer O'Day argued for an alternative to this chaos: standards-based reform that could promote both excellence and equity.[4] Smith and O'Day outlined a systemic reform in which all horses—standards, curriculum, textbooks, tests, teacher training, and teacher development—pulled in the same direction. Directing everything was a "curriculum framework" or content standard of "what students should know and be able to do." The actual curriculum, materials, and state assessments would flow from the standards. Teacher licenses would be based on demonstrating the skills needed to teach the agreed-upon content. Finally, students and educators would be held accountable for mastering the content as measured by student assessments.[5]

Obstacles to Education Standards

The coalition opposed to standards, testing, and accountability (especially national standards) was formidable, and included liberals and conservatives: education-school academics, the NEA, civil-rights groups, some middle-class parents, and advocates of state and local control. The

groups lodged ten main objections to the standards, testing, and accountability scheme:

- Many education-school professors opposed establishing content
  standards because they feared a return to the day when students
  memorized facts rather than learning problem-solving skills and
  critical thinking. Many teachers also opposed specifying content
  standards because they wanted to be free to teach the content that
  interested them or their students.
- Some academics and civil-rights groups worried that the "content"
  standards would be biased toward Europeans, particularly in the
  subject of history. As a result, the tests were also likely to be culturally biased.
- Meanwhile, some conservatives pointed to the long American tradition of local control of education in their opposition to national
  content standards (or even state standards). Some religious conservatives saw in the standards movement an effort to impose secular
  and liberal values on their children.
- Some education-school professors worried that a system of testing
  would hurt the self-esteem of struggling students, which in turn
  would hinder their ability to learn. In earlier years, the NEA claimed
  that standardized tests "maim children" and ran campaign ads showing a child crying after having failed a test.[6]
- The NEA (along with many academics) argued that standards and
  assessments would require teachers to teach to the test and rob them
  of their creativity.[7]
- Some middle-class parents, meanwhile, feared that state or national
  performance standards would be set low, leading teachers to spend
  all their time on struggling students, ignoring more gifted children.
- Some educators were opposed to the use of consequences for students, which they considered crass. John Dewey opposed the use of
  "fear" and "bribes," preferring instead to instill a love of learning in
  students.[8]
- The NEA did not want tests used to judge the performance of teachers, citing research suggesting that home and family environment
  were more responsible for learning than the teacher.[9]
- Some feared that performance standards would be set impossibly
  high and that high rates of test failure among public school students

would simply fuel the demand for tuition tax credits and private-school vouchers.

- Civil-rights groups often argued that the accountability portion of standards-based reform was racially discriminatory. Because poor and minority students were consigned to generally inferior schools, high-stakes tests that came with consequences (such as denial of a diploma) were unfair.

For many years, this coalition of the left and right kept national standards, testing, and accountability off the radar screen. Publication of the *A Nation at Risk* report, however, began to spur new discussion. The business community, worried about U.S. competitiveness in a global economy, and centrist governors, particularly in the South, came together to suggest that Americans should know more about what they were getting in return for their investment in education. Business leaders, in particular, were attracted to the idea of setting measurable goals and targets for education, just as they routinely did in the corporate world.

Shanker's Support for Standards

As the battle shaped up between education-school professors, the NEA, civil-rights groups, and local-control conservatives on the one hand, and business groups and governors on the other, Shanker broke with his colleagues in education and wholeheartedly embraced standards-based reform. Many of America's competitors in Europe and Japan had systems of national standards, rigorous testing, and student accountability, and Shanker saw that these systems were providing higher levels of student achievement. The systems were coherent and made life more predictable for both teachers and students. Everyone knew in advance what was expected of them, and the system turned teachers and students from adversaries into allies. "It's like the Olympics," Shanker said. "There's an external standard that students need to meet, and the teacher is there to help the student make it."[10] A national curriculum, of the type used in Japan, also made the teacher's job more manageable: teachers would no longer be responsible for both writing the script and performing it; they could, like actors, focus on interpretation and delivery. In the words of professors Harold Stevenson and Jim Stigler, teachers could get together and "polish the stone."[11]

Shanker also argued that common content standards were egalitarian because they sought to teach children knowledge that is required to do well in mainstream society. While middle-class children usually pick up some of that knowledge on their own at home, poor kids rarely do, Shanker said.[12] Content standards also promote equity by making clear to all what measures students were going to be judged by. When the content standards are murky, the upper middle class will figure them out and work toward them, while poor and working-class kids remain mystified, Shanker said.[13] Standards also prevented poor children from receiving a less challenging curriculum.[14] He argued, "in a system without standards, they often go to schools where little or nothing is expected of them."[15] Looking internationally, Shanker argued that systems in Germany, France, and Japan did better with low-income students because they have high standards: "equity is better served by demanding a lot of all students—and helping them meet those demands."[16]

In addition to making an affirmative case for standard-based reform, Shanker responded, point by point, to the objections lodged by most of the education establishment.

Facts Versus Critical Thinking

To begin with, Shanker disagreed with education school professors who favored general thinking skills over gaining specific-content knowledge.[17] He believed students needed both, and that John Dewey's education theories had been misinterpreted by some "progressive" educators. "Dewey had reacted against the old-time education which thought that you just take a kid and just stuff his brain," said Shanker. But "Dewey himself was shocked when he went into some of these progressive schools and saw what was going on in his name."[18]

In the 1980s, Shanker became an early advocate of University of Virginia English Professor E. D. (Don) Hirsch Jr.'s argument that American students needed to be "culturally literate"—to master a body of facts that literate Americans know—in order to be successful in mainstream society. A full two years before Hirsch's bestselling book *Cultural Literacy* became a phenomenon, Shanker embraced Hirsch's view that knowing subject matter was important to reading comprehension because reading is not just a formal skill, transferable to any text, but depends on having the requisite background knowledge particular to each text.[19] An Englishman reading a sports page in an American newspaper might be able to decode the words but might not fully understand the meaning without knowing the full context.[20] "To read well you need background information that is culture-specific," Shanker argued.[21] Students needed to be taught Shakespeare and mythology so they could understand common cultural references.

Shanker was also taken by Hirsch's argument that when students know particular content matter, their interest and curiosity are more likely to be aroused. A student who knows something about dinosaurs is more likely to pick up a book on dinosaurs when browsing through the library. "Subject matter," Shanker argued, "is the life's breath of learning."[22] While some "progressive" educators dismissed Hirsch's approach as emphasizing "mere facts," Shanker wrote thirteen separate columns mentioning Hirsch's theory, invited Hirsch to speak at the AFT's biennial QuEST Conference, and featured Hirsch on the cover of *American Educator*.[23]

Eurocentric Curriculum

Shanker also disagreed with those who charged that content standards were culturally biased if they did not provide "equal time" for every ethnic group. While Shanker had long pushed for the inclusion of various ethnic contributions into the history curriculum, he believed that the core knowledge of the dominant culture was essential for all students to master if they wished to advance socioeconomically within the society. Shanker cited Hirsch's research, which found that in West Germany and France, the children of low-income Turkish guest workers and other immigrants did much better academically than low-income Americans in part because they were exposed from a very early age to the key elements of the dominant culture.[24] Pointing to the work of the Italian radical political theorist and activist Antonio Gramsci, Hirsch noted that if the poor are going to flourish, they need to learn the skills of those with power and to master the traditional culture.[25] Shanker argued:

> Some people have been very critical of Hirsch's proposals on the grounds that they try to impose the dominant culture on groups that would rather have their children learn their own culture. But the thrust of Hirsch's proposal is egalitarian. He believes that by starting early and by giving all children the same core knowledge to learn, we can prevent the creation of an educational underclass.[26]

The Hirsch/Shanker argument came under attack from some minority advocates who blamed low minority-student achievement on the "Eurocentric" nature of the public-school curriculum. The issue came to a head in 1989, when the New York State Education Commissioner Thomas Sobol was asked to implement the recommendations made in the report "A Curriculum of Inclusion," which called for a greater recognition of the contributions of nonwhites in the New York State curriculum, in part to raise the self-esteem and achievement of minority students.[27]

Shanker worried that some multiculturalists were pushing to distort the content of the curriculum. Shanker acknowledged that historically, black history had been slighted in the American history curriculum, but he argued that the Sobol report went too far. The authors, Shanker said, are "not primarily interested in contributions that various groups have made to our history. They want to make sure minority students get told nice stories about themselves. . . . And the authors also want to make sure everybody gets equal time."[28] In his "Where We Stand" column, Shanker reprinted an essay by Diane Ravitch, Arthur Schlesinger Jr., and others, who noted that the New York Task Force contained no historians and charged that the report saw history "as a form of social and psychological therapy whose function is to raise the self-esteem of children from minority groups."[29] Shanker said he worried that some multiculturalists were willing to sacrifice "accuracy for diversity."[30]

For their criticisms of extreme forms of multiculturalism, Shanker, Schlesinger, Ravitch, and Hirsch were branded as racists. In New York, City College Professor Leonard Jeffries called the attack on multiculturalism "a war against the African" and said that Ravitch, a "Texas Jew," was the "ultimate, supreme, sophisticated, debonair, racist."[31] Jeffries identified Shanker as one of Ravitch's "several partners," who had "been holding her hand for some time, and now he's at the door of the governor, beating him up, saying you've got to go against this latest report."[32] Hirsch was also labeled a racist for emphasizing the Western roots of American culture.

Elizabeth McPike, editor of *American Educator*, told the *Washington Post* that Shanker and Hirsch were "two people with a passion for equality, equity and civil rights, and both had been called racist. That is something that bound them together, on an emotional and intellectual level."[33] Both men were former Socialists who cared deeply about poor and minority students. They had a shared belief that political liberals, concerned about social mobility, needed to be educational conservatives, concerned about ensuring that all students learned the core elements of Western culture.[34] (Shanker also opposed extreme forms of multiculturalism for undermining the assimilating function of public schools, a topic discussed in chapter 18.)

Local Control

By the same token, Shanker rejected the views of many conservatives that a system of content standards imposed by states or even nationally was an unjustified usurpation of local control. Going back to Ocean Hill–Brownsville, Shanker argued that local control often allowed bigotry to flourish. And just as he rejected the views of extreme multiculturalists on the left—that middle-class culture shouldn't be imposed on children— so he rejected the views of the extreme right, which opposed the teaching of Charles Darwin or other texts they felt undermined their parental authority.

In 1987, when a federal judge excused the children of fundamentalist parents in Tennessee from being required to read "The Wizard of Oz," which they believed promoted witchcraft, and "The Diary of Anne Frank," which they believed suggested that all religions were equal, Shanker opposed the move, saying a shared understanding of literature and history were important. The fundamentalists, taking a page from progressive educators, said children could learn to read with other books; they were to be taught "how to think," not "what to think." Invoking Hirsch, Shanker said: "There are a lot of kids who can decode words, but can't read very well by the eighth or ninth grade because there are certain things they haven't read. If you excuse kids from having to handle this material, you are condemning them to be illiterate."[35]

The conservative local-control argument also ignored the reality that the United States is an extremely mobile society, so having "fifty different education systems" and fifteen thousand districts caused trouble when students moved, Shanker said.[36] The local-control right wing and multicultural left wing might not like the implication that we have a common American culture, he later argued, but Shanker asked: "Is an understanding of the Constitution or the way to write a decent paragraph more important for students in some communities than in others? Should children in Alabama learn a different kind of math or science from children in New York?" Shanker understood that there would

be some variation based on locality. "It would be a great mistake to ignore regional and local history and literature and culture, and there is
no need to do that." He argued for a system in which 50 to 70 percent of
the time was spent on a national curriculum, with the rest for state and
local options.[37]

Self-Esteem

Shanker also fundamentally disagreed with the reigning education-school
theory (also embraced by some civil-rights groups) that a rigorous system of standards, testing, and student accountability might be counter-
productive because it would undermine the self-esteem of struggling students. The emphasis on self-esteem led some districts to advance students
who failed classes (social promotion), to eliminate recognition of academic excellence (such as the honorific title of class valedictorian), and to
employ a distorted multicultural curricula in which students would be
taught inflated claims about their ancestors in order to feel better about
themselves. Some school districts began issuing report cards without
grades.[38] In 1987, the California legislature created a Task Force to Promote Self Esteem.[39]

But Shanker argued there was no real evidence that self-esteem improved learning. The relationship of causation was the reverse. He said,
"if it is achievement we are after, we ought to stop wasting time trying to
make Johnny 'feel good' about himself so that he can learn. Rather, we
should work immediately at getting him to learn, because when he does,
he will feel good about himself."[40] Shanker noted that South Korean students, who ranked high in math and science, spoke less well of their math
abilities than American students, who ranked near the bottom.[41] And
within the United States, black student self-esteem was generally higher
than that of whites, but this did not translate into higher levels of achievement for blacks.[42]

Shanker ridiculed the "smiley-face approach to education," in which
high schools are so wary of comparing students that they eliminate hon-
oring valedictorians. He rejected the view that "it is somehow unfair to
acknowledge that some students have achieved more academically than
others. (This is seldom a problem when it comes to sports.)" He blasted a
high school that had the students elect the valedictorian. "It's as though a
basketball team decided that the high scorer for the year should be
elected," he said.[43]

Teacher Creativity

Shanker also rejected the idea that a system of standards and testing would cramp teacher creativity and require them to "teach to the test." This would be a problem if states used unsophisticated multiple-choice tests, which put an emphasis on drilling and test-taking skills. But it was possible to develop excellent assessments, carefully tied to underlying curriculum, as was done in other high-achieving countries. Shanker argued: "Teaching to the test is something positive when you have really good tests."[44] Indeed, Shanker was worried about an overemphasis on teacher creativity when it came to curriculum and teaching techniques. Professionals have certain protocols, based on research. He argued: "An ailing patient wouldn't want a doctor who said, 'I know what's usually done in situations like yours. But I like to be creative.' "[45] Instead, Shanker said, teachers, like doctors, should normally follow the protocols of pedagogy and apply creativity only in the hard cases when traditional methods did not work.[46]

Dumbing Down

In response to the concern that low performance standards would ignore the needs of more gifted students, Shanker urged the adoption of more than one standard.[47] Shanker wanted to move all parts of the achievement distribution upward, as other nations with standards sought to do, with graduated performance standards that gave incentives for children in all ranges to excel.[48] A single performance standard would inevitably be set low, Shanker argued, because "the political system can't support a high rate of failure."[49]

Shanker was quick to point out that while performance standards should never be set differently for groups of students (minorities versus whites; poor versus rich), there would always be individual variability, and the system of standards ought to reflect that reality.[50] The popular slogan that "all children can learn to the same high levels," he said, "is news to parents, teachers and the public; it defies everything we know and appreciate about human differences."[51] There should be a single set of content standards and curriculum, he said—everyone would be exposed to *Julius Caesar*, for example—but students would learn the material at different rates and at different levels.[52]

Bribery

Shanker also disagreed with progressive educators who opposed the stakes portion of standards-based reform on the theory that students should be motivated by a love of learning rather than bribes. "I once hoped for such a world—one that didn't rely on crass incentives," where kids "would pick up a book by Shakespeare and say, 'Gee, I'd love to read this,'" but that is not the way the world works, Shanker said.[53] Going back to his days as a teacher, Shanker said, "whenever I gave an examination or a quiz or told kids to bring in an essay, the whole class shouted out, 'Does it count? Does it count?' We have an educational system in this country in which nothing counts."[54]

While many people assumed that students had plenty of reason to work hard in high school in order to get into a good college, Shanker pointed out that only a small sliver of the high-school population had this incentive. Many students never went on to college at all, and of America's thousands of colleges, a relatively small proportion were selective.[55] While students aiming at selective colleges had strong incentives to work hard, for the vast majority of students, doing well in high school was not all that important. "Teachers and parents tell kids to work hard in school because their futures depend on it," Shanker said. "But the kids aren't fooled. Doing well in school doesn't make much difference" for those not attending selective institutions of higher education.[56] American employers rarely looked at high-school grades, unlike firms in Europe, Japan, Canada, and Australia, where job applicants were required to show academic performance.[57] As a result, poor and working-class kids were disproportionately robbed of the powerful incentives that wealthy parents of college-bound kids relied upon to motivate their children.

Teacher Accountability

While Shanker acknowledged that it was unfair to hold teachers responsible for the differing family environments of their students, he favored accountability for teachers so long as two conditions were met. First, in comparing schools, Shanker said apples must be compared with apples; schools with similar demographic makeups should be compared, given the powerful effect of home environments on student achievement.[58] Once that is done, he said, persistently failing schools should be closed.[59]

Second, teachers should only be held accountable if kids are too. Shanker argued: "Students won't learn more unless they work harder—come to school, pay attention, and do their homework. But they are unlikely to work harder when they've been told that if they don't, their teachers will be punished."[60]

Facilitating Vouchers

Shanker also disagreed with the view that a system of testing and account-ability would reveal public-school failure and spur the movement toward private-school vouchers. Quite the opposite: he came to believe stan-dards-based reform would save public education by applying needed market-based accountability—external pressure—to public schools with-out changing the essentially public nature of public education. In a state-ment often cited by conservatives, Shanker conceded that the public sys-tem needed more incentives. "It's time to admit that public education operates like a planned economy, a bureaucratic system in which every-body's role is spelled out in advance and there are few incentives for in-novation and productivity. It's no surprise that our school system doesn't improve: it resembles the communist economy more than our own mar-ket economy," he wrote.[61] The statement, however, was not an endorse-ment of privatization but rather a move to prevent it. Standards within the public-school system represented Shanker's synthesis, combining the marketplace's notion of incentives with democracy's need for education to have a public character.

Indeed, a tough system of standards and accountability could bolster the argument for public schools. Shanker knew that many private schools, accustomed to operating freely, would chafe at a system of public testing. If public schools adopted accountability measures, the public would see the comparative danger of putting public money toward unaccountable private schools. Whereas Franklin Roosevelt sought to reform capitalism from the left (injecting democratic modifiers) in order to save it, Shanker sought to reform democratic public education from the right (injecting incentives), in order to save the public enterprise.

Discriminatory Tests

So too, Shanker disagreed with civil-rights advocates who worried that a system of standards, testing, and consequences would hurt minority students. While it was true that minority students as a group did less well on many tests, he argued that throwing out the tests as a result was "roughly equivalent to throwing out the thermometer because it shows the patient has a fever."[62] America's capitalist economy ruthlessly insists on high standards, Shanker said, so it is better to address inequality early on.[63]

While it was true that tests tended to examine students based on a curriculum that required a mastery of mainstream culture, this was the world into which students would be delivered as adults, he said, so it was important to give all students the tools to navigate it successfully. When critics complained, for example, that an inner-city elementary school in Baltimore was using a "rich man's curriculum," Shanker approvingly quoted the principal: "I wouldn't look for a poor man's curriculum."[64]

As the standards movement began to pick up steam in the late 1980s, Shanker found himself virtually alone among members of the education establishment ready to join governors and business leaders in support.[65] The NEA stood out as particularly opposed.[66] But principals, school boards, and professional educators were also unenthusiastic.[67]

There was also strong opposition to Shanker within the AFT. Shanker "took tremendous heat" for embracing the accountability portion of standards-based reform, says Jim Kelly.[68] "He did have to do a heavy lift inside the AFT" on accountability, says Eugenia Kemble, because teachers "were afraid that these standards were going to get set and their kids weren't going to be able to meet them," and that they would be blamed and might lose their jobs.[69] Accountability was particularly risky for AFT teachers, education-policy analyst Michael Cohen says, because "his members were teaching in urban schools that were, by and large, not producing results" compared to the suburban districts, which were largely represented by the NEA.[70]

But Shanker made a critical calculation that standards-based reform was the single best way to preserve public education, and he made that case directly to his skeptical membership. Shanker sought to motivate people by invoking a "big enemy," says Rachelle Horowitz, and there was no bigger enemy than school vouchers.[71] "He felt that he could move people if they felt threatened," says Eugenia Kemble. "That was kind of fundamental to Al's way of thinking."[72]

It would have been unusual enough for Shanker, as a teachers' union leader, to join the standards and accountability movement that made so many of his members nervous. But what was truly astounding to many was that he became the widely recognized leader of the movement. The *Los Angeles Times* labeled Shanker "the earliest and loudest voice for establishing and raising universal curriculum standards."[73] Chester Finn called Shanker "the nation's foremost advocate of real academic standards."[74] Others were very important: business leaders, presidents, and governors were instrumental. But for them, education reform had to compete with running a corporation or reducing crime and balancing the budget; it was "not their daily existence," says former AFT staffer Scott Widmeyer. For Shanker, "this was his livelihood."[75] And, says Finn, among educators who were advocates of standards-based reform, Shanker had "a bigger megaphone" than others.[76]

In the last eight years of his life, on behalf of standards, he would blast away on that instrument for all it was worth.

The National Education Summit in Charlottesville

Most observers peg the beginning of the modern standards movement to September 1989, when the new president, George H. W. Bush, called for a summit of the nation's governors on the topic of education. Unlike Ronald Reagan, who sought to abolish the Department of Education and curtail the federal role in education, Bush campaigned to be the "education president." The summit, which took place in Charlottesville, Virginia, represented only the third time in the nation's history that a president had assembled the nation's governors on a particular topic, and the first time they addressed education. (The previous summits were called by Theodore Roosevelt on conservation and Franklin Roosevelt on the Great Depression.)[77] The summit came at a time of growing public support for national standards. An August 1989 Gallup poll found that 70 percent of Americans favored "requiring . . . schools . . . to conform to national standards and goals," and 69 percent supported a "standardized national curriculum."[78]

At the September Education Summit, forty-nine of the fifty governors attended, as did all the members of Bush's cabinet. Education officials were not invited, nor were members of Congress.[79] (Shanker, citing his "Where We Stand" column, attended as a member of the "press.")[80] At the summit, the governors and White House agreed to establish broad national goals. "We believe that the time has come, for the first time in U.S. history, to establish clear, national performance goals, goals that will make us internationally competitive," the parties said. The goals would be set in seven areas: school readiness, performance on international achievement tests, dropout rates, adult literacy, workforce training, qualified teachers, and safe, disciplined, drug-free schools. Shanker called the agreement on national goals a "historic turning point" in education reform because the goals would "drive what happens in the schools."[81]

Shanker applauded Bush. "For the first time we have a President who is using the word 'national' when he is talking about education, instead of passing the buck to the states."[82] Shanker received a handwritten note of thanks from Bush. His secretary efficiently stamped it with a received date, much to Shanker's amusement.[83]

In October 1990, President Bush appointed Shanker to the Competitiveness Policy Council, where Shanker pushed for a recommendation, eventually endorsed by the council, that a uniform high-school transcript be adopted for employers to look at in making hiring decisions.[84] Alan Wurtzel, the CEO and chairman of the board of Circuit City, who served with Shanker on the council, remembers Shanker speaking about consequences and accountability for students and for adults, which was "music to a businessman's ear."[85]

Shanker also served on President Bush's Education Policy Advisory Panel, chaired by Paul O'Neill, who was then the chairman and chief executive office of Alcoa. In January 1991, the panel recommended the creation of national examinations at the elementary and secondary levels, a recommendation that was influential with Education Secretary Lamar Alexander as he helped put together Bush's education proposal to Congress.[86] In April 1991, Bush unveiled his new plan, called America 2000, which proposed, among other things, a system of national standards and voluntary national exams in five core subject areas in grades 4, 8, and 12. Shanker called the plan "bold and comprehensive. More so than any President or Secretary has come up with yet."[87]

In June 1991, Congress created the National Council on Education Standards and Testing (with the unfortunate acronym NCEST). Chaired by governors Roy Romer (D-Colo.) and Carroll Campbell (R-S.C.), the group included Shanker and NEA president Keith Geiger, among many others.[88] In January 1992, the panel, noting that the United States was the only industrialized country in the world without explicit minimum national standards by grade level and subject, recommended a system of voluntary national standards and tests. Education Secretary Alexander predicted that students would take the first voluntary national tests within two to three years.[89] Shanker commented: "That all these people could agree is some sort of miracle."[90] In an editorial, the *Washington Post* noted that the creation of national standards, "an idea once considered looney," was catching on.[91]

Bush's America 2000 plan, however, began to crumble when he insisted on pushing a plan for private-school vouchers. Shanker was furious and warned: "If they want to pick a fight, they've picked one."[92] In 1992, a Democratic version of America 2000 (standards minus vouchers) passed the House and Senate, but the conference report was filibustered by conservatives worried about federal intrusion into local education policy.[93] It was an enormous setback for the movement toward national standards.

Bill Clinton's Goals 2000 and the "Opportunity to Learn" Debate

The standards movement was hardly dead, however, as the November 1992 election brought to Washington an ardent champion of the movement: Bill Clinton. As we shall see in the next chapter, Shanker worked hard for Clinton's election and was elated with the new president on a number of issues beyond education. But education policy and education standards were at the center of their relationship, and more than any other time since coming to Washington during President Ford's term nearly two decades earlier, Shanker had the White House's ear.[94]

Shanker and Clinton had a special relationship, says former Clinton advisor Michael Cohen, based on intellectual respect. As governor of Arkansas and head of the National Governors Association, Clinton would often call Shanker about education issues. The relationship was clearly based on his regard for Shanker's abilities, given the minimal presence of the AFT in Arkansas.[95] So close was the association that Shanker was a long-shot candidate for education secretary—something unheard of for a teacher's union boss.[96] Shanker was not named to the post—former South Carolina Governor Richard Riley was. But Shanker's influence remained strong. It appeared from the outside, says NPR's Claudio Sanchez, that "Clinton talked to Shanker almost as much as to his Secretary of Education."[97]

Significantly, Clinton appointed Shanker's friend Marshall Smith as a key official in the Department of Education to oversee standards. Shanker's association with Smith, going back to the Carter Administration, was strengthened by their mutual belief that standards-based reform would help marry equity and quality and by their discussions, beginning in 1990, at the Pew Forum for school reform, an influential group that backed higher standards.[98] "If there were any two people who" had created the standards movement, "it was the two of them," says Eugenia Kemble.[99] In a late January 1993 profile in the *Washington Post* about Shanker, a reporter noted that Shanker's ideas about education standards held great sway with Clinton and quoted Smith saying: "There aren't many truly significant figures in American education right now. But Al Shanker is huge. . . . His influence is everywhere in education."[100]

The Clinton Administration soon found it needed a powerful ally like Shanker to help fend off attacks from both the right and the left on its proposal for standards-based reform. In late January 1993, the Administration announced that the very first piece of legislation Clinton would send to Capitol Hill was a standards-based reform package, a modified version of Bush's America 2000 plan, which Clinton called Goals 2000.[101] One key difference was that, given its defeat in Congress the previous year, Clinton had dropped Bush's call for national standards.

The draft bill, based largely on Mike Smith's writings, would establish a National Education Standards and Improvement Council (NESIC) to certify content standards and state assessments, and provide $420 million in funding to help states establish systems of standards.[102] Many liberals were none too pleased. They finally had a Democratic administration after twelve years, and its first piece of legislation did not provide for more education spending but rather was a modified version of what Bush had proposed. Liberals wanted to reauthorize the Elementary and Secondary Education Act (ESEA) first, then consider the issue of standards. And before students were held accountable for performance, liberals argued, they needed resources—an "opportunity to learn." Otherwise, high-stakes tests would simply punish poor children for attending lousy schools.

In February 1993, Education Secretary Riley attended a "stormy meeting" with House Democrats, who raised these issues forcefully.[103] But the administration held firm for the most part. With Shanker's strong support, Clinton kept the sequencing of the legislation, focusing on standards first, to ensure that ESEA would reinforce standards rather than ignore them.[104] And Clinton officials say they envisioned "opportunity-to-learn" standards very narrowly—are kids being taught what they will be tested on?—rather than as equal resources.[105]

But on the issue of "high-stakes" testing—whether students could be held back or denied a diploma based on failure—Clinton sided with

House Democrats, who insisted that Goals 2000 include a ban on such use of testing. Shanker argued that the research suggested that adopting consequences would not hurt low-income and minority students. Students are normally given multiple chances to pass high-stakes tests and will work harder if they know it counts, he argued.[106] Minimum-competence tests, he said, did not lead to a substantial increase in high-school dropout rates.[107] (Subsequent research largely confirmed this point.)[108] Shanker was angered by the administration's agreement to ban high-stakes testing.[109]

Overall, however, Shanker was very supportive of the bill and said it was the first step in a process that might take fifteen to twenty years to perfect. NEA president Keith Geiger, by contrast, was more cautious, and worried: "We've been raising the high bar without worrying about who can jump it in the first place."[110] As the bill moved to the legislature, there were lots of groups that said they were generally supportive of the legislation, says Michael Cohen, but only a few—such as the AFT and the Business Roundtable—strongly believed in it.[111]

The major battle was over the question of "opportunity-to-learn" (OTL) requirements. In May 1993, the House Education Subcommittee on Elementary and Secondary Education adopted an amendment sponsored by Congressman Jack Reed (D-R.I.), providing that states would lose federal funding if they did not take corrective action to provide resources to ensure the opportunity to learn.[112]

The NEA, civil-rights groups, and most of the education establishment supported OTL requirements.[113] But Shanker came out in strong opposition, arguing that OTL standards could "torpedo needed school reforms."[114] Shanker said he was strongly supportive of pursuing the goals of fairness—including proper health care for pregnant mothers, high-quality early childhood programs, and education spending equity—"but if we have to wait until we attain them before trying to establish national standards and assessments, we'll wait forever. It's like saying we have to wait until our society is perfect before trying to improve it."[115] The important work of establishing standards should not be postponed, he argued. "We don't abolish medical school exams because not everyone has had the opportunity for top-notch pre-med education."[116]

Shanker suspected that, in part, the OTL movement was a deliberate ploy to "blow up the whole operation" by those who "basically don't want any standards at all."[117] State governors were livid about the idea of being told to equalize funding, and they convinced members of Congress to oppose any bill that included OTL.[118] Killing standards-based reform would be a disaster, Shanker argued, particularly on the grounds of equity, about which OTL supporters cared so much. The whole notion of standards required a focus on results, not just inputs, which was ultimately a radical concept. Sandra Feldman, who disagreed at the time with Shanker about OTL, later came to believe that Shanker was right to say standards-based reform was an equity issue. The standards movement declared, for the first time, that poor kids and students of color were expected to meet high performance standards, so the achievement gap began receiving much greater attention.[119] Shanker wasn't anti-equity; he believed that as a strategic matter, additional resources would not be forthcoming until accountability measures were put in place. Indeed, Shanker argued, once standards were put in place, they would highlight the need to invest more, particularly in low-income schools. Standards could bring "strong political pressure and legal action to provide the school conditions that matter in student learning."[120]

Clinton agreed with Shanker's position on OTL, and in the end, most Democrats went along with the compromise: no high-stakes tests and no OTL. In October 1993, the House passed Goals 2000 by a solid vote of 307 to 118, with primary opposition coming from conservative Republicans who saw the bill as a threat to local control.[121] On February 8, 1994, the Senate passed Goals 2000 by a vote of seventy one to twenty-five. Competing versions of the legislation were then reconciled, and in April 1994, Clinton signed the legislation—eleven years after *A Nation at Risk* was published.[122]

Shanker called Goals 2000 "the most significant piece of education legislation we've ever had." By itself, Shanker said, Goals 2000 "won't solve the problems of our education system, but it provides a structure without which we can't begin to solve them."[123] Goals 2000 supplied a framework in which states would establish standards and provide assessments in a coherent fashion. Many states had already been developing standards, but Goals 2000 put the federal government in the position of helping to stimulate those efforts, to the point where forty-nine states (all but Iowa) adopted standards.[124] Goals 2000 also helped create the environment in which a more aggressive set of follow-up reforms could be enacted.[125]

In May 1994, Shanker gave an address at the Brookings Institution in Washington, D.C., laying out where he thought the standards movement should go following passage of Goals 2000. He continued to pound away at three major points: the movement needed to incorporate incentives and stakes for students, the standards needed to be national in scope, and the assessments needed to be of the highest quality. In all three cases, we needed to move toward the European and Japanese model, Shanker said, something Goals 2000 did not do as completely as he had hoped.[126]

The Improving America's Schools Act

If Shanker was calling for a European-style system of national standards, consequences for students, and high-quality tests, the next stage in the American standards movement—the reauthorization of the Elementary and Secondary Education Act (ESEA)—was headed in a different direction. Clinton's proposed version of the bill, called the Improving America's Schools Act (IASA), drew heavily on the recommendations of a commission chaired by educator David Hornbeck, which argued that federal ESEA money could be withheld if states did not require schools to make "adequate yearly progress"—prescribed advances on student achievement on tests—or face sanctions.[127] In the draft legislation, the sanctions for failing to have all low-income students make "adequate yearly progress" toward advanced achievement included the right to transfer out of failing schools to a better public school and the task of reconstituting the staff. In a July 1994 column, Shanker outlined two main objections to the proposed legislation.[128] The objections are significant in light of IASA's successor, the No Child Left Behind Act of 2001.

First, the goal set was impossibly high, calling for "miraculous progress." He wrote: "Given the wide range of natural endowments, it would be absurd to expect all children—or even the majority—anywhere to achieve at an advanced level." Noting that in countries with higher achievement than the United States no more than one-third of all students achieve at advanced levels, he asked: "How can we expect Chapter 1 [low-income] schools and teachers to take kids, most of whom are achieving in the bottom quarter, and make them all equal to the best students anywhere in the world?"[129]

Second, unlike European-style systems, the proposed bill put all the sanctions on the adults. "It places all the responsibility on teachers and schools and none on students," Shanker said. "Imagine saying we should shut down a hospital and fire its staff because not all of its patients became healthy—but never demanding that the patients also look out for themselves by eating properly, exercising, and laying off cigarettes, alcohol, and drugs. Is tightening the thumbscrews on the doctors and the hospital the best way to help the patients?"[130] The AFT sought to modify what it saw as unreasonable adequate yearly progress requirements, and the final bill was more to its liking.[131]

Over the years, Shanker's position on consequences was attacked as being in favor of "accountability for everyone except teachers."[132] Shanker responded that he had long supported accountability for teaching—including peer review to weed out failing teachers and the closing and reconstituting of failing schools.[133] But the successful European model, he noted, held students, not teachers, accountable.[134] Shanker argued: "In none of the other countries is there any system of accountability for adults. Now, I am not arguing against adult accountability. I favor it. But I am saying that we will totally oppose any system that says kids can do nothing and move along and not be held accountable, but the teachers and other adults will be held accountable."[135] In October 1994, Clinton signed the IASA.[136] It contained weak accountability provisions for schools and none at all for students.

Cancer Strikes

Amidst all the battles over Goals 2000 and IASA, Shanker received some devastating news. In the fall of 1993, while going for other tests, doctors discovered that he had bladder cancer.[137] In November 1993, Shanker had a tumor removed from his bladder in an operation at George Washington University Hospital. The doctors were encouraged that the cancer did not appear to have invaded the wall of the bladder. But in a subsequent visit, the doctors discovered that the cancer had returned.[138] In March 1994, Shanker had to have his entire bladder removed.[139] Shortly thereafter, Eadie Shanker decided to retire from her job at the City University of New York to spend more time with her husband.[140]

In July 1994, Shanker ran for reelection as AFT president, saying his doctors had given him a "very good prognosis" for a full recovery. He was going through chemotherapy, however, and joked at the convention about his "new hairdo." He thanked the delegates for their flowers and cards and said, "it's been a very tough year, but it meant a lot." He was reelected unanimously.[141] Celebrating his twentieth anniversary as president of the

AFT, Shanker had much more work he wanted to do. But the standards fight was a tough one, and in the fall of 1994, the national movement was beset by difficulties.

In late October 1994, national history standards were published and greeted with harsh condemnation.[142] The standards, written by the National Center for History in the Schools at UCLA under a federal grant dating back to the first Bush Administration, were roundly condemned for painting a very negative picture of American history. The standards mentioned Joseph McCarthy and McCarthyism nineteen times and the KKK seventeen times, but did not mention Paul Revere, Thomas Edison, or Alexander Graham Bell.[143] Shanker called the history standards "a travesty," arguing they embodied a "leftist point of view" that "white people" are "evil and oppressive, while Genghis Khan is a nice, sweet guy just bringing his culture to other places."[144] Shanker said the draft "requires substantial revision."[145] Clinton Administration officials distanced themselves from the standards, noting they had not commissioned them.[146] The U.S. Senate later voted ninety-nine to one to condemn the standards.[147] Advocates worried the controversy would severely damage the standards movement as a whole.[148]

In the five years from 1989 to 1994, Albert Shanker helped lead the beginnings of a stunning transformation in American education. Allied with business leaders, governors, and two presidents, Shanker helped overcome longstanding opposition from the NEA, education professors, civil-rights groups, and conservative local-control advocates to move the United States, in some measure, toward a system of content standards, tests, and accountability of the type used by most of the leading educational systems in the world. It was only a beginning, and Shanker had serious concerns about the level of the performance standard being proposed, the failure to make students accountable for achievement, and the lack of national standards. But now, as returns from the November 1994 elections came in, standards-based reform would face its biggest challenge yet.

18

The Rise of the Angry White Males
and the Gingrich Revolution

1992–1995

T HE Gingrich revolution of 1994—the loss of about fifty Democratic seats and the Republican takeover of the House of Representatives led by Congressman Newt Gingrich—was not supposed to happen to Bill Clinton's Democratic Party. Clinton had run as a
different kind of Democrat, one who appealed to the very group responsible for the Gingrich ascendancy—the "angry white males." Much of the
reason Shanker was so taken by Clinton—apart from their affinity on
education issues—was his rejection of the "soft" liberalism that was so
anathema to Reagan Democrats. But on matters of race, even Clinton
took positions that disappointed Shanker. And during the early years of
the Clinton Administration, Shanker continued to tangle with—and lose
to—a soft liberal worldview within the NEA and the AFL-CIO. Stun-
ningly, Shanker's tough liberalism would become increasingly marginalized even within organized labor.

Clinton: A New Kind of Democrat

Governor Bill Clinton's candidacy in 1992 was the closest the Democrats
had come in a long time to Scoop Jackson. Clinton was a (partial) eco-

nomic populist, a (partial) national security hawk, and a moderate on social issues. He was for civil rights but opposed quotas and was tough on
crime. Shanker especially liked Clinton's idea of a "new covenant," reciprocal rights and responsibilities, which was analogous to Shanker's idea in
education that students should receive the help that they needed but also
be held responsible for achieving.[1] Given Clinton's overall worldview, his
intelligence, and his positions on education, Shanker became a very early
proponent of his candidacy and was one of three union leaders to give
early support to Clinton when most of the labor world was backing Iowa
Senator Tom Harkin for the Democratic nomination.[2]

On economic issues, while many labor leaders were concerned with
Clinton's affiliation with the Democratic Leadership Council and his support for free trade, Clinton also ran as a strong economic populist, promising to support striker-replacement legislation and to lift the ban on the
hiring of those air traffic controllers who had been dismissed for striking
by Reagan twelve years earlier. He was also for better health care and increasing the minimum wage.[3]

As the field narrowed to Clinton and former Massachusetts Senator
Paul Tsongas, the economic case became even clearer. In early March 1992,
Shanker sent a memo to AFT leaders arguing that Clinton was a far preferable candidate to the neoliberal Tsongas. Emphasizing key economic concerns, Shanker said: "Tsongas supports private school vouchers, opposes
legislation to prevent striker replacement, looks to the marketplace to solve
the health care crisis, and centers his economic policies on cuts in the capital gains tax."[4] By contrast, Shanker noted in an April 1992 column just
prior to the New York Democratic primary, Clinton had an economically
populist platform that spoke to both working-class whites and blacks,
"pulling together the first biracial coalition in decades."[5]

In the general election, Shanker also liked what Clinton and his running
mate, Tennessee Senator Al Gore, were saying in the campaign about international affairs, an area where Shanker had broad agreement with Clinton's
DLC. Clinton embraced Reagan's defense buildup, saying it had helped
bring about the fall of the Soviet Union. And Clinton attacked Bush for not
responding strongly enough to the Chinese Tiananmen Square massacre.[6]

During the general election campaign, Shanker joined a number of
Democratic hawks who signed an advertisement in the *New York Times*
entitled "Bill Clinton: A leader for America in the post–Cold War era."
The ad said that while Democrats in the recent past had often lacked
"clear understanding and firm purpose in world affairs," the Clinton-

Gore foreign policy was "coherent and firm, yet infused with the demo-cratic spirit."[7] It lauded Clinton for opposing "the brutal and archaic communist dictatorship in Beijing," for resisting "those at home—and in his own party—who propose reckless cuts in our national defense capa-bilities," and for supporting "increased pressure to end the rule of Cuba's Fidel Castro," among other things.[8] At another point, Shanker joined an ad sponsored by Vietnam-era hardliners who supported Clinton. "We did not agree with the stand Bill Clinton took toward the Vietnam War as a young man," the group wrote. But Clinton's "firm support for the demo-cratic and anti-communist movements in the former Soviet Empire and in China make him a distinctly preferable candidate to George Bush, who in modern times has shown himself far too willing to cooperate with dic-tators, and to turn a blind eye to human rights abuses."[9]

Finally, Shanker liked what Clinton and the DLC were saying on social issues with racial dimensions that were exploited by Republicans to at-tract working-class whites. Shanker was pleased, in 1991, when the DLC, chaired by Clinton, endorsed a policy of equal individual opportunity over a policy of equal racial group results.[10] Like Shanker, Clinton was a strong supporter of civil rights, but in 1992, his campaign book stated its strong opposition to quotas and emphasized race-neutral programs that would disproportionately help minorities.[11] Unlike previous Democratic candidates, Clinton came across as tough on crime.[12] And like Shanker, Clinton advocated a tough approach on student discipline. Both men, having grown up in economically distressed neighborhoods, knew the chaos of poverty and the importance of making schools places that are safe, predictable, and where discipline is maintained.[13]

Shanker advised Clinton that he needed to distance himself from Jesse Jackson, whom previous Democratic presidential candidates, like Gover-nor Michael Dukakis, had been fearful to challenge. The opportunity came in June 1992, when Clinton appeared before Jackson's Rainbow Co-alition convention. The previous night, Jackson had invited rap singer Sister Souljah to participate on a panel. Souljah had aroused controversy by telling the press, following the Los Angeles riots: "If black people kill black people every day, why not have a week and kill white people?" Clin-ton said during his speech: "You had a rap singer here last night named Sister Souljah. . . . Her comments before and after Los Angeles were filled with a kind of hatred you do not honor." Clinton noted that "if you took the words 'white' and 'black' and reversed them, you might think David Duke was giving that speech."[14]

In sum, Clinton was a tough liberal who had inoculated himself against the charge of "softness" on issues such as defense and crime.[15] On most issues, Shanker and Clinton saw eye to eye. The two men, says Ed McElroy, "were probably as close as they could possibly be intellectually."[16]

The night of the 1992 election, Mary Farran recalls, Shanker was ecstatic. A group that included Shanker, Farran, Rachelle Horowitz, Tom Donahue, and Bella Rosenberg was going to watch the returns, and "Al just reached over and hugged me because he was so excited," Farran recalls. "I was floored because I had never been hugged by Al."[17]

In his eighteen years as president of the AFT, Shanker had never had a president to whom he felt so close. From Shanker's perspective, Ford had been conservative on budget matters; Carter had been wrong on foreign policy, quotas, and the budget; Reagan had been wrong on vouchers and education spending and labor, as had George H.W. Bush. Clinton was congenial to Shanker on most issues, and his coalition of support among working-class whites and blacks was proof that a Democrat could hold on to both critical groups with a race-neutral, economically populist, and pro-defense agenda.

Differences with Clinton on Race

After Clinton took office, however, Shanker worried that the president would lose support among white working-class voters over issues of race. In March 1994, for example, the Clinton Administration's Department of Education's Office of Civil Rights began investigating Ohio's requirement that students pass an exit exam in four subjects to graduate from high school, because the white pass rate was higher than the African American pass rate. The investigation examined whether the test violated Title VI of the Civil Rights Act. Shanker wrote a blistering column on May 1, 1994, noting that the four exit tests students were required to pass were designed to measure eighth-grade proficiency. He pointed out that students had eight chances to pass the tests, beginning in the eighth grade, and that they would have a ninth chance that month. Shanker worried that striking down the test would punish students who worked hard. Cleveland had offered remedial summer sessions, but only 10 percent showed up the first time. He said that "the ones who failed the first or second or third time but worked hard and finally made it will get the message that they're chumps." Shanker argued that the OCR investigation was in tension with the Clinton Administration's stated intent on raising academic standards and thereby performance through Goals 2000.[18] Shanker's column was followed by a letter from Representative Bill Goodling and thirteen other Republican members of the House Education and Labor Committee to Secretary Riley complaining about the investigation and charging that it undermined the standards movement. In the end, with help, 98 percent of Ohio seniors ended up passing the test, and in October 1994, OCR finished its investigation and concluded that the Ohio exam was legal.[19]

The second issue was more serious and came to a head in September 1994, when the Clinton Administration's Department of Justice decided to file papers in support of a race-based layoff of a teacher in Piscataway, New Jersey.[20] The case went back to 1989, when the Piscataway school board needed to lay off a teacher in its business-education department and had to choose between two teachers with equal seniority—Sharon Taxman, who was white, and Debra Williams, who was black. On other such occasions in the district, teachers with equal seniority drew lots to determine who would be laid off. But the school board decided to dismiss Taxman to promote racial diversity, as Williams was the only black teacher in the business department of her school. There was no record of past discrimination in the school district—indeed, African Americans were overrepresented compared with the available teacher pool. When Taxman sued, the Bush Administration sided with her, but in September, the Clinton Justice Department shifted sides.[21]

Shanker weighed in with a tough column, chastising his friend. Clinton had run against quotas in the election, Shanker said, so what was the Justice Department up to?[22] The issue of teacher layoffs by race hit home to Shanker, who had fought such policies in Ocean Hill–Brownsville, the Boston teacher case, and the Mississippi *Wygant* case. Using race to promote diversity in hiring was unpopular, but using race to decide a layoff was toxic.

Shanker could not fathom why Clinton, who had made so much progress uniting working-class whites and blacks, would weigh into this thicket with such a weak legal and factual case. In the end, civil-rights groups raised money to settle the case with Taxman in order to keep her from having her case heard by the U.S. Supreme Court, where they fully expected to lose.[23]

Two months after Clinton's actions in the Piscataway case, Newt Gingrich and the Republicans took over the House of Representatives for the first time in forty years, with the strong support of a group that the media described as "angry white men." The white male vote went Republican by an overwhelming 62 to 38 percent margin.[24] Political analysts pointed to many factors in the election—Clinton's support for gays in the military, the failure of Clinton's health-care plan, Clinton's tax hike—but race was high on the list. In the postelection period, Shanker participated in a series of meetings with labor leaders and others about what President Clinton could do differently. He argued that Clinton had been brilliant in the 1992 campaign in deciding to "treat Jesse Jackson as a human being" who makes mistakes like everyone else. "That was a very strong signal, and it was part of the reason white males moved over for the first time since the election of Richard Nixon." Then came issues like Piscataway, and "a large portion of the American people felt betrayed," sensing that Clinton was not a new kind of Democrat after all.[25]

Affirmative Action Review

The White House, too, saw affirmative action as a crucial factor in the 1994 results and worried as it looked ahead to 1996, when the state of California was likely to have an initiative on the ballot calling for an end to state-sponsored discrimination against or preferences for minorities. Polls suggested there was strong support for Proposition 209, the California Civil Rights Initiative.

In February 1995, Clinton announced a "review" of affirmative-action programs—a defensive step, journalist Nicholas Lemann notes, that no president since Lyndon Johnson had taken, "even those Republicans who had campaigned against affirmative action."[26] In an early March 1995 press conference, Clinton suggested that affirmative action should be based on economic need rather than race, a move urged by presidential pollster Dick Morris.[27] Clinton said: "I want to emphasize need-based programs where we can because they work better and have a bigger impact and generate broader support." The *Washington Post* headline declared, "In Shift, President Supports Affirmative Action Based on Needs."[28]

Shanker applauded Clinton's emphasis on class, saying: "It would be fairer to do it based on individual advantage or disadvantage or class."[29] Providing a leg up to individuals based not on race or gender but economic status, he said, "would disproportionately help minorities." And, he said, "it would change things so that a millionaire African-American's son would not get preference. For my own thinking," he said, "I would take that into account if I had two people who were equal and one of them grew up with private tutors and one, well he came over on the boat. I would say that the kid who had overcome all sorts of odds, if they are the same in all other points, I would say the one is really a much harder worker and is more deserving."[30]

Shanker had long argued that affirmative action, properly understood, could include "extra consideration for economic disadvantage."[31] A long line of Shanker's heroes—Martin Luther King, Bayard Rustin, and A. Philip Randolph—had long championed economic programs to help those most in need and to preserve the working-class coalition. Clinton himself seemed to have in mind reuniting the white and black blue-collar coalition he had put together in 1992.

But when Clinton floated his trial balloon about class-based affirmative action, no major figure in the civil-rights community came to his side. King was gone. Randolph was gone. Rustin was gone. Jesse Jackson threatened to challenge the president for the Democratic nomination if he did not "stand firm" on race-based affirmative action.[32] In earlier days, labor would have jumped at the idea of class-based measures, because the last thing labor wanted was to divide working-class people by race. But Shanker noted with disdain that when Clinton flirted with the idea of class-based affirmative action, the AFL-CIO sent a "very strong letter to the President urging him to maintain his full support" for current race-based policies.[33] "I may be the only person in labor circles today" to oppose racial preferences, he said in 1995. "That doesn't mean others are for it, it just means that everybody shut up, because it's politically incorrect."[34] Jesse Jackson's threatened run effectively punctured the class-based balloon. A serious primary challenge, Clinton aide George Stephanopoulos noted, was "the surest predictor of a single-term presidency."[35] In July 1995, Clinton's review of affirmative-action policies concluded they should be "mended not ended." In practice, the slogan meant little in the way of curtailing racial preferences.[36]

In the end, the only political leaders to embrace class-based affirmative action were conservatives like Newt Gingrich, who employed the rhetoric but showed little evidence of really believing in programs to help poor and working-class families of all races.[37] A huge gap had emerged between public opinion on the one hand and American leadership on the other. Polling showed Americans wanted to help the disadvantaged, but not with racial preferences.[38] Shanker backed this approach, but among mainstream liberal and conservative elected officials, no one emerged to represent the views of ordinary Americans.

During the Clinton presidency, Shanker's frustration with his fellow unionists extended far beyond the issue of affirmative action, as he struggled with two major union issues that had implications for the future of American liberalism: first, a renewed effort to merge the AFT and NEA nationally; and second, a large-scale fight within the AFL-CIO over the direction of the federation in years to come.

NEA Merger Talks

By 1993, the case for an NEA-AFT merger was strong, even stronger than it had been in the 1970s, when the last serious attempt at a national merger was made. The NEA had grown to 2.1 million members and the AFT to 820,000 members; the combination would involve the largest union merger in history. For years, the division had diverted money to fights between the organizations, Shanker said.[39]

And the truth was that the rivalry sometimes distorted each union's thinking. To take one example, in 1993, Shanker strongly opposed a lawsuit in Connecticut to require desegregation of city and suburban students.[40] The suit, *Sheff v. O'Neill*, based on the state constitution, was highly unusual, because integration would take place across school-district lines. This was important because the mixing would not be limited to poor whites and poor blacks—as in places like Boston—but would involve middle-class students as well. Shanker had long argued that the research suggested that economic mixing would promote student achievement.[41]

Nevertheless, Shanker opposed the measure. Publicly, he worried that integration might drive whites from the public-school system. But privately, he was also concerned that the plan would hurt the local AFT in Hartford and help the NEA in Connecticut. In a letter to George Springer, president of the AFT state affiliate, the Connecticut Federation of Teachers, Shanker said: "The *Sheff* case could have disastrous effects on the Connecticut Federation of Teachers." He argued that under a regional school system "we may be looking at the end of the union as we know it in Connecticut." In Wilmington, Delaware, where a regional integration plan was put in place, Shanker said, "our union was wiped out and replaced by the NEA which had contracts with the school districts that surrounded ours." Shanker did not mention that the Wilmington integration was considered successful largely because it was regional in character and involved middle-class whites.[42] Shanker's letter noted, correctly, that "the single most important correlation to poor learning is economic isolation, not racial isolation," but ignored the fact that *Sheff* would reduce both by including affluent suburban schools.[43] Shanker's argument against vouchers and against extreme forms of multiculturalism, bilingual education, and community control were all fundamentally founded on the importance of the integrated "common" school, so it is hard to explain his position in *Sheff* without reference to AFT/NEA politics.[44]

Changes in the leadership of the NEA also strengthened the case for merger. Following the election to the presidency of the NEA in 1989 of Keith Geiger, a math teacher from Michigan with strong ties to the labor movement, the organization began allowing local mergers in Minnesota and elsewhere.[45] In 1992, the NEA representative assembly voted to open the door on the issue of AFL-CIO affiliation, modifying its opposition, which had sunk the earlier merger attempt.[46]

A promising precedent was set in January 1993, when, with Shanker's backing, the international organizations to which the NEA and AFT belonged—the WCOTP and the IFFTU—merged into a new organization known as Education International.[47] Shanker was insistent that the merged organization be a member of ICFTU—the international equivalent of the AFL-CIO—and when the NEA agreed, it was a welcome harbinger.[48] Educational International became the largest federation of trade unions organized within a specific industry or occupational group within ICFTU.[49]

But Shanker had a larger motivation behind merger with the NEA. Yes, he thought it would be good for teachers to be unified. But he also had bigger fish to fry. Shanker wanted to transform the AFL-CIO, which he believed had become moribund and needed to change. In particular, Shanker believed the AFL-CIO needed to do much more to reach professional workers. But, he told AFT staff, "I can't do it alone. We need partners." The merger talks with NEA, Shanker said, were ultimately about "whether the NEA can be that partner."[50] A merged AFT-NEA would be a major force within the AFL-CIO and could help reorient the whole federation.

Shanker had watched with growing alarm as union membership as a percentage of the nonagricultural workforce fell from 33 percent in the

1950s to half that level.[51] With it, labor's political power shrank. Labor was being surpassed by evangelical churches as the most important grassroots organization in the country.[52] Where once there were entire sections of bookstores on Labor, this changed, as Thomas Geoghegan noted, to Self-Help and Sex.[53] Part of the decline was due to structural changes in the economy.[54] Part of the problem was the failure of labor-law reform and the union-busting example set by Ronald Reagan during the air traffic controllers' strike. But Shanker also thought part of labor's problem was self-inflicted. Just as Shanker was public education's biggest defender and toughest critic, so he privately complained about the intellectual flabbiness and rigidity of the American labor movement.[55] Shanker thought labor looked too much like a regular interest group, unconcerned about the quality of the product it produced, whether cars or high-school graduates.

In addition, the work world was changing, growing more white collar, Shanker said, but labor had not caught up. He said in an interview, "if you try to promote a trade unionism which is based on a sweatshop where you work 75 or 80 hours a week and where the Triangle Shirt Factory goes on fire, that's not truth in most people's experiences today. So the trade union movement itself has to change its orientation or otherwise it's going to lose out."[56] Shanker felt that the AFL-CIO "had become so fossilized," says Phil Kugler, that it was "incapable of change."[57] Bella Rosenberg recalls: "He pretty much hated going to AFL-CIO meetings," because of the lack of debate. "It was stultifying," she says. "He was just so frustrated."[58]

In particular, Shanker thought the labor movement needed to do three things: recognize the changing makeup of the work force and aggressively organize the growing professional class; appeal to workers on the basis of quality—that the union could give them voice to contribute ideas and produce a better product; and try new approaches to appeal to workers, such as associate memberships, reduced-dues arrangements that could eventually lead to full membership. Shanker believed in these strategies because he had found each of them to be successful within the AFT.

Shanker had for years been arguing that the future of unionism lay in organizing growing white-collar professional fields.[59] While the romantic view held that labor only organized the downtrodden, in fact it was the craft unions and the relatively well-paid auto workers who were at the center of trade unionism. Shanker believed janitors and farm workers and strawberry workers all deserved unions, but the focus had to be on professionals and the "knowledge workers" who were part of the postindustrial economy. Once professionals were organized, a stronger labor movement would be in a better position to organize less affluent workers.[60] Shanker knew that many professionals looked down on unions, but he also knew from organizing teachers in New York City that the objection could be addressed.

Shanker also argued that the appeal to workers, especially professionals, had to go beyond the self-interested model (we'll improve your wages) to include an appeal to quality (we'll help you have a greater voice to do a better job). Part of the appeal of the Saturn auto plant, Shanker said, was that workers gained dignity when they took responsibility for ensuring quality on their own, rather than relying on inspectors and supervisors.[61] Teachers did this when they backed reforms like the National Board for Professional Teaching Standards and peer review. He concluded: "The quality issue is the dignity issue updated."[62]

Shanker said that unions had to be open to new types of memberships, including reduced-dues "associate" memberships of the type the AFT used in Texas. By doing so, unions got their foot in the door, associate members would start receiving union publications, and there was a chance they might later join as full members.[63] It was a technique analogous to one Shanker used in New York City, when he attracted teachers to a talk about the new pension law and would end with a pitch for the union.

Many of these ideas were contained in reports put out by the AFL-CIO's Evolution of Work Committee, which was chaired by the AFL-CIO's Secretary Treasurer Tom Donahue.[64] Shanker, who was a member of the committee, was deeply discouraged when Lane Kirkland did not fight very hard to have some of the Donahue recommendations adopted.[65] While Shanker and Kirkland had "a tremendous rapport" on foreign policy, Ed McElroy says, Shanker was "somewhat critical, and rightly so, of Kirkland in terms of how he ran the labor movement."[66] To people on the outside, says Will Marshall of the DLC, Shanker stood out in his commitment to quality compared with many other union leaders, who were more interested in industrial featherbedding. "The AFT under Shanker seemed like an intellectual center; frankly, it seemed like the only intellectual center in the labor movement in the '80s and early '90s."[67]

To Shanker, merger with the NEA just might change the dynamic within the AFL-CIO to bring about some change. A combined NEA and

AFT would dwarf the AFL-CIO's other unions, and would by itself represent 40 percent of public-sector unionized workers and twenty percent of all union members.[68] Shanker knew that in those states where the NEA and AFT had merged, teachers were a powerful force within labor circles.[69] For Shanker, who believed a revived labor movement was crucial for the country, merger with the NEA represented an enormous possibility.

Negotiations between Shanker and his AFT colleagues and Geiger and his NEA team began on September 20, 1993, in Washington, D.C.[70] The three main sticking points remained from the aborted 1970s negotiation: AFL-CIO affiliation, racial quotas in leadership positions, and issues related to governance and the exercise of power (the secret ballot and the question of term limits for officers). To this, a fourth issue was added: would the merged organization include non-educators (such as nurses), as the AFT allowed, or be limited to educators, the NEA model?[71]

As the negotiations dragged on through 1994, the NEA's attitudes toward labor, quotas, and power simply mirrored the larger divide between the two organizations on a host of educational, social, and foreign-policy issues. The NEA took a far different view of America's role in the world, symbolized by its support during the cold war of the nuclear freeze.[72] The NEA applauded efforts to make it harder to suspend disruptive children, while Shanker took a tough stance on disruption.[73] The NEA supported race-based layoffs in the *Wygant* and *Piscataway* cases, while Shanker supported seniority.[74] The NEA favored an extreme form of bilingual education, which delayed language integration, while Shanker criticized it. The NEA fought against the testing of teachers and students while Shanker fought for it.[75] Says Jim Kelly: "The idea that they would merge made about as much sense to me as Turkey and South Africa merging, or Brazil and Canada, or Finland and Texas. I couldn't even imagine it."[76]

In the early 1990s, two new political issues arose that divided the unions. The first was the push for "full inclusion" of disabled students in the classroom. The NEA was supportive but Shanker raised serious objections.[77] Shanker explained that he favored the mainstreaming of as many disabled students as possible but was opposed to full inclusion of all students no matter their level of disability. Teachers were not trained to handle certain tasks, such as suctioning mucus from a child's lungs or administering a medical enema. And they were ill-equipped to deal with emotionally disturbed students who throw chairs or kick or bite with no apparent provocation. He rejected the idea that anything but full inclusion was "immoral" and a new form of "segregation," like the racial segregation of old. The analogy is faulty, he argued, because black children were excluded for racist reasons that were "totally irrelevant" to education. Placements, he said, ought to depend on the nature of the disability and not be made "according to some ideological theory." Shanker argued that politically correct liberals had allied with stingy conservative interests who supported full inclusion in order to save money by reducing the number of special-education teachers.[78]

The other new issue that divided the AFT and NEA was multiculturalism. It was even more contentious than full inclusion, because it went directly to the fundamental justification for public schools, in Shanker's view. Shanker opposed distorted versions of multiculturalism that were designed to artificially inflate the self-esteem of minority students. But he had a second concern, which ran even deeper.

The new "multiculturalism," Shanker argued, had changed from the sensible idea that students should learn about all different groups to the narrow view that minority students should mainly learn about their own group's accomplishments and learn history from the point of view of their own group.[79] Extreme multiculturalism, Shanker said, maintains, "paradoxically, that groups need to be interested only in their own history." The new multiculturalism, he said, "isn't really multiculturalism at all but ethnocentrism."[80] By calling common history a sham, extreme multiculturalism, Shanker said, would undercut the central rationale for public education:

> Americans have always seen public schools as places where children from various groups would learn to live together and value each other and where they would become acquainted with the common civic culture. If public schools become places where children learn that, fundamentally, they are not American, there will be no reason for taxpayers to continue supporting them. And there will be little to hold society together.[81]

In a speech to the U.S. Education Department in the early 1990s, Shanker talked about the important role public schools play in Americanizing students. "You are born a Kurd and I don't know how anybody in this room would go about becoming a Kurd," he said. "But one is not born into something that makes you an American. It is not by virtue of birth but by accepting a common set of values and beliefs that you become an

American. There is no word comparable in any other language with 'to Americanize.'" Shanker argued that common schools were crucial. "If public schools don't transmit common values and shared culture, why should taxpayers pay for them?" he asked.[82]

To Shanker's way of thinking, the NEA's embrace of extreme multiculturalism undercut the very best argument for preserving the public-school system. In an Executive Council meeting, Shanker remarked that the "strongest argument" against vouchers, and the one that underlies the public opposition, was that the public schools prevent Balkanization. He said that to form a "common culture," the public schools had to be more inclusive than in the past, when they taught a strict Eurocentric curriculum, but they should not go too far in the other direction. "That's obviously a recipe for social destruction."[83]

The multiculturalists and the voucher supporters were cut from the same cloth, Shanker believed. Both had a view that schools were about promoting the narrow values and culture of the families of the students, as opposed to exposing students to broader horizons and diverse ideas. It was not surprising that Howard Fuller, the former Milwaukee superintendent who heads the pro-voucher Black Alliance for Educational Options, was, in the late 1980s, a proponent of a separate black school district in Milwaukee.[84]

To Shanker, the public schools, by embracing an assimilationist vision rather than an extreme multicultural one, had wrought nothing short of a miracle. "A Martian who happened to be visiting Earth soon after the United States was founded would not have given the country much of a chance of surviving," he wrote.

> He would have predicted that this new nation, whose inhabitants were of different races, who spoke different languages, and who followed different religions, wouldn't remain one nation for long. They would end up fighting and killing each other. . . . But that didn't happen. Instead, we became a wealthy and powerful nation—the freest the world has ever known. . . . Public schools played a big role in holding our nation together.[85]

By advocating extreme multiculturalism, the NEA forfeited the common-culture argument for public schools, leaving public-school advocates with two weaker and more debatable propositions. One was that public schools do a better job of promoting academic achievement and preparing children, including poor children, to become workers in a market-based economy. While the evidence for vouchers was thin, the debate became one of dueling studies on student outcomes. The second argument, highlighted by the NEA, was that vouchers divert scarce money from the public schools. But this left public-school advocates vulnerable to bargains in which voucher programs are coupled with greater expenditure for public schools.[86] To Shanker, the argument for public education in a pluralist democracy ran much deeper than academic achievement or resources.

Lamar Alexander recalled attending a conference of education leaders and business people at which the president of Notre Dame, "Monk" Malloy, "brought the discussion to a complete stop by posing this question: 'What is the rationale for the public school?'" Alexander recalls: "After what seemed like an eternity of embarrassed silence," Shanker spoke up and "provided the answer: to teach children what it means to be an American."[87] Shanker believed that with their embrace of extreme multiculturalism, the NEA got the answer wrong on the most fundamental of questions.

In the end, the ideological chasm between the AFT and NEA—as manifested in merger issues such as AFL-CIO affiliation and quotas in leadership positions—proved too great. Shanker pursued the merger because he thought it would be good for teachers and kids and that the NEA might help transform the AFL-CIO, but the differences remained enormous. Within the AFT delegation, Sandy Feldman and Phil Kugler were strong advocates of merger. But at points, as it became clear to Shanker that the NEA had not changed sufficiently, he began asking whether there was some value to having two teacher organizations.[88] Shanker had many big reasons to favor merger, but he also had strong philosophical and cultural reasons to oppose it.[89] After more than a year's negotiation, in December 1994, merger talks collapsed for the moment over AFL-CIO affiliation, minority quotas, term limits, and a host of other issues.[90]

Battle Within the AFL-CIO

A month after the merger struggle ended, Shanker was thrust into another clash with strong ideological overtones—a battle for control of the AFL-CIO. Although the press reported the fight as fresh new leadership versus a decrepit, lethargic old guard, Shanker saw the dispute quite differently: between an AFL-CIO with a distinct internationalist and hawkish perspective versus new leadership that represented an isolationist and dovish view of the world.

The opening salvo came on the morning of January 28, 1995, with a front-page story in the *Washington Post* entitled "Key Union Leaders Want Kirkland to Leave."[91] The attack on Lane Kirkland, the president of the AFL-CIO, was unprecedented in labor circles. In the 109-year history of the AFL-CIO and its predecessors, no one had ever successfully challenged an incumbent president. Columnist Harold Meyerson notes that during this period, there had been twenty presidents and nine popes, but only five AFL presidents (one of whom served just a year.)[92]

The opposition to Kirkland, led by AFSCME president Gerald McEntee and Service Employees International president John Sweeney, lodged several complaints. Fundamentally, opponents were upset that Kirkland had not halted labor's precipitous decline, with the concomitant loss in political power, symbolized by Newt Gingrich's takeover of the House of Representatives. Labor needed more militancy and better organizing, they said, pointing to Sweeney's tactics (blocking bridges) and his success in organizing as a counterpoint to Kirkland's record.[93]

Critics also complained that Kirkland was not energetic enough about communicating labor's message and that he did not go on television talk shows. Said McEntee: "You watch 'Face the Nation' and you are likely to see Newt Gingrich and the head of the National Association of Manufacturers. You never hear someone speak on behalf of the workers."[94] Others complained that Kirkland had not done enough to reach out to women, minorities, and low-wage workers.[95] Finally, critics complained that Kirkland spent too much time on international affairs. He should "come home," said one union leader.[96] Thomas Geoghegan, a Sweeney supporter, explained the view: "I'd be against any labor leader who thought foreign policy was important. I mean, labor's going down the tubes here, and the notion that we're supposed to go around being an advisor and patron to other labor movements in other countries when we're in this terrible shape is just hypocritical and preposterous."[97]

Shanker agreed with some of the criticisms of those seeking change. He agreed that labor needed to do a better job organizing, and Shanker's AFT grew each year. He agreed that the AFL-CIO needed to communicate better, and Shanker had a widely read column and appeared regularly on television and radio. Shanker agreed that labor needed to reach out to women, minorities, and low-wage workers, and he led a female-dominated profession, promoted many women to the highest ranks, and called his organizing of the heavily minority low-wage paraprofessionals in New York City his proudest achievement.[98]

But, despite Shanker's dissatisfaction with the AFL-CIO, he became a staunch defender of Kirkland and his second in command, Tom Donahue. While Sweeney and his colleagues said they were for better and more creative organizing, Shanker did not believe it. "I don't see anyone with new ideas," he said of the challengers.[99] Indeed, said Shanker, the creative ideas about organizing that were part of the Donahue Commission had been rejected by the very people who backed Sweeney.[100]

At bottom, the real substantive battleground was Kirkland's foreign-policy endeavors and his hawkish pro-democratic policy.[101] Once in the mainstream of the Truman-Kennedy Democratic Party, labor had become an anomaly in foreign policy, as the old New Politics views came to dominate the party. The AFL-CIO was the outlier, and the veterans of the New Politics movement wanted to do something about it, in Shanker's view.

Jack Joyce, former president of the Bricklayer's Union, also argues that what really drove the opposition to Kirkland was international policy. "It wasn't about organizing and it wasn't about Lane should appear on talk shows and that other kind of crap." Those were not issues that were brought up in Executive Council meetings. He says: "There may have been other motivations involved, but the energy came from the international ideological part of it."[102] Sweeney backers like Paul Buhle agree, noting Kirkland's defeat was the paved by "fifteen years of grassroots organizing by anti-war and other people who came out of the New Left and the generation following."[103] "There's a fascinating story about how the sixties generation took over the labor movement," says Geoghegan. "And they were behind Sweeney."[104] Indeed, the AFL-CIO leadership fight broke down along the same lines as the old split between the Shachtmanite Social Democrats and the Harringtonite Democratic Socialists of America, with the SDs supporting Kirkland and Donahue, and the Democratic Socialists supporting Sweeney.[105] Shanker saw this very clearly. "Al never wanted to see the left take over organized labor," Arch Puddington says. "And he saw the staff people that were helping to mobilize this anti-Lane movement as being the political left coming in," including people he had fought over Central American policy.[106]

Shanker was deeply troubled by Sweeney's isolationist impulses and the "come home" rhetoric of his backers. It was specious to argue that there

was a tradeoff between promoting democracy abroad and helping workers at home, he said, especially in the context of globalization, where the
wages of workers abroad affect the wages of American workers. Critics said
one-third of the AFL-CIO's budget went to foreign affairs, but Shanker
noted the vast bulk of the money came from U.S. funding (through NED,
USAID, and the like) and less than 1 percent of the AFL-CIO's own budget
was spent on its four international-affairs institutes.[107]

In May, after meeting with Sweeney, Shanker shot off a letter on the issue. The AFL-CIO's International Affairs Department is a very small budget item, Shanker said, and it was misleading to suggest that much organizing could be done "if only we stopped doing international work."
Shanker wrote: "You do the workers of America no good by preaching
isolationism. . . . Would our workers and our country be better off today
if we had not helped Polish Solidarity, Russian miners and South African
trade unionists to overcome their oppressive regimes?"[108] The cold war
was over, but Shanker believed there was much work to be done by the
AFL-CIO in strengthening unions abroad and supporting fledgling
democracies.

Pulling back now, Shanker thought, would simply confirm the view
that labor was a special-interest group concerned only with its own members. Part of what made labor a moral instrument, not just an economic
one, was its heroic role during the cold war in fighting Communism, and
Shanker wanted that role to continue in different forms in the post–cold
war era. Going beyond self-interest was always controversial within labor
circles—as it had been when Shanker involved the UFT in the civil-rights
movement in the 1960s, as well—but ultimately, labor would be stronger
and more appealing to the public if it engaged in promoting international
human rights, Shanker argued.

Moreover, if part of what motivated Sweeney backers was the need to
recalibrate following the loss of the House of Representatives to the Republicans, then adopting a New Politics attitude toward international
matters that was further to the left was a very curious strategy. To reach
angry white males, the last thing to do would be to adopt weaker foreign-
policy positions. Likewise, in organizing workers, adopting positions that
might be perceived as anti-American was unlikely to help the cause of labor in Middle America and the South.

By May 1995, it was becoming clear that the Sweeney forces had a genuine shot at ousting Kirkland. Shanker estimated "each side has about 45
percent of the vote. And both sides are fighting over the remaining 10

percent."[109] In June, Kirkland announced his retirement and threw his support to his successor, Tom Donahue. To Shanker, the case against Sweeney was now even stronger: Donahue was as good as Kirkland on foreign policy and he was much better on union-reform issues than Kirkland.[110] Shanker became, says Donahue, "one of my staunchest, if not the staunchest supporter."[111]

But by the time of the AFL-CIO convention in October 1995, it was clear that Sweeney had the vote wrapped up. Shanker came to the microphone shortly after the opening session on October 24 to make the case for Donahue. The pro-Sweeney forces, who had bused in people to sit in the galleys of the convention, booed Shanker heartily. "It was a convention unlike any AFL-CIO convention I have ever attended," said Joyce. "What kind of malevolence, what kind of malice is involved in this when you've already got the votes?"[112]

The next day, Sweeney was elected president by a margin of 7.3 million to 5.7 million member votes cast. Donahue recalls that he did not wish to sit in the chair at the time of Sweeney's election and have to listen to "pious words" said about him, so he asked Shanker, who was the most senior of the vice presidents, to sit in the chair at the time power was exchanged. Shanker handed Sweeney the gavel. "No public congratulations were proffered," the *Washington Post* noted.[113] Some say Shanker "winced visibly" when he handed the gavel to Sweeney.[114] Puddington says when Kirkland was ousted, "the loudest cheers came from those who had been demanding a reversal in labor's foreign policy."[115] To Shanker, the decline of American labor under Kirkland was a great American tragedy. Sweeney, he feared, would only make things worse.

In the years after Sweeney took power, he made good on his promise of pulling back on international matters. The Social Democratic vision, which had animated Kirkland and the AFL-CIO staff, went by the wayside. Instead, Sweeney's international agenda focused almost entirely on trade issues. The AFL-CIO's "international orientation is but a shell of what it was," Kugler says.[116]

As Shanker predicted, pulling back internationally did not translate into great organizing gains domestically. Instead, under Sweeney, labor continued to decline, to the point, says Arch Puddington, that American labor is now "more marginal and less respected than at any time since the 1920s."[117] Ironically, in 2005, Sweeney faced his own rebellion, as one-third of the AFL-CIO's membership withdrew to form a new organization, called Change to Win.[118]

By pulling back on foreign matters, labor lost something very important. The Sweeney victory, Will Marshall argues, meant "the end of the most attractive features of Kirkland-Shankerism, which was this kind of assertive internationalist policy."[119] Labor's distinctive voice on the left, favoring a robust foreign policy, was stilled. For Shanker, the loss was devastating. The AFL-CIO, which had been the great bulwark against the extreme left in the Democratic Party, had now itself been lost.

The first three years of the Clinton Administration were not particularly good ones for Al Shanker's view of the world. Bill Clinton's handling of racial issues as president, coupled with the 1994 Gingrich revolution, the failure of the AFT merger talks with the NEA, and the change in the leadership of the AFL-CIO, represented a series of defeats for tough liberalism. Clinton was supposed to be a new kind of Democrat, but his embrace of racial preferences helped hand the House of Representatives, liberalism's stronghold, to the right wing. The NEA, the most powerful teachers' union in the world, remained committed to opposing AFL-CIO affiliation, supporting racial quotas, and embracing a separatist form of multiculturalism. The AFL-CIO, meanwhile, for many years the primary constituency in the Democratic Party supportive of a tough foreign policy, had jettisoned that legacy. Blue-collar white males were angry at liberals and there was no sign that any of the great liberal institutions Shanker worked with—the Democratic Party, the NEA, and the AFL-CIO—planned to do anything about the sources of their discontent.

19

Reviving the Education-Standards Movement and the Final Days

1995–1997

I N the twilight years of his life, Shanker continued to battle for the education-standards movement that he believed was so important to improving public education and that was now under attack from the right. He also made a spirited defense of teachers' unions, which would be singled out by 1996 Republican presidential nominee Bob Dole as bad for education. In death, he would receive tributes from across the political spectrum, and liberals and conservatives would fight over his legacy.

Reviving Standards: Student Discipline and the Palisades Summit

While Shanker was engaging in a bruising battle with the isolationist left over control of the AFL-CIO, he was simultaneously doing battle with the far right over the fledgling standards movement. Newt Gingrich, the new Speaker of the House, had opposed Goals 2000 as a member of the minority party in 1993 and now he sought to kill it outright.[1]

Just as the extreme multiculturalists on the left did not like standards-based reform, the extreme religious right wanted parents to be able to design a particular curriculum for their child, making common standards anathema. Ultimately, many opted for home schooling. Shanker's response to both groups was the same: "Bringing together a diverse group of children to learn the same thing is essential in creating a common civic culture. If the schools are forced to abandon this role and bow to the particular demand of every parent, we will lose the glue that has held our society together."[2]

The tides were clearly turning. Lamar Alexander, who had supported national goals as secretary of education but was contemplating a bid for the 1996 Republican presidential nomination, now began complaining that Goals 2000's creation of the National Education Standards and Improvement Council (NESIC) was tantamount to "a sort of national school board that overrides local control."[3] In March 1995, a Gingrich proposal for a 43 percent cut to Goals 2000 funding passed the House as part of a larger set of spending cuts. Shanker denounced the cuts and Clinton vetoed the bill. In July 1995, Gingrich proposed eliminating Goals 2000 funding entirely.[4] As a compromise, Goals 2000 continued to be funded, but NESIC was abolished.[5]

Against this onslaught from the right, Shanker and the AFT sought to forge ahead with three initiatives in 1995 to help shore up the standards movement: a report comparing American tests to international exams, a report analyzing the strength of various state standards, and a campaign aimed at linking the issues of standards with student discipline.

Shanker remained concerned that while many governors and educators were now embracing the rhetoric of standards, the assessments used to test whether students were learning were quite weak. In July 1995, the AFT released a report that examined rigorous national tests taken by students in Germany, France, and Scotland, and Shanker said the United States should adopt something similar for its high-school students.[6] Shanker believed it was important "to be very concrete about what we meant by high standards," says Liz McPike. "There's so much educationese and abstract talk" that Shanker wanted to lay out the facts clearly, and so the AFT published the actual exams.[7]

Publishing tests from abroad had a big effect on business leaders, says Milt Goldberg. "They didn't know what kinds of assessments were being given to these fifteen year olds in other countries." The practice later became commonplace, and it was Shanker, Goldberg says, who "created the appetite for examining the way in which other countries assess their youngsters and thinking seriously about how to accommodate that to the American scene."[8] Shanker's call for a national high-school exam was received less enthusiastically, however, by the Clinton Administration, which said the federal government should limit itself to providing educational guidance to the states.[9]

The AFT's second initiative, also published in July 1995, provided an analysis and scorecard of the standards movement in each of the fifty states. Under Goals 2000, virtually all states were adopting standards, but they varied widely in quality. No one was monitoring the strength of these standards, so the AFT decided to do it on its own.[10] Coming up with a set of criteria by which to judge state standards was an enormous task.[11]

The AFT study, "Making Standards Matter: A 50-State Progress Report on Efforts to Raise Academic Standards," offered the first nationwide information about which states were developing academic standards; their quality, clarity, and specificity; whether the standards were tied to assessments; and whether the standards had teeth and held students accountable.[12] The quality of standards was very important because vague admonitions that did not clearly point to specific grade-by-grade curriculum were worthless. The ratings received a fair amount of attention, particularly in individual states. Initially, some state officials largely ignored the AFT requests for information, but when they saw the attention that was paid, they began providing information and offering critiques of the methodology.[13] The ratings became an annual event for the AFT.[14]

The AFT's third initiative, a campaign to link standards and student discipline through a Bill of Rights and Responsibilities for Learning, was kicked off in September 1995.[15] Shanker had for years argued for fair and strict discipline, back to the 1967 New York City strike, but now there was a new reason: teachers were telling Shanker that unless discipline problems were addressed, students would never reach high standards of performance. "Al, we can't do anything when these kids are preventing us from teaching," they would tell him.[16] Shanker recalibrated his position in order to reflect his members' views. He argued: "It's increasingly clear that the biggest roadblock to improving the achievement of U.S. students is violence and disorder in our schools."[17]

In the clear language of someone who had experienced the problem at first hand, Shanker explained what happens in the classroom. "A second-grade youngster has an outburst—maybe he curses at the teacher or throws something at another kid, and nothing happens. At recess, he taunts his buddies, tells them how tough he is and how chicken they are. One kid, then another, reacts to the challenge, and pretty soon you've got a classroom that's unmanageable."[18] The AFT cited research finding that

160,000 children missed school each day out of fear, and that one in eleven teachers said they had been attacked in school.[19]

Many people understood what Shanker was saying. In an address to the AFT in 1995, President Clinton said he read the AFT's Bill of Rights and Responsibilities and agreed with it completely. It encapsulated both sides of the "values" argument, Clinton said: both the idea that bad behavior should be punished and the notion that government needed to help individuals who are under great economic pressure.[20]

But not everyone agreed with Shanker. In September 1995, Shanker gave an address to a conference of the Council of Great City Schools in Oklahoma City and drew a very hostile response. In a three-page letter released to the press, Executive Director Michael Casserly wrote, "the Council strongly objects to the notion of excluding children from school because they have been disruptive," and objected to Shanker's "national campaign of exclusion."[21] Shanker shot back with a six-page response to Casserly. First, he noted, "I did not propose 'excluding children from school because they have been disruptive.' . . . I did propose alternative educational settings for students who are violent and regularly so disruptive that they prevent all the other children from learning."[22]

While painting himself a champion of the poor, Casserly took a position that was likely to kill off public education, Shanker said. "If an enemy wanted to destroy public education, he could do no better than place a chronically disruptive child in each classroom and then count on your equivocations in the name of educating 'all' children to finish off his job." Shanker concluded: "The public will not give us much more time. The overwhelming majority, across all demographic groups, favor placing violent and chronically disruptive students in alternative educational settings so that all children can learn and be helped. The public is sick and tired of hearing that nothing can be done or should be done because there really isn't much of a problem in the first place."[23] In a column entitled, "Common Sense? Not to Some," Shanker contrasted Casserly's elite liberal position with that of both black and white parents—since 76 percent of white parents and 79 percent of African American parents said disruptive children should be removed from the class, according to Public Agenda, a nonprofit research organization.[24]

On numerous occasions, Shanker pointed out that while in some cities black students might disproportionately be expelled under a tough discipline policy, "the overwhelming percentage of children denied an education in disorderly and even violent classrooms will also be black. That's the real crime of this story."[25] In one column, he pointed to the story of Cedric Jennings, a sixteen-year-old African American honors student at a tough D.C. public high school who was jeered and bullied for doing well academically. "Every inner-city school, no matter how blighted and hopeless, has a core of Cedrics," he wrote. "It's immoral to leave them in a situation where their efforts to learn—to do what society wants them to do—will harm them." He concluded: "We need to help violent kids, but letting them rule the schools isn't helping them, and it's destroying the kids who want to save themselves. That's not decent, wise or practical."[26]

Shanker also continued to work closely with business leaders to keep the standards movement alive in the face of the Gingrich revolution. After the 1994 election, many in the business community feared that the standards movement was "in big trouble," Stanley Litow of IBM recalls. "States that stuck their neck out were stopping. Governors were somewhat intimidated, and the opposition was both from the right and the left," he says. "It was almost over," he says. "People were really concerned."[27]

In response, businesspeople, led by former IBM CEO Louis Gerstner, worked with Shanker to plan a national summit of governors and business leaders to be held in late March 1996 in Palisades, New York.[28] The meeting was hosted by Gerstner of IBM and Tommy Thompson (R-Wis.), head of the National Governors Association.[29] More than forty governors attended, each with a top business executive, along with about forty educators, including Shanker.[30] Shanker was on a panel with Lynne Cheney, Chester Finn, and Jim Hunt, and even among this group of heavy hitters, Shanker dominated, Litow says. It was an audience of mostly Republicans—CEOs and governors—but you could see lots of heads nodding when Shanker spoke, Litow recalls.[31] Shanker repeated his favorite line about stakes, recalling that when he gave students homework, they all asked, "Does it count?" Among those in the audience was President Clinton, who recounted Shanker's line in a speech to the group the next day, adding, "the truth is that in the world we live in today, 'does it count' has to mean something."[32]

One of the governors in attendance was George W. Bush of Texas, whom Shanker ran into at the conference, AFT press aide Jamie Horwitz recalls. "Bet you're a New York Yankees fan," Bush said. Shanker, who knew nothing about sports, replied that no, he wasn't. Shanker sought to engage Bush in an education-policy discussion, and Bush had real fear in his eyes, Horwitz recalls, even though Bush was then deeply immersed in education reform. Here were two men who had almost nothing in common, Horwitz says, with Shanker utterly incapable of making small talk and Bush seeking to avoid policy talk.[33] Neither knew the critical role Bush would later play in the standards movement.

The conference agreed to establish an "external, independent non-governmental entity" to serve as a clearinghouse for state standards. The group, Achieve, was established in order to help states develop good standards and assessments in part by showcasing the best.[34] The spring 1996 issue of *American Educator* was devoted entirely to articles on high standards, including several excerpts from the Palisades Summit.[35] The cover read: "Spring Brings New Life to the Standards Movement."[36]

Cancer Returns

In April 1996, Shanker was dealt an enormous setback when cancer was discovered in his lungs.[37] He began intensive chemotherapy and radiation treatment, but he tried to carry on his active schedule. He continued to travel overseas, and would research the local hospitals in advance in case he ran into trouble. He also kept writing his Where We Stand column. Eadie Shanker remembers, "Al would be home in bed. His column would be read to him over the phone and he'd go back and forth with Marcia Reecer about it."[38] Eadie says, "staying president of the union is what kept him alive."[39]

He became more reflective about his family and in the summer of 1996, when he attended a Pew Forum meeting in Jackson Hole, Wyoming, the group did something unusual: all the members starting talking about their personal lives. Shanker opened up and talked about some of his own children, who had struggled academically but got back on their feet. It was an illustration of how America gives kids a second chance in life, Shanker said.[40]

In July 1996, one of Shanker's important goals was achieved when the AFT and NEA, which had returned to the bargaining table in 1995, finally hammered out a national agreement not to raid one another's locals. Under the agreement, the unions were free to organize new members but would not go after each other's existing union representation. It was not a merger, but it was an important step.[41]

As the AFT national convention in Cincinnati approached in early August 1996, Shanker considered not seeking reelection but eventually decided to run.[42] He was scheduled to give his regular State of the Union speech on August 2, but was too ill. The next day, however, he rallied his strength. A reporter from the *Los Angeles Times* wrote: "thousands of teachers jumped to their feet when Shanker, obviously ill, slipped out unannounced from behind a heavy curtain and made his way slowly across the stage. Their applause thundered across the immense hall, and tears streamed down some faces." He delivered "a rousing, hourlong keynote speech."[43]

Shanker covered a number of topics, but is most remembered for saying two things. The first was a spirited defense of trade unions. He declared: "We've got a good story to tell. We've got a great historic institution to preserve. . . . We've overcome tremendous odds, and we've done it against money and animosity and power. . . . "[44] The second point was that teachers' unions needed to fully engage in education reform. He told delegates: "It is as much your duty to preserve public education as it is to negotiate a good contract."[45] Many were moved by the sight of a completely bald man, who was transported around the convention in an electric cart and delivered his address sitting down, telling delegates, once again, that teachers needed to go beyond their narrow self-interest to preserve an institution so fundamental to democratic society.[46] "That convention was very solemn," Lorretta Johnson recalls, but also inspiring. "For him to come to the convention with no hair and preside over that convention showed the true leadership and the love that he had for the AFT in his last years."[47] Although he could hardly walk, Myron Lieberman says, he was in complete control of the convention.[48]

Bob Dole's Attack on Teachers' Unions

Less than two weeks later, another convention was held, this one for Republican delegates to nominate Bob Dole as their presidential candidate—and the attitude toward teachers' unions at that convention was worlds apart. In his acceptance speech on August 15, Dole said he had no quarrel with teachers, but he thundered at teachers' unions: "If education were a war, you would be losing it. If it were a business, you would be driving it into bankruptcy. If it were a patient, it would be dying." He continued: "And to the teacher unions I say, when I am president, I will disregard your political power, for the sake of the parents, the children, the schools, and the nation."[49]

Much of Dole's attack could be dismissed as politics. Setting aside the issue of whether teachers' unions were good or bad for education, they were very close to the Democratic Party. Both the NEA and AFT were major Democratic donors and gave less than 10 percent of donations to Republicans.[50] But not all the criticism of teachers' unions could be attributed to partisan politics. As Thomas Toch noted in an article published in *U.S. News* that year, unions made it time-consuming at best and virtually impossible at worst for administrators to fire incompetent teachers.[51] The average cost of dismissing a teacher in New York State, he reported, was $200,000.[52] Others complained that teachers' unions went on strike too often, demonstrating their lack of concern for children, who lost valuable instruction time.[53] Still others complained that union seniority rules were bad for education.[54] In some places, critics charged, seniority transfers delayed the hiring of new teachers, as positions must first be made available to senior teachers to take or refuse.[55] And some alleged that seniority rules meant that low-income students in tough schools who need the best teachers most often ended up with the least experienced.[56] Finally, Toch and other critics said union opposition to merit pay made it difficult to reward (and retain) great teachers, who often left the classroom for higher-paying jobs in school administration.[57]

Of course, Shanker had spent many years formulating answers to these criticisms—championing peer review, the National Board for Professional Teaching Standards, and the like. But some alleged that Shanker's rhetoric was not matched by the actions of AFT locals.[58] Chester Finn said in 1996, "look, I agree with Al Shanker four days out of every five. But he's not representative of his union. He is way ahead of his membership."[59]

Shanker, in the twilight of his life, noted with some amusement the tension between Dole's argument and Finn's. Finn's charge, Shanker noted, was not consistent with "what Dole and other Republicans say. They say it's the union leaders who are awful and the members who are wonderful." Moreover, Shanker rejected the dichotomy between teachers and their unions. He asked: "Who started teacher unions? Who pays the dues that keep them going? Who elects the officers and determines union policies?"[60]

On one level, Dole's convention attack was a nice capstone to Shanker's career. When Shanker joined the AFT some forty years earlier, it would have been inconceivable for a presidential candidate to attack teachers' unions. They were not on the radar screen. In that sense, Dole's decision to single out teachers' unions was the highest compliment: a recognition that they had made it big in the world of politics.[61] In the midst of labor's long decline, teachers' unions had survived, flourished, and grown, and become a prime target of the right.

On the merits, Shanker had several responses to the Dole/Finn/Toch critiques. While teachers' unions were not perfect, he argued, they had sprung up for very good reasons, and they accomplished a lot of good for teachers and for students. He wrote: "Unions developed because teachers thought they needed them" to raise salaries and lift up the dignity of the profession.[62] Would teacher quality really increase if teachers' unions were abolished and teachers were paid less and lost their strong voice?

The evidence clearly suggested that teachers' unions increased teacher salaries and fringe benefits significantly, above what they would have been in the absence of collective bargaining.[63] This boost in wages came at a particularly important time—just as barriers to women in other fields declined and the need to attract high-quality candidates to teaching increased.[64] Shanker also argued that teachers' unions reduced turnover, not only by boosting pay but by giving all employees a voice and a remedy other than simply exiting the profession altogether.[65] There was also strong evidence that teachers' unions improved education by succeeding in reducing class size, which most studies find helps students learn better.[66] Teachers' unions also fought for greater preparation time and for staff development funds, which, if used well, could improve education.[67] Teachers' unions bargained and lobbied for tougher discipline policies for students, which research suggested was good for education.[68] Teachers' unions fought patronage hiring and promoted standards for the profession.[69] And finally, teachers' unions, by gaining better treatment of teachers from principals and administrators, helped promote the democratic message of public education. "For teachers," said Shanker, being treated with dignity is "especially important because they're models for all the kids in our society."[70]

Could one seriously argue that education would be better off in a world without teachers' unions—with lower pay, larger class sizes, less professional development, weaker discipline of students, and less dignity for

teachers? In fact, said Shanker, we know such a world. In response to
Toch's article, Shanker said, "the utopia that *U.S. News* longs for, where
teachers have neither collective bargaining rights nor due process and
school boards and principals can pretty much do what they like, already
exists. It's called the American South." So why were places like Texas, Alabama, and Mississippi not performing better than Japan, "where teachers
get tenure the day they are hired and unions are far more powerful than
ours."[71]

Shanker openly conceded that teachers' unions pursue their members'
self-interest. "Guilty as charged," he said. But teacher and student interests were more often closely aligned than the interests of students and
other adults in the system.[72] On the issue of student discipline, for example, management wanted less strict discipline procedures, because they
did not want to be sued by parents and have their schools to look bad
when statistics were compiled on school suspension and expulsion rates.
And in many jurisdictions, administrators opposed innovations like
peer review because they saw it as a management prerogative to evaluate
and fire teachers. Some administrators junked promising education reforms they inherited from previous administrations because they could
not take credit for them.[73] The other major group of adults in the system—parents—might want what is good for their own child but not push
for what is good for the majority of students in the schools. The point was
not that teachers' interests always aligned with those of children. But the
reality was if teachers did not have power through the union, power
would not devolve directly to children but rather to other adults whose
interests might be even further removed.

What about Chester Finn's critique that local unions rarely followed
Shanker's line on education reform? Here the picture is mixed. On some
matters—like the issue of teacher strikes—the criticism is off base. After
a flurry of early strikes in the 1960s and 1970s to gain union recognition
and collective bargaining, the number of strikes declined precipitously.
By 1986, teacher strikes had dropped 90 percent in ten years.[74]

Likewise, certain jurisdictions did implement many of the reforms
backed by Shanker. In Rochester, for example, the local's president,
Adam Urbanski, pushed reforms involving seniority, peer review, and
differentiated pay for teachers. Automatic transfers based on seniority
were replaced with a system in which faculty committees would make
decisions about transfers. Teachers who received the toughest assignments—the "Clint Eastwoods"—were promised the highest salaries.[75]

And peer review was adopted despite the opposition of administrators.[76] Other leading reform unions include Toledo, Dade County (Miami), New York City, Syracuse, Albuquerque, Pittsburgh, Corpus Christi (Texas), Minneapolis, and Cincinnati.[77] In 1995, a number of reform unions banded together to form the Teacher Union Reform Network (TURN). Led by Urbanski, TURN issued a manifesto, "Standards for Responsible and Responsive Teacher Unions," which was largely motivated, Urbanski says, "by Shanker's ideas and work."[78]

But the truth is that the vast majority of AFT's 2,200 autonomous locals did not pick up on the most controversial reforms.[79] Stanford professor Michael Kirst asks: "Where are these great reform unions? Philly? D.C.? Baltimore? Chicago? . . . Detroit? . . . I didn't see anything going on in those places that reflected the kind of things Al was projecting in the *New York Times* or on the lecture circuit."[80] Peer review, in particular, noted scholars Charles Kerchner, Julia Koppich, and Joseph Weeres, started "with a flurry of interest, and then [did] not spread."[81] "That was tough to sell," Sandra Feldman acknowledged. "It didn't take hold."[82] Shanker himself told Toch: "Convincing people to change has been a damn difficult thing to do. I would go into a state, talk up reform and as soon as I left, the union attorney would come in and say, 'We've got a great tenure law, let's keep it.'"[83]

Not that Shanker didn't try. He worked hard in meetings with the Executive Council to bring AFT vice presidents around to his views, often running such gatherings like a college seminar. There was a constant parade of outside speakers—business leaders, foreign educators, and others—as part of Shanker's efforts to bring AFT leaders toward his views on education policy.[84] To Shanker, educating union leaders and members was essential to reducing the tension between his role as democratically elected union leader and education reformer.

While Toch claims that by the early 1990s Shanker "stopped crusading for teacher reforms and made higher student standards his first priority" in part because he "wasn't making much progress in convincing his rank and file to buy into his union-reform agenda," this criticism seems unfair.[85] Shanker continued to push for high teacher standards under the NBPTS through the 1990s.[86] Indeed, in September 1996, the National Commission on Teaching and America's Future (NCTAF), on which Shanker served, concluded that more than 25 percent of new teachers had inadequate skills or training, and called for stricter licensing of teachers, extra funds for excellent teachers, an easier process for dismissing bad teachers, and the closing of failing schools of education—all Shanker staples.[87]

Final Days

By the fall of 1996, Shanker was running out of time for his education-reform agenda, as his cancer continued to spread. But as the end neared, he could be satisfied to know that his contributions to education were being recognized in the press. He was featured in two lengthy articles—a piece by Sara Mosle on national standards that made the cover of the *New York Times Magazine* in late October, and a cover story by Elaine Woo about Shanker in the *Los Angeles Times Magazine* in December.[88] In another article that year, Diane Ravitch said: "Right now, he's probably the most influential person in American education."[89]

Although seriously ailing, Shanker remained feisty, and in January 1997, he blasted a decision of Oakland's school board to teach Black English, or Ebonics. Ebonics was basically "a self-esteem strategy," an attempt to say that using Black English is not wrong, it's "just different," said Shanker. But this attitude, he said, would hurt the very children it was meant to help by delaying the mastery of standard English.[90] E. D. Hirsch, Jr., recalls appearing on a radio show with Shanker on the topic. Confronted with a black militant, Hirsch, the guilty white southerner, gave a mealy-mouthed reply; Shanker, who was very sick at the time, said bluntly that Ebonics was a terrible idea.[91]

On consecutive days in early February, not long before he died, Shanker received two tributes—one from the president of the United States and one from the president of the National Education Association. Neither mentioned Shanker by name publicly at the time, but there was little question about who inspired both sets of remarks.

Following his defeat of Bob Dole, Clinton had set out his goals for his second term, and mentioned in a speech to the Democratic Leadership Council and an interview with the *Wall Street Journal* that "we need national standards." This took Clinton education officials like Richard Riley and Michael Cohen by surprise. Cohen's view was that states were moving forward on standards and the federal government should support them and declare victory, but Clinton had never given up on the idea of national standards.[92]

On February 4, 1997, Clinton devoted most of his State of the Union address to education, which he called his "number-one priority" for his second term. Clinton laid out a ten-point plan for education, the most important of which was a call for voluntary national tests by 1999. The tests would be given to fourth graders in reading and eighth graders in math. The federal government would pay for the creation of the tests. Standards themselves would continue to be set by states, and the national tests would be voluntary—states would not be required to use them.[93] The vision of national tests rather than national standards was not precisely what Shanker had advocated, but it was a big step in the right direction.

Shanker watched the speech on television from his hospital bed and commented that Clinton was "the best that we're ever going to do."[94] Shanker's son Michael says: "Just being able to see the look on my father's face, even though he was sick . . . of basically his life's work being brought to the State of the Union Address . . . was pretty amazing."[95] After the speech, Clinton called Shanker and told him: "You know, I hope you feel good now, because you've been telling us to do this for years and years and years, and finally your crusade will be America's crusade."[96]

Shanker returned the compliment in one of his last columns. It began: "With his State of the Union speech, President Clinton demonstrated that he is indeed the education president. The American public has been demanding higher academic standards. They are right, and with the President's leadership, we are now far closer to reaching that goal." Clinton knew that it is not "somehow kinder and more humane to expect less of poor kids in low-achieving schools."[97]

The second tribute came on February 5, the day after Clinton's speech, when Bob Chase, the newly elected president of the NEA, gave an extraordinary address at the National Press Club, acknowledging NEA errors.[98] He conceded that "in some instances, we have used our power to block uncomfortable changes, to protect the narrow interests of our members, and not to advance the interests of students and schools." He called for a "New Unionism," which puts "issues of school quality front and center at the bargaining table." He said the union must now embrace such reforms as peer review, or America would end up with a system of private-school vouchers. "We must revitalize our public schools from within, or they will be dismantled from without," he declared.[99]

The speech was motivated in part by an internal Kamber Group report entitled *An Institution at Risk*, which argued that the NEA needed to become active in education reform and not just stick to traditional union activities.[100] But it had Shanker's fingerprints all over it. Toch notes: "It was exactly the same message that Albert Shanker had delivered . . . twelve years earlier."[101] Chase later acknowledged his debt to Shanker. "Al taught us that we can defend public education without defending public education's status quo," he said. For those at the NEA, Chase commented, Shanker was a "tough teacher."[102]

As February progressed, Shanker knew the end was near. Lying in a hospital bed in his apartment, he took his wife Eadie's hand and told her, "you are really a special person." He told her that when she died, he would like it if they were buried in the same grave. Two days later, he was rushed to Cabrini Hospital and eventually transferred to Memorial Sloan Kettering.[103] As Shanker lay in the hospital, his sister Pearl came to visit for the last time. He told her if he had to live his life over again, there was not much he would do differently. And he said "the one thing that hurt him the most was the accusations [of racism] around Ocean Hill–Brownsville."[104]

He began to drift in and out of consciousness, and on February 22, 1997, Al Shanker died with much of his family by his side.

Tributes

Upon hearing of Albert Shanker's death, President Clinton issued a statement praising his accomplishments. "Al spent his life in pursuit of one of the noblest of causes—the improvement of our public schools. He challenged teachers to provide every child the very best education possible and made a crusade out of the need for educational standards."[105] It was one of many such statements that would follow in the coming days.

Shanker's body was cremated on February 24, and on February 27, his remains were buried in the King David section of the Rose Hill Cemetery in Putnam Valley, New York. A small group of about forty family and friends gathered at the chapel. Shanker's sister Pearl said a prayer, and his son Carl said Kaddish, the Hebrew prayer for the dead.[106]

Later, a UFT memorial for Shanker was set next to Shanker's grave with an image of a book. On the left hand, the page read, "Albert Shanker 1928–1997." On the right hand, the page read: "President of the UFT and the AFT. Philosophy. Public Education. Free Trade Unions. Civil and Human Rights. Democracy for all people. A visionary and fiery union leader loved by family, friends and colleagues."[107] A small memorial service of about 250 union staff, friends, and family was held on February 28, at Stuyvesant High School, which Shanker had attended a half century earlier.[108]

Almost a month later, Shanker was remembered at a UFT ceremony of more than two thousand people at Lincoln Center in New York City. Participants included Senator Ted Kennedy, former mayor Ed Koch, New York City chancellor Rudy Crew, AFL-CIO president John Sweeney—and Fred Nauman, one of the nineteen educators involuntarily transferred from Ocean Hill–Brownsville.[109] Eadie Shanker, who had been preoccupied arranging a funeral for her sister, Sylvia, who died two weeks after Al Shanker, was distressed that Koch and Sweeney spoke, given Shanker's tangles with them.[110] One of the nicest tributes came not from a speaker but from a former New York City teacher who did not know Shanker well. Rhoda Cohen told the *New York Times*: "He made teachers go from being people who took orders, who had very little impact on their careers, and who felt threatened by administrative authority, to being people who were respected and who gained self-respect."[111]

On April 9, 1997, the AFT sponsored a Washington, D.C., memorial attended by seven hundred people at George Washington University with tributes from President Clinton, Senator Moynihan, and Lorretta Johnson.[112] AFT Secretary-Treasurer Ed McElroy and UFT President Sandy Feldman gave personal remembrances. Education Secretary Richard Riley spoke of Shanker's commitment to raising education standards, and former AFL-CIO president Lane Kirkland spoke of his commitment to the labor movement. "The central idea that moved him and drew his steadfast loyalty was the great concept of human solidarity," Kirkland said. "He understood it not just as an ideal but a necessity in the face of raw political and economic power far beyond the capacity of anyone to meet alone." Shanker knew that labor was a bulwark against both "the restraining hands of state ministries" in places like Poland and in "private counting houses" at home and abroad.[113] Washington, D.C., Delegate Eleanor Holmes Norton spoke of Shanker's commitment to civil rights and the controversy in Ocean Hill–Brownsville, while NEA President Bob Chase mentioned Shanker's bold leadership in embracing *A Nation at Risk*. There were tributes from a Polish activist, a National Board–certified teacher, and other educators and unionists. Vice President Al Gore, who did not know Shanker very well, asked to be included as a speaker, a testament to the power of the union that Shanker had built.

Gore then introduced President Clinton, whose speech concluded the lengthy service.[114]

There were also laudatory op-eds in various newspapers and magazines from moderates such as Diane Ravitch, Arch Puddington, Arnold Beichman, Ben Wattenberg, and E. D. Hirsch, Jr. and conservatives such as Chester Finn and Linda Chavez. They emphasized Shanker's embrace of high standards, hard work, and discipline and his opposition to Communism, distorted multiculturalism, moral relativism, Afrocentrism, extreme forms of bilingual education, and racial quotas.[115]

Not all the published remembrances of Shanker were favorable. A signed *New York Times* editorial written by Steven Weisman blamed Shanker for waging an all-out war over Ocean Hill–Brownsville, "whose victory came at the cost of deepening the city's hatreds." Weisman concluded: "Mr. Shanker believed that total victory was essential. That is what he got, but it was after a war that lacerated the city and left wounds that have never fully healed."[116] Brown University lecturer Paul Buhle wrote a scathing obituary for the Socialist publication *New Politics* entitled "Albert Shanker: No Flowers," which accused Shanker of fomenting racial hatred and suggested links to the CIA.[117]

This then, was the strange reaction that Shanker inspired: praise from mainstream liberals (Clinton and Kennedy), further praise from moderates (Ravitch) and some conservatives (Finn), and utter disdain and hatred from elements of the left (Buhle).

In early May, the AFT chose as Shanker's successor Sandy Feldman, who, as one official noted, "grew up at the foot of the master."[118] An active Social Democrat who backed high educational standards, Feldman pledged to pursue Shanker's "unfinished agenda."[119] Working in the shadow of Shanker's memory was a daunting task for Feldman, as the tributes continued to flow in.

On January 15, 1998, Shanker was posthumously awarded the Medal of Freedom, the nation's highest civilian honor, by President Clinton. Eadie Shanker accepted the medal in a reception in the East Room of the White House. Among the fifteen honored that day were James Farmer, Sol Linowitz, Robert Coles, Elliot Richardson, and David Rockefeller. When it came time to speak about Shanker, Clinton was very personal in his remarks: "Albert Shanker illuminated our nation's path toward educating our children with devastating honesty, sharp wit, and profound wisdom," Clinton said.

He was one of the most important teachers of the twentieth century. In 1983, when the *Nation at Risk* report challenged us to do far more to raise educational standards for all of our children, Al Shanker was one of the very first to answer the call. That began for me, a young governor who cared a lot about education, one of the most remarkable working relationships of my entire life; for Al Shanker was for me, and so many others, a model, a mentor, a friend, a leader of immense stature who always spoke his mind, no matter how unpopular the thought. We miss him dearly.[120]

In late January 1998, Feldman accomplished what Shanker had planted the seeds for during his lifetime: an agreement with the top leadership of the NEA to merge with the AFT. On the pivotal question of affiliation with organized labor, the agreement provided that the new union would affiliate with the AFL-CIO and pay dues for 1.4 million of the 3.2 million members.[121] Some called it the end of "the thirty years war."[122] But that description proved premature. While AFT delegates ratified the merger, only 42 percent of NEA delegates supported merger at the national convention in July, far short of the two-thirds required.[123] The old issue of AFL-CIO affiliation, polls showed, was pivotal.[124] (Later, in 2006, the NEA and AFL-CIO reached an agreement under which individual NEA locals could affiliate.)[125]

No Child Left Behind

Following Shanker's death, President Clinton's call for a voluntary national test withered. Despite strong business support for standards, a coalition of conservatives and civil-rights groups helped push a ban on the development of national tests, a bar that passed the House by a vote of 295 to 125.[126] It would fall to another president to push the standards movement to the next level.

In the 2000 presidential campaign, Texas Governor George W. Bush campaigned for strong standards and accountability reform in education, and on the stump he frequently quoted Shanker on the need for high standards.[127] Following his election as president, Bush teamed up with Rep. George Miller (D-Calif.) and Shanker's old ally, Senator Ted Kennedy, to forge the No Child Left Behind Act of 2001 (NCLB). The bill represented a bargain: the federal government would invest more money than ever in K–12 public education, and in return, schools would be held accountable, judged against mandatory state tests in reading and math administrated in grades 3 through 8. The act set the goal of making all children "proficient" in reading and math by 2014 and required states to make "adequate yearly progress" (AYP) toward those goals. Schools failing to make AYP would be subject to a set of increasingly serious sanctions. On one level, it was astounding that a Texas Republican was backing a larger federal role in education than ever before.

The AFT was generally supportive of NCLB—far more supportive than the NEA, which later sued to have the program halted. This support was consistent with Shanker's call for greater incentives in education, for greater resources in exchange for greater accountability, and for the federal government to invest in high levels of education for all children. It was also consistent with Shanker's view that as a political matter, teachers needed to embrace reform and help shape it rather than be seen as obstructionist.[128]

Having said that, it is also clear that NCLB fell short of the Japanese and European model Shanker advocated in at least four important respects: it called for accountability for adults but not students, it called for tests linked to state rather than national standards, it provided for one single performance standard for all students rather than multiple standards, and it permitted—some would say encouraged—low-quality tests.

NCLB had consequences for schools and teachers (including the reconstitution of failing schools) but no direct consequences for students. A number of states on their own have adopted student accountability—in 2006, twenty-two states, educating 65 percent of the nation's high-school students, required students to pass state tests before graduating.[129] But NCLB itself did not answer Shanker's basic question for children: "Does it count?" This left teachers in the difficult position of being held accountable for the performance of students, many of whom were aware that failing the test had no personal consequences for them.

Likewise, while NCLB asserted a new, strong, federal role in education, it largely left to the fifty states the setting of standards and assessments.[130] States with the highest performance standards were effectively punished because they were more likely to look like failures in the eyes of the public.[131] This fell short of Shanker's call for national standards as they are established in most other countries with effective education systems.

NCLB also set one standard for all American students—proficiency in twelve years, again in contrast to the European model Shanker favored, which recognized that humans vary in abilities and set multiple standards so that each portion of the academic distribution would have an incentive to work hard.[132] "Al believed in eradicating achievement gaps, group distinctions," Bella Rosenberg says. "But Al knew that since the beginning of time, there had been individual variability," so a performance standard which requires 100 percent proficiency by a certain date "is just a human impossibility."[133] Shanker predicted that the result of a single standard was either enormous failure rates, which were designed to undermine public schools and pave the way for private-school vouchers; or a dumbed-down standard, which could be achieved but provided no challenge to the students in the higher part of the distribution.[134]

Finally, NCLB allowed the use of low-quality commercial tests rather than European-style assessments, which often allow for open-ended, sophisticated responses. Because NCLB required so much testing—in every grade for grades 3 through 8—many states used multiple-choice tests, which are cheaper and quicker to administer. Of twelve states that Achieve was asked to benchmark prior to 2003, it found only one (Massachusetts) that had rigorous standards and high-quality assessments.[135] This was a far cry from what Shanker called for during his lifetime: a carefully designed program of clearly articulated standards and a sophisticated curriculum that is aligned with sophisticated assessments, all pulling in the same direction.[136]

Shanker knew that getting standards-based reform right was going to be very difficult, and would take decades to perfect.[137] Many educators wished that he had stayed around longer to help guide the process.

III

LEGACY

20

The Legacy of Albert Shanker

TODAY, roughly a decade after his death, it is possible to begin assessing Shanker's contributions and his legacy. In education circles, Shanker's name is frequently invoked in discussions and arguments, and his ultimate legacy will continue to evolve over time. But it is certainly possible to ask the question: how would our world be different if Al Shanker had gone on, as he planned, to become a professor of philosophy rather than a leader of teachers, an education reformer, a union activist, and a public writer?

Shanker's impact can be considered in three areas: his influence on education (which was great), his short-term influence on fights over the definition of American liberalism (which was minimal), and his long-term legacy of ideas about education and liberalism (which could, conceivably, prove significant in the future).

Shanker's Education Legacy

Although Albert Shanker's policy endeavors ranged broadly—from racial quotas to Poland to labor affairs—his biggest contributions came in the area of education. As a founding father of collective bargaining for teachers and a leading education reformer, he is the single person most responsible for reshaping and preserving public education in the last half of the twentieth century.

A Founding Father of Modern Teacher Unionism

His first accomplishment, which by itself would have earned him a place in the history of American education, was to help win the first significant right to bargain collectively for teachers in the United States. The *Washington Post* and *Education Week* both called him "the father of the teacher unions," which does not give proper credit to others.[1] But he was one of a handful of founders of modern teacher unionism—which moved from collective begging to collective bargaining—and he alone among the group had the ability to take the UFT to the next level. Eugenia Kemble, who knew other early leaders, says "they were nowhere near him" in leadership abilities.[2] Shanker's timing was right—collective bargaining for public employees was in the air in the late 1950s and early 1960s—but Shanker and the UFT were in the vanguard, and as pioneers, they set important precedents about how collective bargaining for teachers would work. The New York City model of bargaining for elementary, middle, and high-school teaching in one citywide unit was adopted by school districts across the country. Shanker also set an important precedent in 1968, when he stood up to efforts to emasculate the union during the Ocean Hill–Brownsville crisis. Had Shanker backed down, the fledgling teachers' union movement might have gone in a very different—and much weaker—direction than it did.

Had Shanker and his UFT colleagues merely transformed their parent organization, that would have been significant. But they did much more than that. The tiny AFT tail wagged the much larger NEA dog, causing the administrator-dominated NEA (ten times the size of the AFT) to turn itself into a real union or die. During Shanker's years in teachers' unions, the AFT membership rose from 70,821 in 1961 to 947,000 in 1997. The NEA, having come around to AFT-style collective bargaining, increased its membership from 766,000 to 2.2 million in 1997.[3] In 1959, when Shanker signed on as an organizer with the AFT, only a tiny percentage of teachers were organized. Today, more than 70 percent of public-school teachers are covered by collective-bargaining agreements—ten times the rate of private-sector workers.[4] Public-school teaching is among the most highly unionized occupations in the country.[5]

While trade unionism was crumbling all around them, the teachers' unions thrived. The larger numbers translated into power. In 1960, says Myron Lieberman, teachers' unions were politically irrelevant.[6] Today, the NEA and AFT, says Lieberman, are "among the most powerful interest groups in U.S. society."[7] Shanker helped transform the AFT from an organization that in 1968 refused to endorse Hubert Humphrey because delegates believed teachers' unions should not be involved in politics to one that by the 1980s would consistently send more delegates to the Democratic National Convention than any other union in the AFL-CIO.[8] While they do not always win policy battles, teachers' unions are widely regarded today as the most powerful political forces in education.[9] And usually—though not always—the rising power of teachers' unions has had positive benefits.

Teacher collective bargaining, which Shanker helped establish, had a significant effect on the social mobility of hundreds of thousands of teachers and their children. Historically, teachers have generally come from blue-collar families, and that was especially true in New York City.[10] (Shanker once joked that the UFT should merge with the International Ladies Garment Workers Union and call it "The ILGWU and Their Children.")[11] In some measure because of collective bargaining, between 1961 and 2001, the average annual salary of public-school teachers (adjusted for inflation) rose from $33,413 to $48,043.[12] By raising the standard of living of teachers, Shanker enabled their offspring to go further in their educations—many becoming professionals. After Shanker's death, a son of a former New York City teacher called an AFT staffer and said, "if it weren't for him, I wouldn't be a doctor."[13] For teachers themselves, the union brought greater dignity, respect, and self-confidence, the initial goals that galvanized Shanker when he was a teacher to join the union.

Taken together, raising both teachers' salaries and their dignity had a profound effect on education, attracting better candidates than would have been available in the absence of unions. Teachers' unions reduced the student-teacher ratio, which most studies find is beneficial to learning.[14] In innumerable ways—mostly, but not always, good—teachers' unions have changed the face of public education.

Having said that, Shanker failed—in the 1970s and again in the 1990s—to create an even greater teacher voice through a merger of the AFT and NEA. Shanker was generally smarter and more agile than the leadership of the NEA, but he was never able to persuade them to come around to his views on key ideological questions and to join in the larger labor movement—a major disappointment to him. Likewise, in the AFT's representation battles with the NEA, Shanker and his colleagues never came close to catching up, either by displacing NEA locals or by conquering the South, as Shanker originally set out to do. The NEA remains the dominant teachers' union in most states. And the NEA's budget is three times the size of the AFT's.[15] The AFT remains a largely urban northeastern and Midwestern union in a country that has been moving to the suburbs and the South and the West.[16] Still, the AFT and NEA separately remain very powerful, and Shanker did live to see the end of the infighting, with the 1996 no-raid agreement.

Education Reformer

Shanker's second major contribution to education was as a reformer, a role in which he championed the professionalization of teaching, an early version of charter schools, and standards-based reform. Shanker asserted that it was in the enlightened self-interest of his union members to improve public education, because without it, he argued, union members would be hurt. This was extraordinary, says union critic Chester Finn; if it weren't for Shanker, he said, conservatives and business leaders would not expect anything from a union leader other than to pursue what was in his members' most narrow interests.[17]

One of Shanker's biggest contributions, says Adam Urbanski, was giving unionism a good name. People were startled and impressed, he says, by "living proof of a unionist who is a brilliant intellectual" and "had so much courage to change . . . the culture of teacher unionism."[18] It was one thing to build a powerful union, Sandra Feldman said, but Shanker did more, by building an "intellectually potent teachers' union. About some other organizations," she noted, "you could say they're large, strong and effective, but not intellectually potent."[19]

If "phase one" was to build a strong union, said the AFT's Tom Mooney, in "phase two, he liberated us from a strict adherence to the industrial unionism model and encouraged us and taught us to blend unionism and professionalism."[20] In seeking to turn the teaching *occupation* into a teaching *profession*, his greatest success was creation of the National Board for Professional Teaching Standards. He was able to transform the traditional union position of both the AFT and NEA—that teachers should be paid equally for equal education, experience, and duties, and that it was difficult to measure who was a better teacher—and create a system of board certification that some preliminary research suggests can identify teachers who are effective at raising academic achievement.[21]

Shanker was far less effective in promoting peer review to weed out bad teachers: only a relative handful of innovative districts adopted the practice. On some levels, the failure is understandable. Teachers' unions are particularly decentralized in the world of organized labor, reflecting the decentralization of the American public-school system, which has 15,000 separate districts.[22] Shanker could no more force autonomous locals to adopt Toledo's peer-review plan than he could have stopped Toledo from using the plan.[23] Leading a million-member democracy was far different than being a CEO who could bark a command and expect others to follow.[24] (Indeed, Shanker may have wished at times he had more of the authoritarian power his critics accused him of having.) And in many cases, school boards resisted peer-review policies that teachers' unions championed. But the failure of peer review to catch on was a major disappointment. Of all the charges raised against teachers' unions, the one that has the most staying power is that unions defend terrible teachers. Shanker latched on to a brilliant response but proved unable to overcome resistance from many locals.

What Shanker did do was create an environment in which innovative local union leaders were given room to maneuver. Stanford's Linda Darling-Hammond notes that the creative leaders in the AFT—people such as Adam Urbanski, Tom Mooney, and Dal Lawrence, "could have been made to feel like outcasts."[25] Shanker's pronouncements in favor of reform did the opposite. "It was inordinately important for Shanker to make the speeches," says Urbanski, "because without him making those speeches the culture of unionism was such that you would not have had the needed cover for those who would even want to do it." Shanker made it possible for local leaders to engage in "heretical thinking," and, indeed, he modeled it.[26]

After the professionalization of teaching, Shanker's second major proposal as an education reformer was charter schools. On one level, his proposal was a tremendous success—after standards, charters are probably the second most important education reform ongoing today. But by Shanker's own reckoning, the movement was hijacked by conservatives who transformed many charter schools into a mechanism to weaken union protections of teachers and, in some cases, allow for-profit institutions a chance to draw from public coffers. Given strong union opposition to the existing regime of charter schools, it is possible that the movement could return to Shanker's original vision—creative teacher-led schools that reach children in new ways. Some charter schools embody that vision today. But for the moment, the charter-school movement that Shanker helped unleash is a far cry from the reform he sought. This was disappointing to Shanker, but when staff would complain to him that his charter-school idea had been twisted, he would respond: "What do you want me to do? Stop coming up with ideas?"[27]

Surely Shanker's biggest legacy as an education reformer was his third initiative: to move the United States toward a European and Japanese system of standards. No other education reform today is nearly as significant as standards-based reform, and no other individual had as important an influence on getting the country to move toward a system of education standards as Albert Shanker. That education standards are the touchstone for all education-reform discussions is an extraordinary development in a country where most every element of the education-policy community—the NEA, education-school professors, civil-rights groups, administrators—showed varying degrees of hostility toward the standards movement.

By deciding to break with the educational establishment and join with business people and governors to put in place a system of standards and accountability, Shanker became, by many lights, the single most influential person in the movement.[28] Former NBPTS president Jim Kelly, for example, argues Shanker "created from scratch the educational standards movement and . . . brought into that movement an extremely resistant education establishment."[29] He pounded away at standards in his column.[30] He lobbied hard for legislation like Goals 2000. And through force of argument and example, he slowly brought around others in the education establishment to the point where they became at least neutral.[31]

Once he latched onto the standards idea, he was relentless. Marshall Smith, whose articles provided much of the intellectual infrastructure of the standards movement, says that among those with political power, Shanker was unique. While Bill Clinton pushed hard for standards, he also got caught up in "the reform du jour" and moved from standards to class size, "so we were never able to get up a steady drumbeat for good implementation." Shanker, by contrast, "was the one steady drum beat" and "the most public nationally understood spokesman for it."[32] Diane

Ravitch, another important intellectual force behind the idea of education standards, argues: "During the early 1990s, the person who influenced the nation's discussion of school quality more than anyone else was Albert Shanker," pointing to his role in the standards movement.[33] Many in the business community agree. Stanley Litow of IBM says Shanker's embrace "was vital because if the teachers in both major unions had been against it, I don't think it would have been able to be as successful."[34]

Of course, the ultimate shape of the standards movement remains a moving target. Shanker would have had quarrels with several of the specific provisions of the No Child Left Behind Act, and it is conceivable that if the standards, testing, and accountability movement produces extremely high rates of school failure, it could undermine Shanker's goal of preserving public education. But the early evidence suggests Shanker was right to push for standards: they are likely to promote greater equity and to strengthen rather than undercut public education.

On the equity issue, there is currently a split within the civil-rights community about whether or not the current manifestation of standards-based reform—the No Child Left Behind Act—is helping poor and minority children.[35] But the preliminary evidence supports Shanker's view that poor and minority students will benefit from the larger standards movement embraced by states over the last decade and a half. Math scores for fourth-grade black and Hispanic students, for example, shot up nearly two grade levels between 1992 and 2005.[36] And the standards movement is providing the evidence necessary for new political reform and school-finance lawsuits seeking an "adequate" education for students.[37]

The preliminary evidence also supports Shanker's view that standards would ward off the private-school voucher movement rather than facilitate its success. It is true that in some places, students in schools identified as failing to meet standards have been provided vouchers to attend private schools. But it still appears more likely that Shanker's embrace of standards made vouchers less politically viable, not more. By embedding market-type incentives and accountability into the public system, standards-based reform kept the business community largely engaged in public-school reform and kept it from being diverted to private-school voucher proposals. In 2002, when the U.S. Supreme Court for the first time upheld the constitutionality of vouchers for religious schools, the floodgates did not open, and testing and standards remain the central focus of education reform.

Preserver of Public Education

Indeed, in looking at Albert Shanker's contributions and legacy in education in total—as a union leader building teachers' unions into a powerful force and as an education reformer working on the professionalization of teaching and raising academic standards—his biggest accomplishment of all was surely to preserve a system of public education against those who would like to see it dismantled in favor of a system of private-school vouchers.

This was no small feat. The United States has the most market-oriented economy in the world, and yet 90 percent of its students continue to attend what critics call "government-sponsored" public schools. While some other countries have implemented private-school voucher systems, the number of students in the United States attending private schools with public funds represents less than one-tenth of one percent.[38] Even as the argument for markets has transformed the world and shaped social policy in the United States, our public-school system remains a notable outlier. In no small part, this was Albert Shanker's doing. Says Myron Lieberman, a strong proponent of vouchers: "Al was the single most effective opponent of any kind of privatization in education."[39] He kept vouchers at bay in three ways.

First, by helping to create the modern teachers' union movement and forcing the NEA to join it or risk irrelevance, he helped forge the single most powerful political obstacle to school vouchers. Other groups in public education—school boards, principals, parents—also oppose vouchers, but it is the teachers' unions that have had the political muscle to defeat all but a tiny number of voucher initiatives and legislative proposals. Teachers' unions are the ones who run ads, man phone banks, and provide political contributions to preserve public education. All the other national education associations lack the strategic and organizational capacity to push back against vouchers, experts say.[40]

But if Shanker and the teachers' unions had relied solely on their raw political power, vouchers might have made more inroads. It was Shanker's insight that in order to preserve public education, teachers' unions had to demonstrate a willingness to abandon an appearance of opposition to all reform. Shanker, says union critic Myron Lieberman, "did more than anyone to counter the idea that teacher unions are an obstacle to education reform." He was, says Lieberman, "an anomaly—a public sector union leader with tremendous prestige among conservatives."[41]

This was a unique combination, says Chester Finn. Groups like the NEA were good at the external defense strategy but cared little about internal reform. And a lot of public-education reformers were also supporters of private-school vouchers. But Shanker "was a smart enough guy to figure out that he needed to do both." He was a "brawler" who sought to "smite the enemies of public education" and a "statesman" who sought to ensure that public education was an "institution worthy of preservation."[42]

Finally, by beating back the movement to impose a divisive form of multiculturalism on public education in the early 1990s, Shanker preserved the single most important argument in favor of public education: their role in helping educate students from all different backgrounds about a common American culture. Had the extreme multiculturalists prevailed, as the NEA and others had hoped, the underlying argument for public schools would have been substantially weakened.

The Most Important Educator Since Dewey

Shanker's trio of contributions—helping to create modern teachers' unions, helping to reform public education, and helping to preserve public education—made him the most important voice in education in the past half century. He had a greater impact, says Diane Ravitch, than any of the commissioners of education or secretaries of education in the second half of the twentieth century.[43] This is not to say Shanker solved the major problems of American education; indeed, the schools that many of his members taught at, especially in struggling urban centers, remain in deep trouble.[44] But he was in the thick of the major efforts to address the problems and fought off a number of bad ideas that would have made things worse.

When journalist Sara Mosle called Shanker "our Dewey," she offered up an interesting comparison. On the one hand, their contributions were quite different. Dewey was an academic whose books on philosophy and pedagogy spawned entire schools of thought and continue to be read by thousands of students every year. Shanker was much more a man of action, who wrote no books and chose to leave academics to organize teachers. Unlike Dewey, Shanker was elected by teachers to lead a million-member union, and he engaged in the rough and tumble of politics.

On the other hand, both Dewey and Shanker were public intellectuals who sought to marry ideas and action. Dewey was not just a philosopher and writer, he was a union activist and a critical figure in the New York City Teachers Union. Shanker, likewise, was not just a union leader, he was a philosophy graduate who read widely, taught courses at Harvard and Hunter, treated his union's executive committee like a college seminar, and produced 1,300 newspaper columns.

And both were committed to a constellation of big ideas. They were strong anti-Communists who believed that the labor movement was critical to advancing the interests of working-class people. Both believed deeply in public education as the incubator of American democracy. Both sometimes saw their ideas twisted—Dewey's by some progressive educators and Shanker by some charter-school advocates. But in the end, both, in their own ways, outpaced the contributions of their contemporaries to help shape American public education.

Shanker was able to be the most influential educator since Dewey in part because he was able to bridge the worlds of power and ideas, of liberals and conservatives, of education and business, and of unionists and education reformers. Bridging the liberal and conservative divide—agreeing with Ronald Reagan on school discipline one day and with the NEA on school vouchers the next—kept lines of communication open no matter who was in power. And his ability to work not only with educators and unionists but also with business leaders enhanced his effectiveness, says Michael Usdan. Because most educators did not bridge those worlds, Shanker served as a critical "ambassador" for education to business.[45] Finally, Shanker's success in the education-reform world was related to his earlier role as a militant unionist. He could remain credible to his members as an education statesman because he had earned his stripes as a diehard unionist willing to go to jail for his members.

There were other qualities that enhanced his influence. One was Shanker's professional longevity. He presided over the AFT as president for twenty-three straight years and had run the UFT for ten years before that. During that period, presidents, education secretaries, and NEA presidents came and went. Shanker remained.

Another quality was his ability to communicate. He could best the strongest of debaters.[46] And through the use of analogies and other devices, he could communicate with even those who understood issues only on a very basic level. Dal Lawrence says "so many bright people can't translate what they know," but Shanker "had the ability to take an idea and present it in a way that made it understandable to the dumbest people in the world."[47] The format of his Where We Stand column has been copied by many education leaders, but its clarity has never been duplicated.

Shanker had core ideas that motivated him—democracy, public education, unionism—but he also understood the importance of adapting to changing circumstances. John Cole, an AFT vice president from Texas, recalls, "Al had a saying, 'The worst crime a leader can commit is to go on playing by the same rules of the game when the game and the rules have changed.'"[48] He saw, says Scott Widmeyer, that while in the 1960s it was necessary to be militant to establish the union, in later years, with the rise of conservatism in the country, it was necessary to shift the focus to education reform.[49] He was a pragmatist, Linda Chavez says, who knew that to be effective you had to "recognize that there were social forces at work that were bigger than you and you'd better learn how to deal with it."[50]

Ultimately, though, it was Shanker's ability to know when not to go with the flow that helped him stand out as an education leader with a lasting influence. Shanker stood out in his willingness to "risk being unpopular," says Diane Ravitch.[51] In Ocean Hill–Brownsville, for example, he was willing to buck the perceived wisdom of the intelligentsia. "Al was not afraid of anything or anybody," says the AFT's Greg Humphrey. On racially charged issues like bilingual education or quotas, some people were "scared to death" to take a stand for fear of being labeled racist. "You could not get him to move off that conclusion by *ad hominem* attacks, which is how a lot of it gets done. And he was fearless in that sense."[52] On the question of standards-based reform, with virtually all the education establishment against him, he was willing to take a stand in favor.

The marriage of ideas and power, idealism and pragmatism, was perhaps his greatest strength. Not many union leaders are ABD in philosophy at Columbia. And not many intellectuals command a union membership of one million. Shanker had both. No one questioned his brains. Stanford's Michael Kirst says Shanker could "hold his own with any intellectual firepower this country has to offer in the area of education and social policy."[53] But unlike many intellectuals, he was very comfortable wielding power and exercising judgment. While intellectually curious, he was decisive and "seldom was ambivalent or confused," says Diane Ravitch.[54] He could have the big ideas and vision but also have a sense of how to get from A to B. In pushing standards, for example, Shanker saw the larger issue, says AFT staffer Burnie Bond, "that there was this big hole in the middle of American education and all of the reform efforts were going to fall into it unless" there were clearly defined goals. But he also was able to think tactically: securing allies and delineating short-term objectives.[55]

He was book smart and street smart, a thinker and a fighter, a great mind and a great general. "Al was the warrior poet," says Greg Humphrey. "Al was the samurai who could do the tea ceremony and wield a sword in combat."[56] It was an exceedingly rare combination, one found in Shanker, Daniel Patrick Moynihan, and few others.[57] Sometimes, he took this quality too far. He could be polarizing, contentious, and confrontational.[58] But his willingness to have the union go it alone when important principles were at stake, even when under attack, was an essential reason why he was able to make a difference.

Shanker's Short-Term Legacy for Liberalism

While Shanker was hugely influential in education debates, he and his like-minded colleagues were far less successful in waging the larger battle over the future of American liberalism. In their intramural fights within the Democratic Party, their argument on behalf of tough liberalism failed on key issues of national security, race, and labor. For the moment, at least, Shanker's political legacy is only faintly visible.

In international affairs, Shanker believed in three things: the need to fight Communists and other dictators who wished to curtail human freedom and crush free trade unions, the need to actively promote and nurture democracy abroad, and the need to have a strong American military ready to help accomplish the first two objectives. Today, Shanker's worldview—the view of Roosevelt, Truman, Kennedy, and Scoop Jackson—is not dominant in the Democratic Party. Chastened by Vietnam and more recently by Iraq, many liberals see promoting democracy and projecting American power as futile at best and arrogant and imperialistic at worst. As Peter Beinart noted in 2004: "When the *Times* asked Democratic delegates whether the 'United States should try to change a dictatorship to a democracy where it can, or should the United States stay out of other countries' affairs,' more than three times as many Democrats answered 'stay out,' even though the question said nothing about military force."[59] Democrats are in danger of replacing Republicans as the party of isolation.

Part of the issue is that many liberals, says liberal writer George Packer, have adopted a cultural relativism that does not want to impose

"Western" values particularly on "poorer and darker skinned peoples."[60] Instead, liberals tend to emphasize humanitarian concerns, like famine in Africa, while ignoring democratic movements in the continent.[61] While the U.S. experience in Iraq gives ample ground for being skeptical of conservative adventurism, liberals are in danger of swinging to the opposite extreme of retreating from the fight for democracy. In October 2005, more than half of Democrats (compared with a quarter of Republicans) agreed that the "U.S. should mind its own business internationally."[62]

On issues of race, from his days at the University of Illinois, through Ocean Hill–Brownsville, up to the Piscataway teacher layoff case, Shanker believed in nondiscrimination in any direction and an affirmative role for government to help low-income people, a disproportionate share of whom are members of minority groups. Today, that view is completely out of fashion among Democratic policymakers, who view the issue of racial preferences simply as a matter of being on the side of beleaguered minorities against privileged whites. Bill Clinton moved to the center on the racially charged issues of crime and welfare, but on affirmative action, he largely defended the use of preferences, his rhetoric about "mend it don't end it" notwithstanding. While many rank-and-file Democrats remain very uneasy about racial preferences, Democratic party leaders are virtually unanimous in support. So universal is the stance among liberal leaders that in 2003 even the AFT executive council voted to support an *amicus* brief favoring of a system of racial preferences at the University of Michigan when it was challenged by a white working-class student before the U.S. Supreme Court.[63]

Finally, Shanker and his colleagues essentially lost the argument that organized labor and the working class of all races should be at the very center of the Democratic Party's progressive coalition. Labor is no longer dominant in part because of its declining size. When Shanker joined the AFT in the early 1950s, labor represented 36 percent of nonagricultural private-sector workers; that dropped to about 10 percent by the time of Shanker's death.[64] Reflecting on fifty years of reporting on Congress, *Washington Post* columnist David Broder recently said the biggest change was that for years, labor unions were more influential than business or trade associations, but today, the opposite is true.[65] Today, labor is seen as a special interest, and 61 percent of Americans hold a negative or neutral view of it, compared to the 1950s, when labor enjoyed a 75 percent approval rating.[66]

Of course, Shanker himself cannot be blamed for the decline of labor and its unpopularity: the AFT grew each year and Shanker worked hard to defy the idea that a teachers' union was a special interest unconcerned about children. But the argument that Shanker and others made within the AFL-CIO, that labor needed to reform itself, largely lost out. Shanker's personal effort to have the AFT make strong inroads in the South failed. Instead, Southern anti-union attitudes largely conquered much of the rest of the country. But perhaps the biggest failure was the effort of Shanker and others within labor circles to convince fellow liberals of the importance of labor and the working class for the Democratic coalition. Shanker and his colleagues were unable to persuade fellow liberals to go to the mat for them during the critical fight over labor-law reform in the late 1970s, and to the very end of Shanker's life, he had trouble making other liberals realize the importance of labor. At a February 1996 AFT Executive Committee meeting, Shanker complained: "You've got these right-wing groups that want to kill us because essentially we form the strongest liberal base in the country for a lot of liberal issues, and if they get us, they're a lot more likely to get elected year after year than if we're around. But the liberals don't realize who their friends are."[67]

Many young liberals do not understand why protecting the ability to organize a union is a human-rights issue.[68] Labor lawyer Thomas Geoghegan explains: "You meet other [liberal] activists, go to their meetings. They understand each other's causes, but have no sense of yours."[69] While Democrats ensure representation at the national convention for identity groups—blacks, Hispanics, women—working-class Americans are not part of the equation. Among the delegates to the 2004 Democratic national convention, 53 percent had postgraduate degrees, compared with 11 percent of voters, and 61 percent made more than $75,000 a year, compared with 29 percent of voters.[70] The national Democratic Party has largely replaced the old black-labor coalition with the Lindsay coalition of elites and minorities. In 2005, Democratic National Committee Chair Howard Dean reportedly called socially liberal and economically affluent "Merlot Democrats" the base of the Democratic Party.[71] While the military used to be full of Democrats and the Ivy League full of Republicans, notes economist Anthony Carnevale, now the reverse is true.[72]

Today, Shanker's Social Democratic vision—the Scoop Jackson/Bayard Rustin strain of economically populist, socially moderate, and internationally engaged Democrats—is virtually absent from liberal discourse. Shanker's "entire career," Arch Puddington notes, "suggests a road that

liberalism might have taken but did not."[73] Many mainstream liberals today believe the opposite of what Shanker did. Drawing on impulses from
both the New Politics of the 1960s and neoliberalism of the 1980s, they are
skeptical of American intervention abroad, politically correct on social
policies like racial preferences, not particularly interested in economic redistribution, and very critical of organized labor.[74] Indeed, the New Politics movement has been so successful in defining modern liberalism that
adherents are no longer called New Politics, but simply liberal.

The DLC's New Democrats, meanwhile, reflect two-thirds of the
Shanker vision. The DLC has long been skeptical of identity politics, racial preferences, and a soft approach to crime. And they continue to fight
for Shanker's vision of a muscular liberal internationalism that actively
promotes democracy abroad. But on economic issues, Shanker and the
DLC often split. The DLC always had close ties to business interests and
was accused of being "Democrats for the Leisure Class."[75] When the DLC
railed against "special interests" in the Democratic Party, they included
not only those pushing for quotas but also organized labor.[76]

Over time, moreover, the DLC shifted away not only from labor, but
also from white working-class voters. In the late 1980s, the DLC talked
about the importance of these swing voters, but a decade later, they had
shifted their attention to the more affluent "learning class," "wired workers," and "soccer moms."[77] Some have spoken of Senator Joe Lieberman, a
longtime DLC leader, as the next Scoop Jackson, despite Lieberman's far
more conservative approach to economic issues—a willingness to explore
Social Security privatization, support private-school vouchers, and cut
the capital-gains tax.[78] The claim merely underlines the absence of a genuine Social Democratic approach in today's politics.

Finally, organized labor itself has abandoned its once distinctive role in
synthesizing international involvement with economic populism. After
Shanker lost his fight on behalf of Tom Donahue against John Sweeney,
the labor movement became indistinguishable from the liberal wing of
the Democratic Party. The AFL-CIO has embraced racial preferences, no
matter how wealthy the beneficiaries, and labor's foreign-policy agenda
has virtually been reduced to the self-interested issue of world trade.[79]
Labor no longer crosses over to forge partnerships with conservatives on
issues of national security and nondiscrimination; it toes the Democratic
party line across the board.

Today, the Democratic Party has economic populists such as organized
labor in one camp and advocates of a tough foreign policy and main-

stream American values such as the DLC in another, but no one—like Al
Shanker—who stands for both. Today, Shanker's cold war international
orientation, his colorblind outlook, and his redistributionist economic
policy is seen as "outdated" in a post–cold war world of increasing racial
diversity and market-based thinking.

Shanker's Long-Term Legacy for Liberalism

While it is true that Shanker was mostly unsuccessful in shaping modern
liberalism and his presence is very weakly felt in current debates, the long-
term prospects for the legacy of his ideas may be more positive. While
times have changed, Shanker's tough liberalism is not obsolete; its rele-
vance to social realities continues to grow. And if American liberalism
continues to be viewed as weak and sometimes incoherent, it is conceivable—though hardly probable—that Shanker's greatest legacy, in the end,
may be his social democratic vision.

A Relevant World View

The terms used to describe Shanker's ideology—"cold war liberalism"
and "New Deal liberalism"—are tied to bygone eras, while the various
movements he disagreed with tried to use fresher sounding names—the
New Left, the New Politics, the New Democrats, neoliberalism, and neoconservatism. Today, "liberal" is an unfashionable label, the cold war is a
piece of history, unions are seen as remnants of an industrial era, and colorblindness sounds positively quaint in an era of rising racial diversity
and identity politics.

But a case can be made that the unfashionable elements of Shanker's
tough liberalism—engaged internationalism, race-neutrality, and a strong
labor movement—are more closely attuned to social realities than those
principles now in vogue among liberals.

Although Communism is largely dead, totalitarianism is not. The "war
on terror," as many have noted, is not really directed against the tactic of
terrorism but rather against a totalitarian ideology.[80] Thomas Friedman
argues: "September 11 amounts to World War III—the third great totalitarian challenge to open societies in the last 100 years." If the Nazis tried
to create the "perfect race" and the Soviets the "perfect class," then Is-
lamists are trying to impose the "perfect faith."[81] The Taliban in Afghani-

stan fit neatly into the history of totalitarian regimes, banning hobbies, sports, and dictating women's dress, notes Peter Beinart.[82] Of course, there are important differences between Communists and jihadists.[83] But the fundamental premise of Shanker's tough liberalism—that totalitarianism must be fought vigorously and relentlessly—is highly relevant in an era where nondemocratic states can serve as training grounds for those who would inflict terror.

Likewise, Shanker's case for nondiscrimination grows more relevant, not less, with the passage of time. As Latinos replace African Americans as the largest minority group in America, the case for racial and ethnic preferences as a remedy for past segregation and slavery weakens. Intermarriage increasingly complicates the calculus of who constitutes a minority.[84] And with the passage of time, the legacy of past *de jure* segregation and discrimination recedes, and a new generation will ask with increasing impatience: why should we continue to pay for the sins of our grandparents?

So too, while the received wisdom tells us that unions are obsolete remnants of the old economy, Shanker's call for workers to have greater a voice to improve quality is just as relevant in the new economy. Moreover, there is a growing need for institutions to counter rampant inequality. In 2004, income inequality was near all-time highs, with 50 percent of income going to the top 20 percent of households.[85] The wealthiest 300,000 Americans had more income than the bottom 120 million.[86] U.S. inequality is greater than in any advanced country—our society is twice as unequal as Sweden's.[87] No institution in all of American society is as well equipped to address growing inequality as is the trade-union movement.

A Politically Attractive Liberalism

It must be acknowledged that there are large structural obstacles to a re-emergence of Shanker-like tough liberalism within the Democratic Party. Scoop Jackson's presidential candidacy and the attempt by the Coalition for a Democratic Majority to take back the party both failed in part because of the power of certain liberal groups. Peace activists will oppose an assertive foreign policy; civil-rights groups will oppose any effort to revise racial preference policies. Likewise, the people who fund Democratic political campaigns tend to come from the wing of the party that is the mirror image of the tough liberals: "well-off social liberals" who are skeptical of America's role in the world and do not have much use for labor unions.[88] In the short run, there is a third obstacle to tough liberalism's emergence: President George W. Bush's embrace of the rhetoric of democracy in the Iraq War. Just as the excesses of McCarthyism and Vietnam discredited anti-Communism, so Bush's bungling in the Iraq War may harm the promotion of democracy as a central goal of U.S. foreign policy.

But, in the long haul, if liberal candidates continue to have difficulty attracting America's broad working-class vote, tough liberalism may get a second look. Today, white working-class voters—those lacking a four-year college degree—constitute 51.5 percent of all voters.[89] White working-class voters were a key constituency in the Democrats' glory years from Franklin Roosevelt through Harry Truman, John Kennedy, and Lyndon Johnson. By contrast, Al Gore lost whites with less than a four-year college degree by 17 points, and John Kerry by 23 points.[90]

To begin with, liberals face what Will Marshall calls the "national security confidence gap."[91] The only times the Democrats have won the presidency since the Vietnam War—Carter's 1976 election and Clinton's 1992 and 1996 elections—were instances when the country turned inward, away from international affairs, and domestic concerns prevailed.[92] Rather than engaging the threats to America, liberals often change the subject to domestic matters. And there is a danger, as with Vietnam, that Democrats will use the legitimate critique of the war in Iraq in order to retreat from the larger and justified war against totalitarianism.[93] Democratic losses at the presidential level cannot universally be attributed to national security, but the issue remains an Achilles' heel for liberals politically.

Likewise, on racial issues, the Democrat's wholesale embrace of identity politics has had enormous political costs, as Shanker argued.[94] While there is a consensus of sorts among elites on the need for racial preferences, the Democrats are wildly out of step with the broader American public. A 2001 survey by the *Washington Post*, Harvard, and the Kaiser Family Foundation found that 92 percent of respondents (including 86 percent of blacks and 88 percent of Hispanics) said "no" when asked: "In order to give minorities more opportunity, do you believe race or ethnicity should be a factor" in job hiring or college admissions.[95] Politically, the problem with identity politics has always been that it encourages a form of white identity politics, in which white working-class Americans vote their race rather than their class. The failure to provide unity between working-class whites and working-class blacks and Latinos is one of the great missed opportunities of the past century. Working-class African Americans, Latinos, and whites would surely benefit from a swing toward the untried class-based liberalism of the type that Shanker, Bayard Rustin, and Martin Luther King articulated many years earlier.

Tough liberalism's emphasis on democratizing economic gains is also a potential winner, even among many voters who now are casting ballots for Republicans. Initiatives to raise the minimum wage, for example, are popular among voters of both political parties.[96] The economic issue is critical because it goes to the heart of Republican vulnerabilities with working-class and middle-class voters.[97] It is possible for Democrats to shift to the center on international affairs and race—they were, for many years, the party of international strength and nondiscrimination. But it does not seem possible that the Republicans would embrace labor and the economic populism of the "radical center." To do so would contradict the very nature of conservatism.

None of this is to say that Shanker's tough liberalism would draw back all elements of the white working class to the Democratic Party. The underlying idea of democracy and nondiscrimination argues for equality in marriage rights for gay and heterosexual couples, a concept that remains unpopular among many working-class voters. Abortion, prayer in school, and other issues held dear by working-class religious conservatives will remain draws to the Republican Party, even if Democrats adopt a tough-liberal approach. But other "values issues"—hard work, discipline, and patriotism—were staples of Shanker's tough liberalism and allowed him to open a dialogue with religious conservatives.

More powerful than the individual elements of Shanker's tough liberalism may be the appeal of the package: a principled, democratic vision that addresses the key vulnerabilities of contemporary American liberalism: its image of being soft, elitist, out of touch, and incapable of understanding the realities of the way the world works.[98]

Shanker's liberalism was tough on defense, tough on student discipline, tough on standards, and skeptical of soft ideas like the importance of self-esteem. It was also tough on inequality, tough on management when it was unwilling to grant higher wages, tough enough to go on strike and risk jail time if necessary, and unafraid to exercise power. Nor could Shanker's tough liberalism be accused of elitism or snobbery—another critical liability of contemporary liberalism. Conservatives have made great hay out the image of Ivy League–educated liberals looking down on working- and middle-class Americans.[99] The theme of "democracy" directly targets liberalism's most salient problem. In Shanker's lifelong battles, he invariably took the nonelitist side. He fought the NEA, over affiliating with the AFL-CIO; fellow teachers over allowing the paras to join the union; education-school professors over the needs of low-income students for a safe, disciplined environment and a core curriculum; and New Politics intellectuals over George Meany's anti-Communism. Tough liberalism, whose central theme is democracy, would address the snobbery issue that some say is liberalism's "besetting sin."[100]

Because Shanker's tough liberalism was straightforward and anchored by a coherent message about democracy, it also answers the debilitating charge that contemporary liberalism doesn't stand for anything.[101] Democrats are seen as offering either poll-driven, mushy centrism on the one hand or interest-group driven politics on the other. While Democrats are good at offering ten-point policy plans, Shanker had a larger vision that united domestic and foreign policy: a truly democratic society with strong public schools for social mobility and social cohesion; a vibrant labor movement that represented the voice of ordinary workers in the economy and checked unfettered corporate power; a universalist view of human rights, where individuals are not judged by race but by merit; and a robust engagement in the world in order to spread democratic rights to people across the globe. An explicit philosophy grounded in democracy will offend certain constituencies but should resonate with those looking for a party with core values and are put off by a floating philosophy aimed at appeasing various interest groups.

Finally, Shanker's tough liberalism blended a politically appealing idealism with a healthy dose of realism. His brand of liberalism understood the importance of human nature and the need for incentives on the one hand, but he also rejected both the left's pessimism about defeating Communism and promoting democracy abroad and the right's malaise about tackling issues like poverty and economic inequality, which they saw as foreordained. Shanker rejected both the "feeling that nothing can be done to solve major social problems" and the feeling "that we should not show concern for violations of human rights and rights in other countries."[102]

For the last few decades, American liberalism has largely given up on "radical centrist" voters—especially blue-collar white males—preferring to target upscale "moderate middle" voters. The decision represents a great political tragedy. On the whole, "cold war" liberalism, with its working-class base, was highly successful. The pro-labor, colorblind, anti-

Communist Democratic party was dominant from 1932 through 1968. Since then, we have experienced a mostly conservative era—of Nixon, and Reagan and Bush, and Bush—with interludes of moderate Southern Democrats like Carter and Clinton, neither of whom fully embodied the tough liberalism Shanker championed.

Tough liberalism does not just offer improved chances of winning elections. Once elected, Democrats would have a grand and noble goal to accomplish, at home and abroad: the improvement of America's great experiment in democracy. During his lifetime, Shanker sowed the seeds of something very promising. It remains to be seen whether the fruit will ever be harvested.

In one lifespan, Albert Shanker helped to create the institution of collective bargaining for teachers, giving them greater dignity and voice in how they would be treated. He then used that power to engage in a series of critical education reforms that proved instrumental in improving and preserving the institution of public education. Both accomplishments served the larger goal he cherished above all others: strengthening American democracy. His failure to convince fellow liberals to extend their support of democracy more broadly—to racial policy, international affairs, and their views of the labor movement—leaves open the question: what might society look like if we tried?

ACKNOWLEDGMENTS

T H I S book could never have been written without the help and generosity of many friends, family members, and colleagues.

Albert Shanker did not fit neatly into existing ideological boxes, so it is perhaps unsurprising that a work to describe his life drew financial support from foundations across the political spectrum. For their generous support, I thank Paul Brest and Marshall Smith at the William and Flora Hewlett Foundation; Eli Broad, Dan Katzir, Erica Lepping, and Wendy Hassett at The Broad Foundation; Richard Leone, Carol Starmack, and Greg Anrig at The Century Foundation; and Chester Finn and Justin Torres at the Thomas B. Fordham Foundation. The views expressed are my own and not those of any of these foundations.

I also wish to give thanks to a number of librarians and archivists whose help was invaluable to my research: Daniel Golodner and Mike Smith at the Wayne State University's Walter P. Reuther Library (which houses the papers of the American Federation of Teachers and the Shanker archives), Evan Daniel and Michael Nash at New York University's Tamiment Institute Library at the Robert F. Wagner Labor Archives (which houses the papers of the United Federation of Teachers), Ellen D. Swain and John Franch at the University of Illinois, Urbana-Champaign's Archives Research Center (which houses papers on the University of Illinois), David Strader of the Rare Book Manuscript and Special Collections division in the Perkins Library at Duke University (which houses the papers of Social Democrats USA), Lynda J. DeLoach and Christine Kohn of the University of Maryland's George Meany Memorial Archives (which houses the papers of the AFL-CIO), and Roberta Saltzman of the Dorot Jewish Division of the New York Public Library (which houses papers on Judaica). A special thanks to Dan Golodner and Evan Daniel, who allowed me advance access to the AFT and UFT papers before their official openings. Thanks also to Miles Ryan, who provided important advice about gaining documents from government sources under the Freedom of Information Act.

A number of individuals also shared with me papers about Albert Shanker from their personal files. Thanks to Ted Kolderie, Myron Lieberman, Herb Magidson, Liz McPike, Marcia Reecer, Bella Rosenberg, Edith Shanker, and Fred van Leeuwen for their generosity in doing so.

In researching this book, I had the opportunity to interview a number of Albert Shanker's friends, family, colleagues, critics, and adversaries, some of them many times. Thanks to the following for their time, generosity, and insights: George Altomare, Gordon Ambach, Judy Bardacke, Rebecca Beagle, Arnold Beichman, Herman Benson, Maurice Berube, Burnie Bond, Lloyd Bond, Paul Buhl, Don Cameron, Sunny Castanza, Vincent Castanza, Robert Chanin, Bob Chase, Linda Chavez, Mark Chaykin, Eric Chenoweth, Karin Chenoweth, Michael Cohen, John Cole, Antonia Cortese, Linda Darling-Hammond, Midge Decter, Vito De Leonardis, Tom Donahue, David Dorn, Mary Farran, Lillian Feldman, Sandra Feldman, Chester Finn, Edward Flower, Albert Fondy, Rita Freedman, Mary Futrell, Keith Geiger, Thomas Geoghegan, Carl Gershman, Rich Gibson, Milton Goldberg, Victor Gotbaum, Pearl Harris, Norman Hill, Velma Hill, E. D. Hirsch Jr., Tom Hobart, Rachelle Horowitz, Jamie Horwitz, Greg Humphrey, Sol Hurwitz, Sandra Irons, Lorretta Johnson, John Joyce, James Kelly, Eugenia Kemble, Penn Kemble, Irena Kirkland, Michael Kirst, Ted Kolderie, Israel Kugler, Phil Kugler, Paul Kurtz, Nat LaCour, Dal Lawrence, Myron Lieberman, Stanley Litow, Melvin Lubin, Richard Magat, Herb Magidson, Will Marshall, Ed McElroy, Liz McPike, John Merrow, Bruce Miller, Tom Mooney, Sally Muravchik, Fred Nauman, Arch Puddington, Ronald Radosh, Diane Ravitch, Richard Ravitch, Marcia Reecer, Mary Ellen Riordan, Bella Rosenberg, Fritz Rothschild, Richard Rothstein, Alan Ruby, Carl Sabath, Gerald Sabath, Lee Sabath, Claudio Sanchez, Elaine Sanders, Arthur Schlesinger Jr., Donna Shalala, Adam Shanker, Albert Shanker, Edith Shanker, Jennie Shanker, Michael Shanker, Joan-Marie Shelley, Marshall Smith, Naomi Spatz, Stephen Joel Trachtenberg, Marc Tucker, Adam Urbanski, Michael Usdan, Fred van Leeuwen, Ruth Wattenberg, Lois Weiner, Randi Weingarten, Scott Widmeyer, Dieter Wunder, and Alan Wurtzel.

I want to give special thanks to Bella Rosenberg and Eugenia Kemble, who were especially generous with their time in making room for repeated conversations. For her excellent job of transcribing the interviews, thanks to Sally Millwood.

Along the way, I had a number of superb research assistants. Thanks to Amy Berg, Melissa Cline, Paul Esformes, Sonya Hoo, Gilbert Lee, Erin Martin, Laura Newland, Kristen Oshyn, Ramesh Padman, Manish Patel, Greg Suber, Tony Sutton, and Rob Wiygul.

For important advice and discussions about Albert Shanker and the project, I want to thank Morton Abramowitz, Greg Anrig, Michael Calabrese, Anthony Carnevale, Brewster Denny, Ted Fiske, Dennis Gaffney, William Galston, Jessica Gingerich, Beverly Goldberg, Patricia Graham, Jennifer Grimaldi, Thad Hall, Leif Wellington Haase, Rick Hess, Christy Hicks, Jack Jennings, John Judis, Michael Kazin, Mary Temple Kleiman, David Kusnet, Richard Leone, Jeffrey Mirel, Sara Mosle, Jason Renker, Andy Rotherham, Jack Schierenbeck, Carol Starmack, Ronald Steel, Leonard Steinhorn, Bob Tate, Ruy Teixeira, Thomas Toch, Ron Unz, Bernard Wasow, Jay Winik, and Lyric Winik.

Many thanks to those who provided comments on drafts of the book: Greg Anrig, Pat Daly, David Dorn, Rita Freedman, Daniel Golodner, Robert Gordon, Wendy Hassett, Rachelle Horowitz, Jeannette Kahlenberg, Rebecca Kahlenberg, Eugenia Kemble, Ted Kolderie, Phil Kugler, Richard Leone, Erica Lepping, Elizabeth McPike, Bella Rosenberg, Andy Rotherham, Eadie Shanker, and Ruth Wattenberg.

I also want to thank my excellent agent, James Levine, for his terrific advice and help. At Columbia University, thanks to Alan Brinkley and Peter Dimock for their wise counsel, and to Rob Fellman for his helpful and careful copyediting.

Above all, I want to give thanks to members of my family, who supported me throughout this long project. My teenage daughters, Cindy, Jessica, and Caroline, put up with hearing stories about Albert Shanker when they were far more interested in other matters. And during the writing of this book, my wonderful wife and best friend, Rebecca, gave birth to our fourth daughter, Amanda, and still managed to provide tremendous love, help, and understanding during my long nights and weekends away from the family. I can't thank her enough.

My parents, Richard W. Kahlenberg and Jeannette Kahlenberg, were enormously supportive and helpful. My father, who in his later years was a schoolteacher and regularly clipped Albert Shanker's "Where We Stand" columns from the *New York Times*, died while I was writing this volume. I miss having the chance to talk with him about it and so many other things, and I dedicate this book to his memory.

ABBREVIATIONS

Organizations

AFT: American Federation of Teachers
NYSUT: New York State United Teachers
UFT: United Federation of Teachers

Archives

NYU: New York University, Tamiment Institute Library at the Robert F. Wagner Labor Archives (housing the UFT archives)

WSU: Wayne State University, Walter P. Reuther Library (housing the AFT archives)

WWS: "Where We Stand" column by Albert Shanker, in the Sunday *New York Times* "Week in Review" section, available at http://www.nysut.org/shanker/index.html.

Newspapers and Periodicals

NYT: New York Times
PDK: Phi Delta Kappan
TNR: The New Republic
WP: Washington Post
WSJ: Wall Street Journal
WT: Washington Times

NOTES

Introduction

1. *NYT*, 2/23/97, sect. 1, p. 1.
2. *NYT*, 11/19/68, p. 1; *NYT*, 2/23/97, sect. 1, p. 1.
3. Spatz interview, p. 45.
4. Memorial Service transcript, 4/9/97, pp. 24, 26.
5. Memorial Service transcript, 4/9/97, p. 21.
6. Memorial Service transcript, 4/9/97, p. 19.
7. Memorial Service transcript, 4/9/97, p. 19.
8. Albert Shanker interview with Shore, p. 8.
9. Shanker, "Reflections," *PDK*, p. 328.
10. Albert Shanker interview with Shore, p. 9.
11. Mooney interview, p. 36.
12. Memorial Service transcript, 4/9/97, p. 21.
13. Brimelow, *The Worm in the Apple*, p. 52 (quoting Lamar Alexander); See also Toch, "A Speech That Shook the Field," *Education Week*, 3/26/97.
14. See, e.g., Thomas Toch, "Why Teachers Don't Teach," *U.S. News & World Report*, 2/26/96, p. 62.
15. *Education Week*, 3/5/97.
16. Center for Education Reform, 10/05.
17. *American Educator*, special issue, "The Power of Ideas," Spring–Summer 1997, 74.
18. Toch, "A Speech That Shook the Field," *Education Week*, 3/26/97.

19. Hirsch, op. ed., *WP*, 3/1/97, p. A23. See also *American Teacher*, 4/97, p. 3, quoting Hirsch: "No other person in recent years has contributed more to the advancement of education in the United States."

20. Mosle, *TNR*, 3/17/97. See also *PDK*, 11/00: "The closest thing to a national education leader of the past generation."

21. Memorial Service transcript, 4/9/97, p. 26.

22. See Lenny Glynn, "The Neanderthal Liberal," *Learning*, 9/73, p. 98, in NYU Archives. Shanker didn't mind the label, and in June 1974, the AFT sought permission to reprint the article, which included an interview with Shanker.

23. Eadie Shanker interview, 10/24/02, p. 1 (enemies on the left); Sara Mosle, *TNR*, 3/17/97, p. 12 (pay for his ideas). In addition to Shanker's mention in Woody Allen's *Sleeper*, he was referenced in a 1996 episode of "Mad About You." Paul Reiser, a New York City resident, giving directions over the telephone, says, "You'll see Zero Mostel Place, and Albert Shanker Circle. All right. Now, be careful 'cause it's tricky around the circle. And then it's the third building on the right. Now, if you hit Bella Abzug, you went . . ." Transcript, *Mad About You*, NBC, 3/24/96, in WSU Archives, box 1, folder 16.

24. *NYT*, 9/4/86, p. B13.

25. Memorial Service transcript, 4/9/97, p. 4.

26. Beinart, *The Good Fight*, p. ix.

1. The Early Years:
Rising from Humble Beginnings and Establishing Values (1928–1952)

1. Lillian Feldman interview, p. 3; Podair, *The Strike That Changed New York*, p. 107 (photo showing birthmark on right side); Constanza interview, p. 81–83 (red); Bella Rosenberg interview, 3/13/06.

2. *U.S. Newswire*, 2/23/97.

3. Pearl Harris interview, 5/6/03, p. 2; Eadie Shanker interview, 9/17/02, p. 10; Albert Shanker interview with Shore, p. 1.

4. Pearl Harris interview, 5/6/03, p. 2; NPR Shanker-Harris debate, 1/17/75, p. 2. See also Albert Shanker interview with Cowan, p. 2.

5. Pearl Harris interview, 5/6/03, pp. 3, 37. Eadie Shanker interview, 10/18/02, p. 9; Shanker family chronology provided by Eadie Shanker, 11/03; Lillian Feldman interview, p. 2; Jennie Shanker interview, p. 10.

6. Howe, *World of Our Fathers*, pp. 5, 26.

7. Pearl Harris interview, 5/6/03, pp. 4, 2; Pearl Harris interview, 8/23/06.

8. Pearl Harris interview, 5/6/03, p. 4.

9. Dorman, *Arguing the World*, p. 26; Howe, *World of Our Fathers*, p. 82.

10. Pearl Harris interview, 5/6/03, pp. 12, 39.

11. *People*, 11/3/75, p. 15; *NYT*, 2/23/97.

12. Pearl Harris interview, 5/6/03, p. 12.

13. Eadie Shanker interview, 9/17/02, p. 10; Eadie Shanker interview, 10/18/02, p. 6.

14. Pearl Harris interview, 5/6/03, p. 2. Eadie Shanker interview, 10/24/02, p. 3, re: birth date; Albert Shanker interview with Shore, p. 1.

15. Pearl Harris interview, 5/6/03, pp. 2–3. Shanker interview with Sara Mosle, part 1.

16. Pearl Harris interview, 5/6/03, p. 3; Telephone interview with Pearl Harris, 11/16/05; Howe, *World of Our Fathers*, p. 219.

17. Pearl Harris interview, 5/6/03, pp. 4–5, 26; Shanker family chronology (Mamie Shanker born 5/14/1894; Morris born 6/7/1897), Eadie Shanker papers.

18. Lillian Feldman interview, pp. 4, 9. See also *NYT*, 8/22/74, p. 40. Hill, *Education Week*, 2/21/96; Noah, "Albert Shanker, Statesman," *TNR*, 6/24/85, pp. 17–19; *U.S. Newswire*, 2/23/97.

19. Pearl Harris interview, 5/6/03, p. 4. For name, see Shanker family chronology from Eadie, 11/03; Eadie Shanker interview, 10/18/02, p. 6.

20. Albert Shanker interview with Shore, p. 1; *NYT*, 8/22/74, p. 40.

21. Eadie Shanker, 12/1/03, p. 17; Hill, *Education Week*, 2/21/96; Noah, "Albert Shanker, Statesman," *TNR*, 6/24/85, pp. 17–19; *U.S. Newswire*, 2/23/97.

22. Pearl Harris interview, 5/6/03, p. 18. See also Eadie Shanker interview, 12/1/03, p. 18.

23. Pearl Harris interview, 5/6/03, p. 16.

24. Eadie Shanker interview, 10/18/02, p. 7; Eadie Shanker letter to author, 12/5/03. See also Jennie Shanker interview, p. 9.

25. Pearl Harris interview, 5/6/03, p. 16.

26. Eadie Shanker interview, 10/18/02, p. 7.

27. Jennie Shanker interview, p. 9.

28. Pearl Harris interview, 5/6/03, pp. 16–17.

29. Pearl Harris interview, 5/6/03, p. 5.

30. Schierenbeck, *Class Struggles*, part 8; Hill, *Education Week*, 2/21/96; *NYT*, 2/23/97, p. A1.

31. Albert Shanker interview with Shore, p. 2.

32. Pearl Harris interview, 5/6/03, pp. 5–6.

33. Pearl Harris interview, 5/6/03, p. 17.

34. *NYT*, 2/23/97.

35. Vincent Castanza interview, p. 7.

36. Hill, *Education Week*, 2/21/96; Gaffney, *Blackboard Warriors*, draft, p. 9.

37. *NYT*, 2/23/97, p. A1.

38. Jennie Shanker interview, p. 11.

39. Pearl Harris interview, 5/6/03, pp. 15–16, 30–31.

40. David Dorn interview I, p. 7.

41. Pearl Harris interview, 5/6/03, p. 7.

42. Pearl Harris interview, 5/6/03, p. 17.

43. *NYT Magazine*, 9/3/67, p. 5.

44. Pearl Harris interview, 5/6/03, p. 7.

45. Eadie Shanker interview, 10/18/02, p. 10.

46. Albert Shanker interview with Shore, pp. 2–3.

47. Eadie Shanker interview, 9/17/02, p. 1.

48. Shanker interview with Schierenbeck, *American Educator*, Fall 2000, p. 40.

49. Lillian Feldman interview, pp. 4, 15.

50. Pearl Harris interview, 5/6/03, p. 8.

51. UFT Website, "Al Shanker: A Passionate Teacher."

52. Pearl Harris interview, 5/6/03, p. 6.

53. Pearl Harris interview, 5/6/03, p. 5. See also Eadie Shanker interview, 10/18/02, pp. 6, 11.

54. Horowitz interview, p. 70.

55. Eadie Shanker interview, 10/18/02, p. 21; Eadie Shanker memo, 3/3/06.

56. Vincent Castanza interview, p. 43.

57. Pearl Harris interview, 5/6/03, p. 28; Eadie Shanker interview, 10/18/02, pp. 10–11.

58. Albert Shanker interview with Shore, p. 1.

59. Eadie Shanker interview, 10/18/02, pp. 10–11; Eadie Shanker memo, 3/3/06.

60. Schierenbeck, *Class Struggles*, part 8.

61. *Bill Moyers' Journal*, 4/16/74, p. 15.

62. Alan Brinkley, *Voices of Protest*, pp. x, 83, 107, 119, 124–125, 140, 168, 266–267.

63. *NYT Magazine*, 9/3/67, p. 28; *NYT*, 2/23/97.

64. Pearl Harris interview, 5/6/03, pp. 8–9, 50.

65. Pearl Harris interview, 5/6/03, p. 48.

66. Pearl Harris interview, 5/6/03, p. 15.

67. Albert Shanker interview with Shore, p. 2.

68. Jennie Shanker journal excerpts, p. 1.

69. Pearl Harris interview, 5/6/03, pp. 8, 10.

70. Albert Shanker interview with Shore, p. 2.

71. *American Teacher*, 4/97, p. 12 (that the incident occurred when he was eight).

72. Pearl Harris interview, 5/6/03, p. 9; Eadie Shanker memo, 3/3/06.

73. Pearl Harris interview, 5/6/03, p. 50. See also *NYT*, 10/28/72, p. 36; *NYT Magazine*, 9/9/73, p. 72; Albert Shanker interview with Shore, p. 2; Braun, *Teachers and Power*, pp. 155–156.

74. Eadie Shanker interview, 10/18/02, p. 12; Eadie Shanker memo, 3/3/06.

75. Sandra Feldman interview, pp. 2–3.

76. Velma Hill interview, p. 32.

77. Pearl Harris interview, 5/6/03, p. 42.

78. WWS, 5/9/82.

79. *NYT*, 2/23/97; quote *American Teacher*, 4/97, p. 20.

80. Schierenbeck, *American Teacher*, 4/97, p. 7. See also Lillian Feldman interview, pp. 5, 12.

81. Albert Shanker interview with Shore, p. 2; *NYT*, 1/5/89, sect. 4a, p. 34.

82. Albert Shanker interview with Shore, p. 3.

83. Schierenbeck, *Class Struggles*, part 8.

84. WWS, 1/5/92; Howe, *World of Our Fathers*, p. 304.

85. *NYT Magazine*, 9/3/67, p. 28; Noah, "Albert Shanker, Statesman," *TNR*, 6/24/85, pp. 17–19 (Hillman); Hill, *Education Week*, 2/11/96 (seventy hours); Lipset and Marks, *It Didn't Happen Here*, p. 213; Schierenbeck, *Class Struggles*, part 8.

86. Pearl Harris interview, 5/6/03, p. 4; Albert Shanker interview with Cowan, p. 4.

87. Albert Shanker interview with Cowan, p. 3. See also *U.S. Newswire*, 2/23/97.

88. Pearl Harris interview, 5/6/03, p. 12; *NYT Magazine*, 9/9/73, p. 72.

89. *NYT Magazine*, 9/3/67, p. 28.

90. *NYT Magazine*, 9/3/67, p. 28. See also *NYT*, 11/5/89, sect. 4a, p. 34.

91. Jack Schierenbeck, *American Teacher*, 4/97, p. 7.

92. Morgan, *A Covert Life*, p. 7.

93. Joshua Muravchik, *Heaven on Earth*, p. 1.

94. Dorman, *Arguing the World*, p. 4.

95. Dorman, *Arguing the World*, p. 50.

96. Schierenbeck, *Class Struggles*, part 8.

97. Mel Lubin interview, pp. 14–16.

98. Pearl Harris interview, 5/6/03, pp. 13–14. See also Lillian Feldman interview, pp. 4, 10.

99. Vincent Castanza interview, pp. 8–9.

100. Pearl Harris interview, 5/6/03, pp. 35–36.

101. Pearl Harris interview, 5/6/03, p. 38.

102. Pearl Harris interview, 5/6/03, p. 27; Albert Shanker interview with Shore, p. 1.

103. *NYT*, 10/28/72, p. 36; Albert Shanker interview with Shore, p. 1.

104. Ed Flower interview, p. 6; Eadie Shanker interview, 10/18/02, p. 10.

105. George Altomare interview II, p. 36.

106. *NYT*, 10/28/72, p. 36.

107. Eadie Shanker interview, 10/18/02, p. 57; Albert Shanker interview with Shore, p. 1 (that he became relatively nonpracticing by age fifteen or sixteen). See also *NYT*, 10/28/72, p. 36.

108. Pearl Harris interview, 5/6/03, p. 28. See also Albert Shanker interview with Reecer, n.d., in Bella Rosenberg papers, pp. 11–12; Ora Weisman, *Hed Hachinuch*, 8/19/71, in NYU Archives and UFT Web site, "Al Shanker: A Passionate Teacher," available at http://www.uft.org/about/history/makers/shanker_albert/index4.html.

109. Pearl Harris interview, 5/6/03, p. 29.

110. Ed Flower interview, p. 9; Pearl Harris interview, 5/6/03, p. 32; Vincent Castanza interview, p. 3.

111. Pearl Harris interview, 5/6/03, pp. 17, 32.

112. Ed Flower interview, pp. 9–10.

113. Pearl Harris interview, 5/6/03, p. 50.

114. Eadie Shanker memo, 3/3/06.

115. Pearl Harris interview, 5/6/03, p. 10; see also *NYT*, 11/5/89, sect. 4a, p. 34; Eadie Shanker memo, 3/3/06. Shanker interview with Mosle, part 1.

116. Ed Flower interview, p. 13; Eadie Shanker interview, 10/18/02, p. 11; Shanker interview with Schierenbeck, *American Educator*, Fall 2000, p. 40.

117. Schierenbeck, *Class Struggles*, part 8; Mosle, *TNR*, 3/17/97. See also *NYT*, 2/23/97 (that Shanker recruited members).

118. Shanker interview with Schierenbeck, *American Educator*, Fall 2000, p. 40.

119. Ed Flower interview, p. 20.

120. Vincent Castanza interview, pp. 4–5.

121. Ed Flower interview, p. 21; Vincent Castanza interview, p. 6.

122. Eadie Shanker interview, 10/18/02, p. 11.

123. Pearl Harris interview, 5/6/03, p. 32; Pearl Harris interview, 3/30/04, pp. 1–2. See also Jennie Shanker interview, p. 1.

124. Ed Flower interview, pp. 18–19; Albert Shanker application, U.S. Civil Service Commission, Security Investigation Data for Sensitive Position, in Eadie Shanker papers.

125. Ed Flower interview, p. 17.

126. Ed Flower interview, pp. 6–7, 9, 17.

127. *NYT*, 11/5/89, sect. 4a, p. 34.

128. Ed Flower interview, p. 46.

129. Vincent Castanza interview, pp. 8, 43.

130. Shanker interview with Marcia Reecer, n.d., in Bella Rosenberg papers; Ora Weisman, *Hed Hachinuch*, 8/19/71, in NYU Archives; *NYT*, 11/5/89, sect. 4a, p. 34.

131. Pearl Harris interview, 5/6/03, p. 49. (By contrast, Pearl went to a test-in school after sixth grade.) See also Lillian Feldman interview, p. 14.

132. Schierenbeck, *Class Struggles*, part 8; Schierenbeck, *American Teacher*, 4/97, p. 7.

133. Ed Flower interview, pp. 35, 40–41. See also Albert Shanker interview with Shore, p. 3. Albert Shanker ledger card, University of Illinois Archives (re: Stuyvesant rank). Others have him 125th out of 625. See *NYT*, 11/5/89, sect. 4a, p. 34. See also Hill, *Education Week*, 2/21/96.

134. Bard, *PDK*, 3/75, p. 468. See also Schierenbeck, *Class Struggles*, part 8.

135. Pearl Harris, 5/6/03, pp. 18–19; Spatz interview, p. 54.

136. *NYT*, 11/5/89, sect. 4a, p. 34. See also Albert Shanker interview with Reecer, n.d., in Bella Rosenberg papers, p. 11.

137. *U.S. Newswire*, 2/23/97.

138. Albert Shanker interview with Reecer, n.d., in Bella Rosenberg papers, p. 11. See also Eadie Shanker interview, 10/18/02, p. 9; Ed Flower interview, p. 14.

139. Shanker interview with Reecer, n.d., in Bella Rosenberg papers, p. 12.

140. *University of Illinois Campus Facts*.

141. Albert Shanker interview with Shore, p. 3.

142. Albert Shanker interview with Shore, p. 3; Braun, *Teachers and Power*, p. 152.

143. Jennie Shanker interview, p. 13.

144. Shanker interview with Reecer, n.d., in Bella Rosenberg papers, p. 11. See also Albert Shanker ledger card, University of Illinois Archives (summer sessions 1948, 1949, and 1950).

145. Ora Weisman, *Hed Hachinuch*, 8/19/71, in NYU Archives.

146. Gerald Sabath interview, p. 21.

147. Shanker interview with Marcia Reecer, n.d., in Bella Rosenberg papers; Ora Weisman, *Hed Hachinuch*, 8/19/71, in NYU Archives.

148. Shanker ledger card, University of Illinois Archives.

149. Shanker interview with Reecer, n.d., in Bella Rosenberg papers, p. 11.

150. Max Fisch letter to Shanker, 4/20/50, in WSU Archives, Shanker personal box 11.

151. Shanker, Testimony, Senate Judiciary Committee, in WSU Archives, box 63, folder 77. See also *American Teacher*, 4/97, p. 12.

152. Hill, *Education Week*, 2/21/96.

153. Hill, *Education Week*, 2/21/96; *NYT Magazine*, 9/9/73, p. 72; Albert Shanker interview with Cowan, p. 97; Braun, *Teachers and Power*, p. 152.

154. D'Emilio, *Lost Prophet*, p. 154.

155. *NYT Magazine*, 9/3/67, p. 28. Noah, "Albert Shanker, Statesman," *TNR*, 6/24/85, pp. 17–19; *U.S. Newswire*, 2/23/97; *NYT Magazine*, 9/3/67, p. 28. Sandra Feldman, *NY Teacher*, 3/10/97; Braun, *Teachers and Power*, p. 152; Podair, *The Strike That Changed New York*, p. 42.

156. Pearl Harris interview, 5/6/03, p. 19; Pearl Harris interview, 3/30/04, p.1; George Altomare interview II, p. 7.

157. Bard, *PDK*, 3/75, p. 469.

158. Dorman, *Arguing the World*, p. 116.

159. Ebert, *An Illini Century*, p. 177.

160. Shanker, letter to Dean of Men, 10/8/48, in University of Illinois Archives.

161. Fred Turner letter to Shanker, 10/22/48, denying MacDonald.

162. Albert Shanker, "Symbolism, Mathematical Exponents, and Socialism," May 19, 1948, in Eadie Shanker papers.

163. Gerald Sabath interview, pp. 20–21.

164. Ora Weisman, *Hed Hachinuch*, 8/19/71, in NYU Archives.

165. Pearl Harris interview, 5/6/03, p. 28–29. See also Eadie Shanker interview, 10/18/02, p. 57; and Pearl Harris interview, 5/6/03, p. 28 (re: later staunch supporter); and Bella Rosenberg e-mail, 12/22/04.

166. Ed Flower interview, p. 48.

167. Pearl Harris interview, 5/6/03, p. 22 (that she was pretty and older); University of Illinois ledger card (she was born July 29, 1926). See also Shanker Security Investigation Data (re: her age).

168. Gerald Sabath interview, pp. 2–5, 10–11, 13; Leon Sabath interview, pp. 4–6.

169. Gerald Sabath interview, pp. 6, 16; Leon Sabath interview, pp. 2, 5.

170. Leon Sabath interview, p. 8 (that they were both tall).

171. Carl Sabath interview, p. 5.

172. Ebert, *An Illini Century*, p. 172.

173. Altomare interview II, p. 27.

174. Golodner e-mail, 3/21/06.

175. Pearl Harris interview, 3/6/03, p. 22. See also Carl Sabath interview, p. 5.

176. Ed Flower interview, pp. 27–28; Gerald Sabath interview, p. 37.

177. Sunny Castanza interview, p. 32.

178. Mel Lubin interview, pp. 3–4; Paul Kurtz interview, pp. 1, 6. Dewey taught at Columbia from 1905 until he retired in 1930, and taught as an emeritus at Columbia until he fully retired in 1939. See http://dewey.pragmatism.org and Berube, *American School Reform*, p. 34 (Dewey retired in 1930).

179. Mel Lubin interview, pp. 4, 18, 20; Paul Kurtz interview, p. 1, 5; Fritz Rothschild interview, p. 9. Confirmation re: John Herman Randall Jr., a Dewey disciple, comes from http://www.pragmatism.org/geneology/columbia.htm.

180. Berube, *American School Reform*, pp. 31, 35; Eadie Shanker interview, 9/18/02, p. 1; Adam Shanker interview II, p. 12.

181. Isserman, *The Other American*, pp. 227, 267.

182. Group Watch, "League for Industrial Democracy."

183. Kaufman, *Broken Alliance*, p. 145; Mosle, *TNR*, 3/17/97; *American Educator*, special issue, "The Power of Ideas," Spring–Summer 1997, p. 59.

184. Pearl Harris interview, 5/6/03, pp. 33–34; Bard, *PDK*, 3/75, p. 469.

185. Vincent and Sunny Castanza interview, pp. 16–17, 85. See also Altomare interview I, p. 18.

186. Schierenbeck, *Class Struggles*, part 8; Beichman, *WT*, 2/25/97, p. A20.

187. *NYT*, 6/26/72, p. 35; *New York Magazine*, 8/25/75, p. 10, in NYU Archives.

188. Dan Golodner, WSU Archives, 1/17/06; Dan Golodner e-mail, 3/21/06.

189. Shanker interview with Reecer, n.d., in Bella Rosenberg papers, p. 13.

190. Gerald Sabath interview, p. 41.

191. Shanker interview with Reecer, n.d., in Bella Rosenberg papers, p. 13. Gaffney, *Blackboard Warriors*, draft, p. 11.

192. Walter Guttshalk, letter to Shanker, 2/26/51, in WSU Archives, Shanker personal box 11.

193. Hill, *Education Week*, 2/21/96. This is a phrase he repeated in many interviews. See Albert Shanker interview with Shore, p. 2 ("ran out of money and out of patience"); Albert Shanker interview with Cowan, p. 5 ("ran out of money and patience").

2. Creating the United Federation of Teachers (1952–1962)

1. Albert Shanker interview with Cowan, pp. 1, 69–70; Schierenbeck, *American Teacher*, 4/97, p. 7; *U.S. Newswire*, 2/23/97; Albert Shanker application, U.S. Civil Service, Security Investigation Data for Sensitive Position, in Eadie Shanker papers; Albert Shanker, speech to Social Democrats USA, 1990, reprinted in *The Social Democrat*, 2/91, p. 5.

2. Shanker interview with Reecer, n.d, p. 14, in Bella Rosenberg papers.

3. Schierenbeck, *American Teacher*, 4/97, p. 7.

4. *NYT Magazine*, 9/3/67, p. 29.

5. Shanker, in Drucker, *Managing the Nonprofit Organization*, p. 134.

6. WWS, 10/22/95.

7. Shanker interview with Reecer, n.d., in Bella Rosenberg papers, p. 14.

8. *NYT Magazine*, 9/3/67, p. 29; Hill, *Education Week*, 2/21/96. Eadie Shanker interview, 5/24/05, p. 2; Memorial Service transcript, p. 1; Schierenbeck, *American Teacher*, 4/97, p. 7.

9. Schierenbeck, *New York Teacher*, 2/25/04, p. 9.

10. *NYT Magazine*, 9/3/67, p. 29.

11. Shanker, "Teacher Unionism and Education," in Marcus and Rivlin, *Conflicts in Urban Education*, p. 135.

12. Stern, *Breaking Free*, pp. 103–104.

13. *NYT*, 6/26/72, pp. 35, 47; Albert Shanker interview with Cowan, p. 1.

14. Albert Shanker interview with Cowan, p. 2.

15. Albert Shanker interview with Cowan, p. 1; Pearl Harris interview, 5/6/03, p. 41.

16. Albert Shanker interview with Cowan, p. 5; Altomare interview I, pp. 16–18, 27.

17. Eadie Shanker interview, 12/1/03, pp. 15–16. Eadie Shanker taught at this school the year after Al Shanker left; Altomare interview II, p. 4.

18. Eadie Shanker interview, 12/1/03, p. 15, referencing the Shanker Exhibit; Eadie Shanker memo, 3/3/06.

19. Altomare interview I, p. 4.

20. *NYT*, 2/23/97.

21. Memorial Service transcript, 4/9/97, p. 1.

22. Shanker, in Pew Forum Supplement, *Education Week*, 5/14/97, p. 35.

23. Shanker, in Pew Forum Supplement, *Education Week*, 5/14/97, p. 35.

24. Memorial Service transcript, 4/9/97, p. 1; Noah, "Albert Shanker, Statesman," *TNR*, 6/24/85, pp. 17–19. See also *NYT*, 1/15/75, p. 59 ($42 a week); and *NYT*, 2/23/97 ($38 per week).

25. Gaffney, *Blackboard Warriors*, draft, p. 12.

26. Altomare interview I, pp. 3–5; Altomare interview II, pp. 1–4.

27. Hill, *Education Week*, 2/21/96.

28. Urban, *Why Teachers Organized*, p. 111; Cameron, *The Inside Story*, pp. 65–66.

29. Cameron, *The Inside Story*, p. 77.

30. Cameron, *The Inside Story*, p. 74.

31. Braun, *Teachers and Power*, p. 48; Berube, *American School Reform*, p. 33; *NYT Magazine*, 9/3/67, p. 29; Israel Kugler interview, p. 8; AFT, "Fighting for the Profession: A History of AFT Higher Education," 3/03, p. 3; Urban, *Why Teachers Organized*, p. 99; Berube, *American School Reform*, p. 133; Daniel Golodner, e-mail, 3/21/06.

32. Ryan, *John Dewey*, pp. 295–296.

33. Braun, *Teachers and Power*, p. 32; Urban, *Why Teachers Organized*, p. 134; Shanker in Braun, *Teachers and Power*, p. 136. See also Shanker, "Address to Institute for Education Policy Studies," 3/10/80, pp. 1–2, in WSU Archives, box 63, folder 47.

34. Perlstein, *Justice, Justice*, p. 18.

35. AFT Amicus Brief, *Brown v. Board of Education*, available at http://curiae.law.yale. edu/html/347–483/018.htm. Murphy, *Blackboard Unions*, p. 197; *American Educator*, special issue, "The Power of Ideas," Spring–Summer 1997, 56; McElroy, *American Teacher*, 4/97, p. 2. See also WWS, 5/22/94.

36. Schierenbeck, *Class Struggles*, part 9.

37. Murphy, *Blackboard Unions*, p. 204; Lieberman, *The Teacher Unions*, p. 239.

38. Perlstein, *Justice, Justice*, p. 24.

39. AFT, "Fighting for the Profession," 3/03, p. 4.

40. Braun, *Teachers and Power*, p. 55; Rosenberg interview I, p. 14.

41. Ryan, *John Dewey*, p. 155; Martin, *The Education of John Dewey*, p. 274.

42. Morgan, *A Covert Life*, p. 370.

43. Bell, in Dorman, *Arguing the World*, p. 115.

44. Iversen, *Communists and the Schools*, pp. 20, 33.

45. Iversen, *Communists and the Schools*, p. 366.

46. *NYT*, 7/11/80, p. B1; Altomare interview I, p. 6.

47. Iversen, *Communists and the Schools*, p. 202; Shanker interview with Reecer, n.d, in Bella Rosenberg papers, p. 17.

48. Taft, *United They Teach*, pp. 46, 56; Braun, *Teachers and Power*, p. 55.

49. Zitron, *The New York City Teachers Union*, p. 34.

50. WWS, 12/15/85.

51. Altomare interview I, pp. 9–10.

52. UFT Web site, "Al Shanker: A Passionate Teacher." Available online at http://www.uft .org/about/history/makers/shanker_albert/index4.html.

53. Altomare interview I, pp. 9–10.

54. Albert Shanker interview with Shore, p. 2.

55. Altomare interview I, pp. 10, 13.

56. Albert Shanker interview with Cowan, p. 11.

57. Albert Shanker interview with Cowan, p. 11.

58. *NYT*, 4/16/64, p. 75; Maurice Berube interview, p. 4 (Cogen a socialist). Farran interview, p. 17; Braun, *Teachers and Power*, p. 62.

59. Biographical Fact Sheet, Charles Cogan, in WSU Archives, box 9, folder 64. See also Israel Kugler interview, p. 7.

60. Rebecca Beagle interview, p. 1; *NYT*, 10/3/84, p. D27.

61. Braun, *Teachers and Power*, pp. 132–134; Altomare interview I, p. 14.

62. Altomare, in Bernhardt, *Ordinary People, Extraordinary Lives*, p. 156; Berube interview, p. 4 (socialist).

63. Rebecca Beagle interview, pp. 1–2; *Forward*, 2/28/97.

64. *NYT*, 2/23/97; Mosle, *NYT Magazine*, 1/4/98, p. 38.

65. Altomare interview I, p. 15; Altomare interview II, pp. 8, 12; Albert Shanker interview with Cowan, p. 11.

66. Daniel Beagle interview, pp. 4–6, 8–9, 19, 34–36, 38.

67. *WP*, 6/26/05.

68. Isserman, *If I Had a Hammer*, pp. 191–192.

69. Murphy, *Blackboard Unions*, pp. 197–198, 200; Perlstein, *Justice, Justice*, p. 24; Albert Shanker interview with Shore, p. 2 (that there were fifty thousand members when he joined); Daniel Golodner e-mail, 3/21/06.

70. Schierenbeck, *Class Struggles*, part 9.

71. Hendrik Hertzberg, "Socialism: What Happened, What Now?", 5/1/02, transcript, p. 4. Available online at http://www.socialdemocrats.org/MayDayTranscript.html.

72. Perlstein, *Justice, Justice*, p. 18.

73. Puddington, *Lane Kirkland*, p. 68.

74. Daniel Beagle interview, pp. 24–26.

75. Horowitz interview, p. 67. See also quote in Meyerson, in Mort, *Not Your Father's Union Movement*, p. 3.

76. Taft, *United They Teach*, p. 93; Zitron, *The New York City Teachers Union*, p. 220.

77. Zitron, *The New York City Teachers Union*, p. 220.

78. Taft, *United They Teach*, pp. 48, 93–94; Zitron, *The New York City Teachers Union*, pp. 247–248.

79. Taft, *United They Teach*, p. 48.

80. Schierenbeck, *Class Struggles*, part 8.

81. George Altomare interview I, p. 30–31; Eadie Shanker interview, 10/24/03, p. 4; Phil Kugler interview, p. 2.

82. Altomare interview I, pp. 31–33.

83. Altomare interview I, p. 31.

84. Ed Flower interview, pp. 26–27, 29; Altomare interview II, pp. 27–28; Elaine Sanders interview, p. 5.

85. Gerald Sabath interview, pp. 17, 29, 45.

86. Jennie Shanker journal excerpts, p. 2.

87. George Altomare interview II, pp. 28–30.

88. Vincent Castanza interview, p. 39; George Altomare interview II, p. 16.

89. Eadie e-mail, 10/9/03. See also Carl Sabath interview.

90. Carl Sabath interview, pp. 5–6; Shanker interview with Schierenbeck, *American Educator*, Fall 2000, p. 41; Salvatore, *Eugene V. Debs*, pp. xi, 183, 258; Schierenbeck, *Class Struggles*, part 8.

91. Lillian Feldman interview, p. 9.

92. Rebecca Beagle interview, p. 12, 16; Daniel Beagle interview, p. 13.

93. Murphy, *Blackboard Unions*, p. 102.

94. Goulden, *Jerry Wurf*, p. 26.

95. Murphy, *Blackboard Unions*, p. 162.; Lee Anderson, "All Should Be Free to Choose," *Chattanooga Times Free Press*, 6/1/99, p. B7; Murphy, *Blackboard Unions*, p. 148.

96. Murphy, *Blackboard Unions*, p. 99; Urban, *Why Teachers Organized*, p. 85 (Chicago); Braun, *Teachers and Power*, pp. 29–33 (Cleveland and Chicago); Taft, *United They Teach*, p. 8 (Seattle).

97. Shanker, "Reflections," p. 326.

98. Murphy, *Blackboard Unions*, pp. 87–88.

99. Urban, *Why Teachers Organized*, p. 15.

100. Shanker, "Reflections," p. 327.

101. Shanker interview with Reecer, n.d., p. 20, in Bella Rosenberg papers.

102. Mosle, *NYT Magazine*, 1/4/98, p. 38; Lieberman, *The Teacher Unions*, p. 18; Shanker, address to Institute for Education Policy Studies, pp. 2–3, in WSU Archives, box 63, folder 47.

103. Auletta, *The Streets Were Paved with Gold*, pp. 45–46; Freeman, *Working-Class New York*, p. 203; Goulden, *Jerry Wurf*, pp. 53–54.

104. Murphy, *Blackboard Unions*, p. 214 (1959); Fuller et al., "Collective Bargaining in Milwaukee Public Schools," p. 121; Chavez, *Betrayal*, p. 93 (says 1958).

105. Fuller et al., "Collective Bargaining in Milwaukee Public Schools," p. 121.

106. Shanker, address to Institute for Education Policy Studies, pp. 2–3, in WSU Archives, box 63, folder 47.

107. Altomare interview I, pp. 21–25; Altomare in Bernhardt, *Ordinary People, Extraordinary Lives*, p. 156; Selden, *The Teacher Rebellion*, p. 31; Gaffney, *Blackboard Warriors*, draft, pp. 25–26.

108. George Altomare interview I, p. 28; Albert Shanker interview with Cowan, p. 7.

109. Murphy, *Blackboard Unions*, p. 215; Selden, *The Teacher Rebellion*, pp. 29–30.

110. Freeman, *Working-Class New York*, p. 99.

111. See, e.g., Barone, *Hard America, Soft America*, p. 30.

112. Barone, "Foreword," in Green, *Epitaph for American Labor*, p. ix.

113. Magat, *Unlikely Partners*, p. 72; Puddington, *Lane Kirkland*, p. 205.

114. See, e.g., Lipset et al., *Union Democracy*.

115. Geoghegan, *Which Side Are You On?*, p. 40.

116. Eadie Shanker interview, 10/18/02, p. 48.

117. Albert Shanker interview with Cowan, p. 9.

118. Mosle, *NYT Magazine*, 1/4/98, p. 38; Albert Shanker interview with Cowan, p. 9.

119. Hill, *Education Week*, 2/21/96.

120. Freeman, *Working-Class New York*, p. 202.

121. *American Educator*, special issue, "The Power of Ideas," Spring–Summer 1997, 14.

122. Albert Shanker interview with Cowan, p. 37.

123. Eadie Shanker interview, 10/18/02, handnotes, pp. 1–2; Altomare interview II, p. 32.

124. Eadie Shanker interview, 10/18/02, pp. 2–3; Eadie Shanker interview, 2/27/04, p. 1; Eadie Shanker, address at the Labor International Hall of Fame Ceremony, 4/8/03, in Eadie Shanker papers, p. 4; Eadie Shanker memo, 3/3/06.

125. Eadie Shanker memo, 3/3/06; Eadie Shanker conversation, 3/3/06.

126. Shanker, "Reflections," p. 327; see also *American Educator*, special issue, "The Power of Ideas," Spring–Summer 1997, 1.

127. *American Educator*, special issue, "The Power of Ideas," Spring–Summer 1997, 16.

128. Gaffney, *Blackboard Warriors*, draft, pp. 20–21.

129. Altomare interview I, p. 19.

130. Altomare interview I, p. 19; Freeman, *Working-Class New York*, p. 203.

131. Altomare interview I, pp. 19, 41; Selden, *The Teacher Rebellion*, p. 3; Taft, *United They Teach*, p. 77.

132. Altomare interview I, pp. 40–41, 43–45; Altomare in Bernhardt, *Ordinary Lives, Extraordinary People*, p. 156.

133. Altomare interview I, p. 43–44.

134. Altomare interview I, p. 47; Albert Shanker interview with Cowan, pp. 16–17.

135. Abe Levine, "The Legacy of Albert Shanker," unpublished statement, n.d.

136. Altomare interview I, pp. 42, 53; Schierenbeck, *American Teacher*, 4/97, p. 8; Abe Levine, "A Day to Remember."

137. Hill, *Education Week*, 2/21/96.

138. Albert Shanker interview with Cowan, p. 17; Selden, *The Teacher Rebellion*, p. 40; Taft, *United They Teach*, p. 107.

139. Taft, *United They Teach*, p. 107.

140. Albert Shanker interview with Shore, p. 7; Hill, *Education Week*, 2/21/96.

141. *NYT Magazine*, 9/3/67, p. 30.

142. Altomare interview I, pp. 35–37, 55.

143. De Leonardis interview, pp. 8, 10.

144. Altomare interview I, p. 35.

145. Altomare interview I, p. 57; Altomare interview II, p. 60; Taft, *United They Teach*, p. 108; Gaffney, *Blackboard Warriors*, draft, p. 34.

146. Albert Shanker interview with Cowan, p. 19; *NYT Magazine*, 9/3/67, pp. 29–30; George Altomare interview I, p. 22; Gaffney, *Blackboard Warriors*, draft, p. 34, citing *NYT*, 11/7/60.

147. Altomare interview I, pp. 56–57; Altomare interview II, pp. 9–10.

148. Freeman, *Working-Class New York*, pp. 204; Selden, *The Teacher Rebellion*, p. 47.

149. Ruffini, *Harry Van Arsdale*, pp. 144–145.

150. De Leonardis interview, p. 11.

151. Altomare interview I, pp. 61–62.

152. Altomare interview I, p. 60. In addition to the strikers, two thousand teachers called in sick. Altomare interview II, p. 5.

153. Altomare interview II, p. 6.

154. Albert Shanker interview with Cowan, p. 40.

155. Ruffini, *Harry Van Arsdale*, p. 244.

156. *NYT*, 11/8/76, pp. 1, 28 (on sixteenth anniversary of 1960 strike); Ruffini, *Harry Van Arsdale*, p. 145.

157. Altomare interview I, p. 39.

158. *NYT*, 11/8/76, pp. 1, 28; Taft, *United They Teach*, p. 110.

159. Albert Shanker interview with Cowan, p. 20.

160. Taft, *United They Teach*, pp. 111, 113.

161. Albert Shanker interview with Cowan, p. 20.

162. Eadie Shanker interview, 3/24/04, p. 1; Eadie Shanker memo, 3/3/06.

163. Eadie Shanker interview, 11/18/05; Eadie Shanker memo, 3/3/06.

164. Hill, *Education Week*, 2/21/96; Selden, *The Teacher Rebellion*, p. 52.

165. *American Educator*, special issue, "The Power of Ideas," Spring–Summer 1997, p. 16.

166. UFT, "Class Struggles: The UFT Story," part 6, "The Struggle for Recognition—1961"; Hill, *Education Week*, 2/21/96; Albert Shanker interview with Cowan, p. 28; Selden, *The Teacher Rebellion*, p. 52.

167. Cameron, *The Inside Story*, p. 74.

168. Stern, *Breaking Free*, p. 103; Selden, *The Teacher Rebellion*, p. 63.

169. Albert Shanker interview with Cowan, p. 24.

170. Altomare interview I, p. 56.

171. De Leonardis interview, p. 12.

172. A few years later, in 1964, the NEA had 900,000 members, while the AFT had 90,000. *NYT*, 4/16/64, p. 75.

173. Albert Shanker interview with Cowan, p. 24.

174. Albert Shanker interview with Cowan, pp. 24–25.

175. Schierenbeck, *American Teacher*, 4/97, p. 8; Lieberman, *The Teacher Unions*, p. 13; Selden, *The Teacher Rebellion*, p. 64; Taft, *United They Teach*, p. 117; Braun, *Teachers and Power*, p. 64.

176. Albert Shanker interview with Cowan, p. 40.

177. Albert Shanker interview with Cowan, p. 22.

178. George Altomare interview II, p. 11; Selden, *The Teacher Rebellion*, p. 71.

179. *NYT Magazine*, 9/3/67, p. 30.

180. Murphy, *Blackboard Unions*, p. 216; Albert Shanker interview with Cowan, p. 32; *NYT*, 3/31/66, pp. 1, 32; Taft, *United They Teach*, p. 127.

181. *NYT Magazine*, 9/3/67, p. 30; Albert Shanker interview with Cowan, pp. 34–35; Braun, *Teachers and Power*, pp. 64–65.

182. Gaffney, *Blackboard Warriors*, draft, p. 40; "Reflections," *PDK*, 328; Albert Shanker interview with Cowan, pp. 37–38, 66.

183. Taft, *United They Teach*, p. 121.

184. Albert Shanker interview with Cowan, p. 66.

185. Albert Shanker interview with Cowan, p. 47.

186. Hill, *Education Week*, 2/21/96; *U.S. Newswire*, 2/23/97; *American Educator*, special issue, "The Power of Ideas," Spring–Summer 1997, p. 14.

187. American Federation of Teachers, *Building on the Past for a Better Future* (Washington, D.C.: AFT, 1990), film; Daniel Golodner e-mail, 3/21/06.

188. Toch, "A Speech That Shook the Field," *Education Week*, 3/26/97.

3. Rising Within the UFT: Labor and Civil Rights Together (1962–1965)

1. Albert Shanker interview with Cowan, pp. 27, 82.

2. Eadie Shanker memo, 3/3/06.

3. Schierenbeck, *Class Struggles*, part 7; George Altomare interview II, pp. 12–13.

4. Freeman, *Working-Class New York*, p. 204.

5. Schierenbeck, *Class Struggles*, part 9.

6. Murphy, *Blackboard Unions*, p. 224.

7. Selden, *The Teacher Rebellion*, p. 115.

8. Cameron interview, pp. 3–4, 23.

9. Murphy, *Blackboard Unions*, p. 224.

10. Usdan interview, p. 5. See also, Stern, *Breaking Free*, p. 117.

11. Murphy, *Blackboard Unions*, p. 220.

12. *Business Week*, 12/30/61, quoted in Perlstein, *Justice, Justice*, p. 21.

13. Green, *Epitaph for Labor*, p. 163.

14. Goulden, *Jerry Wurf*, p. 110.

15. Memorial Service transcript, 4/9/97, p. 21.

16. Wreszin, *A Rebel in Defense of Tradition*, pp. 376–378; Harrington, *Fragments of the Century*, p. 173.

17. Anderson, *A. Philip Randolph*, pp. xv, 312; Puddington, *Lane Kirkland*, pp. 42–43.

18. D'Emilio, *Lost Prophet*, pp. 326–327.

19. Anderson, *A. Philip Randolph*, p. 324.

20. D'Emilio, *Lost Prophet*, p. 343.

21. Marable, *Black American Politics*, p. 93.

22. Puddington, *Lane Kirkland*, pp. 43–44; Goulden, *Meany*, p. 322. See also Norman Hill interview, pp. 4–5; Rachelle Horowitz e-mail to author, 1/31/06.

23. Perlstein, *Justice, Justice*, p. 87; Rachelle Horowitz e-mail to author, 1/31/06.

24. *American Teacher*, 4/97, p. 12.

25. Shanker letter to Carl Megel, 7/24/63, in NYU Archives.

26. Selden, *The Teacher Rebellion*, p. 146.

27. Anderson, *Bayard Rustin*, p. 255.

28. Goulden, *Jerry Wurf*, pp. 171–172; Maget, *Unlikely Partners*, p. 85.

29. WWS, 8/15/93.

30. Taylor, *Knocking at Our Own Door*, p. 116.

31. Albert Shanker interview with Cowan, pp. 54–55.

32. Shanker interview with Reecer, n.d., in Bella Rosenberg papers, p. 9.

33. Taylor, *Knocking at Our Own Door*, pp. 125–126, citing UFT statements from July and December 1963.

34. Perlstein, *Justice, Justice*, pp. 25, 87; Taylor, *Knocking at Our Own Door*, pp. 2–3.

35. Editorial, *NYT*, 1/13/64, p. 26.

36. Perlstein, *Justice, Justice*, p. 194 n. 27; Taylor, *Knocking at Our Own Door*, pp. 140, 132.

37. Horowitz interview, pp. 8–9.

38. Perlstein, *Justice, Justice*, pp. 25, 87; Taylor, *Knocking at Our Own Door*, pp. 2–3; Perlstein, citing Executive Board Minutes in *United Teacher*, 1/24/64, p. 7.

39. Wasserman, *The School Fix*, p. 315.

40. Rogers, *110 Livingston Street*, p. 195.

41. Altomare interview II, pp. 61–63.

42. Rogers, *110 Livingston Street*, p. 132.

43. Taylor, *Knocking at Our Own Door*, pp. 137–138.

44. Taylor, *Knocking at Our Own Door*, pp. 141–142; D'Emilio, *Lost Prophet*, p. 367.

45. Rogers, *110 Livingston Street*, pp. 140–141; Mayer, *The Teachers Strike*, p. 109.

46. Rogers, *110 Livingston Street*, p. 195; Freeman, *Working-Class New York*, p. 199 (on *NYT* poll).

47. Schierenbeck, *Class Struggles*, part 9.

48. King, "Out of a Mountain of Despair," NYU Archives. See also UFT at 25 (1985), p. 11.

49. Wasserman, *The School Fix*, p. 309.

50. De Leonardis interview, pp. 11–12; Hill, *Education Week*, 2/21/96; *NYT*, 2/23/97; *NYT Magazine*, 9/3/67, p. 5; Chavez, *An Unlikely Conservative*, p. 114; Velma Hill interview, p. 31; Eadie Shanker interview, 10/18/02, p. 56; McElroy interview, p. 27; Cortese interview, pp. 6, 23; Spatz interview, p. 44; Altomare interview II, pp. 22–23; Rosenberg interview I, p. 11; *NYT*, 11/5/89, sect. 4a, p. 34; Hurwitz interview, p. 21; Dorn interview I, p. 24; Weiner interview, p. 44.

51. *NYT*, 2/23/97.

52. Sandra Feldman interview, p. 3.

53. O'Neill, in Rubinstein, *Schools Against Children*, p. 176; Selden, *The Teacher Rebellion*, pp. 90–92.

54. *NYT*, 4/16/64, p. 75.

55. Eadie Shanker interview, 10/18/02, p. 4; Eadie Shanker interview, 4/23/04. See also Jennie Shanker journal excerpts, p. 2.

56. *NYT*, 4/16/64, p. 75; *NYT*, 5/12/64, p. 34; De Leonardis interview, p. 15; Taft, *United They Teach*, p. 138.

57. *NYT*, 4/16/64, p. 75.

58. Albert Shanker interview with Cowan, pp. 74–75.

59. *NYT Magazine*, 9/3/67, p. 4.

60. Berube interview, p. 14.

61. Albert Shanker interview with Cowan, pp. 84–87. See also "Reflections," *PDK*, 328; Taft, *United They Teach*, p. 146.

62. UFT press release, 6/22/63, in NYU archives; Mosle, *TNR*, 3/17/97; *American Teacher*, 4/97, p. 2; *NYT Magazine*, 9/9/73, p. 72; Stern, "'Scab' Teachers," p. 179; Selden, *The Teacher Rebellion*, p. 146.

63. Schierenbeck, *Class Struggles*, part 9; Hine, *Eyes on the Prize*, pp. 167–168.

64. Hampton and Fayer, *Voices of Freedom*, pp. 209–210, 227, 230, 236; Levine, *Bayard Rustin*, p. 182.

65. Branch, *At Canaan's Edge*, p. 64.

66. Branch, *At Canaan's Edge*, p. 75.

67. Flyer, "UFT Gives King 1st Stationwagon for Alabama Registration Drive," in NYU Archives; Schierenbeck, *Class Struggles*, part 9. See also John O'Neill, "Memo to Staff members re: Selma, Alabama, 3/16/65," in NYU papers; Shanker letter to Bernard Donovan re: March to Montgomery, 3/23/65, in NYU papers.

68. Shanker, letter to the editor, *New York World Telegram & Sun*, 4/5/65, in NYU archives.

69. Schierenbeck, *American Teacher*, 4/97, p. 9.

70. Schierenbeck, *Class Struggles*, part 9.

71. Harrington, *Fragments of the Century*, p. 77.

72. Barsh oral history, UFT, 11/21/86, p. 3, NYU Archives.

73. Stern, "'Scab' Teachers," p. 182 (mentor to Harrington and Rustin); Diggins, *The Rise and Fall of the American Left*, p. 203 (Harrington and Howe). See also Isserman, *If I Had a Hammer*, pp. 37, 40–41, 61–62, 121, 186.

74. Barsh oral history, UFT, 11/21/86, p. 1, NYU Archives.

75. Horowitz interview, pp. 31–32; Alan Wolfe, *TNR*, 4/3/00.

76. Horowitz interview, pp. 33–34.

77. Miller interview, pp. 17, 25.

78. Adam Shanker interview II, p. 7; Jennie Shanker interview, p. 15.

79. *NYT*, 8/26/83, p. B2; *NYT*, 9/6/83, p. B2; *NYT*, 3/7/91, p. B1; *NYT*, 9/29/95, p. B1; Sandra Feldman interview, pp. 5, 13; Hampton and Fayer, *Voices of Freedom*, p. 489.

80. Eugenia Kemble interview I, pp. 1, 12.

81. D'Emilio, *Lost Prophet*, p. 230.

82. D'Emilio, *Lost Prophet*, p. 248.

83. D'Emilio, *Lost Prophet*, pp. 246, 266.

84. Levine, *Bayard Rustin*, p. 175; Perlstein, *Justice, Justice*, p. 89.

85. *American Teacher*, 4/97, p. 12. See also Perlstein, *Justice, Justice*, p. 89, on the UFT's crucial support for APRI.

86. LaCour interview, p. 26.

87. *American Teacher*, 4/97, p. 12.

88. Bayard Rustin, "From Protest to Politics," *Commentary*, 2/65, reprinted in Rustin, *Down the Line*, pp. 111–122.

89. Albert Shanker interview, pp. 5–6.

90. King, *Why We Can't Wait*, pp. 134–138.

91. In Kahlenberg, *The Remedy*, pp. 3–9.

92. Anderson, *A. Philip Randolph*, p. 344; D'Emilio, *Lost Prophet*, p. 430; Harrington, *Fragments of the Century*, pp. 203–204.

93. Drucker, *Max Shachtman*, pp. 287, 294; Harrington, *Fragments of the Century*, pp. 203–204.

94. Shanker, "Teachers Should Support Freedom Budget," *United Teacher*, 5/5/67, p. 5.

95. O'Neill, in Rubinstein, *Schools Against Children*, p. 174.

96. Cannato, *The Ungovernable City*, p. 68.

97. George Altomare interview II, handnotes at end.

98. Lindsay letter to Shanker, 11/23/65, in NYU Archives.

4. Black Power and the 1967 Teachers' Strike (1966–1968)

1. Freeman, *Working-Class New York*, p. 210.

2. Albert Shanker interview with Shore, p. 7; Shanker in Urofsky, *Why Teachers Strike*, p. 186.

3. Cannato, *The Ungovernable City*, pp. 167–168, 183.

4. Freeman, *Working-Class New York*, p. 216.

5. Schierenbeck, *American Teacher*, 4/97, p. 9.

6. Mayer, *The Teachers Strike*, p. 109.

7. Schierenbeck, *Class Struggles*, part 9. See also Podair, *The Strike That Changed New York*, p. 45.

8. Perlstein, *Justice, Justice*, pp. 61–62.

9. Schierenbeck, *Class Struggles*, part 9.

10. Cannato, *The Ungovernable City*, pp. 167–168, 183; Freeman, *Working-Class New York*, p. 216; Neier, *Taking Liberties*, p. 25.

11. Beinart, *The Good Fight*, p. 39.

12. Branch, *At Canaan's Edge*, p. 549.

13. Carson, *In Struggle*, pp. 3, 197–200, 204, 209–210, 227, 231; Albert Shanker interview with Cowan, p. 93; D'Emilio, *Lost Prophet*, p. 426; Fantini, *Community Control and the Urban School*, p. 16; Salzman, in Salzman and West, *Struggles in the Promised Land*, p. 188; Martin, in Salzman and West, *Struggles in the Promised Land*, p. 345.

14. Carson, *In Struggle*, pp. 210, 219–221.

15. Siegel, *The Future Once Happened Here*, p. 40; Branch, *At Canaan's Edge*, p. 464.

16. Jacoby, *Someone Else's House*, p. 159.

17. Drucker, *Max Shachtman*, p. 295; Harrington, *Fragments of the Century*, p. 117.

18. D'Emilio, *Lost Prophet*, p. 428.

19. King, *Where Do We Go from Here?*, pp. 51–52, cited in Marable, *Race, Reform, and Rebellion*, p. 95.

20. Berube, *American School Reform*, pp. 75–76; Fantini, *Community Control and the Urban School*, p. 16.

21. Albert Shanker interview with Cowan, p. 93.

22. Fantini, *Community Control and the Urban School*, pp. 5, 8.

23. Berube and Gittel, *Confrontation at Ocean Hill–Brownsville*, p. 13.

24. Albert Shanker interview with Cowan, p. 94; Albert Shanker interview with Shore, p. 3.

25. Carter, *Pickets, Parents, and Power*, p. 13; Ravitch, *The Great School Wars*, p. 301; *NYT*, 9/30/66, p. 1.

26. Podair, *The Strike That Changed New York*, p. 41.

27. *NYT*, 9/30/66, pp. 1, 30.

28. Carter, *Pickets, Parents, and Power*, p. 14.

29. Carter, *Pickets, Parents, and Power*, p. 14.

30. Wasserman, *The School Fix*, p. 227.

31. Albert Shanker interview with Cowan, p. 95.

32. Albert Shanker interview with Cowan, p. 97. For a similar story, see Schierenbeck, *American Educator*, special issue, "The Power of Ideas," Spring–Summer 1997, p. 40. See also Albert Shanker interview with Shore, p. 3.

33. *NYT*, 9/30/66, pp. 1, 30.

34. Podair, *The Strike That Changed New York*, p. 159.

35. Albert Shanker interview with Cowan, p. 101.

36. Albert Shanker interview with Cowan, p. 97.

37. Albert Shanker interview with Cowan, p. 98; Kaufman, *Broken Alliance*, pp. 45–46.

38. Albert Shanker interview with Cowan, pp. 99–100.

39. *NYT*, 10/4/66, p. 48.

40. Karp, in Berube and Gittel, *Confrontation at Ocean Hill–Brownsville*, p. 65; Carter, *Pickets, Parents, and Power*, p. 19; Ravitch, *The Great School Wars*, p. 308.

41. Ravitch, *The Great School Wars*, p. 308.

42. Cannato, *The Ungovernable City*, pp. 343–344; Ravitch, *The Great School Wars*, p. 337.

43. Carter, *Pickets, Parents, and Power*, pp. 27–28; *NYT*, 6/24/80, p. A1; *NYT*, 1/9/69, p. 72 (referencing spring 1967); Albert Shanker interview with Cowan, p. 104.

44. Karp, in Berube and Gittel, *Confrontation at Ocean Hill–Brownsville*, p. 63.

45. Stern, in Berube and Gittel, *Confrontation at Ocean Hill–Brownsville*, p. 178.

46. Kaufman, *Broken Alliance*, p. 139.

47. Podair, *The Strike That Changed New York*, p. 19.

48. Mayer, *The Teachers Strike*, p. 18.

49. Karp, in Berube and Gittel, *Confrontation at Ocean Hill–Brownsville*, p. 64; Freeman, *Working-Class New York*, p. 219.

50. Albert Shanker interview with Cowan, pp. 101–102; Podair, *The Strike That Changed New York*, p. 82; Berube and Gittel, *Confrontation at Ocean Hill–Brownsville*, p. 13; Urofsky, *Why Teachers Strike*, p. 12.

51. Taft, *United They Teach*, p. 169.

52. McCoy, in Berube and Gittel, *Confrontation at Ocean Hill–Brownsville*, p. 52.

53. *NYT*, 1/9/69, pp. 67, 76; Shanker, in Urofsky, *Why Teachers Strike*, p. 177.

54. *NYT*, 1/9/69, p. 72; Berube and Gittel, *Confrontation at Ocean Hill–Brownsville*, p. 335.

55. Berube and Gittel, *Confrontation at Ocean Hill–Brownsville*, pp. 13–14; Ravitch, *The Great School Wars*, p. 316.

56. Bundy, *Reconnection for Learning*, p. ix; Berube and Gittel, *Confrontation at Ocean Hill–Brownsville*, pp. 336–337.

57. Fantini, *Community Control and the Urban School*, p. 101; Freeman, *Working-Class New York*, p. 218; Jacoby, *Someone Else's House*, p. 160.

58. Jacoby, *Someone Else's House*, p. 161.

59. Bundy, *Reconnection for Learning*, p. v.

60. Freeman, *Working-Class New York*, p. 218; John Lindsay letter to Jules Kolodny, 5/10/67, acknowledging Kolodny's letter, in NYU Archives.

61. Bundy letter to Shanker, 5/5/67, in NYU archives.

62. Podair, *The Strike That Changed New York*, p. 83; Berube and Gittel, *Confrontation at Ocean Hill–Brownsville*, p. 24.

63. D'Emilio, *Lost Prophet*, pp. 54, 427.

64. *NYT*, 12/23/02, p. B7.

65. *NYT*, 6/24/67, p. 25; *NYT Magazine*, 9/3/67, p. 5; Carson, *The Education of Sonny Carson*, pp. 141–143.

66. Carson, *The Education of Sonny Carson*, pp. 145–147; Jacoby, *Someone Else's House*, p. 173; Murphy, *Blackboard Unions*, p. 237.

67. Niemeyer Report, in Berube and Gittel, *Confrontation at Ocean Hill–Brownsville*, p. 25.

68. Carter, *Pickets, Parents, and Power*, p. 32; Freeman, *Working-Class New York*, pp. 219–220.

69. Kemble, in Berube and Gittel, *Confrontation at Ocean Hill–Brownsville*, p. 36.

70. Carter, *Pickets, Parents, and Power*, p. 32.

71. Kaufman, *Broken Alliance*, pp. 144–145; Mayer, *The Teachers Strike*, p. 26.

72. Berube and Gittel, *Confrontation at Ocean Hill–Brownsville*, p. 336; and *NYT*, 9/17/68, p. 41.

73. Carter, *Pickets, Parents, and Power*, pp. 33–34.

74. Albert Shanker interview with Cowan, p. 106.

75. Jacoby, *Someone Else's House*, p. 178.

76. Kemble, in Berube and Gittel, *Confrontation at Ocean Hill–Brownsville*, p. 40.

77. Mayer, *The Teachers Strike*, p. 26.

78. Jacoby, *Someone Else's House*, p. 180.

79. Podair, *The Strike That Changed New York*, p. 90.

80. Jacoby, *Someone Else's House*, p. 179.

81. Podair, *The Strike That Changed New York*, p. 87; Berube and Gittel, *Confrontation at Ocean Hill–Brownsville*, p. 336.

82. Carter, *Pickets, Parents, and Power*, p. 38; Mayer, *The Teachers Strike*, p. 23.

83. *NYT Magazine*, 11/18/68, in Berube and Gittel, *Confrontation at Ocean Hill–Brownsville*, p. 84.

84. Kaufman, *Broken Alliance*, pp. 129–133; Sleeper, *Closest of Strangers*, p. 100.

85. Carter, *Pickets, Parents, and Power*, p. 39.

86. Niemeyer Report, in Berube and Gittel, *Confrontation at Ocean Hill–Brownsville*, p. 25; Kemble, in Berube and Gittel, *Confrontation at Ocean Hill–Brownsville*, pp. 36–37; Nauman, in Hampton and Fayer, *Voices of Freedom*, pp. 490–491.

87. George Altomare interview I, p. 22.

88. Albert Shaker interview with Cowan, p. 110.

89. *NYT Magazine*, 9/3/67, p. 29.

90. *NYT Magazine*, 9/3/67, p. 4. See also Hill, *Education Week*, 2/21/96.

91. Albert Shanker interview with Cowan, pp. 59–60, 62, 65; Shanker, in Urofsky, *Why Teachers Strike*, p. 176; Sandra Feldman interview, pp. 15–16; Eadie Shanker memo, 3/3/06.

92. Albert Shanker interview with Cowan, pp. 63–64; WWS, 4/1/73. See also Goldbloom, in Berube and Gittel, *Confrontation at Ocean Hill–Brownsville*, p. 251.

93. *NYT*, 12/15/66, pp. 1, 24.

94. Braun, *Teachers and Power*, p. 161.

95. Lieberman, *The Teacher Unions*, p. ix; Brimelow, *The Worm in the Apple*, p. 56. Lieberman also takes the extreme position that even negotiating teacher wages and hours is antidemocratic. Lieberman, *The Teacher Unions*, p. 64.

96. Lieberman, *The Teacher Unions*, p. 15.

97. Kerchner, Koppich, and Weeres, *United Mind Workers*, pp. 7, 186.

98. *NYT Magazine*, 9/3/67, p. 29.

99. Taft, *United They Teach*, p. 149 (citing *NYT*, 9/20/67.)

100. Magidson interview, p. 10.

101. *NYT*, 9/7/67, p. 30 (Man in the News); and *NYT Magazine*, 9/3/67, pp. 4ff.

102. *NYT Magazine*, 9/3/67, p. 4.

103. *NYT Magazine*, 9/3/67, p. 5.

104. *NYT*, 9/8/67, p. 1.

105. *NYT*, 9/12/67, p. 1.

106. Eugenia Kemble interview I, p. 9; Wasserman, *The School Fix*, p. 332.

107. Albert Shanker interview with Cowan, p. 112.

108. Rubinstein, *Schools Against Children*, p. 267.

109. Podair, *The Strike That Changed New York*, p. 163.

110. Wasserman, *The School Fix*, pp. 316–317.

111. Albert Shaker interview with Cowan, pp. 112–113.

112. Murphy, *Blackboard Unions*, p. 237.

113. Perlstein, *Justice, Justice*, p. 137; Taylor, *Knocking at Our Own Door*, p. 188.

114. Meier, *Mainstream*, 12/67, p. 42.

115. Kaufman, *Broken Alliance*, p. 145.

116. Kaufman, *Broken Alliance*, p. 146.

117. Podair, *The Strike That Changed New York*, p. 162.

118. *NYT*, 9/12/67, pp. 1, 40.

119. Mayer, *The Teachers Strike*, p. 31; Shanker, in Urofsky, *Why Teachers Strike*, p. 166.

120. Braun, *Teachers and Power*, p. 162.

121. *NYT*, 9/16/67, pp. 1, 18.

122. Advertisement, "Martin Luther King, Jr. Backs New York City Teachers," *NYT*, 9/16/67, p. 12.

123. Kahlenberg, *The Remedy*, p. 10.

124. D'Emilio, *Lost Prophet*, pp. 453–454, 460.

125. Kahlenberg, *The Remedy*, p. xxvii.

126. *NYT*, 9/3/67, p. 30.

127. *NYT*, 9/23/67, pp. 1, 15. See also *NYT*, 9/25/67, pp. 1, 51.

128. *NYT*, 9/27/67, pp. 1, 32.

129. *NYT*, 10/1/67, sect. 4, p. 9.

130. Albert Shanker interview with Cowan, p. 113.

131. *NYT*, 9/29/67, pp. 1, 43.

132. *NYT*, 10/1/67, sect. 4, p. 9.

133. *NYT*, 9/29/67, pp. 1, 43.

134. *NYT Magazine*, 4/20/69, p. 123.

135. *NYT*, 9/28/67, p. 50; Berube, *American School Reform*, pp. 76–77; Wasserman, *The School Fix*, p. 250.

136. *NYT*, 9/29/67, p. 43.

137. *NYT*, 9/28/67, p. 50.

138. *NYT*, 9/29/67, p. 43.

139. Bundy, *Reconnection for Learning*, pp. v, xiv, 26, 44–46, 69; *NYT*, 11/8/67, p. 1.

140. Levin, *Community Control of Schools*, p. 276.

141. Buhle and Kelley, in Salzman and West, *Struggles in the Promised Land*, p. 216.

142. UFT Policy Statement, in Berube and Gittel, *Confrontation at Ocean Hill–Brownsville*, p. 219.

143. *NYT*, 12/4/67, p. 32.

144. Golin, *The Newark Teachers Strike*, p. 126.

145. *NYT*, 1/9/69, pp. 67, 76.

146. Goldbloom, in Berube and Gittel, *Confrontation at Ocean Hill–Brownsville*, p. 274.

147. WWS, 4/2/72; Hentoff, *Village Voice*, 9/26/68, in Berube and Gittel, *Confrontation at Ocean Hill–Brownsville*, p. 124, citing Shanker in *NYT*, 9/20/68.

148. Siegel, *The Future Once Happened Here*, p. 33.

149. Fantini, in Levin, *Community Control of Schools*, p. 42.

150. *NYT*, 10/19/68, p. 26.

151. UFT Policy Statement, in Berube and Gittel, *Confrontation at Ocean Hill–Brownsville*, p. 219; Ravitch, *The Great School Wars*, p. 335.

152. Shanker, in Jacoby, *Someone Else's House*, p. 193.

153. Shanker, in Podair, *The Strike That Changed New York*, p. 44.

154. Berube, *American School Reform*, p. 74.

155. Richard Ravitch interview, p. 4.

156. Shanker, Address, West Side Montessori School (n.d., but prior to 10/20/67, when transcript had been prepared), WSU Archives, box 63, folder 1.

157. *The Nation*, 2/17/03 (review of Podair book), pp. 40ff; Podair, *The Strike That Changed New York*, p. 21.

158. WWS, 6/27/71.

159. Harrington, *The Long Distance Runner*, p. 76.

160. Oliver, in Marcus and Rivlin, *Conflicts in Urban Education*, pp. 115–116.

161. Podair, *The Strike That Changed New York*, p. 14, 93; Berube, *American School Reform*, p. 73.

162. Podair, *The Strike That Changed New York*, p. 155.

163. Rosenberg interview III, p. 29.

164. Shanker, Testimony, U.S. Civil Rights Commission, 2/72, p. 112.

165. Shanker, *TNR*, 11/15/69, p. 28.

166. Shanker, Testimony, U.S. Civil Rights Commission, 2/72, p. 117.

167. Berube interview, pp. 13, 15.

168. Berube interview, pp. 13, 15; Anderson, *Bayard Rustin*, pp. 331–332; Sandra Feldman interview, p. 21; Carter, *Pickets, Parents, and Power*, p. 91; Gittel, in Levin, *Community Control of Schools*, pp. 120, 293–294, citing *NYT*, 9/16/68; Braun, *Teachers and Power*, pp. 223, 226–227.

169. Moskow and McLennan, in Levin, *Community Control of Schools*, p. 192.

170. Ravitch, *The Great School Wars*, pp. 349–350; Harrington, in Berube and Gittel, *Confrontation at Ocean Hill–Brownsville*, p. 134; Harnett, in Berube and Gittel, *Confrontation at Ocean Hill–Brownsville*, p. 208.

171. Podair, *The Strike That Changed New York*, p. 7.

172. Moskow and McLennan, in Levin, *Community Control of Schools*, p. 209; *NYT*, 12/4/67, p. 32.

173. Mayer, *The Teachers Strike*, p. 109; UFT, *NYT* advertisement, 11/24/68, in Berube and Gittel, *Confrontation at Ocean Hill–Brownsville*, p. 152; Feldman, in Berube and Gittel, *Confrontation at Ocean Hill–Brownsville*, p. 142; Harrington, in Berube and Gittel, *Confrontation at Ocean Hill–Brownsville*, pp. 134–135.

174. *NYT*, 10/5/67, p. 1.

175. *NYT*, 12/21/67, pp. 1, 54.

176. *NYT*, 12/21/67, pp. 1, 54; Braun, *Teachers and Power*, p. 146.

177. Albert Shanker interview with Cowan, pp. 115–118; *NYT*, 12/22/67, p. 21; Eadie Shanker interview, 10/18/02, p. 65; *NYT*, 1/4/68, p. 25.

178. Albert Shanker interview with Cowan, pp. 115–118; Hobart interview, p. 16.

179. Albert Shanker interview with Cowan, pp. 115–118.

180. Eadie Shanker interview, 10/18/02, p. 65. See also *NYT*, 12/21/67, p. 54.

181. *NYT*, 12/26/67, p. 31.

182. Albert Shanker interview with Cowan, p. 118; Sarah Lubin interview, p. 26.

183. Memorial Service transcript, 4/9/97, p. 2.

184. Eadie Shanker memo, 3/3/06.

185. *NYT*, 12/28/67, p. 32.

186. Spatz interview, p. 23; WWS, 12/19/71.

187. Eadie Shanker interview, 10/18/02, p. 67.

188. Magidson interview, p. 11.

189. Memorial Service transcript, 4/9/97, p. 3.

190. *NYT*, 1/4/68, p. 25.

191. Albert Shanker interview with Cowan, p. 113–114; Hill, *Education Week*, 2/21/96.

192. "Albert Shanker: Labor's Educator," Exhibit, 9/12/02.

193. Horowitz interview, p. 21.

194. Harrington, *Fragments of the Century*, p. 120.

195. UFT news release, 4/5/68, in NYU Archives. See also Albert Shanker, statement on King's death, reprinted in UFT pamphlet, "King, Out of the Mountain of Despair the Son of Hope," in NYU archives.

196. UFT news release, 4/5/68, in NYU Archives.

197. Stern, in Berube and Gittel, *Confrontation at Ocean Hill–Brownsville*, p. 179; Podair, *The Strike That Changed New York*, p. 105.

198. UFT news release, 4/5/68, in NYU Archives.

199. Nauman, in Hampton and Fayer, *Voices of Freedom*, pp. 485–486; Jacoby, *Someone Else's House*, p. 188.

200. Goldbloom, in Berube and Gittel, *Confrontation at Ocean Hill–Brownsville*, pp. 270–271; Carter, *Pickets, Parents, and Power*, p. 59; Jacoby, *Someone Else's House*, p. 188; Kaufman, *Broken Alliance*, p. 149.

201. Siegel, *The Future Once Happened Here*, p. 70.

202. Hampton and Fayer, *Voices of Freedom*, p. 469.

203. Horowitz interview, p. 34; Perlstein, *Justice, Justice*, pp. 81–84, 93–94.

204. Rustin, "Integration Within Decentralization," in NYU Archives, pp. 6–7, 9, 12–13, 14–15.

205. Horowitz interview, p. 34; Perlstein, *Justice, Justice*, pp. 81–84, 93–94.

5. The Ocean Hill–Brownsville Strike and the Liberal Assault on Labor
(1968)

1. *NYT*, 5/10/68, pp. 1, 38. See also Ravitch, *The Great School Wars*, p. 352.

2. Podair, *The Strike That Changed New York*, p. 101. Shanker, in Urofsky, *Why Teachers Strike*, p. 150; Jacoby, *Someone Else's House*, p. 191; Kaufman, in Salzman and West, *Struggles in the Promised Land*, p. 113; Traub, *NYT Magazine*, 10/6/02, p. 71.

3. Mayer, *The Teachers Strike*, p. 51; *NYT*, 9/16/68, pp. 1, 52; Ravitch, *The Great School Wars*, pp. 358–359.

4. *NYT*, 5/10/68, p. 1, 38; Berube and Gittel, *Confrontation at Ocean Hill–Brownsville*, p. 33.

5. Nauman, in Hampton and Fayer, *Voices of Freedom*, p. 508; Jacoby, *Someone Else's House*, p. 176.

6. Nauman interview, p. 2.

7. Nauman interview, pp. 7–9, 13–14.

8. Nauman interview, pp. 17–18. See also Nauman, in Hampton and Fayer, *Voices of Freedom*, p. 501.

9. Ravitch, *The Great School Wars*, pp. 355–356.

10. Kaufman, *Broken Alliance*, p. 153.

11. McCoy, in *NYT*, quoted in Goldbloom, in Berube and Gittel, *Confrontation at Ocean Hill–Brownsville*, p. 272. See also McCoy in *NYT*, cited in UFT advertisement, *NYT*, 11/24/68, in Berube and Gittel, *Confrontation at Ocean Hill–Brownsville*, p. 149; Jacoby, *Someone Else's House*, p. 191; Ravitch, *The Great School Wars*, pp. 357–358.

12. Carter, *Pickets, Parents, and Power*, p. 75. See also Podair, *The Strike That Changed New York*, p. 101, 108.

13. Freeman, *Working-Class New York*, p. 22; Jacoby, *Someone Else's House*, p. 194.

14. Taft, *United They Teach*, pp. 175–179, citing *NYT*, 5/14/68, 5/15/68, 5/22/68, 5/24/68; Shanker, in Urofsky, *Why Teachers Teach*, p. 151.

15. Jacoby, *Someone Else's House*, p. 192.

16. Podair, *The Strike That Changed New York*, pp. 104–105; Taft, *United They Teach*, p. 175, citing *NYT*, 5/15/68.

17. Podair, *The Strike That Changed New York*, p. 109; Freeman, *Working-Class New York*, p. 22; Jacoby, *Someone Else's House*, p. 194.

18. Braun, *Teachers and Power*, p. 242.

19. Karp, in Berube and Gittel, *Confrontation at Ocean Hill–Brownsville*, pp. 74–75, 184; Braun, *Teachers and Power*, p. 214; *NYT*, 6/13/68, p. 38;

20. Carter, *Pickets, Parents, and Power*, pp. 68–69.

21. *NYT*, 5/25/68, pp. 1, 20; Stern, in Berube and Gittel, *Confrontation at Ocean Hill–Brownsville*, p. 184.

22. *NYT*, 6/16/68, sect. 4, p. 13.

23. Braun, *Teachers and Power*, p. 214.

24. Mayer, *The Teachers Strike*, p. 51.

25. Berube and Gittel, *Confrontation at Ocean Hill–Brownsville*, pp. 79, 83; Feldman, in Berube and Gittel, *Confrontation at Ocean Hill–Brownsville*, 140; Sandra Feldman interview, p. 20; Jacoby, *Someone Else's House*, pp. 194–196; Podair, *The Strike That Changed New York*, p. 108.

26. Lichtenstein, *State of the Union*, p. 2–3.

27. Toch, "A Speech that Shook the Field," *Education Week*, 3/26/97; Barsh oral history, 11/21/86, p. 7, in NYU Archives; Eadie Shanker interview, 10/18/02, p. 15; Eadie Shanker interview, 2/27/04, p. 2; Adam Shanker interview I, p. 3; WWS, 11/5/89.

28. Mayer, *The Teachers Strike*, p. 244.

29. *NYT Magazine*, 9/3/67, p. 5.

30. *NYT*, 6/10/68, p. 31.

31. Eadie Shanker interview, 10/18/02, p. 8; Eadie Shanker interview, 12/1/03, pp. 1–3, 8; *NYT Magazine*, 9/3/67, p. 5.

32. Eadie Shanker interview, 12/1/03, p. 6.

33. Eadie Shanker interview, 10/18/02, pp. 8, 13; Elaine Sanders interview, pp. 6, 8.

34. Eadie Shanker memo, 3/3/06.

35. Eadie Shanker interview, 12/1/03, p. 5.

36. Eadie Shanker memo, 3/3/06.

37. Hampton and Fayer, *Voices of Freedom*, p. 498; Murphy, *Blackboard Unions*, pp. 243–244; Ravitch, *The Great School Wars*, p. 363.

38. Ferretti, in Berube and Gittel, *Confrontation at Ocean Hill–Brownsville*, p. 286; Mayer, *The Teachers Strike*, p. 59.

39. *NYT*, 9/7/68, pp. 1, 19.

40. *NYT*, 9/8/67, pp. 1, 30.

41. *NYT*, 9/8/67, pp. 1, 30.

42. *NYT*, 9/8/68, pp. 1, 30.

43. *NYT*, 9/9/68, p. 1.

44. *NYT*, 9/10/68, p. 36.

45. *NYT*, 9/11/68, pp. 1, 34.

46. *NYT*, 9/11/68, pp. 1, 34.

47. Mayer, *The Teachers Strike*, p. 70.

48. *NYT*, 9/12/68, pp. 1, 52. See also Diane Ravitch, *The Great School Wars*, pp. 367–368.

49. *NYT*, 9/12/68, pp. 1, 52.

50. Feldman, in Berube and Gittel, *Confrontation at Ocean Hill–Brownsville*, p. 141; Carter, *Pickets, Parents, and Power*, p. 93; *NYT*, 10/23/68, pp. 1, 32; Noah, "Albert Shanker, Statesman," *TNR*, 6/24/85, pp. 17–19; Jacoby, *Someone Else's House*, p. 199; Mayer, *The Teachers Strike*, p. 70; Podair, *The Strike That Changed New York*, p. 117.

51. *NYT*, 9/12/68, pp. 1, 52. See also Goldbloom, in Berube and Gittel, *Confrontation at Ocean Hill–Brownsville*, p. 277; Mayer, *The Teachers Strike*, p. 71.

52. Albert Shanker interview with Shore, p. 4; *NYT*, 2/23/97; *NYT*, 12/20/96, p. B3; Albert Shanker interview with Cowan, p. 149.

53. *NYT*, 9/12/68, pp. 1, 52; *NYT*, 9/16/68, p. 52.

54. *NYT*, 9/16/68, pp. 1, 52; Editorial, *NYT*, 9/16/68, p. 46.

55. Horowitz interview, p. 20.

56. Rustin oral history, p. 8.

57. *NYT*, 9/18/68, pp. 1, 32.

58. *NYT* advertisement, 9/19/68, p. 39, cited in D'Emilio, *Lost Prophet*, pp. 469–470.

59. Levine, *Bayard Rustin*, p. 210.

60. Anderson, *A. Philip Randolph*, p. 313.

61. *NYT Magazine*, 2/16/69, p. 25.

62. *NYT Magazine*, 2/16/69, pp. 25, 107. See also D'Emilio, *Lost Prophet*, p. 471.

63. Levine, *Bayard Rustin*, p. 207.

64. Anderson, *A. Philip Randolph*, pp. xi, 261, 288, 298, 302, 319. See also Goulden, *Meany*, pp. 311–312.

65. Anderson, *A. Philip Randolph*, pp. 313–314; *American Teacher*, 4/97, p. 13. See also *American Educator*, special issue, "The Power of Ideas," Spring–Summer 1997, p. 44.

66. Horowitz interview, pp. 23–25.

67. *American Educator*, special issue, "The Power of Ideas," Spring–Summer 1997, p. 50.

68. Anderson, *Bayard Rustin*, p. 332.

69. *American Educator*, special issue, "The Power of Ideas," Spring–Summer 1997, p. 59.

70. "The Freedom to Teach," paid advertisement, *NYT*, 9/20/68, p. 39. See also advertisement reprinted in Berube and Gittel, *Confrontation at Ocean Hill–Brownsville*, p. 120; Alan Wolfe, *TNR*, 4/3/00.

71. D'Emilio, *Lost Prophet*, pp. 326–327; *NYT*, 12/17/67, p. 1 (on growing white liberal support for Black Power).

72. Neier, *Taking Liberties*, p. xix.

73. Ravitch, *The Great School Wars*, pp. 365–366.

74. *NYT*, 10/11/68, p. 50.

75. Glazer, in Berube and Gittel, *Confrontation at Ocean Hill–Brownsville*, pp. 104–105, 117.

76. Berube and Gittel, *Confrontation at Ocean Hill–Brownsville*, pp. 4–6.

77. Levin, *Community Control of Schools*, p. 298.

78. *NYT*, 10/6/68, p. 40. See also D'Emilio, *Lost Prophet*, p. 469.

79. Breslin, quoted in Berube and Gittel, *Confrontation at Ocean Hill–Brownsville*, p. 147.

80. Stern, in Berube and Gittel, *Confrontation at Ocean Hill–Brownsville*, p. 179.

81. Stern, in Berube and Gittel, *Confrontation at Ocean Hill–Brownsville*, p. 181.

82. Podair, *The Strike That Changed New York*, p. 129.

83. Epstein, in Berube and Gittel, *Confrontation at Ocean Hill–Brownsville*, pp. 320–322.

84. Harrington, *Long Distance Runner*, p. 78.

85. Carter, *Pickets, Parents, and Power*, p. 114.

86. Harrington, in Berube and Gittel, *Confrontation at Ocean Hill–Brownsville*, pp. 132–133.

87. *NYT*, 9/30/68, pp. 1, 50.

88. *NYT*, 9/30/68, pp. 1, 50.

89. *NYT*, 9/30/68, pp. 1, 50; *NYT*, 10/9/68, p. 36.

90. *NYT*, 10/8/68, pp. 1, 38; *NYT*, 10/9/68, pp. 1, 36.

91. *NYT*, 10/15/68, pp. 1, 38.

92. *NYT*, 10/13/68, p .1. See also Ravitch, *The Great School Wars*, p. 374.

93. *NYT*, 10/15/68, pp. 1, 38.

94. *NYT*, 10/15/68, pp. 1, 38.

95. *NYT*, 10/15/68, p. 1.

96. UFT advertisement, *NYT*, 10/15/68, p. 57.

97. Kaufman, *Broken Alliance*, p. 137.

98. Sleeper, *Closest of Strangers*, pp. 77, 90.

99. Kaufman, *Broken Alliance*, p. 137.

100. Puddington, *Commentary*, 7/97; Puddington interview, pp. 9–11.

101. Berube and Gittel, *Confrontation at Ocean Hill–Brownsville*, pp. 165–166; Podair, *The Strike That Changed New York*, p. 124.

102. Shanker, letter to Conigliaro, 10/31/68, in NYU Archives.

103. *NYT*, 10/23/68, pp. 1, 32.

104. Kaufman, *Broken Alliance*, p. 153; Jacoby, *Someone Else's House*, p. 208; Selden, *The Teacher Rebellion*, p. 153; Podair, *The Strike That Changed New York*, p. 124.

105. Berube and Gittel, *Confrontation at Ocean Hill–Brownsville*, p. 168.

106. Kaufman, *Broken Alliance*, p. 154.

107. Jacoby, *Someone Else's House*, p. 209.

108. Ravitch, *The Great School Wars*, p. 369.

109. Jacoby, *Someone Else's House*, p. 210.

110. *NYT*, 12/22/96, p. D5.

111. Berube, *American School Reform*, p. 79, citing Shanker, in Urofsky, *Why Teachers Strike*, p. 160.

112. Shanker, in Urofsky, *Why Teachers Strike*, p. 157.

113. Shanker, in Urofksy, *Why Teachers Strike*, p. 159.

114. Advertisement, *NYT*, 11/11/68, p. 55.

115. Jacoby, *Someone Else's House*, p. 209; Kaufman, *Broken Alliance*, p. 156.

116. Podair, *The Strike That Changed New York*, p. 125.

117. *NYT*, 10/23/68, pp. 1, 32; Jacoby, *Someone Else's House*, p. 214.

118. *NYT*, 10/30/68, p. 1, 16.

119. *NYT*, 11/4/68, p. 52. See also Elaine Sanders interview, p.1.

120. Albert Shanker interview with Shore, p 5

121. *NYT*, 11/9/68, p. 20.

122. *NYT*, 11/9/68, p. 20.

123. Spatz interview, p. 21.

124. Jacoby, *Someone Else's House*, p. 211.

125. Jacoby, *Someone Else's House*, p. 212.

126. Carter, *Pickets, Parents, and Power*, p. 122.

127. Horowitz interview, p. 19.

128. *NYT*, 11/24/68, sect. 4, p. 9.

129. *NYT Magazine*, 2/16/69, pp. 24–25.

130. Urofsky, *Why Teachers Strike*, pp. 24–25.

131. *NYT*, 11/17/68, pp. 1, 47.

132. *NYT*, 11/18/68, pp. 1, 50; *NYT*, 11/20/68, pp. 1, 32 (on identity of the three).

133. *NYT*, 11/18/68, pp. 1, 50.

134. *NYT*, 11/18/68, pp. 1, 50.

135. *NYT*, 11/18/68, pp. 1, 51; Podair, *The Strike That Changed New York*, p. 139.

136. *NYT*, 11/19/68, p. 1; Mosle, *NYT*, 10/27/96, p. 45ff; Fantini, Gittel, and Magat, *Community Control and the Urban School*, p. xiii ("the longest school strike in the nation's history"). WWS, 12/17/95, called it "the longest teacher strike in U.S. history." See also WWS, 12/16/90, "the longest teacher strike in U.S. history." Shanker, interview with Reecer, 2/91, pp. 5–6 ("at that time the longest strike in teacher history"); *International Workers Bulletin*, 3/17/97.

137. Braun, *Teachers and Power*, p. 261.

138. WWS, 8/24/75; Braun, *Teachers and Power*, p. 69.

6. Ocean Hill–Brownsville: The Fallout (1969)

1. *NYT*, 12/12/68, p. 58.

2. *NYT*, 1/16/69 (referencing the December 26 incident).

3. *NYT*, 1/16/69, p. 48; Jacoby, *Someone Else's House*, p. 218.

4. *NYT*, 1/20/69, p. 22.

5. *NYT*, 1/31/69, pp. 1, 77.

6. *NYT*, 1/4/69, p. 56.

7. *NYT*, 1/5/69, p. 43. See also Perlstein, *Justice, Justice*, p. 6.

8. *NYT*, 1/9/69, p. 23.

9. *NYT*, 1/26/69, pp. 1, 59 (citing editorial "last week").

10. *NYT*, 1/17/69, pp. 1, 19. See also the Botein Report, in Berube and Gittel, *Confrontation at Ocean Hill–Brownsville*, p. 174.

11. *NYT*, 1/23/69, pp. 1, 51.

12. *NYT*, 1/26/69, pp. 1, 59.

13. *NYT*, 2/17/69, p. 68.

14. Harris and Swanson, pp. 98 (table 83), 110–111 (table 90).

15. *NYT Magazine*, 4/20/69, p. 124.

16. WWS, 3/23/75.

17. *NYT*, 2/2/69, p. 36.

18. Magat, *Education Week*, 3/26/97.

19. WWS, 10/17/71.

20. WWS, 12/8/74.

21. *NYT*, 2/17/69, pp. 1, 21.

22. Neier, *Taking Liberties*, p. xxviii; Ravitch, *The Great School Wars*, p. 397.

23. Podair, *The Strike That Changed New York*, p. 149.

24. Cannato, *The Ungovernable City*, p. 2; David Halberstam, *Harper's*, 1/69, p. 2.

25. *NYT Magazine*, 4/20/69, p. 124; Kelly interview, pp. 4–5, 7.

26. Cannato, *The Ungovernable City*, p. 428.

27. Eadie Shanker memo, 3/3/06.

28. Podair, *The Strike That Changed New York*, pp. 117–119.

29. Diggins, *The Rise and Fall of the American Left*, p. 232.

30. Stern, in Berube and Gittel, *Confrontation at Ocean Hill–Brownsville*, p. 182.

31. Eadie Shanker interview, 10/24/02.

32. Wrezlin, *A Rebel in Defense of Tradition*, p. 84.

33. Macdonald, *New York Review of Books*, in Berube and Gittel, *Confrontation at Ocean Hill–Brownsville*, pp. 222–228.

34. Harrington, *New York Review of Books*, in Berube and Gittel, *Confrontation at Ocean Hill–Brownsville*, pp. 229–236.

35. *NYT Magazine*, 4/20/69, pp. 121–122.

36. *NYT*, quoted in Hill, *Education Week*, 2/21/96.

37. *American Educator*, special issue, "The Power of Ideas," Spring–Summer 1997, p. 30.

38. Hill, *Education Week*, 2/21/96. See also Albert Shanker interview with Cowan, p. 124; *NYT*, 2/6/69, p. 35; *WP*, 1/28/93, p. A3.

39. Eadie Shanker interview, 10/18/02, p. 36.

40. Sandra Feldman interview, p. 36.

41. *NYT Magazine*, 4/20/69, p. 25.

42. *NYT*, 4/17/69, p. 32.

43. *NYT*, 5/4/69, p. 84; *NYT*, 5/2/69, p. 29 (Marchi a principal architect of the final bill).

44. *NYT*, 5/4/69, p. 84; *NYT*, 6/25/69, p. 26.

45. *NYT*, 6/25/69, p. 26.

46. *NYT*, 1/10/71, p. 1 (referencing earlier dispute).

47. WWS, 11/26/72.

48. Siegel, *The Future Once Happened Here*, p. 44.

49. *NYT*, 5/2/69, p. 29.

50. Braun, *Teachers and Power*, p. 222.

51. Gittel, in Levin, *Community Control of Schools*, p. 117.

52. Kaufman, *Broken Alliance*, p. 161; Sleeper, *Closest of Strangers*, p. 100.

53. Albert Shanker interview with Shore, p. 5.

54. *NYT*, 6/24/80, p. A1; *NYT*, 6/27/80, p. A1.

55. WWS, 2/13/72; Hentoff, *Village Voice*, in Berube and Gittel, *Confrontation at Ocean Hill–Brownsville*, p. 125; Podair, *The Strike That Changed New York*, p. 152.

56. *NYT*, 6/24/80, p. A1; *NYT*, 6/28/80, p. A1.

57. *NYT*, 12/20/96, p. B3.

58. Traub, *NYT Magazine*, 10/6/02, pp. 71–72.

59. O'Neill, in Rubinstein, *Schools Against Children*, p. 183.

60. *NYT*, 10/26/68, p. 25. See also Podair, *The Strike That Changed New York*, p. 232.

61. Braun, *Teachers and Power*, pp. 10, 13.

62. Stern, *Breaking Free*, pp. 8, 23.

63. Shanker interview with Reecer, 2/91, p. 3.

64. Albert Shanker interview with Cowan, p. 123.

65. Lieberman interview, p. 57.

66. Ravitch, *The Great School Wars*, p. 378.

67. Pearl Harris interview, 5/6/03, p. 45.

68. *NYT*, 10/16/68, p. 30; *NYT*, 10/28/68, p. 40 (James Buckley); *NYT*, 10/30/68, p. 33 (Nixon); Berube, *American School Reform*, p. 78 (Nixon); Jacoby, *Someone Else's House*, p. 211.

69. Albert Shanker interview with Shore, p. 3; Albert Shanker interview with Cowan, p. 103.

70. Murphy, *Blackboard Unions*, pp. 230–231, 250.

71. Hill, *Education Week*, 2/21/96.

72. Albert Shanker interview with Shore, p. 5.

73. Shanker, in Urofsky, *Why Teachers Strike*, pp. 186–187.

74. *NYT Magazine*, 2/16/69, p. 105.

75. Rustin, "The Blacks and the Unions," *Harper's*, 5/71, p. 81.

76. Siegel, *The Future Once Happened Here*, p. 42.

7. Rebuilding:
Recruiting the Paraprofessionals, Launching the "Where We Stand" Column, and Seeking Teacher Unity (1969–1972)

1. Phil Kugler interview, p. 3.

2. Shanker interview with Reecer, n.d., p. 1, in Bella Rosenberg papers.

3. *NYT*, 6/25/69, pp. 1, 26; *NYT*, 1/17/69, p. 1.

4. *NYT*, 6/25/69, p. 26; *NYT*, 6/26/69, pp. 1, 30; Albert Shanker interview with Cowan, p. 124.

5. *NYT*, 6/30/69, pp. 1, 27; Carter, *Pickets, Parents, and Power*, p. 154; WWS, 4/2/72.

6. *NYT*, 6/25/69, pp. 1, 26, 27; WWS, 4/2/72.

7. *NYT*, 6/25/69, pp. 1, 26, 27; WWS, 4/2/72; *NYT*, 6/26/69, pp. 1, 30; *NYT*, 6/30/69, pp. 1, 27; Carter, *Pickets, Parents, and Power*, p. 154.

8. *NYT*, 6/25/69, p. 1, 26, 27; *NYT*, 6/26/69, p. 1, 30; Nauman interview, pp. 19–20; Eadie Shanker memo, 3/3/06.

9. *NYT*, 6/25/69, p. 1, 26, 27; *NYT*, 6/26/69, p. 1, 30.

10. Editorial, *NYT*, 6/26/69, p. 40.

11. *NYT*, 6/26/69, pp. 1, 30.

12. *NYT*, 4/23/70, p. 36; Albert Shanker interview with Cowan, p. 136.

13. *NYT*, 4/21/70, pp. 1, 39. See also Eugenia Kemble interview I, p. 17.

14. Albert Shanker interview with Cowan, pp. 143–144.

15. Albert Shanker interview with Cowan, pp. 143–144.

16. Magat, *Unlikely Partners*, p. 115.

17. Eadie Shanker interview, 6/11/02, p. 1.

18. Lipset and Marks, *It Didn't Happen Here*, pp. 88–91.

19. Albert Shanker interview with Cowan, p. 136. See also Decter, *New York Magazine*, 10/25/71, p. 3; *NYT*, 4/21/70, pp. 1, 39; Eadie Shanker interview, 10/18/02, p. 25.

20. Taft, *United They Teach*, p. 219; *American Teacher*, 4/97, p. 14; Eugenia Kemble interview I, pp. 15–16; Magidson interview, p. 21; Barsh oral history, 11/21/86, p. 11, in NYU Archives.

21. Eugenia Kemble interview I, p. 14.

22. Velma Hill oral history, 6/19/86, p. 4, in NYU Archives.

23. Goulden, *Jerry Wurf*, pp. 125, 142, 176.

24. Velma Hill interview, pp. 1, 5–6

25. Albert Shanker interview with Cowan, p. 137; Schierenbeck, *American Teacher*, 4/97, p. 9; Velma Hill interview, p. 14; Decter, *New York Magazine*, 10/25/71, p. 3; Woo, *LA Times Magazine*, 12/1/96, pp. 17ff.

26. Woo, *LA Times Magazine*, 12/1/96, pp. 17ff; *United Teacher*, 6/29/69, p. 2; Albert Shanker interview with Cowan, p. 137.

27. Woo, *LA Times Magazine*, 12/1/96, pp. 17ff; Albert Shanker interview with Cowan, pp. 137–138. See also WWS, 12/15/85; *American Educator*, special issue, "The Power of Ideas," Spring–Summer 1997, p. 15.

28. Velma Hill interview, p. 9.

29. *NYT*, 4/21/70, pp. 1, 39.

30. Albert Shanker interview with Cowan, pp. 138–139.

31. Oliver and McCoy, Letter to Para Professionals of the Ocean Hill Brownsville School District, 4/22/70, in NYU Archives.

32. *NYT*, 4/23/70, p. 46.

33. *NYT*, 4/21/70, pp. 1, 39; Eadie Shanker interview, 10/18/02, p. 25.

34. Bernard Bard, *New York Post*, 5/16/70, p. 22, in NYU Archives.

35. Albert Shanker interview with Cowan, p. 139.

36. Shanker, Letter to UFT Members, 5/19/70, pp. 4, 5, 7, in WSU Archives; *United Teacher*, 5/31/70, pp. 1–2.

37. *NYT*, 6/5/70, p. 12.

38. *NYT*, 6/3/70, p. 48; *NYT*, 8/4/70, p. 28; *UFT News*, 8/7/70, in NYU Archives.

39. Velma Hill oral history, 6/19/86, p. 13, in NYU Archives.

40. *U.S. Newswire*, 2/23/97; UFT Web site, "Al Shanker: A Passionate Teacher," available at http://www.uft.org/about/history/makers/shanker_albert/index4.html.

41. Albert Shanker interview with Cowan, pp. 140–141.

42. Johnson interview, pp. 14–15; Freedman interview, pp. 34–35.

43. Penn Kemble interview, p. 23.

44. Velma Hill interview, p. 16.

45. Weiner, *The Nation*, 9/24/77, p. 276.

46. Johnson interview, pp. 3–4; *WP*, 11/17/88, p. A11.

47. WWS, 12/15/85; *American Educator*, special issue, "The Power of Ideas," Spring–Summer 1997, p. 15.

48. *NYT Magazine*, 9/9/73, p. 74.

49. Paul Buhle, *Taking Care of Business*, pp. 9, 17–18.

50. Penn Kemble interview, pp. 9–10.

51. Penn Kemble interview, pp. 10–11.

52. Christine Kohn, Archives Fellow, George Meany Memorial Archives, conversation with Laura Newland, 5/12/05; Penn Kemble biography, available at USIA Web site: http://dosfan.lib.uic.edu/usia/usiahome/regdirs.htm.

53. Ruth Wattenberg interview, pp. 1–2.

54. Penn Kemble interview, p. 11.

55. Kemble, *Commentary*, 4/71, p. 49.

56. Harrington, *Fragments of the Century*, p. 221; Puddington, *Lane Kirkland*, pp. 49, 137.

57. WWS, 7/25/71.

58. *NYT*, 7/15/69, p. 35.

59. *NYT*, 1/12/70, p. 66.

60. *NYT*, 10/11/69, p. 40.

61. "Albert Shanker: Labor's Educator," WSU, 9/12/02.

62. *NYT*, 10/21/69, p. 47.

63. *NYT*, 6/26/72, p. 47.

64. Eugenia Kemble interview, 6/14/06.

65. *NYT*, 12/16/69, p. 42.

66. Decter, *New York Magazine*, 10/25/71, p. 9.

67. Decter, *New York Magazine*, 10/25/71, p. 20.

68. *NYT*, 2/24/71, pp. 43, 82.

69. Decter, *New York Magazine*, 10/25/71, p. 17.

70. Decter interview, p. 3.

71. *NYT*, 3/20/72, p. 48. See also Perlstein, *Justice, Justice*, p. 45; Shanker, *United Teacher*, 7/31/69, in NYU archives.

72. Perlstein, *Justice, Justice*, p. 44.

73. Letter from Michael Leinwand, president of Jewish Teachers Association, to Shanker, 3/24/72, in NYU Archives.

74. Advertisement, "Statement of UFT President Albert Shanker on the school situation in Canarsie," *NYT*, 10/30/72, p. 20; *NYT*, 10/30/72, p. 25.

75. WWS, 5/20/73.

76. Advertisement, "Statement of UFT President Albert Shanker on the school situation in Canarsie," *NYT*, 10/30/72, p. 20; *NYT*, 10/30/72, p. 25; WWS, 5/20/73.

77. Advertisement, "Statement of UFT President Albert Shanker on the school situation in Canarsie," *NYT*, 10/30/72, p. 20; *NYT*, 10/30/72, p. 25.

78. WWS, 5/20/73. See also Taft, *United They Teach*, p. 232 (Shanker appeared personally in Canarsie).

79. Shanker, in *Learning*, 9/73, p. 103, in NYU archives.

80. *NYT*, 11/2/72, p. 54.

81. *NYT*, 10/30/72, p. 25.

82. Berube interview, pp. 17–18; WWS, 12/13/70; Berube, *American School Reform*, p. 80.

83. *Bill Moyers' Journal*, 4/16/74, p. 4; Podair, *The Strike That Changed New York*, p. 126.

84. Arnold Beichman interview, pp. 2–3; Spatz interview, pp. 1–2. See also *American Teacher*, 4/97, p. 18.

85. Jennie Shanker interview, p. 25.

86. WWS, 12/16/90.

87. WWS, 12/16/90.

88. *NYT*, 12/12/70, p. 35.

89. Urbanski interview, pp. 16–17.

90. Shanker interview with Reecer, n.d., p. 3, in Bella Rosenberg papers.

91. Ravitch, *New Leader*, 2/24/97, 4.

92. Hirsch, op-ed, *WP*, 3/1/97, p. A23.

93. *American Educator*, special issue, "The Power of Ideas," Spring–Summer 1997, p. 1 (on the number of columns); Hill, *Education Week*, 2/21/96 (12/13/70 as starting date); *NYT*, 2/23/97.

94. Eadie Shanker interview, 10/18/02, p. 23.

95. Eadie Shanker interview, 2/27/04, pp. 4, 9; Eadie Shanker memo, 3/3/06.

96. Eadie Shanker interview, 3/22/04, p. 3. See also *NYT Magazine*, 9/3/67, p. 5.

97. Radosh interview, p. 44; Eadie Shanker memo, 3/3/06.

98. Eugenia Kemble interview II, p. 24.

99. *NYT*, 11/5/89, sect. 4a, p. 34.

100. Lawrence interview, p. 24.

101. Adam Shanker interview II, p. 11.

102. Adam Shanker interview II, pp. 10–11; Jennie Shanker interview, p. 39.

103. Velma Hill interview, p. 22.

104. Johnson interview, p. 30.

105. Eugenia Kemble interview I, p. 2.

106. Reecer interview, pp. 10–11; Rosenberg interview I, pp. 16–17.

107. Reecer interview, p. 22; WWS, 12/16/90.

108. Reecer interview, p. 14.

109. See e.g., WWS, 9/10/72.

110. WWS, 12/20/70; WWS, 12/27/70.

111. Reecer interview, p. 2.

112. Kelly interview, p. 37.

113. *NYT*, 8/22/74, p. 40; Hobart interview, p. 21.

114. Spatz interview, pp. 3, 54.

115. Chavez interview, p. 30; Chavez, *An Unlikely Conservative*, p. 248 n. 8.

116. Marcia Reecer interview, p. 1; Rosenberg interview I, pp. 12–13; Eadie Shanker interview, 10/18/02, pp. 47, 49; Eadie Shanker interview, 2/27/04, p. 3; Rita Freedman interview, p. 28; memo from Scott Widmeyer to Albert Shanker, 1/23/86, re: Where We Stand column, WSU Archives, box 4, folder 24.

117. Reecer interview, p. 8.

118. Reecer interview, pp. 1–2, 4–5, 9, 20. See also Eadie Shanker interview, 4/22/03, p. 4; Rosenberg conversation, 4/10/03 (regarding PhD in English literature).

119. Eadie Shanker interview, 10/18/02, p. 49.

120. Eadie Shanker interview, 10/18/02, p. 51.

121. Reecer interview, p. 3. See also Cameron interview, p. 1; Freedman interview, p. 28.

122. Reecer interview, p. 3.

123. Reecer interview, p. 19.

124. Eadie Shanker interview, 10/18/02, p. 48.

125. Reecer interview, p. 8.

126. Reecer interview, pp. 3, 5, 12–13.

127. Sandra Feldman, *NY Teacher*, 3/10/97.

128. Rosenberg interview I, p. 10. See also Spatz interview, p. 52.

129. Trilling, introduction to Orwell, *Homage to Catalonia*, pp. xxi, xix, and xxii.

130. Rosenberg interview III, p. 47.

131. WWS, 12/16/90.

132. *WP*, 1/28/93, p. A3.

133. Woo, *LA Times Magazine*, 12/1/96, pp. 17ff.

134. Lieberman, *The Teacher Unions*, p. 202.

135. Arnold Beichman interview, p. 4.

136. *WP*, 1/28/93, p. A3.

137. Maurice Berube interview, p. 22.

138. *NYT*, 1/15/75, p. 59.

139. Lieberman, *The Teacher Unions*, p. 202.

140. Spatz interview, p. 2.

141. Eadie Shanker interview, 9/17/02, p. 10.

142. LaCour interview, p. 9.

143. Urbanski interview, p. 17.

144. Sanchez interview, pp. 11–12, 33–34.

145. Hobart interview, pp. 1, 8.

146. Gaffney, *Blackboard Warriors*, draft, p. 136.

147. Cortese interview, p. 1.

148. WWS, 6/6/71.

149. Cortese interview, p. 1.

150. Cortese interview, p. 5.

151. *NYT*, 11/8/71, p. 34.

152. *NYT*, 11/16/71, p. 40; Hobart interview, p. 3; *NYT*, 4/1/72, p. 31.

153. Hobart interview, pp. 1, 4–5.

154. *NYT*, 4/1/72, p. 31; Hobart interview, p. 3.

155. *NYT* 4/23/72, p. 44; Hobart interview, pp. 7–8.

156. *NYT*, 5/19/72, p. 39.

157. *NYT*, 6/6/72, p. 49. See also Tom Hobart remarks, "Al Shanker's Induction Into the Labor Hall of Fame," 4/8/03, in Eadie Shanker papers. (Co-president from 5/1/72 through 5/1/73).

158. *NYT*, 3/26/73, p. 35; *NYT*, 7/2/73, pp. 1, 19; *NYT*, 7/17/73, p. 39; Chanin interview, pp. 8, 12.

159. WWS, 4/9/72.

160. *NYT*, 6/26/72, p. 35.

161. *NYT*, 6/29/72, p. 42; Gaffney, *Blackboard Warriors*, draft, pp. 262–264.

162. *NYT*, 7/6/73, p. 20.

163. *NYT*, 6/6/72, p. 35.

164. Selden, *The Teacher Rebellion*, p. 190.

8. Becoming President of the American Federation of Teachers and Battling the New Politics Movement (1972–1974)

1. WWS, 8/30/87; *American Educator*, special issue, "The Power of Ideas," Spring–Summer 1997, p. 50.

2. Penn Kemble interview, pp. 1–6.

3. Penn Kemble interview, pp. 2–3; *United Teacher*, 6/3/66.

4. Foner, *U.S. Labor and the Vietnam War*, pp. 34–36, 163. See also Freeman, *Working-Class New York*, pp. 240–241.

5. Edmund F. Wehrle, "Labor's Longest War," p. 52.

6. Penn Kemble interview, p. 4; Edmund F. Wehrle, "Labor's Longest War"; Kemble, *Commentary*, 4/71, p. 52.

7. Foner, *U.S. Labor and the Vietnam War*, p. 41.

8. Barsh oral history, UFT, 11/21/86, p. 5, in NYU archives.

9. "Executive Board Dissents from AFL-CIO Vietnam Policy," *United Teacher*, 3/15/67, p. 2; "Majority Reports of Adcom for DA to Defeat Resolution on Vietnam," *United Teacher*, 3/15/67, p. 2. In the *United Teacher*, 5/5/67, p. 23, the vote is recorded as 22 to 19.

10. Shanker, letter to the editor, *United Teacher*, 5/5/67, p. 4. See also Jack Mallon, "UFT Flunks President on the Viet War," *The News*, 3/12/67, p. 100, in NYU archives.

11. Shanker, "Arguments in Favor of Position C, Referendum IV," *United Teacher*, 4/70, p. 7 (referring to earlier delegate assembly and referendum on the Vietnam War).

12. Altomare interview II, p. 52.

13. Foner, *U.S. Labor and the Vietnam War*, pp. 57–58, 61.

14. Braun, *Teachers and Power*, pp. 143, 164–165; Selden, *The Teacher Rebellion*, p. 161.

15. Jack Schierenbeck, "Seeing All Sides," UFT Web site.

16. *NYT Magazine*, 9/9/73, p. 83.

17. *NYT Magazine*, 9/9/73, p. 64.

18. Beagle oral history, 8/16/85, pp. 22, 24, in NYU Archives.

19. Goulden, *Jerry Wurf*, p. 187; Foner, *U.S. Labor and the Vietnam War*, pp. 22, 32.

20. Altomare interview II.

21. Drucker, *Max Shachtman*, p. 294.

22. D'Emilio, *Lost Prophet*, pp. 438–439.

23. Levine, *Bayard Rustin*, pp. 189–190.

24. Drucker, *Max Shachtman*, p. 295; Harrington, *Fragments of the Century*, p. 95; Anderson, *A. Philip Randolph*, p. 344.

25. Horowitz interview, p. 66; Rustin, guest WWS, 7/20/75.

26. *NYT*, 6/7/67, p. 15; Kaufman, *Broken Alliance*, pp. 200–201.

27. Puddington interview, p. 4.

28. Foner, *U.S. Labor and the Vietnam War*, p. 45.

29. *NYT*, 10/27/67, pp. 1, 2; *NYT*, 10/30/67, p. 19; *NYT Magazine*, 12/3/67, pp. 49, 177, 179, 184, 194, 195.

30. Mary Temple Kleiman conversation, 10/1/05.

31. Penn Kemble interview, pp. 3–4, 16; Eugenia Kemble interview I, p. 45; Sandra Feldman interview, p. 24; Ronald Radosh interview, p. 23.

32. Foner, *U.S. Labor and the Vietnam War*, pp. 51, 65.

33. Paul Hollander, *Political Pilgrims*, 273.

34. Dorn interview II, p. 13; Michael Lind, *Vietnam*, pp. xi–xii.

35. Perlstein, *Justice, Justice*, p. 62.

36. Berube interview, p. 9.

37. Drucker, *Max Shachtman*, pp. xvi, 1.

38. Eric Chenoweth interview, p. 13. See also Freedman interview, pp. 6–7; Dorn interview I, p. 9; Horowitz interview, p. 32. See also Horowitz interview, pp. 32–33.

39. Diggins, *The Rise and Fall of the American Left*, p. 204; Isserman, *If I Had a Hammer*, p. 57.

40. Lieberman interview, p. 61.

41. Eadie Shanker interview, 10/18/02, pp. 30–31.

42. Shanker, "Statement against Position B," *United Teacher*, 4/70, pp. 6–7.

43. Beichman interview, pp. 11; quoted in David Brooks, "The Happy Cold Warrior: The First 90 Years of Arnold Beichman," *Weekly Standard*, 5/19/03.

44. Beichman interview, p. 18; Beichman, *Washington Times Book Review*, 10/17/04.

45. Lind, *Vietnam*, pp. xv, 76–77, 137–38, 258.

46. John Roche, "Indochina Revisited: The Demise of Liberal Internationalism," *National Review*, 5/3/85.

47. *NYT*, 2/24/71, p. 43.

48. Howe, *TNR*, 9/7/74, p. 9; draft letter to the editor in response to Howe's *TNR* article, NYU Archives.

49. Benson interview, pp. 9–12; Lieberman interview, p. 66. See also Weiner interview, p. 2; Weiner, *New Politics*, Fall 1976, p. 53; Weiner, *Contemporary Education*, Summer 1998, 196ff (citing Lieberman, *The Teacher Unions*).

50. Braun, *Teachers and Power*, p. 143; Selden, *The Teacher Rebellion*, pp. 168–170.

51. Braun, *Teachers and Power*, p. 70, 144; Golin, *The Newark Teachers Strike*, p. 184; Murphy, *Blackboard Unions*, p. 257; Selden, *The Teacher Rebellion*, p. 170.

52. Feldman interview, pp. 30–31.

53. Phil Kugler interview, pp. 13–14; Fondy interview, p. 20 (Miesen); Murphy, *Blackboard Unions*, p. 257; Selden, *The Teacher Rebellion*, p. 171.

54. Shanker, letter to UFT members, 3/18/72, in WSU Archives, box 7, folder 1.

55. Benson interview, p. 13; Chavez interview, p. 9.

56. Selden, "Fight for Union Democracy," *American Teacher*, January 1974, in NYU Archives; Israel Kugler interview, pp. 21–22.

57. H. W. Benson, letter to Albert Shanker, 1/25/74, with article enclosed, in NYU archives.

58. Benson interview, pp. 4–7.

59. Phil Kugler interview, pp. 13–14; Fondy interview, p. 20 (Miesen); Murphy, *Blackboard Unions*, p. 257.

60. Fondy interview, pp. 18–19. See also Sandy Feldman interview.

61. Riordan interview, p. 3.

62. Pat Daly memo, 5/12/06.

63. Braun, *Teachers and Power*, pp. 125, 129.

64. Braun, *Teachers and Power*, pp. 69–70. See also Golin, *The Newark Teachers Strike*, p. 183.

65. Altomare interview II, pp. 48–49; Sandra Feldman interview, pp. 30; Eugenia Kemble interview I, p. 30; Weiner interview, p. 20; Beagle oral history, n.d., NYU Archives, pp. 19–20; Braun, *Teachers and Power*, p. 11.

66. Pat Daly memo, 5/12/06.

67. Kelly interview, p. 17.

68. Kelly interview, p. 37.

69. Merrow interview, p. 9.

70. Sanchez interview, p. 24.

71. Lieberman, *The Teacher Unions*, p. 194; See also Rachelle Horowitz e-mail to author, 7/26/06, that Shanker "liked" Daly.

72. *NYT*, 4/30/72, p. 48.

73. Kaufman, *Henry M. Jackson*, pp. 226, 229.

74. Schlesinger, *The Vital Center*, p. 49; Diggins and Lind, in Diggins, *The Liberal Persuasion*, p. 4.

75. Kaufman, *Henry M. Jackson*, pp. 236–237. See also Lichtenstein, *State of the Union*, p. 188.

76. Shanker, as part of CDM Task Force, press release 2/8/74; Puddington, *Lane Kirkland*, p. 74.

77. Cited in Radosh, *Divided They Fell*, p. 139.

78. Drucker, *Max Shachtman*, p. 308.

79. Selden, *The Teacher Rebellion*, p. 195.

80. WWS, 9/24/72.

81. Horowitz interview, p. 38.

82. Selden, letter to Shanker, 10/25/72, in WSU Archives, box 7, folder 1.

83. WWS, 9/24/72; WWS, 10/22/72.

84. WWS, 9/24/72.

85. WWS, 10/22/72; Shanker, "Commission on Delegate Selection," 9/21/73, in NYU Archives.

86. Shanker, "Commission on Delegate Selection," 9/21/73, in NYU Archives.

87. Green, *Epitaph for American Labor*, p. 124.

88. Harrington, *Fragments of the Century*, pp. 195, 224.

89. Harrington, *Long Distance Runner*, pp. 19–22; Radosh, *Commies*, pp. 138–139; *WP*, 3/25/79, p. D1; Israel Kugler interview, p. 23.

90. Radosh interview, p. 43.

91. Freedman interview, pp. 7–9; *NYT*, 12/31/72, p. 36.

92. Isserman, *The Other American*, p. 299; Drucker, *Max Shachtman*, p. 311.

93. *WSJ*, 12/8/72.

94. Puddington interview, p. 14; Phil Kugler interview, pp. 8–9 (Meany said it was a waste of time for Kugler to go to Selden's AFT, but was impressed when he found out Kugler was going to work for Shanker).

95. Selden, *The Teacher Rebellion*, pp. 196–197; *NYT*, 2/8/73, p. 50.

96. *NYT*, 8/26/73, sect. 4, p. 7.

97. Buhle, *Taking Care of Business*, pp. 93–94; Goulden, *Meany*, p. 7; Muravchik, *Heaven on Earth*, p. 244.

98. Eugenia Kemble, 6/14/06; Goulden, *Meany*, p. 122.

99. Gotbaum interview, p. 9.

100. Golden, *Jerry Wurf*, pp. 8, 56–58, 189–192, 219.

101. Irving Howe, *TNR*, 9/7/74, p. 9.

102. *NYT*, 1/15/75, p. 59; *American Teacher*, 4/97, p.16.

103. Hill, *Education Week*, 2/21/96; *NYT Magazine*, 9/9/73, p. 64. See also Rosenberg interview III, p. 31; Gotbaum interview, p. 10; Horowitz interview, p. 76; Eugenia Kemble interview I, pp. 25–26; *NYT Magazine*, 9/9/73, p. 64; *NYT Magazine*, 9/3/67, p. 30; Eadie Shanker interview, 10/18/02, p. 36; De Leonardis interview, pp. 28–29; Donahue interview, p. 9; Sandra Feldman interview, p. 31.

104. WWS, 3/3/74.

105. Shanker, Executive Council, AFT, 5/10/90, p. 3 in WSU Archives, box State and Fed A-I, folder FEA United 1990–1996.

106. Shanker, in *Bill Moyers' Journal*, 4/16/74, p. 14.

107. Selden, *The Teacher Rebellion*, p. ix.

108. *NYT*, 7/6/73, p. 20.

109. Memorial Service transcript, 4/9/97, p. 4.

110. WWS, 10/28/73.

111. Urban, *Why Teachers Organized*, p. 138.

112. NYSUT History, part 16, "Hand in Hand," available at http://www.nysut.org/history/16hand.html.

113. Shanker, in Marcus and Rivlin, *Conflicts in Urban Education*, p. 147.

114. Hobart interview, p. 5; Gaffney, *Blackboard Warriors*, p. 185.

115. *NYT*, 7/6/73, p. 20.

116. WWS, 7/16/72.

117. Lieberman et al., *The NEA and AFT*, p. 116; Lieberman, *The Teacher Unions*, p. 239. Cameron, *The Inside Story*, p. 69.

118. Shanker, in John Merrow, *NPR*, 1/17/75, p. 15.

119. Lieberman et al., *The NEA and AFT*, p. 117.

120. Shanker in John Merrow, *NPR*, 1/17/75, pp. 15–16.

121. Lieberman et al., *The NEA and AFT*, p. 119; WWS, 1/21/79.

122. *NYT*, 7/1/73, p. 18; *NYT*, 7/2/73, pp. 1, 19; *NYT*, 7/17/73, p. 39

123. *NYT*, 7/17/73, p. 39.

124. *NYT*, 7/2/73, pp. 1, 19.

125. *NYT*, 7/2/73, pp. 1, 19; *NYT*, 7/8/73, sect. 4, p. 7.

126. Selden, *The Teacher Rebellion*, p. 206.

127. Eadie Shanker interview, 4/23/04; Braun, *Teachers and Power*, p. 68; Lieberman et al., *The NEA and AFT*, pp. 107–108.

128. *NYT*, 8/25/73, p. 16.

129. *NYT*, 10/30/73, p. 50.

130. *NYT*, 12/11/73, p. 29; Selden, *The Teacher Rebellion*, pp. 219–220; *WP*, 12/17/73, pp. A1, A25.

131. Dave Selden, *The Teacher Rebellion*, p. 219; *NYT*, 1/15/75, p. 59.

132. *NYT*, 12/20/73, p. 11.

133. AFT Executive Council transcript, 1/20/74, p. 5, in WSU Archives, box 7, folder 4.

134. "Response of the Executive Council to Dave Selden's Attack on the Executive Council and the Policies of the AFT," in WSU Archives, box 7, folder 6.

135. Pearl Harris interview, 5/6/03, p. 46.

136. *NYT*, 3/1/74, p. 61; *NYT*, 3/9/74, p. 18.

137. *NYT*, 4/16/74, p. 35.

138. *NYT*, 8/21/74, p. 16.

139. Eugenia Kemble interview, 6/14/06.

140. *NYT*, 8/21/74, p. 16.

141. Farran interview, p. 24.

142. *NYT*, 8/23/74, p. 32; Selden, *The Teacher Rebellion*, p. 223.

143. Eadie Shanker interview, 10/18/02, p. 37, 41.

144. Newfield and DuBrul, *Permanent Government*, pp. 199–200.

145. Eadie Shanker memo, 3/3/06; Bella Rosenberg interview, 4/4/06; Daly memo, 5/12/06.

146. Ed Flower interview, p. 59.

147. Velma Hill interview, pp. 27–28.

148. Pat Daly memo, 5/12/06.

9. "A Man by the Name of Albert Shanker":
Sleeper and the Controversy of Power (1973–1975)

1. *American Teacher*, 4/97, p. 4; Phil Kugler interview, p. 16; Farran interview, p. 23; Eugenia Kemble interview I, p. 3.

2. Farran interview, p. 2.

3. Farran interview, pp. 3–4, 10–13.

4. *NYT*, 8/23/74, p. 32; Report on 1974 AFT Convention, box 7, folder 6, WSU Archives.

5. Humphrey interview, pp. 1–4.

6. Eugenia Kemble interview, 6/14/06.

7. Shanker, address, Institute for Education Policy Studies, 3/10/80, p. 4, in WSU Archives, box 63, folder 47; Humphrey interview, pp. 6–7; Cameron, *The Inside Story*, p. 38.

8. WWS, 8/22/76; Shanker, Address, Institute for Education Policy Studies, 3/10/80, in WSU Archives, box 63, folder 47.

9. Newfield and DuBrul, *The Permanent Government*, p. 72.

10. *NYT Magazine*, 9/9/73, p. 64.

11. *NYT Magazine*, 9/9/73, p. 67.

12. Albert Shanker interview with Cowan, pp. 130–131.

13. Horowitz interview, p. 26.

14. AFT, *Building on the Past for a Better Future* (video) (1990).

15. Horowitz interview, p. 38. See also Phil Kugler interview, p. 11.

16. McElroy interview, p. 12.

17. Horowitz interview, pp. 10–11, 41–42.

18. Farran interview, p. 14.

19. Humphrey interview, pp. 10–13.

20. Phil Kugler interview, p. 5.

21. Phil Kugler interview, p. 17; Shanker, quoted in *U.S. News & World Report*, 4/5/76, p. 90.

22. WWS, 10/28/73.

23. Phil Kugler interview, p. 45.

24. Cole interview, pp. 6–9.

25. Cole interview, pp. 9–10, 13, 20.

26. Cole interview, pp. 10–12.

27. Cole interview, pp. 10–12.

28. Chaykin interview, p. 22.

29. *NYT*, 8/28/77, p. 30; Weiner, *The Nation*, 9/24/77, p. 276.

30. Rosenberg interview III, p. 4; Lieberman, *The Teacher Unions*, p. 26 (497,237 of 907,430, or 54.8 percent were current K–12 teachers).

31. Shanker, address, National Press Club, 9/24/74, in WSU Archives, box 63, folder 9, pp. 1–2, 7–8, 10; *NYT*, 9/25/74, p. 45.

32. WWS, 9/8/74.

33. Humphrey interview, pp. 9–10; Kelly interview, pp. 11–12; Kirst interview, p. 15; Eugenia Kemble interview II, pp. 59–60.

34. Shanker, "Public Schools and Preschool Programs: A Natural Connection," 6/5/75, pp. 3, 6, 11; *NYT*, 6/6/75, p. 36.

35. Morgan, *Journal of Policy History* 13, no. 2 (2001), p. 237.

36. *NYT*, 7/14/75, p. 17.

37. WWS, 11/11/90; WWS, 11/3/96, citing Hirsch.

38. Kirst interview, pp. 15–16.

39. *NYT*, 8/22/74, p. 40.

40. *NYT Book Review*, 5/2/04, p. 16.

41. *NYT*, 6/8/83, p. A23.

42. *NYT*, 4/16/74, p. 79.

43. WWS, 4/14/74.

44. Jennie Shanker interview, p. 25.

45. *Bill Moyers' Journal*, 4/16/74, pp. 1–2.

46. *Bill Moyers' Journal*, 4/16/74, pp. 8, 12.

47. *Bill Moyers' Journal*, 4/16/74, p. 13.

48. *Bill Moyers' Journal*, 4/16/74, p. 16.

49. Bard, *PDK*, 3/75, p. 467.

50. *Time*, 9/22/75.

51. *NYT*, 1/15/75, p. 59.

52. *NYT*, 8/22/74, p. 40.

53. Eugenia Kemble interview I, p. 25; Eugenia Kemble interview II, p. 59.

54. *NYT Book Review*, 5/2/04, p. 16.

55. *Bill Moyers' Journal*, 4/16/74, p. 15.

56. Benson interview, pp. 7–8. See also Weiner, *Union Democracy Review*, 5/85, p. 4.

57. Lipset et al., *Union Democracy*, p. 9.

58. *NYT Magazine*, 9/3/67, p. 5.

59. Irons interview, p. 14.

60. Magidson interview, p. 40.

61. Lipset et al., *Union Democracy*, pp. 11, 414; Benson interview, p. 20.

62. Benson interview, p. 12. See also Benson, UDR #36, cited in Weiner, letter to the editor, *Union Democracy Review*, 5/85, p. 4.

63. Spatz interview, p. 45.

64. Diane Ravitch interview, pp. 13–14.

65. Lieberman, *The Teacher Unions*, p. 194.

66. Chaykin interview, p. 21.

67. Dorn interview, p. 29.

68. Farran interview, p. 35.

69. Muravchik interview, pp. 16–17; Bardake interview, p. 32.

70. Burnie Bond interview, pp. 6, 19.

71. Eric Chenoweth interview, pp. 16–17.

72. Horowitz interview, p. 77.

73. Chavez interview, pp. 16–18.

74. Chavez interview, pp. 16–18.

75. Judy Bardacke interview, p. 31.

76. Burnie Bond interview, p. 10. See also Velma Hill interview, pp. 10–11, 22.

77. Rosenberg interview I, p. 58.

78. Humphrey interview, p. 4.

79. Eugenia Kemble interview II, p. 26.

80. Rosenberg interview III, pp. 37, 42. See also Chavez interview, p. 16.

81. Murphy, *Blackboard Unions*, pp. 265–266.

82. Horowitz interview, p. 79.

83. Dorn interview I, p. 26. *NYT*, 2/23/97. Mosle, *NYT Magazine*, 1/4/98, p. 38. Dorn interview I, p. 27. Adam Shanker interview II, p. 8.

84. *NYT*, 11/5/89, sect. 4a, p. 34. See also Eadie Shanker interview, 10/18/02, pp. 22–23.

85. Goldberg interview, p. 12.

86. Memorial Service transcript, 4/9/97, p. 8.

87. Hobart interview, p. 20.

88. Rosenberg interview III, pp. 42–43.

89. Reecer interview, p. 19.

90. Eadie Shanker interview, 10/18/02, p. 3.

91. Rosenberg interview I, pp. 48–49.

92. Lieberman, *The Teacher Unions*, p. 192.

93. Cameron interview, p. 10.

94. Eugenia Kemble e-mail to author, 4/19/06.

95. Pat Daly memo, 5/12/06.

10. Losing Power:
The New York Fiscal Crisis and the Decline of Labor (1974–1976)

1. Schierenbeck, "Union Made a World of Difference," p. 13.

2. *NYT Magazine*, 9/9/73, pp. 72, 74.

3. Albert Shanker interview with Cowan, p. 130; Eugenia Kemble interview, 6/14/06.

4. Newfield and DuBrul, *Permanent Government*, pp. 158, 160.

5. Editorial, *NYT*, 7/22/75, p. 30.

6. WWS, 8/17/75. See also *NYT*, 8/18/75, p. 48.

7. *NYT*, 9/9/75, pp. 1, 30; *NYT*, 12/12/74, p. 1. See also *NYT*, 7/2/85, p. A1 (first city layoffs since the Depression).

8. *NYT*, 9/5/75, p. 20.

9. *NYT*, 9/30/75, p. 30. See also Feldman, *NY Teacher*, 3/10/97 (Shanker had great doubts regarding 1975 strike).

10. WWS, 9/14/75.

11. Sandra Feldman interview, pp. 34–35.

12. *NYT*, 9/9/75, pp. 1, 30. See also WWS, 9/14/75.

13. Albert Shaker interview with Cowan, pp. 133–134.

14. *NYT*, 9/17/75, pp. 1, 28; *NYT*, 7/2/85, p. A1 (ten-year anniversary); Freeman, *Working-Class New York*, p. 265.

15. Newfield and DuBrul, *Permanent Government*, p. 158.

16. Newfield and DuBrul, *Permanent Government*, pp. 159–160.

17. *NYT*, 9/17/75, pp. 1, 28; *NYT*, 7/2/85, p. A1 (ten-year anniversary); Freeman, *Working-Class New York*, p. 265.

18. *NYT*, 9/17/75, pp. 1, 28.

19. *NYT*, 9/17/75, pp. 1, 28.

20. *NYT*, 10/8/75, pp. 1, 38. See also Newfield and DuBrul, *Permanent Government*, p. 160.

21. Editorial, *NYT*, 10/10/75, p. 36.

22. *NYT*, 10/13/75, p. 1.

23. *NYT*, 10/18/75, pp. 1, 18.

24. *NYT*, 10/18/75, pp. 1, 18; *NYT*, 10/18/75, pp. 1, 16; *NYT*, 12/27/02, p. B1; Richard Ravitch interview, p. 7; *Newsweek*, 10/27/75, pp. 16ff.

25. *Newsweek*, 10/27/75, pp. 16ff.

26. *NYT*, 10/18/75, pp. 1, 16.

27. *NYT*, 10/18/75, p. 1, 18; *NYT*, 10/18/75, pp. 1, 16; *NYT*, 12/27/02, p. B1; *Newsweek*, 10/27/75, p.16ff.

28. *NYT*, 10/18/75, p. 1, 18.

29. *NYT*, 10/18/75, pp. 1, 16.

30. Ravitch interview, p. 8.

31. *NYT*, 10/18/75, p. 1, 18; *NYT*, 10/18/75, pp. 1, 16; *NYT*, 12/27/02, p. B1; *Newsweek*, 10/27/75, pp. 16ff.

32. *NYT*, 10/18/75, pp. 1, 16.

33. *Newsweek*, 10/27/75, p. 16ff.

34. Freeman, *Working-Class New York*, p. 268.

35. Newfield and DuBrul, *Permanent Government*, pp. 56–57.

36. *NYT*, 12/27/02, p. B1.

37. *NYT*, 10/18/75, pp. 1, 16.

38. *NYT*, 10/18/75, pp. 1, 16.

39. WWS, 10/19/75.

40. *International Workers Bulletin*, 3/17/97. Gibson interview, p. 5.

41. Magidson interview, p. 22.

42. *NYT*, 10/5/01, p. B10.

43. Freeman, *Working Class New York*, p. 267.

44. Referred to in *New York Daily News*, 10/20/02.

45. WWS, 11/2/75.

46. Albert Shanker interview with Cowan, p. 133.

47. Podair, *The Strike That Changed New York*, p. 194; Lois Weiner, *The Nation*, 9/24/77, p. 276.

48. Murphy, *Blackboard Unions*, p. 266.

49. Freeman, *Working-Class New York*, p. 266.

50. WWS, 12/7/75.

51. WWS, 4/18/76.

52. WWS, 5/9/76; WWS, 8/8/76; WWS, 8/29/76.

53. *NYT*, 8/6/77, p. 20; Auletta, *The Streets Were Paved with Gold*, pp 185–186, 299.

54. Albert Shanker interview with Cowan, pp. 131–132.

55. Albert Shanker interview with Cowan, p. 135.

56. Geiger interview, p. 17.; Gaffney, *Blackboard Warriors*, draft, pp. 306, 321–322.

57. Gaffney, *Blackboard Warriors*, draft, pp. 315–321.

58. Cortese interview, p. 11.

59. WWS, 1/11/76.

60. Gaffney, *Blackboard Warriors*, draft, p. 323.

61. Chaykin interview, p. 29.

62. Hobart interview, pp. 16–17.

63. Shanker, "Keep the Clock," 3/6/76, pp. 10–11, 15.

64. Gaffney, *Blackboard Warriors*, draft, p. 325.

65. Shanker, "Keep the Clock," 3/6/76, pp. 15–16.

66. Cortese interview, p. 12.

67. Gaffney, *Blackboard Warriors*, draft, p. 327. See also Hobart interview, p. 17.

68. Hobart interview, pp. 13–14; *NYT*, 3/7/76, p. 31.

69. *Education Week*, 5/17/06, p.5

70. Bard, *PDK*, 3/75, p. 467; *People*, 11/3/75, pp. 14–15.

71. Eadie Shanker memo, 3/3/06.

72. Eadie Shanker interview, 10/18/02, p. 37.

73. Adam Shanker interview I, pp. 1, 3–4, 7–8, 11–12, 23, 34.

74. Eadie Shanker interview, 10/18/02, p. 16; Jennie Shanker interview, pp. 5–6, 28.

75. *WP*, 11/5/89, p. E2; *NYT*, 11/5/89, sect. 4a, p. 34.

76. Farran interview, pp. 33–35.

77. Eadie Shanker interview, 10/18/02, p. 52.

78. Eadie Shanker interview, 10/18/02, p. 31; Jennie Shanker interview, pp. 33–34, 47; Eadie Shanker memo, 3/3/06.

79. Albert Shanker interview with Cowan, p. 84.

80. Michael Shanker interview, pp. 1, 3, 18.

81. Eadie Shanker interview, 10/18/02, p. 20.

82. Adam Shanker interview I, pp. 4, 7; Adam Shanker interview II, pp. 6, 10; Eadie Shanker memo, 3/3/06.

83. Jennie Shanker interview, p. 3.

84. Michael Shanker interview, pp. 1, 4.

85. Michael Shanker interview, pp. 5–6.

86. Adam Shanker interview I, p. 4.

87. Michael Shanker interview, p. 20.

88. Eadie Shanker interview, 10/18/02, p. 19; Carl Sabath interview, p. 10; Adam Shanker interview I, p. 9.

89. Adam Shanker interview I, p. 10.

90. Eadie Shanker, in joint foreign policy interview, p. 28.

91. Albert Shanker interview with Cowan, pp. 82–83.

92. Jennie Shanker interview, pp. 3–4, 12, 47.

93. Judy Bardacke interview, p. 23.

94. Adam Shanker interview I, pp. 7, 12, 26.

95. Michael Shanker interview, p. 2, 7, 12–14.

96. Michael Shanker interview, pp. 20–22.

97. Eric Chenoweth interview, pp. 34–36.

98. Eadie Shanker interview, 10/18/02, p. 19.

99. Jennie Shanker interview, pp. 33–34, 47.

100. Weiner interview, pp. 25–26; Feldman interview, p. 44. The allegation that Shanker had extramarital affairs was also raised by a number of union staff members in interviews. All insisted on anonymity.

101. Eadie Shanker memo, 3/3/06.

102. Michael Shanker interview, p. 7.

103. Eadie Shanker memo, 3/3/06.

104. Michael Shanker interview, p. 2.

105. Adam Shanker interview I, pp. 31, 33.

106. Baer, *Reinventing Democrats*, p. 25.

107. Ruy Teixeira, *Public Opinion Watch*, 7/28/04.

108. Decter, letter to Albert Shanker, 11/7/72, in NYU Archives.

109. CDM, "Come Home Democrats," in NYU Archives.

110. Memo from Bardacke re: CDM, 2/2/73, in NYU Archives.

111. Shanker, statement submitted to the DNC's Commission on Delegate Selection and Party Structure, 9/21/73, in NYU Archives.

112. Radosh, *Divided They Fell*, pp. 131, 176.

113. Shanker, statement submitted to the DNC's Commission on Delegate Selection and Party Structure, 9/21/73, in NYU Archives.

114. California Teachers Association, "Fed Facts," 3/75, p. 2, in WSU Archives, box State Fed A-I; folder CA Fed Teachers 1974–6.

115. Penn Kemble interview, p. 14.

116. WWS, 12/22/74. See also WWS, 1/26/75.

117. *NYT*, 12/9/74, pp. 1, 45. See also Shanker, in John Merrow, NPR, 1/17/75, p. 17.

118. Kaufman, *Henry M. Jackson*, p. 314.

119. WWS, 12/22/74. See also WWS, 1/26/75.

120. Spatz interview, p. 52.

121. *DeFunis v. Odegaard*, 416 U.S. 312, 324 (1974); Fishkin, *Justice, Equal Opportunity*, p. 90.

122. WWS, 5/13/73.

123. WWS, 7/16/72.

124. Buhle, *Taking Care of Business*, p. 189.

125. Aronowitz, *How Class Works*, p. 125.

126. *DeFunis v. Odegaard*, 416 U.S. 312, 313 (1974).

127. WWS, 8/25/74.

128. *DeFunis v. Odegaard*, 416 U.S. 312, 331 (1974).

129. *NYT*, 8/21/76, p. 18.

130. Shanker, interview, *USA Today*, 2/15/83, p. 11A. See also WWS, 1/26/75.

131. Lukas, *Common Ground*, pp. 245, 269, 499.

132. Rosenberg interview I, pp. 20–21.

133. Rosenberg interview I, p. 20; Spatz interview, p. 47.

134. *NYT*, 1/15/75, p. 59.

135. *NYT*, 7/16/75, p. 32.

136. Sandra Feldman interview, pp. 25–26; Horowitz interview, pp. 12–14, 30.

137. Kaufman, *Henry M. Jackson*, pp. 302, 316.

138. Kaufman, *Henry M. Jackson*, photos.

139. *Bill Moyers' Journal*, 4/16/74, p. 8; *NYT*, 3/9/74, p. 33.

140. Prochnau and Larsen, *A Certain Democrat*, pp. 127, 133–34, 346.

141. Prochnau and Larsen, *A Certain Democrat*, p. 344.

142. Kaufman, *Henry M. Jackson*, pp. 110, 216–217.

143. Kaufman, *Henry M. Jackson*, p. 318–327.

144. *NYT*, 3/25/76, p. 30.

145. *NYT*, 3/25/76, p. 30.

146. WWS, 4/4/76; Kaufman, *Henry M. Jackson*, pp. 327–328.

147. Kaufman, *Henry M. Jackson*, pp. 329–330.

148. Kaufman, *Henry M. Jackson*, pp. 5–6, 302.

149. Prochnau and Larsen, *A Certain Democrat*, pp. 156–157, 179.

150. Kaufman, *Henry M. Jackson*, p. 321.

11. Jimmy Carter and the Rise of the Reagan Democrats (1976–1980)

1. *NYT*, 8/20/76, p. 25.

2. WWS, 6/5/77.

3. WWS, 6/12/77.

4. NCES, *Digest of Education Statistics 2005*, table 156.

5. WWS, 11/12/78.

6. Puddington, *Lane Kirkland*, p. 78.

7. White, in Guttman, *Freedom of Association*, pp. 336–338; Guttman, in Guttman, *Freedom of Association*, pp. 29–30.

8. Kahlenberg, *American Prospect*, 9/11/00.

9. Geoghegan, *Which Side Are You On?*, p. 255.

10. Puddington, *Lane Kirkland*, p. 259.

11. Puddington, *Lane Kirkland*, pp. 83, 102.

12. Puddington, *Lane Kirkland*, p. 259.

13. Puddington, *Lane Kirkland*, p. 85; WWS, 2/26/78; Geoghegan, *Which Side Are You On?*, pp. 278, 284.

14. AFT Convention, Boston, 8/77, in *American Educator*, special issue, "The Power of Ideas," Spring–Summer 1997, p. 10.

15. AFT Convention, Boston, 8/77, in *American Educator*, special issue, "The Power of Ideas," Spring–Summer 1997, p. 8.

16. Humphrey interview, p. 31.

17. Donahue interview, p. 5.

18. Rustin, guest WWS, 7/17/77.

19. Puddington interview, p. 7; Freeman and Medoff, *What Do Unions Do?*, p. 204; Lind, in Fraser and Gerstle, *Ruling America*, p. 273; Puddington, *Lane Kirkland*, p. 87.

20. Freeman and Medoff, *What Do Unions Do?*, p. 204, table 13-4.

21. AFT Convention Proceedings, 8/78, in *American Educator*, special issue, "The Power of Ideas," Spring–Summer 1997, p. 12.

22. WWS, 11/2/80.

23. Joyce interview, p. 10. See also Puddington, *Lane Kirkland*, p. 78.

24. WWS, 10/7/79.

25. Finn interview, p. 3.

26. Pearl Harris, 5/6/03, p. 47.

27. Ed Flower interview, pp. 59–60.

28. *American Teacher* 4/97, p. 24; *American Educator*, special issue, "The Power of Ideas," Spring–Summer 1997, p. 112.

29. Califano, *Governing America*, p. 306; WWS, 10/12/80; WWS, 8/6/78.

30. Finn interview, p. 4; WWS, 3/5/78; Califano, *Governing America*, p. 305.

31. Eugenia Kemble interview II, p. 5; *American Teacher*, 4/97, p. 4.

32. WWS, 3/5/78; WWS, 3/12/78; Califano, *Governing America*, p. 302.

33. WWS, 11/2/81.

34. WWS, 11/2/81.

35. *American Teacher*, 4/97, p. 3.

36. WWS, 3/5/78.

37. WWS, 10/12/80.

38. WWS, 4/16/78.

39. WWS, 1/25/81; *American Educator*, special issue, "The Power of Ideas," Spring–Summer 1997, p. 102.

40. *NYT*, 8/22/78, p. 56.

41. Humphrey interview, pp. 28–30. See also Lawrence J. McAndrews, "Late and Never," 467ff (quoting Rachelle Horowitz: "A candidate who supports tuition tax credits will not get AFT backing" in 1982 elections).

42. Califano, *Governing America*, p. 307. WWS, 10/12/80.

43. Bell, *The Thirteenth Man*, pp. 91 92.

44. Califano, *Governing America*, pp. 274–275.

45. Humphrey interview, pp. 33–34.

46. WWS, 3/4/79; Cross, *Political Education*, p. 62; Heffernan, *Cabinetmakers*, p. 195.

47. Quoted in Califano, *Governing America*, p. 284.

48. Heffernan, *Cabinetmakers*, p. 410.

49. Cross, *Political Education*, p. 58.

50. Heffernan, *Cabinetmakers*, p. 321.

51. Heffernan, *Cabinetmakers*, p. 37.

52. Humphrey interview, pp. 33–34.

53. WWS, 7/11/76. See also Heffernan, *Cabinetmakers*, p. 37.

54. Heffernan, *Cabinetmakers*, p. 76.

55. Califano, *Governing America*, p. 278.

56. Heffernan, *Cabinetmakers*, p. 351.

57. WWS, 6/12/77.

58. WWS, 7/11/76.

59. WWS, 4/29/79.

60. Califano, *Governing America*, p. 288.

61. Obey article, circulated by Rachelle Horowitz, 5/17/78, in WSU Archives, box 1, folder 26; See also Heffernan, *Cabinetmakers*, p. 436.

62. Califano, *Governing America*, p. 277; Heffernan, *Cabinetmakers*, pp. 80–81.

63. Califano, *Governing America*, pp. 276–277; Cross, *Political Education*, pp. 56–57.

64. Califano, *Governing America*, p. 277.

65. Califano, *Governing America*, pp. 281–283; Heffernan, *Cabinetmakers*, p. 82.

66. Cross, *Political Education*, p. 58.

67. Heffernan, *Cabinetmakers*, pp. 162–163.

68. Heffernan, *Cabinetmakers*, p. 75.

69. Califano, *Governing America*, p. 285; Cross, *Political Education*, p. 64; Heffernan, *Cabinetmakers*, pp. 387–392, 402–403.

70. Humphrey interview, p. 8; Heffernan, *Cabinetmakers*, p. 317.

71. Smith interview, pp. 11–12, 15; *WP*, 6/27/79, p. A1.

72. Smith interview, pp. 11–12, 15; *WP*, 6/27/79, p. A1; Califano, *Governing America*, p. 287.

73. Smith interview, pp. 13–16; Califano, *Governing America*, pp. 288–290.

74. *WP*, 6/27/79, p. A1; Editorial, *WP*, 7/1/79; Califano, *Governing America*, p. 287.

75. Califano, *Governing America*, p. 291; Cross, *Political Education*, p. 64; Heffernan, *Cabinetmakers*, p. 461.

76. Phil Kugler interview, p. 59.

77. Kelly interview, p. 11.

78. Raspberry, quoted in WWS, 4/27/80.

79. WWS, 3/16/80.

80. Jeffries, *Justice Powell*, p. 455.

81. Califano, *Governing America*, p. 242.

82. *NYT*, 8/19/77, p. 13; Murphy, *Blackboard Unions*, p. 264; Kelly interview, p. 7.

83. Chanes, "Affirmative Action: Jewish Ideals, Jewish Interests," p. 303.

84. Kahlenberg, *The Remedy*, p. 25.

85. *NYT*, 9/25/77, pp. 1, 28.

86. *NYT*, 9/25/77, pp. 1, 28.

87. Chanes, "Affirmative Action: Jewish Ideals, Jewish Interests," p. 303.

88. WWS, 3/27/77.

89. WWS, 9/25/77; *American Educator*, special issue, "The Power of Ideas," Spring–Summer 1997, p. 41.

90. *NYT*, 9/25/77, pp. 1, 28.

91. *NYT*, 8/24/77, pp. A1, A12.

92. WWS, 7/9/78.

93. Diggins, *The Rise and Fall of the American Left*, p. 213.

94. WWS, 9/25/77; *American Educator*, special issue, "The Power of Ideas," Spring–Summer 1997, p. 42.

95. *U.S. Steelworkers of America v. Weber*, 443 U.S. 193 (1979).

96. *WP*, 12/22/78, p. E2.

97. Albert Shanker interview, p. 3.

98. Albert Shanker interview, p. 3.

99. Green, *Epitaph for American Labor*, pp. 10, 106–107.

100. WWS, 5/20/79.

101. *NYT*, 10/3/77, p. 27.

102. *NYT*, 9/25/77, p. 32.

103. WWS, 9/11/77.

104. *NYT*, 9/25/77, p. 32.

105. *NYT*, 9/25/77, p. 32; *NYT*, 10/3/77, p. 27; *NYT*, 12/2/77, sect. 2, p. 3.

106. *NYT*, 9/25/77, p. 32; *NYT*, 10/3/77, p. 27; WWS, 10/2/77.

107. *NYT*, 12/7/78, pp. A1, B15; *NYT*, 6/27/80, p. A1.

108. *NYT*, 12/2/77, sect. 2, p. 3.

109. *NYT*, 12/7/78, pp. A1, B15.

110. WWS, 8/24/80.

111. *NYT*, 7/16/75, p. 32; Rogers and Chung, *110 Livingston Street Revisited*, p. 21. See also WWS, 6/18/72 (on job insecurity and bilingual education).

112. WWS, 8/24/80; *American Educator*, special issue, "The Power of Ideas," Spring–Summer 1997, p. 90.

113. Humphrey interview, pp. 31–32.

114. WWS, 11/3/74.

115. Califano, *Governing America*, p. 313.

116. WWS, 8/24/80; Chavez, *An Unlikely Conservative*, p. 134.

117. *American Educator*, special issue, "The Power of Ideas," Spring–Summer 1997, p. 89; WWS, 8/24/80.

118. Califano, *Governing America*, p. 313; WWS, 4/10/83; WWS, 9/24/80, p. A9.

119. Chavez, *An Unlikely Conservative*, pp. 10–11.

120. Kaufman, *Henry M. Jackson*, pp. 352, 358. See also Baer, *Reinventing Democrats*, p. 31.

121. Kaufman, *Henry M. Jackson*, pp. 369–370; Gershman interview, pp. 20–21; Magidson interview, p. 33; Miller interview, p. 11; Kaufman, *Henry M. Jackson*, pp. 5, 353, citing Muravchik, *The Uncertain Crusade*, pp. 1–4.

122. Kaufman, *Henry M. Jackson*, p. 353; Shanker, address to Social Democrats USA, 12/5/82, pp. 1–2, in WSU Archives, box 63, folder 71.

123. Kaufman, *Henry M. Jackson*, p. 354. See also Leo Cherne, speech accepting John Dewey Award, 5/20/78, p. 13, in NYU Archives.

124. *American Educator*, special issue, "The Power of Ideas," Spring–Summer 1997, p. 41.

125. Shanker, quoted in *American Teacher*, 4/97, p. 10.

126. WWS, 12/30/79.

127. WWS, 5/11/75.

128. Shanker, letter to Cherne, 3/13/78; Cherne speech accepting John Dewey Award, 5/20/78, in NYU Archives.

129. Levine, *Bayard Rustin*, p. 234.

130. WWS, 12/31/78.

131. WWS, 10/21/79.

132. Eugenia Kemble interview.

133. Kaufman, *Henry M. Jackson*, p. 355.

134. Shanker, address to Social Democrats USA, 12/5/82, pp. 1–2, in WSU Archives, box 63, folder 71.

135. Chenoweth interview.

136. Puddington, *Lane Kirkland*, p. 108; Califano, *Governing America*, p. 292; *WP*, 1/21/80, p. A5.

137. *U.S. News & World Report*, 11/26/76, p. 91.

138. Phil Kugler interview, p. 58.

139. Horowitz interview, pp. 51–52.

140. Jimmy Carter Library and Museum, President's Daily Diary, available online at http://www.jimmycarterlibrary.org/documents/diary/index.phtml.

141. Horowitz interview, p. 53.

142. Horowitz interview, p. 53.

143. *NYT*, 7/11/80, p. B1; *NYT*, 3/17/80, pp. A1, A16.

144. WWS, 3/23/80.

145. *NYT*, 7/11/80, p. B1.

146. *NYT*, 7/11/80, p. B1.

147. *NYT*, 6/26/83, sect. 4, p. 22; Califano, *Governing America*, p. 292.

148. *NYT*, 8/13/80, p. B2.

149. *WP*, 8/16/80, p. A11.

150. *NYT*, 8/15/80, p. B3.

151. *NYT*, 8/22/80, p. B7; *WP*, 8/22/80, p. A3.

152. *WP*, 8/23/80, p. A5; *NYT*, 8/23/80, p. A8; *NYT*, 3/17/80, p. A1.

153. Chavez interview, p. 10; Kaufman, *Henry M. Jackson*, pp. 398–399; Kristol, *Neoconservatism*, p. 37; Simms, *Workers of the World Undermined*, p. 47.

154. WWS, 10/24/82.

155. *American Educator*, special issue, "The Power of Ideas," Spring–Summer 1997, p. 106; Eadie Shanker interview, 10/18/02, p. 34; Pearl Harris interview, 5/6/03, p. 47; Sandra Feldman interview, p. 38.

156. Rosenberg interview III, pp. 40–42.

157. Branch, *At Canaan's Edge*, p. 400.

158. Puddington, *Lane Kirkland*, p. 227.

159. Shanker, address to Social Democrats USA, 12/5/82, pp. 2–4, in WSU Archives, box 63, folder 71.

160. Shanker, letter to the editor, *NYT*, 9/27/81, sect. 4, p. 18.

161. Lipset, cited in Harrington, *Toward a Democratic Left*, p. 9.

162. Teixeira, *Donkey Rising*, 7/24/04 (Reagan won an average of 61 percent of white working-class voters in 1980 and 1984).

163. Rieder, *Canarsie*, p. 5.

164. Lind, in Fraser and Gerstle, *Ruling America*, pp. 258–262.

12. Being a Social Democrat Under Ronald Reagan: Domestic Policy (1980–1988)

1. *NYT*, 2/20/81, p. A10; WWS, 2/22/81.

2. WWS, 10/10/71.

3. WWS, 10/17/71.

4. *NYT*, 3/5/81, p. B12.

5. WWS, 6/7/81.

6. WWS, 5/29/83.

7. WWS, 4/11/82.

8. *WP*, 3/5/83, p. A5.

9. *NYT*, 11/11/80, p. A1.

10. *NYT*, 1/4/81, sect. 12, p. 1.

11. *NYT*, 6/2/81, p. B11.

12. WWS, 10/12/80.

13. WWS, 4/11/82.

14. *WP*, 9/23/81, p. A8.

15. WWS, 4/18/82.

16. See, e.g., Senator Chafee, in *WP*, 5/25/83, p. A8.

17. WWS, 9/19//82.

18. WWS, 3/17/85.

19. *NYT*, 8/16/83, p. A12.

20. *WP*, 11/17/83, p. A1.

21. WWS, 5/10/81. See also Matthew Miller, *The Two Percent Solution*, p. 153; Horowitz interview, p. 73; Bella Rosenberg conversation, 6/6/03.

22. WWS, 11/17/85.

23. Shanker, letter, *Reason*, 10/92, p. 6.

24. Cross, *Political Education*, pp. 86–87.

25. *WP*, 7/6/83, p. A3.

26. Puddington, *Lane Kirkland*, pp. 112, 118–120.

27. Puddington, *Lane Kirkland*, pp. 122–128; Aronowitz, *How Class Works*, p. 23.

28. Puddington, *Lane Kirkland*, pp. 122–128; Aronowitz, *How Class Works*, p. 23.

29. Shanker, in Merrow, *NPR*, 1/17/75, p. 14; Cooper, "An International Perspective on Teachers Unions," pp. 262–263.

30. WWS, 8/16/81; WWS, 3/18/90.

31. WWS, 4/12/92.

32. Jim Smith, "AFL-CIO's Last Cold Warrior," *Z Magazine*, 7–8/95.

33. *NYT*, 10/14/85, p. B3. See also AP, 9/26/85.

34. *WP*, 7/7/85, p. A13.

35. WWS, 10/13/85.

36. *WP*, 6/24/82, p. A7; William Raspberry, editorial, *WP*, 7/2/82, p. A19.

37. *WP*, 6/24/82, p. A7.

38. *WP*, 6/24/82, p. A7; William Raspberry, editorial, *WP*, 7/2/82, p. A19.

39. WWS, 6/20/82; *American Educator*, special issue, "The Power of Ideas," Spring–Summer 1997, pp. 47–48.

40. "Questions and Answers on the Boston Case," in Liz McPike papers, p. 6; AFT News release, "AFT Blasts NEA Position on Seniority Rights," 2/24/83, in Liz McPike papers.

41. *NYT*, 7/7/82, p. B3.

42. Miller interview, pp. 4–5. See also AP, 7/5/83.

43. AFT *amicus curiae* brief, *Wygant vs. Jackson Board of Education*, 6/24/85, in WSU Archives, box 3, folder 2.

44. Letter from K. Preston Oade Jr. to Bruce A. Miller, 7/1/85, in WSU Archives, box 3, folder 2.

45. Unsigned and undated memo, WSU Archives, box 3, folder 2.

46. *Wygant v. Jackson Board of Education*, 476, U.S. 267, 276, 282–283 (1986).

47. *WP*, 5/26/83, p. A2.

48. WWS, 7/17/83.

49. WWS, 6/5/83.

50. Meet the Press transcript, 5/29/83, p. 6, in WSU Archives, box 8, folder 5. (The show was preempted on television and was broadcast by NBC Radio.)

51. *WP*, 7/27/83, p. A3; *NYT*, 7/27/83, p. A16; Shanker, testimony before Senate Judiciary Committee, on Abram/Bunzel/Chavez, in WSU Archives, box 63, folder 77.

52. Shanker, testimony before Senate Judiciary Committee, on Abram/Bunzel/Chavez, in WSU Archives, box 63, folder 77.

53. WWS, 1/17/82; WWS, 10/17/82; WWS, 6/5/83.

54. WWS, 11/22/87.

55. *NYT*, 3/10/85, p. D24.

56. *American Educator*, special issue, "The Power of Ideas," Spring–Summer 1997, p. 40.

57. WWS, 5/23/82; Levine, *Bayard Rustin*, pp. 219–220.

58. WWS, 12/21/80.

59. WWS, 9/20/81.

60. WWS, 6/27/82.

61. WWS, 8/30/87; *American Educator*, special issue, "The Power of Ideas," Spring–Summer 1997, pp. 49–50.

62. Bayard Rustin, "The King to Come: The Holiday and the Future Racial Agenda," *New Republic*, 3/9/87, pp. 19–21.

63. See, e.g., *NYT*, 9/18/71, p. 17.

64. *NYT*, 4/17/75, p. 11; *NYT*, 6/30/81, p. C3; *WP*, 1/26/84, p. C2.

65. *NYT*, 2/12/84, p. D5.

66. Chavez, *An Unlikely Conservative*, pp. 4, 130.

67. *WP*, 1/30/84, p. B1.

68. *NYT*, 4/10/84, p. C1.

69. *NYT*, 8/28/84, p. C1.

70. NYT, 8/23/84, p. A19.

71. *PR Newswire*, 8/5/85; Chaykin interview, pp. 23–24.

72. WWS, 12/6/81.

73. WWS, 5/9/82.

74. WWS, 9/23/90.

75. WWS, 8/1/82; *NYT*, 7/3/82, p. A25.

76. *American Educator*, special issue, "The Power of Ideas," Spring–Summer 1997, p. 95.

77. WWS, 9/23/90.

78. WWS, 1/1/84.

79. Ruth Wattenberg interview, p. 14; Hook, *Commentary*, 7/84, pp. 17–22.

80. Dorn interview II, p. 30.; Liz McPike e-mail, 8/30/06.

81. Diggins, *The Rise and Fall of the American Left*, pp. 158–159.

82. Hook, letter to Shanker, 8/10/71, in NYU Archives.

83. Ruth Wattenberg interview, pp. 14–17, 19; WWS, 9/30/84.

84. *WP*, 5/20/87, p. A14; "Education for Democracy: A Statement of Principles" (AFT, 5/87).

85. *WP*, 5/20/87, p. A14; Ruth Wattenberg interview, p. 17.

86. "Highlights/Accomplishments, Education for Democracy," AFT memorandum, WS Archives, box 5, folder 19.

87. "Education for Democracy: A Statement of Principles" (AFT 5/87); Ruth Wattenberg interview, p. 18; *NYT*, 7/30/87, p. A20; *WP*, 7/30/87, p. D3.

88. *WP*, 5/20/87, p. A14.

89. Ruth Wattenberg interview, p. 22.

13. Being a Social Democrat Under Ronald Reagan:
Foreign Policy (1980–1988)

1. Richard Ravitch interview, p. 13.

2. Tom Donahue interview, pp. 18–19.

3. Buhle interview, p. 3.

4. Dorn interview I, p. 19.

5. Dorn interview II, p. 14.

6. Altomare interview II, p. 65. See also Dorn interview I, p. 19.

7. Dorn interview II, pp. 34–36; Eugenia Kemble interview I, p. 43; IFFTU, "1987 Annual Report to the Executive Board," p. 1.

8. Dorn interview I, p. 15; Dorn interview II, pp. 36–37; van Leeuwen interview, pp. 2, 6.

9. van Leeuwen interview, pp. 5–6.

10. Education International was created in a merger between the IFFTU and the WCOTP in 1993.

11. van Leeuwen interview, pp. 5–6, 14.

12. Dorn interview I, p. 32.

13. Dorn interview II, pp. 32–33; Magidson interview, pp. 26–27.

14. Pat Daly memo, 5/12/06.

15. Johnson interview, p. 20.

16. Dorn interview I, p. 15.

17. Dorn, in joint foreign policy interview, p. 11; and Eugenia Kemble, in joint foreign policy interview, p. 12.

18. Mooney interview, pp. 39–40; Ruby interview, p. 4.

19. Eugenia Kemble interview I, p. 48.

20. Burnie Bond interview, p. 17; Shanker, Memorial Service transcript, 4/9/97, p. 4; Dorn interview I, p. 10; WWS, 10/28/84.

21. Morgan, *A Covert Life*, pp. x, 352, 370.

22. Morgan, *A Covert Life*, pp. 175, 177–178, 351–352.

23. Dorn interview II, pp. 34–36; Eugenia Kemble interview I, p. 43.

24. Dorn interview I, p. 10; Eugenia Kemble interview, 6/14/06.

25. WWS, 12/31/95.

26. Eugenia Kemble interview II, p. 57.

27. Arnold Beichman, "Shanker's Heroic War for Labor," *Washington Times*, 2/25/97, p. A20.

28. Puddington, *Lane Kirkland*, p. 163.

29. WWS, 10/4/81.

30. Puddington, *Lane Kirkland*, p. 168.

31. Puddington, *Lane Kirkland*, pp. 166–168.

32. WWS, 8/31/80.

33. *NYT*, 9/8/81, p. A3.

34. WWS, 10/4/81.

35. Schmidt, *The American Federation of Teachers and the CIA*, p. 9.

36. Dorman, *Arguing the World*, p. 114; Kristol, *Neoconservative*, pp. 23, 458–459; Morgan, *A Covert Life*, pp. 197, 217, 339–340; Schmidt, *The American Federation of Teachers and the CIA*, pp. 11–15, 21–22; Goulden, *Jerry Wurf*, p. 103; Goulden, *Meany*, pp. 328–329; Lichtenstein, *State of the Union*, p. 248; Dorn interview I, pp. 3, 34.

37. Morgan, *A Covert Life*, p. 340.

38. UPI, "Moscow Claims CIA Runs Solidarity Office," *Los Angeles Times*, 9/30/81; AFT News Release, 9/29/81, in WSU Archives, box 4, folder 23; WWS, 10/4/81.

39. Dorn interview I, p. 35; Eugenia Kemble interview I, pp. 38–39.

40. Sanchez interview, pp. 1–4; Buhle interview, pp. 3–4.

41. WWS, 10/4/81 (last part quotes the *Wall Street Journal*).

42. Puddington, *Lane Kirkland*, pp. 173–175.

43. Puddington, *Lane Kirkland*, p. 233.

44. WWS, 12/20/81.

45. WWS, 12/27/81.

46. Eric Chenoweth, "Albert Shanker's Involvement in International Affairs," unpublished mimeograph in Eadie Shanker papers.

47. Puddington, *Lane Kirkland*, p. 182.

48. Ravitch, *New Leader*, 2/24/97, p. 4.

49. *American Teacher*, 4/97, p. 10.

50. Eric Chenoweth, "Albert Shanker's Involvement in International Affairs," unpublished mimeograph in Eadie Shanker papers; Eric Chenoweth, "Poland Today: Democracy Aborning," *Freedom at Issue*, November–December 1988, pp. 10–14.

51. Sandra Feldman interview, pp. 39–40.

52. Puddington, *Lane Kirkland*, p. 164.

53. Puddington, *Lane Kirkland*, p. 263.

54. WWS, 11/12/89.

55. Shanker, address to Social Democrats USA, 12/5/82, p. 10, in WSU Archives, box 63, folder 71.

56. WWS, 10/28/84. See also Puddington, *Lane Kirkland*, p. 132.

57. Lawrence Kaplan, *TNR*, 6/10/02, p. 16.

58. *American Teacher*, 4/97, p. 10; *TNR*, 6/22/87.

59. Eric Chenoweth, "Albert Shanker's Involvement in International Affairs," unpublished mimeograph in Eadie Shanker papers; Puddington, *Lane Kirkland*, p. 222.

60. WWS, 2/2/92.

61. NED, "Twentieth Anniversary," 11/6/03; Gershman interview, pp. 3, 21–22.

62. Gershman interview, pp. 6–7.

63. Carl Gershman bio, NED, available online at http://www.ned.org/about/president .html.

64. Eugenia Kemble interview I, pp. 4–5.

65. *NYT*, 8/15/84, p. A21; Puddington, *Lane Kirkland*, p. 223.

66. *NYT*, 8/15/84, p. A21; Puddington, *Lane Kirkland*, p. 223.

67. Gershman interview, p. 12.

68. WWS, 6/24/84

69. WWS, 2/19/89.

70. *WP*, 11/15/84, p. A27.

71. *NYT*, 10/30/85, p. B6; *WP*, 10/30/85, p. A25; Puddington, *Lane Kirkland*, p. 207.

72. Radosh, *Divided They Fell*, p. 233.

73. Shanker, "Higher Education Breakfast," AFT Convention, July 1986, in *American Educator*, special issue, "The Power of Ideas," Spring–Summer 1997, p. 49.

74. Murphy, *Blackboard Unions*, p. 272.

75. AP, 4/24/87.

76. WWS, 4/19/97.

77. WWS, 10/28/84.

78. *American Teacher*, 4/97, p. 11. See also Magidson interview, p. 37.

79. van Leeuwen interview, pp. 8–9. See also Dorn, in joint foreign policy interview, pp. 20–21.

80. *American Teacher*, 4/97, p. 11.

81. Dorn interview II, p. 16; *American Teacher* photos, 4/97, p. 10.

82. Gaffney, *Blackboard Warriors*, draft, p. 432.

83. *American Teacher*, 4/97, p.11.

84. Dorn interview II, p. 8.

85. Memorial Service transcript, 4/9/97, p. 13.

86. Dorn interview I, pp. 17–18; Dorn interview II, pp. 21–22; Dorn, in joint foreign policy interview, pp. 15–16.

87. Magidson interview, p. 33.

88. Puddington, *Lane Kirkland*, p. 234.

89. Kaufman, *Henry M. Jackson*, p. 3.

90. Penn Kemble, "Notes online: a newsletter for the social democratic community in the United States," June 2004, available online at http://www.socialdemocrats.org/Notesonline June2004.html.

91. Muravchik, *Heaven on Earth*, p. 244.

92. Puddington interview, p. 13.

93. Eric Chenoweth interview, pp. 9–10.

94. Email from Lynda J. DeLoach, archivist, George Meany Memorial Archives, 4/5/05. See also *NYT*, 11/5/89, sect. 4a, p. 34.

95. *PR Newswire*, 3/28/92; Sandra Feldman interview, p. 39; Humphrey interview, p. 13.

96. Dorn, in joint foreign policy interview, p. 35.

97. WWS, 4/22/90.

98. WWS, 2/2/92.

99. WWS, 6/10/90.

100. WWS, 2/2/92.

101. Shanker, in AFT video, "The Road to Democracy," 7/30/90.

102. Ruth Wattenberg interview, p. 23.

103. AP, 1/25/90; *US Newswire*, 1/25/90.

104. Phil Kugler interview, p. 26.

105. Widmeyer interview, p. 8; Chavez interview, p. 11.

106. Horowitz interview, p. 56.

107. Phil Kugler interview, pp. 4–5.

108. Dorn interview I, p. 25; Horowitz interview, p. 56.

109. *NYT*, 7/2/83, p. A25; Judy Bardacke interview, p. 26.

110. *NYT*, 7/5/83, p. A15; *WP*, 7/6/83, p. A3; Greg Humphrey interview, p. 22; Selden, *The Teacher Rebellion*, p. 245.

111. Dorn interview I, p. 25.

112. *Public Papers of the President: 1983*, Book II, p. 1012; *WP*, 7/6/83, p. A3; *NYT*, 7/6/83, p. A12.

113. *Public Papers of the President: 1983*, Book II, pp. 1012–1013; *WP*, 7/6/83, p. A3; *NYT*, 7/6/83, p. A12.

114. *WP*, 7/6/83, p. A3; *NYT*, 7/6/83, p. A12.

115. *WP*, 6/9/83, p. A3.

116. *NYT*, 7/6/83, p. A12.

117. *Public Papers of the President: 1983*, Book II, p. 1013; *WP*, 7/6/83, p. A3; *NYT*, 7/6/83, p. A12.

118. Cameron interview, pp. 12–13; AP, 6/25/83; AP, 7/9/83.

119. *NYT*, 7/6/83, p. A12.

120. Geiger, in Woo, *Los Angeles Times Magazine*, 12/1/96, p. 17ff.

121. Chavez, *An Unlikely Conservative*, pp. 142–3.

122. Chavez interview, p. 10.

123. Hook, Social Democrats speech, 7/76.

124. Phil Kugler interview, p. 57.

125. Smith interview, p. 6.

126. Albert Shanker interview with Shore, p. 10.

127. Putnam, *Bowling Alone*, pp. 80–81, 337, 456, 494–496.

128. Lipset et al., *Union Democracy*, pp. 13–14, citing Aristotle *Politics* 4.11.

129. Madrick, "Inequality and Democracy," in Packer, *The Fight Is for Democracy*, pp. 260–262.

130. Hook, Social Democrats speech, 7/76.

131. Hook, "A Response to Conservatism," 1978, available online at http://www.social democrats.org/HookResponse.html.

132. *NYT*, 3/10/85, p. D24.

133. Albert Shanker, meeting with AFT Human & Civil Rights Committee regarding California Civil Rights Initiative, in Marcia Reecer papers, 4/4/95.

134. Puddington, *Lane Kirkland*, p. 215.

135. Beinart, *TNR*, 12/13/04, p. 23.

136. Shanker speech to SDUSA, 12/5/82, in WSU Archives, box 63, folder 71.

137. WWS, 8/31/80.

138. Shanker, speech to SDUSA, 11/12/90, in *The Social Democrat*, 2/91, in Duke University Archives.

139. Shanker, speech to SDUSA, 11/12/90, in *The Social Democrat*, 2/91, in Duke University Archives.

140. Eric Chenoweth interview, pp. 1–2; David Samuels, *Harper's Magazine*, 5/95, p. 47ff.

141. Sandra Feldman interview, p. 7.

142. Eadie Shanker interview, 10/18/02, p. 40 (identifying Orwell, Rustin, and Randolph as heroes).

143. Interviews with Miller, pp. 9–11; Eugenia Kemble I, pp. 18–19; Rita Freedman, pp. 2–3; Chavez, pp. 2, 12; Eric Chenoweth, p. 14; Muravchik, p. 4; Horowitz, p. 59; McPike, pp. 1, 5, 16; Bardacke, pp. 28–29; Phil Kugler, p. 38; Radosh, pp. 18–19; Dorn I, pp. 1–3, 6; Wattenberg, pp. 6, 37; Bond e-mail, 6/20/06.

144. Ruth Wattenberg interview, pp. 38–39.

145. Shanker, speech to SDUSA, 11/12/90, in *The Social Democrat*, 2/91, in Duke University Archives.

146. See, e.g., AFT Executive Committee minutes, 10/25–26/74, in WS Archives, box 7, folder 3; Shanker Affiliations, Eadie Shanker papers.

147. Decter interview, p. 8.

148. Puddington interview, p. 4.

149. Miller interview, pp. 9–11.

150. Meeting of Executive Council of the AFT, 7/30/87, vol. 2, transcript, pp. 50–106, WSU Archives. See also Phil Kugler interview, pp. 38–39; David Dorn interview II, pp. 1–4. Massing, *TNR*, 6/22/87, pp. 18ff.

151. Siegel, *The Future Once Happened Here*, p. x.

152. Shanker, letter to the editor, *National Review*, 5/29/81, p. 586.

14. Education Reform:
A Nation at Risk, Merit Pay, and Peer Review (1983–1984)

1. Ambach interview, p. 6.

2. Gaffney, *Blackboard Warriors*, draft, p. 409 (quoting Ravitch).

3. *NYT*, 4/27/83, p. A1; *WP*, 5/5/83, p. A25; Goldberg interview, pp. 2, 24.

4. National Commission on Excellence in Education, *A Nation at Risk: The Imperative for Educational Reform*, reprinted in Gordon, *A Nation Reformed?*, pp. 165–194; *NYT*, 4/27/83, A1; *WP*, 4/27/83, p. A1; *Education Week*, 5/18/83; Bell, *The Thirteenth Man*, p. 132; Grossman, in Gordon, *A Nation Reformed?*, p. 70.

5. Goldberg interview, p. 5.

6. *Public Papers of the Presidents*, 19 Weekly Comp. Pres. Doc. 592, 4/26/83; Goldberg interview, p. 5; Bell, *The Thirteenth Man*, pp. 128–131.

7. *American Teacher*, 4/97, p. 4; Humphrey interview, p. 21.

8. Kelly interview, p. 14.

9. Toch, *In the Name of Excellence*, pp. 29, 155; Woo, *LA Times Magazine*, 12/1/96, pp. 17ff.

10. Goldberg interview, pp. 8, 23.

11. Cameron, *The Inside Story*, p. 106, 109.

12. Bob Chase interview, p. 5.

13. WWS, 5/9/71. See also WWS, 5/21/72.

14. WWS, 7/28/74; Shanker, on Merrow, NPR, 1/17/75, p. 5; WWS, 3/4/79; WWS, 6/15/80; WWS, 11/29/81; WWS, 12/5/82.

15. WWS, 10/16/77.

16. WWS, 5/19/74; WWS, 3/2/75.

17. *NYT*, 11/23/69, p. 69.

18. Mooney interview, p. 8. Usdan interview, p. 22.

19. Mosle, *NYT Magazine*, 10/27/96.

20. Spatz interview, p. 12.

21. Shanker, speech to NYSUT, 4/30/83, transcript, p. 368, from NYSUT Library, Albany; *NYT*, 5/1/83, p. A1.

22. *American Educator*, special issue, "The Power of Ideas," Spring–Summer 1997, p. 68.

23. Mooney interview, p. 13.

24. *NYT*, 4/28/83, p. B15.

25. WWS, 5/1/83.

26. NYSUT speech, pp. 358, 373; *NYT*, 5/1/83, p. A1.; Shanker, "Address to Institute for Education Policy Studies," 2/10/80, p. 10, in WSU Archives, box 63, folder 47; WWS, 7/12/81; *NYT*, 11/5/89, sect. 4a, p. 34.; NYSUT speech, p. 351; *NYT*, 5/1/83, p. A1.

27. Shanker speech to NYSUT assembly, p. 371.

28. WWS, 5/1/83. See also WWS, 1/29/84.

29. Shanker, AFT Convention, 7/4/83, in *Vital Speeches of the Day*, 9/15/83; *American Educator*, special issue, "The Power of Ideas," Spring–Summer 1997, p. 64. See also Shanker, NPC Speech, 9/12/83, p. 5.

30. WWS, 4/16/89; WWS, 1/14/90; WWS, 7/29/90; *St. Petersburg Times*, 10/30/88, p. 1D.

31. Rosenberg interview I, pp. 62–64. See also *Education Week*, 4/24/91 (Shanker applauding Bush effort not just to target special problems like poor minorities and the handicapped, but to "improve American education overall.")

32. *American Teacher*, 4/97, p. 4.

33. Sandra Feldman interview, p. 46.

34. Memorial Service transcript, 4/9/97, p. 11.

35. *American Teacher*, 4/97, p. 4.

36. Ellen Goodman, "Grading Time," *WP*, 5/10/83, p. A19.

37. Goldberg interview, p. 7.

38. Schwartz, in Gordon, *A Nation Reformed*, pp. 132–133.

39. Goldberg interview, p. 19.

40. Gaffney, *Blackboard Warriors*, draft, p. 413.

41. See, e.g., WWS, 4/23/89, 1/14/99, 7/29/90, 11/3/91, 8/30/92, 7/7/96, 2/5/89, and 1/14/90.

42. Rothstein, *American Prospect*, 11–12/96, pp. 82ff. See also Berliner and Biddle, *The Manufactured Crisis*.

43. Rothstein, *American Prospect*, Spring 1993, pp. 20ff.

44. WWS, 1/17/93.

45. Cameron interview, pp. 9–10.

46. Bell, *The Thirteenth Man*, p. 131.

47. Vinoukis, in Gordon, *A Nation Reformed?*, p. 123.

48. Tucker interview, pp. 12–13.

49. Chase interview, pp. 18–19.

50. Cole interview, p. 5.

51. Usdan interview, pp. 10–11; Michael Usdan, "The New State Politics of Education," National Association of State Boards of Education, Spring 2002, pp. 15–18.

52. Usdan interview, pp. 13, 31.

53. WWS, 3/15/87.

54. Rosenberg interview I, pp. 1–8, 59. See also Rosenberg e-mail, 1/13/03 (*Risk* report "led to his hiring me"); Eugenia Kemble interview, 6/14/06.

55. Shanker, *United Teacher*, 11/8/70, p. 11A, in Magidson papers.

56. Lieberman interview, pp. 40, 78.

57. Lieberman, *The Teacher Unions*, p. 213.

58. WWS, 3/2/75.

59. WWS, 10/23/83.

60. WWS, 10/20/85.

61. *WP*, 6/4/83, p. A4; *NYT*, 6/9/83, p. A1; *NYT*, 6/17/83, p. A17.

62. *NYT*, 5/1/83, p. A1.

63. Finn, "Teacher Unions and School Equality: Potential Allies or Inevitable Foes," pp. 113–114; *Education Week*, 6/15/83; *NYT*, 6/17/83, p. A17; William Raspberry, *WP*, 6/17/83, p. A19; *WP*, 8/3/83, p. C1.

64. Toch, *In the Name of Excellence*, p. 172; *WP*, 6/4/83, p. A4; *NYT*, 6/17/83, p. A17; *NYT*, 6/21/83, p. C7; *WP*, 8/3/83, p. C1.

65. WWS, 7/24/83.

66. Stern, *Breaking Free*, p. 24.

67. Toch, *U.S. News and World Report*, 2/26/96, pp. 62ff; Stern, *Breaking Free*, p. 24; Brimelow, *The Worm in the Apple*, p. 41.

68. Gaffney, *Blackboard Warriors*, draft, p. 81.

69. *Time*, 12/23/91, p. 64.

70. Cameron, *The Inside Story*, p. 31.

71. WWS, 1/22/84; WWS, 9/15/96.

72. WWS, 1/22/84; WWS, 7/28/96.

73. WWS, 4/25/93.

74. See, e.g., WWS, 8/21/83.

75. *WP*, 11/6/94, p. R5.

76. Johnson interview, p. 11; WWS, 6/22/86.

77. Cameron interview, pp. 5, 10, 21. See also Geiger interview, p. 18.

78. Eadie Shanker interview, 10/18/02, p. 24.

79. Lawrence interview, pp. 1–4.

80. Lawrence interview, pp. 5–7; *American Teacher*, 4/97, pp. 4–5. See also *Chicago Tribune*, 2/10/85, p. C1.

81. Lawrence interview, pp. 9–10.

82. Lawrence interview, pp. 10–12.

83. Lawrence interview, pp. 12–13; *American Teacher*, 4/97, pp. 4–5. AFT Executive Council transcript, 5/8/82, pp. 160–208, in WSU archives.

84. Liz McPike memorandum to Al Shanker and others, November 30, 1983, in McPike papers.

85. McPike interview, p. 31.

86. Lawrence interview, p. 14.

87. McPike interview, p. 32.

88. WWS, 2/5/84.

89. McPike interview, p. 31; *American Educator*, Spring 1984, pp. 22–29.

90. Lawrence interview, pp. 14–15; Kerchner et al., *United Mind Workers*, p. 96.

91. Shanker speech, AFT Convention, 8/84, in *American Educator*, special issue, "The Power of Ideas," Spring–Summer 1997, p. 27.

92. Johnson interview, pp. 9–10.

93. Jennie Shanker journal excerpts, p. 3.

94. *NYT*, 8/21/84, p. A15.

95. WWS, 2/9/86; Kerchner and Koppich, "Organizing Around Quality: The Frontiers of Teacher Unionism," pp. 304–305.

96. Shanker speech, AFT Convention, August 1984, in *American Educator*, special issue, "The Power of Ideas," Spring–Summer 1997, p. 26.

97. Shanker speech, AFT Convention, August 1984, in *American Educator*, special issue, "The Power of Ideas," Spring–Summer 1997, p. 26.

98. *WP*, 8/21/84, p. A3; *NYT*, 8/21/84, p. A15.

99. *NYT*, 12/14/85, p. A29.

100. Kerchner et al., *United Mind Workers*, p. 99.

101. Mooney interview, pp. 20–21 (saying this was Shanker's argument).

102. *WP*, 8/21/84, p. A3; *NYT*, 8/21/84, p. A15.

103. WWS, 2/25/90.

104. *American Educator*, special issue, "The Power of Ideas," Spring–Summer 1997, p. 36; *Time*, 12/23/91, p. 64; Mooney interview, pp. 17–18; WWS, 9/15/96. See also Kerchner et al., *United Mind Workers*, p. 90.

105. Johnson and Kardos, "Reform Bargaining and Its Promise for School Improvement," p. 29.

106. Mooney interview, p. 19; WWS, 9/15/96; Kerchner and Koppich, "Organizing Around Quality: The Frontiers of Teacher Unionism," p. 290.

107. Lawrence interview, pp. 16–18; *Cleveland Plain Dealer*, 11/11/02, p. B3; Darling-Hammond interview, pp. 4–5.

108. *American Teacher*, 4/97, p. 5.

109. Rosenberg interview II, pp. 31–32; WWS, 2/25/90; Kerchner and Koppich, "Organizing Around Quality: The Frontiers of Teacher Unionism," pp. 288, 291. See also WWS, 1/25/87.

110. Lawrence interview, p. 22.

111. *NYT*, 4/22/84, sect. 1, p. 17; *NYT*, 7/4/84, p. A8; Editorial, *NYT*, 3/19/86, p. A26.

112. *WP*, 9/28/83, p. A3; *NYT*, 11/20/83, sect. 1, p. 62.

113. *NYT*, 8/28/84, p. C1.

114. *WP*, 7/11/85, p. A22.

115. *NYT*, 2/5/85, p. C7; Cole interview, pp. 21–22.

116. *NYT*, 7/4/84, p. A8.

117. *NYT*, 8/28/84, p. C1.

118. Cole interview, pp. 2–3.

119. Cole interview, p. 3.

120. *WP*, 7/13/85, p. A3.

121. *NYT*, 7/14/85, p. A18.

122. *NYT*, 8/28/84, p. C1.

15. Beyond Special Interest: Making Teaching a Profession (1985–1987)

1. *WP*, 2/27/83, p. A1.

2. Will Marshall interview, pp. 4–5.

3. Puddington, *Lane Kirkland*, p. 146.

4. Rachelle Horowitz e-mail to author, 2/13/06.

5. Geoghegan, *Which Side Are You On?*, p. 247; Geoghegan interview, pp. 17–18.

6. Magat, *Unlikely Partners*, p. 191.

7. WWS, 3/25/84. See also WWS, 12/2/79.

8. Baer, *Reinventing Democrats*, p. 33; See, e.g., Weiner, *New Politics*, Fall 1976, p. 55.

9. Puddington, *Lane Kirkland*, p. 140.

10. *NYT*, 6/23/93, p. B7; Johnson and Kardos, "Reform Bargaining and Its Promise for School Improvement," p. 13.

11. *American Educator*, special issue, "The Power of Ideas," Spring–Summer 1997, p. 27.

12. *NYT*, 4/16/85, p. C1.

13. *WP*, 1/30/85, p. A7; *American Educator*, special issue, "The Power of Ideas," Spring–Summer 1997, pp. 28–30; Noah, "Albert Shanker, Statesman," *TNR*, 6/24/85, pp. 17–19; *Education Week*, 2/6/85.

14. Shanker, *NPC*, 9/12/83, p. 19. See also WWS, 12/18/83.

15. *American Educator*, special issue, "The Power of Ideas," Spring–Summer 1997, p. 24; WWS, 3/14/82.

16. *Education Week*, 2/6/85; *American Educator*, special issue, "The Power of Ideas," Spring–Summer 1997, pp. 28–30; *NYT*, 4/16/85, p. C1.

17. *WP*, 1/30/85, p. A7; *Education Week*, 2/6/85.

18. Shanker, QuEST Conference, 7/8/83, in *Vital Speeches of the Day*, 9/1/93, p. 680.

19. Rosenberg interview III, p. 30.

20. *NYT*, 4/16/85, p. C1.

21. WWS, 5/19/85.

22. WWS, 3/17/96.

23. *WP*, 3/13/85, p. A8.

24. Widmeyer memo to AFT Executive Council and others, 7/3/85, in WSU Archives, box 4, folder 24; WWS, 5/19/85.

25. WWS, 6/19/83; Ballou and Podgursky, "Gaining Control of Professional Licensing and Advancement," pp. 76–79.

26. *NYT*, 7/1/85, p. A13; Futrell interview, pp. 23–24.

27. *NYT*, 7/4/85, p. A10.

28. *NYT*, 7/7/85, p. D7.

29. Lee Shulman, correspondence with author, 8/23/06.

30. Shanker, *The Making of a Profession*. See also *NYT*, 4/28/85, p. A1. See also Hill, *Education Week*, 2/21/96.

31. Shanker, *The Making of a Profession*.

32. *NYT*, 4/28/85, p. A1.

33. Toch, *In the Name of Excellence*, p. 134.

34. Shanker, *The Making of a Profession*; Bella Rosenberg interview.

35. Shanker, *The Making of a Profession*.

36. Shanker, *The Making of a Profession*. See also *NYT*, 4/28/85, p. A1.

37. Toch, *In the Name of Excellence*, p. 144.

38. *NYT*, 7/12/85, p. A1.

39. *NYT*, 7/12/85, p. A1; *WP*, 7/12/85, p. A2; *American Teacher*, 4/97, p. 5; Shanker, "The Dangers of Not Having Any New Ideas," Remarks, AFT QuEST Conference, 7/11/85, pp. 12–16, in WSU Archives, box 64, folder 3.

40. *NYT*, 7/12/85, p. A1; *WP*, 7/12/85, p. A2; *WWS*, 7/28/85; Lieberman interview, pp. 23–25; Shanker, "The Dangers of Not Having Any New Ideas," Remarks, AFT QuEST Conference, 7/11/85, pp. 12–16, in WSU Archives, box 64, folder 3.

41. Carnegie Forum, *A Nation Prepared*, pp. 97–98; WWS, 1/15/95.

42. WWS, 7/28/85.

43. *NYT*, 7/23/85, p. C9.

44. UPI, 5/24/85.

45. Carnegie Forum, *A Nation Prepared*, pp. iv–v. See also *NYT*, 5/16/86, p. A17.

46. Tucker interview, pp. 1–4, 8.

47. Tucker interview, pp. 4, 6–7.

48. Tucker interview, p. 6.

49. *NYT*, 5/16/86, p. A1.

50. Carnegie Forum, *A Nation Prepared*, p. 3; See also *NYT*, 5/16/86, p. A1; *WP*, 5/19/86, p. A7; *NYT*, 7/1/86, p. C8; *NYT*, 7/5/86, p. A10.

51. Kelly interview, p. 14.

52. *NYT*, 5/16/86, p. A1; AP, 5/16/86.

53. Carnegie Forum, *A Nation Prepared*, pp. 117–118.

54. *WP*, 5/18/86, p. A4.

55. *WP*, 5/19/86, p. A7.

56. *NYT*, 5/16/86, p. A1; *WP*, 5/14/86, p. A23.

57. Tucker interview, p. 7.

58. Cameron, *The Inside Story*, pp. 150–151.

59. Futrell interview, pp. 12–13; *NYT*, 7/5/86, p. A10; *WP*, 7/5/86, p. A2.

60. *NYT*, 7/3/86, p. A19; *WP*, 7/7/86, p. A5.

61. *WP*, 7/7/86, p. A5.

62. *WP*, 5/16/87, p. A1; *NYT*, 5/16/97, p. A9.

63. WWS, 5/17/87.

64. Lloyd Bond interview, pp. 5–6; Rosenberg e-mail, 3/21/03.

65. Lloyd Bond interview, pp. 6, 9–12.

66. Lloyd Bond interview, pp. 4, 8, 9, 14.

67. Kelly interview, pp. 20–22.

68. National Board for Professional Teaching Standards, *Raising the Standard*, p. 10; Kelly interview, p. 30.

69. Humphrey interview, p. 37.

70. WWS, 1/15/95.

71. National Board for Professional Teaching Standards, "Quick Facts," 11/04.

72. Kelly interview, pp. 26–28.

73. *American Teacher*, 4/97, p. 5.

74. *NYT*, 8/26/83, p. B2; *NYT*, 9/6/83, p. B2.

75. *NYT*, 9/19/85, p. A1.

76. *NYT*, 12/15/85, p. A1; *NYT*, 12/14/85, p. A29.

77. WWS, 12/15/85.

78. Editorial, *NYT*, 1/2/86, p. A18.

79. *NYT*, 1/10/88, p. D6.

80. *NYT*, 12/15/85, p. A1.

81. Phil Kugler interview, pp. 6, 18–19.

82. *WP*, 5/27/88, p. A16.

83. *NYT*, 11/5/89, sect. 4a, p. 34.

84. Kirst interview, pp. 5–6.

85. Kelly interview, p. 18.

86. Rosenberg interview I, p. 14.

87. Usdan interview, p. 34.

88. Kelly interview, p. 18.

89. Kugler interview, p. 24.

90. *WP*, 7/2/86, p. A4.

91. McPike interview, pp. 21–22.

92. Chaykin interview, p. 9, 11–12, 21.

93. Brimelow, *The Worm in the Apple*, p. xv.

94. Ruth Wattenberg interview, p. 11.

95. See, e.g., Noah, "Albert Shanker, Statesman," *TNR*, 6/24/85, p. 17; *WSJ*, 11/21/87.

96. *U.S. News & World Report*, 2/8/88, p. 64.

97. Quoted in WWS, 1/29/89.

98. *WP*, 8/5/84, p. A2; *WP*, 8/6/84, p. B2; *WP*, 3/31/85, p. A3.

99. *NYT*, 6/3/83, p. B3; *NYT*, 5/24/85, p. B2.

100. *NYT*, 9/10/86, p. B7; Shalala interview, p. 1.

101. Shivers, *Education Week*, 3/12/97.

102. Jonathan Kozol, letter to Shanker, 1/20/92, in WSU Archives, box Pubs A–W, file Misc.
1991–1992.

103. Magat, *Education Week*, 3/26/97. See also Magat, *Unlikely Partners*, p. 189. The Twentieth Century Fund was later renamed The Century Foundation, an organization for which
the author works.

104. Rosenberg interview III, pp. 19–20.

105. *NYT*, 11/5/89, sect. 4a, p. 34; Hurwitz interview, pp. 9–12.

106. Hurwitz interview, pp. 20–21, 29.

107. Shalala interview, pp. 5–6; *Denver Post*, 2/15/98, p. A1.

108. Diane Ravitch interview, p. 13.

109. Dorn interview II, pp. 53–54.

110. Ted Kolderie interview, pp. 1–2, 18.

111. Kirst interview, pp. 5–6.

112. *WP*, 12/12/86, p. A3; Marshall interview, p. 9.

113. Tucker interview, p. 11.

114. Geiger interview, p. 9. See also Geiger interview, p. 21; Hobart interview, p. 15.

115. Freedman interview, p. 49.

16. Charter Schools and School Restructuring (1988–1997)

1. WWS, 12/13/87.

2. WWS, 4/3/88.

3. Shanker, National Press Club, 3/31/88, in *Vital Speeches of the Day*, 8/15/88, p. 666; Shanker, National Press Club, 3/31/88, transcript, in Bella Rosenberg papers, p. 7.

4. Albert Shanker interview with Shore, p. 6.

5. Bella Rosenberg interview, 5/17/06.

6. *NYT*, 4/26/88, p. A23.

7. WWS, 1/10/88.

8. WWS, 12/17/89.

9. William Raspberry, op-ed, *WP*, 8/1/88, p. A13 (quoting Shanker's review).

10. Rosenberg interview I, pp. 31–32.

11. WWS, 4/19/92; WWS, 1/31/93; WWS, 4/26/87.

12. Bella Rosenberg interview.

13. WWS, 1/10/88.

14. *A Nation at Risk*, in Gordon, *A Nation Reformed*, pp. 181 182.

15. WWS, /15/84. See also Shanker, *Education and Urban Society*, 2/85, p. 218.

16. WWS, 11/25/84; WWS, 3/30/86; WWS, 3/8/92. See also WWS, 1/10/88.

17. Shanker, *PDK*, 1/90, p. 347. See also WWS, 5/28/95; and Shanker, ETS speech, 10/28/89, referencing Bowsher's appearance before an AFT Executive council meeting "last June."

18. Kahlenberg, *All Together Now*, p. 148.

19. Albert Shanker, National Press Club address, 3/31/88, in *Vital Speeches of the Day*, 8/15/88, pp. 664–669; WWS, 7/10/88.

20. *NYT*, 4/1/88, p. A16.

21. *NYT*, 1/4/89, p. B10. See also *NYT*, 3/22/89, p. B6.

22. Shanker, *Peabody Journal of Education*, Spring 1988, p. 98.

23. Shanker, NPC Speech, 3/31/88, transcript in Bella Rosenberg papers, p. 9. In another context, Shanker cited a RAND study which found strong teachers' unions are most likely to be innovative. See WWS, 9/8/96.

24. Shanker, Pew Forum Supplement, *Education Week*, 5/14/97, p. 38.

25. *NYT*, 4/1/88, p. A16.

26. WWS, 7/17/88; Finn interview, pp. 8–9.

27. *NYT*, 7/5/88, p. A15; *NYT*, 7/6/88, p. B5; WWS, 7/10/88; Albert Shanker, "Charter Schools," p. 72.

28. *NYT*, 1/3/99, sect. 4, p. 3; Kolderie interview, pp. 6–7; Ted Kolderie, Center for Policy Studies, "Minnesota's New Program of 'Charter Schools,'" June 1991.

29. Moe, *Schools, Vouchers, and the American Public*, p. 33.

30. Chubb and Moe, *Politics, Markets, and America's Schools*.

31. Kolderie, "Beyond Choice to New Public Schools."

32. Kolderie interview, pp. 12–13. See also Finn, Manno, and Vanourek, *Charter Schools in Action*, p. 43.

33. WWS, 9/27/92.

34. Kolderie interview, p. 24; Ravitch, *New Leader*, 2/24/97, p. 4; Wattenberg, *WT*, 2/27/97, A15.

35. Finn, Manno, and Vanourek, *Charter Schools in Action*.

36. *NYT*, 1/19/94, p. B9; *Boston Globe*, 1/9/94; WWS, 7/17/94.

37. Rosenberg interview I, pp. 38–39.

38. Horowitz interview, p. 65.

39. Sandra Feldman interview, p. 51.

40. WWS, 11/7/93.

41. WWS, 7/3/94. See also WWS, 12/11/94.

42. U.S. Department of Education, *Evaluation of Public Charter School Program: Final Report* (2004), p. 32.

43. WWS, 12/18/94.

44. WWS, 11/19/95.

45. Shanker op-ed, *WP*, 12/27/94, p. A14.

46. WWS, 12/22/96.

47. WWS, 12/22/96.

48. *NYT*, 1/3/99, sect. 4, p. 3.

49. WWS, 7/3/94.

50. *NYT*, 9/22/96, p. A14.

51. Rosenberg interview III, p. 53.

52. Brimelow, *Worm in the Apple*, p. 141.

53. Shanker, AFT Executive Council transcript, 2/14/96, pp. 9, 15, 17, in Marcia Reecer papers.

54. Shanker, Pew Forum Supplement, *Education Week*, 5/14/97, p. 38.

55. Shanker, "The Task Before Us," p. 95.

56. Mooney interview, p. 11.

57. Marshall interview, p. 1.

58. Rosenberg interview, 3/13/06.

59. *NYT*, 3/22/92, p. A22; Shanker, speech to NYSUT, 3/21/92, in WSU Archives, box 65, folder 13.

60. WWS, 12/1/96.

61. WWS, 10/16/88.

62. Shanker op-ed, *WP*, 12/27/94, p. A15.

63. WWS, 12/18/94.

64. Shanker op-ed, *WP*, 12/27/94, p. A15. See also WWS, 12/8/96.

65. Bella Rosenberg e-mail, 12/10/06.

66. Reecer interview, pp. 24–25; McPike interview, p. 33.

67. Shanker, in Pew Forum Supplement, *Education Week*, 5/14/97, p. 43.

68. WWS, 6/26/94.

69. Randi Weingarten, "What Matters Most," *NYT*, 12/17/06.

70. Shanker, Executive Committee of AFT, 2/14/96, p. 37, in Marcia Reecer papers.

17. The Early Education-Standards Movement (1989–1994)

1. Finn, op-ed, *WP*, 7/16/89, p. B7.

2. McPike e-mail to author, 9/12/06.

3. Finn, op-ed, *WP*, 7/16/89, p. B7. See also Bella Rosenberg e-mail, 12/10/06.

4. Cross, *Political Education*, p. 149.

5. Bella Rosenberg interview; O'Day and Smith, "Systemic Reform"; Smith and O'Day, "Systemic School Reform." See also Cross, *Political Education*, p. 149.

6. Shanker, ETS Speech, 10/28/89. See also Gordon Ambach interview, p. 11; McPike interview, p. 10; Rosenberg interview I, p. 57; AFT, "The AFT v. the NEA" (12/83), p. 5, citing various NEA resolutions and statements from 1972 to 1981, in Bella Rosenberg papers.

7. Gibson, quoted in *Detroit News*, 11/27/00, p. 1C; Kirst interview, p. 12 (describing NEA attitude).

8. Hook, "Introduction," in Dewey, Democracy and Education, p. xi.

9. Califano, *Governing America*, p. 295.

10. *American Educator*, special issue, "The Power of Ideas," Spring–Summer 1997, p. 76. See also WWS, 12/6/92; Shanker, "The Task Before Us," p. 91. Shanker was heavily influenced on this point by the work of Cornell professor John Bishop.

11. Liz McPike e-mail to author, 9/7/06; James Stigler and Harold Stevenson, "How Asian Teachers Polish Each Lesson to Perfection," *American Educator*, Spring 1991, pp. 12–30.

12. *American Educator*, special issue, "The Power of Ideas," Spring–Summer 1997, p. 55.

13. Karin Chenoweth e-mail to author, 11/8/04; Bella Rosenberg interview II, p. 16. See also WWS, 12/15/91; WWS, 10/8/95.

14. WWS, 12/15/91.

15. WWS, 3/12/95.

16. WWS, 4/3/94; WWS, 4/24/94. See also WWS, 5/29/94; and *American Educator*, special issue, "The Power of Ideas," Spring–Summer 1997, p. 74.

17. Shanker, *NPC*, 9/12/83, p. 21.

18. Shanker interview with Schierenbeck, *American Educator*, Fall 2000, p. 42.

19. WWS, 6/9/85.

20. WWS, 8/4/85; see also WWS, 6/9/85.

21. *NYT*, 8/2/87, sect. 12, p. 20.

22. WWS, 12/29/96.

23. Hirsch interview, pp. 14–15; Ruth Wattenberg interview, p. 49.

24. WWS, 12/15/91.

25. Hirsch, *The Schools We Need*, pp. 6–7.

26. WWS, 12/15/91.

27. *NYT*, 2/7/90, p. A1; WWS, 1/28/90; WWS, 8/12/90.

28. WWS, 1/28/90.

29. WWS, 8/12/90.

30. *American Educator*, special issue, "The Power of Ideas," Spring–Summer 1997, pp. 91, 106.

31. *Newsday*, 8/19/91, pp. 3ff.; *NYT*, 12/1/96, sect. 13, p. 3.

32. *Newsday*, 8/19/91, pp. 3ff.

33. *WP Magazine*, 11/11/01, p. W24; Hirsch interview, pp. 2, 8.

34. Hirsch, *The Schools We Need*, pp. 6–7; Hirsch interview, 10.

35. *NYT*, 8/2/87, sect. 12, p. 20. Bates, *Battleground*, pp. 227, 273–275.

36. *American Educator*, special issue, "The Power of Ideas," Spring–Summer 1997, p. 75. See also Hirsch, *The Schools We Need*, p. 35.

37. WWS, 4/28/96.

38. Toch, "A Speech That Shook the Field," *Education Week*, 3/26/97.

39. Ravitch, *Left Back*, p. 428.

40. WWS, 7/29/79; *American Educator*, special issue, "The Power of Ideas," Spring–Summer 1997, p. 88; McPike interview, pp. 18–19; Ravitch, *Left Back*, p. 428.

41. WWS, 1/28/90; WWS, 2/23/97; Barone, *Hard America, Soft America*, p. 113.

42. *American Educator*, special issue, "The Power of Ideas," Spring–Summer 1997, p. 87; Thernstrom and Thernstrom, *No Excuses*, p. 198.

43. WWS, 6/16/96. See also *NYT*, 7/7/96, p. B6 (citing WWS).

44. WWS, 5/17/92.

45. Shanker, *Education Week*, 12/6/95.

46. Bella Rosenberg interview.

47. UPI, 1/25/90.

48. Eugenia Kemble interview II, p. 46; Rosenberg interview II, p. 5; Diane Ravitch interview, p. 16; WWS, 5/9/93.

49. Peter Schrag, *Atlantic Monthly*, 8/00, p. 19ff (paraphrasing Shanker).

50. Rosenberg interview II, p. 5.

51. Shanker, *Daedalus*, Fall 1995, pp. 50–51.

52. WWS, 8/22/82.

53. *American Educator*, special issue, "The Power of Ideas," Spring–Summer 1997, p. 75.; Rosenberg interview III, p. 68.

54. *American Educator*, special issue, "The Power of Ideas," Spring–Summer 1997, p. 74.

55. Shanker, "A Landmark Revisited," 5/9/93, cited in Barone, *Hard America, Soft America*, p. 111.

56. *NYT*, 11/15/89, p. B12. See also WWS, 3/5/89.

57. WWS, 3/5/89.

58. Bella Rosenberg interview; WWS, 7/23/89; WWS, 8/13/89.

59. Shanker, letter to Casserly, 10/10/95, in Bella Rosenberg papers.

60. WWS, 7/10/94. See also Bella Rosenberg, Supplemental Statement, Commission on Chapter 1, Making Schools Work for Children in Poverty, December 1992, p. 99.

61. WWS, 7/23/89, cited, for example, in Richman, op-ed, *WP*, 2/9/96, p. A21.

62. WWS, 6/14/81.

63. *American Teacher*, 4/97, p. 6.

64. *American Educator*, special issue, "The Power of Ideas," Spring–Summer 1997, pp. 78–79.

65. Lemann, *New Yorker*, 9/25/00, pp. 89ff.

66. Chavez and Gray, *Betrayal*, pp. 112, 134.

67. Usdan interview, pp. 3–4.

68. Kelly interview, p. 13.

69. Eugenia Kemble interview II, p. 39.

70. Cohen interview, p. 4.

71. Horowitz interview, pp. 75–76.

72. Eugenia Kemble interview II, p. 40.

73. Woo, *LA Times Magazine*, 12/1/96, pp. 17ff.

74. Finn, "Pew Forum Supplement," *Education Week*, 5/14/97, p. 44.

75. Widmeyer interview, p. 12.

76. Finn interview, p. 11.

77. WWS, 9/17/89.

78. *WP*, 8/25/89, p. A14.

79. Cross, *Political Education*, p. 93.

80. Horwitz interview, p. 6.

81. *WP*, 9/29/89, p. A3; *NYT*, 9/29/89, p. A10.

82. *NYT*, 9/30/89, p. A9.

83. Horwitz interview, pp. 6–7.

84. Public Papers of the President, 10/5/90; Alan Wurtzel, Congressional Testimony, 2/2/95; *NYT*, 3/17/93, p. D2.

85. Wurtzel interview, pp. 1–4.

86. Cross, *Political Education*, p. 100.

87. Cross, *Political Education*, pp. 100–101; *WP*, 4/19/91, p. A1; *NYT*, 4/20/91, p. A1; WWS, 4/21/91.

88. *NYT*, 12/18/91, p. B9.

89. *NYT*, 12/18/91, p. B9; *WP*, 1/25/92, p. A1.

90. *LA Times*, 1/3/92, p. A1.

91. Editorial, *WP*, 3/3/92, p. A16.

92. *NYT*, 7/22/91, p. A12; *NYT*, 7/12/91, p. A13; Jennings, *Why National Standards and Tests?*, p. 28.

93. Cross, *Political Education*, pp. 102–103. See also Jennings, *Why National Standards and Tests?*, pp. 30–31.

94. Eugenia Kemble interview II, p. 18.

95. Michael Cohen interview, p. 6.

96. *National Journal*, 11/21/92, p. 2676; *WP*, 1/28/93, p. A3; Jennie Shanker interview, pp. 18–20.

97. Sanchez interview, p. 10.

98. E-mail from Marshal Smith, 3/18/02; Smith interview, pp. 20–21; *Education Week*, 11/13/91; "A Tribute to Al Shanker," *Education Week*, 5/14/97, p. 34.

99. Eugenia Kemble interview II, p. 17.

100. *WP*, 1/28/93, p. A3.

101. Cross, *Political Education*, p. 105. See also Jennings, *Why National Standards and Tests?*, p. 42.

102. *Boston Globe*, 4/22/93, p. 13; WWS, 5/23/93.

103. Julie Miller, *Education Week*, 3/31/93; Bill Galston conversation, 10/1/05.

104. Cross, *Political Education*, p. 108; Bill Galston conversation, 10/1/05. See also Jennings, *Why National Standards and Tests?*, p. 114.

105. Michael Cohen interview, pp. 6–10.

106. WWS, 5/1/94.

107. WWS, 3/29/92.

108. WWS, 8/14/94; *American Educator*, special issue, "The Power of Ideas," Spring–Summer 1997, pp. 77–78. See also McPike interview, p. 20 (citing data); WWS, 5/14/95; and Barone, *Hard America, Soft America*, p. 58, citing *NYT*, 4/23/03.

109. Jennings, *Why National Standards and Tests?*, p. 50.

110. *Boston Globe*, 4/22/93, p. 13; WWS, 5/23/93.

111. Cohen interview, p. 17.

112. Jennings, *Why National Standards and Tests?*, p. 56.

113. Cross, *Political Education*, pp. 106–107; Rosenberg interview II, pp. 12–13; Jennings, *Why National Standards and Tests?*, p. 50.

114. WWS, 5/23/93; WWS, 5/30/93.

115. WWS, 3/29/92. See also WWS, 5/30/93.

116. WWS, 5/30/93.

117. *National Journal*, 7/3/93, pp. 1688ff.

118. Darling-Hammond interview, pp. 30–31.

119. Sandra Feldman interview, p. 48.

120. WWS, 5/30/93.

121. Cross, *Political Education*, p. 107; *Heritage Foundation Reports*, 7/14/93.

122. Jennings, *Why National Standards and Tests?*, pp. 91, 107–108. See also Cross, *Political Education*, p. 107; and *WP*, 5/11/94, p. A21.

123. WWS, 4/24/94.

124. Cohen interview, pp. 12–14.

125. Cohen interview, pp. 14–16.

126. *American Educator*, special issue, "The Power of Ideas," Spring–Summer 1997, p. 73. See also *WP*, 8/21/84, p. A3; WWS, 1/4/87; WWS, 4/24/88; WWS, 4/23/89; *NYT*, 10/29/89, p. A34; WWS, 10/29/89; WWS, 4/21/91.

127. Cross, *Political Education*, pp. 108–110. See also Cohen interview, pp. 14–16.

128. WWS, 7/10/94.

129. WWS, 7/10/94.

130. WWS, 7/10/94.

131. Bella Rosenberg e-mail to author, 11/1/05.

132. Casserly, letter to Shanker, 10/2/95, in Bella Rosenberg papers.

133. Shanker, letter to Casserly, 10/10/95, in Bella Rosenberg papers; WWS, 11/22/92; Shanker, *PDK*, 1/90, p. 355. See also Shanker, in "Pew Forum Supplement," *Education Week*, 5/14/97, p. 37.

134. WWS, 5/9/93.

135. Shanker, QuEST speech, 7/8/93, reprinted in *Vital Speeches of the Day*, 9/1/93, p. 679.

136. Cross, *Political Education*, pp. 111–113.

137. Eadie Shanker interview 3/1/04, p. 1. See also AP 7/16/94.

138. Eadie Shanker interview, 10/18/02, pp. 70–71.

139. Eadie Shanker interview, 2/27/04, p. 7; Eadie Shanker interview, 3/1/04, p. 1.

140. Eadie Shanker memo, 3/3/06.

141. *NYT*, 7/20/94, p. B7; AP, 7/16/94.

142. *WT*, 10/27/94, p. A2; *MacNeil/Lehrer Newshour*, 10/26/94.

143. Ravitch, *Left Back*, p. 434.

144. TNR, 1/2/95, quoting *WSJ*, 11/11/94.

145. *Rocky Mountain News*, 10/30/94, p. 102A.

146. *U.S. Newswire*, 10/27/94.

147. *Society*, 1/11/97, pp. 20ff.

148. *Education Week*, 4/12/95.

18. The Rise of the Angry White Males and the Gingrich Revolution (1992–1995)

1. Bella Rosenberg interview.

2. Horowitz interview, p. 62; *Chicago Tribune*, 2/20/92; Green, *Epitaph for American Labor*, p. 133; *NYT*, 3/22/92, p. A22; *WP*, 2/15/93, p. A10.

3. *WP*, 2/15/93, p. A10.

4. Shanker, memo to AFT Leaders, 3/4/92, in WSU Archives, box 9, folder 17.

5. WWS, 4/5/92. See also WWS, 6/12/94, on Shanker's support for universal health care.

6. Dionne, *Stand Up, Fight Back*, pp. 125–126.

7. Stephen Rosenfeld, op-ed, *WP*, 8/28/92, p. A23.

8. *U.S. Newswire*, 8/17/92.

9. *U.S. Newswire*, 10/9/92.

10. *WP*, 5/7/91, p. A8; *WP*, 5/8/91, p. A7.

11. Clinton and Gore, *Putting People First*, p. 64.

12. Dionne, *Stand Up, Fight Back*, p. 124.

13. Andy Rotherham discussion, 8/20/03.

14. Radosh, *Divided They Fell*, p. 218.

15. Dionne, *Stand Up, Fight Back*, p. 126.

16. McElroy interview, p. 17.

17. Farran interview, p. 38.

18. WWS, 5/1/94; *American Educator*, special issue, "The Power of Ideas," Spring–Summer 1997, p. 56; *Cleveland Plain Dealer*, 3/23/94, p. 1B; *WT*, 5/27/94, p. A3; *WT*, 10/5/94, p. A4.

19. *WT*, 5/27/94, p. A3; *Cleveland Plain Dealer*, 10/4/94.

20. *WP*, 9/7/94.

21. WWS, 9/4/94; *Taxman v. Bd. of Ed. of Piscataway* (3rd Cir., 1996).

22. WWS, 9/4/94.

23. *WP*, 11/22/97, p. A1.

24. *NYT*, 11/13/94, sect. 1, p. 24.

25. Albert Shanker interview, p. 4.

26. Lemman, *The Big Test*, p. 271.

27. Stephanopoulos, *All Too Human*, p. 365.

28. *WP*, 3/4/95, p. A1.

29. Albert Shanker interview, p. 2.

30. Albert Shanker, meeting with AFT Human & Civil Rights Committee regarding California Civil Rights Initiative, in Marcia Reecer papers, 4/4/95.

31. See, e.g., WWS, 12/17/78. See also WWS, 3/27/77, "Help for Disadvantaged, But not Quotas."

32. Stephanopoulos, *All Too Human*, p. 364.

33. Albert Shanker interview, pp. 3–4.

34. Albert Shanker interview, p. 2.

35. Stephanopoulos, *All Too Human*, p. 336.

36. Richard D. Kahlenberg, "Class-Based Affirmative Action," *California Law Review* 84 (1996), pp. 1037, 1048–1056.

37. Kahlenberg, *The Remedy*, pp. 118, 271, n. 183.

38. See, e.g., *NYT*, 12/14/97, p. A1.

39. *NYT*, 6/23/93, p. B7.

40. WWS, 4/4/93.

41. See, e.g., Goldbloom, in Berube and Gittel, *Confrontation at Ocean Hill–Brownsville*, p. 274; WWS, 4/2/72; Hentoff, *Village Voice*, 9/26/68, in Berube and Gittel, *Confrontation at Ocean Hill–Brownsville*, p. 124, citing Shanker in *NYT*, 9/20/68; WWS, 4/18/82; WWS, 1/26/75; Shanker interview, *USA Today*, 2/15/93, p. 11A.

42. Kahlenberg, *All Together Now*, p. 154.

43. Albert Shanker letter to George Springer, 4/1/93, in WSU Archives, box State Fed A-J, folder CT FT 1987–97. See also Springer letter to Shanker, 4/12/93, in WSU Archives, box State Fed, folder CT 1987–1997.

44. See, e.g., WWS, 4/2/72; WWS, 4/18/82; WWS, 1/26/75; *USA Today*, 2/15/83, p. 11A; Decter, *NY Magazine*, 10/25/71, p. 17; WWS, 1/25/81.

45. *WP*, 7/4/90, p. A8; *Washington Times*, 5/5/92, p. A1.

46. *Washington Times*, 7/6/92, p. A3.

47. Chanin interview, p. 12; *WP*, 1/28/93, p. A3.

48. van Leeuwen interview, pp. 12–13; Dorn in joint foreign policy interview, p. 34.

49. Eric Chenoweth interview, p. 27.

50. Rosenberg interview III, pp. 3–4, 6–7, 9–11.

51. Putnam, *Bowling Alone*, pp. 80–81.

52. Lind, in Fraser and Gerstle, *Ruling America*, p. 252.

53. Geoghegan, *Which Side Are You On?*, p. 40.

54. Putnam, *Bowling Alone*, p. 82, 456, n. 4 (citing numerous studies).

55. Rosenberg interview I, p. 4; Rosenberg interview III, pp. 8, 31; Humphrey interview, p. 43.

56. Albert Shanker interview with Shore, pp. 9–10.

57. Phil Kugler interview, p. 53.

58. Rosenberg interview III, p. 5. See also McElroy interview, p. 27; Eric Chenoweth interview, p. 34; Dorn interview II, p. 29; Puddington interview, p. 13.

59. See, e.g., WWS, 12/23/79, "What Collar Unions Wave of the Future?"

60. Phil Kugler interview, p. 53; Marshall interview, pp. 3, 15, 18; Rita Freedman, e-mail, 5/2/06.

61. Shanker, op-ed, *WP*, 9/1/86, p. A15; Phil Kugler interview, 11/29/05.

62. Shanker, op-ed, *WP*, 9/1/86, p. A15.

63. Rosenberg interview III, pp. 7–8.

64. *NYT*, 2/22/85, p. A10; *NYT*, 2/24/85, p. D5; *WP*, 2/25/85, p. A5.

65. Eugenia Kemble interview I, p. 26.

66. McElroy interview, p. 21.

67. Marshall interview, pp. 2–3.

68. Lieberman, Haar, and Troy, *The NEA and the AFT*, p. 134; Stern, *Breaking Free*, p. 117; Hill, *Education Week*, 2/21/96; Geoghegan, *Which Side Are You On?*, p. 320; Buhle interview, pp. 15–16.

69. LaCour interview, p. 32.

70. *U.S. Newswire*, 9/21/93.

71. Bella Rosenberg interview.

72. *Newsweek*, 6/13/83, p. 53; Beichman interview, p. 21.

73. WWS, 2/9/75. See also Raspberry, op-ed, *WP*, 9/1/95, p. A23.

74. Chanin interview, pp. 10, 23–24.

75. Finn, letter to the editor, *Commentary*, 6/98, p. 5ff.

76. Kelly interview, p. 18–19.

77. *WT*, 7/4/94, p. A6.

78. Shanker, AFT Conference, 1/14/94, printed in *Vital Speeches of the Day*, 3/1/94; Shanker, *Exceptional Parent*, 9/94, pp. 39–40; Shanker, *Educational Leadership*, Winter 1994–1995, p. 18.

79. Ravitch, *Left Back*, p. 421; Stern, *Breaking Free*, p. 121.

80. WWS, 12/9/90. See also WWS, 2/17/91.

81. WWS, 2/23/92. See also Schlesinger interview, p. 10.

82. Shanker, multiculturalism speech at Department of Education, 10/8/91, in Reecer papers, pp. 1, 3.

83. Shanker, AFT Executive Council Meeting, 2/14/96, pp. 44–45, 50.

84. Raspberry, "Solidly for Vouchers," *WP*, 8/6/01, p. A15.

85. *American Teacher*, 4/97, p. 24; *American Educator*, special issue, "The Power of Ideas," Spring–Summer 1997, p. 112.

86. Brimelow, *Worm in the Apple*, p. 140.

87. Alexander, *The Journal of American Citizenship Policy Review*, November/December 1998, pp. 18ff.

88. Phil Kugler interview, pp. 27–28; Eadie Shanker interview, 4/22/03, p. 3; Diane Ravitch interview, p. 11; Fondy interview, pp. 13, 21; Bella Rosenberg interview.

89. Finn interview, p. 15.

90. Brimelow, *Forbes*, 2/13/95, pp. 121ff; AP, 12/22/94; Cameron, *The Inside Story*, pp. 165–166.

91. *WP*, 1/28/95, p. A1.

92. Meyerson in Mort, *Not Your Father's Union Movement*, pp. 4–5.

93. Geoghegan interview, p. 2; *WP*, 10/25/95, p. A1.

94. *NYT*, 5/11/95, p. A26.

95. Geoghegan interview, pp. 1–2. See also, Geoghegan, *Which Side Are You On?*, p. 292; Buhle interview, p. 16. See also *WP*, 1/28/95, p. A1.

96. *NYT*, 5/11/95, p. A26; *WP*, 1/28/95, p. A1.

97. Geoghegan interview, p. 3.

98. Mort, *Not Your Father's Union Movement*, pp. v–vi; Moody, *New Politics*, Winter 1996.

99. *NYT*, 5/11/95, p. A26. See also *Cleveland Plain Dealer*, 5/14/95, p. 1H.

100. Shanker, *Think Tank*, 11/2/95.

101. Shanker, *Think Tank*, 11/2/95.

102. Joyce interview, pp. 17–20. See also Irena Kirkland interview, p. 7.

103. Buhle interview, p. 15.

104. Geoghegan interview, p. 25.

105. Taylor Dark, *Labor History*, 8/99, p. 11. See also Irena Kirkland interview, p. 8; Kim Moody, *New Politics*, Winter 1996; Puddington, *Lane Kirkland*, pp. 76, 305; Chavez and Gray, *Betrayal*, pp. 19, 48.

106. Puddington interview, p. 22.

107. Shanker, letter to the editor, *Business Week*, 3/6/95, p. 4.

108. Shanker, letter to Sweeney, 5/26/95, in Bella Rosenberg papers.

109. *Cleveland Plain Dealer*, 5/14/95, p. 1H.

110. *NYT*, 6/13/95, p. A16.

111. Donahue interview, pp. 15–16, 19, 22.

112. *WP*, 10/25/95, p. A1; Joyce interview, pp. 20–22.

113. *WP*, 10/26/95, p. A1; Puddington, *Lane Kirkland*, p. 304. See also Donahue interview, pp. 23–24.

114. Buhle, *Taking Care of Business*, p. 204.

115. Puddington, *Lane Kirkland*, p. 212.

116. Phil Kugler interview, pp. 39–40. See also Dorn interview II, p. 15; Puddington, *Lane Kirkland*, p. 212.

117. Puddington, *Lane Kirkland*, p. 10.

118. *NYT*, 9/15/05, p. A14.

119. Will Marshall interview, pp. 16–18.

19. Reviving the Education-Standards Movement and the Final Days (1995–1997)

1. AP, 7/22/93.

2. WWS, 2/25/96.

3. WWS, 10/9/94.

4. *WT*, 3/17/95, p. A2; *Boston Globe*, 7/12/95, p. 3; WWS, 3/5/95.

5. Cross, *Political Education*, p. 115.

6. *NYT*, 7/6/95, p. A15; *U.S. Newswire*, 6/29/95. See also WWS, 10/29/95.

7. McPike interview, p. 18.

8. Goldberg interview, pp. 13–14; *U.S. Newswire*, 6/29/95.

9. *NYT*, 7/6/95, p. A15.

10. Cohen interview, pp. 19–20.

11. Ruth Wattenberg interview, pp. 25, 27.

12. WWS, 7/30/95.

13. Ruth Wattenberg interview, pp. 26.

14. Mosle, *NYT Magazine*, 9/8/96, p. 41. *Making Standards Matter* was published by the AFT annually from 1995 through 2001. See AFT, *Smart Testing: Let's Get It Right*, July 2006, p. 3.

15. *U.S. Newswire*, 9/6/95; *M2 Presswire*, 9/4/95.

16. Eugenia Kemble interview II, p. 41.

17. WWS, 2/19/95; Eugenia Kemble interview, 6/14/06.

18. *NYT*, 7/6/95, p. A15.

19. *NYT*, 9/20/95, p. B11.

20. Bill Clinton, "Remarks to the American Federation of Teachers," 7/28/95, in *Public Papers of the Presidents*.

21. Casserly, letter to Shanker, 10/2/95, in Bella Rosenberg papers.

22. Shanker, letter to Casserly, 10/10/95, in Bella Rosenberg papers.

23. Shanker, letter to Casserly, 10/10/95, in Bella Rosenberg papers.

24. WWS, 10/22/95.

25. WWS, 1/16/94.

26. WWS, 6/19/94.

27. Litow interview, pp. 6–7.

28. Litow interview, p. 7.

29. Cohen interview, p. 20; *U.S. Newswire*, 3/24/96.

30. Cross, *Political Education*, pp. 115–116; Jennings, *Why National Standards and Tests?*, p. 165; *American Educator*, Spring 1996, p. 15.

31. Litow interview, pp. 7–8.

32. President Clinton speech, 3/27/96, in *American Educator*, Spring 1996, p. 11.

33. Horwitz interview, pp. 4–5.

34. *NYT*, 3/28/96, p. B10; Schwartz, in Gordon, *A Nation Reformed?*, p. 144.

35. McPike interview, p. 24.

36. *American Educator*, Spring 1996.

37. Mosle, *NYT Magazine*, 10/27/96; Eadie Shanker interview, 2/27/04. See also AP, 5/14/96.

38. Eadie Shanker interview, 10/18/02, pp. 68, 71; Eadie Shanker memo, 3/3/06.

39. Eadie Shanker interview, 2/27/04, p. 8.

40. Smith interview, pp. 25–26; Eadie Shanker interview, 10/18/02, p. 18.

41. AP, 7/1/96; *WP*, 1/28/98, p. A3.

42. Mosle, *NYT Magazine*, 10/27/96.

43. Woo, *LA Times Magazine*, 12/1/96, p. 17ff.

44. *American Educator*, special issue, "The Power of Ideas," Spring–Summer 1997, p. 112.

45. Ann Bradley, "End of an Era," *Education Week*, 3/5/97. See also Memorial Service transcript, 4/9/97, p. 5.

46. Lieberman interview, p. 34; Woo, *LA Times Magazine*, 12/1/96, pp. 17ff; Chaykin interview, p. 28.

47. Johnson interview, p. 30.

48. Lieberman interview, p. 92.

49. Bob Dole acceptance speech, 8/15/96, available at http://www.pbs.org/newshour/convention96/floor_speeches/bob_dole.html.

50. Lieberman, *The Teacher Unions*, pp. 2, 84, 87; Chavez and Gray, *Betrayal*, p. 119, citing Charles Lewis.

51. Thomas Toch, "Why Teachers Don't Teach," *U.S. News and World Report*, 2/26/96, pp. 62ff. See also Fuller, Mitchell, and Hartmann, "Collective Bargaining in Milwaukee Schools," p. 128; Stern, *Breaking Free*, p. 24.

52. Toch, *U.S. News*, 2/26/96.

53. Finn, quoted in Fiske, *NYT*, 11/5/89, sect. 4A, p. 34.

54. Toch, *U.S. News*, 2/26/96.

55. Goldhaber in *Collective Bargaining*, p. 147.

56. Lieberman, *The Teacher Unions*, p. 221.

57. Toch, *U.S. News*, 2/26/96; Caroline Hoxby and Andrew Leigh, "Pulled Away or Pushed Out? Explaining the Decline of Teacher Aptitude in the United States," http://post.economic.harvard.edu/faculty/hoxby/papers.hoxbyrackoff.pdf. Note that some argue that the single salary schedule is not necessarily attributable to collective bargaining. The single salary schedule exists in nonbargaining states as well. Kerchner and Koppich, "Organizing Around Quality," p. 293. See also Lieberman, *The Teacher Unions*, p. 214. And the practice has been around for one hundred years, long before the advent of collective bargaining for teachers. See Lewis Solomon, "Recognizing Differences: Let's Reward Good Teachers," *Education Next*, Winter 2005, p. 16.

58. Finn, *Commentary*, 10/94, pp. 30ff.

59. Mosle, *NYT Magazine*, 10/27/96, pp. 45ff.

60. WWS, 9/8/96; *American Educator*, special issue, "The Power of Ideas," Spring–Summer 1997, pp. 19–20.

61. Adam Shanker interview II, p. 17.

62. WWS, 9/8/96.

63. Joe A. Stone, "Collective Bargaining and Public Schools," pp. 49–51; U.S. Department of Education, National Center for Education Statistics, *Digest of Education Statistics, 2003*, table 69, p. 89. This research is consistent with studies finding a significant wage and benefits premium for union members as a whole. See Freeman and Medoff, *What Do Unions Do?*, pp. 46–48.

64. Boyd et al., "The Preparation and Recruitment of Teachers," pp. 152–153.

65. WWS, 12/2/79, citing Freeman and Medoff. See also Freeman and Medoff, *What Do Unions Do?*, pp. 7–8, 20–21.

66. Johnson and Kardos, "Reform Bargaining," p. 13; U.S. Department of Education, National Center for Education Statistics, *Digest of Education Statistics, 2002*, table 65, p. 77; Stone, "Collective Bargaining and Public Schools," p. 51; See, e.g., Mishel and Rothstein, *The Class Size Debate* (with contributions by Alan B. Krueger, Eric A. Hanushek, and Jennifer King Rice).

67. Johnson and Kardos, "Reform Bargaining and Its Promise for School Improvement," p. 13; Stone, "Collective Bargaining and Public Schools," p. 51; Kerchner and Koppich, "Organizing Around Quality," pp. 295–296 (describing staff development contractual provisions in Dade County, Minneapolis, and New York); Elmore and Burney, "Investing in Teacher Learning: Staff Development and Instructional Improvement in Community School District #2, New York City."

68. Barton, "Unequal Learning Environments," pp. 235–236 (Texas and West Virginia), 246 (Minneapolis), 229–234 (relationship between discipline and achievement). For reference to New York's early contract provisions on discipline, see Hechinger, "School and Teacher—Repercussions of the Strike," *New York Times*, October 1, 1967, sect. 4, p. 9.

69. Bella Rosenberg interview. See also the discussion in chapter 4 regarding the UFT's opposition to patronage hiring under New York City's school-decentralization program.

70. Interview with Albert Shanker, 1988, The New York Public Library—American Jewish Committee Oral History Collection, Dorot Jewish Division, The New York Public Library, p. 9.

71. WWS, 3/3/96. See also WWS, 7/21/96; WWS, 5/3/87; Shanker, Pew Forum, August 1993, in "Pew Forum Supplement," *Education Week*, 5/14/97, p. 35.

72. WWS, 3/3/96.

73. Rosenberg interview II, p. 32; Rosenberg interview III, pp. 24–25; Darling-Hammond interview, pp. 7–8.

74. Mooney interview, pp. 5–6; Chaykin interview, p. 4; UPI, 1/12/86.

75. WWS, 8/23/87; *WP*, 12/21/87.

76. Urbanski interview, pp. 8–9; *National Journal*, 11/17/90, p. 2819; *U.S. News & World Report*, 12/24/90, p. 52; *WT*, 1/21/91, p. A3; *WP*, 2/21/88, p. H5; Toch, *In the Name of Excellence*, p. 146.

77. Litow interview, pp. 11–12; Rosenberg interview III, p. 23; Darling-Hammond interview, p. 6; Sandra Feldman interview, pp. 54–55; Kerchner et al., *United Mind Workers*, pp. 87–88; Finn, "Teacher Unions and School Equality," pp. 122–123; Bella Rosenberg interview.

78. Urbanski interview, pp. 12, 14; *Chicago Tribune*, 8/18/02, p. C10.

79. Widmeyer interview, p. 21 (regarding the number of locals); Chanin interview, p. 18.

80. Kirst interview, p. 11.

81. Kerchner et al., *United Mind Workers*, p. 4.

82. Sandra Feldman interview, p. 52.

83. Thomas Toch, "America's 'Most Militant Teacher' Calls for Reform," *U.S. News & World Report*, 2/26/96, p. 70.

84. Ruth Wattenberg memo.

85. Toch, *Education Week*, 3/26/97.

86. Diane Ravitch interview, p. 17; Urbanski interview, p. 10.

87. *NYT*, 9/13/96, p. A1; *NYT*, 9/13/96, p. A1; Darling-Hammond interview, pp. 20–23.

88. *NYT Magazine*, 10/27/96, p. 45ff; *LA Times*, 12/1/96, p. 17ff.

89. David Hill, *Education Week*, 2/21/96.

90. WWS, 1/5/97.

91. Hirsch interview, pp. 12–13; *USA Today*, 1/13/97, p. 6D.

92. Michael Cohen interview, p. 19.

93. *NYT*, 2/5/97, p. A1; *NYT*, 2/5/97, p. A21.

94. Adam Shanker interview II, p. 21.

95. Michael Shanker interview, pp. 23–24; Adam Shanker interview II, p. 21.

96. Memorial Service transcript, 4/9/97, p. 25.

97. WWS, 2/9/97.

98. *WP*, 5/7/97, p. A2.

99. Bob Chase, "The New NEA: Reinventing the teacher unions for a new era," *Vital Speeches of the Day*, 4/1/97, pp. 372–375.

100. Cameron, *The Inside Story*, p. 172.

101. Toch, *Education Week*, 3/26/97.

102. Memorial Service transcript, 4/9/97, p. 12.

103. Eadie Shanker interview, 2/27/04, p. 8; Eadie Shanker memo, 3/3/06.

104. Harris interview, 5/6/03, p. 51. See also Harris interview, 3/30/04, p. 2.

105. *WP*, 2/23/97, p. B5.

106. Eadie Shanker interview, 11/1/02 p. 1; Eadie Shanker interview, 10/24/03; Eadie Shanker interview, 3/18/04; Elaine Sanders interview, p. 9. Eadie Shanker comments at Stuyvesant, 2/28/97; Eadie Shanker memo, 3/3/06.

107. Visit to gravesite during Elaine Sanders interview, p. 10.

108. *American Teacher*, 4/97, p. 7; Eadie Shanker interview, 3/18/04; Eadie Shanker memo, 3/3/06.

109. *NYT*, 3/25/97, p. B7.

110. Eadie Shanker interview, 10/18/02, p. 44; Eadie Shanker memo, 3/3/06.

111. *NYT*, 3/25/97, p. B7.

112. Eadie Shanker memo, 3/3/06.

113. Kirkland speech, Memorial Service transcript, 4/9/97, p. 10.

114. Dorn interview II, pp. 52–53; McElroy interview, p. 19.

115. Ravitch, *New Leader*, 2/24/97; Chester Finn, *WSJ*, 4/9/97, p. A14; Chavez, *Chicago Tribune*, 2/26/97; Arch Puddington, "Missing Albert Shanker," *Commentary*, July 1997; Beichman, *WT*, 2/25/97, p. A20; Wattenberg, *WT*, 2/27/97, A15; E. D. Hirsch, op-ed, *WP*, 3/1/97, p. A23.

116. Weisman, editorial, *NYT*, 3/1/97, p. A22.

117. Paul Buhle, "Albert Shanker: No Flowers," *New Politics*, Summer 1997.

118. *NYT*, 3/30/97; *NYT*, 5/7/97, p. B14.

119. *NYT*, 7/30/97, p. B8.

120. Remarks by President Clinton, Federal News Service, 1/15/98.

121. *NYT*, 1/27/98, p. A12.

122. *Times-Picayune*, 7/3/98, p. A1 (citing union officials).

123. *WP*, 7/6/98, p. A1.

124. McElroy interview, p. 15; Futrell interview, pp. 28–29; Weiner interview, pp. 38–39.

125. *Education Week*, 3/8/06, p. 1.

126. Cross, *Political Education*, pp. 118–119; *Los Angeles Sentinel*, 10/1/97, p. 8; Michael Cohen interview, p. 16.

127. *NYT*, 3/31/00, p. A22; *WP*, 5/23/00, p. C1.

128. Tucker interview, pp. 15 17; Sandra Feldman interview, pp. 48–49; Ambach interview, handnotes, pp. 9–11, 15.

129. Center on Education Policy, "State High School Exit Exams: A Challenging Year," August 2006, pp. 1–2.

130. Cross, *Political Education*, p. 139. While the fifty states set their own standards, there is a vague federal check against the National Assessment of Education Progress (NAEP).

131. Ambach interview, handnotes, pp. 9–11, 15.

132. Cross, *Political Education*, pp. 139–140.

133. Rosenberg interview III, pp. 54–58.

134. Fondy interview, p. 36; Irons interview, p. 9; Cohen interview, p. 21; Rosenberg interview II, p. 6.

135. Schwartz, in Gordon, *A Nation Reformed*, pp. 11, 145; Cross, *Political Education*, pp. 138–139.

136. *LA Times*, 5/26/91, p. A1.

137. *Boston Globe*, 4/22/93, p. 13.

20. The Legacy of Albert Shanker

1. *WP*, 2/23/97, p. B5; *Education Week*, 3/5/97.

2. Eugenia Kemble interview II, p. 55.

3. Lieberman, *The Teacher Unions*, p. 1.

4. Lieberman, Haar, and Troy, *The NEA and The AFT*, p. 1; Lichtenstein, *State of the Union*, p. 185.

5. Toch, *In the Name of Excellence*, p. 135.

6. Lieberman, *The Teacher Unions*, p. 2.

7. Lieberman, *The Teacher Unions*, p. 4.

8. Rachelle Horowitz, e-mail to author, 2/14/06; *American Teacher*, 9/84; *American Teacher*, 9/88.

9. Kerchner et al., *United Mind Workers*, p. 13; Ballou and Podgursky, "Gaining Control of Professional Licensing and Advancement," 86; Lieberman, *The Teacher Unions*, p. 4; Brimelow, *The Worm in the Apple*, p. 171; Toch, "Why Teachers Don't Teach," *U.S. News & World Report*, 2/26/96, pp. 62ff; Terry Moe, "No Teacher Left Behind," *WSJ*, 1/13/05, p. A12.

10. Murphy, *Blackboard Unions*, p. 4.

11. Memorial Service transcript, 4/9/97, p. 15.

12. U.S. Department of Education, National Center for Education Statistics, *Digest of Education Statistics, 2005*, table 76, p. 115.

13. Rosenberg interview III, pp. 48–49.

14. Stone, "Collective Bargaining," p. 51; See, e.g., Mishel and Rothstein, *The Class Size Debate* (with contributions by Alan B. Krueger, Eric A. Hanushek and Jennifer King Rice).

15. Toch, *In the Name of Excellence*, p. 152; James Parks, "NY Teacher's Unions Set to Merge," *AFL-CIO NOW*, 5/18/06.

16. Kirst interview, p. 7.

17. Finn conversation, 10/18/05.

18. Urbanski interview, pp. 13–14.

19. Sandra Feldman interview, p. 59. See also Horowitz interview, p. 71.

20. Mooney interview, p. 36.

21. Linda Jacobson, "First Major Study Suggests Worth of National 'Seal,'" *Education Week*, 3/17/04, p. A; Goldhaber and Anthony, "Can Teacher Quality Be Effectively Assessed?" 4/27/04 (updated from 3/8/04 paper), available online at http://www.urban.org/Uploaded PDF/410958_NBPTSOutcomes.pdf.

22. Bob Chase interview, p. 17; Phil Kugler interview, p. 23.

23. Lawrence interview, p. 21.

24. Litow interview, p. 13; McElroy interview, p. 6; Ruth Wattenberg interview, p. 45.

25. Darling-Hammond interview, p. 25.

26. Urbanski interview, p. 10.

27. Bella Rosenberg conversation, 5/9/05.

28. *WP Magazine*, 11/11/01, p. 28.

29. Kelly e-mail to author, 11/30/04.

30. Kelly interview, p. 16.

31. Kelly interview, p. 16.

32. Smith interview, pp. 21–22.

33. Ravitch, *Left Back*, p. 430.

34. Litow interview, p. 13.

35. *Education Week*, 8/31/05, p. 1.

36. "Quality Counts," *Education Week*, 1/5/06, p. 6.

37. Smith interview, p. 34.; Wurtzel interview, pp. 7–8.

38. Ryan and Heise, *WP*, 7/3/02, p. A23.

39. Lieberman interview, p. 42. See also Finn interview, p. 16.

40. Darling-Hammond interview, p. 12.

41. Lieberman, *The Teacher Unions*, pp. 196, 205.

42. Finn interview, pp. 16–17.

43. Diane Ravitch interview, p. 15.

44. Gibson interview, p. 10.

45. Usdan interview, p. 34.

46. Finn interview, pp. 5–6.

47. Lawrence interview, pp. 22, 26.

48. Cole interview, p. 20.

49. Widmeyer interview, pp. 6–7.

50. Chavez interview, pp. 27–28.

51. Diane Ravitch interview, p. 24.

52. Humphrey interview, pp. 7, 32–33.

53. Kirst interview, p. 27.

54. Diane Ravitch interview, p. 4.

55. Burnie Bond interview, p. 16.

56. Humphrey interview, pp. 41–43.

57. Eugenia Kemble interview II, p. 53.

58. Sandra Feldman interview, p. 2; Darling-Hammond interview, p. 2; Mooney interview, p. 37.

59. Beinart, *TNR*, 12/13/04, p. 24.

60. George Packer, *New Yorker*, 2/16&23/04, pp. 103, 106.

61. Jean-Claude Shanda Tonme, op-ed, *NYT*, 7/15/05, p. A19.

62. Beinart, *The Good Fight*, pp. 187–188

63. AFT Executive Council resolution "To Support the Affirmative Action Policy at the University of Michigan Before the U.S. Supreme Court," available at http://www.aft.org/about/resolutions/2003/affirmative_action.htm.

64. Lieberman, *The Teacher Unions*, p. 1.

65. Broder, *WP*, 9/9/04, p. A27.

66. Dean, *Toward a More Perfect Union*, draft, p. 28.

67. Shanker, AFT Executive Committee meeting, 2/14/96, p. 18, in Marcia Reecer papers.

68. Arch Puddington, Sidney Hook and American Democracy conference, 10/1/05.

69. Geoghegan, *Which Side Are You On?*, pp. 7, 269, 278, 284.

70. NYT/CBS News poll, in *NYT*, 7/25/04, pp. 1, 9.

71. *WP*, 10/16/05, p. A5.

72. Anthony Carnevale interview, 7/26/06.

73. Puddington, *Commentary*, 7/97.

74. Baer, *Reinventing Democrats*, pp. 32–33.

75. Baer, *Reinventing Democrats*, p. 7.

76. Baer, *Reinventing Democrats*, p. 67.

77. Kahlenberg and Teixeira, "A Better Third Way," *The Nation*, 3/5/01, pp. 15ff. See also Frank, *What's the Matter With Kansas?*, p. 243; and Reich, "Dead Center," *NYT*, 1/29/04.

78. Kaufman, *Henry M. Jackson*, pp. 432–433, 446; David Corn, "Gore's Surrender," *The Nation*, 8/21/00, p. 4.

79. Michael Allen, Sidney Hook and American Democracy conference, 10/1/05.

80. George Packer, *New Yorker*, 2/16&23/04, p. 106.

81. Thomas Friedman, *NYT*, 1/8/04.

82. Beinart, *Blueprint Magazine*, 10/21/05.

83. Robert Leiken, Sidney Hook and American Democracy conference, 10/1/05; Zbigniew Brzezinski, *WP*, 12/4/05, p. B2.

84. See Skrentny, *Color Lines*.

85. Editorial, "Life in the Bottom 80%," *NYT*, 9/1/05.

86. *NYT*, 12/10/06, sect. 3, p. 3.

87. Sebastian Mallaby, *WP*, 11/14/05, p. A21.

88. *WSJ*, 7/29/04, pp. A1, A4.

89. Ruy Teixeira, *Public Opinion Watch*, 6/8/05.

90. Ruy Teixeira, "It's the White Working Class, Stupid," *Public Opinion Watch*, 2/16/05.

91. Will Marshall interview, pp. 4–5, 8. See also Carville and Begala, *Take It Back*, p. 85.

92. Beinart, *Blueprint Magazine*, 10/21/05. See also William A. Galston and Elaine C. Kamarck, *The Politics of Polarization: A Third Way Report*, October 2005, p. 18, chart 2. Available online at http://www.third-way.com/data/product/file/16/politics_of_polarization.pdf.

93. Weisberg, *Slate*, 8/9/06.

94. Packer, *Blood of the Liberals*, pp. 306–307.

95. Chait, *TNR*, 2/3/03, p. 14.

96. Jerome R. Stockfisch, "Minimum Wage Rises; High Speed Rail Fails," *Tampa Tribune*, 11/3/04, p. 2.

97. Ross Douthat and Reihan Salam, "The Party of Sam's Club," *Weekly Standard*, 11/14/05.

98. Packer, *Blood of the Liberals*, p. 300.

99. Siegel, Sidney Hook and American Democracy conference, 10/1/05.

100. David Brooks, *NYT*, 10/21/03.

101. John Halpin and Ruy Teixeira, "The Politics of Definition," *The American Prospect*, May 2006.

102. WWS, 7/4/76.

BIBLIOGRAPHY

Ad Hoc Committee to Defend the Right to Teach. "The Freedom to Teach." In *Confrontation at Ocean Hill–Brownsville: The New York School Strikes of 1968*, edited by Maurice Berube and Marilyn Gittell, 120–122. New York: Praeger, 1969.

Ad Hoc Committee for Justice in the Schools. "Due Process, Civil Liberties, and the Public Schools." In *Confrontation at Ocean Hill-Brownsville: The New York School Strikes of 1968*, edited by Maurice Berube and Marilyn Gittell, 148–155. New York: Praeger, 1969.

Advisory and Evaluation Committee on Decentralization (Niemeyer Committee). Excerpts from the "Final Report Submitted to the New York City Board of Education." In *Confrontation at Ocean Hill–Brownsville: The New York School Strikes of 1968*, edited by Maurice Berube and Marilyn Gittell, 24–32. New York: Praeger, 1969.

Anderson, Jervis. *A. Philip Randolph: A Biographical Portrait*. Berkeley: University of California Press, 1986.

———. *Bayard Rustin: Troubles I've Seen*. New York: Harper Collins, 1997.

Aronowitz, Stanley. *How Class Works: Power and Social Movements*. New Haven, Conn.: Yale University Press, 2003.

Auletta, Ken. *The Streets Were Paved with Gold: The Declined New York—an American Tragedy*. New York: Vintage Books, 1980.

Baer, Kenneth. *Reinventing Democrats: The Politics of Liberalism from Reagan to Clinton*. Lawrence: University Press of Kansas, 2000.

Ballou, Dale, and Michael Podgursky. "Gaining Control of Professional Licensing and Advancement." In *Conflicting Missions? Teachers Unions and Educational Reform*, edited by Tom Loveless, 69–109. Washington, D.C.,: The Brookings Institution Press, 2000.

Barone, Michael. *Hard America, Soft America: Competition Versus Coddling and the Battle for the Nation's Future.* New York: Crown Forum, 2004.

Barton, Paul E. "Unequal Learning Environments: Discipline That Works." In *A Notion at Risk: Preserving Public Education as an Engine for Social Mobility*, edited by Richard D. Kahlenberg. New York: Century Foundation Press, 2000.

Bates, Stephan. *Battleground: One Mother's Crusade, the Religious Right, and the Struggle for Control of Our Classrooms.* New York: Poseidon Press, 1993.

Beinart, Peter. *The Good Fight: Why Liberals—and Only Liberals—Can Win the War on Terror and Make America Great Again.* New York: Harper Collins, 2006.

Bell, Terrel. *The Thirteenth Man: A Reagan Cabinet Memoir.* New York: The Free Press, 1988.

Bensinger, Richard. "When We Try More, We Win More: Organizing the New Workforce." In *Not Your Father's Union Movement*, edited by J. Mort, 27–42. New York: Verso, 1998.

Berliner, David C., and Bruce J. Biddle. *The Manufactured Crisis: Myths, Fraud, and the Attack on American Public Schools.* New York: Perseus Books, 1995.

Bernhardt, Debra. *Ordinary People, Extraordinary Lives: A Pictorial History of Working People in New York City.* New York: New York University Press, 2000.

Berube, Maurice. *American School Reform: Progressive, Equity, and Excellence Movements, 1883–1993.* Westport, Conn.: Praeger, 1994.

Berube, Maurice, and Marilyn Gittell, eds. *Confrontation at Ocean Hill–Brownsville: The New York School Strikes of 1968.* New York: Praeger, 1969.

Boyd, Donald, Hamilton Lankford, Susanna Loeb, and James Wyckoff. "The Preparation and Recruitment of Teachers." In *A Qualified Teacher in Every Classroom? Appraising Old Answers and New Ideas*, edited by Frederick M. Hess, Andrew J. Rotherham, and Kate Walsh. Cambridge, Mass.: Harvard Education Press, 2004.

Branch, Taylor. *At Canaan's Edge: America in the King Years, 1965–1968.* New York: Simon and Schuster, 2006.

Braun, Robert. *Teachers and Power: The Story of the American Federation of Teachers.* New York: Simon & Schuster, 1972.

Brimelow, Peter. *The Worm in the Apple: How the Teacher Unions Are Destroying American Education.* New York: Harper Collins, 2003.

Brinkley, Alan. *The End of Reform: New Deal Liberalism in Recession and War.* New York: Vintage Books, 1995.

———. *Voices of Protest: Huey Long, Father Coughlin, and the Great Depression.* New York: Vintage Books, 1982.

Buhle, Paul. *Taking Care of Business: Samuel Gompers, George Meany, Lane Kirkland, and the Tragedy of American Labor.* New York: Monthly Review Press, 1999.

Buhle, Paul, and Robin Kelley. "Allies of a Different Sort: Jews and Blacks in the American Left." In *Struggles in the Promised Land: Toward a History of Black-Jewish Relations in the United States*, edited by Jack Salzman and Cornel West, 197–230. New York: Oxford University Press, 1997.

Bundy, McGeorge. *Reconnection for Learning: A Community School System for New York City (Mayor's Advisory Panel on Decentralization of the New York City Schools).* New York: n.p., November 9, 1967. In *Confrontation at Ocean Hill–Brownsville: The New York School*

Strikes of 1968, edited by Maurice Berube and Marilyn Gittell, 217–219. New York: Praeger, 1969.

Bunzel, John. *Anti-Politics in America: Reflections on the Anti-Political Temper and Its Distortions of the Democratic Process.* New York: Alfred A. Knopf, 1967.

Califano, Joseph. *Governing America: An Insider's Report from the White House and the Cabinet.* New York: Simon and Schuster, 1981.

Cameron, Don. *The Inside Story of the Teacher Revolution in America.* Lanham, Md.: Scarecrow Education, 2005.

Cannato, Vincent. *The Ungovernable City: John Lindsay and His Struggle to Save New York.* New York: Basic Books, 2001.

Carnegie Forum on Education. *A Nation Prepared: Teachers for the Twenty-First Century (The Report of the Task Force on Teaching as a Profession).* New York: Carnegie, 1986.

Carson, Clayborne. *In Struggle: SNCC and the Black Awakening of the 1960s.* Cambridge, Mass.: Harvard University Press, 1981.

———. "Black Jewish Universalism in the Era of Identity Politics." In *Struggles in the Promised Land: Toward a History of Black-Jewish Relations in the United States,* edited by Jack Salzman and Cornel West, 177–196. New York: Oxford University Press, 1997.

Carson, Sonny (Mwlina Imiri Abubadika). *The Education of Sonny Carson.* New York: W. W. Norton, 1972.

Carter, Barbara. *Pickets, Parents, and Power: The Story Behind the New York City Teachers' Strike.* New York: Citation Press, 1971.

Carville, James, and Paul Begala. *Take It Back: Our Party, Our Country, Our Future.* New York: Simon & Schuster, 2006.

Chanes, Jerome. "Affirmative Action: Jewish Ideals, Jewish Interests." In *Struggles in the Promised Land: Toward a History of Black-Jewish Relations in the United States,* edited by Jack Salzman and Cornel West, 295–322. New York: Oxford University Press, 1997

Chavez, Linda. *An Unlikely Conservative: The Transformation of an Ex-Liberal.* New York: Basic Books, 2002.

Chavez, Linda, and Daniel Gray. *Betrayal.* New York: Crown Forum, 2004.

Chester, Eric. *Covert Network: Progressives, the International Rescue Committee, and the CIA.* Armonk, N.Y.: M. E. Sharpe, 1995.

Chubb, John, and Terry Moe. *Politics, Markets, and America's Schools.* Washington, D.C.: Brookings Institution Press, 1990.

Clark, Kenneth. Introduction to *Community Control and the Urban School,* by Mario Fantini, Marilyn Gittell, and Richard Magat. New York: Praeger, 1970.

Clinton, Bill, and Al Gore. *Putting People First: How We Can Change America.* New York: Times Books, 1992.

Cooper, Bruce. "An International Perspective on Teachers Unions." In *Conflicting Missions? Teachers Unions and Educational Reform,* edited by T. Loveless, 240–280. Washington D. C.: The Brookings Institution Press, 2000.

Council of Supervisory Associations. "Hate Literature." In *Confrontation at Ocean Hill–Brownsville: The New York School Strikes of 1968,* edited by Maurice Berube and Marilyn Gittell, 165–167. New York: Praeger, 1969.

Counts, George. *Dare the Schools Build a New Social Order?* New York: Arno Press/New York Times, 1969.

Cross, Chris. *Political Education: National Policy Comes of Age.* New York: Teachers College Press, 2004.

Dawidoff, Nicholas. *The Fly Swatter: How My Grandfather Made His Way in the World.* New York: Pantheon, 2002.

Dean, Amy. *Toward a More Perfect Union.* Manuscript.

D'Emilio, John. *Lost Prophet: The Life and Times of Bayard Rustin.* New York: The Free Press, 2003.

Dewey, John. "Democracy and Education 1916." In *The Middle Works of John Dewey: 1899–1924*, vol. 9, edited by J. Boydston. Carbondale: Southern Illinois University Press, 1985.

———. *The Moral Writings of John Dewey*, edited by J. Gouinlock. Amherst, N.Y.: Prometheus Books, 1994.

Diggins, John Patrick. *The Rise and Fall of the American Left.* New York: W. W. Norton, 1992.

Diggins, John Patrick, and Michael Lind. "The Vital Historian." In *The Liberal Persuasion: Arthur Schlesinger, Jr., and the Challenge of the American Past*, edited by J. Diggins. Princeton, N.J.: Princeton University Press, 1997.

Dionne, E. J. *Stand Up, Fight Back: Republican Toughs, Democratic Wimps, and the Politics of Revenge.* New York: Simon & Schuster, 2004.

Dorman, Joseph. *Arguing the World: The New York Intellectuals in Their Own Words.* New York: The Free Press, 2000.

Drucker, Peter. *Max Shachtman and His Left: A Socialist's Odyssey Through the "American Century."* New Jersey: Humanities Press, 1994.

Drucker, Peter F. *Managing the Nonprofit Organization: Practices and Principles.* New York: Harper Collins, 1990.

Ebert, Roger, ed. *An Illini Century: One Hundred Years of Campus Life.* Urbana: University of Illinois Press, 1967.

Elmore, Richard. "Change and Improvement in Educational Reform." In *A Nation Reformed? American Education Twenty Years After* A Nation at Risk, edited by David Gordon, 23–38. Cambridge, Mass.: Harvard Education Press, 2003.

Elmore, Richard, and Deanna Burney. "Investing in Teacher Learning: Staff Development and Instructional Improvement in Community School District #2, New York City." National Commission on Teaching and America's Future, August 1997.

Epstein, Jason. "The Brooklyn Dodgers." In *Confrontation at Ocean Hill–Brownsville: The New York School Strikes of 1968*, edited by Maurice Berube and Marilyn Gittell, 314–326. New York: Praeger, 1969.

Fantini, Mario. "Community Control and Quality Education in Urban School Systems." In *Community Control of Schools*, edited by H. Levin, 40–75. Washington, D.C.: The Brookings Institution, 1970.

Fantini, Mario, Marilyn Gittell, and R. Magat. *Community Control and the Urban School.* New York: Praeger, 1970.

Feldman, Sandra and Maurice Berube. "An Exchange of Views: Challenge and Reply." In

Confrontation at Ocean Hill–Brownsville: The New York School Strikes of 1968, edited by Maurice Berube and Marilyn Gittell, 139–148. New York: Praeger, 1969.

Ferretti, Fred. "Who's to Blame in the School Strike." In *Confrontation at Ocean Hill–Brownsville*, edited by Maurice Berube and Marilyn Gittell, 283–313. New York: Praeger, 1969.

Finn, Chester E., Jr. "Teacher Unions and School Equality: Potential Allies or Inevitable Foes." In *Challenge to American Schools: The Case for Standards and Values*, edited by J. Bunzel, 99–124. New York: Oxford University Press, 1985.

Finn, Chester E., Jr., Bruno V. Manno, and Gregg Vanourek. *Charter Schools in Action*. Princeton, N.J.: Princeton University Press, 2000.

Fishkin, James. *Justice, Equal Opportunity, and the Family*. New Haven, Conn.: Yale University Press, 1983.

Foner, Philip. *U.S. Labor and the Vietnam War*. New York: International Publishers, 1989.

Fox, Richard. *Reinhold Neibuhr: A Biography*. Ithaca, N.Y.: Cornell University Press, 1996.

Frank, Thomas. *What's the Matter with Kansas? How Conservatives Won the Heart of America*. New York: Henry Holt, 2004.

Fraser, Steve. *Labor Will Rule: Sidney Hillman and the Rise of American Labor*. New York: The Free Press, 1991.

Fraser, Steve, and Gary Gerstle. *Ruling America: A History of Wealth and Power in a Democracy*. Cambridge, Mass.: Harvard University Press, 2005.

Freeman, Joshua. *Working-Class New York: Life and Labor Since World War II*. New York: The New Press, 2000.

Freeman, Richard, and James Medoff. *What Do Unions Do?* New York: Basic Books, 1984.

Fuhrman, Susan. "Riding Waves, Trading Horses: The Twenty Year Effort to Reform Education." In *A Nation Reformed? American Education Twenty Years After A Nation at Risk*, edited by David Gordon, 7–22. Cambridge, Mass.: Harvard Education Press, 2003.

Fuller, Howard, George Mitchell, and Michael Hartmann. "Collective Bargaining in Milwaukee Public Schools." In *Conflicting Missions? Teachers Unions and Educational Reform*, edited by T. Loveless, 110–149. Washington, D.C.: The Brookings Institution, 2000.

Gaffney, David. *Blackboard Warriors: How New York State United Teachers (NYSUT) Learned to Unite, Elect Senators, and Reform Education*. Manuscript: Draft Copy.

Geoghegan, Tom. *The Secret Lives of Citizens: Pursuing the Promise of American Life*. New York: Pantheon Books, 1998.

———. *Which Side Are You On? Trying to Be for Labor When It's Flat on Its Back*. New York: Farrar, Straus & Giroux, 1991; New York: New Press, 2004.

Gittell, Marilyn. "The Balance of Power and the Community School." In *Community Control of Schools*, edited by H. Levin, 115–137. Washington, D.C.: The Brookings Institution, 1970.

Glasser, Ira, and approved by the New York Civil Liberties Union Board of Directors. "The Burden of the Blame." In *Confrontation at Ocean Hill–Brownsville: The New York School Strikes of 1968*, edited by Maurice Berube and Marilyn Gittell, 104–119. New York: Praeger, 1969.

Glotzner, Albert. *Trotsky: Memoir and Critique*. Buffalo, N.Y.: Prometheus Books, 1989.

Goldbloom, Maurice. "The New York School Crisis." In *Confrontation at Ocean Hill–Browns-ville: The New York School Strikes of 1968*, edited by Maurice Berube and Marilyn Gittell, 247–283. New York: Praeger, 1969.

Goldhaber, Dan. "Are Teachers Unions Good for Students?" In *Collective Bargaining in Education: Negotiating Change in Today's Schools*, edited by Jane Hannaway and Andrew J. Rotherham. Cambridge, Mass.: Harvard Education Press, 2006.

Golin, Steve. *The Newark Teachers Strike: Hopes on the Line.* New Brunswick, N.J.: Rutgers University Press, 2002.

Gordon, David, ed. *A Nation Reformed? American Education Twenty Years After* A Nation at Risk. Cambridge, Mass.: Harvard Education Press, 2003.

Goulden, Joseph. *Jerry Wurf: Labor's Last Angry Man.* New York: Athenaeum, 1982.

———. *Meany.* New York: Athenaeum, 1972.

Graham, Patricia. Foreword to *A Nation Reformed? American Education Twenty Years After* A Nation at Risk, edited by David Gordon. Cambridge, Mass.: Harvard Education Press, 2003.

Green, Max. *Epitaph for American Labor: How Union Leaders Lost Touch with America.* Washington, D.C.: AEI Press, 1996.

Grossman, Pam. "Teaching: From *A Nation at Risk* to a Profession at Risk?" In *A Nation Reformed? American Education Twenty Years After* A Nation at Risk, edited by David Gordon, 69–80. Cambridge, Mass.: Harvard Education Press, 2003.

Gutmann, Amy. "Freedom of Association: An Introductory Essay." In *Freedom of Association*, edited by Amy Gutmann, 3–34. Princeton, N.J.: Princeton University Press, 1998.

Hampton, Henry, and Steve Fayer. *Voices of Freedom: An Oral History of the Civil Rights Movement from the 1950s Through the 1980s.* New York: Bantam Books, 1990.

Harnett, Patrick. "Why Teachers Strike: A Lesson for Liberals." In *Confrontation at Ocean Hill–Brownsville: The New York School Strikes of 1968*, edited by Maurice Berube and Marilyn Gittell, 205–214. New York: Praeger, 1969.

Harrington, Michael. *Fragments of the Century: A Social Autobiography.* New York: Saturday Review Press, 1973.

———. "The Freedom to Teach: Beyond Panaceas." In *Confrontation at Ocean Hill–Browns-ville: The New York School Strikes of 1968*, edited by Maurice Berube and Marilyn Gittell, 129–136. New York: Praeger, 1969.

———. *The Long Distance Runner: An Autobiography.* New York: Henry Holt & Company, 1988.

———. "An Open Letter to Men of Good Will (with an Aside to Dwight MacDonald)." In *Confrontation at Ocean Hill–Brownsville: The New York School Strikes of 1968*, edited by Maurice Berube and Marilyn Gittell, 229–237. New York: Praeger, 1969.

———. *Toward a Democratic Left: A Radical Program for a New Majority.* New York: Macmillan, 1968.

———. Foreword to *Why Is There No Socialism in the United States?*, by Werner Sombart. White Plains, N.Y.: International Arts and Sciences Press, Inc., 1976.

Harris, Louis, and Bart Swanson. *Black-Jewish Relations in New York City.* New York: Praeger Publishers, 1970.

Heffernan, Robert. *Cabinetmakers: Story of the Three-Year Battle to Establish the U.S. Department of Education.* New York: Writer's Showcase, 2001.

Hentoff, Nat. *Does Anybody Give a Damn?* New York: A. A. Knopf, 1977.

———. "Ad Hoc Committee on Confusion." *Village Voice*, September 26, 1968. Quoted in Maurice Berube and Marilyn Gittell, eds., *Confrontation at Ocean Hill–Brownsville: The New York School Strikes of 1968*, 122–129. New York: Praeger, 1969.

Hine, D. C., ed. *Eyes on the Prize: Civil Rights Reader (Documents, Speeches, and Firsthand Accounts from the Black Freedom Struggle).* New York: Penguin Books, 1991.

Hirsch, E. D., Jr. *The Schools We Need; And Why We Don't Have Them.* New York: Doubleday, 1996.

Hitchens, Christopher. *Why Orwell Matters.* New York: Basic Books, 2002.

Hollander, Paul. *Political Pilgrims.* 4th ed. New Brunswick, N.J.: Transaction Publishers, 1998.

Holmes, Steven. *Ron Brown: An Uncommon Life.* New York: John Wiley and Sons, 2000.

Hook, Sidney. *Out of Step: An Unquiet Life in the Twentieth Century.* New York: Harper & Row, 1987.

Horowitz, Helen. *Campus Life: Undergraduate Cultures from the End of the Eighteenth Century to the Present.* New York: A. A. Knopf, 1987.

Howe, Irving. *World of Our Fathers: The Journey of the Eastern European Jews to America and the Life They Found and Made.* New York: Harcourt Brace Jovanovich, 1976.

Isaacs, Charles. "A JHS 271 Teacher Tells It Like He Sees It." In *Eyes on the Prize: Civil Rights Reader (Documents, Speeches, and Firsthand Accounts from the Black Freedom Struggle)*, edited by D. C. Hine, 362–376. New York: Penguin Books, 1991.

Isserman, Maurice. *The Other American: The Life of Michael Harrington.* New York: Public Affairs, 2000.

———. *If I Had a Hammer … : The Death of the Old Left and the Birth of the New Left.* New York: Basic Books, 1987.

Iversen, Robert. *The Communists and the Schools.* New York: Harcourt, Brace and Company, 1959.

Jacoby, Tamar. *Someone Else's House: America's Unfinished Struggle for Integration.* New York: The Free Press, 1998.

Jeffries, John C., Jr. *Justice Lewis F. Powell, Jr.: A Biography.* New York: Scribner's, 1994.

Jennings, John. *Why National Standards and Tests? Politics and the Quest for Better Schools.* Thousand Oaks, Calif.: SAGE Publications, 1998.

Johnson, Susan, and Susan Kardos. "Reform Bargaining and Its Promise for School Improvement." In *Conflicting Missions? Teachers Unions and Educational Reform*, edited by T. Loveless, 7–46. Washington, D.C.: The Brookings Institution Press, 2000.

Kahlenberg, Richard D. *All Together Now: Creating Middle-Class Schools Through Public School Choice.* Washington, D.C.: The Brookings Institution Press, 2001.

———. *The Remedy: Class, Race, and Affirmative Action.* New York: Basic Books, 1996.

Karp, Richard. "School Decentralization in New York." In *Confrontation at Ocean Hill–Brownsville: The New York School Strikes of 1968*, edited by Maurice Berube and Marilyn Gittell, 63–78. New York: Praeger, 1969.

Kaufman, Jonathan. *Broken Alliance: The Turbulent Times Between Blacks and Jews.* New York: Charles Scribner's Sons, 1988.

————. "Blacks and Jews: The Struggle in the Cities." In *Struggles in the Promised Land: Toward a History of Black-Jewish Relations in the United States,* edited by Jack Salzman and Cornel West, 107–122. New York: Oxford University Press, 1997.

Kaufman, Robert. *Henry M. Jackson: A Life in Politics.* Seattle: University of Washington Press, 2000.

Kelley, Robin. *Race Rebels: Culture, Politics, and the Black Working Class.* New York: The Free Press, 1994.

Kemble, Eugenia. "Ocean Hill–Brownsville." In *Confrontation at Ocean Hill–Brownsville: The New York School Strikes of 1968,* edited by Maurice Berube and Marilyn Gittell, 33–51. New York: Praeger, 1969.

Kerchner, Charles and Julia Koppich. "Organizing Around Quality: The Frontiers of Teacher Unionism." In *Conflicting Missions? Teachers Unions and Educational Reform,* ed. T. Loveless, 281–316. Washington, D.C.: The Brookings Institution Press, 2000.

Kerchner, Charles, Julia Koppich, and Joseph Weeres. *United Mind Workers: Unions and Teaching in the Knowledge Society.* San Francisco: Jossey-Bass Publications, 1997.

King, Martin Luther, Jr. *Why We Can't Wait.* New York: New American Library, 1964.

Kolderie, Ted. "Beyond Choice to New Public Schools." Available online at http://www.ppionline.org/ndol/print.cfm?contentid=1692.

Kristol, Irving. *Neoconservative: The Autobiography of an Idea.* New York: Free Press, 1995.

Kusnet, David. "The 'America Needs a Raise' Campaign: The New Labor Movement and the Politics of Living Standards." In *Not Your Father's Union Movement,* edited by J. Mort, 167–178. New York: Verso, 1998.

Lemann, Nicholas. *The Big Test: The Secret History of American Meritocracy.* New York: Farrar, Straus & Giroux, 1999.

Levin, Henry. "Summary of Conference Discussion." In *Community Control of Schools,* edited by Henry Levin, 275–309. Washington, D.C.: The Brookings Institution Press, 1970.

Levine, Daniel. *Bayard Rustin and the Civil Rights Movement.* New Brunswick, N.J.: Rutgers University Press, 2000.

Lichtenstein, Nelson. *The Most Dangerous Man in Detroit: Walter Reuther and the Fate of American Labor.* New York: Basic Books, 1995.

————. *State of the Union: A Century of American Labor.* Princeton, N.J.: Princeton University Press, 2002.

Lieberman, Myron. *The Teacher Unions: How the NEA and AFT Sabotage Reform and Hold Students, Parents, Teachers, and Taxpayers Hostage to Bureaucracy.* New York: The Free Press, 1997.

Lieberman, Myron, Charlene Haar, and Leo Troy. *The NEA and the AFT: Teacher Unions in Power and Politics.* Crockport, Mass.: Pro Active Publications, 1994.

Lind, Michael. *Vietnam: The Necessary War.* New York: The Free Press, 1999.

Lipset, Seymour Martin, and Gary Marks. *It Didn't Happen Here.* New York: W. W. Norton, 2000.

Lipset, Seymour Martin, Martin Trow, and James Coleman. *Union Democracy: The Internal Politics of the International Typographical Union*. Glencoe, Ill.: The Free Press, 1956.

Lukas, J. Anthony. *Common Ground: A Turbulent Decade in the Lives of Three American Families*. New York: A. A. Knopf, 1985.

MacDonald, Dwight. "An Open Letter to Michael Harrington." In *Confrontation at Ocean Hill–Brownsville: The New York School Strikes of 1968*, edited by Maurice Berube and Marilyn Gittell, 222–228. New York: Praeger, 1969.

Madrick, Jeff. "Inequality and Democracy." In *The Fight Is for Democracy*, edited by George Packer. New York: Harper Perennial, 2003.

Magat, Richard. *Unlikely Partners: Philanthropic Foundations and the Labor Movement*. Ithaca, N.Y.: Cornell University Press, 1999.

Marable, Manning. *Black American Politics: From Washington Marches to Jesse Jackson*. London: Verso, 1985.

——. *Race, Reform, and Rebellion: The Second Reconstruction in Black America, 1945–1990*. 2nd ed. Jackson: University Press of Mississippi, 1991.

Martin, Jay. *The Education of John Dewey: A Biography*. New York: Columbia University Press, 2003.

Martin, Waldo, Jr. "'Nation Time!': Black Nationalism, the Third World, and Jews." In *Struggles in the Promised Land: Toward a History of Black-Jewish Relations in the United States*, edited by Jack Salzman and Cornel West, 341–356. New York: Oxford University Press, 1997.

Mattson, Kevin. *When America Was Great: The Fighting Faith of Postwar Liberalism*. New York: Routledge, 2004.

Mayer, Martin. *The Teachers Strike: New York, 1968*. New York: Harper & Row, 1969.

McCoy, Rhody. "The Formation of a Community Controlled School District." In *Community Control of Schools*, edited by H. Levin, 169–190. Washington, D.C.: The Brookings Institution, 1970.

——. "The Year of the Dragon." In *Confrontation at Ocean Hill–Brownsville: The New York School Strikes of 1968*, edited by Maurice Berube and Marilyn Gittell, 52–62. New York: Praeger, 1969.

Meyerson, Harold. "A Second Chance: The New AFL-CIO and the Prospective Revival of American Labor." In *Not Your Father's Union Movement*, edited by J. Mort, 1–26. New York: Verso, 1998.

Miller, Matthew. *The Two-Percent Solution: Fixing America's Problems in Ways Liberals and Conservatives Can Love*. New York: Public Affairs, 2003.

Mishel, Lawrence, and Richard Rothstein, eds. *The Class Size Debate*. Washington, D.C.: Economic Policy Institute, 2002.

Moe, Terry M. *Schools, Vouchers, and the American Public*. Washington, D.C.: The Brookings Institution Press, 2001.

Morgan, Ted. *A Covert Life: Jay Lovestone: Communist, Anti-Communist, and Spymaster*. New York: Random House, 1999.

Mort, JoAnn. "Finding a Voice: The AFL-CIO Communicates." In *Not Your Father's Union Movement*, edited by J. Mort, 43–54. New York: Verso, 1998.

Moskow, Michael, and Kenneth McLennan. "Teacher Negotiations and School Decentraliza-
     tion." In *Community Control of Schools*, edited by H. Levin, 191–218. Washington, D.C.:
     The Brookings Institution Press, 1970.

Mungazi, Dickson. *Where He Stands: Albert Shanker of the American Federation of Teachers.*
     Westport, Conn.: Praeger, 1995.

Muravchik, Joshua. *Heaven on Earth: The Rise and Fall of Socialism.* San Francisco: Encoun-
     ter Books, 2002.

———. *The Uncertain Crusade: Jimmy Carter and the Dilemmas of Human Rights Policy.*
     Lanham, Md.: AEI Press, 1988.

Murphy, Marjorie. *Blackboard Unions: The AFT and the NEA, 1900–1980.* Ithaca, N.Y.: Cor-
     nell University Press, 1990.

National Board for Professional Teaching Standards. *Raising the Standard: A Fifteen-
     Year Retrospective.* Arlington, Va.: National Board for Professional Teaching Standards,
     2002.

National Commission on Excellence in Education. "A Nation at Risk." In *A Nation Reformed?
     American Education Twenty Years After* A Nation at Risk, edited by David Gordon, 165–
     194. Cambridge, Mass.: Harvard Education Press, 2003.

Neier, Aryeh. *Taking Liberties: Four Decades in the Struggle for Rights.* New York: Public Af-
     fairs, 2003.

Newfield, Jack, and Paul DuBrul. *The Permanent Government: Who Really Runs New York.*
     New York: Pilgrim Press, 1981.

Norton, Eleanor Holmes. *Fire in My Soul.* New York: Atria Books, 2003.

Nussbaum, Karen. "Women in Labor: Always the Bridesmaid?" In *Not Your Father's Union
     Movement*, edited by J. Mort, 55–68. New York: Verso, 1998.

O'Day, Jennifer, and Marshall S. Smith. "Systematic Reform and Educational Opportunity."
     In *Designing Coherent Education Policy*, edited by S. Fuhrman. San Francisco: Jossey-Bass,
     1993.

Oliver, Rev. C. Herbert. "Community Control of Schools." In *Conflicts in Urban Education*,
     edited by S. Marcus and H. Rivlin, 111–132. New York: Basic Books, 1970.

Orwell, George. *Homage to Catalonia.* New York: Harcourt Brace & Company, 1952.

Packer, George. *Blood of the Liberals.* New York: Farrar, Straus and Giroux, 2000.

———. *The Fight Is for Democracy: Winning the War of Ideas in America and the World.* New
     York: Harper Perennial, 2003.

Pearl, Arthur, and Frank Reissman. *New Careers for the Poor: The Nonprofessional in Human
     Service.* New York: The Free Press, 1965.

Perlstein, Daniel. *Justice, Justice: School Politics and the Eclipse of Liberalism.* New York: Peter
     Lang, 2004.

Pfautz, Harold. "The Black Community, the Community School, and the Socialization Pro-
     cess: Some Caveats." In *Community Control of Schools*, edited by H. Levin, 13–39. Wash-
     ington, D.C.: The Brookings Institution, 1970.

Podair, Jerald. *The Strike That Changed New York: Blacks, Whites, and the Ocean Hill–Browns-
     ville Crisis.* New Haven, Conn.: Yale University Press, 2002.

Prochnau, Will, and Richard Larsen. *A Certain Democrat: Senator Henry M. Jackson—A Political Biography.* Englewood Cliffs, N.J.: Prentice-Hall, Inc., 1972.

Puddington, Arch. *Lane Kirkland: A Champion of American Labor.* New York: Wiley, 2005.

Putnam, Robert. *Bowling Alone: The Collapse and Revival of American Community.* New York: Simon & Schuster, 2000.

Radosh, Ronald. *Commies: A Journey Through the Old Left, the New Left, and the Leftover Left.* San Francisco: Encounter Books, 2001.

———. *Divided They Fell: The Demise of the Democratic Party, 1964–1996.* New York: The Free Press, 1996.

Ravitch, Diane. *The Great School Wars: A History of the New York City Public Schools.* New York: Basic Books, 1988.

———. *Left Back: A Century of Failed School Reforms.* New York: Simon and Schuster, 2000.

———. *The Troubled Crusade: American Education, 1945–1980.* New York: Basic Books, 1983.

Reich, Robert. *Locked in the Cabinet.* New York: Random House, 1997.

Rieder, Jonathan. *Canarsie: The Jews and Italians of Brooklyn Against Liberalism.* Cambridge, Mass.: Harvard University Press, 1985.

Rivers, Francis. "Rivers Report." In *Confrontation at Ocean Hill–Brownsville: The New York School Strikes of 1968*, edited by Maurice Berube and Marilyn Gittell, 83–101. New York: Praeger, 1969.

Rogers, David. *110 Livingston Street: Politics and Bureaucracy in the New York City Schools.* New York: Random House, 1968.

Rogers, David, and Norman Chung. *110 Livingston Street Revisited: Decentralization in Action.* New York: New York University Press, 1983.

Rosenthal, Steve. "Building to Win, Building to Last: The AFL-CIO Political Program." In *Not Your Father's Union Movement*, edited by J. Mort, 99–112. New York: Verso, 1998.

Rubinstein, Annette. *Schools Against Children: The Case for Community Control.* New York: Monthly Review Press, 1970.

Ruffini, Gene. *Harry Van Arsdale Jr.: Labor's Champion.* Armonk, N.Y.: M. E. Sharpe, 2003.

Rustin, Bayard. *Down the Line: The Collected Writings of Bayard Rustin.* Chicago: Quadrangle Books, 1971.

Ryan, Alan. *John Dewey and the High Tide of American Liberalism.* New York: W. W. Norton, 1995.

———. "The City as a Site for Free Association." In *Freedom of Association*, edited by A. Gutmann, 314–329. Princeton, N.J.: Princeton University Press, 1998.

Salvatore, Nick. *Eugene V. Debs: Citizen and Socialist.* Urbana: University of Illinois Press, 1982.

Salzman, Jack. Introduction to *Struggles in the Promised Land: Toward a History of Black-Jewish Relations in the United States*, edited by Jack Salzman and Cornel West, 1–20. New York: Oxford University Press, 1997.

Schierenbeck, Jack. *Class Struggles: The UFT Story.* United Federation of Teachers, Feb. 2, 2005. Available online at http://www.uft.org/about/history/uft_story_part1/index1.html.

———. *Union Made a World of Difference: Reflections on the Revolution at Forty*. New York: United Federation of Teachers, 2000.

Schlesinger, Arthur, Jr. *The Vital Center: The Politics of Freedom*. Boston: Houghton Mifflin Company, 1949.

Schmidt, George. *The American Federation of Teachers and the CIA*. Chicago: Substitutes United for Better Schools, 1978.

Schwartz. Robert. "The Emerging State Leadership Role in Education Reform: Notes of a Participant-Observer." In *A Nation Reformed? American Education Twenty Years After A Nation at Risk*, edited by D. Gordon, 131–152. Cambridge, Mass.: Harvard Education Press, 2003.

Selden, David. *The Teacher Rebellion*. Washington, D.C.: Howard University Press, 1985.

Shachtman, Max. *The Bureaucratic Revolution: The Rise of the Stalinist State*. New York: The Donald Press, 1962.

Shanker, Albert. "Chapter 6." In *Why Teachers Strike: Teachers' Rights and Community Control*, edited by Melvin Urofsky, 149–188. Garden City, N.Y.: Anchor Books, 1970.

———. *The Making of a Profession*. Washington, D.C.: American Federation of Teachers, 1985.

———. "Reflections on Forty Years in the Profession.," in *Reflections: Personal Essays by Thirty-Three Distinguished Educators*, edited by Derek L. Burleson. Bloomington, Ind.: Phi Delta Kappa Educational Foundation, 1991.

———. "The Task Before Us." In *The State of the Nation's Public Schools: A Conference Report*, edited by Stanley Elam, 88–107. Bloomington, Ind.: Phi Delta Kappa, 1993.

———. "Teacher Unionism and Education." In *Conflicts in Urban Education*, ed. S. Marcus and H. Rivlin, 133–148. New York: Basic Books, 1970.

Siegel, Fred. *The Future Once Happened Here: New York, D.C., L.A., and the Fate of America's Big Cities*. New York: The Free Press, 1997.

Sifton, Elizabeth. *The Serenity Prayer: Faith and Politics in Times of Peace and War*. New York: W. W. Norton & Company, 2003.

Simms, Beth. *Workers of the World Undermined: American Labor's Role in U.S. Foreign Policy*. Boston, Mass.: South End Press, 1992.

Skrentny, John David, ed. *Color Lines: Affirmative Action, Immigration, and Civil Rights Options for America*. Chicago: University of Chicago Press, 2001.

Sleeper, Jim. *Closest of Strangers: Liberalism and the Politics of Race in New York*. New York: W. W. Norton & Company, 1990.

Smith, Marshall S., and Jennifer O'Day. "Systemic School Reform." In *The Politics of Curriculum and Testing*, edited by Susan Fuhrman and Betty Malen, 233–267. Bristol, Penn.: The Falmer Press, 1990.

Sombart, Werner. *Why Is There No Socialism in the United States?* Translated by Patricia Hocking and C. T. Husbands. White Plains, N.Y.: International Arts and Sciences Press, Inc., 1976. Originally published in 1906.

Special Committee on Racial and Religious Prejudice. "Excerpts from the 'Botein Report.'" In *Confrontation at Ocean Hill–Brownsville: The New York School Strikes of 1968*, edited by Maurice Berube and Marilyn Gittell, 174–176. New York: Praeger, 1969.

Stephanopoulos, George. *All Too Human: A Political Education*. New York: Little, Brown & Co., 1999.

Stern, Sol. *Breaking Free: Public School Lessons and the Imperative of School Choice*. San Francisco: Encounter Books, 2003.

———. "'Scab' Teachers." In *Confrontation at Ocean Hill–Brownsville: The New York School Strikes of 1968*, edited by Maurice Berube and Marilyn Gittell, 176–192. New York: Praeger, 1969.

Stevenson, Harold, and James W. Stigler. *The Learning Gap: Why Our Schools Are Failing and What We Can Learn from Japanese and Chinese Education*. New York: Simon & Schuster, 1992.

Stigler, James W., and James Hiebert. *The Teaching Gap: Best Ideas from the World's Teachers for Improving Education in the Classroom*. New York: The Free Press, 1999.

Stone, Joe. "Collective Bargaining and Public Schools." In *Conflicting Missions: Teachers Unions and Educational Reform*, edited by T. Loveless, 47–68. Washington, D.C.: The Brookings Institution Press, 2000.

Taft, Philip. *United They Teach: The Story of the United Federation of Teachers*. Los Angeles: Nash Publishing, 1974.

Tamir, Yael. "Revisiting the Civic Sphere." In *Freedom of Association*, edited by A. Gutmann, 214–238. Princeton, N.J.: Princeton University Press, 1998.

Taylor, Clarence. *Knocking at Our Own Door: Milton A. Galamison and the Struggle to Integrate New York City Schools*. New York: Columbia University Press, 1997.

Thernstrom, Abigail, and Stephan Thernstrom. *No Excuses: Closing the Racial Gap in Learning*. New York: Simon & Schuster, 2003.

Toch, Thomas. *In the Name of Excellence: The Struggle to Reform the Nation's Schools, Why It's Failing, and What Should Be Done*. New York: Oxford University Press, 1991.

Tomasky, Michael. *Left for Dead: The Life, Death, and Possible Resurrection of Progressive Politics in America*. New York: The Free Press, 1996.

Trilling, Lionel. Introduction to *Homage to Catalonia*, by George Orwell. New York: Harcourt Brace & Company, 1952.

United Federation of Teachers. Excerpts from the "UFT Policy Statement on Decentralization." In *Confrontation at Ocean Hill–Brownsville: The New York School Strikes of 1968*, edited by Maurice Berube and Marilyn Gittell, 219–221. New York: Praeger, 1969.

Urban, Wayne. *Why Teachers Organized*. Detroit: Wayne State University Press, 1982.

Urofsky, Melvin. "Reflections on Ocean Hill." In *Why Teachers Strike: Teachers' Rights and Community Control*, edited by Melvin Urofsky, 1–34. Garden City, N.Y.: Anchor Books, 1970.

Vinovskis, Maris. "Missed Opportunities: Why the Federal Response to *A Nation at Risk* Was Inadequate." In *A Nation Reformed? American Education Twenty Years After* A Nation at Risk, edited by David Gordon, 115–130. Cambridge, Mass.: Harvard Education Press, 2003.

Walzer, Michael. "Blacks and Jews: A Personal Reflection." In *Struggles in the Promised Land: Toward a History of Black-Jewish Relations in the United States*, edited by Jack Salzman and Cornel West, 401–410. New York: Oxford University Press, 1997.

Wasserman, Miriam. *The School Fix, NYC, USA.* New York: Simon & Schuster, 1970.

Wehrle, Edmund F. "Labor's Longest War: Trade Unionists and the Vietnam Conflict." *Labor's Heritage* 9, no. 4 (Winter/Spring 2002): 50–65.

White, Stuart. "Trade Unionism in a Liberal State." In *Freedom of Association*, edited by A. Gutmann, 330–356. Princeton, N.J.: Princeton University Press, 1998.

Wildavsky, Ben. *U.S. News and World Report's Ultimate Guide to Becoming a Teacher.* Naperville, Ill.: Sourcebooks, Inc., 2004.

Wreszin, Michael. *A Rebel in Defense of Tradition: The Life and Politics of Dwight Macdonald.* New York: Basic Books, 1994.

Zitron, Celia Lewis. *The New York City Teachers Union: 1916–1964: A Story of Educational and Social Commitment.* New York: Humanities Press, 1968.

Interviews

Unless otherwise noted, all other interviews were conducted by the author. A full list of those interviewed can be found in the acknowledgments.

Barsh, Yetta, interview with Epstein, Renee. United Federation of Teachers. 1986. NYU Archives.

Beagle, Simon, interview with Epstein, Renee. United Federation of Teachers. 1985. NYU Archives.

Hill, Velma, interview with Epstein, Renee. United Federation of Teachers. 1986. NYU Archives.

Rustin, Bayard, interview with Epstein, Renee. United Federation of Teachers. 1985. NYU Archives.

Shanker, Albert, interview with Cowan, Neil. United Federation of Teachers. 1985. NYU Archives.

Shanker, Albert, with Mosle, Sara. New York: N.Y. 1996. Wayne State University Archives.

Shanker, Albert, interview with Reecer, Marcia. N.d. Bella Rosenberg papers.

Shanker, Albert, interview with Shore, Miriam. American Jewish Committee. 1988. Dorot Jewish Division of the New York Public Library.

INDEX